The
Universal
Kabbalah

Also by Leonora Leet

The Kabbalah of the Soul: The Transformative
Psychology and Practices of Jewish Mysticism

Renewing the Covenant: A Kabbalistic
Guide to Jewish Spirituality

The Secret Doctrine of the Kabbalah:
Recovering the Key to Hebraic Sacred Science

The
Universal
Kabbalah

Deciphering the Cosmic Code
in the Sacred Geometry
of the Sabbath Star Diagram

LEONORA LEET

Inner Traditions
Rochester, Vermont

Inner Traditions
One Park Street
Rochester, Vermont 05767
www.InnerTraditions.com

LIBRARY OF CONGRESS CATALOGING-IN-PUBLICATION DATA

Leet, Leonora.
The universal kabbalah : deciphering the cosmic code in the sacred geometry of the sabbath star diagram / Leonora Leet.
p. cm.
Includes bibliographical references and index.
ISBN 0-89281-189-7 (hardcover)
1. Cabala. 2. Cabala—Mathematical models. 3. Jewish cosmology. 4. Tree of life. 5. Magen David.
I. Title.
BM525.L325 2004
296.1'6—dc22

Printed and bound in the United States by Sheridan Books, Inc.

10   9   8   7   6   5   4   3   2   1

Text design and layout by Virginia Scott Bowman
This book was typeset in Galliard and Futura

To the

tradition of

my grandmother

Pessie Neznir and to

the cherished memory of

my mother, Tania Neznir Leet,

and to my most beloved daughters

Susannah Rachel Brodwin and

Tamar Brodwin Goodman

and the special blessing

of my granddaughters

Stephanie Caroline

and Sarah Julia

Goodman

a Tree

of Life

in Israel

Contents

Foreword *by Dr. Julian Ungar-Sargon*   ix

Note from the Publisher   xii

Preface   xiii

PART ONE
Introducing a New Model for the Kabbalah

1 The Star and the Tree   2

Hebraic and Pythagorean Sacred Science   2

The Hexagram and Hebraic Sacred Science   7

The Hexagram: An Esoteric Key to Genesis and the *Zohar*   10

The Hexagram of Creation   13

A Further Study of Jewish Cosmology   20

2 The Sabbath Star Diagram   28

Discovering the Geometric Source of the Tree of Life Diagram   28

The Science of Expressive Form   44

A General Preview   48

PART TWO
A New Model for Kabbalistic Cosmology

3 Generation of the Fourth-World Diagram   56

A Summary Introduction to the Fourth-World Diagram   56

Generating the Fourth-World Diagram   58

The Fourth-World Diagram and the Fall   68

The Fourth-World Diagram and the Transformative Moment   81

The Sabbatical Model of Redemption   83

The Trivalent Logic of the Sabbath Star Diagram   87

4 **The Evolution of the Fourth World**   90

    Preliminary Definition of the Sabbath Stars   90

    The Sabbath Stars of Yetzirah   91

    The First Sabbath Star of Asiyah and the Minerals   98

    The Second Sabbath Star of Asiyah and the Plants   106

    The Third Sabbath Star of Asiyah and the Animals   112

    The Fourth Sabbath Star of Asiyah and Man   118

5 **The Fifth-World Diagram and the Messianic Age**   126

    Introduction to the Fifth World Diagram   126

    The Fifth-World Sabbath Stars and the Messianic Age   131

    Stages of Ruach Consciousness   144

6 **The Sixth-World Diagram and the World to Come**   148

    A Manual for Sixth-World Diagram Construction   148

    The Laws of Diagram Construction and Number Theory   162

    The Construction Elements and Gender   165

    The Construction Elements and the Partzufim   169

7 **The Culminating Diagram of the Cosmic Octave**   181

    Construction Elements of the Octave Diagram   181

    The Unification of the Name   186

    The Working of the Chariot   189

    The Octave Diagram and the Tzimtzum   197

    The Angels of Aravot   204

PART THREE

A New Model for Kabbalistic Soul Psychology

8 **The Fourth-World Matrix Model of the Nefesh Soul**   214

    Understanding the Hexagram Matrix   214

    The Dual Spiral Matrix in Its Unfallen and Fallen Forms   220

    Temptations beyond the Matrix Border   228

9 **The Fifth-World Matrix Model of the Ruach Soul**   236

    Primary Definition of the Fifth-World Matrix   236

    The Ruach Matrix Model of Meditation   247

    The Levels of Ruach Master Power   249

10 **The Sixth-World Matrix Model of the Neshamah Soul**   256

    The Completed Pattern of the Spiral Tree   256

    The Matrix Partzufim   262

    The Sefirot and the Path of the Soul   267

The Spiral Tree as Psychological Model   269

The Fourth- and Fifth-World Matrix Models of the Nefesh and Ruach Souls   270

The Sixth-World Matrix Model of the Neshamah Heart   273

The Sixth-World Matrix Model of the Neshamah Mind   279

11 Forbidden Crossings and the Illusion of Knowledge   288

Introduction: Tohu or Tikkun?   288

Beyond the Fourth-World Matrix Borders   289

Beyond the Fifth-World Matrix Border   294

Beyond the Sixth-World Matrix Border   300

Light Units and the Illusion of Knowledge   308

12 The Octave Matrix of the Chayah Soul   313

Cherubs and Trees   313

The Double Spiral Tree: Redemption through the Other Side   319

The Sixfold Cherub Tree and the Measure of the Body   329

PART FOUR
A New Model for the Infinite

13 Exploring the Geometry of the Infinite beyond the Cosmic Circle   336

The Seventh World   336

The Eighth World   346

The Ninth World   353

14 Charting the Infinite Future   358

Extrapolating the Matrix to Infinity   358

The Relationship of Construction and Matrix Elements   362

15 The Final Model of Infinity: The Sabbath Star System   373

The Periodic Decimal Sequence   373

The Converging Decimal Sequence   380

Convergence and the Law of Complex Magnitudes   390

APPENDICES
A New Universal Model

A Scientific Implications of the Hexagram Matrix   402

B A Systems Model of Sociology   409

C Systematic Linguistics   427

D A Gender Model of Human History   444

Notes   464

Index   486

Foreword

Leonora Leet received her Ph.D. from Yale University and was, until her untimely death in the spring of 2004, professor of English at St. John's University. Her other books on the Kabbalah are *Renewing the Covenant, The Secret Doctrine of the Kabbalah,* and *The Kabbalah of the Soul.* Given her training in classical English literature and that the subject of her Ph.D. dissertation was Elizabethan drama, we might have expected further work along the lines of her celebrated scholarship on Marlowe and Elizabethan love tragedy, but this was not to be, for about twenty years ago she had a sudden spiritual awakening that was to change her life and her written work. Having experienced being touched by an Indian mystic, she went back to sources in esoteric Judaic texts in an attempt to discover the roots and trajectory of her own tradition. Her discoveries are published in this volume, the fruit of twenty years of research.

It is with great sadness that I write this posthumous tribute. It was only a few months before publication of *The Universal Kabbalah* that I received the news of her untimely death. I am, however, encouraged by the fact that she lived to see all but the final stages of the publication of this culmination of her life's work and mission. I was involved in translating and reviewing its Hebrew citations from original material and researched some of the more obscure sources on her behalf, so I had the pleasure and privilege of working with her over the last few years more closely than anyone, I believe. I was moved by her honesty, passion, diligence, and perseverance. She had an uncanny intuitive sense about the connection between the divine and humanity, and having had a profound spiritual experience, went about finding the tools by which to express this enormous insight.

I know of no other scholar who single-handedly tackled a field so foreign to her own primary area of expertise. Yet she doggedly pursued the source material in fields such as mathematics, geometry, and Kabbalah until she had mastered them with the same acumen as she did her literary studies. Leet's major claim is that within the Jewish esoteric tradition humankind plays a pivotal role in the perfection of the divine personality by uniting the finite with the infinite. Working from an original synthesis of the major kabbalistic traditions of cosmology derived from the Hechalot literature, the Zohar, and the school of Isaac Luria, Leet attempted to erect a new framework for understanding the mechanism of the transformative spiritual work that enables the human soul to reach increasingly higher dimensions of consciousness.

Her voice reached many, both in her classes and through her previous books. As is evident from general sales of esoteric literature and expanded course offerings in esoteric subjects, increasing numbers of people are seeking a more direct connection with spirituality. As part of this phenomenon, Leet, in her *Renewing the Covenant,* provides access to Jewish spirituality as a means for achieving higher consciousness, a path that could deepen the devotions of both nonobservant and traditionally observant Jews. This process of "covenant renewal" begins with effective kabbalistic techniques of meditation, combining mantra with visualization; proceeds through the return to a "reconstructed Sinai-Sabbath"; and arrives at the culminating practice of ritual prayer, the performance of which can fulfill the kabbalistic purpose of creation. When undertaken in the steps outlined in her book, this process has helped many to discover forms of spiritual practice precisely tailored for the modern world, as well as a new appreciation for the rich spiritual heritage of Judaism.

Leet explores the false temptations of worldly power and pleasure that lead to the fall of the soul and then the means of its redemption. She develops a powerful meditative technique called the Transformative Moment, the workings of which are exemplified by Jacob and Joseph and which allow the individual to progress through all the higher levels of the soul, even possibly to attain the miraculous powers of the legendary spiritual masters. She further correlates the hierarchy of soul levels with Ezekiel's throne vision to show the various paths the soul may travel toward self-realization: sex, love, power, knowledge, holiness, and unification. The first four paths relate to the four-faced living creatures (Chayot) of Ezekiel's throne vision—the bull-ox, lion, eagle, and man. The final two paths correlate to the prophet and the envisioned man on the throne that he recognizes to be his divine higher self—the knowledge that defines the secret doctrine of the whole of the Jewish mystical tradition culminating in the Kabbalah.

Leet's twenty-year quest and departure from classical Western literature produced a vast reconstruction of the knowledge of the ancient Jewish priest-scientists, with vital implications for contemporary spirituality and science. She cast Kabbalah as an ancient Hebrew sacred science that used geometry, sound, and number to link the finite world of human experience with the infinite realm of the divine, and she attempted to make use of teachings extending back thousands of years to explicate key concepts of quantum physics and quantum cosmology.

Unlike previous, purely historical explorations of the Jewish esoteric tradition, Leet's work in *The Secret Doctrine of the Kabbalah* resurrects this ancient body of knowledge to reveal eternal truths that can have a profound and positive impact on contemporary spirituality. In this text she explores new experimental methods of practicing Hebraic sacred science that explain as never before the meaning of the central cosmological diagram of the entire Western esoteric tradition—the kabbalistic Tree of Life. Leet shows that the Kabbalah and its central diagram enshrine a key to the purpose of the cosmos, a key that has vast implications for modern physics and cosmology. She takes what has always been considered a two-dimensional model of the famous kabbalistic tree of anthropos and insists on a three-dimensional projection more common to other hermetic traditions. In a final synthesis she envisions a culmination in which the universe and its divine child, perfected humanity, achieve that unification of the finite and infinite that has ever been the secret doctrine of the Kabbalah.

The acceptance of *The Universal Kabbalah* for publication turned out to be a moment of glory and grace for Leonora Leet, for to her this book marked the acme of her life's work. Reviewers of her writings, which included those well connected to the world of theoretical kabbalistic study as well as practical therapists and mystics, noted the depth and significance of her ideas. Gerald Epstein, M.D., director of the American Institute for Mental Imagery, commented: " . . . a daring and innovative exposition of the secret doctrines and practices of traditional Jewish mysticism uniquely applicable to the present."

Nevertheless, I encouraged her to return to her old familiar archive to reconcile the more scientific aspects of her highly technical sacred science and the inner connection of longing and desire that she so eloquently described in her literary work.

In her literary scholarship there were subtle similarities as yet to be unfolded between what she evoked in her analysis of mythic themes running through literature and Kabbalah. She was interested, for instance, in the characters of the unconditional lover and the warrior, both of whom were involved with the conversion of love into power, albeit with a difference: The lover's selfless concern to empower the powerless diffuses his or her power, while the self-possession of the spiritual knight concentrates it. It is this concentration that is needed to direct spiritual power into manifestation, a concentration that depends upon possessing rather than losing the self. Such possession is also different from the self-confidence of the ordinary hero, for where the power of the merely brave warrior relies on his faith, that of the master warrior is recognized as a product of his own consciousness. He is not dependent on but is the maker of his moods. In possessing himself, he has brought all the levels of his being into the light and control of his conscious will. Such power is certainly formidable and, if placed in the service of a diseased will, can become most dangerous.

Viewed through her kabbalistic work, in the fight between those whose use of power is good and those whose use is for evil, the good master will always win because the right that goodness adds to power will make it the more attractive. The good master will be more relaxed and graceful in his manner, will exude an air of freedom exhilarating to all, offering the double attraction of power and beauty in one fully realized being. Where the evil or false master is coercive, whipping his followers into an obsessional frenzy, the good and true master is liberating, lifting his followers into creative joy. Offered a choice between two such masters, few would choose to serve the egomaniac. But the choice is more often between the modes of power presented by the diseased master and the Ruach path of the heart, and in such a contest it is the warped master of evil who will win. For he offers a more direct source of power than does love, one already mature rather than the seedling offered by unconditional love. Because any form of power is vitalizing, even coercive and destructive power will draw adherents where there is a power vacuum, such warped vitality being predictable to none insofar as it can organize otherwise dissipated energies into the production of some form of nourishment.

It is not love that can fight such evil power but only a form of equally masterful power ranged on the side of holiness. And this is true not only of a fallen world but of the whole structure of cosmic consciousness. To win the spiritual battle on the side of right, the devotees of spiritual love must be ready to accept power so that they may perfect the world as they perfect themselves on the Neshamah path of power. This is particularly important for the work of the Tikkun that, like power, is future-oriented. The master in the arena of power is always figuring a few moves ahead and working with future probabilities. And his or her ultimate concern is for some form of divine communion without loss of self. The concept of the Tikkun has been primarily associated with the forward thrust of spiritual evolution, that reconstitution by which the cosmos, like humans, can become twice-born, and it requires the spiritual mastery of the uses of power with which we have here been concerned.

I looked foward to Leonora Leet's scholarship to come: her bringing to bear on the works of classical English literature her experience with and understanding of the Western esoteric tradition. But it was not to be. She has left that kind of connection for us, her students, to continue.

JULIAN UNGAR-SARGON, M.D., PH.D.

Note from the Publisher

Throughout a lifetime of work, every publisher has the opportunity to engage with an author who is indomitable in spirit, fortitude, exactitude, and purpose. Such an author was Leonora Leet. When she first submitted her manuscript to us in 1994, we were stunned by the enormity of the task she had set before herself and convinced her to allow us to release portions of her work in several smaller books, each of which would have a more narrowly defined topic and focus. This request resulted in our publication of her first three books on the Kabbalah: *Renewing the Covenant: A Kabbalistic Guide to Jewish Spirituality* (1999), *The Secret Doctrine of the Kabbalah: Recovering the Key to Hebraic Sacred Science* (1999), and *The Kabbalah of the Soul: The Transformative Psychology and Practices of Jewish Mysticism* (2003).

It had always been Leonora's hope and desire to publish *The Universal Kabbalah* as her first and definitive work on this topic, but as with all innovative thinkers, her ideas were still growing and expanding in complexity and depth. We now have the pleasure and honor to see with this publication her complete opus brought to fruition. This book represents her more than twenty years of study and synthesis in deciphering the sacred geometry of kabbalistic cosmology derived from the Tree of Life and her own geometric model, the Sabbath Star Diagram. In order for readers to grasp the full measure of the progression of her new scientific model of the laws of cosmic manifestation, some of the foundational components that were explored in her previous books will by necessity appear in *The Universal Kabbalah* as well.

Preface

Thomas More expressed my situation best when, in detailing the professional and family obligations that had left only stolen time for his writing, he said: "Slowly, therefore, because this time is but little, yet finally, because this time *is* something, I have finished *Utopia*. . . ." My similar reasons for the thirteen years it has taken me to complete the writing and illustration of my work and the following thirteen years to prepare it by stages for publication may also explain, if not excuse, its length. For had I been able to complete at least the writing of this project in one unbroken block of time, it would doubtlessly have been the simpler work I had originally envisioned. But the vacation periods and even two research leaves were never long enough to do more than individual sections of the work, and the intervening periods of teaching left me just enough time to research yet another unexpected area suggested either by my own ongoing analysis or the developments in a variety of related fields, with the result that the work expanded with the ever richer complexity that also characterizes its subject. This work centers on a self-generating geometric construction I have named the Sabbath Star Diagram that, in addition to the interesting combination of predictable and unpredictable elements that endows each of its regular expansions with unique qualities, also seems expressive of cosmological meanings, particularly those of the Jewish esoteric tradition known as the Kabbalah.

It was in June of 1978 that I stumbled upon the discovery of the geometric construction I would name the Sabbath Star Diagram that was to demand my unremitting efforts at that joint labor of construction and cosmological interpretation I have named the Science of Expressive Form. But when I had completed the more creative part of this labor in 1991, the main analysis of the Sabbath Star Diagram had become overgrown with a flora of supplementary analyses that more than doubled the size of what I had earlier thought of as a single-volume work, bringing it to three volumes totaling 2,600 pages. Because it appeared that important supplementary chapters would be buried under the sheer weight of the total work, I decided to present in independent books those related analyses that could be largely separated from the Sabbath Star Diagram model, the clearer focus thus given the themes of these studies compensating for their loss of the larger cosmological context for their reflections they had previously enjoyed in terms of this geometric model. These first supplementary analyses were published in 1999 by Inner Traditions under the titles *The Secret Doctrine of the Kabbalah: Recovering the Key to Hebraic Sacred Science* and

Renewing the Covenant: A Kabbalistic Guide to Jewish Spirituality. But though preceding and hopefully arousing interest in the foundational work now finally appearing, it should be realized that all of these prior analyses were inspired by various aspects of the geometry and interpretation of the Sabbath Star Diagram contained in the present work. This is particularly true of my most significant contribution to an understanding of the history of the Jewish mystical tradition, that "secret doctrine of the Kabbalah" whose key only emerged from certain mathematical features of the seventh expansion of the Sabbath Star Diagram.

As these earlier published analyses had, however, lost the references to parts of *The Universal Kabbalah* on which some of them had depended, it has become necessary to present again a portion of the material appearing in these earlier books, leading to some duplication in the present volume. This is particularly true with much that is to follow in this preface as well as with the first two chapters of this book, the latter of which appeared in only slightly modified form as chapter 6 in, and the former as the preface of, *The Secret Doctrine of the Kabbalah.* This original introduction to my three-volume work is a necessary foundation for the present volume, and all of the repeated material from *The Secret Doctrine of the Kabbalah* is presented again to validate two main points of this analysis, the ancient Hebraic association with the hexagram and the long history of a seven-world cosmic model in the history of Jewish thought, the subjects of chapter 1. Even more important is the subject of chapter 2, the elementary derivation of the Sabbath Star Diagram from that of the Tree of Life. Small portions of chapter 5 and chapter 9 also appeared previously in *Renewing the Covenant.*

My third book published by Inner Traditions, *The Kabbalah of the Soul: The Transformative Psychology and Practices of Jewish Mysticism,* which appeared in 2003, focused primarily on the modeling of kabbalistic soul psychology and contained both supplementary analyses and analyses directly modeled on the less-expanded forms of the Sabbath Star Diagram that could be separated from this original and more precise model. Chapters 3, 4, and 8 contain material from chapter 2 of *The Kabbalah of the Soul,* and chap-

ters 5 and 9 reprise material from chapter 3 of that same book. The solution for separating these analyses from the modeling of the Sabbath Star Diagram that had originally inspired their distinctive features was to invent a new theoretical three-dimensional cosmic model that could be imaginatively projected and would contain the essential characteristics on which much of the original analyses had been based, a model that proved to have its own power to illuminate this material. But in adapting the material appearing in chapters 2 and 3 of *The Kabbalah of the Soul* to the new model developed in its first chapter, some regularizing of these analyses was necessary to fit them to this new model, and so there are some minor inconsistencies between these adapted analyses and the original forms that will be met here. Unlike the supplementary analyses in its fourth and fifth chapters, those in its second and third chapters could not be cut from the present volume since they are essential to both the geometric development of the Sabbath Star Diagram and its primary modeling of the Kabbalah. But readers of *The Kabbalah of the Soul* should be interested to see how precisely its analyses are supported by the geometry of the Sabbath Star Diagram. In general, the principle that I adopted as to what portion of these earlier published studies to include and what to cut from the present book was, in the interest of reducing the excessive size of this volume, to cut everything not germane to the just-stated purpose of this work, its new modeling of the Kabbalah by the successive expansions of the Sabbath Star Diagram, especially if such material could be referred to in notes. Thus the material appearing in chapters 2 and 3 of *The Kabbalah of the Soul* is both richer in detail and poorer in the precise modeling that can benefit by comparison with the original form of these analyses appearing in this book.

To aid readers of my previous books in navigating through the varied streams of analysis in the present work, I have added footnotes at the beginning of repeated sections advising them of these repetitions. But for analyses integral to the development of the Sabbath Star Diagram as a geometric model for kabbalistic cosmology and soul psychology, I have felt it would not be fair to new readers of my work to simply relegate such material to note references. I hope the use of footnotes to alert readers to material repeated largely verbatim from earlier books will help those readers familiar with these works in progressing through this book as well as interest new readers in exploring the often richer development of parallel passages in these other books.

The following volume develops a new form of experimental geometry that can equally provide a powerful new model for the Kabbalah and also one for complexity theory and for the various other fields modeled in the appendices. In terms of the Kabbalah, the construction elements of the Sabbath Star Diagram are correlated with its "outer" cosmological stages, and the matrix produced within each diagram expansion by these construction elements is correlated with the "inner" soul levels corresponding to these "cosmic worlds." The construction elements are the subject of part 2, which provides a new scientific model for kabbalistic cosmology, whose seven dimensions or worlds can integrate the past orientation of the *Zohar* and the future orientation of Luria with biblical cosmology; and its third part, whose subject is the expanding matrix, provides a new model for the multileveled spiritual psychology of the Kabbalah. Finally, part 4 takes its experimental geometric model beyond the circumference of the Lurianic cosmos in a numerical extrapolation to infinity that finally leaves the Sabbath Star Diagram behind to develop the Sabbath Star System that can provide a fuller model for complexity theory with its own cosmological implications.

As rewarding to me as the final publication of this foundational basis of my previous books and the work I consider the most important is the opportunity it provides to give thanks to the various people whose help through my long years of work on this project has been especially appreciated. My discovery in 1978 of a key to the geometric derivation of the kabbalistic Tree of Life Diagram, the major cosmological diagram of Western esoteric thought, was partly the result of my initial exposure to Pythagorean geometry two years earlier. It was in the fall of 1976 that I took a course in such geometry with Robert Lawlor, this at a place called Lindisfarne, an institution of esoteric learning founded by William Irwin Thompson that flourished for two and a half years in New York

City. Lawlor's explanations of the meaningfulness of geometric forms and processes both inspired me and gave a foundation for what would become the major work of my life, and I am most indebted to him. His parting advice to me was that I do actual geometric drawing. And so it was that on a fateful June day in 1978 I attempted to diagram the generation of the Platonic solids in a manner more symmetrical than the various versions I had seen. I need not elaborate on the details of that construction because its true importance for me was something quite unexpected, the fact that the Tree of Life Diagram with almost all of its paths popped out at me from the particular two-dimensional arrangement of these solids I had made. Though there seemed no way to generate the missing lines on the basis of my original Platonic solids diagram, I realized that this could be done if the various orthogonally drawn solids were first redrafted in the simplified form of the expanding series of hexagrams, Stars of David, they could be seen to suggest. It was the Tree of Life Diagram, then, that finally led me both to the form of the hexagram and the modes of its expansion by which not only its own geometric derivation could be explained but also the basis on which the reciprocally derived Sabbath Star Diagram could become self-generating.

By the time I made this initial geometric discovery in June of 1978, my exploration of various Western and Eastern esoteric traditions had finally brought me to the Kabbalah, with its strange, seemingly arbitrary diagram, and it was the convergence of these two streams of sacred geometry in my own awareness that enabled me to recognize both the fact and the importance of my chance discovery of this geometric key to the Tree of Life Diagram. By the end of that summer, my initial study of the Sabbath Star Diagram and of the Kabbalah convinced me that there was a book I had to write on this association of a particular cosmology with a self-generating geometric construction. Though I was not the scholar of the Kabbalah that I was of Renaissance English literature, my skills as a literary critic proved to be just the hermeneutical tools needed to do the mode of modern kabbalistic geometry I have called the Science of Expressive Form. And the structure of the Sabbath Star Diagram, as I successively generated each of its regular expansions, provided the guideposts necessary to give direction to my exploration of the Kabbalah, enabling me to find those cosmological concepts that could be precisely modeled by the geometry of this diagram in a way that seemed mutually validating.

As I began the serious study of the Kabbalah, I sought a teacher, and I almost immediately found myself in the classes that Aryeh Kaplan was conducting in his Brooklyn home on the *Sefer Yetzirah*. Kaplan approached the Kabbalah not only as the scholar he assuredly was but as a Kabbalist, one who believes it to be an ancient though developing tradition that enshrines a coherent key to cosmic functioning, a sacred science whose rigor can be brought into coherence with modern secular science. And it is just such a Kabbalist that I was to become. Not only did Kaplan's sense of the meaningfulness of the Kabbalah have a profound influence upon me, but he was also of immense help to me both directly and indirectly, pointing me to the textual sources of certain materials that I needed and, in his works, providing me with a wealth of newly translated texts that, however differently I may have interpreted them from his own surrounding commentary, became the basis of much of my own analysis of this tradition. My indebtedness to Kaplan is apparent in the multitude of my quotations from his works. I am also grateful to Seymour Applebaum, a psychiatrist and fellow student in Kaplan's classes, for having made certain of his posthumous manuscripts available to me.

Of the various other individuals for whose support and aid I am particularly grateful, the first I wish to acknowledge is Reb Zalman Schachter-Shalomi, a major figure in the world of Jewish spiritual renewal, whose great heart immediately intuited the nature and importance of my project and gave it his unstinting support. His high and extended recommendation of the manuscript was of especially great help to me in finding a publisher for my unusual work. Through most of the long years that I have been engaged on this work, I have also been most beholden to my best friend, Esse Chasin, whose subtle knowledge of Hebrew was a treasure I could always call upon at need. More recently, I have been much indebted to

Dr. Julian Ungar-Sargon for his enthusiastic support of my work and the help he has given me in understanding the Hebrew subtleties of certain talmudic and kabbalistic texts, for being, in truth, my *chavrusa,* study companion, though unfortunately at long distance. Finally, I would like to thank my mathematician colleague Maurice Machover for sharing with me something of his knowledge of the latest developments in science and especially for the most valuable contribution he made to the final numerical extrapolation of the diagram, in the culminating chapter of this work, by discerning in my calculations the workings of a formula through which the expansion of the diagram could more easily be taken to infinity.

There are a few additional scholars whose personal suggestions or comments to me I have acknowledged in notes, most prominently Stanley Krippner, Martin Samuel Cohen, and Gerald Epstein. I would also now like to acknowledge the following individuals for their various appreciated contributions to this work: Darren P. Rosa for the art work in figure 10.4; James White for an early interpretative suggestion; Robert Stein for helping me to crystallize certain ideas; John Anthony West, Maia Gregory, Richard Falk, Deborah Foreman, and, most crucially, Gerald Epstein for their help in securing a publisher for my works.

Of the many individuals at Inner Traditions who have variously helped with the production of my books for this press, I would like especially to single out Jon Graham for his sensitive appreciation of my efforts and unstinting support of them through the more than six years of my involvement with this press, years during which I twice revised what was originally a two-volume version of this work until it finally achieved its present superior form that best suited it for publication; and for their equally sensitive editorial overseeing of my work, I would like to express my deep appreciation to Cannon Labrie, Jeanie Levitan, and Elaine Sanborn, Cannon particularly for his careful and knowledgeable line editing of my previous two books as well as of this; and finally I must thank Peri Champine for her creativity in designing the beautiful covers of my previous two books and this last and most important work.

Finally, I would like to acknowledge my great

debt to St. John's University for its generous support of my research, including various research leaves and course reductions, and to give special thanks for the support given me by former Graduate Dean and Vice President Paul T. Medici, the late Fr. Thomas Hoar, C.M., and my former chairperson, Angela Belli. I would also like to give special thanks to the Word Processing Center at St. John's University for the priority that was given to my enormous and constantly revised manuscript in an earlier three-volume format and to that best of typists, Kathy Leander. Perhaps even more important was the help given me on the computer graphics for this work by the Faculty Support Center, most substantially by its former director, Fr. Frank W. Sacks, C.M., who not only taught me how to use the Superpaint program on the Macintosh computer but, recognizing my need for a triangular grid on which to draft my diagrams with greater accuracy than the Superpaint program could otherwise afford, laboriously constructed such grids as could be hidden in the final printing for the fourth-through seventh-diagram expansions, the grids provided in the text for the fourth and sixth expansions being largely his own work. Also of great help to me has been another of its former directors, Robert Lejeune, particularly for enlisting the aid of a systems analyst at the University Computer Center, Paul Karagianis, who programmed the IBM mainframe computer with the formula devised by Dr. Mackover for generating an infinite periodic decimal out of a central diagram function, one that, taken to 6,300 formula iterations at 1,500 decimal places each, provided the raw data for the final numerical extrapolation of the diagram developed in the culminating chapter of this volume. This final development of the Sabbath Star System into a model for complexity theory is one that would never have been possible without the computer technology and resources made available to me through the university during the final phase of its initial manuscript preparation, 1989–91. I would also like to give thanks to all those at the university E Studio who have recently helped me in drafting some new black and white figures to complement the color diagrams that could not appear directly in the text, particu-

larly Rammy Joudeh for all his efforts at finding a version of Superpaint for me that enabled me to open up and work on my old files and for his other invaluable aid that made these figures possible.

Two points about my stylistic practice should also be noted. The first involves the practice I adopted with regard to Hebrew words. Whether wisely or not, I decided not to italicize the multitude of such words appearing in my text and yet to give them the slighter distinction of capitalizing their initial letters, a compromise to be sure. I also decided not to note in most cases the editions from which I took classical literary quotations, as in the quotation beginning this preface.

There are a few final comments I would like to make on the intentions and hopes I have concerning this work. The attempt of this work to validate the substance of the Kabbalah in terms of the precise symbolic expression it can give to the archetypal truth of a self-generating geometric model is one that goes counter to the direction of academic scholarship on the Kabbalah, whose primary concern is with the circumstances of kabbalistic texts and schools in terms largely of cultural history. For though I have both made use of this research and will hopefully contribute something to it at various points in my analysis, my primary concern has been to reveal as best I could the vital meaning of this ancient esoteric lore and to synthesize its various aspects into one coherent structure of cosmic understanding. It is a structure that I also hope will interest scientists as a new model for complex systems. And while I understand that my previously published studies might more readily draw readers interested in broader theoretical and practical concerns and wary of even such a nonspecialist approach to geometric models as here essayed, I also hope that, if not sooner, then finally, their greatest appreciation will be for the Sabbath Star Diagram, whose very geometric modeling may not only serve to validate kabbalistic cosmology and soul psychology through the meaningful structure it can impart to them, but further provide the needed new paradigm that can synthesize sacred and secular science into a coherent cosmology acceptable to the modern mind.

PART ONE

Introducing a New Model
for the Kabbalah

CHAPTER ONE
The Star and the Tree

HEBRAIC AND PYTHAGOREAN SACRED SCIENCE

At the heart of most sacred traditions lies a holy diagram in which the knowing can read a record of cosmological history, the ritual use of such forms of illumination attesting to the understanding, long before Kepler, that "God forever geometrizes." In the *Zohar*, the central work of the Jewish mystical tradition broadly designated as the Kabbalah, allusion is made at the very beginning to a diagram underlying all creation, a diagram whose existence in the supernal thought is said to have been first disclosed through the direct revelation of Elijah:

> This mystery was only revealed one day when I was at the seashore. Elijah . . . said to me, "Rabbi, the word was concealed with the blessed Holy One, and he revealed it in the Academy on High. Here it is:
> 'When Concealed of all Concealed verged on being revealed, it produced at first a single point, which ascended to become thought. Within, it drew all drawings, graved all engravings, carving within the concealed holy lamp a graving of one hidden design, holy of holies, a deep structure emerging from thought. . . . called by no name . . . Through this mystery, the universe exists.'"[1]

The fact that this most "hidden design" is said to be "called by no name" suggests that it is not the famous Tree of Life Diagram, a detailed geometric design that forms the basis of most later kabbalistic thought and that would already have been known by the author or final redactor of the *Zohar* in thirteenth-century Spain. It is just such a more hidden diagram that is the subject of this work, one that was discovered through the key of the Tree of Life Diagram and that, because it features a unique configuration of seven hexagrams, or Stars of David, has been named the Sabbath Star Diagram. In its form and derivation it serves to combine the two major geometric expressions of the Kabbalah—the Star of David and the Tree of Life Diagram, the star and the tree—whose symbolic association spans the millennia from the cartouche proclaiming the pharaoh to be king of Lower Egypt[2] to the decorative motifs identified with the Christmas celebration, an association that seems to express the universal spiritual understanding that all that grows on earth is fertilized from above. Initially constructed from the mysterious arrangement of hexagrams required to explain the geometric derivation of the Tree of Life Diagram, this underlying cosmological construction not only provides a geometric demonstration of the principles of kabbalistic cosmology but a geometric model applicable both to kabbalistic concepts of the soul and modern scientific theories, a model that lends support to the esoteric belief that matter and spirit are homologous structures of a coherent cosmos.

Unlike the seemingly arbitrary arrangement of the Tree of Life Diagram,[3] the Sabbath Star Diagram becomes a self-generating geometric construction following its own discoverable laws of expansion. Whatever may be the source of the Tree of Life Diagram, it can, in fact, be argued that its purpose was not only to model the esoteric cosmology identified with the Kabbalah but to serve as an initiatic key to unlocking this more complex but also more intelligible geometric construction, one whose geometric processes appear to encode with uncanny precision the archetypal principles of cosmic development. Whether or not the Tree of Life Diagram has ever been previously used to unlock this more hidden diagram, it enabled me to discover both the geometric laws of its construction and the methodology appropriate to interpret its implications.

As shown in chapter 6 of *The Secret Doctrine of the Kabbalah*,* the Tree of Life Diagram is not simply an arrangement of various circles and the lines connecting them, its parts are named and their spatial arrangements given an associative mythological interpretation. Thus the kabbalistic geometry of the Tree is distinguished by what shall later be shown to be a "quasi-Talmudic" approach to geometric form as something very much like a literary "text" whose meanings must be grasped not through logical demonstration but mythological association.[4] The question of the methodology of kabbalistic geometry, the methodology of this work, will be addressed in chapter 2, and it should serve to validate this linguistic method of geometric interpretation, explain-ing how it is possible to "read" a geometric form as a sign, to construe its meaning and translate its absolute truth into a secondary order of mythological explanation. For in addition to such use of precise geometric processes to model creation as this chapter will demonstrate can be found in the *Zohar* as well as in Genesis, the Kabbalah developed its distinctive approach to geometry in which form could not be separated from cosmological interpretation. It is this method that will be further employed in chapter 2, in which the Sabbath Star Diagram is derived from the key of the Tree of Life Diagram in an elementary version that, though not yet self-generating, is expressive at every stage of its development of cosmological implications consistent with the basic principles of kabbalistic cosmology, here especially its concept of four cosmic worlds.

The remarkable coherence between the Sabbath Star Diagram and the Kabbalah will be the primary focus of this work, as each expansion of the diagram takes us to new worlds and levels of consciousness. In the process, the Kabbalah of the Tree of Life Diagram will be both elucidated and shown to be coherent with the broader Jewish esoteric tradition originating with the Bible. All aspects of this tradition will find their place in the Sabbatical cosmic structure that the seven expansions of the Sabbath Star Diagram can so well model, a structure that derives from Genesis 1 and can contain both the four worlds of emanation of the Kabbalah developed in fourteenth-century Spain and the future worlds of rectification projected by the normative Messianic tradition as well as the Lurianic Kabbalah of sixteenth-century Palestine. The development of such a seven-dimensional cosmic model wholly interpreted in terms of Jewish esoteric cosmology and its correlated concept of soul levels should contribute to the new understanding of the Kabbalah now emerging, providing the scientific foundation for the Sabbatical cosmology presented in my earlier books that was derived from the geometric modeling now to be developed.[5] In addition, this work both represents an approach to the interpretation of geometric form that is new to modern mathematical science and also a new form of experimental geometry that in its fully self-generated form can

---

*As explained in the preface, much of part 1 appeared almost verbatim in chapter 6 of *The Secret Doctrine of the Kabbalah*, and readers may wish to skip ahead to the new material in this first part. In this chapter the new material will be found in the final section entitled "A Further Study of Jewish Cosmology"; in chapter 2 it is the "General Preview" section that is new.

provide a model for the theory of complex systems.

But however wide this focus may be, encompassing all aspects of the Kabbalah and its fuller tradition, it never ranges too far from its geometric base. For it is geometry in general, and the geometry of the Sabbath Star Diagram in particular, that can provide the meaningful structure to cosmological and related areas of speculation that seems to partake of absolute truth, the truth inherent in the processes and forms of geometric construction. That geometry is particularly expressive of cosmological meaning was understood as well by the Greeks, Plato developing his cosmology on the basis of the earlier geometric insights of Pythagoras. As such a core of geometrically encoded knowledge is to be found in the whole of the Western esoteric tradition, including that of the Kabbalah, further consideration should first be given to the reason for the remarkable association of geometry with such philosophy as attempts to bring the precise workings of matter and spirit together in one comprehensive explanation.

If geometry holds a central position in Western esoteric thought, it is because of its unique ability to supply an explanation, a blueprint, of those laws of existence that seem to apply equally to the processes of immaterial thought and to the material objects of such thought, an explanation of how consciousness and the world of material solids can be but different aspects of a coherent cosmos ordered by intelligible functions. Average liberally educated people of today have, however, so lost touch with the discipline of geometry that, even if interested in the Jewish branch of esoteric mysticism, they will not normally be attracted to its geometric aspect and, if they are, will feel themselves ill prepared to engage in its study. To overcome such hesitancy, there can be no more inspiring introduction to the spiritual importance of geometric constructs than the lines of the Romantic poet Wordsworth as he meditates on the special attraction of "geometric science":

With Indian awe and wonder, ignorance
pleased
With its own struggles, did I meditate
On the relation those abstractions bear

To Nature's laws . . . there, recognized
A type, for finite natures, of the one
Supreme Existence, the surpassing life,
Which . . . hath the name of God. . . .

. . . .

In verity, an independent world,
Created out of pure intelligence.
(THE PRELUDE, 6.115–67)

Though not even a rudimentary knowledge of classical geometry will be necessary to follow the discussions of geometric form and meaning in this text, the reader should come to share something of Wordsworth's awe at the power of geometry to convey ultimate truths.

It is this unique power of geometry to provide an archetypal explanation of the functioning of cosmic consciousness that explains the long hold its principles and practice have had in all the Western esoteric traditions; and to the extent that the Eastern and Western traditions can be distinguished, it is largely due to the absence or presence of the Pythagorean leaven. Though there would seem to have been a native tradition of Hebraic sacred science, the later kabbalistic tradition was as imbued with Pythagoreanism as the gnostic systems that, like it, were fertilized in the rich spiritual soil of the late Hellenistic period. Indeed, the association of the Jewish esoteric tradition with Pythagoreanism goes even further back. Josephus tells us that the Essenes were Pythagorean;[6] Philo Judaeus is known to have employed Pythagorean numerology in his biblical exegesis;[7] and the most noted contemporary scholar of kabbalistic literature, Gershom Scholem, considers the first extant work of the Kabbalah, the *Sefer Yetzirah*, to have been written as early as the third century C.E. by "a Jewish Neo-Pythagorean."[8]

As I proposed in *The Secret Doctrine of the Kabbalah*, the Jewish esoteric tradition was schooled in the same sacred sciences as informed the Pythagorean tradition—geometry, harmonics, and number—a proposition that will be demonstrated in the reading of the first chapter of Genesis offered later in this chapter. And this will show that the Hebraic sacred science of this early period, which was probably conserved and developed by the Zadokite priesthood of the Second Temple,[9] was as sophisticated as its Pythagorean counterpart, despite its different focus. For the key to the ordering of the Genesis creation account will prove to be none other than these same three elements comprising the core understanding of Pythagorean sacred science, that there is a precise and inverse relationship, expressible in numerical ratios, between the length of the string and the frequency of the tonal pitch it will produce when plucked, that geometrical length is convertible into musical sound through an inversion of fixed numerical ratios, one in which the Pythagoreans also saw a more ultimate relationship of space to time, of the limited to the limitless.[10]

Evidence has just been noted of the continuous association of the Jewish esoteric tradition with Pythagorean geometry; but before the Renaissance, the geometric content of kabbalistic thought was rendered largely by verbal description or metaphorical allusion. Even the profoundly geometric *Sefer Yetzirah* gives only verbal directions, and these couched in an obscurity probably meant to be penetrated only by the initiate, for what appears to be the construction of a cosmological diagram. The same obscurity marks the geometric aspect of the *Zohar*. It is possible, nonetheless, to recognize the Pythagorean quality of geometric description in these two monuments of kabbalistic thought by the primary geometric concepts they employ. As we shall be focusing on Zoharic geometry in the next section, we shall now just briefly note the Pythagorean core of the *Sefer Yetzirah*.

On one level, the *Sefer Yetzirah* describes the process of constructing the cube of infinite space. In *The Secret Doctrine of the Kabbalah* I provided a full discussion of the *Sefer Yetzirah* Diagram that not only showed the *Sefer Yetzirah* to begin with the ascription to language of the same central aspects of Pythagorean sacred science—shape, sound, and number—but a proposed solution of its geometric enigma, one that explains the relationship of the "twelve diagonals" of the text to the previously defined cube of space and how this relationship permits the cosmic expansion of the cube.[11] This matter will be further discussed later in this chapter, it

being sufficient at this point simply to observe that the author seems to have derived the structure of his cosmos from contemplation of the mysterious relationship of the diagonal to the side of a cube. This mystery emerges from the fact that when the side of a square is a whole number, such as 1, the diagonal will be the irrational number $\sqrt{2}$, and that it is this irrational element that provides the square with its potential for growth, the new base through which it can multiply its size. It was the incommensurability of the diagonal to the side that was the great secret the Pythagorean initiate was vowed to keep, not, as generally taught, because this fact destroys the rationality of Pythagorean geometry, but precisely because it is a revelation of the vital necessity of the suprarational, infinite element in all finite structures, that the square root contains a power whose nature is, in truth, unutterable in terms of finite measure and that points to the deepest of cosmic mysteries.[12]

The basic principles of Pythagorean cosmology are contained in Pythagoras's great mystical symbol, the Tetractys, and because there would seem to be evidence that the Kabbalists of medieval Provence and Spain were practicing geometers with knowledge of this prime Pythagorean symbol, some elucidation of the Tetractys would be helpful. In this symbol, the association of geometry, number, and musical harmonics, which forms the essence of Pythagoras's sacred science, is graphically presented. Its ordering of ten "pebble" points in the shape of an equilateral triangle not only provides the numerical ratios of the musical consonant intervals—2:1 of the octave, 3:2 of the fifth, and 4:3 of the fourth—but also a diagram of the emanation of four successive "worlds" or dimensions:

The single pebble on the top signifies the mathematical point, which represents the first world of unity. The two points on the second line signify the mathematical line that can be drawn between them and represent the second world of duality, of multiplicity. The three points on the third line signify the minimal surface of the triangle, which requires three such points, and are representative of the harmonizing third world. Finally, the four points on the bottom line signify the minimal solid, the four-pointed tetrahedron composed of four equilateral triangles,

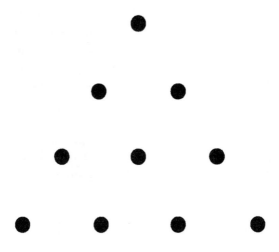

Figure 1.1. The Tetractys

which represents the fourth world of manifest solids. The addition of the pebbles or dots that make up the four "worlds" of the point (1), the line (2), the surface (3), and the solid (4), equals the ten points of the Tetractys.

Gershom Scholem has summarized some of the evidence of geometric concepts employed by the medieval Spanish Kabbalists of Gerona:

> In the Zohar, as well as in the Hebrew writings of Moses de Leon, the transformation of Nothing into Being is frequently explained by the use of one particular symbol, that of the primordial point. Already the Kabbalists of the Geronese school employed the comparison with the mathematical point, whose motion creates the line and the surface, to illustrate the process of emanation from the "hidden cause."[13]

The use by Geronese Kabbalists of the point, line, and surface "to illustrate the process of emanation" might well indicate a knowledge of the Tetractys. More significant, however, is the emergence of the related concept of four cosmic worlds in such late-thirteenth- and early-fourteenth-century Spanish texts as the *Tikkunei Zohar* and the *Ma'asekhet Atzilut,* a subject to be considered more fully near the close of this chapter. The connection of this four worlds concept with that of the ten Sefirot[14] of the Tree of Life Diagram, in the form first appearing in

the twelfth century Provençal *Sefer ha-Bahir*, is one seen and elaborated upon by almost the whole of the later kabbalistic tradition. The pervasiveness of this union of four worlds with ten constituents in this tradition indicates something of the importance it must have accorded to the practice of Pythagorean geometry.

For more than one thousand years, then, from the emergence of the *Sefer Yetzirah* as early as the third century to the golden age of Spanish Kabbalism in the thirteenth century, there seems to have been some core of geometric practice and understanding in the kabbalistic tradition. Indeed, the continuation of this practice in the later Kabbalah is indicated by the reference to what "we know from the science of geometry,"[15] made by Chayyim Vital, the chief expounder of the system of cosmology developed in the sixteenth century by Isaac Luria, known as the Ari or lion. Such a practice provides the force of concrete demonstration that can allow the mystic to harmonize his intuitive experience with his rational mind. This is particularly true for the geometric construction of the hexagram, which involves basic geometric processes that can be associated with the primary processes of creation and that we shall see to have a special significance for Jewish esotericism. The next sections of this chapter should explain something of the importance of actual geometric practice to the adepts of Western esoteric mysticism through its study and construction of the hexagram.

But first we must consider the problematic relationship of the hexagram to the early history of the Jewish esoteric tradition.

THE HEXAGRAM AND HEBRAIC SACRED SCIENCE

Variously called the Shield of David (Magen David), the Star of David, and Solomon's Seal, the hexagram has come to be the symbol most identified with the Jewish people. Composed of two oppositely pointed equilateral triangles whose apexes are defined by the six radial arc points of a circle, this six-pointed star is an important esoteric symbol, associated with the heart chakra in Tantric yoga and discovered in the ground plan of Stonehenge.[16] It has long been thought that it was Arabic alchemy that in the West most popularized this symbol of equilibrium between the opposed archetypal forces of fire (the expansive force represented by the upward-pointing triangle) and water (the contractive force represented by the downward-pointing triangle). Since it was only in the early Middle Ages that the hexagram began to be featured prominently in Jewish magical texts and amulets, most modern historians have concluded that it was probably through this Arabic source that the hexagram was most directly transmitted to the medieval Spanish Kabbalists. But since in the Arabic literature employing this symbol the hexagram is normally given a Hebrew derivation through the terms "Solomon's Seal" or "Shield of David" by which it is called,[17] it may well be that there was a continuous association of the Jewish esoteric tradition with this esoteric symbol of David and Solomon that preceded Islam. The Talmudic reference to the hexagram engraved on the seal ring of Solomon[18] supports the possibility of an early association of the hexagram with Jewish esoteric understanding and practice reaching as far back as the biblical period, and this chapter will provide further grounds for such an association.

Gershom Scholem supports the contrary view that "the hexagram is not a Jewish symbol."[19] He does admit that this figure and its names "Seal of Solomon and Shield of David . . . go back to pre-Islamic Jewish magic,"[20] but considers that the hexagram "had one and only one purpose in its career as magic: to serve as protection against demons."[21] More allegorical treatment of the hexagram by the few later Jewish authors he cites is set down by him to the "use of alchemistic symbolism,"[22] apparently of Arabic origin. But Raphael Patai, in his important recent work *The Jewish Alchemists*, has traced a very different history for the alchemical tradition that must cause a major revision of the received opinion concerning the relationship of Jews to alchemy and its hexagram symbol. As he reveals:

> The first nonfictitious alchemists of the western world lived, as far as can be ascertained, in Hellenistic Egypt. And the earliest among them was Maria Hebraea, Maria the Hebrew, or Maria the Jewess, for whom our chief source is Zosimus the Panopolitan. Zosimus is the first Greek alchemical author whose actual writings have survived. He lived in Hellenistic Egypt, about 300 C.E. . . .We can thus tentatively assign her to the early third century C.E. at the latest.[23]

In the quotations from Maria's teachings, cosmological principles appear that have been thought to emerge only later in the Kabbalah:

> "One becomes two, two becomes three, and by means of the third and fourth achieves unity; thus two are but one.". . . "Join the male and the female, and you will find what is sought.". . . "If you do not render the corporeal substances incorporeal, and the incorporeal substances corporeal, and if you do not make the two bodies one, nothing of the expected will be produced.". . . She [Maria] said: "The philosopher (Pseudo-) Democritus said . . . 'Transform nature, and make the spirit which is hidden inside this body come out. . . . Destroy the body, and make it become water, and extract that which is in it.'". . . "The 'water' which I have mentioned is an angel, and descends from the sky, and the earth accepts it on account of its [the earth's] moistness. The water of the sky is held by the water of the earth."[24]

Maria Hebraea reveals alchemy to be a sacred science much like the more theoretical sacred sciences of geometry, harmonics, and number, the precise procedures of metallurgy, the first human technology, being studied and valued not only for their mundane usefulness but for what they can reveal of the principles governing both natural law and cosmic possibility. Her first quoted rule, which we are told "the Hebrew prophetess shrieked,"[25] seems to foreshadow the kabbalistic doctrine of the Partzufim, the divine personalities. Appearing in the *Bahir*, fully defined in the Idra Zuta section of the *Zohar*, and informing the later Lurianic Kabbalah, are the five main such Partzufim related to the ten circles, called Sefirot, of the Tree of Life Diagram. Though discussion and illustration of the forms of the Tree of Life Diagram will be deferred to chapter 2, a brief summary of its associations is necessary here to appreciate the significance of Maria Hebraea's formulations.

The Tree is a diagram composed of ten circular Sefirot and the twenty-two paths connecting them. The names of the ten Sefirot both define the attributes of a single divine figure and the five Partzufim into which they are transformed in the course of cosmic history. These names are: Keter (Crown), Chokhmah (Wisdom), Binah (Understanding), Chesed (Mercy), Gevurah (Judgment), Tiferet (Beauty), Netzach (Eternity), Hod (Splendor), Yesod (Foundation), and Malkhut (Kingdom). As Partzufim, Keter is identified with Arikh Anpin (Long Face), the original Partzuf who is the source of the next two Partzufim, Abba (Father), identified with Chokhmah, and Imma (Mother), identified with Binah, whose continuous mating is responsible both for the continuous process of creation and the generation of the originally androgynous Ze'ir Anpin (Short Face), the son figure identified with the six Sefirot from Chesed to Yesod, from whom the daughter-bride Partzuf of the Nukvah (Female), identified with Malkhut, separates in order to mate intermittently with Ze'ir Anpin and so both direct the course of Providence and generate the higher souls of the righteous. The six-Sefirot Partzuf of the son is clearly the most important, and may be said to combine a divine upper triad (Chesed-Gevurah-Tiferet) with a human lower triad (Netzach-Hod-Yesod), a unification of the infinite and finite that fulfills and models the purpose of Creation. This purpose is the generation both of the supernal son and those higher human souls who can recognize their identity with the supernal son and so achieve the unification of these two levels of divine sonship, a cosmic purpose I have earlier presented as the priestly secret doctrine of the son.[26]

Let us now apply the kabbalistic concept of the Partzufim to Maria Hebraea's statement: "One [Arikh Anpin (the long face)] become two [Abba (father) and Imma (mother)], two [Abba and Imma] becomes three [Ze'ir Anpin (the short face and son)], and by means of the third [Ze'ir Anpin] and fourth [the Nukvah (female of Ze'ir Anpin and daughter-bride)] achieves unity [a metaphorically sexual unification]; thus two are but one." The meaning of this "unification" of the transcendent or "incorporeal" with the immanent or "corporeal" is well understood by what the tenth-century Arab alchemist Ibn Umail understood Maria to mean by the descending water or angel through which nature can be transformed to realize the spirit within it: "And as for her statement '[The water] descends from the sky,' she meant by this the child which they say will be born for them in the air, while conception had taken place in the lower [region]; this being [through] the higher celestial strength which the water has gained by its absorption of the air."[27] The sexual model, imputed not only to humans but to metals, is important because it sees the object of the Great Work of alchemy to be such a unification of the opposing metallurgic procedures for dissolving the fixed and coagulating the volatile as can generate a more precious new being, "the child which they say will be born for them in the air," one whose perfection consists precisely in the conjunction of both of these purified qualities—truly a new definition of what I have elsewhere shown to be the Hebraic secret doctrine of the son.

Maria Hebraea's alchemy also seems already to suggest use of the hexagram model, the descending "water of the sky" not only denoting the descending triangle of the hexagram but also the concept of the upper and lower waters in the Genesis creation account, which we shall later see can also be modeled by the hexagram and in a way whose clarification of otherwise inexplicable features of the biblical account reinforces the early association of the hexagram with the sacred science of the Hebraic priesthood. The alchemical revelations of Maria Hebraea would seem, then, to be a direct outgrowth of an earlier and continuing Hebraic sacred science and to provide a link to the later theoretical elaborations of this tradition in the more sexually generative form of kabbalistic myth.

Patai provides much evidence to show "that Jewish alchemists were the teachers of both Muslim and Christian alchemists in the Middle Ages, just as they had been of Hellenistic alchemists in antiquity."[28] One Arab work, falsely attributed to Khalid Ibn Yazad, is particularly indebted to Maria Hebraea, as can be seen in the following quotation:

> But this dissolution and congelation, which I mentioned, is the dissolution of the body and the congelation of the spirit, and they are two but have one single operation, because the spirit cannot be congealed except with the dissolution of the body, and similarly the body cannot be dissolved except with the congelation of the spirit. And the body and the soul, when they are joined at the same time, each acts on its partner, making it similar to itself. . . . For the composition in this artifice or magisterium is the conjunction or matrimony of the congealed spirit with the dissolved body. . . .[29]

Again this essential alchemical marriage of opposites seems suggestive of the hexagram model, the "dissolved body," signified by its ascending triangle, "joined at the same time" to the "congealed spirit," signified by its descending triangle, a conjunction that represents the culmination of the Great Work of alchemy, the production of the "Philosophers' Stone." As Patai indicates, in considering the alchemical legends surrounding Solomon:

> The close association between Solomon and the philosophers' stone is shown by the fact that the materia prima of the stone was sometimes repre-

sented as the two interlaced triangles of "Solomon's seal.". . . the sign of the "fiery water," since it consists of a combination of two symbols: that of fire, which rises upward and hence is symbolized by the upward pointing triangle, and that of water, which descends from the sky and is represented by the downward pointing triangle. The old midrashic interpretation of the Hebrew word for heaven, *shamayin*, namely that it is a combination of the words *esh*, fire, and *mayim*, water, was known and restated by the alchemists.[30]

Recognition of the coherence between the doctrines of alchemy and the Kabbalah appears in a Jewish sixteenth-century treatise entitled *Esh M'Saref* (The Refiner's Fire):

> But know that the mysteries of this wisdom [i.e., alchemy] do not differ from the supernal mysteries of the Kabbalah. For just as there is a reflection of predicaments in sanctity, so there is also in impurity. And the sefirot which are in Asilut [the first kabbalistic world] . . . are also in 'Asiya [the fourth kabbalistic world of matter] . . . yea, even in that kingdom which is commonly called Minerals, although on the supernal plane their excellence is always greater. . . . Gehazi, the servant of Elisha, is of the type of the vulgar students of nature who set about contemplating the valleys and profundities of nature, but do not descend into its secrets, wherefore they labor in vain and remain servants forever. They give counsel about procuring the son of the wise, whose generation is impossible for nature, 2 Kings 4:14. But they can contribute nothing to this generation. . . .[31]

The great secret shared by both the Kabbalah and alchemy is that which I have termed the secret doctrine of the son, that "son of the wise, whose generation is impossible for nature," and who unites the essential qualities of the higher and lower planes, of the infinite and the finite. And they would seem to share this secret doctrine because both are similarly derived from an earlier Hebraic priestly culture.

In arguing that in the Western esoteric tradition the hexagram had a Hebrew origin as well as a

Hebrew name, I have shown that the imputed alchemical source for its spiritual symbolism not only does not preclude a Jewish source earlier than that of Arabic alchemy but demands it. In the Maria Hebraea of second or third century C.E. Alexandria, we may see a union of Hebraic esoteric teachings with some seed elements of an Egyptian Hermetic practice of metallurgy that bore the new ideological fruit of alchemical formulation.

But at the same time in Palestine there was a parallel theoretical development that showed a similar concern with the opposing qualities of fire and water and so with the possible employment of the hexagram to symbolize their union. This is in the most important text of Hebraic sacred science, the *Sefer Yetzirah*, in which fire is correlated with the mother letter Shin and the head, water with the mother letter Mem and the abdomen, and the air, which mediates between these opposed elements and their upper and lower locations, is correlated with the mother letter Aleph and the chest. As in alchemy, though differently, this text defines the process of generating the cosmic man. Given that in the later alchemical tradition, the circumstances of upper fire and lower water betoken the model of the hexagram, it does not seem too much to find a similar hidden reference to the hexagram in the *Sefer Yetzirah*, concerned as they both are with the same sacred scientific quest to study those features of theoretical or technological science whose precise processes appear to reveal the structure and purpose of existence. One difference between these teachings, however, is that Maria Hebraea synthesizes Hebraic sacred science with some earlier development of metallurgy in Egypt while in the *Sefer Yetzirah* Hebraic sacred science is synthesized with the Pythagorean sacred science of Greece. But the most important point to be made is that sometime during the second and third centuries C.E. there was a separate flowering of Hebraic sacred science both in post-Temple Palestine and diaspora Alexandria whose similarities would seem to imply the same source.

This source is most likely to have been the members of the priesthood deprofessionalized after the destruction of the Temple, who would have become private teachers of what must have been a long tradition of Temple sacred science. And one feature of this ancient science that appears to have surfaced alike in the teachings of Maria Hebraea and the *Sefer Yetzirah* is a peculiar joint definition of a fire above and water below, which in the later alchemical tradition was identified with the figure of the hexagram and given a Hebrew origin in the names by which it was known, Solomon's Seal and the Shield of David. As with the discovery of Troy just where Homer had claimed it to be, so it seems reasonable to conclude from the long association of the hexagram with the Hebrew kings that this geometric figure was, indeed, a particular aspect of the Jewish esoteric tradition going back at least to the Temple priesthood. The remainder of this chapter will not only assume this to be true but add important new evidence to support this thesis. It is appropriate at this point to review the method by which the hexagram is geometrically constructed. As will be seen, it is a method that recreates the primal acts of creation as they are defined from these very geometric processes in the esoteric traditions that have a geometric base.

THE HEXAGRAM: AN ESOTERIC KEY TO GENESIS AND THE ZOHAR

We begin with that marvelous instrument, the compass, whose features the poet John Donne thought a fitting symbol for the mysteries of spiritual love[32] and that the poet John Milton employed in his depiction of the creation, a depiction that already seems conversant with the Lurianic concept of the Tzimtzum, the divine withdrawal that left a spherical space for a finite cosmos:

> *One foot he centred, and the other turn'd*
> *Round through the vast profundity obscure,*
> *And said, Thus far extend, thus far thy*
> > *bounds,*
> *This be thy just Circumference, O World.*
> *Thus God the Heav'n created, thus the Earth,*
> *Matter unform'd and void:*
> > (*PARADISE LOST*, 7.228–33)

Observing with Milton the creative workings of the compass, we can begin with the fact that the compass is an instrument that unites in a larger functional whole a fixed foot and a moving foot, the fixed foot pointing always to the unmanifest center of unity represented by the mathematical point and the moving foot creating the mathematical line, which measures the shortest distance it has traversed in its movement away from the center. The compass, which can be taken as a symbol of the One from whom all creation emanates, defines its threefold nature as: (1) the point or unitary center established by the fixed foot; (2) the line or extension into duality, difference, and multiplicity, produced by the movement of the movable foot; and (3) the circular plane, a third, larger whole that contains and harmonizes the polarity of point and line into the complementarity of circular line, and that is produced by rotating the moving foot about the point to form a circumference.

Having produced a bound expanse, the first primordial space, through its three successive manifestations as contracted point, expansive line, and harmonizing circle, for its second action, the One may be said to multiply itself as point through the interaction of its other two aspects as (2) line or radius and (3) circumference, which is why the growth process would seem to require these other two aspects of unity. The generative interaction of the second and third aspects or steps, in other words, the measuring of radial arcs on the circumference by moving the fixed foot successively to each new marked-off point on the circumference, results in the production of six and only six points, the multiplication of 3 by 2 equaling 6. It is precisely because the compass, without changing the established distance of the radius between its two hinged feet, will mark off exactly six equidistant points on the circumference of a circle that the number six is accorded such a high place in numerology. It is thought of as the number of perfection not only because it is the sum of its factors but also because it is the first and closest expression of the perfection of the circle, the geometric shape that has been universally accepted as a symbol of the divine. It is also the number of creation because it is from these six points that the first manifest lines can be drawn.

The work of the compass has been to establish the basis for manifestation, but all its actions may be associated with a premanifest level of that creation which can be modeled by such diagram construction. For once these six points have been determined, the circle needed for their establishment can be erased. At this point the work of creation can be handed over from the compass to the straightedge, which will be used for drawing straight lines between the already established points and adding extensions of these lines to newly established vertices. The switch from the geometry of the circle to that of straightedged surfaces, from what might be considered the unmanifest to the manifest aspects of creation, is required for precision because the circle and any curved line is, in every sense of the word, immeasurable. The world of the determinate is the world of straight lines, and such straight lines can be found within the general curvature of nature, in the crystalline form of all chemical substances and in the lines that can be drawn between the centers of circular cells in organic matter to reveal its determining geometric structure.[33]

From the six points that have been established through the use of the compass, our divine geometer or its human counterpart will now most logically draw the hexagram, for it is the figure that most perfectly represents the six-pointed product of 3 × 2, the unmanifest operations of unity just detailed. As the union of two triangles, the hexagram represents both twoness and threeness around a center, the inner hexagon. It further represents two essential principles of the cosmos, the threefold manifestation of unity in the form of the triangle—which incorporates the contraction of the point, the expansion of the line, and the harmonizing surface that contains them—and the principle of the inverse. The upward-pointed triangle can also be taken to represent heaven, the downward-pointed triangle the earth, and the hexagram the symbol of their interconnection. From the preceding discussion, it should now be clear how the process of constructing the hexagram could become symbolic of the primordial acts of creation to a practicing geometer, and the hexagram, itself, the paramount symbol of the creation.

With this understanding of the basic geometric processes involved in the construction of the circle and the hexagram, we should be better able to appreciate the geometric descriptions of creation in the *Zohar*. At the start of section "Bereshit," the basic geometric progression from point, through line, to circle, and then to the marking of radial arc points is described in relation to the first processes of creation: "a single, concealed, supernal point shone. . . . so it is called רֵאשִׁית (Reshit), *Beginning*. . . . Then this *beginning* expanded, building itself a palace. . . . With this *beginning*, the unknown concealed one created the palace. . . . From here on בְּרֵאשִׁית בָּרָא שִׁית (Be-reshit—bara shit), He created six . . . six directions extending from the supernal mystery through the expansion that He created from the primordial point."[34] The interpretation of the first word of the Torah, *bereshit*, as signifying "he created six," has a long tradition prior to the *Zohar*, going back at least to the *Baraita de Ma'aseh Bereshit* (ca. eighth century): "In the beginning God created the heaven and the earth; you shouldn't read BERESIT as *in the beginning* but BERA SIT, *He created six*. And in effect you will find that it is written *He created six*."[35] In *Bereshit Rabba* we may see a similar effort to assert that "six things preceded the creation of the world."[36] That the number is more important than what it may signify is shown by the fact that two different lists are provided.[37]

Earlier in the *Zohar* there is a geometric elaboration of the interpretation of *bereshit* as *bara shit*:

What is בְּרֵאשִׁית (Be-reshit)? With Wisdom. This is the Wisdom on which the world stands—through which one enters hidden, high mysteries. Here were engraved six vast, supernal dimensions, from which everything emerges, from which issued six springs and streams, flowing into the immense ocean. This is בָּרָא שִׁית (*bara shit*) created six, created from here. Who created them? The unmentioned, the hidden unknown.[38]

In this reference, the meaning "[The hidden unknown] created six" ascribed to *bereshit* deconstructed into *bara shit* is directly identified with the

"six vast, supernal directions, from which everything emerges." It has, then, a geometric meaning and derivation. But since these "supernal directions" precede existence, they cannot be identified with the world of created solids, with the six directions that define the sides of a cube: up, down, east, west, north, and south. Rather, the "six vast, supernal directions" would have to be those defined by the six points inscribed on the circumference of the primal circle in the regular progression of geometric growth.

It will be remembered that in the earlier discussion of the primary geometric processes, the work of the compass was distinguished from that of the straightedge, the former being the instrument of immeasurable unity and the latter the instrument of precise measure, that through which the second linear world can be constructed. The previous two quotations from the *Zohar* depict the creative work of the compass by the "hidden unknown," leading through the successive stages of point, line, and circle to the final work of premanifest, primordial creation, the fixing or creation of the six radial arc points on the circle by measuring the distance between the two hinged feet of the compass or of a two-branched twig.

The next stage being here suggested for the creation process, the joining of these six radial arc points in the form of the hexagram, would also seem to be suggested in the *Baraita de Ma'aseh Bereshit*:

HE EXTENDS THE HEAVENS AS A VEIL. Why are these called heavens? It is because the Holy One, blessed be He, had mingled the fire with the water, spreading out the one with the other in creating the heavens, as it is said: IT IS MY HAND WHICH HAS FOUNDED THE EARTH AND MY RIGHT HAND WHICH HAS STRETCHED OUT THE HEAVENS. You shouldn't read it as "heavens" but as "fire and waters." He formed seven abodes on high . . . He stretched the heavens above. . . .[39]

As this work had interpreted *bereshit* as signifying the composite of *bara* and *shit*, whose meaning is

"He created six," so does it interpret the word for heavens, *shamayim*, as signifying a composite of *aesch*, meaning "fire," and *mayim*, meaning "water," a linguistic meaning that has become standard in the Jewish esoteric tradition. But we have seen that it is precisely the composite of fire and water that is signified by the hexagram in this prime alchemical symbol going back to an apparent Hebraic source. If the hidden meaning of this text is that the process of stretching out the heavens, of which we shall hear more in the following sections, is signified by the hexagram form and that there are to be seven of these, then we have encoded here the precise cosmic model of the Sabbath Star Diagram, whose sevenfold expansion of the hexagram form will be developed in this book.

But the creation of the first hexagram requires a dualistic instrumentality, that which is or uses the straightedge. This creative instrument is, in the *Zohar* as in Genesis, given the plural divine name Elohim. Continuing an earlier quotation that detailed the progression from supernal point through its extension into a palace (geometrically the circle), we can see the identification of Elohim with this third manifestation of the "hidden unknown" as circle: "This palace is called אֱלֹהִים (*Elohim*), God. The secret is: בְּרֵאשִׁית בָּרָא אֱלֹהִים (*Be-reshit bara Elohim*), *With beginning, _____ created God* (Genesis 1:1)."[40] The interpretation just given of the first three words of Genesis, *Bereshit bara Elohim* presents the startling but by no means unusual esoteric conception that the creator God of the heavens and the earth is not the ultimate source of all being, here the mysterious Ein Sof, but a derived aspect of its plurality harmonized with its unity (the symbolic meaning of the circle), here called Elohim. But if *bereshit*, normally translated "In the beginning," is understood in its other kabbalistic interpretation as "He created six," then a preliminary reading of the first seven words of Genesis could be: "The hidden unknown created six; Elohim created the heavens and the earth." Now if these six are given the simple geometrical significance of the six points made by the compass on the circumference of the circle for which it provided the radius, then the form of the heavens and the earth created by the straightedge would most logically be the hexagram joining these six points in the interrelated ascending triangle, signifying the heavens or the spiritual fire that is their source, and the descending triangle, signifying the earth or its source in the spiritual waters. The hexagram is, then, a fitting supernal symbol of the process of creation defined in the first sentence of Genesis: "*Bereshit bara* [created] *Elohim et ha-shamayim* [the heavens] *ve-et ha-aretz* [and the earth].*" From the foregoing analysis, it thus becomes possible to give the following completely geometric reading to the first seven words defining creation: "By means of the six [points] He [the "hidden unknown"(?)] had created, Elohim created the heavens [signified by the ascending triangle of the hexagram] and the earth [signified by the hexagram's descending triangle]." The Zoharic treatment of the first seven words of Genesis relates them, then, to the basic geometric processes thought to have been involved in the process of cosmic creation. And it also shows how the hexagram can provide the geometric model of the creation: "Come and see. When it arose in the will of the Holy One, blessed be He, to create the world, He brought out a single flame from the spark of blackness, and blew spark upon spark. It darkened and was then kindled. And He brought out from the recesses of the deep a single drop, and He joined them together and with them He created the world. . . . They became intertwined. . . ."[41] Here the "intertwined" forms of fire and water can only refer to the famous alchemical symbol of the hexagram, and the next section will bring the Hebraic provenance of this symbol as far back as the opening chapter of Genesis to reveal how it could become the instrument for ideally conceptualizing how "He created the world."

THE HEXAGRAM OF CREATION

If the first verse of Genesis provides a summary of the creation that may be modeled by the hexagram, the remainder of its first chapter can be understood as a progressive revelation of this hexagram form. Such a progressive revelation of the work of the first day in the following days of creation is again suggested in the *Zohar*: "Rabbi Judah bar Shalom said: On the very same day that the heavens and earth were created, all their products were made as well. . . . and afterward He revealed them day by day, and explains each one of them on the day that it was revealed."[42] But it is not only the sacred geometry of the hexagram that Genesis 1 has encoded. The esoteric nature of the creation account can be demonstrated by its apparent employment of two organizing keys drawn from the most essential of esoteric sciences, geometry and music. We shall begin this exploration with the latter and then conclude by analyzing the geometry of the full creation account.

The key to the peculiar chronological order of creation is so remarkably simple that it is a wonder no one has ever recognized it before. It is none other than the overtone or harmonic series. When a tone is sounded (1), its first overtone or second harmonic will be the octave (2), followed by the fifth (3), the next octave (4), the third (5), the next fifth (6), and the minor seventh (7). This can be represented by the following chromatic Solfeggio names and tones in the key of C: (1) Do-C_1, (2) Do-C_2, (3) Sol-G_1, (4) Do-C_3, (5) Mi-E_1, (6) Sol-G_2, (7) Tay-Bb_1. An important aspect of the harmonic series is the distinction it makes between the odd and even harmonics, a distinction that the Pythagorean tradition related to its central notions of the limited and the limitless. For whereas each odd number introduces a new tone, it is the function of the even numbers to resonate this tone in the doubling geometric progression through a potentially infinite number of octaves. Thus the odd numbers are each identified with their own unique tone while the even numbers relate this limited particularity to the limitless through a progression that they neither initiate nor can end. Now what is astonishing about this series in conjunction with the creation account is that the first, second, and fourth positions in which the Do tone is sounded are the same chronological positions in which reference is made to heavenly creation; the third and sixth positions in which the Sol tone is sounded are the same in which reference is made to earthly creation; and the remaining tones of the fifth and seventh positions relate to neither of these creation categories. Let us now

follow the account through the days of creation.

The first day can be associated with heaven (Do) insofar as it involves the creation of the supernal light. In the second day, the firmament that is created is specifically called "Heaven"[43] (Do). The third day gives us the creation of the dry land called "earth" (Sol). The fourth day returns us to the creation of the "lights in the firmament of the heaven" (Do). The fifth day takes us to the creation of the creatures inhabiting the flowing elements of water and air (Mi). The sixth day returns us to the earth (Sol) with the creation of the animals and man. And the seventh day brings us to that Sabbath sanctification that may well be associated with the modulating interval of the minor seventh, what in harmonic theory is more precisely defined as that flatter interval of the septimal seventh. Thus the peculiar reversal of the third and fourth days, in terms of which the logical progression of heavenly creation is interrupted by that of earthly vegetation, can be explained and would seem to have been motivated by the overriding consideration of the parallel to the harmonic series of overtones. The importance of such a parallel would further suggest that Hebrew cosmology is like the Hindu in tracing the creation back to an original sound. For Hindu cosmology it is the sound OM or AUM; in the biblical account it is the sound produced by the voice of God, an original vibration resulting in a form of supernal energy that can be associated with light. If all of the creation is implicit in the creative activity of the first day, as the opening seven words would suggest, then this original sound, which may be what Israel is twice daily called upon to "hear" in its prayers, would implicitly contain the harmonic series that is to be progressively expressed through the remaining days of creation and provide its order of manifestation.

The immediate translation of sound waves into a patterning of light, ascribed to the first day of creation, reveals an esoteric understanding of the relationship of musical harmonics to geometric form that is being increasingly substantiated by modern experimentation. The work of Hans Jenny in the study of wave forms he has called Cymatics is particularly important in this regard. When Jenny subjected certain substances such as oils or powders to specific sound frequencies, they assumed special geometric forms that could only be called forth by those frequencies. As he explains:

> we see in front of us the result of complex periodic vibration, a musical tone becoming a "visible" figure in which one or more intervals are featured. One must always bear in mind that these phenomena are generated by sound. If the sound is removed the whole picture along with its dynamics will disappear and return again immediately the sound is restored. These phenomena are subject to definite laws and are repeatable at any time. . . . The resultants of harmonic vibrations are at all times so strictly law-ordered that it is possible to draw up a systematology of morphogenesis. What one must bear in mind is that under this or that quite specific set of conditions Nature produces this form only and no other. Nothing here is diffuse and indeterminate; everything presents itself in a precisely defined form. The more one studies these things, the more one realizes that sound is the creative principle. It must be regarded as primordial.[44]

Among the beautiful photographs taken of such symmetrical patterning is the one shown in figure 1.2 that reveals a clear hexagram form.

The ability of the hexagram form to provide such a secondary key to the Genesis account further suggests that it was precisely the sound which could "cymatically" produce the hexagram that was understood to have been emitted by the divine voice "in the beginning." This final proof of the esoteric

Figure 1.2. A Cymatic Hexagram Form. From Hans Jenny, Cymatics, *2 vols. (Basel: Basilius Press, 1974), vol. 2, p.106.*

nature of the biblical creation account and of its particular association with the hexagram form has now to be demonstrated.

If the creation of the heaven and the earth referred to in the first verse can be understood to denote the resonating of the fundamental tone of creation, then this tone would not only have implicit within it the whole series of overtone harmonics related to its frequency but also a precise geometrical form. If we can further postulate that this implicit or virtual form is that of the hexagram, then we should be able to observe its progressive spatial unfolding through the days of creation in the same way that these days revealed the chronological phenomenalization of the harmonic series. The earlier analysis of the first seven words showed that these could be read as defining the six radial arc points on the circumference of a circle and their interconnection in the hexagram form. If these are now understood to refer to a premanifest circle and a virtual hexagram, then we can begin the progressive manifestation of the hexagram whose form is already virtually present.

We begin, then, with a circle that represents "the face of the deep" and that is filled with "waters" that are "without form and void" (Gen. 1:2). Into this circle, a ray of light may be thought to emerge from the uppermost radial arc point to fill and manifest the upper subtriangle of the hexagram and to complete the creative process of the first day. On the second day, the firmament that divides the upper from the lower waters can be said to manifest the upper and lower bars of the hexagram and to fill the space between them. It is the special circumstances of the third day that spatially as well as temporally argue strongly for the esoteric keys being here provided: "And God said, Let the waters under the heaven be gathered together unto one place, and let the dry land appear" (Gen. 1:9). In terms of the hexagram model, the place of the lower waters would be beneath the lower bar of the hexagram, which is the base of its full ascending triangle, and the "one place" where they can be gathered would be in the hexagram's lowest subtriangle, the point of its full descending triangle. The lower two subtriangles of the full ascending triangle would then pro-

vide the twin mountain forms in which the "dry land" could appear. Continuing with the account, the fourth day would now complete the manifestation of the hexagram form, the remaining two upper subtriangles of the full descending triangle providing the spaces within the firmament in which the sun and moon can be set. The circumstances of the fifth day can be better understood if the descending triangle is thought to overlay the ascending triangle in a single unbroken form, for the fish and fowl created on this day can then be placed within the water of its lower subtriangle and the air that can be understood to fill the adjoining inner hexagon. With the sixth day, the separated earthly mountains, which had earlier been covered with vegetation, can now be given the animal and human inhabitants that complete the work of creation. Though the Sabbath adds no new elements, its holiness is suggested in the final design of the Hexagram of Creation (fig. 1.3) by the way the fourth-day elements are illustrated. The simultaneous appearance of the setting sun and three stars is meant to suggest that most holy twenty-fifth hour of the Sabbath occupying the period from just before sunset, when the Sabbath began on the previous evening, to the time at which the first three stars can be seen, which officially closes the Sabbath.

The Hexagram of Creation does more than reveal the geometric structure of the Genesis account. It also provides a key to understanding much of biblical imagery as well as major aspects of the Jewish and other esoteric traditions. The first is particularly true of the scheme it provides for the elements of the third day. Its graphic representation of two mountains separated by water is echoed by the position accorded these elements in biblical narrative, law, and prophecy. For Jewish history can be viewed as progressing from one mountain to another, from Mount Sinai where the Law was given to the Holy Mountain of Messianic Jerusalem where it is to be fulfilled. To move from the first to the second mountain, however, requires a spiritual purification both symbolized and facilitated by the ritual bath of the *mikvah*.

The manner in which the hexagram can arrange the elements of the whole creation account also sug-

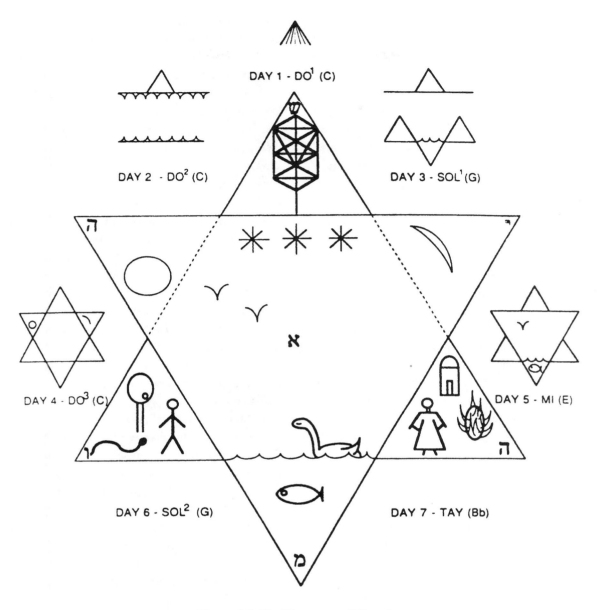

Figure 1.3. The Hexagram of Creation

gests a parallel between this account and the cosmology that has been ascribed to the more universal shamanic tradition, a parallel that this Hexagram of Creation can enable us to perceive. For its descending triangle, associated as it is with the flowing elements of water and air, can be related to the shamanic lower world, and its ascending triangle, associated with the elements of mountains and fire, can be related to the shamanic upper world.[45] The forms of these two major triangles can also deepen the usual interpretation of them by which the descending triangle is identified with divine descent and the ascending triangle with human ascent, showing the unity of the divine flowing force and the segmented nature of human ascent, its movement from the mountain of fallen man through the waters of purification to the mountain of perfected man and finally to the transcendent mountain of divine light. As we shall later see, the descending triangle can also be associated with a "lower world" of Ruach consciousness and the ascending triangle with an "upper world" of Neshamah consciousness, the former associated with the Way of God, the *Derekh ha-Shem*, and the latter with that which is above and directs its flow, the former with submergence in this flow and the latter with spiritual dominion. Such an association of Ruach consciousness with a "lower world" that is not hellish but represents a higher spiritual state may perhaps explain the standard references to mystical experience in the Merkabah tradition as a "descent."[46] The association of the uppermost subtriangle, and so the entire ascending triangle, with light or fire and of the lowest subtriangle, with the entire descending triangle of which it is a part, with water shows further coherence between the hexagram model of creation and its use in alchemy, again suggesting that it was not from Arabic alchemy that medieval Kabbalists were introduced to the hexagram but that this alchemical tradition was correct in attributing an earlier Hebrew origin to this form.

In the artistic design of the Hexagram of Creation, the uppermost subtriangle of fire is designated by the Hebrew letter shin, the lowermost subtriangle of water by the letter mem, and the central point of the air by the letter aleph. As was earlier indicated, these three letters were given these connotations in the *Sefer Yetzirah*, which classifies them as the three "mother letters." To complete the design, the remaining four subtriangles have each been correlated with one of the letters of the Tetragrammaton. Trees also figure in each of the ascending subtriangles, the Tree of Knowledge, on the left mountain of fallen man, the burning bush, on the right mountain of perfected man, and the Tree of Life Diagram on the central mountain of transcendent light, that diagram that will provide the further key by which the Hexagram of Creation can generate the more complex and precise cosmological model whose construction and interpretation will constitute the major subject and contribution of this work.

We come finally to what may be the most significant fact about the hexagram modeling of the cre-

ation account, the fact that the full manifestation of the hexagram is completed by the fourth day of a seven-day process. This permits us to integrate the four-stage process of later kabbalistic cosmology within the larger Sabbatical structure that Genesis projects for the cosmos and that would seem to be the more authentic cosmological model of the Jewish esoteric tradition.[47] But associating the four days of creation needed to manifest the hexagram form with the four cosmic worlds of the later Kabbalah, which lead to the manifestation of the physical world, will call for a radical reinterpretation of the biblical account. The four worlds doctrine enters the Kabbalah in the thirteenth century, primarily in the writings of Azriel of Gerona, and achieves its definitive form in such fourteenth-century additions to the *Zohar* as the *Tikkunei Zohar* as well as in the *Massekhet Atzilut*, though it does not appear in the main body of the *Zohar*. In this doctrine the four worlds descend from purest spirit to grossest matter and are defined as Atzilut (Emanation), Beriah (Creation), Yetzirah (Formation), and Asiyah (Making).

Associating the first world of Atzilut with the first day offers no problem since both may be said to represent a divine emanation not really separable from its divine source. It is with the second world of Beriah that creation may be said properly to begin from the kabbalistic perspective, and the separation of creation from Creator would also seem to be the function of the firmament created in the second day. The identification of the garden world of the third day with Yetzirah can also be supported since this world is kabbalistically associated with the Garden of Eden and the Fall of man leading to the materialization of the fourth world. The major problem that arises is with the fourth day, the day identified with the creation of the sun and the moon. But an observation made by the *Zohar* on this text can help to resolve this problem: "Come and see: Stars and constellations endure through a covenant, which is indeed *the expanse of heaven* (Genesis, ibid., 15). . . . There are seven planets corresponding to seven heavens."[48] If the major lights of the sun and the moon can be related to the stars and planets of the heavens, which is what they are, indeed, then the fourth day can be understood astronomically to represent all the physical components of the cosmos, that which is precisely correlated with the fourth kabbalistic world as well as the vital or Nefesh level of the soul with which it can also be associated. This leaves the last three days of creation to define the more subtle dimensions of consciousness that can be associated with the concept of the Tikkun, the cosmic process of Return or Reconfiguration developed by the sixteenth-century Kabbalist Isaac Luria. The fifth day can be associated with the flowing Ruach dimension of consciousness and the sixth day with the achievement of that dominion characteristic of Neshamah consciousness, beyond which is the holiness of the Sabbath with its promise of Devekut, divine communion. Thus the first and last three days would define supernal creations with only the fourth day representing the physical dimension of creation.

The progressive unfolding of hexagram elements during the first three days also reveals a numerological progression through geometrically defined worlds or dimensions. The first day may be said to disclose a single point of light that radiates forth a certain distance into the medium of chaotic waters. The second day not only brings us to the second world of the line but of the number two, for it manifests the two horizontal bars of the hexagram. Since these bars are meant to clear the area between them of "waters," they may be further thought of as providing some form of directional heat or magnetic attraction that might cause the intervening medium to collect about them. In the process, the upper bar would close off the portion of the upper "waters" that may be thought to have transformed the fundamental tone of creation into a ray of light. Finally, with the third day we arrive at both the third world of the triangular plane and the triple number of such triangles, the arrangement of which also suggests the quality of balance associated with the triadic. It is the unfolding of these three supernal worlds— defining the archetypal elements of unity, duality, and balance—that allows the fourth world of solids, informed by these functions, to be manifested.

Beyond this, the creation account may be understood to project the virtual fields of higher consciousness. The Zoharic Kabbalah understands the soul to be composed of three basic levels, those of the Nefesh, the Ruach, and the Neshamah, and these may be related to the fourth, fifth, and sixth cosmic worlds or days of a Sabbatical cosmic structure. If the fourth day is now to be identified with the fourth cosmic world of the later Kabbalah, then it would not only represent the mineral elements of creation but all the constituents living in the physical world in accordance with their natural endowments. For man, this natural spiritual endowment is the Nefesh or animal soul. In the biblical account, the fourth day contributes a level of creation under "rule" (Gen. 1:18), one that may be supposed to exhibit matter under the control of natural law and spirit needing to control the instinctual animal appetites. This latter defines the Nefesh level of the soul. The fifth and sixth days bring us to two higher soul levels both of which are termed "blessed" (Gen. 1:22, 28). As earlier suggested, the fifth day and world may be understood to define the Ruach soul dimension as that which enters into the divine flow and the sixth day and world as that in which man has moved from a condition of being controlled, through one of participating in such control, to a final state of spiritual "dominion" (Gen. 1:26). In such a state, man can enter into the Sabbatical day and world to experience the fullness of that holiness with which he has been briefly visited each earthly Sabbath.

We have seen that the first chapter of Genesis is informed by esoteric keys of musical harmonics and geometric form that reveal a deeper logic underlying and ordering the progression of its elements, and its whole seven days can be understood to develop the plan of cosmic history, to program the perimeters within which the creation can achieve actualization. That this program can not only be modeled but decoded by the hexagram form would seem further to demonstrate that the association of the Jewish esoteric tradition with the hexagram goes back to its earliest biblical origins, and it goes far to validate my earlier thesis that there was a sophisticated core of Hebraic sacred science that was probably conserved by the Zadokite priesthood of the Second Temple.

As the Sabbath Star Diagram that will begin to be developed in the next chapter will be wholly composed of hexagrams, all of its parts, whether those hexagrams involved in its outward construction or its inner matrix, may be said to contain the Hexagram of Creation holographically within them. It is not, then, just the initial hexagram that may be said to contain the whole of creation enfolded within it, but each part of the unfolding whole, however specific its position and meaning, may also be said to holographically encode the archetypal model and plan of the whole.[49] The discussion of the Hexagram of Creation has shown this form to be the basis of a Sabbatical cosmic structure whose progression is outlined in the first chapter of Genesis. But we have finally to consider the further historical developments that establish this Sabbatical structure as the most authentic form of Jewish cosmology.

A FURTHER STUDY OF JEWISH COSMOLOGY

The foregoing analysis is not the first attempt to derive a Sabbatical cosmic structure from the creation account in Genesis. Such a structure appears most importantly in the Talmud, in the talmudic resolution of the two creation accounts in Genesis 1 and 2 that understands the seven days of the Genesis account to involve a spiritual creation preceding physical manifestation and providing its plan of development. In the Talmud (*Eruvin* 18a and *Berakhot* 61a), the concept that there were two creations is articulated, the first in thought, wherein Adam and Eve were created simultaneously, and the second in deed, wherein Eve was created from Adam's rib. The coherence of such a view with esoteric understanding is clear and accounts for its adoption by, among others, Isaac Luria, as seen in the *Pri Eitz Chayyim* (The Fruit of the Tree of Life) of his disciple Chayyim Vital, in the section on the Rosh Hashanah service. Most importantly, it is the seven-day creation account that is accepted as representing a creation in "thought,"[50] a spiritual rather than physical creation, though one that provided a model and frame for the subsequent evolution of the physical universe. More than this, it may be viewed as providing the spiritual structure of a

seven-dimensional cosmos in which the physical universe is to form but one level. Thus the creation in deed of the expanding universe may be thought to give physical form to a layer of the multidimensions already in place, a median layer incorporating the logically prior worlds of emanation as its operating principles and being itself contained within higher dimensions of consciousness waiting to be personalized by the evolving consciousness of man. The most significant contribution of the Sabbath Star Diagram and its explication to an understanding of this tradition may well be in this movement beyond the four cosmic worlds of the later Kabbalah to the larger cosmic structure of seven worlds that ultimately derives from Genesis 1.

But the major association of the Talmud with a Sabbatical cosmic structuring appears in its developing concept of the Sabbaticals (*shemitot*) as world-eras. This represents a continuation of what can be considered either the first biblical elaboration of the sevenfold account of creation or its analogue, the institution of the Jubilee cycle:

> Six years thou shalt sow thy field. . . . But in the seventh year shall be a sabbath of rest unto the land, a sabbath for the Lord. . . . And thou shalt number seven sabbaths of years unto thee, seven times seven years. . . . And ye shall hallow the fiftieth year, and proclaim liberty throughout all the land unto all the inhabitants thereof: it shall be a jubile unto you. (Lev. 25:3–4, 8, 10)

By the time of the pseudepigraphical *Book of Jubilees*, the Jubilee cycle had been further elaborated to account for all of biblical history, past and projected. But it is in the Talmud that the Jubilee cycle of Shemitot becomes a cosmic principle, most importantly in Rosh Hashonah 31a: "R. Katina said: The world is to last six thousand years, and one thousand it will be desolate."[51] An alternate view appears in Avodah Zarah 9a: "The Tanna debe Eliyyahu taught: The world is to exist six thousand years; the first two thousand years are to be void, the next two thousand years are the period of the Torah, and the following two thousand years are the period of the Messiah."[52] Sanhedron 97a refers to both of these views of Sabbatically structured history, using the identical language of the other accounts. These two accounts can be synthesized if to the understanding of the school of the Tanna Eliyyahu, which defines three two-thousand-year divisions of the six thousand years of the world's existence is added the period of the seven-thousandth year of desolation defined by Rabbi Katina. It is, however, the simpler formulation of Rabbi Katina whose influence has persisted in the tradition, to be given its fullest kabbalistic reformulation in the fourteenth-century *Sefer ha-Temunah*, which develops a full Jubilee cycle of cosmic eras correlated with the lower seven Sefirot.[53]

But there was an equally if not more important elaboration of Genesis 1 in terms of cosmic space that appears in the main Hekhalot texts of late antiquity, the *Hekhalot Rabbati* and the *Hekhalot Zutrati*, which project a structure of seven cosmic "palaces" (*hekhalot*) or "firmaments" (*rekion*), in the seventh of which, named Aravot, the mystic achieves the goal of his ascent and enters before the Throne of Glory. As with the elaboration of the Genesis seven-day creation account first into a structure of seven one-thousand-year eras and then into a Jubilee cycle of seven such *shemitot*, so its elaboration into a cosmic structure of seven palaces, firmaments, or heavens was to persist at least into the thirteenth-century period of greatest kabbalistic creativity, the period of the main portion of the *Zohar*.

It is in the *Sefer Yetzirah*, however, that these two traditions of Sabbatically structured cosmic space and time are finally synthesized into a larger structure associated with the word for "worlds," *olamot*, the plural of *olam*. Before we can appreciate this synthesis, we should review something of the contents of this work. Perhaps most important is the key to the creation it provides through its division of the twenty-two Hebrew letters, which are the instruments of creation, into the categories of the three mother letters, the seven double letters, and the twelve single letters, most importantly the latter two categories. The seven double letters clearly define the six sides of the cube of cosmic space: "Up and down[,] east and west[,] north and south[,] and the Holy Palace precisely in the center" (4:4).[54] But

as I have elsewhere shown, the specifications of "the twelve diagonal boundaries" of 5:2 can only be satisfied if they are understood to refer to an octahedron, the dualing Platonic solid of the cube and a means for its doubling, an unsolved problem throughout the history of the Platonic academy and one for which the author of the *Sefer Yetzirah*, or of the priestly tradition of Hebraic sacred science from which it most probably derived, would seem to be offering a solution.[55] So if I am right that the twelve diagonals represent the means of expanding the cube, we can better appreciate the expansion of the single cubic structure of the cosmos in 4:4 into the concept encountered in 4:15, that for which we have been searching in the tradition, the concept of "seven worlds" (*shevah olamot*).[56] This appears in the text followed directly by: "seven firmaments, seven lands, seven seas, seven rivers, seven deserts, seven days, seven weeks, seven years, seven sabbaticals, seven jubilees, and the Holy Palace. Therefore, He made sevens beloved under all the heavens." Since the Hebrew word *olam* can refer both to the more spatial concept of "world" and more temporal, really atemporal, concept of eternity, it is not surprising to find it followed by five categories of space (firmaments, lands, seas, rivers, and deserts) and five categories of time (days, weeks, years, Sabbaticals, and Jubilees), these two sets of five equaling the number of the ten *sefirot belimah* (signifying abstract numbers) of chapter 1 of the *Sefer Yetzirah*, particularly in the distribution of 1:3: "five opposite five." So we have here the recognition that these two traditions of Jewish esoteric cosmology are complementary and can be combined under the larger rubric of "worlds," still more, that both are required. For in 4:7–14, the author divides all of creation into three basic categories, the spatial category of "world" (*olam*), the temporal category of the "year" (*shanah*), and the spiritual category of "soul" (*nefesh*). As so defined, the cosmos is understood to be extended in space and time and permeated by soul. It is only after so defining its three aspects that we come, in 4:15, to the further understanding that the process of such extension involves the seven stages that can be called "worlds" and that require the dual Sabbatical cosmologies of space and time that only this text has been able to synthesize, a synthesis that will continue to influence Jewish cosmological thinking for at least a millennium.

Appearing in Palestine hundreds of years after the *Sefer Yetzirah*, probably in the eighth century, is the important rabbinical text that serves as a clear bridge to the *Zohar* in the thirteenth century, one thousand years after the *Sefer Yetzirah* is thought to have been written, also in Palestine. This suggests that there was a continuing study in Palestine of the *Sefer Yetzirah* from the time of its composition to that of the text we are now to explore. This text is the *Pirke de Rabbi Eliezer*, in whose eighteenth chapter we find a cosmological elaboration of the Sabbatical creation account of Genesis, beginning with the image "He put forth His right hand and stretched out the heavens," a reference to the verse in Psalm 104:2 earlier encountered that has had a continuing influence on early Jewish cosmology, and coming to the important words: "The Holy One, blessed be He, created seven worlds and of all of them He chose the seventh world. Six of them come and go and one is totally Sabbath and eternally at rest."[57] Here I would suggest that the difficult phrase "come and go"[58] can be taken to refer to the ever more purified but still finite cosmic worlds, while the Sabbatical world is that of the infinite. What is of equal importance to the use here of the *Sefer Yetzirah* phrase "seven worlds" (*shevah olamot*) is its context. For it is preceded by the statement, "The Holy One, blessed be He, created seven firmaments, and He chose from all of them only Aravot for the place of the Throne of Glory of His kingdom," as well as references to the creation of "seven lands," "seven deserts," and "seven seas"; and it is followed by references to the creation of "seven days" and "seven years." The inclusion here of six out of the ten sevens following the words "seven worlds" (*shevah olamot*) in *Sefer Yetzirah* 4:15 shows beyond a doubt that the reappearance of this all-important phrase in chapter 18 of the *Pirke de Rabbi Eliezar* derives directly from the *Sefer Yetzirah* and represents a continuing tradition.

Turning now to the *Zohar*, we are told by Scholem that "the oldest parts, relatively speaking, are sections of the Midrash ha-Ne'lam . . . which

established Eliezer b. Hyracanus also, following the Hekhalot and the *Pirkei de-Rabbi Eliezer*, as one of the main heroes of mystical thought. This section contains the basis of many passages in the main body of the Zohar, which quotes statements to be found only there and develops its themes, stories, and ideas more expansively."[59] In a Zoharic passage we read:

> [Rabbi Eleazar] began by quoting: "The Lord is in His holy palace" . . . (Habakkuk 2:20). When the Holy One, blessed be He, wished to create the world. . . . He looked at the first light, and clothed Himself in it and created the heavens, as it is written "Puts on light like a garment" (Psalm 104:2) and then "stretches out the heavens like a curtain" (ibid.). He looked to make the lower world. He made another palace and entered it, and from it He looked and sketched before Him all the worlds below, and created them. This is the meaning of "The Lord is in His holy palace."[60]

Here we have a concept of cosmic "worlds" associated with more than one "palace." Such a cosmological use of the word for "worlds," here the Aramaic *almin* and its singular *alma*, derives in a direct line from the *Sefer Yetzirah* and the *Pirke de Rabbi Eliezar*, and, though no number is given, its association with the term for "palace," here the Aramaic *hakhala*, reinforces the correlation of this term in Hekhalot literature with the number seven This correlation becomes explicit in a later passage from *Zohar* 2, 164a–65a, which again begins with a reference to the beautiful image of the creative process from Psalm 104:2, the "stretching out" of each of the heavens through the power of the divine light, which produces the "seven firmaments," the Aramaic *rak-i'in*, with the seventh raised above the lower six:

> Rabbi Hiyya began by quoting "[He] covers Himself with light as with a garment, stretching out the heavens like a curtain" (Psalm 104:2). They have interpreted this verse [to mean] that when the Holy One, blessed be He, created the world, He wrapped Himself in the primal light, and with it created the heavens (*Bereshit Rabbah* 3:4). . . . And seven firmaments are stretched out,

concealed in the celestial treasury, as they have explained, and one firmament stands above them.[61]

Thus we see that, from the first two centuries of the common era that produced the Hekhalot literature through much of the *Zohar* in the thirteenth century, as also of the *Temunah* in the fourteenth century, Jewish cosmological thinking was primarily devoted to elaborations of the seven-stage account of creation in the first chapter of Genesis, that it is such a derived doctrine of seven worlds that is the most authentic form of Jewish mystical cosmology. It is only in the fourteenth century that the rival doctrine of four worlds fully emerges in the late additional sections to the *Zohar* entitled the *Ra'aya Meheimna* and the *Tikkunei Zohar*, in the writings of Isaac of Acco, and most importantly in the anonymous *Massekhet Atzilut*, finally to be adopted by the Safed Kabbalists Cordovero and Luria; and through the influence of the Lurianic reformulation of the Zoharic Kabbalah on the subsequent centuries of Jewish mystical development, it has come to be thought of as the only model for Jewish cosmology.

In discussing the development of the four-worlds doctrine, Scholem first asserts that "The use of the term 'world' in the sense of a separate spiritual unit, a particular realm of being, came to the halakhic kabbalists from the heritage of neoplatonism" and that "medieval philosophy knew of three worlds." But then he says:

> However, this did not occur in the development of the Spanish Kabbalah, where the doctrine of the four worlds originated. Rather it had its origin in speculations connected with the interpretation of Isaiah 43:7: "Everything called by my name— for my glory I have created it, have formed it, yea I have made it." The three words used here, creation, formation, and making or achieving (*beri'ah, yezirah, asiyyah*), were interpreted by many authors as pointing to the progressive stages of divine activity.[62]

But in both of these derivations Scholem only shows a basis for three such worlds.[63]

Though the standard Neoplatonic cosmology of emanation can be construed to define four worlds if, to its three spiritual worlds—those of the One, the Divine Mind or Logos, and the World Soul—the material world be added, I would suggest that it is not so much from this standard Neoplatonic model that the Spanish Kabbalists derived their quite different four-worlds doctrine but from that which it carried within it from its Platonic roots and which continued to exert an independent influence, the Pythagorean central concept of the tetrad or Tetractys, earlier illustrated and discussed.

It was Pythagoras who originated the Greek word *kosmos*,[64] whose Latin translation is *mundus* and whose meaning is conveyed through the Hebrew word for world, *olam*. As has been shown:

> The tetractys was held in such reverence by so many, in fact, that syncretists attempted to associate it with the sacred symbols of other religions. Iamblichus early identified it with the oracle at Delphi (*De vita Pythagorae*, xviii), while Johann Reuchlin saw it as the tetragrammaton, J[e]h[o]v[a]h, the four-lettered name of God among the Hebrews. Christian apologists soon noted that the tetractys is an equilateral triangle and used it as the symbol of the Trinity. . . . is the proper number for cosmos because it is the first number with three-dimensional extension; geometrically speaking, it is the smallest number by which the full range of physical extension can be represented. . . . Plato patiently explains the mathematics of the tetrad in the *Timaeus* (31B–32C). . . . explicit delineation of specific tetrads begins in the second century A.D. with . . . Theon of Smyrna. . . . But from then on, the tetrad enjoyed a continuous and prolific tradition, culminating for the renaissance . . . in Agrippa's *De occulta philosophia*. . . .[65]

It is unfortunate that the Pythagorean tradition is today so little recognized that even Scholem—who, as earlier seen, categorized the *Sefer Yetzirah* as the work of a "Jewish Neo-Pythagorean"—failed to see the continuing influence of the Pythagorean tradition on the Kabbalists of fourteenth-century Spain, as on all of Western esoteric traditions. It is also to be lamented that today's leading Kabbalah scholars are largely unconcerned with the subject of kabbalistic cosmology here being centrally addressed.

But the fourteenth-century Kabbalists who adopted the four worlds of Pythagorean cosmology had to confront and overcome the rival kabbalistic cosmology of seven worlds going back, via the *Pirke de Rabbi Eliezar* and the *Sefer Yetzirah,* to Genesis. This they did by integrating these seven worlds-firmaments-heavens-palaces-aeons into their new four-worlds cosmology, assigning them to the second world of Beriah to which the Throne of Glory was also assigned. As Scholem has shown, it is the *Massekhet Atzilut,* the first to clearly call its cosmic divisions "four worlds," that so defines "the world of *beri'ah,* creation, which is essentially the sphere of the throne of God and the seven palaces surrounding it."[66] In the same manner have I integrated these four worlds of the later Kabbalah into my reformulation of the more authentic seven-world model for Jewish cosmology. And this work is devoted to generating a precise geometric model for the Kabbalah that can include both the past orientation of the *Zohar* and the future orientation of Luria within its seven worlds. But this is not the only way in which this work relates the four worlds of the later Kabbalah to the original Jewish cosmology of seven worlds. In chapter 7 we shall see that these two models can be directly correlated with each other. And in chapter 15, which develops a numerical extrapolation to infinity of a central function of the Sabbath Star Diagram, we shall see that the seven worlds of this geometric model also form the lowest division of the four-level structuring of the infinite, the two central numbers of Jewish cosmology again changing places.

If Genesis 1 is the fount of Jewish cosmological thinking continuing to the present day, the fount of Jewish cosmogony, the study not of the order but of the process of creation, is a passage often encountered in this discussion and that surely represents the earliest source of Jewish cosmogony, the ubiquitously repeated verse from Psalm 104:2 in which the Lord God of verse 1, in my translation of verse 2, "wears light like a garment, stretches the heavens

like a curtain." In the Bible it is to be found in various prophetic texts: Jeremiah 10:12 and 51:15; Isaiah 40:22, 42:5, 44:24, and 51:15; and Zechariah 12:1; as well as Job 9:8. In the Bereshit section of the *Midrash Rabba,* it can be found in 1:3, 1:6, 3:4, and 5:5. In the *Pirke de Rabbi Eliezar,* it not only appears in the previously quoted passage from chapter 18 but also in chapter 3. We have already encountered it in two quotations from the main work of the Kabbalah, the *Zohar;* and in what may be considered the earliest formulation of the Kabbalah, that of the *Bahir* in twelfth-century Provence, it appears in verses 22 and 24. It can be found, then, in most references to the creation in both the exoteric and esoteric traditions of Judaism. But though all of these later references add little to the original formulation of Psalm 104:2, this verse can nevertheless be seen to hold the essence of that further articulation to which both the Zoharic and Lurianic Kabbalah are devoted. The following discussion of this verse will not only complete this study of Jewish cosmology, the term that will generally be understood to include cosmogony, but show its coherence with modern scientific cosmology.

What this verse from Psalms would seem most importantly to accomplish is the division of the Godhead into both immanent and transcendent forms. In the image that God "wears light like a garment" lies the kernel of the thought that Luria would most fully develop in his concept of the Tzimtzum, the divine "contraction." For to wear a garment is to fit within its delimitations, which for God must involve a contraction. As the *Zohar* develops this concept of contraction: "A spark of impenetrable darkness flashed within the concealed of the concealed, from the head of Infinity—a cluster of vapor forming in formlessness, thrust in a ring. Deep within the spark gushed a flow . . . concealed within the concealed of the mystery of *Ein Sof.* It split and did not split its aura, was not known at all, until under the impact of splitting, a single, concealed, supernal point shone."[67] The initial process of contraction, beginning with the flash of an impenetrably dark "spark" from the innermost recess of Ein Sof, which thrusts itself "in a ring," ends with the shining forth of a supernal point within the enclosure of this ring. In the Zoharic understanding, the further process of cosmic development involves the successive extensions of this *point* of primordial light into a larger *field* of primordial light:

> The primordial point is inner radiance—there is no way to gauge its translucency, tenuity, or purity until an expanse expanded from it. The expansion of that point becomes a palace, in which the point was clothed—a radiance unknowable . . . yet not as gossamer or translucent as the primordial point. That palace expanded an expanse: primordial light . . . From here on, this expands into this, this is clothed in this. . . . Although a garment, it becomes the kernel of another layer.[68]

This primordial point is not only composed of "inner radiance" but contains all the light that is to extend, in formed "palaces," into the residual or outermost field of "primordial light." Such an infinitely condensed ball of primal matter extending outward to fill cosmic space would seem very much like the current scientific cosmology of the big bang.

But this process is significantly described in the verse from Psalms not simply as an extension but as a stretching. Though Isaiah 40:22, 42:5, and 44:24, have parallel passages relating the word for "stretches," *noteh*, with that for "spreads," *rakia*, a word related to the word for "firmament," and our verse from Psalms is mistranslated thus in the JPS edition of the Hebrew Bible, these terms would seem to define conflicting notions, *rakia* a process of spreading from within, of pushing outward, and *noteh* a process of stretching from without, of an outward pulling. Here it would be the field of "primordial Light" that is exerting an attractive energy upon the innermost ball of light, causing it to stretch into the seven firmaments of the Hekhalot tradition and its successors, the creative process thus involving an interaction of the immanent and transcendent aspects of the divine.

This is the most profound implication of our verse and it accords with the central insight demonstrated in all forms of sacred science,[69] the understanding conveyed through the first of Pythagorean writers, Philolaus: "The world's nature is a harmonious compound of Limited and Unlimited elements; similar is the totality of the world in itself, and of all it contains."[70] This is the idealized relationship we have earlier seen to hold between the side and the diagonal of the square, between the rational and the irrational aspects of number. But what our verse from Psalms adds to this understanding is the further identifications of the "Limited" elements with substance and of the "Unlimited" elements with process, the process of stretching that our verse would seem to be telling us is derived from the field surrounding the central globe from which all the matter of the universe is to be drawn, a relationship enshrined in the basic union that language also makes between the subject and the verb.

We shall soon see that an even closer analogue to scientific cosmology is provided by the Lurianic concept of Tzimtzum, which more clearly than the *Zohar* involves first a contraction of the divine to a point and then its withdrawal around that point:

> You should know that at the beginning . . . there was no empty or open space; the light of the Infinite was everywhere. . . . So the infinite contracted itself in the middle of its light, at its very central point, withdrawing to the circumference and the sides, leaving an open space in between. . . . This empty space is circular, the same on all sides, and the World of Emanation and all the other worlds are to be found inside that circle, with the light of the Infinite uniformly surrounding it.[71]

To complement the Zoharic "inner radiance," we here have the divine contraction "in the middle of its light," and so a point also composed of the infinite light. Similarly, the Zoharic field of "primordial light," is comparable to the Lurianic "surrounding" "light of the Infinite" with the difference that the Zoharic field extends without limit from the central point while the Lurianic original light has been withdrawn to surround the finite sphere produced by the process of the Tzimtzum. If we now adopt the Lurianic version, then between the two sources of light[72] of our synthesized cosmic model, the innermost light at the central point and the surrounding light, is the "empty space," termed the *tehiru*, which still holds a minute residue of the surrounding light that had been largely exhausted in the process of its withdrawal, this residue termed the *reshimu*. In this case it would be this *reshimu* that could be thought to exert a stretching energy upon the central ball of light. But before we review the analogue to this process provided by the latest news from outer space, there is another element of our verse to be considered.

The final observation in our verse from Psalms is the comparison of the heavens thus stretched out to a "curtain" or, as we have seen it translated in one of our earlier quotations, to a veil, the latter suggesting a wide-meshed or netted, gauzelike cloth. But if the *tehiru* has been largely exhausted of its light, its blackness would show through such a veil, *dok*, giving its stretched-out heavens the gray color that seems more appropriate to their subsequent definition as firmaments, that which also conceals what is behind it.

This largely vacuum state of the Lurianic cosmic space may finally be compared to the vacuum thought to permeate outer space in the scientific model of cosmology. And what is true of this scientific vacuum in the latest version of quantum cosmology is that it is now held responsible for the accelerating expansion of the universe, the result of applying Einstein's "cosmological constant," a force of cosmic antigravity supposed to counteract the force of gravity, to the observations of supernovae in 1998 that seem to reveal such cosmic acceleration:

> Einstein's cosmological term . . . does not depend on position or time—hence the name "cosmological constant." The force caused by the constant operates even in the complete absence of matter or radiation. Therefore, its source must be a curious energy that resides in empty space. The cosmological constant endows the void with an almost metaphysical aura. . . . the calculated vacuum energy is roughly 120 orders of magnitude larger than the energy contained in all the matter in the universe.[73]

It is the force of antigravity, which "resides in empty space," that is now thought to have overcome the force of gravity to produce "an accelerating expansion of the universe."[74] Though the formulations of scientific cosmology do not allow for the concept of an infinite surrounding light that I have elsewhere shown to provide the most intellectually satisfying solution of some of the problems of quantum cosmology,[75] its latest reformulation seems particularly coherent with the Lurianic concept of the *tehiru* or cosmic space as a virtual vacuum and, particularly in its understanding that "The energy of the universe is dominated by empty space,"[76] suggests how Luria's cosmic space could operate to "stretch the heavens" in accordance with Psalm 104:2.

It is the synthesis of the Zoharic central point of cosmic expansion and reservoir of its substance with the Lurianic circumscription of this expansion within the cosmic space produced through the Tzimtzum that can best explain the cosmological insight of Psalm 104:2, one that has inspired so much repetitive confirmation of its meaningfulness in the history of Jewish thought, and it also provides a framework of Jewish cosmology both coherent with the latest scientific evidence and with the model to be generated in this work, one taken to the seven geometric expansions whose number derives from what we have seen to be that most authentic form of Jewish cosmology defined in the opening chapter of Genesis.

The main attempt of this section has been to develop a clearer history of kabbalistic cosmology prior to its adoption of the four-worlds doctrine, and it has shown its central model to be one of seven worlds, a model deriving from all the earlier forms of Jewish cosmology going back to the first chapter of Genesis. The earlier discussion of the Hexagram of Creation has further shown the hexagram to be integrated with this Sabbatical cosmic structure. In the development of the Sabbath Star Diagram that is to follow, we shall see how the hexagram can precisely model all seven of the cosmic worlds or dimensions whose pervasiveness in earlier Jewish cosmology we have just been tracing, doing so in ways that seem uncanny in their correlations with major principles of the Kabbalah.

Because the new model for the Jewish mystical tradition that will be developed in this work is composed wholly of hexagrams taken to the seventh expansion of this form, it has first been necessary to establish the ancient Hebraic provenance of this geometric form and of the cosmology of seven worlds. We are now to see how this six-pointed Jewish star may be integrated with the kabbalistic Tree of Life Diagram to provide a new model for the Kabbalah.

CHAPTER TWO

The Sabbath Star Diagram

DISCOVERING THE GEOMETRIC SOURCE OF THE TREE OF LIFE DIAGRAM

If God is a geometer, as Kepler surmised, the principles of His operations can be taught to an intelligent kindergarten class, as indeed Rudolph Steiner has shown in the practice of the Waldorf schools he founded.* The best place to begin such a geometric study of the nature and evolution of the cosmos is with the hexagram, which chapter 1 has shown to be traditionally associated both with the processes of creation and the Jewish esoteric tradition since the beginning of Genesis. In the geometric analyses to follow, all that will be required is the ability to distinguish between two geometric figures, the hexagram and the hexagon, and to have that confidence on one's ability to follow a discussion of such simple geometric figures as will focus the mind on the diagram under consideration and perhaps even lead one to attempt its construction.

For the Sabbath Star Diagram, however beautiful its form, is a geometric meditation that reveals its cosmic secrets only to the person who engages in its construction. It is precisely for this reason that esoteric geometry in its most vital form—and in this form it is a great power capable of inspiring a culture to the construction of pyramids and cathedrals—has always been a practice, a form of spiritual discipline. But the geometric forms that have been most enlarging to the consciousness have been the circular, symmetrical mandalas and yantras whose cosmological records the mind can remember when lifted by such geometric meditations to its higher powers. The Sabbath Star Diagram is such a mandala, and its successively more complex versions have their origin in the elemental mandala of the hexagram, honored by so many sacred traditions, that the Jewish people have made their own.

To begin the discovery and development of the new model for the Kabbalah being here proposed, we shall start with the necessary distinction between the hexagram and the hexagon, whose forms and relationship are given in figure 2.1.

---

*The material in this chapter appeared largely verbatim in chapter 6 of *The Secret Doctrine of the Kabbalah*. Readers who feel sufficiently familiar with this material may wish to skip ahead to the final section entitled "A General Preview (see page 48)."

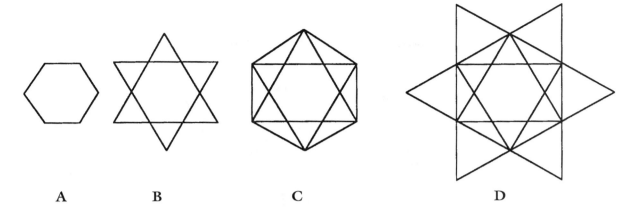

Figure 2.1. A, the hexagon; B, the hexagram; C, a hexagram within a hexagon; D, a second hexagram constructed on the point hexagon of a smaller hexagram.

It is from the simple geometric process of constructing larger hexagrams from the point hexagon or double points of the smaller hexagram contained within its own inner hexagon that the Sabbath Star Diagram may be said to originate. If, as earlier argued, the initial geometric processes associated with creation involve the drawing of a hexagram from the six radial arc points of an original, premanifest circle, then the further acts of creation would fittingly involve the building of ever more complex patterns of hexagrams upon this primordial base. But when a third hexagram is constructed by this process, the remarkable inner pattern shown in figure 2.2 is revealed.

When three hexagrams are constructed one upon the double points of the other, the simplest way of building an enlarging structure of hexagrams, the remarkable inner pattern they form is none other than the Tree of Life Diagram in almost all of its details. As this kabbalistic diagram will provide the key for further construction of the underlying hexagram diagram, it will be necessary now to give a brief review of the history and structure of the Tree of Life Diagram.

The two main elements in the design of the Tree of Life Diagram, the ten Sefirot-named spheres (*sphere* being one etymological derivation of the word *sefirot*, the plural form of the word *sefirah*) and the twenty-two paths or channels connecting them, first make their appearance in the *Sefer Yetzirah*.

There ten such Sefirot are specified, apparently corresponding to the ten basic numbers, and the twenty-two letters of the Hebrew alphabet are divided into the groups of the three "mother letters," the seven double letters, and the twelve single letters that complete the formal elements of cosmic creation, this being the book (*sefer*) of the world of Formation (*yetzirah*). Although the *Sefer Yetzirah* does not go further to give the Sefirot their familiar names or to place them in a drawn diagram clearly associated with the Tree of Life, it does define the two essential elements to which the later-drawn versions will largely hold, the ten spheres called Sefirot and the twenty-two variously lettered paths connecting them. The recognized names of the Sefirot begin to appear in the *Bahir* and the *Zohar*, but it is not until the work of the sixteenth-century Kabbalists in the Safed community of Palestine that the names and diagrammatic positions of the Sefirot and paths are fully and openly disclosed. It is in Moses Cordovero's *Pardes Rimmonim* (Garden of Pomegranates), written in 1548 in Safed and first published in 1591 in Cracow, Poland, that the Tree of Life Diagram finally emerges from the obscurity of at least three hundred years of verbal allusion in its generally accepted modern proportions, the previous 1516 publication of the diagram in Paulus Rincius's *Portae Lucis*, a Latin translation of Joseph Gikatilla's *Sha'arei Orah* (Gate of Light), having eccentric proportions. Cordovero's disclosure is

Figure 2.2. The Emerging Tree of Life Diagram

most important because it combines a detailed commentary on the Sefirot and the channels with a drawn diagram depicting them. I have elsewhere analyzed the discrepancies between this commentary and illustration[1] and shown that together they appear to validate the two major forms of the diagram that have been prominent in the kabbalistic tradition, that which can be associated with Cordovero since it is consistent with his written commentary, and that which is closer to the illustrated diagram and can be associated with Isaac Luria. It was probably the growing influence of the Lurianic version of the Tree in the period intervening between the writing and publication of the *Pardes* that accounts for the presumed editorial tampering with the original Cordovero diagram to bring it into closer conformity with the different version of the Tree popularized by Luria that had gained in authority during this time.

Luria's story is probably the most remarkable in the history of the Kabbalah. He arrived in Safed in the year of Cordovero's death, 1570, and was able to study briefly with the older master before himself attracting a distinguished circle of learned disciples.

Noted for his saintly behavior and spiritual power, he gave oral instruction to his disciples both in his original kabbalistic system and in modes of mystical meditation, and there are suggestions that he believed himself to be the Messiah ben Joseph. Though he was only thirty-eight when he died in an epidemic a brief two years later, the legend of his saintly life and the writings of his disciples on his theoretical teachings had an immense effect on the subsequent history of the Kabbalah, which in the Jewish tradition has been almost entirely Lurianic for the past four hundred years. As developed by his disciples, primarily by Chayyim Vital in the *Eitz Chayyim* (Tree of Life), there are three main principles of the new Lurianic Kabbalah: the Tzimtzum, or "contraction" of the divine light, which is followed by the light's retraction to leave the primordial circular space in which the creation could take place; the Shevirah, or "breaking of the vessels" of the original Sefirot, which enter the cosmic space from the surrounding light on a line of light identified with the singular figure of Adam Kadmon, and which were not strong enough to contain the divine influx; and the Tikkun, the cosmic restoration by which the Sefirot are reconstituted as the five divine personalities or Partzufim. Luria calls the cosmic world of the originally emanated Sefirot the Olam ha-Tohu, the world of chaos, because in his system the Sefirot at this stage existed only as points of light without the connecting paths that could give them structural stability. When asked to explain the difference between his system and that of Cordovero, he answered that Cordovero's concern was with the Olam ha-Tohu while his was with the Olam ha-Tikkun.[2]

Although Cordovero's understanding of the original emanation of the Sefirot is not in accord with that attributed to him by Luria, the basic distinction made by Luria does hold true. Cordovero, who may be considered the culmination of the earlier Zoharic tradition, is primarily concerned with the cosmic process of emanation, and Luria, who begins the later continuous history of Jewish mystical theory and practice that has been largely associated with the Hasidim, is primarily concerned with the cosmic process of reconstruction. It is the breach between these two different foci of attention that the Sabbatical structure developed in chapter 1 hopes to heal by providing the larger cosmic structure that can contain them both.

This distinction does not only hold between the earlier Zoharic Kabbalah and the later Lurianic Kabbalah but also between the two streams of Kabbalah that begin to diverge from each other during the Renaissance. For the Christian scholars who begin the serious study of the Kabbalah at this time[3] are primarily students of the *Zohar* and the *Sefer Yetzirah*, both of which were published in Latin translations before they appeared in the original. Although the transmission of Lurianic concepts was widespread enough for the able Hebrew scholar John Milton to incorporate the doctrine of the Tzimtzum into *Paradise Lost* within only one century,[4] the major "Lurianic" writings were circulated in manuscript, the most authoritative version of the *Eitz Chayyim* not being published until 1784, and they are still largely unavailable in translation.

But it is not only in their primary concepts that the Christian and Jewish Kabbalah begin to diverge at this time; it is also in their versions of the Tree of Life Diagram. While the Christian tradition seems to have largely adopted the model as defined in the textual commentary of Cordovero, the Jewish tradition has used the Lurianic version of the Tree almost as exclusively, the version approximated in the drawn diagram of the *Pardes*. Thus both major versions of the diagram may be said to have made their first public appearance in the 1591 publication of the *Pardes Rimmonim*, a fact that authenticates both versions as belonging to the genuine Jewish kabbalistic tradition. In the following analysis, therefore, both versions of the Tree will be accepted while the difference between them will be maintained, the Cordovero diagram being regarded as the Tree of Emanation and the Luria diagram as the Tree of Return, the way of return being understood not to go backward but forward to the upper Do. Both versions give the same names to the Sefirot: Keter (Crown); Chokhmah (Wisdom); Binah (Understanding); Chesed (Mercy); Gevurah (Judgment); Tiferet (Beauty); Netzach (Eternity); Hod (Splendor); Yesod (Foundation); and Malkhut (Kingdom). But they differ in the positions accorded to some of the paths. The Cordovero diagram contains paths from Malkhut to Netzach and Hod that do not appear in the Luria diagram, while the latter has paths from Chokhmah to Gevurah and from Binah to Chesed that do not appear in the former. Although the writings of Luria's disciples do not contain a drawn version of his diagram, the descriptions of the paths are clear enough, particularly in his commentary on the Talmud and at the end of his edition of the *Sefer Yetzirah*, to enable the construction of such a diagram, and it has appeared without proper identification in more than one modern work on the Kabbalah.[5] As earlier noted, the *Sefer Yetzirah* divides the Hebrew alphabet into the three mother letters, the seven double letters, and the twelve single letters; similarly the Tree of Life Diagram in both versions features three horizontal paths, seven vertical paths, and twelve diagonal paths. Figure 2.3 gives both forms of the Tree of Life Diagram, the Cordovero Tree of Emanation and the Luria Tree of Return or Tikkun.

With this brief introduction to the form of the Tree of Life Diagram, we can now return to the underlying hexagram diagram for whose principles the traditional Tree holds the key and recognize how the developing Sabbath Star Diagram can already unlock one major puzzle of the Tree. This is the relationship to the ten Sefirot of an eleventh non-Sefirah called Da'at, which is placed in many diagrams at the otherwise conspicuously empty spot at the center of the upper kite shape. For Da'at, translated as "Knowledge" and signifying for the Kabbalist the ultimate gnosis at the heart of this mystical tradition, is located at the exact center of the larger diagram from which the Tree would seem to have been derived. Although the particular association of Da'at with Chokhmah and Binah goes back at least as far as the "Idra Rabba" section of the *Zohar* and informs the "Chabad" tradition founded by the original Lubavitcher Rabbi, all those who attempt to make a triad of Chokhmah and Binah with Da'at (the three words whose initial letters compose the name Chabad) rather than with Keter

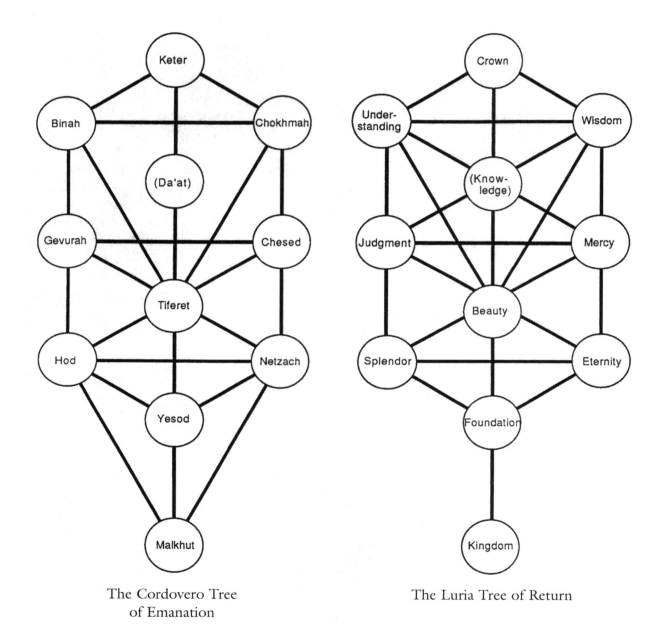

The Cordovero Tree
of Emanation

The Luria Tree of Return

Figure 2.3. The Tree of Life Diagrams

are normally careful not to claim it as a Sefirah. The placement of the non-Sefirah Da'at at this precise spot has never before been satisfactorily explained, nor the reason why it cannot be treated simply as another Sefirah, but it should now be clear that the source of its special treatment lies in its position at the true center of an underlying diagram containing six such trees[6] and that, though this knowledge has been largely lost, there must have been some who once could claim it.

If we look again at the Tree of Life Diagram that emerges from this construction of three hexagrams, it can be seen that it lacks only the Sefirah Yesod, with the two paths connecting it to Netzach and Hod, and the three paths of the central line between Keter and Malkhut. Now, if the Tree of Life Diagram is, indeed, derived from a more basic geometric construction composed only of hexagrams, then it would follow that these missing elements of the Tree diagram should also be somehow produced by hexagrams, though this cannot be accomplished through the simple addition of the fourth hexagram in the previously established mode of progression.

But once the conviction has been reached that the complete diagram underlying that of the Tree is composed entirely of hexagrams, that every line in it must be a line of a hexagram, one can then proceed to construct the necessary additional hexagrams using the Tree of Life Diagram as a key to such further construction.

To do this, one should begin by drawing lines along the paths already established between Netzach and Hod with Yesod, lines that cross Yesod and extend until they meet lines with which they can define a new hexagram, these lines joining them from the other five directions of the diagram to maintain the diagram's symmetry. The hexagram thus formed can be seen in figure 2.4.

As figure 2.4 should show, the hexagram whose construction manifests the previously missing Yesod with its two paths to Netzach and Hod discloses another principle of hexagram construction than that by which the first three hexagrams had been formed. These could be built in an inward or outward direction by the same simple procedure of either inscribing a smaller hexagram within the inner

Figure 2.4. The Yesod Crossing

hexagon formed by an originating hexagram, as in figure 2.1C, or by extending the sides of its outer hexagon until they form a new enlarged hexagram, as in figure 2.1D. We may call this most natural way of building infinitely larger or smaller hexagrams the whole-step progression, and it involves an alternation of orientation at each whole step. This change of orientation is determined by the very structure of the hexagram, whose inner hexagon defines a different orientation from that of its points. Since the outer hexagon formed by aligning two of the hexagram points becomes the inner hexagon of the next larger inclosing hexagram, we are really talking only about the dual-oriented nature of the hexagram, which rotates 90° at each whole-step progression of hexagram construction as shown in figure 2.5.

The Yesod hexagram, however, involves a second important way of constructing hexagrams that may be called the half-step progression inasmuch as it has produced a hexagram that, though larger than the

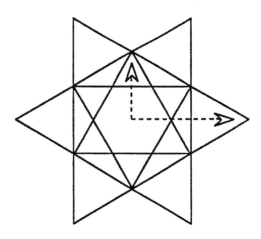

Figure 2.5. Orientations of the Hexagram

previously constructed third hexagram, is not as large as the hexagram that can be formed from the point hexagon or double points of this third hexagram in the regular whole-step method of hexagram expansion. Rather than a product of the third hexagram, it seems to be, like the third hexagram, itself,

built upon the base of the second hexagram, but with a different manner of construction. Figure 2.6B shows that the points of the second largest hexagram fall midway on the lines forming the fourth hexagram, lines that are parallel to the lines of the second hexagram and lie on the same axis of orientation. Although discovered through plotting the Yesod crossing, the hexagram thus formed would seem to be most easily constructed directly from the single points of the second hexagram.

There are, then, two ways of constructing larger hexagrams that are both first demonstrated in relationship to the second hexagram of the elementary version of the Sabbath Star Diagram now being constructed. From this second hexagram, two larger hexagrams can be formed, as shown in figure 2.6.

As can be seen, the whole-step progression (based upon the alignment through two points shown in figure 2.6A) extends the orientation of the smaller hexagram's outer hexagon, while the half-step progression (based upon the alignment through a single point shown in figure 2.6B) extends the orientation of its points. But since the half step is measured as a half step past the previous whole step, it is really one and one-half steps beyond the hexagram on whose single points it is constructed.

What is most significant about this difference in construction, however, is that the whole-step progression produces a more stable hexagram than the half-step progression since the direction of a line connecting two separated points is clearly defined while that based on a single point is uncertain and in terms of construction harder to draw with accuracy. This distinction can be more easily appreciated if we move from a two-dimensional line to a three-dimensional board, such a board obviously being more precariously balanced on one pivot than on two. In terms of visual appearance as well, these lines convey different aesthetic qualities to the symbolic understanding of the mind, the dual-supported line conveying an impression of stable balance and the singly supported line an impression of precarious tension. There is no doubt that something novel is being introduced to the diagram by this fourth hexagram, and its expressive form can help to reveal both its encoded meaning and, through this, the first princi-

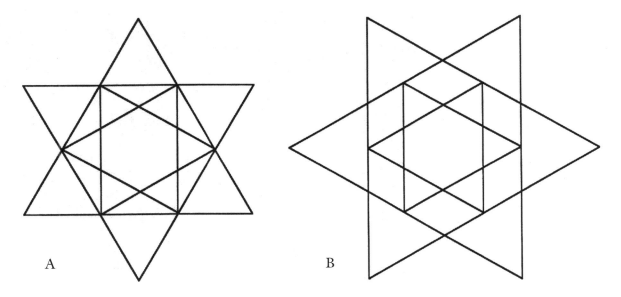

A   B

Figure 2.6. The Two Ways of Constructing Hexagrams

ple of diagram interpretation. For each new form of hexagram that has and will become manifest is most expressive, one whose interpretation will be dependent upon and display a new approach to geometric interpretation.

We have seen that the half-step hexagram following the third hexagram gives an impression of instability and further that it is connected by the key of the Tree of Life Diagram with the Sefirah Yesod. Now, this is the Sefirah that the kabbalistic tradition associates with sex, for in the version of the Tree placed upon the cosmic body of Adam Kadmon, the primordial man, it defines the site of the sexual organ. The association of sex with instability would seem to take us to the myth of the Fall.[7] In the earlier discussion of the creation account, we saw that the garden world was a product of the third day and that this could be associated with the third world of Yetzirah, which is, indeed, where a kabbalistic tradition places the Garden of Eden and the Fall of man. Particularly in the Lurianic system presented in Vital's *Eitz Chayyim*, the Fall of the Adam of Genesis is understood to occur in the spiritual realm of Yetzirah and to be the precipitating cause of the final manifestation of the fourth material world of Asiyah, our world. This would suggest an associa-

tion of the kabbalistic cosmic worlds not only with the days of creation but also with the progression of whole-step hexagrams in the Sabbath Star Diagram.

The first stage, represented by the first hexagram, defines the hexagram, with all its implicit meanings of expansion, contraction, and balance as the model of construction. The stage represented by the second hexagram defines the basic process of growth as the whole-step progression involving a change of orientation. But the dualistic nature of this second hexagram, which its very number implies, would seem to express itself through the two differently oriented hexagrams that it spawns, both of which together form the next stage. This third stage repeats the whole-step progression that had been accomplished by the second stage but adds a new half step, one whose form may be said to manifest an instability already latent within the changed orientation of the second stage.

Now if these stages can be associated with the cosmic worlds, as previously suggested, then the geometric descriptions of the hexagrams just given can also serve as archetypal definitions of the first three of these worlds. Thus the world of Atzilut (Emanation) can be seen to define the basic cosmic functions associated with the hexagram, the world of Beriah (Creation), a basic shift of orientation to a creative dualism, and the world of Yetzirah (Formation) to be made up of its two resulting parts, one stable and one unstable. On this basis, the third hexagram, constructed through the more stable dual supports of the whole-step progression, would seem to be identifiable with the unfallen state of Yetzirah, while the fourth hexagram, constructed through the more precarious single support of the half-step progression, seems to signify a predisposition to the Fall or to be identifiable with it and transitional to the fourth world's further fracturing of unity into multiplicity.

The peculiar characteristics of the fourth hexagram not only suggest an analogy between the developing diagram and the worlds of the Kabbalah but also one to music. For the movement of one whole step from a starting point, followed by another whole step, followed by a half step has an obvious musical analogue in the tonal intervals of the rising diatonic scale, which begins with the similar progression of two whole tones followed by a half or semitone that is easily recognizable through their familiar Solfeggio names: Do, Re, Mi, and Fa. If we can so associate this first tetrachord of the diatonic scale with the hexagrams earlier associated with the first three kabbalistic worlds, this would suggest that the diatonic scale contains a second key for further construction of the hexagram diagram, one that reinforces the earlier implications of the geometric-musical keys to the creation account. Where the creation account appears to associate the hexagram form with a Sabbatical cosmic structure contained within the harmonic series, the diatonic scale would seem to suggest another octave structure to the expanding hexagram diagram that would bring this diagram to the same seventh world of the Sabbath. But if each of the future worlds are to be as tonally complete as the third world, having what can be considered two semitone hexagrams in accordance with this model, this would place the octave within the first half of the seventh such world and give to this seventh world a special character as that which both consummates and transcends the cosmic octave. It further suggests that the developing diagram will have to be extended beyond the four

worlds of the classical Kabbalah in accordance with the two modes of musical progression, harmonic and diatonic, that seem to be part of the esoteric cosmology here being decoded.

Chapter 1 showed that the cosmology of Genesis is based on a triple association of harmonics, geometry, and number, with the mythological interpretation of the laws of sound and form they reveal. In the creation account, a seven-day pattern is inextricably tied to both the harmonic series and the hexagram form; and the further expansion of the single hexagram diagram into one of multiple hexagrams would now seem to relate the progression of hexagrams with the structure of tones appearing in the major diatonic scale, a structure that has been held since Plato's *Timaeus* to contain a cosmic code. In this scale the various tones that emerge in the harmonic series are organized into a particular succession of intervals interjected between the fundamental tone and its first octave overtone. Unlike the discoverable laws of the harmonic series or of "gnomonic" hexagram construction, that in which a geometric expansion results in a form similar to the original, the diatonic scale is like the Tree of Life Diagram in having an apparently arbitrary arrangement of its two tetrachord parts.[8] And it is the apparently arbitrary structures of the Tree of Life Diagram and the diatonic scale that prove to be the twin keys to unlocking the construction principles for the ultimate cosmological diagram here being developed.

Because the diatonic scale appears to be so closely correlated with the hexagram progression of this diagram, and this despite the numerical incongruence of harmonic and $\sqrt{3}$ geometric proportions, the Solfeggio names of its tones will henceforth be adopted to define their hexagram counterparts, a procedure that will not only simplify the identification of hexagrams but also reveal their analogous harmonic relationships. This is particularly useful in the case of the fourth or Fa hexagram at which the twin keys meet. As it was to accommodate the irregular placement of the Sefirah Yesod and its upper paths that its half-step or half-tone method of construction was developed, so it seems not accidental that this Sefirah should mean Foundation; for the Fa hexagram, more clearly designated in figures 2.5 and 2.7, will provide the foundation for the structure of those later Sol, La, and Ti hexagrams, built upon it in whole-step progressions, that, with the upper Do, will form the geometric counterpart to the second tetrachord of the diatonic scale and the dominant hexagrams of their respective worlds.[9]

Its construction, then, also establishes a second whole-step progression that goes back to the beginning and that emanates the principle of duality in ever more manifest forms throughout the evolution of the first three worlds. The drawing of the fourth hexagram may have manifested both the Sefirah Yesod and its two connecting paths, but contemplation of the structure of the diagram will reveal that this Sefirah and its two paths are actually derived from two different sources. Comparison of figures 2.2 and 2.4 should make it apparent that the point of Keter is derived from the first hexagram while its paths to Chokhmah and Binah are derived from the second hexagram. In the same way, it would appear that the Sefirah Yesod is really the product of an unmanifest hexagram in the half-step position after the second hexagram and that it is only the paths to Netzach and Hod that are produced by the fourth hexagram. On the basis of our musical analogy, which should now be extended to the Solfeggio names for the full ascending chromatic scale—Do, Di, Re, Ri, Mi, Fa, Fi, Sol, Si, La, Li, Ti, Do—this unmanifest hexagram would correlate with the Ri tone. The Ri hexagram can be considered unmanifested because it is possible to construct the Tree of Life Diagram without it, the Tree and the diatonic scale here agreeing on the elements essential for creation. In the earlier discussion of the fourth hexagram, it was said to mark a shift from the whole-step progression that seemed to indicate something like a Fall.

We are now better prepared to understand something about the latency of those forces associated in this diagram with the half-step progression. If we divide the first three worlds into the two aspects paralleling the tones of the chromatic or twelve-tone scale, Atzilut would be represented by Do-Di, Beriah by Re-Ri, and Yetzirah by Mi-Fa. Now when the full fourth-world diagram is devel-

oped in the following chapter, the reason why the second half of Atzilut (Di) can be considered unmanifestable will become clear. Though its area becomes defined, it cannot manifest a separate hexagram consistent with the matrix that emerges in this full fourth-world diagram, a matrix that provides the geometry of what may be considered the more interior constituents of reality, its "soul." On the other hand, the development of this full fourth-world diagram does manifest the previously unmanifest Ri hexagram defining the second half of Beriah. We thus have a progression from an *unmanifestable* second stage or aspect of Atzilut, to an *unmanifest* second stage of Beriah, and finally to a *manifest* second stage of Yetzirah. If the Fa hexagram is viewed as signifying an introduction of evil into creation, then the seeds of this evil can be seen to extend at least as far back as Atzilut.

But viewing the diagram in its full geometric complexity and regularity should suggest that this view of the Fall is, itself, limited in vision and that the half-step progression, which had seemed to signify such a Fall, is a necessary aspect of a cosmos geometrically defined from the beginning in terms of diagrammatic surfaces that harmonize the polarity of unified point with the dualistic extension of line, the first stage of each world representing its contracted form and the second stage its expansive form. Furthermore, the different degrees to which this expansive aspect is manifested in these worlds can further help to define their archetypal natures. They reveal Atzilut to be the world of indivisible unity, Beriah to be the world of pure potentiality, and Yetzirah to be the world in which such potentiality finally becomes manifest as form. And since this second aspect evolves thus slowly through the first three worlds only for the ostensible purpose of manifesting the Sefirah Yesod, this should tell us much about the significance of this Sefirah. In the elementary version of the Sabbath Star Diagram derived directly from the Tree of Life Diagram, the unique geometric process needed to define the position of this Sefirah is one that, at all stages, goes counter to the rules of the whole-step progression everywhere else in force. It seems to reveal a process of individuation whose production may well be considered the driving force behind the emanation of the supernal worlds, one that is to become the Foundation (the meaning of Yesod) of the higher work that may also be said to constitute the purpose of the creation. Such an understanding of Yesod as the Foundation of higher spiritual work rather than of sex, or of the conversion of such sexual energy to this spiritual end, is also consistent with the traditional identification of this Sefirah with the biblical Joseph, the Tzaddik ("righteous one," whose category is also traditionally identified with this Sefirah) who resisted sexual temptation.

But though the Fa hexagram is to become the foundation for those later hexagrams whose successive whole-step progressions upon it complete the diagrams of their successive cosmic worlds, it is not on its basis that we are brought to the fourth world of Asiyah by the key of the Tree of Life Diagram. And the way this key will bring us to a fourth-world hexagram form exactly a whole step beyond the third or Mi hexagram will further reinforce the suggestions of a contrary quality to the Fa hexagram arising from this key, particularly the fact that it is the only structural form in the Elementary Sabbath Star Diagram not generated by the whole-step progression from the original Do hexagram. But this is jumping ahead, for we have yet to complete our derivation of the Tree of Life Diagram. There remains the decisive middle pillar or line between Keter and Malkhut.

To derive the missing line between Keter and Malkhut, we should, as earlier, simply proceed to draw it, extending the line beyond Keter as far upward from the central Da'at point as it goes down from it to Malkhut, for symmetry must clearly be a guiding principle of this diagram. This line should extend from point to point of the third hexagram. But since the first rule of this diagram is that all its lines must be parts of a hexagram, we must now construct an equilateral triangle using this line as its base and then cross it with its inverse triangle. This can be easily done by aligning the other two lines of this triangle with two points of the third Mi hexagram and its inverse triangle with the angle formed by a point of the second Re hexagram, as shown in figure 2.7.

This completes the Tree of Life Diagram with lines formed only from hexagrams but it clearly unbalances the diagram. The procedure has obviously to be repeated on the other side of the vertical line forming the middle pillar and then on the other two axes of symmetry passing through the points of the first and third hexagrams, which follow the same orientation, a procedure that will lead to

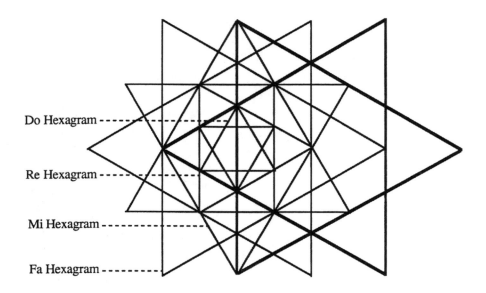

Figure 2.7. Initial Completion of the Hexagram Diagram

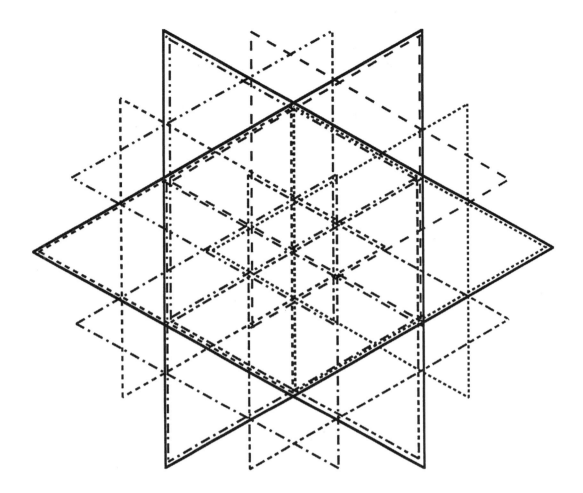

Figure 2.8. The Sabbath Star

the drawing of six hexagrams. But the drawing of these six hexagrams produces a veritable explosion of hexagrams. It looks as though a "big bang" has suddenly taken place in the diagram. And then the wonder of the diagram manifests itself. A seventh star can be seen to form itself without geometric work from the six drawn hexagrams, larger than all of them and located exactly a whole step beyond the third hexagram, the whole step that brings us finally to the kabbalistic fourth world. It seems fitting to name it a Sabbath Star and the diagram after it. It also seems clear that the six worked hexagrams and the seventh embracing star of consummation, which together form the constellation of hexagrams named the Sabbath Star, are symbolic of the creation of the material world as it has been numerologically projected in the first chapter of Genesis. Because of the

importance of the Sabbath Star construct, it will be presented first by itself in a version that will make it easier to distinguish its parts, each of its six component hexagrams being marked by a different form of dashed or dashed-and-dotted lines within the unbroken form of the seventh embracing star.

Though such a construction is not featured in any text of practical or spiritual geometry of which I am aware, it is a potential construction inherent in the recognized geometric progression of one to six to seven: six derived from one will magically produce or contain a seventh. We have already seen how six is the first geometric expression of the unity of the circle. Now, if we join the six points that the radius defines on the circumference of a circle not in the hexagram, as previously, but in a hexagon, and build other hexagons of the same size on each of its sides, we will find that these six close-packed hexagons define the outline of the central hexagon: in a two-dimensional drawing, as opposed to an actual flooring made of hexagonal tiles, the six outer hexagons can be thought of as producing the inner seventh. Six circles will equally enclose a seventh. And this is a geometric property only of sixness. It does not apply to five, seven, or any other number of hexagons or circles. But the magical power of six derived from unity to manifest a seventh is perhaps nowhere so dramatically expressed as in the Sabbath Star we have just seen produced from six symmetrically arranged hexagrams whose bases diametrically connect the six radial arc points of a circle. If Pythagoras was right in asserting that the ultimate nature of reality lies in numbers, by which he meant the various functions and qualities associated with unity, duality, triplicity, and so on, then the manifestation of the One into multiplicity would follow the laws of geometry and in some sense the universe

would have been produced through the workings of six, six acts that together formed the completeness, the harmony, the peace, the sacredness of seven.

Having studied the Sabbath Star separately, we can now place it in the completed Elementary Sabbath Star Diagram, the diagram composed of the minimum number of hexagrams, consistent with symmetry, needed to manifest the Tree of Life Diagram with all its paths and Sefirot. And this also proves to be the number necessary for the Sabbath Star Diagram to define the four kabbalistic worlds culminating in the material world of Asiyah. If we now translate the whole-step progression magically produced by this Sabbath Star construction into the musical terminology of Solfeggio, the tone signified by its larger seventh hexagram would be that termed Fi, and we can speak of the whole construction as the Fi Sabbath Star. And since this Sabbath Star is necessary to complete the derivation of the Tree of Life Diagram from the underlying Sabbath Star

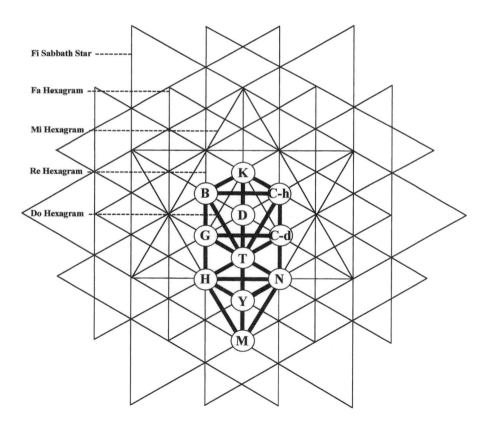

Figure 2.9. The Labeled Sabbath Star Diagram: Elementary Version with the Tree of Emanation

Diagram, it is possible to associate it not only with the big bang of material creation but more specifically with that potential for embodied life in the cosmos ever symbolized by the tree, the very Tree of Life from whose diagram it was discovered.

In figure 2.9, the completed Elementary Sabbath Star Diagram is illustrated with the super-imposed Tree of Emanation but without the further discrimination of its parts that might mar the visual impression of the whole, particularly the way in which the horizontal hexagrams of Re and Fa have been incorporated into an overall matrix design featuring triangles of the same size as the six component triangles of the Re hexagram, an element of the expanded diagram whose significance will be variously developed in the remainder of this work. It should also be noticed that the Fi Sabbath Star overlays the second or Re hexagram signifying Beriah, the world of Creation, and might thus be said to incorporate in manifest form the Berian

archetypes from which the creation was generated.

In the evolving cosmic process conceptually represented by the kabbalistic structure of the four worlds, the archetypes too would seem to evolve through the supernal worlds, chief among which may well be that of the Tree of Life Diagram. For it is in the third world of Yetzirah, the world mythologically represented as Eden in the Kabbalah, that the full outline of the Tree of Life Diagram first most fittingly becomes visible in figure 2.2. Its Yetziric form is clearly that which, in the fourth world, will become the complete Tree of Emanation. Indeed, though figures 2.9 and 2.10 will demonstrate that both forms of the Tree are equally validated by the final process of constructing the Elementary Sabbath Star Diagram, it can also be argued that the fourth-world Sabbath Star effects a change in the Tree diagram, replacing Malkhut's former paths to Netzach and Hod with those of the central column, by which it now has contact with

Figure 2.10. The Sabbath Star Diagram: Elementary Version with the Tree of Return

the upper Tree only through Yesod, and adding the paths criss-crossing Da'at, those from Chokhmah to Gevurah and from Binah to Chesed.

The Sabbath Star Diagram, then, provides a geometric derivation for both major forms of the Tree of Life Diagram that have been present in the kabbalistic tradition since at least sixteenth-century Safed. But in addition it shows that the Tree of Emanation is particularly relevant to the process of emanation up to and including the fourth world of manifest solids and that the Tree of Return has its origin at that very central seventh tone of the spiral octave of creation, after which all is Tikkun. This can be easily seen in the twelve-tone progression of the chromatic Solfeggio scale, in which Fi occupies the central seventh position: Do, Di/ Re, Ri/ Mi, Fa/ **Fi**, Sol/ Si, La/ Li, Ti/Do. It would thus seem that both versions of the Tree are relevant to discussions of the fourth world, but that the Tree of Emanation has more relevance to an understanding of the earlier cosmic worlds, the focus of the Zoharic Kabbalah, while the Tree of Return has more relevance to the future Olam ha-Tikkun, the focus of the Lurianic Kabbalah. These two forms of the Tree are represented consecutively in figures 2.9 and 2.10, the former also marking all its Sefirot as well as all the construction elements and the latter presenting their pure forms; and they are followed by figure 2.11, which also reveals the remarkable coherence between the Elementary Sabbath Star Diagram and the menorah.

Figure 2.11 takes us back to the very first geometric form to be incorporated into the ritual of Jewish observance, the form from which the Tree of Life Diagram itself has been thought to have been derived, that of the menorah. The seven-branched candelabrum can be seen to fit exactly onto the vertical lines that meet at the upper bar of the Mi hexagram. The connection between this earliest external emblem of the Jewish people and the later emblem of its esoteric spirituality, the Tree of Life Diagram, can be seen most immediately by comparing the three essential aspects of both. In both we can find right and left sides and a central shaft that joins and may be said to harmonize them. Moreover, in the description of the menorah given in Exodus

25:31–40, there are further numerical correspondences to be observed. In addition to the shaft and three pairs of branches, there are also ten knobs or spheres and twenty-two bowls. Although there is scholarly dispute about the exact arrangement contemplated by the text and whether the menorah depicted on the Roman Arch of Titus conforms to it, what can be determined from the text is that each branch contains one sphere with flowers and three bowls while the central shaft contains four spheres with flowers and four bowls. Not only do the branches and flowers suggest a tree, then, but the ten spheres suggest the ten Sefirot and the twenty-two bowls the twenty-two paths of the Tree of Life Diagram that, like the menorah, is divided into right, cental, and left parts. Moses was shown the menorah in a vision on Mount Sinai and told that it should be constructed on this visionary pattern: "And look that thou make them [the ark, table, and menorah] after their pattern, which was shewed thee in the mount" (Exod. 25:40). Moses was further instructed to have the menorah made of a single piece of beaten gold by Bezaleel, "in whose heart the Lord had put wisdom" (Exod. 36:2). The menorah, then, was conveyed to Israel through two levels of prophetic vision, first that shown to Moses on the mountain and then that directly communicated to the heart of the inspired craftsman Bezaleel. We can never know the exact nature of the vision on the mount, but it seems not beyond possibility that the "pattern" of the menorah shown to Moses included the underlying Sabbath Star Diagram and revealed the relationship between the menorah and the Tree as both were seen to be contained within it.

In concluding this discussion of the Elementary Sabbath Star Diagram, it will be seen that this representation of the emanation of the four worlds of the medieval Kabbalah was accomplished by the drawing of a special arrangement of exactly ten hexagrams. It will also be remembered that at the very beginning of this work the *Zohar* was quoted as making reference to a "hidden design, holy of holies, a deep structure emerging from thought," which, it was then suggested, might be taken as an allusion to the Sabbath Star Diagram. I should now like to conclude this section with another passage

Figure 2.11. The Menorah within the Elementary Sabbath Star Diagram

from the *Zohar* that seems to describe the basic progression and structure of the Sabbath Star Diagram:

Come and see: With Torah the blessed Holy One created the world. . . . He gazed upon her once, twice, three and four times, then spoke, creating through her. To teach human beings not to err in her, as is written: *Then He saw and declared her, arranged her and probed her. He told humanity* (Job 28:27) . . . The blessed Holy One created what He created corresponding to those four times: *He saw and declared her, arranged her, and*

probed her. Before generating His work, He introduced four words בְּרֵאשִׁית בָּרָא אֱלֹהִים אֵת (*Bereshit bara Elohim et*), *In the beginning God created.* First these four; then הַשָּׁמַיִם the heavens. These correspond to the four times that the blessed Holy One contemplated Torah before actualizing His work of art.[10]

In the Sabbath Star Diagram there are also four processes to be done "before actualizing" the work of creation," the drawing of the four hexagrams that precede the explosion of six hexagrams in the Sabbath

Star signifying this final actualization, all drawn in accordance with the hidden laws (Torah) of this diagram: that all its lines be formed from hexagrams; that the progression be from the first to the second to the third hexagram by the whole-step method; that the progression to the fourth hexagram be by the half-step method; and that this be followed by the remarkable configuration and transmutation of six hexagrams into seven of the Sabbath Star.

If we can accept Zoharic discussion of Sefirot in connection with "paths" and "columns" as denoting a specific diagram because a model of just such a diagram surfaced three hundred years later called the Tree of Life, might we not also find allusions in the Zoharic quotation just referred to that would equally seem to point to the existence and knowledge of the Sabbath Star Diagram had such a diagram ever surfaced before in the tradition? But whether or not such quotations suggest a knowledge of the Sabbath Star Diagram by the author of the *Zohar* and others before him, they should show that there was some geometric model that Kabbalists associated with the processes of creation, that this "mystic and most holy design" existing in the supernal mind not only contained the processes of emanation and material creation but their meaning, and that this divine geometry could be discovered in all levels of the cosmos and reveal its mystic secrets to the knowing. Whatever its origin, the Sabbath Star Diagram seems deeply connected with a basic hexadic geometry at the very heart of the kabbalistic tradition, one that expressed itself most overtly in the two geometric symbols popularized by the Kabbalah since the sixteenth century, the hexagram, or Star of David, and the Tree of Life Diagram. It may perhaps explain the secret of their connection.

THE SCIENCE OF EXPRESSIVE FORM

In relating its major speculations to a specific visual model, the Kabbalah has shown unusual sensitivity to the correlation between form and meaning and to the possibility of conveying this meaning through language. The question of the methodology of kabbalistic geometry, the methodology as well of all the geometric investigations in this work, has now to be more fully considered, and we shall see how the explanation to be given can go far toward validating this linguistic method of geometric interpretation, suggesting how it is possible to "read" a geometric form as a sign, to construe its meaning and translate its absolute truth into the secondary order of mythological explanation that permits it to be verbalized.

If all esoteric traditions have held geometry to be sacred, it is because they understood it to encode the basic principles on which the cosmos is founded, and their geometric practice instructed them in its meaning. This dual practice of construction and interpretation provides a technique for the discovery of cosmic principles that it seems fitting to name the Science of Expressive Form. It can be considered a science because its basis is not arbitrary but determined by the discoverable geometric laws involved in geometric construction. But the forms produced by such construction are also expressive of meanings that go beyond their purely mathematical properties and whose interpretation can be considered an art. The Science of Expressive Form has ever required, then, a synthesis of analytic and intuitive capacities. John Michell, who has himself contributed importantly to modern efforts at recovering the ancient esoteric traditions, has spoken similarly of both its ancient and modern practitioners: "Its masters are both mystics and logicians, insisting that nothing be accepted as true that cannot be proven so in two ways: by reason and poetic intuition." And he further asserts that "there are no esoteric schemes of geometry, no secret laws of mathematics, lost chords or musical harmonies which may not be discovered by searching."[11]

We can begin this attempt to validate the methodology of what is here being called the Science of Expressive Form by considering the now fairly standard distinction between the spatial quality of thought for the Greeks and the contrasting temporal quality of Hebrew thought. As expressed by Thorlief Boman:

It is astounding how far clear thinking depended for the Greeks upon the visual faculty. As evidence we may cite not only Euclid's Geometry,

Aristotle's Logic, and Plato's Doctrine of Ideas, but we should also recall the quite metaphysical significance that Plato accords to the study of geometry—through geometry the highest earthly being is perceived, and true being, i.e. divine being, is betokened. . . . Quite as decided in the Old Testament is the emphasis upon the significance of *hearing* and of the *word in its being spoken*. . . . For the Greeks truth, negatively expressed, is that which is unveiled . . . that which is seen clearly. . . . The corresponding Hebrew concept of truth is expressed by means of derivates of the verb *aman*—"to be steady, faithful." . . . the Hebrews really do not ask what is true in the objective sense but what is subjectively certain, what is faithful in the existential sense. . . . Greek thinking is clear logical knowing; Israelite thinking is deep psychological understanding.[12]

This contrast has been importantly challenged by Elliot R. Wolfson, who has demonstrated that "it is the visual aspect of biblical revelation that informed subsequent mystical (including kabbalistic) hermeneutics. . . . that inspired later Jewish mystics and informed their own revelatory experiences."[13] The Hebraic tradition, then, combines the auditory with the ocular to achieve its deep synthesis of cosmic knowledge, a synthesis that also defines the nature of kabbalistic geometry. For to the spatial logic discernible by the eye, the Kabbalah brings the special interpretative sensitivity of that linguistic logic tied to the laws of hearing that is the characteristic mark of the Hebrew genius. This union of precise geometric construction with a linguistic explication of its felt meaningfulness would also seem to have been true of the Pythagorean mode of philosophical geometry, Pythagoras having been the first to call himself a philosopher as well as being the first independent thinker to ground philosophy on geometric principles. And these principles also inform the cosmology of Plato.

But if on both sides of the Hebrew-Greek divide there were schools of esoteric knowledge that exemplified a synthesis between the orientations of the ear and the eye, finally of time and space, in the later tradition of kabbalistic geometry the Hebraic

approach can be distinguished from the Greek in two important respects. The first is the unique contribution of the Kabbalah to the whole corpus of Western esotericism, that of the Tree of Life Diagram. But it is not alone in its almost exclusive focus on the geometry of the Tree that the Kabbalah can be distinguished from its sister form of sacred geometry practiced by the heirs of Pythagoras. It is also in its peculiarly Jewish mode of interpreting this diagram, a mode that can only be called talmudic in its associative reasoning.

Not only can the methodology of kabbalistic geometry be related to rabbinical hermeneutics but to all forms of literary interpretation. How the practice of interpreting geometric constructs may be related to that of literary texts is further suggested by the analysis of E. D. Hirsch Jr.:

the complex process of construing a text always involves interpretative guesses as well as the testing of those guesses against the text. . . . But the process and psychology of understanding are not reducible to a systematic structure (despite the many attempts to do so), because there is no way of compelling a right guess by means of rules and principles. . . . There can be no canons of *construction*, but only canons [of validation] which help us to choose between alternative meanings that have already been construed from the text. . . . What Schleiermacher calls the "divinatory function" is the productive guess or hypothesis for which no rules can be formulated but without which the process of interpretation cannot even begin.[14]

The modern study of hermeneutics founded by Schleiermacher, though devoted to the divining of sacred texts, has also become a basis of contemporary literary theory, and both may be related to the interpretative processes of kabbalistic geometry. But what is even more surprising is the further similarity between the kabbalistic approach to geometric form and the scientific use of models.

Max Black has shown that the pervasive use of models in scientific theorizing reveals the same process as that involving all symbolic or linguistic thought: "Use of theoretical models resembles the use of metaphors in requiring analogical transfer of a vocabulary. Metaphor and model-making reveal new relationships. . . ."[15] Scientific reasoning begins, then, as a hermeneutic discipline; it must interpret its disordered data through divining their structural similarity to another, more familiar, domain, and this structural similarity can best be apprehended through the cognitive medium of an image, a visual model. Most useful for this purpose is the constructed analogue model:

> An analogue model is some material object, system, or process designed to reproduce as faithfully as possible in some new medium the *structure* or web of relationships in an original. . . . [It is] a symbolic representation of some real or imaginary original, subject to rules of interpretation for making accurate inferences from the relevant features of the model. . . . analogue models must be actually put together. . . . The theoretical model need not be built. . . . The inventor of a theoretical model is undistracted by accidental and irrelevant properties of the model object . . . but he is deprived of the controls enforced by the attempt at actual construction.[16]

It is precisely the controls involved in the actual construction of geometric models that give to such models a truth value lacking in an arbitrarily "invented" theoretical model, such as the one I presented in chapter 1 of *The Kabbalah of the Soul.*[17] And it is also through the attention paid to the "accidental" properties of the model that new insights can be generated regarding the structure of the domain intuitively recognized to be isomorphic to the model: "A promising model is one with implications rich enough to suggest novel hypotheses and speculations in the primary field of investigation. 'Intuitive grasp' of the model means a ready control of such implications. . . . [It can] help us to notice what otherwise would be overlooked, to shift the relative emphasis attached to details—in short, to *see new connections.*"[18] Black's analysis of the scientific use of models, like Hirsch's analysis of the interpretative process, is shown to begin with

"interpretative guesses" and then to move to the canons of validation by which they can be tested: "We can determine the validity of a given model by checking the extent of its isomorphism with its intended application."[19] In its use of models, then, scientific theorizing approximates the interpretative methods used in the construing of a literary text, not the processes of logical syllogism but the more intuitive processes of associative reasoning, a metaphorical apprehension of similarity between apparent dissimilars.

It is such a union of the techniques of literary interpretation with those of geometric construction that may thus be said to define traditional kabbalistic geometry, and this is also true of my own methodology in this work. The geometry practiced here may justly claim a place in the long tradition of kabbalistic geometry for the two reasons that it uses the same methodology and that its own geometric constructions are most specifically derived from the kabbalistic diagram of the Tree of Life. Here, as in earlier kabbalistic works, the main effort has been spent on the association of a particular geometry with biblical and kabbalistic texts, the geometry serving to order and validate concepts of the specifically earlier Jewish tradition and these concepts providing a reciprocal enlargement of the diagram's power of signification by demonstrating its power to model them.

But between the pure geometry of these diagrams and their use to model a linguistically expressed domain that had an original coherence apart from any such geometric modeling, there is the all-important step unique to kabbalistic geometry, the nongeometric naming of geometric elements. Not only this, as these diagrams are configurations expressive of linguistically conceptual meanings, the explication of their significance is as intrinsic to their definition as is the naming of their parts. And since this significance is not limited to the internal laws and rules of their geometric construction but also extends to the cosmological correspondences to these constructions expressible in language, the explication of such geometric constructions cannot be one of logical proof but must be that interpretative method appropriate to linguistic formulations that is based upon association.

Such further associations of the geometry of the Sabbath Star Diagram with kabbalistic cosmology is facilitated by the fact that *we know where we are* at every stage of diagram construction on the basis of the preliminary associations already made, primarily the equation of every double-pointed expansion of hexagrams with a cosmic world and the understanding that this diagram is to be expanded to the seventh such world in accordance with the biblical model of creation. In the following chapter we shall see that generation of the full fourth world of the diagram also produces a matrix in its interior that can be correlated with the soul level appropriate to this world. Thus we know that this fourth expansion will represent both the fourth kabbalistic world of Asiyah identified with the world of solid matter and the lowest level of the soul, that of the Nefesh or vital soul normally associated with it. In each further expansion of the diagram the construction elements can be similarly identified with the chronology or hierarchical nature of a particular "future" world and its matrix with one of the successively higher, kabbalistically defined levels of the soul. Once these initial definitions of construction and matrix elements have been arrived at, the further analytic process of the Science of Expressive Form involves seeing what the specific geometric forms and relationships of the diagram model can suggest regarding the domain whose isomorphism with the geometric model had first suggested the transfer of its terminology to the specific features of this model, primarily that of the larger tradition of Jewish esoteric cosmology and soul psychology.

The methodology of kabbalistic geometry can be considered to be essentially talmudic not only in the associative approach that Susan A. Handelman has shown to characterize talmudic reasoning but also in its conception of the relationship of "text," geometric in this case, to interpretation. As she further shows, in talmudic practice "interpretation is not essentially separate from the text itself—an external act intruded upon it—but rather the *extension* of the text, the uncovering of the connective network of relations, a part of the continuous revelation of the text itself: at bottom, another aspect of

the text."[20] And as interpretation and text form one unity in talmudic understanding, so also is it impossible to separate the geometry of kabbalistic diagrams from the full explication of their meaning, the interpretation being understood, rather, to be an "*extension* of the text," the expression of its geometrically formulated significance. Also talmudic has been the concern evinced in this study to explore every detail of the diagram, including all forbidden but possible constructions. Moreover, it is just such a claim to fundamental and universal significance as is made for the Bible, both internally and by its rabbinical interpreters, and for the Tree of Life Diagram by the sages of the Kabbalah, that I am also claiming for the Sabbath Star Diagram, the double claim that it embodies the cosmic code and that the ultimate source of its uncanny revelations is beyond human understanding or invention. For though I may have discovered the laws governing this geometric construction, I did not invent them.

But whether or not the Sabbath Star Diagram is granted such status, it shares with the biblical text a relationship to its interpretation that we have seen can also be compared with that of models to scientific theory. Indeed, as a geometric construction whose formal expansion follows its own discoverable laws, it is most precisely a mathematical model having its own scientific validation. As such, its use as an analogue model for a clearer structural understanding of a different domain is closer to the method of scientific reasoning than it is to the prophetic mode of discourse more normally associated with anything like a sacred oracle. Most important, the Science of Expressive Form, in its unique synthesis of science, art, and philosophy, combines the best of Pythagorean and kabbalistic approaches to geometry—the Pythagorean concern for the discovery of meaningful geometric laws through precise explorative constructions and the kabbalistic concern to explicate the meanings of a given geometric diagram through the displacement of an essentially talmudic hermeneutics to a visual model, the combination of geometric construction with an associative mode of interpretation that offers a most promising methodology for the apprehension of fundamental truth as well as the best hope for the modern redevelopment of a sacred science.

It is to the ancient sacred science that we must finally turn for the ultimate explanation of the effectiveness of this new sacred science, with its central gnosis involving the reciprocals of space and time. The fact that forms, whose particularities are delimited in space, and sound, whose waves are temporally extended and interact with all other frequency patterns, were demonstrated by the Pythagoreans to be interconvertible through some form of numerical mediation is so important because of the cosmic truth it has seemed to enshrine: that we, like all things, like the cosmos itself, are at one and the same time, now and forever, both limited and limitless.[21] And it is in this same complementarity that all the later developments of language and geometry are rooted whose union still makes both of these branches of thought fully comprehensible.

There is a final point that must be understood about the relationship of geometry to interpretation. As we have seen, analysis of the Elementary Sabbath Star Diagram, as earlier of the Hexagram of Creation, was based on two criteria, its visual appearance and its correlation with a text or tradition that may be said to mythologize its properties and so to provide them reciprocally with verbal descriptions and names. Granted that geometry provides less arbitrary constructions than language, the fact of such persuasive correlations would seem to argue that, to paraphrase a famous law of genetics, *mythology recapitulates geometry*. This is not to deny the truth of such mythology but to recognize it as a second order of truth, one based upon the absolute truths of its geometric models and giving to each systematic interpretation the quality of secondary or symbolic truth. For geometry is, indeed, a form of language that expresses ideas which the deep structures of the mind can recognize intuitively and for the reason that this deepest level of mental perception would seem to be encoded in such geometric archetypes. The persuasiveness with which geometric forms can be associated with mythological symbols further suggests that the mythological and geometric levels of the mind lie close together and that it is in terms of such mythology that the mind first interprets its geometric understanding into linguistic symbols. Whether or not the revelation of such meaning first arises in the mind at the primary geometric level or the secondary level at which geometric forms have already become translated into mythological symbols and narratives, the coherence between such narratives and geometric construction shows that such a geometric base is implicit in these narratives, a fact that serves to validate their mythology as symbolic expressions of absolute truths.

A GENERAL PREVIEW

Before concluding this introductory part, a brief preview of the whole would be advisable. The primary analytic focus of this work will be the mapping of both the outer and inner stages of the cosmic process, the outer stages being modeled by the construction elements of the Sabbath Star Diagram and the inner stages by its emergent matrix. In part 2, the chronology or hierarchy within the various cosmic eras will be determined through analysis of the *construction elements* of a cosmic world, with analysis of its *matrix* being restricted to the expressive nature of its matrix border and some other larger matrix structures. These dual elements will sometimes be further suggestive of psychological meanings, but it is part 3 that will be devoted to this subject, with its matrix modeling of kabbalistic transpersonal psychology, the matrix understood to model the "inner" aspect of each cosmic world, its "soul." Thus part 2 will be focused on kabbalistic cosmology and part 3 on kabbalistic psychology, and they will both show how the Sabbath Star Diagram can provide a scientific model for the Kabbalah that can give coherent form to the full range of kabbalistic doctrines, many of which have hitherto seemed to be in conflict. Part 4 will then take us beyond the cosmic circle defined in the Lurianic Tzimtzum to a new modeling of the infinite through the further numerical extrapolation of the diagram in the fuller Sabbath Star System.

The Elementary Sabbath Star Diagram developed in the first section will be used in chapters 3 and 4 to unlock the cosmic geometry encoded in the first four expansions of the Sabbath Star Diagram, which the analysis of Genesis 1 in chapter 1 has already correlated with the kabbalistic four worlds of emanation. Chapter 3 will be devoted to development of the complete fourth-world diagram. It will first establish how the diagram can become self-generating and then show how the various options of diagram construction can provide both the range of possibilities available for the evolution of life and an explanation of the Fall. Chapter 4 will trace the stages of this evolution in the third and fourth worlds through harmonic analyses of their six construction elements, the two possible third-world Sabbath Stars identified with aspects of the preincarnate Nefesh soul and the four fourth-world Sabbath Stars with the minerals, plants, animals, and man, the latter providing the final embodiment of the Nefesh soul.

Chapter 5 will take us to the fifth world, analysis of its Sabbath Star elements showing how they precisely parallel the traditional chronology projected for the Messianic Age correlated with this world as well as how these stages may be applied to an understanding of the progressive development of the Ruach consciousness with which it may also be associated. The fifth world can further be identified with the moral fifth dimension defined in the *Sefer Yetzirah*,[22] a Way of God working through nature and empowering the Ruach spiritual masters who can enter its flow.

With chapter 6 we arrive at the wholly spiritual sixth dimension of the World to Come, the Olam ha-Ba, one that can be associated both with the Partzufim (the divine personalities) and with Neshamah consciousness. It is in the sixth-world diagram that the cumulative Sabbath Stars can be seen to complete patterns that provide a basis for predicting the exact number of construction elements for all future worlds as well as making a first determination of the laws of diagram construction. The sixth dimension can thus be understood to be that whose revelation of completed pattern can fill the consciousness with a sense of meaningfulness.

The exploration of the seventh dimension of holiness in chapter 7 completes the analyses of part 2, focused on the construction elements of the Sabbath Star Diagram, with a modeling of the octave culmination of divine communion in which form, number, and language combine into a final revelation of cosmic truth. It is one that supports the Lurianic understanding of creation as a process whose purpose is the development of multiple divine personalities. Most important is the personality of that "son" who can bridge and unify the finitude of the cosmic octave with the infinity beyond it, this salvific image not only being the central gnosis of the Jewish esoteric tradition but the final revelation of the Sabbath Star Diagram.

One result of the modeling of the sixth and seventh dimensions by the construction elements of these worlds of the Sabbath Star Diagram is the recognition, developed in the third section of chapter 6, of the way the two construction grids could be correlated with gender, the vertical construction elements with the masculine and the horizontal construction elements with the feminine, a correlation that allows their interaction, as that of the gender-distinguished Partzufim they are also modeling, to be further construed as one of generation in which the sexual metaphor becomes most apt and the matrix is understood to be the son of such parentally correlated construction elements. With this understanding of the correlation of the construction elements to the matrix, this study then turns to analysis of this emergent matrix, which part 3 also takes from the fourth world through the octave. Finally, part 4 extrapolates this functional relationship to the endless sequence of patterning that will provide a new understanding of the infinite.

As the first chapter of part 2 had first to develop the way in which the Elementary Sabbath Star Diagram could become self-generating before its construction elements could be specifically interpreted in that chapter and the next, so must the first chapter of part 3 first explore the matrix to discover its inner structuring before its four structures, in their proper relationships could be interpreted as a model of the multidimensional soul. Beginning with the correlation of the Nefesh soul with the fourth world and continuing through all the correlated levels of kabbalistic soul psychology, the matrix provides a scientific model for the levels of the soul with one most important feature, the distinction at each of its levels of an essential polarity between the collective and the individual, one whose matrix positions lead logically to their designation as "central" or "lateral."

Chapter 8 maintains the distinction developed in chapter 3, that there are two separate forms of the fourth-world diagram, the simpler form produced by the past modeling of its intermediate construction elements, which can be taken to represent its "unfallen" form, and the more complex diagram produced by the future modeling of these intermediate construction elements, which can, from one perspective, be taken to represent its "fallen" form. As the completed matrices of these two forms of the fourth-world diagram can represent both the unfallen and fallen forms of the Nefesh soul, so can the unfinished matrix elements beyond their matrix borders be taken to define the temptations to both forms of the Nefesh soul. Chapter 9 then applies these interpretative approaches to the matrix of the fifth world with analyses that illuminate the nature of the Ruach soul.

But it is chapter 10 on the sixth-world matrix that is the most illuminating portion of this whole work, for the cumulative number of matrix elements at this level permits the matrix to be precisely correlated with the central model of the Kabbalah, a correlation that not only permits its modeling of the Neshamah soul level to model as well the divine mind and heart but permits a reenvisioning of the matrices of the prior worlds into one spectacular structure of meaning. Where chapter 10 introduces us to this astonishing correlation and its various kabbalistic implications, chapter 11 takes this reconceptualization of matrix structure into a study of those elements beyond the matrix borders of the fourth through sixth worlds that provides a full understanding of all the difficulties that beset one on the path to spiritual perfection. Chapter 12 completes part 3 with a deeper understanding of the transcendent image emerging in the octave matrix that represents the Chayah soul, an understanding deeper than was possible in the analysis provided in chapter 7 of just its matrix border. And it also shows how the Sabbath Star Diagram can precisely model that "Measure of the Body," the *Shi'ur Komah* of Merkabah literature, by which the "son of

man" can become a "son of the World to Come."[23]

A correlation was earlier made between the construction elements of the Elementary Sabbath Star Diagram derived directly from the Tree of Life Diagram and the tones of the diatonic scale, a correlation that supports the expansion of the self-generated form of this diagram to the upper Do of the octave and identifies this octave with the first half of the seventh world, a correlation that also permits an identification of such a seven-dimensional cosmos with the "days" of biblical cosmology. It is this correlation of diagram worlds with the diatonic scale that chapter 7 had earlier shown to support an identification of the midpoint of the seventh world with the circle of the Lurianic Tzimtzum, that spherical withdrawal of Ein Sof, the Unlimited One, which provided the "space" for a finite cosmos. Parts 2 and 3 form the heart of this work with their modelings of the outer and inner aspects of the synthesized kabbalistic cosmology here developed that integrates the four worlds of the Kabbalah into the larger seven stages of biblical cosmology needed to provide the room necessary for the future orientation of the Lurianic Tikkun. But part 4 takes us beyond the cosmos into a true exploration of the infinite.

Chapter 13 is primarily concerned with the construction of the full seventh world that provides a modeling of the highest Yechidah soul. Though this was the last expansion possible to be printed clearly with the graphics program used to draft the diagrams of this book, such construction of the full seventh world revealed an apparent inconsistency with a way of counting the values of matrix elements, one derived from an aspect of the sixth-world matrix, that raised the need for some graphic representation of the matrices of first the eighth and then the ninth worlds. Because of this need, a way was found that resolved this issue, leading to a full disclosure of the laws of this geometric construction. And it also showed its full program to be one beginning in chaos and growing in regularity as it gains in complexity. This is as far as geometric exploration of the diagram can or need be taken. But in chapter 14, the emerging regularities in the numbers of matrix elements, in concert with the earlier established regularities in the numbers of construction elements, are finally to lead to the numerical extrapolation of the special functional relationship of construction to matrix elements, which is the one still unpredictable aspect of the diagram. In chapter 15, this function, simplified to an algebraic formula, becomes the basis of a new experimental mathematics of the infinite and the new model for complexity theory that is this work's most significant scientific achievement.

The main concern of the following three parts of this work is with developing both the experimental exploration of the rules of the Sabbath Star Diagram and its modeling of the Jewish mystical tradition from which it was derived. But the ability of the Sabbath Star Diagram to provide a secondary, "mythical" level of understanding that can model other domains is not limited to the Jewish mystical tradition and comparable spiritual traditions. That it is a universal model applicable to other domains is importantly demonstrated in the four appendices to this volume. The first three appendices involve applications of the matrix, appendix A of the fourth-world matrix to quantum physics, appendix B of the matrices of the fourth through sixth worlds to the evolutionary stages of systems theory, with emphasis on sociology, and appendix C applies this same systems modeling of the fourth- through sixth-world matrices to the levels of linguistics. Finally, appendix D applies the construction elements of the third through seventh worlds to a gender modeling of human history.

The higher worlds of the diagram will also provide new solutions to mysteries of the Jewish esoteric tradition. The octave diagram, in particular, may explain the special exemption of the Cherubim from the Second Commandment as well as other mysteries related to the Tetragrammaton, the Tzachtzachot (the three "Splendors"), the Measure of the Body, and the opening paragraph of the *Zohar*. In its uncanny ability to provide graphic demonstration of details of the Jewish esoteric tradition ranging from the Bible through the Talmud, Merkabah mystics, and the Zoharic and Lurianic Kabbalah, the Sabbath Star Diagram reveals them all to be parts of one tradition of esoteric knowledge

based upon geometric models. But chapter 15 will take us even further to develop a new model for complexity theory. The comprehensive analyses of the Sabbath Star Diagram undertaken in this work should establish the significant role it can play in two complementary respects: as a model for a new paradigm that can synthesize science, psychology, esoteric learning, and other fields into one source of universal truth, and as a vehicle whose objective logic can both validate and translate kabbalistic mythology into the modern terms that can once more inspire the seeker with a sense of cosmic meaningfulness. Having briefly outlined the structure of this work, we can finally consider its implications for three broad areas: science, psychology, and the Jewish esoteric tradition.

Most important to the larger scientific contribution of this work will be the study of the systemic aspects of the Sabbath Star Diagram, which will be seen to exemplify many of the characteristics attributed to the systems studied by chaos theorists. Its construction involves a similar type of experimental mathematics and its successive expansions reveal a similar union of determinism with unpredictable emergent properties. For, it is like dynamic chaotic systems in producing a miniature universe whose evolution seems almost organic in its generation of complex patterning and whose trivalent logic permits a certain freedom to explore alternative possibilities of growth. Chaos theorists are also most attentive to visual form and see in their miniature universes a model applicable to the whole cosmos.[24]

But the major contribution of this work to systems theory will be in its final modeling of the theory of complex systems. In chapter 15 the geometric expansion of the diagram will yield to two higher levels of numerical extrapolation based upon a numerical function emerging in the seventh- through ninth-diagram worlds. These two higher levels of what can finally be called the Sabbath Star System involve infinite decimal sequences revealing a remarkable structure of patterning, one that, like the lower-level worlds of the Sabbath Star Diagram, shows a progression from chaotic irregularity to increasing but never perfectly predictable regularity. Study of the experimental mathematics of the

Sabbath Star System will provide a new model for complex systems with major cosmological implications. In this model it is *size* that proves to be the determining factor in driving an expanding complex system to new levels of organization, size that has its own threshold for how much complexity its level of organization can handle. Thus complex systems can be said to be controlled by what I call the Law of Complex Magnitudes, a "complex magnitude" being recognized by the emergence at its start of a new mode of regulating its members. Though we cannot tell at what magnitude the sequence will shift to a new mode of regularity and what this new mode will be, what this model does show can be predicted for all complex systems is that at a very precise magnitude of spatial, temporal, or numerical expansion an older, long-maintained patterning will suddenly yield to a new pattern, the periods of each new level of complexity being increasingly large. Most importantly, in the Sabbath Star System model for complexity theory, chaos is present both at the beginning and in the transitions between phases but is contained, and the growth is toward greater overall regularity rather than entropy. This is the opposite of what happens in the progression to chaos of certain turbulent systems and a major reason for preferring the Sabbath Star Diagram as a model for the growth of such stable complex systems as the cosmos.

What is finally represented by the Sabbath Star Diagram and its two higher levels of numerical extrapolation is a new way of doing both the geometric and numerical branches of mathematics, not in terms of isolated geometric or numerical properties but of dynamically growing systems, the diagram being treated scientifically as a source of experimental data rather than mathematically as subject to logical proofs. Prior study of such systems has largely been a product of the computer, of its graphics modeling of algebraic formulas or of numerical automata. But I believe this to be the first example of such a systems approach to manually constructed two-dimensional geometry and to numerical sequences derived from such construction. The Sabbath Star Diagram is still a product of the original tools of plane geometry, the compass and straightedge, but they have been used to develop a non-Euclidian mode of geometry concerned with the experimental evolution of a construct from a few simple constituents and rules to phases of systemically increasing complexity with their own cosmological implications. Whether or not such an evolving geometric system could be duplicated by other self-similar constructions, systems based perhaps on the pentagram or square, or whether the same or similar formulas applied to another sequence of three of more fractions would yield a similar wealth of complex and meaningful patterning, I do not know. But the system I have discovered does have remarkable properties that have here been studied exhaustively. Thus even if there is nothing further to be learned about the Sabbath Star System, and its characteristics cannot be duplicated by any other originating geometric form, that is, even if it does not open the new avenues for other experimental mathematicians that are the staples of any new branch of science, it should still win acceptance as a unique and significant achievement in the broader new science of dynamic complex systems.

If the Sabbath Star Diagram is both inimitable and particularly suggestive of cosmological implications, this may be because it is based on forms that the esoteric traditions have long recognized to encode such cosmological meaning. It is constituted exclusively of hexagrams, a symbol that many traditions have understood to convey the unification of heaven and earth, fire and water, male and female; and its rules of construction are derived from the interfacing of this hexagram form with the kabbalistic Tree of Life Diagram, the major cosmological diagram of the Western esoteric tradition. So it would seem that these sources of the Sabbath Star Diagram do contain keys to cosmology. For the self-generated construct deriving from them, with or without kabbalistic interpretation, has characteristics that mirror and illuminate the cosmic structure we inhabit, showing how various forms of freedom and unpredictable emergent properties can be generated by a structure both deterministic and evolving to greater regularity, a structure that it must also be said is extraordinarily beautiful. At the center of the

Tree of Life Diagram is the Sefirah Tiferet, which means Beauty, and this is certainly the most immediate impression produced by its derivative hexagram diagram. This is also a characteristic of much of the computer graphics modeling of previous dynamic systems, these evolving systems manifesting a unique synthesis of science and art that has been called the "Beautiful Science." Though the diagrams for each Sabbath Star world are beautiful, it is the spectacular emergences in the matrices of the sixth world and the octave that are particularly awesome.

As the Sabbath Star Diagram can model the emerging paradigm of a new scientific approach to multidimensional nature, so can it provide the model for a new holistic and transpersonal psychology, in so doing providing further evidence for the esoteric principle of coherence between the knower and the known. The Sabbath Star Diagram can be useful to psychology in two respects, first and most importantly as a model of the psyche and secondly as a clue to effective therapeutic techniques. Part 3 will show the matrix to provide the most comprehensive model for transpersonal psychology that I believe has yet been developed. It permits a discrimination between the lower and higher egos as well as between the minds and hearts of the three soul levels associated with the fourth through sixth worlds. These characteristics of the Nefesh, Ruach, and Neshamah soul levels are precisely mapped in the chapters analyzing the matrices of the fourth-through sixth-world diagrams, with the chapters on the seventh-world diagram giving the final form to this model, both extending its mapping of kabbalistic psychology to its two highest soul levels, those of the Chayah and Yechidah levels of the Lurianic Kabbalah, and showing how its overall double-aspecting and three levels are most consistent with the latest brain research. What is more, chapter 3 contains a section showing how the ordering and forms of the Sabbath Stars provide a model of what can be called "The Transformative Moment," a model whose therapeutic use by psychologists can complement their use of the matrix as a theoretical model of the transpersonal psyche.[25] The Sabbath Star Diagram, then, can provide both a theoretical and therapeutic model for psychology, and do this in terms of a geometry expressive of its own significant meanings.

We turn finally to the two main implications of the Sabbath Star Diagram for the Jewish esoteric tradition. The first is that it shows this variegated product of millennia to be both a coherent whole and one informed by the same core of salvational knowledge, the second that it shows it to be based throughout on geometric models. This study begins as does this tradition with the cosmology of the Bible, showing the creation account in Genesis 1 to be directly modeled on the triple esoteric keys of geometry, music, and number. But the greatest significance of the creation account is its disclosure of a Sabbatical structure to the cosmos, a structure whose modeling by the Sabbath Star Diagram can include all aspects of the Jewish esoteric-mystical tradition. It is the Sabbath Star Diagram, itself, that should make the greatest contribution to the Kabbalah, helping to write a new chapter to its long history, and this because it can provide graphic illustration of so many of its formulations, including many that were before inexplicable, as well as fitting all aspects of the Jewish esoteric tradition into one consistent cosmology. Whether the geometry of this archetypal cosmic model was conveyed directly to the great seers of this tradition or in the already translated forms of the mythology with which their writings abound, the present disclosure of the Sabbath Star Diagram should go far to validate the symbolic truth of the mythological systems broadly known as the Kabbalah. For this geometry and mythology are mutually validating and together point to mysterious connections of icons with the sources of their meaning beyond our normal powers of comprehension. Most uncanny is the final revelation of various aspects of the seventh world of the diagram, for this is none other than that which, following upon this discovery, I have isolated throughout the Jewish esoteric tradition and named the secret doctrine of the son.

Because of its ability to provide a comprehensive structure to the various formulations of the Jewish mystical tradition, this expanding geometric construct, both derived from the kabbalistic Tree and interpreted in terms of this mystical tradition, may well provide just the remythologizing of the Kabbalah for which historians of this tradition have recently been calling.

In 1978, the year in which I discovered the Sabbath Star Diagram, Arthur E. Green first issued this call:

> We have seen the theology of despair which comes out of the Holocaust: we must now go beyond it to a renewal of real life. We have lived through the dead end of historicism as an ideology and have been crippled by the conclusions of the critical consciousness; *we must now move from the critical to the post-critical age in our religious formulations.* We have seen the unidimensional flatness and poverty which positivism and historicism have lent to our once sacred existence. The need for demythologizing is past; *a remythologizing of the religious consciousness is what this hour calls upon us to create.* And here it is the Kabbalist, the one who has most successfully accomplished that task in our past, who is to be our historic guide and mentor.[26]

These stirring words are echoed almost exactly by the analysis of the present juncture of Jewish history offered by Yosef Hayim Yerushalmi:

> Much has changed since the sixteenth century; one thing, curiously remains. Now, as then, it would appear that even where Jews do not reject history out of hand, they are not prepared to confront it directly, but seem to await a new, metahistorical myth. . . . it is hard to escape the feeling that the Jewish people after the Holocaust stands today at a juncture not without analogy to that of the generations following the cataclysm of the Spanish Expulsion. They, as we saw, ultimately chose myth over history. . . . There are myths that are life-sustaining and deserve to be reinterpreted for our age.[27]

Though the parallel Yerushalmi draws to the sixteenth-century emergence of the Lurianic Kabbalah in response to the Spanish Expulsion, a historical hypothesis developed by Gershom Scholem, has been questioned in recent years, it is also true that Jews in this post-Holocaust age are again in need of just such a remythologizing as Luria did provide for the Zoharic Kabbalah, a process that may be aided by the model of the Sabbath Star Diagram. But such a remythologizing should understand the Lurianic preoccupation with the Partzufim as pointing a brave new way to human perfectibility, that the reconstitution of the broken cosmic fragments into multiple divine personalities through the spiritual development of humanity constitutes Luria's mythological way of revealing the path of human salvation. Luria's deeper message is that it is man who is to become the divine cosmic child and that human spiritual growth and transformation into a multiplicity of divine personalities represents the purpose of creation, the purpose that has ever been the hidden gnosis of the Jewish esoteric tradition as well as being the culminating revelation of the Sabbath Star Diagram. And it may finally be the objective logic of its geometry that will allow the Sabbath Star Diagram to become the vehicle for the transmission of such sacred truths into the modern world, providing the model that can synthesize secular as well as sacred knowledge into the living ideology required to release the creative energies of the new millennium now upon us.

PART TWO

A New Model for Kabbalistic Cosmology

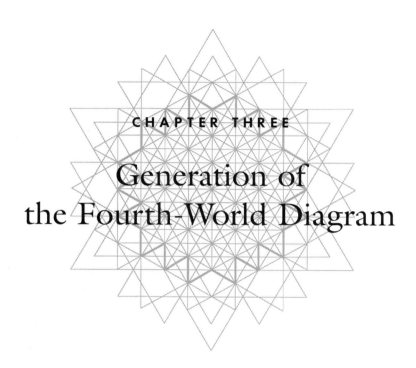

CHAPTER THREE

Generation of the Fourth-World Diagram

A SUMMARY INTRODUCTION
TO THE FOURTH-WORLD DIAGRAM

Study of the full fourth-world diagram should prove most interesting for two reasons: It models the three-dimensional world of consensus reality we all share, and it offers a unique choice between two different forms of construction, both of which can be variously supported by the regularities developing with the sixth and later such worlds, but which provide contrasting versions not only of the fourth world but also of the fifth. As shall shortly be clarified, there is a "past-modeled" method of constructing the self-generated fourth-world diagram and a "future-modeled" method, the former providing a simpler form of this diagram and the latter a form that is more complex. These differences would seem to correspond to the distinction traditionally made between the unfallen and fallen forms of this world, and the third section of this chapter, entitled "The Fourth-World Diagram and the Fall," will arrange the various design choices into a scenario of the Fall at various stages of actualization, a scenario whose principal character is the Nefesh soul in both its third- and fourth-world stages of progressive embodiment; for it is this vital or animal soul level that is correlated with the fourth world or dimension of consciousness to be studied in this chapter and the next. The fact that the self-generated Sabbath Star Diagram shows regularities in the later worlds of the multidimensional cosmos it models but a fundamental irregularity at its fourth-world level as well as a choice between design options may well be the most significant implication of the Sabbath Star Diagram for this crucial cosmic stage, the turning point between the worlds of emanation and of such return or reconfiguration as is signified by the Lurianic concept of Tikkun. But it has other important implications as well.

The most important of these has to do with the very fact of such design choices, choices that define a new form of trivalent logic, one that, in addition to the categories of forbidden impossibilities and permitted possibilities, also has a third category of forbidden possibilities that can allow for the exercise of freedom, a subject discussed at length in the concluding section of this chapter. The fact that the emergent rules of the diagram demonstrate a trivalent logic especially in the construction of the fourth-world diagram shows that this geometric construct seems designed to allow for precisely such freedom at the level correlated with material manifestation. This point has particular significance if this diagram is to be credited with encoding the laws of cosmic evolution, which is the premise of this book and the reason for its detailed analysis.

What distinguishes the future-modeled form of the fourth-world matrix from its past-modeled counterpart is that its larger matrix contains additional elements that would otherwise emerge only with the fifth-world matrix and be identified with elements of its correlated Ruach soul level, a subject largely deferred to part 3. We thus have two alternative forms not only of the fourth world but also of the fifth. If the simpler model of the Nefesh soul may be identified either with its animal embodiment or prelapsarian (also primitive) human state, then the fuller Ruach model would represent the ideal state in which man is supposed to be functioning in this world. If the more complex model of the Nefesh soul is adopted, however, its fuller constituents can be understood in two distinct ways. In the first, which largely adopts the view of the simpler model as preferred, this could explain why man has remained so long in his spiritually undeveloped form and pushed the higher Ruach level off to an ever receding Messianic future. In terms of the simpler model, which could so be considered the *ideal* program for these levels of the Sabbath Star Diagram, man's limited Nefesh soul would have served as a successful preliminary for the more ample Ruach development we would now be enjoying. In terms of the more complex model, which can correspondingly be considered the diagram's program for the *real* nature of these levels, it is the expanded Nefesh soul that represents humanity's present condition, the very enlargement of man's capacities that has permitted his fuller functioning at this lowest of spiritual levels also having lessened his felt need for further spiritual development and so consigned his optimal earthly functioning to the long-delayed future. But there is a final way of viewing the more complex model, not simply as real though unfortunate but as preferable, as accomplishing a transfor-

mation of the Nefesh soul from its retrogressive modeling on the past to that progressive future modeling by which the soul can evolve to the higher future dimensions of the Tikkun through which it can fulfill the purpose of the cosmic process, the development of divine personality.

Though there is no way of choosing between these two versions of the fourth-world diagram at this initial point of diagram self-generation, the question arises as to what the future worlds of the diagram will reveal regarding the proper form of this most important of diagram worlds. The answers, for better or worse, are mixed. Where the fourth world may be viewed as transitional between the past worlds of emanation and the future worlds of Tikkun, so will chapter 7 show the seventh world, divided by the octave, to be equally transitional between the worlds of the finite and the infinite. And these perspectives provide different initial answers to our central question. At the highest full level of finite intelligence, that of the sixth world, which is to provide so many principles of construction, the answer would seem to favor the "ideal" program. But at the lowest full level of infinite intelligence, that of the eighth world, it seems equally to favor the program more consonant both with reality and the law of future modeling everywhere else operative. It is only at the level of the ninth world that the full diagram program is finally revealed, and this both opens up the whole question again and leaves it unresolved.

Just as chapter 6 will show that at the sixth world the increasing numbers for the two grids of construction elements have become regular by the third world, so will chapter 13 show that at the ninth world the rates of increase for the four matrix categories have become regular by the sixth world, this progression from initial irregularity to final regularity defining the nature of the Sabbath Star System and the new model it can contribute to the theory of complex systems, the subject of chapter 15. A backward extrapolation of the formulae for matrix growth, presented in chapter 14, further reveals that at the fourth-world level it is the numbers deriving from the past-modeled version that are most coherent with the later program, while at the fifth-world level it is the numbers resulting from a future modeling of the fourth world, an inconsistency for which there is no resolution.

Thus we end as we began with two equally valid versions of the fourth-world diagram, and these can either be kept separate, as alternate visions of the fourth material world, or sequentially related. It is the latter possibility that will first be adopted in interpreting the unique features of the fourth-world diagram, the implied progression from the simpler past-modeled form to the more complex future-modeled form being understood to express the change in human consciousness that has been traditionally embodied in the myth of the Fall. This will assume that its past modeling represents the ideal form of the fourth world and that, therefore, the movement to future modeling represents the path of transgression into the forbidden. Though recognizing that the final rules of diagram construction do not strictly disallow this future-modeled form, acceptance of it as the fallen form of the fourth-world diagram, and of the alternate form as unfallen, can be justified by its illuminating interpretative results, providing a most coherent account of cosmic development up through the sixth-world level of intelligence, what Plato has called "a likely story."[1]

Though this approach to the two forms of the fourth-world diagram will be followed through much of this chapter and the next, in the section of this chapter entitled "The Sabbatical Model of Redemption" the alternative view of the future-modeled diagram will be developed that sees it positively, as embodying the transformative process necessary for initiating the Tikkun. Since the fourth world of a Sabbatical cosmos may be understood to represent the midpoint of the cosmic process, its past-modeled form, defined by the past modeling of that first intermediate construction element coming just before the cosmic turning point, would give this form a past orientation, while its future-modeled form, defined by the future modeling of that second intermediate construction element coming just after this cosmic midpoint, would similarly give this form a future orientation. This difference also distinguishes the two opposing modes of spiritual under-

standing associated with the East and West, that of the Eastern traditions largely seeing the course of spiritual development as taking the soul back to a past condition of spiritual unity and that of the West, particularly as expressed by the Lurianic Kabbalah, seeing this course as taking the soul forward to a future condition of divine multiplicity.[2] In these terms, the two alternative forms of the fourth-world diagram may also serve to model these contrasting spiritual orientations. In the later sections of this chapter, the future-modeled form will not only be reenvisioned as a model of transformative consciousness but also as a model of rectification produced by a Sabbatical element added from the first stage of the fifth-world diagram.

Chapters 3 and 4 are primarily concerned with the construction elements of the fourth-world diagram, with chapter 3 defining the further self-generation of the diagram and chapter 4 applying its geometric analysis to the evolution of this world. In chapter 4, all possible Sabbath Star formations of the position-defining hexagrams of the third and fourth worlds will be analyzed on the basis of certain geometric considerations for the illumination this can provide of the various stages of cosmic evolution. The analysis of the fourth-world diagram now beginning will show us where we are, how we got here, and where we are to go.

GENERATING THE FOURTH-WORLD DIAGRAM

In chapter 2 of this book, as in chapter 6 of *The Secret Doctrine of the Kabbalah*, a cosmological diagram was derived from the Tree of Life Diagram that seemed to shed new light on the geometry of divine emanation as understood in the kabbalistic tradition. We shall now see, in this most important section for the remainder of this work, how this Sabbath Star Diagram, once conceived, can become self-generating and provide further illumination both of this fourth world of material creation and of the human potential for spiritual growth. Such self-generation can begin from the two main principles of construction by which the Sabbath Star Diagram was derived from the Tree of Life Diagram: It was constructed out of hexagrams in either the simple Star of David or complex Sabbath Star form, and it grew from one such hexagram to the next by either the whole- or half-step progression.

The emergence of the half-step hexagram in the third world, after three prior hexagrams successively enlarged by the double-point or whole-step method, seemed to encode a second key for construction that could take the diagram beyond the limit defined by the key of the Tree of Life Diagram. This was the key of the diatonic scale, which we shall also see to be a key to cosmic creation in Plato's *Timaeus*, whose first four tones (Do, Re, Mi, and Fa) are analogous to the intervals defined by the first four hexagrams of the Elementary Sabbath Star Diagram. And this key suggests both that the diagram be expanded to the octave and that the fourth world should be extended to a hexagram or Sabbath Star corresponding to the diatonic Sol tone. It seems logical, therefore, that the fourth world should perpetuate the third-world division into contractile and expansive stages and that, since the first stage of the material fourth world took the form of a Sabbath Star, a form representative of both the multiplicity and divine nature of material creation, this should also be the form of its second stage. As we shall now see, this logical first step in the self-generation of the Sabbath Star Diagram will lead to all the idiosyncrasies of this cosmic diagram.

For the addition of the Sol Sabbath Star to the Elementary Sabbath Star Diagram produces some surprising results. In the first place it leads to the manifestation of a significant matrix pattern at the center of the diagram, specifically in the area contained within the Re hexagram defining the first and second cosmic worlds. This matrix is formed of equilateral triangles, the macrotriangles with lines running through them that define their threefold symmetry and the interfaced microtriangles with only a single expressed line of symmetry,[3] six macrotriangles filling the points of the Re hexagram and another six filling its inner hexagon and incorporating the Do hexagram that it contains. This matrix pattern is illustrated in figures 3.1 and 3.2. In figure 3.1 the matrix pattern is illustrated in an enlarged version that can provide all the lines necessary for

construction of the fourth-world diagram. This figure is provided as a service for those who wish to construct their own diagrams, its grid lines making such construction possible with an accuracy beyond the normal powers of all but the most skilled draftsmen. The area within its darkened inner hexagon contains all the lines necessary for the fourth-world diagram, while the area extending to the darkened outer hexagon can accommodate the first construction element of the fifth-world diagram, an added element necessary for the final "Sabbatical" version of the fourth-world diagram presented in figure 3.13. The far more condensed grid for the sixth-world diagram will also be provided in figure 6.1 in concert with an instructional guide for constructing that world of the diagram.

In figure 3.2 we can see the original matrix produced within the Re hexagram by addition of the Sol Sabbath Star, its matrix border being outlined for greater visibility. In addition to manifesting the beginnings of a matrix pattern, the drawing of the Sol Sabbath Star leads to another unexpected manifestation, that of the hitherto unmanifest Ri hexagram of the second world, earlier suggested only by the position of the Sefirah Yesod on its as yet concealed tip. In keeping with the use of Solfeggio terminology to define the construction elements of the diagram, here of the twelve-tone or chromatic scale, this hexagram has been given the Solfeggio name of Ri, corresponding to the semitone between Re and Mi. Appearing midway on the vertical grid between the Do and Mi hexagrams, the Ri hexagram has been specially darkened in figure 3.2.

If we look at the effect of this later manifestation of the Ri hexagram upon the Re hexagram that had formerly defined the second world exclusively, we can see that what it, in concert with the whole of the Sol Sabbath Star, contributes to the redefinition of Beriah is the matrix pattern, a pattern of such cosmic significance that it will take all of part 3 to define it adequately. But if the second, third, and fourth worlds all appear now to have second stages, what of the first world? Here again the Sol Sabbath Star provides the answer, for as it produces the Ri hexagram so does the Ri hexagram produce in its inner hexagon the extended area that would correspond to the locus of a Di hexagram, were such a hexagram possible. But such a second stage of Atzilut cannot be manifested without breaking the emerging matrix pattern, as figure 3.3 should show.

Where figure 3.3 shows that the Ri hexagram fits nicely into the emerging matrix pattern of Re-point-size triangles, it also shows that the Di hexagram breaks this emerging matrix pattern by instituting a diminutive version of the matrix macrotriangle—an equilateral triangle with its three lines of symmetry expressed—in the six points of the Do hexagram. However interesting such one-third-sized triangles may be in suggesting an Atzilutic mode of return to the infinitesimal primal point of cosmic origin, they

break the matrix of Creation defined by the triangles in the points of the Re hexagram of Beriah, a matrix that has already succeeded in incorporating the world of divine Emanation, Atzilut. It is because the Ri hexagram is consistent with the emerging matrix while the Di hexagram is not that we can speak of a progression from the *unmanifestable* second stage of Atzilut through the *unmanifest* second stage of Beriah to the *manifest* second stage of Yetzirah. In chapter 2 we saw that the initial mode of emanation, as defined by the Elementary Sabbath Star Diagram, manifested only the second stage of Yetzirah, a stage that broke the whole-step progression of hexagrams to define the Sefirah Yesod. Though this Sefirah

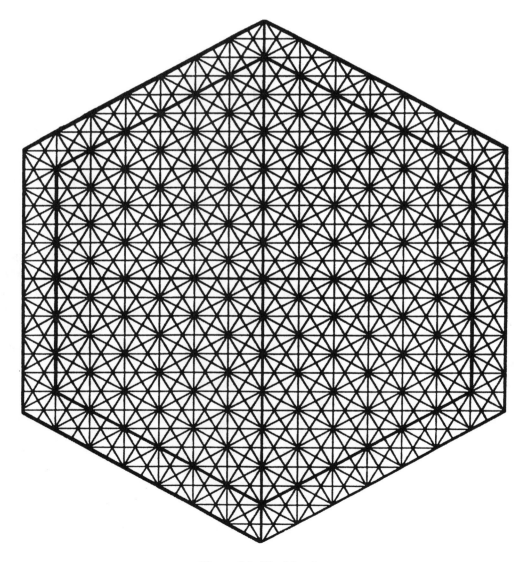

Figure 3.1. The Matrix

A NEW MODEL FOR KABBALISTIC COSMOLOGY

implied the existence of a second stage of Beriah, its Ri hexagram was as yet unmanifest. It is only the later development of the diagram that both reveals its hitherto unmanifest form and proves the permanent unmanifestability of the second stage of Atzilut that such a Di hexagram would signify. We now can recognize that it is the gross materialization of the fourth world that reveals the subtle processes of progressive manifestation in the prior worlds. More than this, there seems to be a reverse cosmological history by which later cosmological events can produce, or at least disclose, earlier cosmological causes, the future, as it were, determining the past, a phenomenon that we shall see

confirmed in chapter 6 on the sixth-world diagram.

A similar reversibility of time has been suggested as a feature of quantum field theory in modern, relativistic physics. Though I have been speaking of a cosmological "history," this is really a simplification of the more mystical understanding of the four worlds signified by this diagram as coexisting in a timeless present, a four-dimensional continuum of space-time that can be read forward or backward in time like the space-time diagrams of quantum physics. In the matrix version of the Sabbath Star Diagram, however, the backward movement in "time" has a more complex character than that theorized in quantum physics, not simple reversibility

Figure 3.2. Addition of the Sol Sabbath Star to the Elementary Sabbath Star Diagram

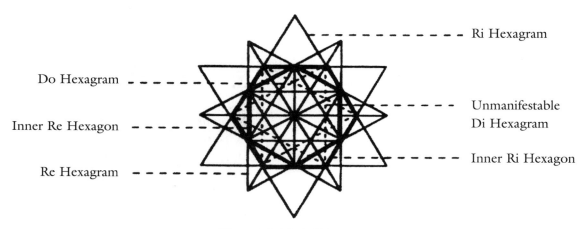

Do Hexagram

Inner Re Hexagon

Re Hexagram

Ri Hexagram

Unmanifestable
Di Hexagram

Inner Ri Hexagon

Figure 3.3. The Di Hexagram

but a precise filling in of a simpler by a more complex pattern. Nonetheless, it is analytically possible to separate the sediment left by each world within the layers that form the later world of a diagram under examination and so to travel back through it to earlier stages of its evolution, as shall soon be demonstrated.

Of the two inherited construction principles with which we began, the second principle involving the half-step progression has both allowed and led us to the construction of a second-stage hexagram for the fourth world and in the Sabbath Star form allowed by the first principle. Since no further half-step progressions can be accepted by the fourth-world diagram, the question arises as to whether any of the previously established simple hexagrams can be converted to Sabbath Star form. The answer is that one of these hexagrams can contain a Sabbath Star consistent with the matrix pattern and with the Sabbath Star form as previously defined by first the Fi and then the Sol Sabbath Stars. This is the Mi hexagram defining the first stage of the third world. The two qualifications just given are important, the first because consistency with the matrix can be considered the first new principle of diagram construction that, though derived from application of the inherited principles, goes beyond them, and the second because a different form of Sabbath Star not yet discovered will later prove to be a possibility for the Fa hexagram consistent with the matrix but not permitted on the basis of other emergent principles.

These later developed principles will also make clear, however, that the Mi Sabbath Star cannot appear in the same diagram with the Sol Sabbath Star, whose final generation will cover all of this third world form except for its position-defining hexagram. But as we shall later also see, the possibility that the Mi hexagram can be reformulated as a Sabbath Star has two important consequences. It provides a model without which one form of Sabbath Star construction at the level of the soon to be defined intermediate fourth-world hexagrams would be impossible, and it becomes a principle means of better understanding not only the third world but also the earlier stages of the fourth world. How it can function as such a model will be seen in the later discussion of figure 3.5 and the following figures, in which it will appear in its correct chronology though without the differentiation of its form later to be illustrated in figure 4.1. But we must now proceed to discover the further rules for generating the first "past-modeled" form of the fourth-world diagram.

We have just seen that extending the previous rules of diagram construction initially led to the addition of the Sol Sabbath Star. Perhaps the most significant effect of this new Sabbath Star was the manifestation of a matrix pattern within the Re hexagram, a matrix that became the creative womb of what might be called the second generation of the Sabbath Star Diagram, one whose rules of construction would have to be discovered in the very process of such construction but whose first new principle would be the consistency of any new construction with the integrity of the matrix.

The second new principle, now to be defined, has to do with the filling in of available positions on the twin grids of the diagram. Observing figure 3.2 once more, it can be seen that there are two grids at right angles to each other, a vertical and a horizontal grid. On the vertical grid there appears to be room between the points of the Mi and Sol Sabbath Stars for two additional hexagrams or Sabbath Stars while this does not appear to be true for the horizontal grid, the points of the Re and Fa hexagrams and the Fi Sabbath Star being evenly spaced along this grid and admitting of no further additions. Establishing these two new vertical stages fills in all possible points on both the vertical and horizontal grids to the final height of Sol and provides both a new description of the fourth world of Asiyah and the new rule that all intermediate positions on the grids culminating in the semitone Sabbath Stars should be occupied by stage-defining hexagrams. This rule will have the most crucial effect on the developing diagram, leading to the numerical differences between its vertical and horizontal grids. It will produce the 3:1 proportion of vertical to horizontal construction elements, which we shall later see to be true for all even-numbered worlds. It is the addition of the Sol Sabbath Star to the Elementary Sabbath Star Diagram whose delayed manifestation of the Ri hexagram and production of the matrix has led to the two new rules requiring the addition of two stage-defining construction hexagrams on the vertical axis, such further additions also being responsible for the idiosyncratic form of the finally developed diagram.

It now seems clear that the fourth world consists of four stages rather than the two earlier assumed on the basis of the third-world pattern. But the nature of these two additional stage-defining hexagrams is not so clear, and for two reasons. The first reason has to do with its tonal analogue. Following more usual musical conceptions, it would be tempting to consider them the quarter tones at which Eastern musicians are so adept. But a careful study of the diagram in figure 3.4 suggests a different interpreta-tion of the spatial intervals among these four hexagrams. If we first look at the area beyond the Fa-point hexagon that defines the fourth world, the area extending to the peak of the Sol Sabbath Star, the distance between these two points can be equated with the whole-tone continuum from Fa to Sol. Turning now to the Fi-point hexagon, it can be seen to bisect exactly the length from the Fa-point hexagon, also the inner hexagon of the Sol Sabbath Star, to the peak of this Sabbath Star, thus justifying its identification with the semitone. But the two new hexagram points are not spaced at the quarter marks of the whole-tone length that would justify identifying them with even-tempered quarter tones. Rather, they exactly trisect this length. They would seem, then, to represent a division of the whole tone, and of the geometric distance corresponding to this musical analogue, into thirds. From this it follows that the twin grids of the diagram are defining a contrapuntal division of the tonally defined space into both halves and thirds, a counterpoint of two against three. This same distinction will continue to appear in the diagrams of the future worlds, the numbers of construction elements on the two grids always being multiples of two and three.

This distinctive feature of the diagram, which we shall see reappearing in many guises, would seem to originate in the very nature of the hexagram, a figure composed of two triangles—of two and three—that encodes the essential cosmic functions of contraction and expansion in balance. What is true of the hexagram as cosmic model, its counterpointing of two and three, can also be seen in Platonic cosmology. For it is from the unfolding powers of even and odd —1, 2, 4, 8, and 1, 3, 9, 27—that Plato derived his cosmos in the *Timaeus*, most particularly the intervals of the diatonic scale that provide an organizing principle of his cosmos.[4] This understanding of the cosmological importance of the numbers 2 and 3 goes still further back to ancient Egyptian civilization. It can be seen in the special treatment given in Egyptian mathematics to the fraction $2/3$. As deciphered by R. A. Schwaller de Lubicz and explained by an interpreter of his thought, John Anthony West, the meaning of the glyph for this fraction is that "'Unity is proportioned as two is to three.' . . . One becomes Two and Three simultaneously."[5] A similar distinction in kabbalistic cosmology can be seen in the concept of the Partzufim, the divine personalities. The five Partzufim can be divided into groups of three and two, the three supernal Partzufim of Arikh Anpin, Abba, and Imma, who are inseparable, and the two lower Partzufim of Ze'ir Anpin and the Nukvah, whose relationship is intermittent, cosmic functioning being explained in terms of just this distinction. Startling cognates of this cosmological counterpointing can be found in the structure of two major human organs, the lungs and the brain. The two lobes of the lungs feature the unexplained asymmetry of their divisions into two and three parts, while the brain is divided into right and left hemispheres and the three developmental levels that trace its evolution from the reptilian through the mammalian phases to the culminating human level of the cerebral cortex. The twin grids of the Sabbath Star Diagram, then, display the significant counterpointing of two and three, even and odd, that would seem to define the nature of manifest reality as also of our organs of breath and thought, of life and its highest development.

As just seen, the four hexagrams of Asiyah give us one-third of the tone, a semitone, two-thirds of the tone, and the whole tone. Since the chromatic scale can provide no Solfeggio counterparts for division of the tone into units smaller than the semitone, the problem arises as to what to name the one-third and two-thirds divisions of the tone to which these two intermediate hexagrams correspond. The simplest solution seems to be to place them most conveniently within the established Solfeggio semitone names without defining their precise fractional nature. Thus the first third of the tone, coming between Fa and Fi, shall be named Fa/Fi, and the second third, coming between Fi and Sol, Fi/Sol, recognizing that these terms do not name spatial positions analogous to quarter tones but thirds of a tone, and waiving for the moment the additional difficulties with naming the further fractions of the tone that will be encountered in the diagrams for the future worlds.

But the appearance of such later fractions of the space or their tonal analogues follows a different development than that of the semitone. As recently shown, it is possible to trace the antecedents of the first semitone to manifest in the elementary diagram, Fa, back through unmanifest and unmanifestable earlier stages, and these antecedents can be reconstituted. The Ri hexagram can be drawn within the inner Fa hexagon, and the inner Ri hexagon, were it not for the restrictions of the matrix design, could accommodate a Di hexagram. But there are no possible antecedent causes for the Fa/Fi or Fi/Sol hexagrams consistent with the established grids of the diagram. It is as though the entire structure of the diagram through the first three worlds is necessary to prepare the way for this new outgrowth, very much like a new level of branching. These new thirds of a tone, in their turn, will provide the base for a new structure of such thirds, which build upon them in whole tone progressions through the following worlds. But in the fifth world a new branching level further dividing the tone into sixths will commence that will support a further structure of these sixths of a tone; and in the sixth world, in addition to the inherited system of whole tones, semitones, thirds, and sixths of a tone, a new generation subdividing the tone into ninths will find a prepared spot from which to branch out. The Sabbath Star Diagram is beginning to resemble the organic principles of growth of a true Tree of Life, from whose diagrammatic representation it was discovered, following geometric laws of branching similar to those encoded in the seed of a living tree.

The complete fourth-world diagram, then, seems to contain four distinct moments of creative evolution, each represented by its own hexagram. Once the meaning of these four hexagrams is framed in this way, the identification of these four stages seems obvious: Fa/Fi should represent the minerals, Fi the vegetables, Fi/Sol the animals, and Sol the crowning achievement of man. With the more subtle analysis provided by these new tonal discriminations, it would now appear that the "big bang" that produced this universe of matter occurred not at Fi, as the elementary diagram had seemed to indicate, but at the more subtle first stage of the fourth world, Fa/Fi, representing the minerals. From the perspective of the Sabbath Star Diagram, however, the second star burst at Fi, marking the introduction of organic life into the material world, has still greater importance; for, as the next section will show, it is at this point that the matrix, the womb of future cosmic history, is first properly manifested in the diagram. So, too, with the other significant stages of evolution on earth, those of the animals and man. The next chapter will be devoted to analyses of these individual Sabbath Stars, at which time all their geometric features and harmonic resonances will be explored.

We come now to the second reason that the stage-defining construction elements for the intermediate vertical positions were earlier said to be hard to define. This is the question of whether these elements should remain as simple hexagrams or be split into the six constituent hexagrams that together can form a Sabbath Star and, if the latter, what the form of such Sabbath Stars should be. This question did not arise previously because the form of the initially developed Fi Sabbath Star provided a model that could be followed by the Mi and Sol Sabbath Stars as well as by all the semitone Sabbath Stars of the future worlds. For its midpoint split through the center of the diagram leaves no possibility for alternate forms of Sabbath Stars. This is not the case, however, with any stage-defining hexagrams for intermediate positions, none of which can be split symmetrically so that the base of its ascending component triangle will pass through the central point of the diagram. This does not mean that these hexagrams cannot be redesigned as Sabbath Stars but rather that there are no clear guidelines as to which, if any, of the alternative methods of possible Sabbath Star construction should be adopted—no clear guidelines, that is, at the level of the fourth-world diagram. One important rule of construction will become clear by the time the sixth world of the diagram has, through much trial and error, finally been correctly constructed in chapter 6, and analysis of the fourth-world diagram will begin with the definition and application of this rule.

The program for the Sabbath Star Diagram that construction of the sixth-world diagram makes clear is one in which earlier elements are covered by later Sabbath Stars in a precise schedule that makes possible an alternate method of reverse construction. In this reverse method, the complete diagram up to the world under construction can be produced through just the required Sabbath Stars of that final world and the hexagrams of the previous world. Thus the sixth-world diagram will feature a certain number of sixth-world Sabbath Stars and just the position-defining hexagrams of the fifth world, with all the construction elements of the first four worlds and the Sabbath Star additions of the fifth world being covered by the sixth-world Sabbath Stars. The fifth-world diagram can similarly be constructed from just the fifth-world Sabbath Stars and fourth-world hexagrams. Skipping the fourth world momentarily and moving further back to the third, we can now understand why the Mi hexagram is programmed to be a Sabbath Star and the Fa hexagram is not. If a later world is supposed to leave the hexagrams of the previous world intact but to cover the construction hexagrams of all worlds prior to that, then the construction elements of the third world will have to cover the Do hexagram but leave the Re hexagram uncovered. Now, the Mi Sabbath Star does just that; it covers the Do hexagram. But the only form of Sabbath Star possible for the Fa hexagram that will be consistent with the matrix is one that will cover the Re hexagram of the previous world, a practice not allowed by the later determined rules of the diagram. Though subsequent analysis in this chapter will make much of the presence of the Mi Sabbath Star both in reinterpreting the third world and in understanding the processes in the earlier stages of the fourth world, the rules just given should make clear that the Mi Sabbath Star cannot survive in the final fourth-world diagram, that in the final form of this diagram it will be once again reduced to the state of a simple hexagram. In chapter 2 we saw that the Fi Sabbath Star covers the Re hexagram and we have recently seen that the Sol Sabbath Star manifests the Ri hexagram. To conform to the diagram program just defined, the Do hexagram must now also be covered by a fourth-world construction element rather than by the Mi Sabbath Star of the third world.

Later analysis in this chapter will show that there are two modes of intermediate Sabbath Star construction that will fulfill the above-stated requirement of covering the Do hexagram. The first is the Sabbath Star reformulation of the Fa/Fi hexagram constructed in the most natural way possible for this first incremental level of the fourth world, by modeling it directly on the Mi Sabbath Star just within it. As the Fa/Fi hexagram comes at the very next step in the vertical grid beyond the Mi hexagram and continues lines earlier defined by the Mi Sabbath Star, so the six component triangles of the Fa/Fi Sabbath Star can each exactly contain a corresponding triangle of the Mi Sabbath Star. Where the base of a component ascending triangle of the Mi Sabbath Star passes horizontally through the central point, the corresponding base of this form of Fa/Fi Sabbath Star passes through a bar of the Do hexagram at the next lower grid line of the matrix. Similarly, where the point of a component descending triangle of the Mi Sabbath Star covers a vertex point of the Do hexagram, the corresponding point of the Fa/Fi Sabbath Star does the same for such a point of the Ri hexagram. Though the resulting Fa/Fi Sabbath Star is not evenly split at the diagram's center as are the semitone Sabbath Stars, it is composed of six perfectly equilateral component hexagrams that together comprise the larger position-defining hexagram of this Fa/Fi Sabbath Star, as shown in figure 4.3. The alternate method of covering the Do hexagram will be considered later.

This first form of the complete fourth-world diagram, then, involves four position-defining hexagrams, at least three of which are to be elaborated as Sabbath Stars, those at the Fi and Sol positions being in the standard semitone Sabbath Star form and, in this first alternative, that at Fa/Fi being in a new form directly modeled on the pattern of the past, on the Mi Sabbath Star. Left to be determined for this first version of the fourth-world diagram is the final form of the Fi/Sol hexagram. This, too, can follow the pattern of the past and be directly modeled on the Fa/Fi Sabbath Star, each of its component triangles exactly containing one such triangle of this previous Sabbath Star. The trouble is that such a past-modeled Sabbath Star would cover the

Mi hexagram, and this is not allowed by the recently defined program for diagram construction, which stipulates that all position-defining hexagrams of the previous world must survive without covering. If aesthetic values can also be considered a ground for graphic validity, then the past-modeled Fi/Sol Sabbath Star can be further disallowed because of its lack of coherence with the culminating Sol Sabbath Star, a circumstance that will later be more fully considered. One way of completing the fourth-world diagram, then, is to have a past-modeled Sabbath Star at the Fa/Fi level and a simple hexagram at the Fi/Sol level. In what follows, this will be considered the ideal form of the fourth-world Sabbath Star Diagram, one that can be correlated with the traditional understanding of the earth as originally unfallen. We shall close this section with this first definition of the "unfallen" fourth world of material manifestation. Other options of intermediate Sabbath Star construction, and the larger diagram forms and matrices to which they contribute, will be defined and discussed as they emerge in an analytic scenario of the Fall exemplifying the mythological level of diagram interpretation, that major element in the hermeneutic methodology employed in this work that I call the Science of Expressive Form. One implication that can already be seen is that in this unfallen version the Fi/Sol hexagram identified with the animal level of evolution is programmed to be under a peculiar constraint.

But the permitted past modeling of the Fa/Fi Sabbath Star is equally surprising insofar as it is the only example of such past modeling that seems to be permitted by the full program of the Sabbath Star Diagram. This gives added support to the musical analogue to the geometry of this diagram. For it is only by recognizing the Fi Sabbath Star as the turning point of the cosmic octave, a characteristic given to it not by anything apparent in its geometry but only by its analogous position in the musical chromatic scale, that we can appreciate why only this Fa/Fi Sabbath Star could be correctly past modeled. If all that precedes the Fi Sabbath Star can be identified with the cosmic past and all that follows it with the cosmic future, then it can be seen that the only intermediate Sabbath Star emerging in the diagram before this cosmic turning point, the only one that can be identified with the past, is this Fa/Fi Sabbath Star that the diagram program allows to be so past modeled.

This uncanny correspondence is not the only one to give added support to the cogency of the musical analogue. Even more significant is the remarkable diagram produced by dividing the seventh-world diagram at the midpoint corresponding to the musical octave, that in figure 7.1, a division only undertaken because of this correspondence and one of major importance in interpreting not only the culminating seventh world of the diagram but the ultimate meaning of the Jewish mystical tradition. The past modeling of the Fa/Fi Sabbath Star ranks, then, with the geometric relationship of the first four hexagrams—that corresponding to the musical intervals Do, Re, Mi, and Fa—and with the nature of the octave diagram in support of the unlikely proposition that the geometry of the Sabbath Star Diagram can, in some unexplained manner, show correspondences with what appears to be the different logic of the musical scale, that the laws of musical sound and geometric form are so related.

The first form of the fourth-world diagram consistent with the developmental code inherent in the Sabbath Star Diagram is, then, that which contains the Mi and Fa hexagrams of the third world as well as the following fourth-world constituents: the Fa/Fi Sabbath Star in the form modeled on that of the now covered Mi Sabbath Star, the Fi Sabbath Star, the unelaborated Fi/Sol hexagram, and the Sol Sabbath Star, these six constituents plus the darkened zigzag form of its matrix border being illustrated in figure 3.4. This is the first of many figures in this chapter that will illustrate the various combinations of construction elements possible at each stage of the self-generated fourth-world diagram, and all will offer the undifferentiated view of their construction elements that can permit a proper apprehension of the matrix patterns they together variously produce, a perception enhanced by the outlining of the always expressive form of each of the matrix borders, which will be a major focus of the analysis in this chapter. Further specification of the individual construction elements would both

overly complicate these diagrams and detract from the aesthetic impression made by the undifferentiated versions here given. Each of the possible Sabbath Stars of the third and fourth worlds will, however, be separately illustrated in the next chapter, and readers who desire more precise understanding of the individual constituents of the present diagrams can use these models to outline their own constituents on copies of these diagrams. But it is the simple outlining of their matrix borders that will prove most meaningful, as with its stunning form in figure 3.4.

The zigzag matrix border of the past-modeled fourth-world diagram, what can be considered its unfallen form, is most suggestive iconographically, for such a symbol has been used worldwide from earliest times to signify water, and it can still be found in the zodiacal sign for Aquarius. If such a suggestion can be accepted and regarded as a key expressive of the intended character of the fourth world, then the original plan for unfallen Asiyah was for a flowing world in which the parts could not be fully distinguished from the whole, like the vortex in a stream. In this world, there was to be a creative union of the material force represented by the Fa/Fi Sabbath Star with the life force represented by the Fi Sabbath Star as these forces joined with the culminating achievement of embodied life represented by the Sol Sabbath Star of humanity. But the remaining element of the fourth world, its animal constituents, was programmed not to permit of further development, to be under that "rule" definitive of fourth-day creation. The problem with the fourth-world diagram, however, is that there is no immediate way of apprehending this rule and the diagram offers more attractive design alternatives. The combination of such a programmed constraint in the face of more inviting design possibilities seems like a geometric description of Eden, and the sequence of such design possibilities defines an archetypal pattern consistent both with the concept of the Fall and its chronological elaboration. The message of the unfallen version of the fourth-world diagram would seem to be, then, that animal behavior, including the animal level of man, should be restricted to the instinctual functions and that any development of

Figure 3.4. The Past-Modeled Fourth-World Diagram

higher emotional and cognitive capacities on the part of a nature not yet emancipated from instinctual responses can only spell disaster for the world of which it is a part. In the following section an attempt will be made to show how the various design options for construction of the fourth-world diagram can be arranged to provide a scenario consistent with the biblical description of the Fall.

THE FOURTH-WORLD DIAGRAM AND THE FALL

If construction of the fourth-world diagram is begun with the working hypothesis that all of its

hexagrams should be Sabbath Stars and be added incrementally in their chronological order, then the most natural way of constructing the Fa/Fi Sabbath Star would be for it to follow the model of the Mi Sabbath Star just within it in the manner outlined in the previous section. Adding the Fa hexagram and Fi Sabbath Star results in a diagram that provides a significant matrix pattern within the limits of the Sabbath Star Diagram as originally defined by the key of the Tree of Life Diagram. This elaboration of the Elementary Sabbath Star Diagram is illustrated in figure 3.5.

Elaborating the full Sabbath Star potentials of the diagram within the limits for expansion set by the Tree of Life Diagram not only leads to the transformation of the Mi hexagram into a Sabbath Star but to the assignment of a stage to the fourth world intermediate between the Fa hexagram and the Fi Sabbath Star that can be identified with the minerals. This first level of material creation is encoded in a unique form of Sabbath Star that, unlike the Mi Sabbath Star on which it is modeled, exhibits an additional six Do-sized hexagrams around the original Do hexagram, which it also covers and embodies. Since six around a seventh can always be taken as a sign of creation, or re-creation, rebirth, this additional Sabbath configuration of the Fa/Fi Sabbath Star would seem to express the creative

potential within the minerals to combine into the ever more complex compounds from which all the higher levels of creation will evolve, to be at once the basis and fuel of this higher evolution. The added Sabbatical configuration of the Fa/Fi Sabbath Star is an emblem of the creative force that unleashed the big bang of cosmic creation, the force inherent in the added level of individual specificity that matter contributes to creation.

The matrix produced by this version of the Mi, Fa/Fi, and Fi Sabbath Stars as well as the Fa hexagram also exhibits a Sabbatical configuration, that of six loose-packed hexagons around a seventh. Such a loose-packed configuration of hexagons is clearly

Figure 3.5. The Mi, Fa/Fi, Fi Matrix: First Version

less economical than that of a close-packed arrangement since it requires an additional six interspersed triangles, those in the points of the Re hexagram, to surround and, as it were, to manifest the central hexagon, and it needs them as well to give a stability to its on-point hexagons that they would otherwise lack. This loose-packed hexagonal matrix is expressive of a quality at once spaced out and precariously balanced, liable to fall.

It is its expansive quality that provides the first clue as to the meaning of this matrix, for this quality in concert with the three Sabbath Stars contributing to it seems to offer a striking parallel to the passage on the creation of man: "And the Lord God formed man of the dust of the ground, and breathed into his nostrils the breath of life; and man became a living soul" (Gen. 2:7). In this description, Adam comes to life when his lungs are fully expanded by the divine breath, in a condition of divine plenitude. The biblical description also seems to be defining the three Sabbath Stars with which we are concerned. The "dust of the ground" (*afar min ha-adamah*) is most easily correlated with the Fa/Fi Sabbath Star of the minerals, and the "breath of life" (*nishmat chayyim*) can also be correlated with the Fi Sabbath Star earlier identified with the emergence of life. This would leave the Mi Sabbath Star to be correlated with the final definition of unfallen man as a "living soul" (*nefesh chayah*), specifically as the Nefesh soul in its early fourth-world manifestation.

Though the full discussion of the soul as kabbalistically understood will be the subject of part 3, it is necessary here to give a brief introduction to the Nefesh level of the soul. This lowest level of the soul is doubly associated with Yetzirah, for it is in the third world that the soul can first be distinguished from the angelic structure characterizing this stage of emanation, and it is in the continuing Gan Eden of Yetzirah that Nefesh souls are thought still to gather while awaiting incarnation in man.[6] On this basis, it would seem reasonable to identify the original Mi hexagram with the angels and its further elaboration as a Sabbath Star with the Nefesh soul. What this first development of the matrix, which is produced at the furthest point of the emanation process and the turning point of the octave spiral,

seems to be defining, then, is the initial condition of the Nefesh Chayah in a dimension transitional between the third and fourth worlds. Its association with Yetzirah is evidenced both by the presence of the Mi Sabbath Star and by the word used in the biblical description, "formed" (*yetzer*). But it goes beyond the third world to a fourth world as yet composed only of dry land and vegetation, the garden world of the third day. This half-formed, not yet fully materialized or inhabited, version of what will eventually become the fourth world can be identified, then, with the scene of the biblical description of Adamic creation. And what that creation would seem to involve is the transformation of the Nefesh soul of Yetzirah into a Nefesh Chayah, a soul imbued with life in its original immortal form and endowed with a body of still etherealized matter. This ghostlike antecedent of man may be imagined as flitting around a crystalline garden of living energy patterns. The triangulation of these Mi, Fa/Fi, and Fi Sabbath Stars thus gives us an Eden in which the rocks and flowers may be thought to possess souls and the souls to possess bodies of fluid and living minerals. In such an Eden the evolution of the kabbalistic four worlds might have come to a conclusion within the limits of the Elementary Sabbath Star Diagram. But it would be an evolution lacking the animals and man, lacking also the higher levels of individual identity whose manifestation and perfection would seem to be the guiding principle of creation.

The object now is to bring the animals and man into the Garden without their suffering and contributing to the Fall of their world. If we again proceed chronologically and fill in the Fi/Sol evolutionary level of the animals with a Sabbath Star constructed, as was the Fa/Fi Sabbath Star, on a past model, a problem, as we saw, arises. Modeling the Fi/Sol Sabbath Star on that of Fa/Fi by again enclosing each major triangle of its component hexagrams within one enlarged to the next lines of the matrix grid results in an evolutionary dead end, like the dinosaurs whose name can be fittingly applied to the diagram it produces when the Sol Sabbath Star is also added, as in figure 3.6.

As can be seen, the form of such a Fi/Sol

Sabbath Star is not only outsized and dispropor-tionate in the relationship of its parts but it provides no basis for the culminating Sol Sabbath Star of man, whose predetermined semitone form is not coherent with this previous form. The unresolved form of such a "Dinosaur Diagram" would seem to require the design revision of earlier constructed Sabbath Stars that can be correlated with the bibli-cal narrative of the Fall. The Dinosaur Diagram, however, can only be considered a quasi-fallen form of the fourth-world diagram since the conversion of the Fa/Fi and Fi/Sol hexagrams to Sabbath Stars based upon the past model of the Mi Sabbath Star does not significantly alter the ideal zigzag matrix

border of this world. The past-modeled Fi/Sol Sabbath Star adds two matrix triangles in the form of a bow tie whose discontinuity with the otherwise connected matrix does not change its functional characteristics.

Each of the intermediate Sabbath Stars on the vertical grid covers and incorporates much of the previous Sabbath Star on which it has been mod-eled, a circumstance that can be better appreciated by observing their illustrations in the next chapter. But unlike the creative form of the Fa/Fi Sabbath Star, this Fi/Sol Sabbath Star exhibits no addi-tional Sabbath configuration of diminutive hexa-grams, its mechanical imitation of past models no

Figure 3.6. The "Dinosaur" Diagram

longer signifying a current of creative vitality. The comparison of its outsized form to the evolutionary dead end of the dinosaurs suggests that this form of the Fi/Sol Sabbath Star might be further identified with the reptilian level of animal evolution, more generally with the egg-laying animals of the fifth day of creation, animals particularly blessed in the Genesis creation account, and more specifically with that familiar figure of ancient myth, the snake. At the stage of the story represented by figure 3.6, the Nefesh Chayah is still unfallen, but it and the animals of Eden live in a state of tension since its evolution is discontinuous from theirs.

We may now imagine that the snake sees a means of evolving to a mammalian form of consciousness by adapting its form to the model of future perfection represented by man, adapting the form of its Sabbath Star to that of the Sol Sabbath Star. In a tremendous burst of creative evolution, it sheds its old skin or form and comes forth in the beautiful shape of a Sabbath Star with the six additional stars shining in its border that appear in figure 4.8. This change of shape, from one built upon past models to one nesting within a future pattern, may now be thought to exert pressure on the previous Fa/Fi Sabbath Star to conform its shape to the new pattern of future evolution. In so doing, this future-modeled Fa/Fi Sabbath Star would lose its former creative form and beauty to become the most ungainly of Sabbath Stars, a massive hexagon with a triangular point protruding from each of its sides, its denser form, shown in figure 4.5, being more suggestive, however, of a crystalline solid. But whether or not it does so, for both forms of the Fa/Fi Sabbath Star are completely covered by the future-modeled Fi/Sol and culminating Sol Sabbath Stars, being sacrificed, as it were, to the future evolution of the fourth world, the denser pattern of the Sabbath Star Diagram produced by the change in the shape of the Fi/Sol Sabbath Star also changes its matrix border to plateaulike forms suggestive of the biblical "dry land." Thus the change in animal consciousness may be said to produce a consequent change in mineral density, leading to the fully physical form of the fallen world as we know it. It is in this change of matrix border, from the zigzag signi-

fier of water to the plateaulike signifier of earth seen in figure 3.7, that something like the Fall can be located.

To present the matter in more mythological form, we may imagine that the fallen but now more subtle snake invites man to accept its revision of border law, saying that, when you do so, "your eyes shall be opened, and ye shall be as gods, knowing good and evil" (Gen. 3:5). On the basis of the Sabbbath Star Diagram, it would first appear that the "gods" being here referred to are none other than the Ruach spiritual masters of the fifth world. For in the Messianic fifth world, it is thought that good and evil would be known differently. From Jeremiah to the *Temunah* it has been taught that the new world of Messianic perfection would be characterized by a new Torah, one both internalized and more lenient, no longer guided by the restrictive spirit of Gevurah. So Adam followed the guidance of the snake in revising the law of the matrix border before its time. Had he waited until construction of the Sabbath Star Diagram was completed from the end backward, as chapters 6 and 7 will show to be a possible mode of construction, those higher powers he coveted would have been his at their correct level of development. There is a tradition that man's sin in eating the forbidden fruit was only that he did so on the sixth day rather than the seventh. Had he waited and eaten it with Sabbath consciousness, it would have been for him a *pri eitz chayyim*, a fruit of the Tree of Life, endowing him with immortality.

Figure 3.7 presents the denser, less energetic form of the fallen fourth-world diagram, a form in which the Fi/Sol and then the Fa/Fi Sabbath Stars are nested within the final form of the Sol Sabbath Star. Since this nesting mode of construction leaves no such unfinished gaps in the diagram's outer border as does the other mode of intermediate Sabbath Star construction, it is clear that this is the preferred mode of diagram construction, and it is one that will properly be followed in the diagrams of the future worlds. But the following future-modeled form of the fourth-world diagram, if taken to model such a scenario of the Fall, shows it to be a direct product of the animal level of evolution.

We have thus far considered the Fall in its bibli-

Figure 3.7. The Future-Modeled Fourth-World Diagram

cal version, with both unfallen Adam and the fallen snake together in the Garden. But a different version is possible by continuing the evolutionary story in chronological stages. If not man, himself, but the idea of man was propelling the force of evolution forward to the point that a proper form might develop in which the Nefesh soul could become embodied, then it is the idea of this future form that would have influenced the course of animal evolution, redirecting it from the dead end it had reached

to more productive channels. In terms of the diagram, the undrawn form of the Sol Sabbath Star could be viewed as the Final Cause, the Aristotelian *telos*, instructing the more knowing elements within animal consciousness to produce a shape on whose basis its own final form could become manifest. This is, of course, a notion that runs counter to Darwinian evolutionary theory.

The diagram offers a graphic illustration of the Fall as represented at the animal level by the shift in the form of the Fi/Sol Sabbath Star. For in the form based upon a past model, the component hexagrams of this Sabbath Star are larger than in that based on a future model, as the dinosaurs were larger than the mammals. Thus the shape of the animal Sabbath Star may be said to have suffered a fall from the former higher position of its component hexagrams within the diagram. If this change in form may be said to cause a retroactive change in the form of the mineral Sabbath Star to the nesting shape coherent with the later development of the diagram from future causes, then an even more significant change

in the matrix is produced. The past-modeled form of the Fi/Sol Sabbath Star, when added to the past-modeled or unfallen Mi, Fa/Fi, Fi matrix, as in figure 3.8, retains the form of its loose-packed hexagonal matrix, earlier outlined in figure 3.5. Nor does the shift to the fallen form of the Fi/Sol Sabbath Star, shown in figure 3.9, change that hexagonal matrix. It is only the additional shift of the Fa/Fi Sabbath Star from its unfallen to its fallen form, seen in figure 3.10, that appreciably changes the evolving fourth-world matrix border, exchanging the former loose-packed hexagonal matrix for a

Figure 3.8. The Past-Modeled Intermediate Sabbath Stars in the Mi-Fi/Sol Matrix Diagram

close-packed hexagonal matrix, each of whose hexagons is surmounted by a crownlike form, a significant expressive form to be considered later. More important, the collapse of the precariously balanced loose-packed hexagonal matrix to the more compact and stable close-packed form seems again to encode the movement from an expansive to a denser patterning that can be taken as a graphic expression of the Fall of spirit into materiality. And since the Fa/Fi Sabbath Star has been identified with the mineral stage of evolution, the more compact but also explosive form of its six component hexagrams

would now seem to give another graphic expression to the concept of a "big bang," whether it is thought to be manifested chronologically or retroactively after the Fall of man or the animals. Figures 3.8, 3.9, and 3.10 map these three penultimate stages of the fourth-world diagram that contain the Mi, Fa/Fi, Fi, and Fi/Sol Sabbath Stars in their various configurations.

Though the only way one can arrive at the nesting rather than enlarging form of the Fa/Fi Sabbath Star is by proceeding backward from the Sol Sabbath Star and the form of the Fi/Sol Sabbath

Figure 3.9. The Transitional Form of Intermediate Sabbath Stars in the Mi-Fi/Sol Matrix Diagram

Figure 3.10. The Future-Modeled Intermediate Sabbath Stars in the Mi-Matrix Diagram

Star nesting within it, if we now were to use this knowledge to construct the fallen form of the Fa/Fi Sabbath Star at an earlier evolutionary stage, its triangulation with the Mi and Fi Sabbath Stars would give us the perfect close-packed hexagonal matrix seen in figure 3.11, one in which six matrix hexagons are close-packed around a central seventh to provide another and more stable Sabbatical formation than that of the loose-packed variety. The generation of this close-packed hexagonal matrix can offer an illuminating view of a still earlier stage of what can be considered the progressive unfolding of

the process of the Fall. This fallen version of the Mi, Fa/Fi, Fi matrix is given in figure 3.11 and should be compared with the earlier version of what can now be considered its unfallen form shown in figure 3.5. Such a comparison provides the purest version of the Fall of the Nefesh soul in that primitive fourth-world Eden completed by the Fi Sabbath Star, one in which the Nefesh soul may be said to suffer a condensation from the more expansive form expressive of inspiration by the divine breath to the more contracted form expressive of the expulsion of that breath, the progression involved both in this act

Figure 3.11. The Mi, Fa/Fi, Fi Matrix Diagram: Second Version

of breathing and that from a loose-packed to a close-packed hexagonal matrix providing comparable symbols of the Fall. And if the future-modeled Fa/Fi Sabbath Star that produces this contracted form of the hexagonal matrix can be considered as the element defining its fallen nature, then the Sol Sabbath Star, which can produce this same matrix when similarly triangulated with the Mi and Fi Sabbath Stars, would also seem to be defined as fallen in its very nature, a point to be further developed in chapter 4 on the individual Sabbath Stars.

Stunning confirmation that this progression of hexagonal matrices is to be associated with the Fall can be seen in figure 3.12, in which there is a triple interfacing of the Tree of Life Diagram with the matrix borders surrounding these dual Sabbatical configurations of hexagons. This shows that the superimposed Tree is wholly contained within the loose-packed hexagonal matrix but that its Malkhut point and vertical path to Yesod is outside of—mythologically exiled from—the close-packed version. As unfallen Adam had free access to the Tree of Life in the Garden, so that expanded matrix form identified with the unfallen spiritual body of the

●●●●●●●●●●● **The Close-Packed**
Matrix Hexagons

— — — **The Loose-Packed**
Matrix Hexagons

Figure 3.12. The Superimposed Hexagonal Matrix Borders

Nefesh soul would seem to be the very Garden that encloses and sustains the Tree; and as fallen Adam was exiled from the Garden specifically to deny him access to the "way" of the Tree—"he drove out the man; and he placed . . . Cherubims . . . to keep the way [*derekh*] of the tree of life" (Gen. 3:24)— so the contracted matrix form identified with the fallen Nefesh soul no longer embodies the "way" of the Tree, the Hebrew word *derekh* for "way" having a similar connotation to the Chinese term *tao*, as can be seen in the title *Derekh ha-Shem* (The Way of God) by the seventeenth-century Italian Kabbalist Moshe Chayyim Luzzatto. In the exclusion of the

Malkhut point from the matrix of fallen Adam, the mutual exile from each other of man and the Shekhinah, the immanent form of the divine identified with this Sefirah, could not be more poignantly illustrated.

It is only the Mi Sabbath Star that, in concert with the Fi Sabbath Star and either of the two forms of the Fa/Fi Sabbath Star, can produce a matrix of precisely six hexagons loose-packed or close-packed around a central hexagon. Since the Mi stage has been identified with Yetzirah, the world of the archetypes, it is in these dual Sabbatical configurations of hexagons that the progression from expansion to contraction is revealed in its most perfect archetypal form. These two Sabbatical configurations will be obscured by the further evolutionary process resulting in man, but within the larger matrix that can be identified with human consciousness both the expansive and contracted forms of man's spiritual inheritance can be understood to be still simultaneously present and interpenetrating. Thus man would seem to have the capacity to return to an earlier stage of prelapsarian expansiveness, to that loose-packed hexagonal matrix in which the Tree of Life is embodied and its Way is seen still to flourish. Like the space-time diagrams of quantum physics, the fourth-world diagram can be read forward or backward in time, forward through the various incremental levels of the Fall or backward to a still present and unfallen Eden.

A similar progression of hexagonal matrices can be produced in another manner signifying a yet earlier stage of cosmic evolution. For if the ungainly form of the future-modeled Fa/Fi Sabbath Star can be deemed acceptable, then it can provide a model by which the Fa hexagram can also be transformed into a Sabbath Star. Though it was earlier argued that such a transformation is forbidden by the developmental program of the diagram, since it would cover the Re hexagram of the world immediately preceding it, if the equally forbidden development of the past-modeled form of the Fi/Sol Sabbath Star and perhaps of the future-modeled Fa/Fi Sabbath Star can be admitted into the discussion of diagram possibilities and illuminate the Fall by providing a geometry of the forbidden, so may this practice be extended to the Fa hexagram, its forbidden Sabbath Star development giving further support to the earlier association of this cosmic level with the Fall. Though the Sabbath Star additions to the Fa hexagram will all be covered by the Fi Sabbath Star, the proposed transformation of the Fa hexagram into a forbidden Sabbath Star can provide our earliest glimpse at the process of matrix diagram transgression that can be equated with the myth of the Fall.

If the progressive transgression of the rules of diagram construction is carried even further back to the self-generation of the forbidden Ri hexagram, then matrix formation becomes possible as far back as the Fa stage of Yetzirah, signifying a Nefesh soul already fallen in the third world, what we shall see to provide the most meaningful scenario of the Fall. This earliest matrix diagram of the Fall is produced by only three elements, the Mi and Fa Sabbath Stars and the Ri hexagram, since the Mi Sabbath Star covers the Do hexagram and the Fa Sabbath Star the Re hexagram. Though not specifically outlined, this matrix can be discerned in figure 4.2, which includes the three aforementioned elements. Though this seed level of the Fall will be largely or wholly obscured in the final version of the fourth-world diagram, the full discussion of it in the second section of chapter 4 will show how its premature manifestation in the third world can be considered responsible for the loss of immortal life.

Several versions of the fourth-world diagram have been illustrated in both completed and incomplete forms, but from the previous discussion we may conclude that there are only two essential forms of the fourth-world diagram, one that has been considered its ideal or unfallen form and the other its real or fallen form. In addition to the Fi and Sol Sabbath Stars shared by both, the unfallen diagram would feature the past-modeled form of the Fa/Fi Sabbath Star and just the Fi/Sol hexagram, while the fallen diagram would feature the future-modeled form of the Fi/Sol Sabbath Star and the survival of just the Fa/Fi hexagram, both forms of the latter Sabbath Star being covered by the upper three Sabbath Stars of the future-modeled version. In all discussions of the fourth-world diagram following this chapter, reference will be made only to these two versions, the past-modeled version being that appearing in figure 3.4 and the future-modeled version that given in figure 3.7.

The Sabbath Star Diagram represents reality at a level more subtle than that at which it is ordinarily apprehended not only because of its geometric form but because its temporal dimension has both chronological and simultaneous aspects depending on how the observer chooses to observe it, whether in terms of the chronology of its construction or of the simultaneity of its final appearance, both of which are valid. This means that whatever scenario is adopted to define the chronology of its construction, in its final appearance all such stages are simultaneously present. Thus the Fall can be understood to take place simultaneously at the mineral, animal, and human stages, the Fa/Fi and Fi/Sol Sabbath Stars moving synchronistically from their past-modeled to their future-modeled forms and, in so doing, altering the final matrix border from its zigzag to its plateau form, from that expressive of water to that expressive of earth. And what is decisive in viewing the final diagram as unfallen or fallen is the Fi/Sol level of evolution. How its change of form from hexagram to nesting Sabbath Star can be related to the scenario of the Fall will be considered more fully in the conclusion to this section.

To recapitulate what has already been shown, figure 3.5 represents the stage at which the Nefesh soul first became a Nefesh Chayah, a soul informed by immortal life and contained within a body of still fluid minerals, what can be considered its unfallen state. With the addition of the quasi-fallen form of the Fi/Sol Sabbath Star in figure 3.8, the Nefesh Chayah would seem to have found further animal bodies of slightly denser substance to inhabit. In another scenario, illustrated by figure 3.11, the Nefesh Chayah would have already developed a more contracted soul body at the earlier mineral stage, its free will being motivated by the desire to acquire ever denser bodies in a manner that will be discussed more fully in the next chapter and that not only signifies its own Fall but entails the emergence of the next stage of animal evolution in an already fully fallen form.

But whether figure 3.10 is understood to follow figures 3.8 and 3.9 or figure 3.11, it is at this stage that the Nefesh Chayah can be understood to have acquired the further specification of a fallen animal body. To complete the mythologizing of the fourth-world diagram, figure 3.10 can now be viewed as the fallen Nefesh Chayah in its animal form, a snake if you will, and that in this form it is offering to the future form of man something it cannot otherwise utilize, a "crown," inviting man to become manifest in the fallen material and animal form that will make possible his further spiritual development to the crowning heights of Keter to become, in a second interpretation of the bibli-

cal words "as gods," as divine personalities of God.

It is the emergence of man's Sol Sabbath Star as the final stage of an already fallen world of desensitized minerals and animals that empowers his natural endowment of self-conscious will with the higher faculties of thought and feeling that chapter 8 will show to be a consequence of the alteration of the matrix border from its zigzag to its plateau shape. Without the evolutionary emergence of man as the final embodiment of the Nefesh soul, the "crown" of Keter, the meaning of this highest Sefirah, would not be available to this animal or vital soul; for it is only the addition of the Sol Sabbath Star to this evolving fallen form of the fourth-world diagram that contains those added matrix elements that distinguish the human from the animal forms of the Nefesh Chayah, both Adam and the animals being equally referred to by this term in Genesis 2:7 and 2:19. Figure 3.7 represents the final spiritual body of the Nefesh Chayah as incarnated in the body of fallen man. Inhabited by a soul already fallen in a fallen world, man must now evolve to the higher worlds of consciousness the hard way, through the portals opening from the physical world.

The previous discussion of all the possible ways of constructing the fourth-world diagram has shown how the Sabbath Star Diagram encodes what would seem to be the precise number of potential modes available for cosmic manifestation, modes that can be arranged into alternate scenarios with remarkable correspondence either to biblical myth or the fossil records depending upon whether the evolutionary impulse is traced from future or prior causes. In either case, it does define a movement toward greater matrix density that seems consistent with traditional understanding of the Fall and may be said to provide a working model that can help to explain many features of the biblical account and of the later traditions deriving from it. Among these features is the particular involvement of the reptilian animal form and the retroactive sequence by which the Fall of animal consciousness is considered to precede the final materialization of this world. But if the fourth-world diagram can provide a model of the Fall of this world, so can it provide one for its proper transformation, as the next section will now show.

THE FOURTH-WORLD DIAGRAM AND THE TRANSFORMATIVE MOMENT

Once the fourth world is understood as the turning point between the worlds of emanation and those of Tikkun, its transformative nature can best be realized in a form of the diagram that would feature the Fa/Fi Sabbath Star based on a past model and the Fi/Sol Sabbath Star based on a future model, as in figure 3.9, but with the addition of the Sol Sabbath Star that would complete this fourth-world diagram. In reviewing these forms of the fourth-world Sabbath Stars, we can see how their final simultaneous appearance can become a model of transformation, particularly of the transformation from a past to a future orientation. When applied to the human consciousness that crowns the fourth-world evolution of the Nefesh soul, this need not be taken to mark the change from an unfallen to a fallen state, but can rather model a life-altering moment of creative insight that can be called the Transformative Moment, a model that will provide a new positive perspective on what is essentially the future-modeled form of the fourth-world diagram.*

For the first phase of development, whether of an individual, an age, or a world, the creative form of the Fa/Fi Sabbath Star modeled on the past form of the Mi Sabbath Star would seem to provide the most vital foundation for further growth, one that has deep roots of continuity with the past. A premature movement to future patterning, before a firm foundation of traditional knowledge and skills has been acquired, can likewise be modeled by the alternate form of the Fa/Fi Sabbath Star. This future-modeled Sabbath Star is unlike its past-modeled counterpart in having no additional Sabbatical configuration of hexagrams, which can be taken as expressive of creativity, but also unlike its counterpart it has direct contact with the center, the points of the descending triangles of its component hexagrams meeting at that center of Knowledge, Da'at, and seeming to explode outward from it in all direc-

tions. Explosive, indelicate, and lacking in true creativity, the Fa/Fi Sabbath Star prematurely based on the pattern of the future can equally model the explosive beginning of the physical universe and the course of adolescent rebellion, and this not only in the case of individual youths but of such artistic movements as Dadaism. At this first stage in the development of an individual, an artistic or scientific tradition, or an age, the most vital and creative efforts will be those that expand upon the resources of the past rather than rebelling too early against its limitations.

By the midpoint of development, however, it should become clear that the vitality is seeping out of the traditional patterns that formerly worked so well. At this point it is possible to get an insight into the inappropriateness of past patterns of behavior for future growth, that the techniques formerly successful in coping with the circumstances of the past have ceased to work positively for the individual and, if continued, will make him increasingly rigid, unable to adapt to changing circumstances like the dinosaur whose name was earlier given to the past-modeled Fi/Sol Sabbath Star.

The Fi Sabbath Star, whose modulating tone comes at the diagram's midpoint, seems most fit to assume the role of mediating consciousness needed at this time to make the shift in consciousness from a past to a future orientation that can keep the course of creative vitality flowing through the second half of a life or era. The association of this Sabbath Star with the plants gives further support to its new role of transformative mediator, for the plants do mediate between the minerals and the animals, converting the minerals into the organic compounds of life and providing both food and breathable air for the animals. If the Fi Sabbath Star can be accepted as the center of transformative consciousness, then we can chart the elements of what can be called the Transformative Moment from its perspective, the moment at which an insight into the inappropriateness of persisting patterns of behavior can produce real change.

Though this moment can occur many times during a lifetime and with more highly developed individuals can become a habit of mind, for many

---

*Much of this material on the Transformative Moment is taken verbatim from *The Kabbalah of the Soul*, pp. 116–21.

individuals it occurs just once, at that midlife crisis for which the fourth-world diagram can also provide the model. In this model, consciousness is alerted at this midpoint to some behavior or situation causing acute pain that is suddenly recognized to be part of a whole pattern of inappropriate behavior. In diagram terms, the pattern recognized is that past modeling of Sabbath Stars that, if persisted in, will result in the displaced growth of such a Fi/Sol Sabbath Star, already well on its way to completion. Recognizing the negative patterning of this projected Fi/Sol Sabbath Star, the next step is to trace it back to its cause, the Fa/Fi Sabbath Star modeled, like it, on the past. This second step is necessary since one cannot be released from the grip of the past until one has learned to understand and accept its former influence, to recognize that such modeling on the past was the only way in which appropriate behavior, form, could have been originally developed but that it is no longer appropriate for further creativity.

The transformative process cannot end, however, with such analysis of past causation. Without a new image of the self that seems attainable, the individual will rather cling to the old self, whose failings and foibles have been so lovingly understood and forgiven in the process of analysis. Two further steps are necessary for true transformation to take place. First a new ideal image of the self must be projected, that represented by the Sol Sabbath Star. But this is not enough, for its very perfection is so far from the recognized imperfection of the self as to be not only daunting but undesirable, undesirable because it seems to offer no continuity to the present personality that could make its attainment appear to be other than the death of the self.

What is necessary is a creative specification of the ideal model to the peculiarities that give one's essential self its identity, a specification that can enable the self to identify with this new image because it can see the continuity of its personality in this new and improved form. This personalized ideal can be identified with the Fi/Sol Sabbath Star based on a future model, that more abstract ideal identified with the Sol Sabbath Star. Now, if the added Sabbatical configuration of the Fa/Fi Sabbath Star based on a past

model could be taken as expressive of a new creation, in this case the birth of the individual self, so would the Sabbatical configuration of this future-modeled Fi/Sol Sabbath Star similarly seem to signify the re-creation or rebirth of the self.

If the creative form of both Sabbath Stars indicates that this is the progression that can ensure continuing vitality, then it would seem that life and all forms of development are programmed to require such a midcourse correction as, in personal terms, can be considered a spiritual rebirth. He who before had been an apprentice can now display the mark of the master, the ability to redefine the tradition with a creative power that not only expresses the original spirit of its creator but of its age. Only such a progression can provide the continuity of a living tradition, that which was received being transformed through a creative refashioning which can leave its own legacy for the future because it is in harmony with its nature. It is only with the projection of a new ideal model (the Sol Sabbath Star) and the creative adaptation of this ideal to fit the personality (the Fi/Sol Sabbath Star based on this future model) that the individual can be released from its past patterning (the Fa/Fi Sabbath Star based on a past model); for as the diagram shows, it is the Sol Sabbath Star and Fi/Sol hexagram that completely cover all of the Fa/Fi Sabbath Star except for its position-defining hexagram.

The Transformative Moment occurs, then, when both the pattern derived from the past is seen to produce a form no longer coherent with the emerging design of the present, and the future form needed to replace it can be envisioned in terms with which the self can identify. It is only with such a creative revisioning of the self that the old self can be sacrificed. Indeed, this creative revisioning effects just such a sacrifice, producing that transformation in which all distinguishing traces of past determinism have been immolated and the essence freed to ascend upwards. These four stages of the fourth-world diagram thus define a transformative process in which past patterning must be sacrificed to permit further creative evolution in accordance with a projected model of future perfection.

Once we take the fourth-world diagram as a

model of transformative change, the purpose of this fourth world of material manifestation would seem to be none other than to turn the cosmic process around, from one that expanded upon past models in a series of emanations consistent with the four cosmic worlds of the classical Kabbalah to one that nests within the virtual dimensions of future, more perfected worlds reaching to that final circle of the Tzimtzum that can enclose the cosmic octave and the future worlds of the Lurianic Tikkun. And it provides as well a model of the process by which one world can be transformed into another, moving from past patterning to find its own identity that, in turn, can provide a foundation for the evolution of further worlds or the higher dimensions of consciousness they can also be understood to represent. For though the fourth-world diagram contains the previous three worlds and its own prior stages still accessible within it, and can be used meditatively to retrace the process of emanation back to its original simplicity, it also contains implicit within it the potentiality for further spiritual development, one that can retain the complex individuality acquired by the soul in the fourth world while purifying it of the gross materiality that impedes the full utilization of its powers. Thus man has the possibility of reorienting himself to the very direction of his future perfection expressed by the form of this fourth-world model of transformative change

If this future-modeled form of the fourth-world diagram is still taken as a model of the Fall, then the Fall must be considered either as "fortunate" or as at least providing the vehicle for its own correction. There is, however, another way in which this model of transformative consciousness may be viewed that does not require our acceptance of such a Fall as the necessary prerequisite for further spiritual development. Rather, we can view the past-modeled and future-modeled forms of the fourth-world diagram as defining a necessary sequence for fourth-world development, one whose movement from a simpler to a more complex form does not imply such a negative construction as the Fall but can be viewed as a further positive stage of evolution. Such a view will receive support from yet another conceptualization of the fourth-world diagram to be developed in the

next section. There we shall see that the addition of the very first construction element of the fifth world provides exactly the same extension of the matrix border as that resulting from construction of the future-modeled Fi/Sol Sabbath Star, thus validating this form of the fourth-world diagram. But once this sanctifying presence is added, it implies that the power of transformation is one truly coming from another world.

THE SABBATICAL MODEL OF REDEMPTION

As the first Sabbath Star to introduce the new tonal division of the sixth, the first construction element of the fifth world establishes the new vibratory level by which the reattunement of the Nefesh soul to that of the fifth world is to be accomplished. Its rectifying presence appears in figure 3.13.

It is this addition of the first fifth-world Sabbath Star to the fourth-world diagram that can truly convert its fallen form, if such it was, into the transformative model recently considered, this Sabbath Star covering precisely all the elements of the past-modeled Fa/Fi and future-modeled Fi/Sol Sabbath Stars, with the exception of their position-defining hexagrams, that define the transformative model of the fourth-world diagram. In figure 3.13, the only design element to be featured is the significant matrix border produced by this addition to the future-modeled fourth-world diagram, any further discrimination of its parts yielding more confusion than light. But this fifth-world Sabbath Star can be seen separately illustrated in figure 5.2, and if further compared with figure 4.3 of the past-modeled Fa/Fi Sabbath Star and figure 4.8 of the future-modeled Fi/Sol Sabbath Star, it can be seen to cover exactly their Sabbath Star elements. What its addition to the fourth-world diagram also shows, however, is that this rectifying Sabbath Star is discontinuous from its fourth-world elements, nesting rather within the still unmanifest forms of future Sabbath Stars, truly a presence coming from another world and sanctifying both its extended plateaulike border and the higher capacities it signifies.

As is apparent by their embodiment in the star of

Figure 3.13. The Sabbatical Diagram

attunement, it is the past-modeled Fa/Fi and future-modeled Fi/Sol Sabbath Stars that are most in tune with the higher energy that may be associated with the future perfection of the self, the mammalian brain level of the limbic system providing the emotional impetus and the expanded Nefesh

Chayah the meditative condition through which this attunement may be perfected. Thus the very future orientation of this animal level, which a previous section told us is responsible for the Fall, is also the level that can first feel and respond to the call to higher attunement that may be considered the catalyst to the Transformative Moment, transforming the fallen diagram as well into a model of rectification. But though figure 3.13 takes us into the first sixth of the fifth world, we may still consider it a model of rectified Nefesh consciousness rather than a full ascension to the Ruach level of the soul, and this because it adds no new powers to those already possessed by man in his future modeling, as can be seen in the identical matrix border it defines. And though the effects of this attunement on the physical nature of man must be most striking, since this fifth-world Sabbath Star covers the same Do and Ri hexagrams covered by the past-modeled Fa/Fi Sabbath Star of the minerals, the heightened harmony and vitality it may be said to impart to the body and world of man does not change the essentially earthy character of man that the plateaus of the matrix border would still seem to signify.

But if this first Sabbath Star of the fifth world is, indeed, added to the fourth-world diagram to transform it into a model of rectification, then it adds a most significant number to this diagram, converting its six construction elements to seven. With this understanding, figure 3.13 can now be regarded as providing a new Sabbatical model of creation. We have seen that this Sabbatical element covers or manifests exactly the same construction lines as those produced by the past-modeled Fa/Fi and future-modeled Fi/Sol Sabbaths Stars, that same combination as in the transformative model just studied. The Sabbatical nature of this extended diagram is further reinforced by the fact that the two Sabbath Star forms covered by this seventh construction element are precisely those that feature a Sabbatical arrangement of six additional hexagrams surrounding the one that is covered. The implication of this is again that the power of transformation is one truly coming from another world, a supernal power so informing the consciousness with additional dimensions of heart and mind that it will be lifted into a Transformative Moment of change, into the beginnings of Ruach consciousness. But even if we accept the fallen nature of the fourth world, we can now understand its transformative form to be the rectification produced by the virtual presence of that added seventh element, that Presence epitomized in the Sabbath that can facilitate a reattunement to higher energy frequencies. It is, indeed, such a power of reattunement as can be identified with the shofar, understood to be the "trumpet of the Messiah," that will be correlated with this first construction element of the fifth world in chapter 5, which also concludes with a discussion of just such possible future influences.

In chapter 1, the creation account in Genesis was reinterpreted as a model for a seven-dimensional cosmos, one that could be geometrically rendered by the full seven worlds of the Sabbath Star Diagram. Now, however, it becomes possible to interpret the seven stages of the expanded fourth-world diagram as providing a model not of such an archetypal cosmos but of the actual world of physical manifestation, with those more limited supernal constituents that this diagram would suggest are part of the natural conditions of undeveloped man. Construction of this Sabbatical diagram involves the Sabbath Stars for Fi, Sol, and that which, coming between the Sol and the Sol/Si Sabbath Stars and closer to Sol than to Si, may be called Sol$_2$/Si, the two intermediate construction elements of the fourth world having been reduced from Sabbath Star form by the additional fifth-world Sabbath Star as had the two of the third world by the Sabbath Stars of the fourth.

The numerical relationship of the Sol and Sol$_2$/Si Sabbath Stars is most significant. For with the sixth construction element of the Sol Sabbath Star we come finally to the element correlated with the manifestation of man that crowns both the divine works and the fourth-world diagram, both also composed of exactly six stages of creation or construction, the four construction elements of the fourth world and the surviving two of the third world. But the addition of the seventh element suggests that man was created not simply for obedience, that his purpose is, rather, to mediate a cosmic transformation from obedience to the dominion that is the privilege of master spirits. For to fulfill this purpose, both of man and the whole of creation, another element is needed, a future influence that can facilitate this transfer from a past to a future orientation. This would seem to be the purpose both of the seventh day and this seventh construction element, both being alike in signifying a power of attunement that can transform consciousness. Their association seems further to imply that this attunement process is accomplished precisely by the very transmission of holiness that defines the Sabbath, the Sol₂/Si Sabbath Star being viewed as the final organ for this transmission from the holiness of the seventh world to the mundane fourth world below, a function metaphorically defined by the identification given it in chapter 5 with the shofar, the ram's horn. What the association of the seventh day with this fifth-world Sabbath Star finally reveals, then, is that the holiness of the Sabbath is not of this world.

We should now see what further illumination it can provide with respect to the spiritual evolution of human consciousness. Contemplating the seven construction elements of the Sabbatical diagram, it is apparent that they can be divided into two different groups of four and three, the former number being esoterically identified with the square of earth and later with the triangle of spirit. In the first instance we may distinguish the four constituents of the fourth world from the three supernal elements, two of which come from the third world and reflect the characteristic dualism associated with the number two while the third comes from the fifth world and, in its singleness, reflects a unifying quality. The four constituents of earth are subject, then, to spiritual influences from both the cosmic past and its future. Associated with the past are those representatives of the third world figured in the Mi and Fa hexagrams, which we shall see in the next chapter can be correlated either with the angels and demons or the Yetzir ha-Tov and the Yetzir ha-Ra, the good and evil inclinations of the Talmud. Arising from the past, these influences are concerned primarily with obedience or disobedience to a deterministic mode of regulation. While the will that can consciously choose to follow its good inclination and restrain its evil inclination can bring the soul back to its unfallen condition, it cannot contribute in this manner to the evolution of the soul's full powers. For this it must answer the call of the influence deriving from the future, the call to that creative liberation of the self by which evolution can move from the material not back but forward to the spiritual.

The vehicle for this evolution may be associated with the second triad of construction elements in the Sabbatical diagram. It will be remembered that this diagram is composed of four simple hexagrams—those for Mi, Fa, Fa/Fi, and Fi/Sol—and three Sabbath Stars—those for Fi, Sol, and Sol₂/Si. And it would seem to be the latter three whose combined creative forms can transform the evolutionary process in this manner from matter to consciousness. The Fi Sabbath Star may perhaps be associated with something like the Bergsonian "élan vital," that there is a vital driving force behind evolution. But if the prior interpretation of the fourth-world diagram according to Murphy's Law has any applicability to the real world, it would suggest that this vital evolutionary force has been primarily concerned to discover what it can do, not what it should do. On the other hand, the supernal force identified with the Sol₂/Si Sabbath Star would seem to convey just this needed sense of higher purpose. Coming between the Fi and Sol₂/Si Sabbath Stars and the forces they define is the Sol Sabbath Star of man; and man's function would seem to be to mediate between them, in his own person taking the blind force of vital evolution—which, like water, fills all the spaces within the preset boundaries of the areas to which it happens to have arrived, in this case discovering all allowable forms within a particular branch of development—and endowing it with purpose. Such an enlightening of vital evolution would transform it from an unconscious to a conscious process, and in so doing transform it as well into a process of consciousness, of the evolution of consciousness, an evolution possible only for those who, by gaining dominion over their lower selves, have freed the will and its true power of creative manifestation.

Figure 3.13 shows us a picture of the fourth world as completely contained within an all-embracing Sabbatical Sabbath Star, one that does not follow the forms of the past but points a new direction to future patterns of growth. But this very lack of coherence between the forms of the Sol and Sol₂/Si Sabbath Stars, the latter built not upon the former but nesting within the future model of the Si

Sabbath Star, indicates that this should not be considered the final form of the fourth-world diagram. For the future-modeled form of the fourth-world diagram, this rectifying first Sabbath Star of the fifth world may be considered only a virtual presence, invisibly sanctifying what might otherwise be considered its fallen matrix border and, through the reattunement of its matrix elements, effecting the rectification of Nefesh consciousness. But whether drawn or understood, the sanction this Sabbatical element gives to the future-modeled form of the fourth-world diagram may provide another way of viewing both fourth-world diagrams, not as signifying an evolution from an unfallen to a fallen state but the proper evolution from the simpler condition of that upright primate, evolving through several small-brained hominid levels for two-thirds of its *Homo sapiens* span, to the modern men and women who some 60,000 years ago left Africa to begin our amazing spiritual journey.

We have thus far been viewing the Sabbatical Diagram in terms of its seven construction elements. But it should be pointed out that there are three additional elements covered by its Sabbath Stars, the Do, Re, and Ri hexagrams. This brings the total number of manifest construction elements to ten, a number whose particular significance in the context of the Tikkun will be developed in chapter 7. There the Lurianic concept of the Tzimtzum, the divine retraction that left a finite space for the creation, will be correlated with the Octave Diagram, whose forty cumulative construction elements will be further identified with the individual Trees of the four cosmic worlds of emanation, a progression going from the Keter of Atzilut at the upper Do to the Malkhut of Asiyah at the lower Do. From the perspective of this Tzimtzum version of the Sabbath Star Diagram, the addition of the first construction element of the fifth-world diagram to the diagram of the fourth world is required to effect the reconfiguration of the Tree of Asiyah to a perfection different from its origin, for it is this element that brings the total number to the necessary ten of its Sefirot. Whether viewed in terms of outward or inward construction, then, this first Sabbath Star of the fifth world has a unique significance for the fourth world. As that

which doubly effects its rectification, it may truly be called the Star of Redemption.

In interpreting the fourth-world diagram from the perspective that considers its past-modeled form to be ideal, we have seen that the movement from a loose-packed to a close-packed configuration of matrix hexagons and from a zigzag to a plateaulike matrix border seems expressive of a progression from a more expansive and fluid state to one more contracted and solid that can be taken to signify the Fall. This progression seems particularly close to biblical descriptions of Adamic history. Adam was originally conceived in a state filled with the divine breath of life. What must follow from this initial condition, however, is the contraction of his being as the breath of life is expelled from his lungs and the action of breathing commenced. So the breath of life was expelled from his lungs, as he from Eden, and a fallen Adam entered the world of history the better to fulfill its purposes, to effect its rectification to a state higher than that from which it fell.

Just as man can only reach his fullest potential by leaving the Garden behind him, so it was only by moving beyond the key of the Tree of Life Diagram that the principles for constructing the full fourth world of the diagram as well as of its later worlds could be discovered; and these show that the fourth world is not the end of the cosmic process but the point at which a new beginning is possible, a redirection that can be accomplished only by humanity and in which it will find the purpose not only of its own existence but of creation.

THE TRIVALENT LOGIC OF THE SABBATH STAR DIAGRAM

The freedom we have just witnessed to draft such alternate forms of the fourth-world diagram as may symbolize either its fall or positive transformation, as well as another form of freedom allowed by this diagram that we are shortly to explore, suggests that this construction, like many of the systems explored by chaos theory[7] with which it may be compared, is informed by a trivalent logic,[8] study of which will provide a culminating understanding of the meaning of this diagram.

Modern systems of trivalent logic have largely rejected the Aristotelian law of the excluded middle, that there is no middle category between true and false. But if the Aristotelian distinction can be rephrased as that between the permitted and the forbidden, rather than the true and false, then it can be seen that it overlaps another distinction between the possible and the impossible that allows for a trivalent system in which the middle is nonetheless excluded or forbidden. In this new Sabbath Star logic, the two extreme categories would give us that which is impossible and therefore necessarily forbidden and that which is both possible and permitted or correct. But between them is the all-important category of the possible but forbidden that establishes the reality of genuine freedom; for, without it, necessity alone would reign, only the permitted being possible and all that is forbidden being impossible to realize. The fourth category of permitted impossibilities is clearly a null classification that can be disregarded since it is immaterial whether or not an impossibility is permitted. A final point about these two overlapping dimensions is that what distinguishes the possible from the impossible can be considered under the character of laws and what distinguishes the permitted from the forbidden under that of rules, a law being defined as that which it is impossible to break and a rule as that which can be broken but at punishing cost. These categories of Sabbath Star logic can be charted as follows:

WORLD	I	II	III
Rules	Forbidden	Forbidden	Permitted
Laws	Impossible	Possible	Possible

Let us now see how these three logical categories can be illustrated through the procedures of diagram construction.

There are first those necessarily forbidden constructions that are impossible because they violate the fundamental laws that define the uniquely patterned Sabbath Star Diagram, that it consist entirely of simple hexagrams or Sabbath Stars whose symmetrical expansions are consistent with the grid lines of a particular matrix pattern. Any scribbles, circles,

and so on, are thus categorically outlawed. But there are possible constructions of hexagrams or Sabbath Stars that do follow the proper matrix grid lines but are forbidden by rules of the diagram that only become clear with the correct construction of the sixth-world diagram.

All three categories can best be illustrated in terms of the initial generation of the half-step progression, a generation that is both impossible and forbidden in the first world, possible but forbidden in the second, and finally both possible and permitted in the third. In the first world it is considered "unmanifestable" because its construction would violate the grid lines of a matrix pattern not yet established in the diagram. In the second it is consigned to an "unmanifest" status, though its construction is possible in terms of the not yet established matrix pattern, because its manifestation would violate a regularity that emerges with construction of the sixth world of the diagram, as analyzed in chapter 6. This is the unique numerical series of correct construction elements for each world that depends on there being only one construction element for the second as well as for the first worlds, the very circumstance resulting from the initial derivation of the Sabbath Star Diagram from that of the Tree of Life and a feature with further esoteric correspondence to the Pythagorean distinction between the monad and the number one.

But with the final permitted possibility of half-step construction in the third world, a new distinction between permitted and forbidden construction possibilities arises involving the possible conversion of the two permitted hexagrams of the third world into Sabbath Stars, a conversion permitted to the whole-step hexagram because its Mi Sabbath Star would correctly cover the Do hexagram of the first world but forbidden to the half-step hexagram because such a Fa Sabbath Star would cover the Re hexagram of the world just prior to it, a circumstance forbidden by the later developed rules of diagram construction. Finally, with the fourth world, the distinction between permitted and forbidden possibilities involves Sabbath Star construction of the newly emergent forms of intermediate hexagrams. Here again rules deriving from the sixth world would seem to specify that the first of these be permitted a uniquely past-modeled form while the second not be permitted such a form because it would incorrectly cover the Mi hexagram of the just previous third world.

Though such possibilities of forbidden construction may be regarded as ending with the commencement of the future worlds, in which the future modeling of intermediate elements becomes both proper and standard, this does not mean that all freedom to follow the forbidden also disappears from the diagram. For part 3 will show that another form of diagram freedom emerges with the fourth world, the freedom to transgress the matrix border. As the cosmic turning point, the fourth world is the only world to contain both forms of freedom, the freedom it shares with the prior worlds of Emanation to follow forbidden or alternative paths of construction and that it shares with the future worlds of the Tikkun to transgress the matrix border, the former involving the process of cosmic manifestation and the latter the evolution of the soul. But it is the allowance of forbidden possibilities for the first four worlds by the laws of diagram construction that now concerns us.

As shown in this chapter, the drafting of these alternative constructions provides a complex model through which a scenario coherent with the myth of the Fall can be mapped with precision. And it would further seem that the Sabbath Star Diagram is logically programmed to make such a scenario of erroneous construction more than probable, with significant implications for the nature of the fourth world in which we live that go beyond the simple charting of logical categories. This is because construction of the fourth-world diagram consistent with the regularities that appear to emerge in the sixth, rules that themselves will have to be qualified by the intelligence coming from still higher dimensions, cannot be made on any rational basis derivable only from its own and past construction. We are

thus faced with the fact that the cosmic world corresponding to our given world of three-dimensional solids seems programmed to allow for choices among various alternatives, a condition revealing what the highest levels of exploration will confirm, the fundamental irregularity of this world.

The first thing that can be said about the rules governing the Sabbath Star Diagram is that there is no way in which they can be arrived at without recourse to some more hidden knowledge. It is not just that an ideal form for the fourth-world diagram can only be given by a shamanic geometer who has been to the diagram of the sixth world and returned to redraft that of the fourth, but that no version of the fourth-world diagram would be possible without the prior construction of the elementary version from the key of the Tree of Life Diagram. And the source of the Tree of Life Diagram is completely lost to history. So for the poor dwellers in the fourth world, the rules that govern our world must be accepted as apodictically known only to the seer who has been to the mountain of the sixth world and come back to reveal its inexplicable truths and commandments.

The process by which the laws of the diagram may be learned can be treated, finally, as a parable of the difficulties attending the trial-and-error quest for true knowledge, a method that would seem to be mandated by the very way in which the diagram defines the fourth world, as a wilderness, indeed, whose irregularity cannot be understood at this level but whose possibilities do permit one to reach the grail of proven correctness through such trial and error. It would seem to be just this irregularity, however, that can ensure the very exercise of freedom that alone gives meaning to the regularities of all the future worlds, that gives to this wilderness the character of a school for the disciplined testing and perfecting of that freedom until, through such efforts as are analogous to the actual construction of the future worlds of the diagram, the way is opened to the promised land.

CHAPTER FOUR

The Evolution of the Fourth World

PRELIMINARY DEFINITION OF THE SABBATH STARS

The program for construction of the Sabbath Star Diagram prescribes growth by either simple hexagram or Sabbath Star, and these lead to very different results Growth by hexagram can occur only in one direction, whether that is outward to infinite size or inward to infinitesimal size. The case of the Sabbath Star, pictured by itself in figure 2.8, is quite different. The outsized hexagram in the Sabbath Star constellation functions like any other position-defining hexagram; it enlarges the diagram to the level that gives it its tonal name. But the six smaller hexagrams, whose combination forms the seventh larger hexagram, function in an altogether different manner. Not only do they contribute to the outward growth, in most cases embroidering the outer design of the diagram with an additional twelve points, but they also grow inwardly, providing a new incremental layer on what has already been deposited and so restructuring an earlier formation along the lines of a newer model of growth.

This restructuring takes the form of a matrix pattern, it being a primary characteristic of the Sabbath Star that it can participate in the process of matrix formation. The matrix of a cosmic world, or portion of a world, is, indeed, an artifact of its Sabbath Stars, one that would seem to delineate the inner structure of its soul. This is not just a figure of speech, for Sabbath Star formation enters the diagram at the same point that the Kabbalah traditionally ascribes to the emergence of the soul, the third world of Yetzirah. In the diagram, it is the Mi Sabbath Star of Yetzirah that has been identified with the pre-incarnate Nefesh soul; and this suggests that a defining characteristic of the soul, as of its Sabbath Star model, is its unique capacity both to participate in the ongoing process of cosmic evolution in which it is to achieve its own perfection while, at the same time, having a reciprocal effect on the earlier worlds responsible for its present state, thus allowing the future-directed action of soul growth to enrich the reconstituted past. It tells us that the process of spiritual redemption must proceed in both directions simultaneously, forward to an individual spiritual mastery that can survive in the collectivity with which it will also be unified in the final convergence of past and future that chapter 15 will map so precisely. But the doubly directed growth of the Sabbath Stars primarily defines the elements and epochs of the cosmic worlds, and these stages can be illuminated by study of the particular resonance of any such evolutionary level with other realms of being, prior or future.

In addition to the system of resonance deriving from the overlaying of previous hexagrams by later Sabbath Stars, a second key to an understanding of the Sabbath Stars is the relative degree of their access to the center. The first thing to be noted with respect to this last consideration is the marked difference in access between the levels defined by the semitones and those defined by the thirds or lesser fractions of the tone. For it is only the semitone levels whose Sabbath Stars go right through the center. This shows that the whole- and half-tone stages— the latter of which can be traced right back to the first world in those successively unmanifestable, unmanifest, and finally manifest forms—continue to maintain their special significance; and this would seem to be to define the polar opposites of contraction and expansion, collectivity and individuation, that function in all the worlds.

A third and final clue to the meaning of a Sabbath Star is its appearance, its expressive form. As was shown in chapter 3, there are various distinctive forms of Sabbath Stars, that of the semitones and those of the past or future modeling of each of the thirds; and these forms will reappear in any future Sabbath Stars built in a whole-step, or double-point, progression upon these earlier Sabbath Stars. The distinctive form of a particular Sabbath Star contributes, then, to its formal definition. But another part of its definition, as earlier suggested, is contextual, the resonance of the precise position it holds in what can be considered the syntax of the diagram. A Sabbath Star can be classified by both its form and context, its relationship to other diagram elements, and this latter involves the two previously defined keys of resonance by overlaying and access to the center. These three keys will be employed in an analysis of each Sabbath Star to have thus far appeared in the diagram, beginning with those of the third world, and will prove an invaluable aid to diagram analysis.

THE SABBATH STARS OF YETZIRAH

Like the Ri hexagram, the Sabbath Stars of Yetzirah are not manifest in the Elementary Sabbath Star Diagram derived from the Tree of Life and can only

be said to appear in their correct chronological order when the Sabbath Star Diagram is self-generated. But unlike the later disclosure of the Ri hexagram by the Sol Sabbath Star and earlier fourth-world Sabbath Stars, the fourth-world diagram covers up any Sabbath Star development of third-world hexagrams and reduces their Sabbath Star elements to what can be considered a virtual status. From the perspective of the complete fourth-world diagram, then, the Sabbath Stars of Yetzirah exist only in a virtual state. Figures 4.1 and 4.2 illustrate the Mi and Fa Sabbath Stars, respectively, outlining their position-defining hexagrams, one of their component hexagrams, and the earlier hexagrams they cover.

As was indicated in chapter 3 but will only be explained in chapter 6, the program for the self-generated diagram would seem to require the construction elements of a world to leave the hexagrams of the previous world intact but to cover those of all worlds prior to that. On this basis, it is only with the emergence of the third world that any prior elements need to be covered, in this case the Do hexagram of

Figure 4.1. The Mi Sabbath Star

Figure 4.2. The Fa Sabbath Star

the first world. Conversely, the Re hexagram of the second world should not be covered by third-world elements. Comparison of figures 4.1 and 4.2 shows that the Mi Sabbath Star is required at this stage of diagram development precisely because it does cover the Do hexagram, while the Fa Sabbath Star violates the rules of the diagram by covering the Re hexagram and should be prohibited. Both the permitted Mi Sabbath Star and forbidden Fa Sabbath Star can be considered manifest in the self-generated third-world diagram, the latter maintaining this manifest state as well through the first third of the fourth world while the former can maintain this state through the second third of that world. As such, study of these Sabbath Stars can tell us much about the third world and earlier stages of the fourth world, and their final virtual status retains a significance for the ultimate human stage of the fourth world.

Let us first try to understand the implications of these permitted and forbidden coverings. If the Do hexagram can be identified with the Hexagram of Creation developed in chapter 1, then it may be said to contain the whole program of creation implicit within it, and any later element that covers it may also be said to embody this code. As the hexagram denoting the cosmic world of Atzilut (Emanation), it also represents a direct emanation of the divine, and this also may be said to be embodied by any element that later covers it. Now, since the Mi Sabbath Star was earlier identified with the Nefesh soul, it would seem to be this soul that comes into being gifted with a spark of the original divine emanation of Atzilut and containing an implicit knowledge of the divine plan or program. Its access to such knowledge is further indicated by the way the bases of the component hexagrams of the Mi Sabbath Star cut right through the Da'at (Knowledge) center of the diagram.

In contrast, the forbidden Fa Sabbath Star covers the Re hexagram of Beriah (Creation), embodying its creative force but without knowledge of the plan contained in the Do hexagram. And though the whole of this Sabbath Star may be said to cross the Da'at center, this is not true of any component hexagrams, the points of their descending triangles just touching this center. Rather, these component hexagrams may be said to be turning their backs to the center and flying off in all directions, exploding with blind, creative force. If such an idea can again be entertained, then we may see a reason why the Re hexagram was not intended to be covered at this stage. For the proper manifestation of the fourth world in due course, it was necessary for the creative element in cosmic evolution to remain in the unitary state that contained only the potential of multiplicity so that it could find its most appropriate vessel, life, the defining characteristic of the Fi Sabbath Star that finally does properly cover it.

It will be remembered that the world of Beriah was largely identified with the state of potentiality because of the initially unmanifest status of its potential Ri hexagram. That the Ri hexagram was intended to remain unmanifest even in the self-generated form of the second world of the Sabbath Star Diagram is indicated not only by the key of the Tree of Life Diagram; it is also demanded by the numerical formula for construction elements in each world that will become clear with the special construction of the sixth-world diagram detailed in chapter 6. But though this apparently correct form of the self-generated second-world diagram would feature only the Re hexagram, the very fact that construction of the forbidden Ri hexagram is possible means that the possibility of such forbidden construction, a possibility included in figure 4.2, enters the diagram at the stage still earlier than that of the even more forbidden Fa Sabbath Star. The admission of such forbidden possibilities into the process of constructing the Sabbath Star Diagram reveals this diagram to be informed by a trivalent logic that allows for the exercise of such freedom, as developed at the close of the previous chapter.

The first possibility of such forbidden construction occurs, then, in the second world, and it involves the question of whether this world should contain hexagrams built upon the Do hexagram in both the double- and single-point methods of construction. With such a forbidden single-point construction of the Ri hexagram, the individuating force, which may be identified generally with such half-step construction elements and most particularly with this seed of the divisive half step, would make a premature entrance onto the cosmic stage, with effects both on its second world, the third, and ours. But when in the third world the possibility of half-step construction finally becomes permitted, a new possibility of forbidden construction emerges with regard to the question of Sabbath Star construction. As we have recently seen, such construction is permitted in the case of the Mi hexagram and forbidden in that of the Fa hexagram. But if the propensity of the half-step position for the forbidden is again actualized in the third world with construction of the forbidden Fa Sabbath Star, this would not only cover the Re hexagram prematurely, that which may be identified with the proper unfolding of the creative process, but leave only the Ri hexagram to exert an independent supernal influence on the third world, individualism being now the only motive for purposeful action.

By developing its forbidden potential for Sabbath Star form, the Fa hexagram effaces the independent power of the Re hexagram and makes possible the development of the matrix at an earlier stage than would otherwise be possible, with the forbidden Ri hexagram at its own Fa stage and without it at the Fa/Fi stage, but in either case before its proper manifestation at the Fi stage of the fourth world. Since in the future-modeled form of the fourth-world diagram both forms of the Fa/Fi Sabbath Star are as covered as those for Mi and Fa, the matrix of which we now speak is as virtual as the three Sabbath Stars that produce it. Without the Fa Sabbath Star, matrix formation is only possible at the Fi stage, and it defines what can be considered the ideal form of the Nefesh Chayah, the living soul. With the Fa Sabbath Star, we come to levels of matrix formation produced without the contribution of the life ideally programmed for the Fi stage of Nefesh development.

In chapter 2 the Mi and Fa hexagrams were

associated with the unfallen and fallen aspects of Yetzirah, and we now have an even better gauge for such a distinction than that apparently sudden intrusion of the half step from which this fallen quality was originally derived. For the aspect that was then thought to signify an unfallen condition is now shown to be capable of permitted Sabbath Star formation, and that aspect earlier associated with a fallen state is now shown to be only capable of a Sabbath Star development that transgresses the rules of orderly manifestation. Whether or not the Fa hexagram is given such license in diagram construction, it carries within it a capacity for engaging in the forbidden that gives support to the earlier association of this hexagram with the introduction into the diagram of some quality suggestive of irregularity or evil. Once it is redesigned as a Sabbath Star, however, the evil of such irregularity becomes more specified as the evil of prematurity. As it is the only Sabbath Star of a semitone hexagram that does not conform to the shape of the semitone Sabbath Stars otherwise everywhere in force, it would seem to represent a premature stage for the half-step hexagram to develop Sabbath Star form. Unlike the beautiful form of the Mi Sabbath Star, its appearance is ungainly, gross—in a word, ugly, and ugly precisely because of its undeveloped Sabbath Star form, its premature manifestation. The beauty of the Mi Sabbath Star and ugliness of its Fa counterpart seem expressive of the moral or spiritual qualities that these forms may be taken to represent, outwardly expressing their inner qualities as the body does the spirit within. And its premature manifestation has effects on the diagram equally premature, too early specifying the creative potential of the Re hexagram and so producing matrix forms not yet endowed with the principle of life. As we shall see more clearly in the following two sections, what the Sabbath Star Diagram encodes as the accomplishment of such premature production of matrices at the Fa/Fi rather than Fi level of Nefesh development, a production only made possible by the forbidden Fa Sabbath Star, is precisely the loss of divine or immortal life, the biblical loss of natural immortality from an engagement with forbidden behavior that the Kabbalah says was wrong only in its prematurity.

This brings us back to the question of how the Fa Sabbath Star is to be mythologically identified, a question that cannot be divorced from the earlier identification of the Mi Sabbath Star as the pre-incarnate Nefesh soul. If we now extend this identification to include both of the Yetziric Sabbath Stars, then the Mi Sabbath Star should be identified with its soul essence and the Fa Sabbath Star with that which the Kabbalah also assigns to Yetzirah, the soul's Tzelem or soul body. As the first half of all the worlds is closer to the center and the second half to the periphery, we can see this primary distinction as characterizing the difference between these two sides of the soul, its inner half still more collective and its outer half more particularized by the embodiment it gives to its soul essence.

The concept of the Tzelem as subtle body derives from the concept of "image" as this term was used in the central biblical text: "Let us make man in our image, after our likeness" (Gen. 1:26).* In the final section of this chapter we shall consider the way in which man may be considered the image of God; but to speak in more general terms, the Tzelem is ordinarily understood to mean the form in which a spiritual essence can be reflected.

An analogous illustration that may clarify this meaning is the mysterious spatial pattern discussed in chapter 1 that can be "formed" by the temporal vibration of a sound. It can be easily demonstrated that if a thin layer of sand is placed on the skin of a drum and a sound is produced at its edge, the sand will form itself into a geometric pattern with infinite shadings to reflect the exact tone and timbre of the formative sound,[1] such a generation of the hexagram form being illustrated in figure 1.2. That is, a particular sound contains a unique spatial form potentially within it that the right circumstances can permit it to manifest. In the same way, it is thought that a spiritual entity can manifest itself in a form that uniquely reflects its essence and thus can be considered its image. As the spatial pattern cannot exist without the generative sound, so is the subtle

---

*Both in this section and the next, there are ideas, words, and quotations on the subject of the Tzelem, the soul body, that earlier appeared in *The Kabbalah of the Soul*, pp. 73–78.

body dependent for its form and subsistence on the spiritual vibration informing it. Such a causative sequence can also be seen in the commonplace of esoteric cosmology that the first activity in the actual process of manifest creation was the production of a cosmic sound or vibration, in the West known as the Marmor (Saying) or the Word and in the East as the sound AUM, space and form being later cosmic developments.

That the Nefesh soul is endowed with the unique capacity for free will is indicated by the way its Mi Sabbath Star, shown in figure 4.1, cuts through the diagram center at right angles to the central line of a superimposed Tree of Life Diagram. But the freedom of the Nefesh soul in its original expansive form, like that of unfallen Adam, may exist only in potential, the actualization of this potential immediately causing a two-stage process leading through something like the myth of the Fall to its final embodiment in man. The first stage would seem to involve a necessitated contraction of its formerly unconstrained soul essence into the Tzelem required to bond this essence to the physical body, and we shall soon consider a further contraction it may be said to suffer at the next stage. But since its function is directed toward physical embodiment, so is it through the Tzelem that the Nefesh soul may be said to begin its purposeful exercise of freedom, freely choosing now to complete the course that will accomplish this. The two different terms that were just applied to these stages, the Fall and embodiment, contain two opposite ways of perceiving the material world, as unfortunate or as desirable. As the myth of Adam incorporates the former vision, so the soul's free choice to incarnate is seen as a positive fulfillment of the purpose for which it was created. The first completion of the soul, which was equated to formation of the Nefesh Tzelem in Yetzirah, would seem, then, to define the capacity for freely willed action, though its only available choice appears to be the acquirement of a denser physical body. As we shall later see, it is only in its human incarnation that the soul can choose another path, can begin to effect a Tikkun to a more complex spiritual state.

But before it gains the capacity for such free choice, it must first have a distinctive, a personal, will. It seems likely, therefore, that the Tzelem which the Nefesh develops at this early stage of Yetzirah should also signify the quality that, for Gershom Scholem, is the defining attribute of the Tzelem, individuality. This can be seen in the fuller context of his discussion of the Tzelem.

> The ẓelem is the principle of individuality with which every single human being is endowed, the spiritual configuration or essence that is unique to him and to him alone. Two notions are combined in this concept, one relating to the idea of human individuation and the other to man's ethereal garment or ethereal (subtle) body which serves as an intermediary between his material body and his soul. Because of their spiritual nature, the neshamah and nefesh are unable to form a direct bond with the body, and it is the ẓelem which serves as the "catalyst" between them. It is also the garment with which the souls clothe themselves in the celestial paradise before descending to the lower world and which they don once again after their reascent following physical death. . . . In Lurianic Kabbalah the nefesh, ru'ah, and neshamah were each assigned a ẓelem of their own which made it possible for them to function in the human body.[2]

The Tzelem gives the soul a power it did not previously possess, its individuality, and it is precisely this acquirement of the soul through the Tzelem that appears to be necessary for it to fulfill its purpose. In creating its individual image through some impress of its unique vibration on the ethereal substance of the second and lower plane of Yetzirah, the Nefesh thus gains an instrument through which it can effect its personal will in the material world, finally through the human body. The Tzelem gives the soul that near-focus lens that permits it to perceive reality under the aspect of concrete particularity that also serves to individuate the soul and would seem to be the purpose of the whole process of cosmic emanation. Though the final version of the fourth-world diagram will once again reduce the Mi and Fa Sabbath Stars to hexagrams, the influences represented by those hexagrams will continue to exert their force on the whole of material creation and especially on man. To understand what these influences may be and how they are to be related to the previous consideration of their Sabbath Star forms, we shall have to review the inhabitants of the kabbalistic supernal worlds.

The three supernal worlds are traditionally associated with two different kinds of entities that first become clearly distinguishable in Yetzirah. The first of these is divine and in Yetzirah is represented by those entities most identified with this third world, the angels. In the process of emanation beginning with the static *sefiratic* points of Atzilut and proceeding through the dynamic archangelic Forces (*kokhot*) or linear vectors of Beriah, the angels of Yetzirah represent the final engineers of the grand design, drawing the detailed two-dimensional blueprints for the myriad types of future materialization or subprograms that translate the more abstract principles they have received into manifestable form. The whole structure of the three earlier worlds may be understood, then, as an organ for transmuting immaterial thought into living matter, and though this organ or organism may be filled with power, knowledge, and joy, its member parts do not have any personal freedom of the will. Nor are they normally thought to be endowed with permanent spiritual bodies.

But alongside of this structure of divine powers are spiritual entities of another type known as souls. The source of these souls is regarded as being higher than that of any of the angels, being rooted in the first world of the Sefirot. Most of these souls are thought to descend from Atzilut to a Yetziric Gan Eden where they await incarnation, but their intermediate history is obscure in both the tradition and the diagram. Prior to Yetzirah, the Sabbath Star Diagram provides no way of distinguishing the spirituality of the soul from the organism of multileveled angelic forces that define the first two cosmic worlds. Thus the Atzilutic Sefirot share the condition of unity that characterizes the first world, as the Forces of Beriah share its state of unmanifest potentiality, what is true of the world being equally true of its members. In Yetzirah, however, we can begin

to distinguish the angelic structure of the world organism, as defined by the progression of hexagrams, from another entity capable of combining into a matrix that had no prior existence. Thus it seems possible to identify the Mi hexagram, as it appears in the elementary and fourth-world diagrams, with the angelic world of Yetzirah and the Mi Sabbath Star, which emerges in the self-generated third-world diagram, with the first distillation of the soul from its earlier suspension in the maternal waters of Creation (Beriah), which occurs to it on the Nefesh level of the soul in Yetzirah. Whatever may be its prior history, then, the spiritual entity of the soul makes its first appearance in the diagram in the world of Yetzirah. But whereas its Sabbath Star forms will be absorbed by the structure of the full fourth-world diagram, its hexagram forms will survive throughout the fourth world. We should now try to understand what role the surviving constituents of Yetzirah are to play in the drama of Asiyah.

In discussing the construction program for the diagram that calls for the survival of the hexagrams of a previous world, it was suggested near the end of chapter 3 that these surviving elements were meant to signify the continuation of an independent higher influence upon the constituents of the next world. Such a suggestion appears most meaningful with regard to the influence of third-world elements on the fourth world since it is consistent with traditional concepts of spiritual influences affecting this world. We have already seen reason to equate the surviving Mi hexagram with the angels, an equation that would give diagram support for the religious conception of angelic influence on and interaction with man. What, then, of the Fa hexagram? The Kabbalah does posit a second class of entities intermediate between the spiritual and physical that are called *shedim* and that would seem, on this model, to be identifiable with the Fa hexagram. Generally translated as demons, the *shedim* are the subject of a rich and varied kabbalistic demonology. I wish, however, to discuss only those aspects of them that seem to be suggested by the Sabbath Star Diagram.

If the Fa hexagram is to be identified first with the lower plane of Yetzirah and then further with the concepts of *shedim* (demons) and Gehennah (hell), there are various points on which the diagram may prove illuminating. The first concerns the genesis and purpose of such evil. Considering its chronological appearance in the elementary diagram, its major cause for being is quite specifically to manifest the Sefirah Yesod. The association of the *shedim* with Yesod is most suggestive since this is the genital Sefirah, and most of the kabbalistic lore concerning *shedim* focuses either on their direct sexual intercourse with humans or indirect participation in unlawful sexual relations, which become a source of *shedim* generation. The *shedim*, then, would be a source of reinforcement to the natural tendency of the Nefesh soul, soon to be again considered, to acquire ever denser bodies through which to express the freedom of its will, reinforcing as well its growing appreciation of the sensual pleasures made possible by its final human body, pleasures that can block all influence coming to inform the human will from the oppositely oriented angelic sources of inspiration.

Once both the angels (*malakhim*) and the demons (*shedim*) are located in the third world of Yetzirah and their influence is understood to extend to the world of Asiyah, such influence can be conceptualized in yet another way that has deep roots in the Jewish religious tradition. This involves the two "inclinations" understood to exist in man, a good inclination, Yetzer ha-Tov, and an evil inclination, Yetzer ha-Ra. If we look at these terms, it can easily be seen that the good (ha-Tov) and evil (ha-Ra) referred to are "formations" somehow related to Yetzirah, the world of forming, Yetzer. Although such an association is not normally made by Kabbalists, it would seem to be implicit in these terms and to signify that there is a good form of Yetzirah and an evil form of Yetzirah, and that man's good and evil urges have their origin there.

Whether identified with good and evil spiritual entities or inclinations, the Mi and Fa hexagrams reveal their own Yetzer ha-Tov and Yetzer ha-Ra through two characteristics of their forms. The first is their derivation from the whole- and half-step progressions, the former based upon the more stable double-point method of hexagram expansion and the latter upon the unstable single-point method. This difference in potential stability is further expressed in the self-generated third-world diagram by the forms of Sabbath Stars they can develop, for, as we have seen, the stable Mi hexagram can be refashioned as a permitted and beautiful Sabbath Star while the refashioning of the unstable Fa hexagram can only be in a form both forbidden and ugly. Thus the soul aspects or types that, in Yetzirah, become distinguishable from the spiritual constituents that compose their cosmic world betray in their Sabbath Star forms the strengths or liabilities inherent in their hexagram sources.

The two forms taken by these Yetziric structures have different cosmic durations, however. As already indicated, the Fa Sabbath Star maintains itself from the second half of Yetzirah through the first half of Asiyah, to have its Sabbath Star elements covered by the Fi Sabbath Star, whereas the Mi Sabbath Star has a duration twice as long, from the beginning of Yetzirah up until the final stage of Asiyah, being finally covered only by the Sol Sabbath Star representing its embodiment in man. Though the cosmic code of the diagram would seem to give evil permission to flourish, it also indicates the final triumph of good. The greater longevity of the forces of good is also exhibited by the hexagrams associated with Yetziric good and evil. As with their Sabbath Star forms, so also is the Fa hexagram shorter lived than the Mi hexagram. It extends from the second half of the third world through the first third of the fifth, finally to be covered by the Sol/Si Sabbath Star later to be identified with the cosmic stage of apocalyptic war. In contrast, the Mi hexagram extends from the beginning of the third world to the midpoint of the fifth, being finally covered and incorporated by the Si Sabbath Star signifying the Messiah or Messianic consciousness. At that point, the Yetzer ha-Ra will be completely eliminated and the Yetzer ha-Tov will become definitive of Ruach consciousness: the law will be written in the heart. Thus in the fourth world, and particularly at the Fa/Fi stage of the minerals in which both of the third-world Sabbath Stars are fully operative, the structures of Yetzirah will continue to play most significant roles.

THE FIRST SABBATH STAR OF ASIYAH AND THE MINERALS

Introduction

The fourth-world diagram can be chronologically developed with either of the alternative forms of the Fa/Fi Sabbath Star correlated with the minerals, its past-modeled or future-modeled form. But it is only in the form of the complete fourth-world diagram containing its past-modeled form that there can be any survival of the Fa/Fi Sabbath Star. The future-modeled form of the Fa/Fi Sabbath Star has only a hypothetical existence at this final stage of the fourth-world diagram since it cannot contribute to that previously considered its unfallen form and is completely covered by that which may be considered either fallen or transformative, a fate it shares in this version with its past-modeled counterpart.

From the perspective of either final diagram, therefore, a fallen form of the mineral Sabbath Star is only a hypothesis. The Sabbath Star Diagram, then, offers us a choice in its fourth-world versions, either of a world whose mineral aspect manifests a Sabbatical holiness, or of a world whose true material dimension is hidden and subject to conflicting interpretations. While many may see matter as God-forsaken, an Isaiah can still perceive the virtual outlines of God's glory.

Figure 4.3 illustrates the past-modeled form of the Fa/Fi Sabbath Star with a darkened outlining of its position-defining hexagram and of one of its component hexagrams. Also outlined with broken lines are the Do and Ri hexagrams that this Sabbath Star covers. Figure 4.4 illustrates another feature of this past-modeled form, the six additional Do-sized hexagrams that encircle the Do hexagram in a

Figure 4.3. The Past-Modeled Form of the Fa/Fi Sabbath Star

Sabbatical configuration, all seven of these mini-hexagrams being outlined with dashes. Finally, figure 4.5 illustrates the future-modeled form of the Fa/Fi Sabbath Star, with its position-defining hexagram and one of its component hexagrams outlined by an unbroken line, while the Ri hexagram it covers is outlined by a broken line.

As can be seen in figures 4.3 and 4.4, the past-modeled form of the Fa/Fi Sabbath Star has a more graceful appearance than the future-modeled form pictured in figure 4.5, though the more crystalline form of the latter is suggestive of the denser form of matter that has been correlated with the concept of the Fall. Both cover the Ri hexagram and may equally be said to embody its potential for individuality, for manifesting the particular. But the past-modeled form also covers the Do hexagram, and

knowledge of the laws of the diagram indicates that this is its primary function, to be a part of the fourth-world diagram that can cover the Do hexagram and thus embody the original plan of creation. The capacity for such a creative manifestation of the laws governing materialization would seem to be further signified by the Sabbatical constellation of Do-sized hexagrams that this Sabbath Star features. But however beautiful this Sabbatical array may be, it cannot mask the fact that this is as close to the center as this Sabbath Star form can come, that it has no direct contact with the Da'at center of Knowledge. The future-modeled form, on the other hand, does touch the center with the point of each of its descending component hexagrams.

As with the Sabbath Stars of Yetzirah, where the Mi Sabbath Star seems more correctly manifested

Figure 4.4. The Additional Sabbatical Constellation of the Past-Modeled Fa/Fi Sabbath Star

Figure 4.5. The Future-Modeled Form of the Fa/Fi Sabbath Star

than that of Fa, so in the first stage of Asiyah the past-modeled version would seem to have greater diagram justification than the future-modeled form, whose very existence can be called into question. What can be considered the fallen version of the Fa/Fi Sabbath Star has the same premature form as the Fa Sabbath Star; and it can be questioned whether it was ever meant to be manifested since this form of the first third Sabbath Star is always covered by later Sabbath Stars of its world. But since it is disclosed in the octave culmination of the diagram, and since it can be similarly disclosed through the reconstruction of the early stages of the fourth world, there would seem to be a

point in illustrating and analyzing its features as well as that of its counterpart.

The Soul and Its Vestments

In its associations with fourth-world Sabbath Stars, parts of the Mi Sabbath Star are successively covered by all of the vertical Sabbath Stars that enclose it, those signifying the minerals, the animals, and man. The latter two are related to the primary definition of the Nefesh soul, signified by the Mi Sabbath Star, as the animal soul, and the first to its physical embodiment. We can thus view the three vertical

Sabbath Stars of the fourth-world diagram as together constituting the three evolutionary levels present in the final human embodiment of the Nefesh soul, the Fa/Fi level representing the material constituents of the physical body with its capacity for sensual experience, the Fi/Sol level the animal inheritance of the psyche with its capacity for emotional experience, and the Sol level the unique contribution of the human neocortex with its capacity for mental experience; and it is in these terms that this lowest level of the fourth world will primarily be considered.

This overlaying feature of the diagram seems comparable to the all-pervasive principle of cosmic construction defined in the *Zohar*:

> The Holy One, blessed be He, found it necessary to create all these things in the world to ensure its permanence, so that there should be, as it were, a brain with many membranes encircling it. The whole world is constructed on this principle, upper and lower, from the first mystic point to the furthest removed of all the stages. . . . Although at first a vestment, each stage becomes a brain to the next stage. The same process takes place below, so that on this model man in this world combines brain and shell, a spirit and body, all for the better ordering of the world.[3]

The Zoharic understanding is that all levels of the macrocosm repeat the same arrangement of spirit to body that is reflected in the human microcosm. In the same way, the Nefesh soul identified with the Mi Sabbath Star may be said to embody the primal emanation comprehended in the Do hexagram, while itself serving as the soul of the successively higher levels of evolution by which it is embodied.

We have seen that the Nefesh soul seems to be endowed with the unique capacity for free will, this graphically indicated by the way its Mi Sabbath Star cuts through the diagram center at right angles to the central line of the interfaced Tree of Life Diagram. But the freedom of the Nefesh soul in its original expansive form, like that of unfallen Adam, may exist only in potential, its actualization immediately causing a two-stage process of descent involv-

ing first the Yetziric acquisition of its Tzelem and then that Asiyic physical body bonded to the Nefesh soul by its Tzelem. But as earlier shown, a matrix at the Fa/Fi level is only possible if not only the Mi but also the Fa hexagram is converted to Sabbath Star form. And since such conversion of the Fa hexagram is forbidden, it can only produce a matrix already fallen at this first stage of Asiyah, a matrix signifying a mortal body. This accords with the traditional view that the Nefesh soul is not immortal but lingers a short time around the grave of its physical body before decomposing into the earth whence it came.

One feature of the Fa/Fi Sabbath Star, in either of its forms, is that it covers precisely that element of the earlier diagram identified with the source or principle of such individuality, the Ri hexagram. Given the identification of the Fa/Fi Sabbath Star with matter, this would seem to define the principle feature of macroscopic matter, the localization in space and time that distinguishes the individuality of every material object in the universe. But in its past-modeled form, this Sabbath Star also covers the Do hexagram, the model or code of the whole creation. The Mi Sabbath Star first overlays this Atzilutic hexagram, and in figure 4.1 it can be seen that its descending component hexagrams cover two of its bars. In contrast, figure 4.4 shows that the base of the ascending component hexagrams of the past-modeled Fa/Fi Sabbath Star covers only one bar of the Do hexagram, its resonance to this primary source being only half that of the Mi Sabbath Star, which it also largely overlays. Here we see that successive, harmonically related elements overlay and may be said to enclothe or embody earlier elements in a series of increasing size. Still considering the Fa/Fi Sabbath Star only as providing the material body of man, we can say that in its past-modeled form the Nefesh body is in resonance with, and thus defined by, two complementary characteristics. It embodies both individuality and the code of its proper functioning. But since the Do hexagram of Atzilut is also identified with the emanation of the divine into cosmic form, it may also represent the indwelling divine spirit or breath. Thus this past-modeled form may be said to contain the divine immanently within it and to give it individuated form.

In discussing the Mi, Fa, Fa/Fi matrices, it was

earlier suggested that either of its forms can be considered to define the material level of creation and of man as impermanent or fallen insofar as it was constructed prematurely, without the Fi Sabbath Star that could have endowed it with divine life, a subject to be more fully developed in the next section. But even in this now mortal condition, it is possible to define more and less expansive forms of this soul level, which may imply that the soul suffers a second Fall at this stage in again moving from an expanded to a contracted form. Like its past-modeled form, the future-modeled form of the Fa/Fi Sabbath Star covers parts of the Mi Sabbath Star and so may also be said to embody the Nefesh soul. But its resonance to this soul is less, since, unlike its counterpart, it does not cover and resonate to the Do hexagram. A further implication of this might be that the body constructed of it would not contain the indwelling spirit of the divine.

This is similar to the Lurianic view that, as a result of the Shevirah, a breakage here occurring in the third world, the soul became imprisoned in the shells or husks, Kelipot, and that it is necessary to rescue the holy sparks within such souls from this godless and demonically influenced material confinement. Such a view can be supported by the fact that the Mi Sabbath Star, representing the Nefesh soul, does still embody the Do hexagram, which may now be identified with the holy spark within the soul, whereas the future-modeled Fa/Fi Sabbath Star, representing its more materialized form, does not and would thus seem comparable to a husk whose only characteristic is its individuation. This lack of resonance might well cause the soul to feel such a material body as an imprisonment.

If the diagram is constructed in accordance with the laws of the diagram that would prohibit a Fa Sabbath Star, then either or both forms of the Fa/Fi Sabbath Star could have triangulated with the Mi and Fi Sabbath Stars to produce the immortal life ideally intended for the Nefesh soul. It would now be at the Fa/Fi stage that the Nefesh soul would construct its more material Tzelem. Such a Tzelem formation seems to be suggested in a passage from the *Ha-Nefesh ha-Chokhmah* (The Wisdom of the Soul) of Moses de Leon, the Geronese Kabbalist to whom authorship of the *Zohar* is generally attributed:

> The purpose of the soul in entering the body is to exhibit its powers and abilities in the world. . . . And when it descends to this world it receives power and influx to guide this vile world and to undergo a *tikkun* above and below, for it is of high rank, [being] composed of all things, and were it not composed in a mystic manner of what is above and below, it would not be complete. . . . And when it is in this world, it perfects itself and completes itself from this lower world. . . . And then it is in a state of perfection, which was not the case in the beginning before its descent.[4]

The passage is primarily concerned to show that the soul's ultimate function in bringing about the Tikkun depends upon the elements of which it is composed, elements combining "what is above and below." It seems to be defining a two-stage process, the first involving the acquirement of its subtle body from what is below and the second its final incarnation in man. If this passage is read in the context of the Sabbath Star Diagram, it seems clear that the first process being referred to is one that concerns a Yetziric entity not before but after the materialization of Asiyah, at its Fa/Fi stage. In some "mystic manner," it suggests, the soul draws upon this matter to construct for itself its subtle image. Since it is thought that the Nefesh souls still congregate in a Yetziric Gan Eden where they clothe themselves in the Tzelem they will continue to wear once they have achieved the further stage of incarnation, this same interaction of Yetziric and Asiyic elements could be considered an ongoing process, the soul completing itself before incarnation with a Tzelem composed in a "mystic manner" of what is below combined with the soul essence that is above.[5]

But this form of interaction between the Yetziric Nefesh soul and the mineral stage of Asiyah would only yield an immortal Tzelem if the soul had not already constructed its Tzelem in Yetzirah with the collaboration of the forbidden Fa Sabbath Star. For whether this Tzelem is completed in Yetzirah with the contribution of the Ri hexagram or at the Fa/Fi stage of Asiyah without it, the legacy of the Fa Sabbath Star would still be of a mortal Tzelem produced before the advent of the Fi Sabbath Star that would have endowed it with immortality. But there would still be an advantage to either original or secondary formation of the Tzelem at the Fa/Fi stage, one that can support De Leon's radical conclusion that in this more physical form, the soul achieves a perfection it did not possess before its descent and that seems to incorporate the whole purpose of cosmic manifestation.

Such a view is especially coherent with the future-modeled form of the fourth-world diagram. For since that version covers both forms of the Fa/Fi Sabbath Star, one can hypothesize that both would still be virtually present, a possibility that need not lead to a choice between these two forms but to the inclusion of both in a pattern of oscillation. Significantly, it is only the diagram level identified with matter that is susceptible to such an interpretation, one that sees it as composed of two oscillating modes, with implications for an understanding of matter to be considered later.

For such oscillation introduces a new cosmic element: process. Though time may be considered to have been introduced by the premature generation of the Fa/Fi matrix by the Fa Sabbath Star that produced a perishable world, within that temporal limitation the physical body may still be regarded as in a static state as long as it was formed only of the past-modeled Fa/Fi Sabbath Star. But it becomes dynamic if it is understood to oscillate between its expansive and contracted modes. In the former mode, based upon past modeling, its individuality would be harmonized by the divine purpose to which it is in resonance, whereas in the latter mode, based upon future modeling, its individuality would be responsive to no prompting beyond its own will. But viewing these modes as in oscillation gives us a view of the soul as moving rhythmically back and forth between the poles of an individuality opaque to all sense of its connectedness and one capable of recognizing itself as part of a cosmic web of interrelationships, thus defining a rhythmic process akin to, or the source of, the alternation of waking and sleeping states in all forms of conscious life, such an

alternation as we shall meet again in the matrix modeling of the Nefesh soul in chapter 8.

This brings us to the next evolutionary level of the Nefesh soul, the level reached with the addition of the Fi Sabbath Star to the diagram. Though analysis of this Sabbath Star must be deferred to the section devoted to it, the important thing to note at this time about this symbol of life is the relationship of the two matrices to which it contributes. As shown in the previous chapter, its triangulation with the Mi and past-modeled Fa/Fi Sabbath Stars produces the loose-packed hexagonal matrix of figure 3.5 and its triangulation with the Mi and future-modeled Fa/Fi Sabbath Stars produces the close-packed hexagonal matrix of figure 3.11, that same progression earlier identified with the inspiration and expiration of the breath in Adam. For what the Fi Sabbath Star may be said to contribute to matter is precisely its endowment of life, and life, as we saw in the inspiration of Adam, is breath, is that which produces the "living soul" called the Nefesh Chayah. Indeed, it is this Nefesh Chayah that can be understood to inhabit the mineral and vegetable stages of the fourth world in such a Gan Eden as can be identified with these stages when considered chronologically. The distinguishing characteristic of the Nefesh Chayah, that soul composed of the divine breath and of earth with which Adam was endowed, is, then, that it breathes, and such breathing can also be diagrammed by the oscillation between the two forms of the Fa/Fi Sabbath Star and the dual forms of the matrix to which this Sabbath Star contributes.

In concluding this discussion either of the material endowment of man or of the earliest Asiyic stage of the Nefesh Chayah, a few final points should be made about the Fa/Fi Sabbath Star and its dual virtual forms. It was earlier suggested that its two forms defined two modes of consciousness, that which saw its individuality as a harmonic part of a larger whole and that which saw only its uniqueness. This distinction was based on the fact that both forms cover the individuating Ri hexagram but that only the past-modeled form also covers the higher code of the Do hexagram. But there are two other aspects of these forms that need to be considered.

The first is that the future-modeled form covers those parts of the Mi Sabbath Star that pass directly through the diagram's center and at a right angle to the harmonizing middle pillar of the Tree of Life Diagram, a circumstance that was associated with free will. Thus modeling upon the future would seem to imply a movement toward an increase in individual freedom, while past modeling would imply a movement backward to greater collectivity. In oscillating between these two poles, the soul would thus move out to a greater but less informed individual freedom and back to a state of harmony with the whole. It is, however, from this harmonious state that the deepest creative potential of the soul would seem to arise, for a special feature of the past-modeled form of this Sabbath Star is that it contains an additional Sabbatical configuration of hexagrams deep within it, a configuration that can be considered expressive of creativity. Since these hexagrams are all Do-sized, they seem to suggest a potential for the creative specification of the cosmic code through all manner of material embodiment. Thus it would seem that the soul can only use the greater freedom of its active phase effectively if it periodically returns to that passive phase from whose harmony true knowledge and creativity arise. The dual-aspected character that the soul will exhibit in its human incarnation would appear to be derived, then, from the properties of its physical body as these are defined by the dual, oscillating, and finally virtual forms of the Fa/Fi Sabbath Star representative of matter. And since this character is not only the most fruitful we have thus far explored but also that given by the future-modeled form of the complete fourth-world diagram, it again suggests that such future modeling is not a way of transgression but the true path the soul is to follow to achieve its highest realization.

An Esoteric Interpretation of Matter

The relationship between the Mi and Fa/Fi Sabbath Stars, the latter particularly in its past-modeled form, may continue to be suggestive when we turn to consideration of the purely material dimension of the fourth world. As matter may be thought to embody the soul, so may the soul be understood to ensoul matter, particularly in its larger astronomical formations. As we have seen, both of these Sabbath Stars overlay the Do hexagram, a fact that has new significance in this context. This significance will emerge from a reconsideration of the earlier discussion of the first sentence in Genesis, "In the beginning God created the heavens and the earth." The burden of the discussion in chapter 1 was to suggest that the esoteric meaning of this sentence is none other than the construction of the hexagram from six premanifest points. If this interpretation be now allowed, the association of the Fa/Fi Sabbath Star with this first hexagram is certainly striking. For if "the heavens and the earth" are taken in their astronomical signification, the mineral composition of the great heavenly bodies and of the earth cannot be denied. But since the Mi Sabbath Star had earlier covered the Do hexagram and is largely overlaid by the form of the Fa/Fi Sabbath Star modeled upon it, the implication is that the astronomical bodies of the heavenly skies and also the earth may have existed first as Nefesh souls and that when these astronomical bodies were later mineralized these spiritual entities continued to ensoul them. Since the component hexagrams of the Mi Sabbath Star overlay two bars of the Do hexagram to the one bar covered by the past-modeled Fa/Fi Sabbath Star, it may even be suggested that the proportion of soul to mineral composition in the earth and heavenly bodies is 2:1. The association of these two Sabbath Stars may also explain the close relationship of astronomy to astrology in the Kabbalah and all esoteric sciences.

From this it may be further suggested that among the varieties of Nefesh souls not created to incarnate in humankind, there are some who chose to form their image directly in or from the planetary and stellar bodies. Such a suggestion differs but slightly from a kabbalistic tradition that claims that the only way the permanent angels, especially archangels, can maintain their identity is through association with a planet or star. This tradition has talmudic roots and is related to the question of whether the angels were created on the second or the fifth day (Bereshit Rabbah 1:3, 3:8), a question resolved by identifying the former with the class of temporary angels, those who exist only to perform a particular task, and the latter with the class of permanent angels, those who have names. In reference to the verse, "He telleth the number of the stars; he calleth them all by their names" (Psalms 147:4), the Midrash relates the different names of the stars to the names of the various angels (Bereshit Rabbah 78:4). Thus the Kabbalist Isaac Abrabanel considers the angels to be like the souls of the stars. The final understanding is that the named angels, those created on the fifth day after the fourth-day creation of the stars, retain their permanent identities through their association with the particular physical bodies of the planets and stars, an association that not only explains the permanent character of the named angels but the influence of the stars, this being the kabbalistic explanation and validation of astrology.[6] I have hitherto tried to distinguish sharply between angels and souls, but the area of astrology may be one place where they overlap and where, as sometimes appears in kabbalistic texts,[7] one may speak of Nefesh angels, of souls that function with an angelic kind of determinism or of angels that have developed individuality through association with the various frequencies and periodicities of the heavenly bodies.[8]

As we have seen, the form of the Sabbath Star of the minerals modeled on that of the Sabbath Star of the soul not only contains the archetype of creation, the Do hexagram, but also the six surrounding Do-sized hexagrams, which may here be taken to signify the creative potential of matter to explicate the model of the heavens and the earth in various forms, each of which will continue to contain the cosmic model enfolded within it. As the Sabbath Star of the heavens and the earth in their manifest state, it has, moreover, the vastest scope of all the fourth-world Sabbath Stars since it embraces the entire physical universe, all of which is composed of relatively similar minerals. But if all forms of material existence can thus be said to be ensouled, then it would seem that the collective soul of the minerals is the most universal in its scope. And it may be because of the true universality of its collective soul that its particular embodi-

ments are so completely lacking in individual will.

But whether or not the planetary bodies are ensouled, they certainly "embody" the archetypal laws of geometry, not only in the resonances their aspects and periods produce but also in their very physical structure. For the minerals do give precise embodiment to the geometric archetypes of creation and are completely subordinate to the laws informing the physical world. The former can be shown in the precise geometric shapes that all chemical elements exhibit in their crystalline state, the latter in the law of octaves that informs the periodic table of these elements. Matter can thus be considered the perfect physical manifestation of the immaterial archetypes that Wordsworth understood to be "created out of pure intelligence," and each of its individual forms encodes the whole. The whole world, as Blake said, can be seen in a grain of sand, and all its power.

The Physics of Matter

The previous analysis of the Fa/Fi Sabbath Star in terms of the esoteric interpretation of matter has focused largely upon its past-modeled form, considered unfallen, since this is the form most coherent with such an interpretation. Similarly, its future-modeled form, considered fallen in this scenario, can provide a model for the contrasting scientific view of matter. Its essentially cubic form gives us an even more perfect emblem of the geometric archetypes informing matter than that of the unfallen form, for the cube has always represented the element of earth in the esoteric tradition.

An important difference between the past-modeled and future-modeled forms of the Fa/Fi and Fi/Sol Sabbath Stars is the more expanded size of both these past-modeled Sabbath Stars and the matrices to which they contribute as opposed to the smaller, denser forms of these future-modeled Sabbath Stars and their matrices. At the Fa/Fi level, the greater density of the future-modeled form is suggestive of matter as the more spread-out form produced by past modeling is suggestive of spirit or its physical analogue, energy. Taken together, they give us models of the convertible forms of macroscopic matter and energy or the quantum forms of particles and waves. Taken in oscillation, they can more precisely reflect the vibratory nature of matter as energy, as rhythmic and oscillating movement, the dual forms of this Sabbath Star now being taken to mark the crests and troughs of the oscillating wave pattern. And on the level of molecular structures, there is also an oscillation in response to both internal and external temperature. Finally, if taken in sequence, they can define an important moment in scientific cosmology. In the chronology of modern cosmology, this moment comes later than that usually assigned to the cosmic beginning, not at that above 100^{32}K, but at a temperature of a mere 3,000K. As Steven Weinberg has remarked: "It is striking that the transition from a radiation to a matter-dominated universe occurred at just about the same time that the contents of the universe were becoming transparent to radiation, at about 3,000K."[9] The two forms of the Fa/Fi Sabbath Star identified with matter may thus be considered to model the sequence going from a radiation-dominated universe to one dominated by matter.[10] But the Sabbath Star Diagram encodes the physical dimension of the cosmos through a Sabbath Star whose dual, and potentially oscillating, forms are only virtual in the complete fallen fourth-world diagram. And it has taken modern physics to reveal the subtle nature of visible matter and so the continuing appropriateness of this aspect of the diagram to the description of material reality.

Study of the peculiarities of these two Sabbath Star forms can reveal a further aspect of matter. We have seen that the future-modeled form of this Sabbath Star can be correlated with individual freedom since it covers the individuating Ri hexagram and that the past-modeled form in addition embodies something not present in the future-modeled form, a higher code (the Do hexagram). This latter combination is suggestive of the macroscopic, molecular level of matter in which quanta may be said to be arranged in accordance with a code to form a dual-leveled system that is distinctive and stable. Given the peculiarities of the two Sabbath Star forms in question, it would seem that what they are also encoding are the defining characteristics and

distinction between the quantum microstructure and atomic macrostructure of matter, the former defined by the smaller future-modeled form and the latter by the larger past-modeled form.[11]

The Sabbath Star Diagram can also be instructive if the two forms of the Fa/Fi Sabbath Star are further equated with the permitted and the forbidden. For the past-modeled form, just correlated with the coding that provides stable atomic and molecular structures, features the additional Sabbatical configuration that may signify such macrostructures to be the forms designed for and appropriate to a blessed creation. Contrariwise, the future-modeled form, here correlated with the complete subatomic level, may be regarded as forbidden precisely because any tampering with atomic structure may prove catastrophic. It may already be proving catastrophic to scientific theory. With modern physics we find an obsessive concentration upon penetrating the secrets of the quantum level and the belief that it explains all phenomena, that all higher levels can be built up from these "basic building blocks" despite the fact that they do not exhibit the coding characteristic of these higher levels. The result of such theoretical imperialism on the part of quantum physicists is to replace our familiar landscape with an unreal terrain governed by laws that will not support life. But still worse is the terrain they will leave behind if Murphy's Law, that whatever can happen will happen, is allowed to operate within the nuclear technology they have unleashed. Then we shall once again learn the price of prematurity as forbidden experimentation leads to a nuclear holocaust bringing the apocalypse to earth before its time, before its more subtle manifestation programmed by the fifth-world diagram. If study of the forbidden elements of the diagram has taught us anything, it is the danger resulting from premature activity. In the next section we shall learn the opposite lesson of patience.

THE SECOND SABBATH STAR OF ASIYAH AND THE PLANTS

We come now to the Fi Sabbath Star, probably the most important such element in the diagram. In the elementary diagram, it is the only Sabbath Star and establishes the principles by which this newly discovered geometric form can be constructed. As developed through the key of the Tree of Life Diagram, it was taken to signify the whole of the fourth world, and in the structure of the fuller fourth-world diagram, it can be more generally identified with the life principle and more particularly with the vegetative level to which it first gives rise, thus also symbolizing the Tree of Life.

In the form of the Sabbath Star Diagram that seems to be intended by its own program, it is at the evolutionary level of the Fi Sabbath Star that the matrix was supposed to have first been manifested. Triangulating with the Mi and past-modeled Fa/Fi Sabbath Stars, it produces the loose-packed hexagonal matrix that can model an unfallen Eden, a Garden either of dry land and vegetation or of living matter that is the setting for the Nefesh Chayah, the living soul, and can be further regarded as its actual embodiment. In such an unfallen world, the biblical story suggests, the life force was to have been eternal. There is first the reference to the "tree of life" from which man might "live for ever" (Gen. 3:22), and then the ambiguous reference in Genesis 6:3 involving the shortening of the human life span and variously translated as follows:

> And the Lord said, My spirit shall not always strive with man, for that he also is flesh: yet his days shall be an hundred and twenty years. (King James Version)
>
> God said, "My spirit will not continue to judge man forever, since he is nothing but flesh. His days shall be 120 years." (Aryeh Kaplan)
>
> And the Lord said: "My spirit shall not abide in man for ever, for that he also is flesh; therefore shall his days be a hundred and twenty years." (J. H. Hertz)[12]

What is at issue here is the word *yedon*, derived from the root of *din* and generally signifying "judgment," and the syllable *va*, meaning either "in" or "with." In the Hertz version, which is the most interesting, the meaning of "in" for *va* is chosen and a meaning given for *yedon* that makes most sense of the

sequence from the reference to the divine spirit to the punishing shortening of man's days. In the previous two versions, which give closer approximations to the meaning of *yedon*, the conciliatory tone of God is not consistent with the punishment meted out. But even if the Hertz version is modified by the substitution of the closer "strive" for "abide," we have an identification of life with the divine spirit that not only makes most sense of the passage but also of the biblical understanding of true life. In this reading, God would be withdrawing His spirit from man after a limit of one hundred and twenty years because of His weariness in the continual strife of His spirit with the inclinations of the flesh within the soul of man. This meaning is reinforced by that most significant biblical definition of life given by Moses in the climactic moment when he exhorts Israel to "choose life" and to understand that the true choice of life entails the choice of God: "for he is thy life, and the length of thy days" (Deut. 30:19–20). The biblical conception of life identifies it with the divine spirit and so with the eternal, an eternity lost as a birthright with the transgression of Adam and Eve. Also characteristic of the divine spirit of life is that it is informed by the Way of God, and the flood that follows the shortening of the period in which this divine spirit would abide or strive in man is sent just because of the abuse of this Way: "for all flesh had corrupted his way upon the earth" (Gen. 6:12).

If the Fi Sabbath Star can be correlated with such an understanding of the meaning of life, then it seems clear that the matrix model programmed for an unfallen world would have animated all of matter with spirit and endowed the Nefesh soul with immortality. For those who believe this still to be the case, the ideal version of the fourth-world diagram can stand as model. But if all remaining design possibilities are realized and the forbidden Fa Sabbath Star is introduced into the diagram, the die is cast, and the addition of the Fi Sabbath Star can do no more than enclose the dual forms of the now mortal Nefesh Chayah in its own loose-packed or close-packed hexagonal matrices. By the time the Fi Sabbath Star is added to the fallen diagram, the life it signifies has already been shortened; but the vegetative forms that it also signifies would seem to have been spared the further corruption that, as we shall see more clearly in the next section on the animals, is attendant upon "all flesh." Though subject to the impermanence visited upon matter, they have not been party to the corruption of "his way upon the earth," a Way they still follow and reveal. How the Fi Sabbath Star and the vegetable kingdom it signifies may by related to the Way of God we shall shortly see. But first there is another aspect of the position of the Fi Sabbath Star in the diagram that needs examination.

This derives from its significant position with respect to what can either be considered the musical analogue or component of the diagram, the fact that its major construction elements can be correlated with the tones of the musical scale, here the twelve-tone or chromatic scale. It is in terms of the latter that the Fi tone correlated with this Sabbath Star is most significant since it occupies the exact center of this scale, the seventh out of the thirteen semitones from Do to Do: Do, Di, Re, Ri, Mi, Fa, **Fi**, Sol, Si, La, Li, Ti, Do. In Greek musical theory, this tone marks the unutterable pause between the two perfect tetrads or fourths of the octave: Do-Fa, Sol-Do. Where the perfect fourth represents the harmonic mean between a tone and its octave double, signified by the proportion 4:3, and the perfect fifth the arithmetic mean, whose proportion is 3:2, the interval Do-Fi, signified by $\sqrt{2}$, represents the geometric mean in terms of the "unutterable" (in Greek, *alogon*) irrational interval[13] that, when sounded, produces a disturbing lack of harmonious resolution. We shall shortly return to the significance of the root power to the plant level of life most specifically signified by the Fi Sabbath Star, but first we must consider the significance of the Fi tone as the unutterable center of the spiral circularity of the octave.

The Fi tone is certainly the pivot point of the twelve-tone scale, signifying the furthest extension out from Do before the return to its higher octave. In the elementary diagram, this furthest outward extension from the center of unity signified the fourth world of manifest creation, a world whose material multiplicity was the furthest removed from its "beginning" in spiritual unity. In the unfallen

form of the properly self-generated fourth-world diagram, the purpose of creation appeared to be manifested by the sudden emergence of the matrix, whose sevenfold hexagonal configurations could be considered symbolic of the Nefesh Chayah, the vehicle for the return to the soul tonic of Do.

Now, all of these aspects of the Fi Sabbath Star can be associated with the numerical equivalent of the Fi musical tone, $\sqrt{2}$. To understand this, we must first review the geometric manifestation of the square root in terms of the doubling of the square. The geometric method by which a square can be doubled in size is by bisecting the initial square with its diagonal and then building a new square on this diagonal base. Repeating this process with the intermediate second square results in a third square whose sides are double the size of the first. If the side of the first square has a numerical value of 1, its diagonal will be $\sqrt{2}$. Similarly, the second square will have a side value of $\sqrt{2}$ and a diagonal value of 2, which then becomes the side value of the third square.

This geometric process is the source of what is called the "geometric proportion," a proportion of three terms with the middle term serving as the mean: *a* is to *b* as *b* is to *c*; $1:\sqrt{2}::\sqrt{2}:2$. From this latter we can see that the process by which unity can be multiplied is through the transformative power of the square root, which doubles a unit through dividing it in half, the same process followed in all cellular growth of living substance. The fact that ancient geometers gave this power of the diagonal in a square the name of "root" shows their awareness of the association of vitalistic processes with the geometry of the square, the most important esoteric symbol of the earth. For the vegetal root performs the same transformative function as the square root. The process it performs is that of decomposition or division upon the minerals in the earth, which it then transforms into the organic compounds through which the plant can grow. The $\sqrt{2}$, then, contains all of the powers associated with the Fi Sabbath Star: It has the power of multiplication implicit in the multiplicity of manifest creation; it accomplishes growth through division, the growth process of all life systems; and this archetypal symbol of the transformative function is most perfectly embodied in the vegetal root.[14] It is surely no coincidence that the division of the musical string necessary to produce the Fi tone in the scale leads to the $\sqrt{2}$ proportion that has such deep associations with those special aspects of the cosmic process signified by the Fi Sabbath Star. It suggests that the Sabbath Star Diagram is the spatial manifestation of a geometry based on the mathematics of the musical octave and that both encode the same truths of cosmology. Let us see what further understanding we can gain of this pivotal evolutionary level through examining figure 4.6 of the Fi Sabbath Star.

Figure 4.6 shows that the base of the ascending triangle of the component hexagram, in this horizontal Sabbath Star more properly denoted as that doubly outlined triangle on the right, goes through the Da'at center, while the point of the outlined descending or left triangle of this component hexagram overlays the Re hexagram. The special resonance that the diagram shows between the Fi and Re Sabbath Stars is again evidence of the special relationship between its geometry and the laws of musical harmony. As with the relationship of the Mi and Do Sabbath Stars, it represents that most harmonious interval of the major third, a part of the resonant overtone system. Thus Do will resonate first with its octave overtone, second with the fifth above that octave, Sol, third with the second octave above Do, and fourth with the major third above

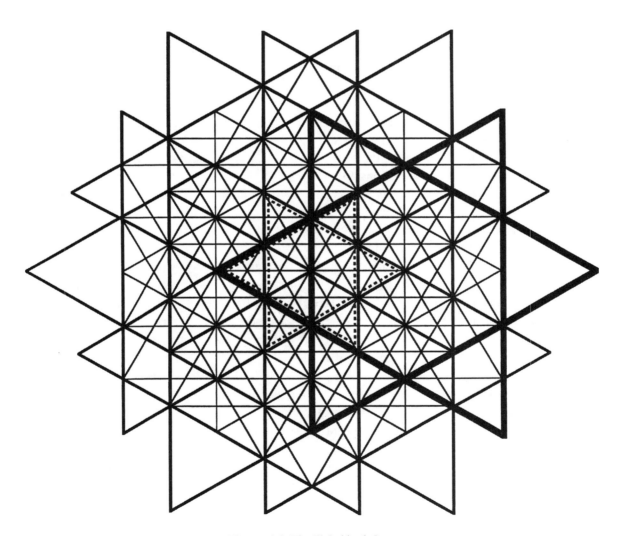

Figure 4.6. The Fi Sabbath Star

the second octave, Mi. In the case of the Re tone, the major third above it is Fi. The harmonic resonance of the Fi Sabbath Star of the plants is thus to the second world of Beriah or Creation. The Fi Sabbath Star represents the life principle in general and its plant form in particular; and it can be said that all of life follows the divine command, significantly couched in the plant metaphor: "Be fruitful, and multiply" (Gen. 1:22). Life in general and the living tree in particular embody the dynamic, transformative, and generative laws representative of Beriah. It is, moreover, to the original wholeness of Beriah, before its potentiality for individualization became manifest with the Ri hexagram, that the vegetative life forms of the Fi Sabbath Star resonate.

We can understand why this should be so by contemplating what is probably the most significant feature of the Fi Sabbath Star, the fact that it crosses through the central Da'at point along the middle pillar of the superimposed Tree of Life Diagram. This would seem to indicate that the plants not only incorporate the Berian archetypes of dynamic transformation, but are also the most perfect created embodiments of the Derekh ha-Shem, the Way of God, or Tao. For the plant seems to be the living part that has the most harmonious relationship to the whole, bending to its varying currents. Indeed, Taoist philosophy considers the distinctive quality of the sage to be the level of understanding that allows him to bend with the wind like a tree. In addition to this perfect adaptation to both seasonal and unseasonal change, the tree, in its stillness, maintains a relationship of perfect peace with its environment. It peacefully draws its sustenance directly from the four elements, its mineral nutrients from the earth, its water from the cyclical relationship of earthly sea to sky, of evaporation and precipitation, its air directly from this higher source of the sky, and its light from a still higher source in the sky, the fiery sun. And through these four hierarchically ranked sources of its nutrients, it is connected to those functional qualities of earth, water, air, and fire that animate all the worlds. Nor it is simply the passive receiver, but also the giver, the transformer of lower to higher energies. It transforms inorganic minerals to organic compounds, carbon dioxide to pure oxy-gen. Thus it provides breathable air for the higher animal life forms and its own body for their food. Because it seems to incorporate a knowledge, Da'at, of the proper way to live, it has served as a spiritual teacher to many sensitive spirits.

The most famous of these is probably Wordsworth, whose continuing love for the woods as a source of spiritual elevation is contained in the following lines from "Tintern Abbey":

> And I have felt
> A presence that disturbs me with the joy
> Of elevated thoughts; a sense sublime
> Of something far more deeply interfused.
> . . . .
> A motion and a spirit, that impels
> All thinking things, all objects of all thought,
> And rolls through all things. Therefore am
>   I still
> A lover of the meadows and the woods,
> . . . .
> . . . well pleased to recognize
> In nature and the language of the sense,
> The anchor of my purest thoughts, the nurse,
> The guide, the guardian of my heart, and
>   soul
> Of all my moral being.
>   (LL. 93–96, 100–103, 107–11)

This belief in the spiritual guidance offered through association with trees and flowers has had proponents in our time. The most notable is probably Dr. Bach, whose distillations of trees and flowers have been sold not simply as remedies for physical and emotional ailments but as inner guides for specific modalities of spiritual development. Like Dr. Bach, the spiritual teacher known as the Mother also believed in the power of flowers to teach high moral and spiritual qualities. The late companion of Sri Aurobindo and, after his death, the leader of a spiritual community called Auroville, founded in southern India to perpetuate his teachings, the Mother instigated the planting of large flower gardens at Auroville where flowers incorporating the functional epitome of certain moral qualities could share their spiritual energies with man.

If proof were needed of the capacity of people such as Dr. Bach and the Mother to be inwardly guided by the plant kingdom to a spiritually enlarging knowledge of the subtler aspects of plants, this would seem to have been provided by Dorothy Maclean and the Findhorn garden. As a founding member of the Findhorn community in Scotland, which may be said to have literally grown up in response to the magic of this garden, Dorothy Maclean was the person responsible for those spiritual contacts with the plant angels or *devas* that guided the efforts of the few original gardeners. Of the *devic* guidance resulting in those enormous vegetables yielded by a previously sandy ground, Dorothy Maclean has written: "It was the reality of the garden growth that brought home to us the reality of the devas. Out of this grew a new way of gardening, and a deeper understanding of life. . . . [T]he devas began to relate more and more as educators. Just as they had taught us to see subtler aspects of Nature, they taught us how to live in touch with subtler aspects of our own beings."[15]

It is nearly impossible, of course, for any Western mind to contemplate the garden as a higher spiritual center without being immediately reminded of the classical locus of this image, the Garden of Eden. It is interesting in this context that the three notable examples just discussed are all from the West, Dr. Bach from England, the Mother from France, and Dorothy Maclean from Canada. This resonance of the unfallen state is always there in the feeling of spiritual healing that so often accompanies a simple walk in the country, away from the jarring noises and pressures of what is then felt to be an unnatural urban life. Although such a response could be set down to fresh air and negative ions, the Sabbath Star Diagram offers another explanation.

It was recently shown that the Fi Sabbath Star has a special resonance with the Re hexagram of Beriah. But it has an even closer association with the Mi hexagram, signifying the third world of Yetzirah or Formation, that additional level of specificity "formed" by the creative forces of Beriah in its original perfection. For the larger Fi hexagram is exactly a full step beyond the Mi hexagram and, were it not for its special generation through the six smaller hexa-

grams of its Sabbath Star, could be said to be generated from it. If, however, we think of the Fi hexagram as being generated from the double points of the Mi hexagram, it presents a different view of this first half-tone stage of the fourth world, as a further development of the Edenic third world of Mi before the Fall from its perfect spiritual flow that can be assigned to the Fa stage. Thus we can think of nature, up through the plant level of development, as representing the higher potentiality within material development for perfect attunement to the direction of the cosmic flow, as in fact, the materialized form of Eden. Similarly man, whose Sol hexagram is a full step beyond the Fa hexagram, would represent that state of exile from the Garden resulting from his generation by a fallen Yetziric Adam. The fourth world, then, can be thought of as containing both fallen and unfallen elements, the way of the woods and gardens of this world really being able to instruct man as to his proper relationship to the cosmos and so guide him in the way of Tikkun by restoring him to his proper spiritual environment for soul growth.

But it has been felt that trees, the whole of the green world, can teach man not only how to adapt to the ebb and flow of cosmic change but also how to return to the still source beyond the realm of transformation, that they are spiritual teachers of meditation. Again this intuition has been articulated most powerfully by the poets. Andrew Marvell, in the poem entitled "The Garden" that epitomizes the consciousness of the Edenic archetype within the natural retreat, takes us from such a retreat first to a higher meditative state—"Annihilating all that's made / To a Green Thought in a green Shade"(ll. 47–48)—and finally to a state of spiritual ecstasy:

> *Here at the Fountains sliding foot,*
> *Or at some Fruit-trees mossy root,*
> *Casting the Bodies Vest aside,*
> *My Soul into the boughs does glide:*
> *There like a Bird it sits, and sings,*
> *Then whets, and combs its silver Wings;*
> *And, till prepar'd for longer flight,*
> *Waves in its Plumes the various Light.*
> *Such was that happy Garden-state. . . .*
>
> (LL. 49–57)

In "Upon Appleton House" Marvell shows that his nature mysticism draws importantly from the Kabbalah, for in a startling image, he seems to be referring directly to the standard kabbalistic understanding of the Tree of Life Diagram as an inverted tree whose root is in Keter: "turn me but, and you shall see / I was but an inverted Tree" (ll. 567–68). Man in his true essence is an inverted tree, for he contains all the Sefirot and all the worlds within him. But he needs to return to nature to experience his transcendent soul and the cosmic whole of which he forms a meaningful part.

Of all the spiritual lessons the plants can teach us perhaps the greatest is that of patience, and this is the lesson as well of the diagram. As the plant ripens at its own pace, so the diagram is ideally programmed to bear its matrix fruit only at the point of the Fi Sabbath Star that defines the patience of the plant nature. If the discussion in this chapter has taught us anything, it is the danger of prematurity. We have seen that the impermanence of matter can be explained in terms of the transformation of the Fa hexagram into a Sabbath Star premature for the horizontal axis in the third world, such development violating the rules of the diagram in a manner that would seem to equate the "sin" of such violation with this very fact of prematurity. But if Paradise can be lost from such a premature eating of the fruit, so can it be regained by learning the lesson of patience the plants have to teach us. So does Shakespeare's Brutus realize that he should arm himself "with patience / To stay the providence of some high powers / That govern us below" (*Julius Caesar*, 5.1.105–7). Though matter and the original Tzelem of the soul may have lost their eternal permanence, the soul, at least, may grow beyond its now mortal Nefesh Tzelem into the immortalizing Tzelem of the Ruach soul, and this by learning to harmonize itself with the ebb and flow of cosmic time that is still the gift of the plant kingdom in this world and the sign of the Ruach consciousness that informs the next epoch of cosmic history. For the key to such growth is embodied in the plant, as Shakespeare recognized in that crowning expression of his wisdom, "Ripeness is all."[16]

THE THIRD SABBATH STAR OF ASIYAH AND THE ANIMALS

If the plants can teach us how to be restored to a condition of harmony with the whole, the animals can teach us what it is we must learn to transcend. For of all the elements of the fourth world, this is the one that lies under the severest constraint, ideally programmed to permit of no Sabbath Star development. What this suggests is that there is something in the animal nature that must be restrained. The soul that dominates fourth-world consciousness is the Nefesh Chayah, that living animal soul man shares with the animals despite his added ability to name them. This soul level, which is applied indifferently to man and the animals in Genesis 2:7 and 2:19, is associated directly with the blood. As can be seen in the laws given after the flood, the Nefesh, translated as "life," is equated with the blood in both man and the animals: "But flesh with the life [Nefesh] thereof, which is the blood thereof, shall ye not eat. . . . Who so sheddeth man's blood, by man shall his blood be shed" (Gen. 9:4, 6). It is the blood, with the heart that drives it and the autonomic nervous system that regulates its circulation and heat, that defines the evolutionary level beyond the vegetative identified with the animals. But at the level of the fourth world, this soul was ideally to be allowed no development beyond this blood-borne circulation of hormonal chemicals that can reproduce the vegetative functions of the plants at the higher level of animal mobility.

It would seem, then, that the simple hexagram prescribed for the Fi/Sol level of unfallen animal development can be identified with the autonomic nervous system driven by the blood and governed by the hypothalamus, the cranial body of the animal brain that regulates the biorhythms that harmonize animal functioning with the solar periodicities of the day and the seasons. Like the plants, the animals were designed to follow the Way of God conveyed through the periodicities of time but with the added capacity for conscious pleasure, whose center is also in the hypothalamus, the pleasure of restored homeostasis achieved through a balancing of self with environment and through satisfying the appetites for food and sex. Since the thalamic region also houses the pineal gland thought to be the inner or third eye of the esoteric traditions, the implication is that a restriction of psychic functioning to this subcognitive level was intended to lead to an opening of higher capacities for intuitive knowledge and for that conscious control of the autonomic nervous system whose inverse product is the empowerment of higher consciousness.[17]

This blissful state of harmony and empowerment was the condition ideally intended for the animal level of evolution by both the diagram and the Bible, as long as it remained obedient to the "rule" (Gen. 1:16–17) of solar and lunar periodicities. But as the Bible tells us, "all flesh had corrupted his way upon the earth" (Gen. 6:12). Man and the animals began to kill, both for pride or territory and for food, thus violating the original commands to "Be fruitful, and multiply" (Gen. 1:22, 28) and to eat only fruit and the "green herb" (Gen. 1:30). This Fall from bliss into anxiety may also be located in the hypothalamus, the seat of the fight or flight mechanism that has largely replaced the harmony of animal biorhythms with the ever anxious state of alarm infecting predator and prey alike. Thus the blood that was to be a constant source of revitalization has become, instead, the conveyor of soul-destroying neurotransmitters urging it on a path of fight or flight that has taken it far into exile from the Garden. It was because of the danger inherent in the blood that the animal nature was laid under an original constraint not to permit of any further fourth-world development until it had naturally ripened into the higher consciousness that may be said to mark the advent of the fifth world. Instead, it followed a "forbidden" course that may be diagramed by the two Sabbath Star forms that the Fi/Sol hexagram can take in violation of the rules of ideal diagram construction.

Though the second third stage is like that of the first third in allowing alternative modes of Sabbath Star construction, it is unlike it insofar as both forms cannot be simultaneously present in the same diagram. Where both forms of the Fa/Fi Sabbath Star can equally be reconstructed in the future-modeled form of the fourth-world diagram, at the Fi/Sol level each of its Sabbath Star forms will affect the final appearance of the diagram in a manner different from that of the other. They provide, rather, two alternative models for animal development. Thus they must be studied separately in their own diagrams for the partial illumination they can shed. Figures 4.7 and 4.8 present the two forms of the Fi/Sol Sabbath Star, the former its past-modeled and the latter its future-modeled form, each again featuring the outlining of its position defining hexagram, one component hexagram and the earlier hexagrams it covers.

As can be seen in figure 4.7, the past-modeled form covers the Ri and Mi prior hexagrams, while the future-modeled form, given in figure 4.8, covers only the Do hexagram, though it reproduces this in an externalized Sabbatical formation also outlined; and the former provides a form from which no evolution to the human stage is possible, while the latter leads to just such evolution: Figure 4.7 presents what can be considered a quasi-fallen stage of animal development since its contribution to the final diagram of two matrix triangles discontinuous with the ideal zigzag matrix border, that seen in figure 3.5, in no way adds to the constituents of the unfallen matrix, as those constituents will be defined in chapter 8. It is not in terms of the matrix, then, that this Sabbath Star form is forbidden but in violating the central diagram law prohibiting the covering of position-defining hexagrams of a just prior cosmic world, here the Mi hexagram.

It will be remembered that a distinction was made at the Mi level between its Sabbath Star form, identified with the Nefesh soul of Yetzirah, and its simple hexagram form, identified with the angels and thus the entire cosmic structure of Yetzirah mythologized as the Garden of Eden. The fact that the past-modeled Fi/Sol Sabbath Star overlays both the Ri and Mi hexagrams indicates that it represents a state of conflicting directions, one between the individualizing tendencies of the first divisive half step, that of the Ri hexagram, and the integrative tendencies of that first harmonious creation, the Garden of Eden, signified by the Mi hexagram. If the plants can be thought of as the materialization of the spiritual Garden that generated and still sustains them, since its Fi Sabbath Star is built in the

Figure 4.7. The Past-Modeled Form of the Fi/Sol Sabbath Star

full-step progression on the Mi hexagram, the animals signified by the past-modeled form of the Fi/Sol Sabbath Star are in an ambivalent position, both in and out of the Garden. They are in the Garden to the extent that they live by the rhythms of nature, know instinctively how to satisfy their needs, and are capable of long periods of inner stillness. But they have left the Garden to the extent that they kill for food and are also the ever anxious prey of other predators.

It is in terms of the identification of the Mi hexagram with the angels that this Sabbath Star is even more revealing. For what it seems to be suggesting is the embodiment of angelic intelligence in those animal species that may be correlated with its form. Such animals may be said to be marked by individ-

ual motion, the Ri hexagram, but not by individual consciousness, rather by the collective consciousness of some overriding spiritual entity, whether it be given the name of angels, *devas*, or elementals, the intelligence denoted by the Mi hexagram. This combination of individual members with collective consciousness seems true of those species like the bees, ants, and termites that live in colonies and seem to act not like individuals but collective wholes. By extension, all forms of insects and reptiles may be included in this category of wholly instinctual animals that seem to be guided more by the need to propagate their species than by individual desire. Such species may be said to have a collective, angelic intelligence that not only guides its individual members' behavior but the course of its

Figure 4.8. The Future-Modeled Form of the Fi/Sol Sabbath Star

evolution in terms of the changing circumstances of its environment.

If covering the Mi hexagram can be considered the sin of this form of Sabbath Star development, then what the diagram seems to be telling us is that animals were not supposed to develop in this manner, that continuing the past modeling appropriate to matter on the animal level could only lead to an individual rigidity inappropriate to an animal. Such overrigidity is given clear physical form in the shells of the crustaceans but its most catastrophic expression was in those giant reptiles whose extinction may be proof of a mechanically proceeding evolution out of touch with the true survival needs not only of its individuals but also of the species. Such

lock-step applications of past models can only lead to the exaggerations of form that produced those ill-fated dinosaurs, whose large size without elegance marked an evolutionary dead end exactly mirrored by the form of the Fi/Sol Sabbath Star that may be said to bear their name. From the ants to the dinosaurs, the wholly instinctual behavior that characterizes the lower animal orders may be explained by the forbidden covering of the Mi hexagram by this past-modeled Fi/Sol Sabbath Star with which they may be correlated. For rather than allowing the continuing angelic presence represented by the surviving Mi hexagram its proper influence on animal intelligence, the premature covering of this hexagram permitted a complete takeover of animal consciousness by this higher spiritual power, a takeover resulting in particular bodies without individual wills, mechanical forms of life whose only semblance of autonomy is itself instinctual, the instinct for survival.

Further proof that this form of animal development is opposite to that required for the evolution of man may be seen in another feature of this Sabbath Star, the nature of the matrix configuration that it uniquely contributes to the diagram, in the sense of being necessary for its completion. This is the point to point configuration of two matrix triangles shaped like a bow tie, which appears in figure 3.6 just beyond the loose-packed matrix hexagons, whose forms they extend. When the Sol Sabbath Star is added to this "dinosaur diagram," another set of these triangles appears at a point discontinuous from the zigzag matrix border, as previously described. But in either case of diagram evolution, the past-modeled Fi/Sol Sabbath Star produces this unique geometric form. In Indian cosmology, this geometric shape, normally visualized in its vertical rather than horizontal form, is called "Shiva's drum," and it refers primarily to the principle of the inverse, a principle that it represents at the most extreme point of opposition, at that point of contact from which diametrically opposed triangles expand to potentially infinite size. This form of extreme inversion appears all the way through the Sabbath Star Diagram, since any triangular peak of a hexagram forms a Shiva's drum with either of its adjacent peaks. But what the hexagram shows is that extreme inversion only forms a fragment of the total design whose main principle is the harmonizing of inverse polarities into a larger unity. For if the two triangles of Shiva's drum begin to encroach on each other's territory until their combined six points touch the six radial arc points of an encompassing circle, they will form the hexagram, symbol of the balancing of the inverse. In the matrix form contributed by this Sabbath Star, however, there is no such harmonizing of the inverse. What its appearance at this point in the diagram seems to be suggesting is that any further evolution from the dead end of reptilian development must be by way of the inverse, that the evolution of man requires a capacity for creative

adaptation that is the inverse of reptilian instinctual responsiveness.

This capacity would seem to be represented in the alternative form of the Fi/Sol Sabbath Star based upon future modeling since its primary feature is that additional Sabbatical configuration of Do-sized hexagrams that may be taken as a symbol of creation or of creativity. If we can accept the scenario projected in the previous chapter in which animal development was understood to proceed in a chronological sequence from the past-modeled to the future-modeled form of the Fi/Sol Sabbath Star, then we may read in this symbol of creativity precisely that inversion from mechanical behavior whose necessity was spelled out in the Shiva's drum symbol deposited by the past-modeled reptilian form. But this scenario also suggests a continuity between the reptilian and later phases of animal evolution by which these later phases would incorporate some elements of reptilian development.

On this basis, we can identify the future-modeled form with the mammals and recognize in its higher level some surviving elements of reptilian consciousness. Thus the future-modeled form may be said to incorporate those reptilian elements that took part in the evolution from reptilian to mammalian species and the past-modeled form to represent the surviving reptilian species after the fork took place from which the mammals branched out from the parent trunk. The past-modeled and future-modeled versions of the fourth-world diagram up to the Fi/Sol level give us, then, separate illustrations of the two main levels of animal evolution that may be correlated with the reptiles and the mammals, the former revealing the collective consciousness underlying the behavior of all the purely instinctual species and the latter the individual creativity that marks some species of mammals.

If the future-modeled form can be identified with the mammals, then it must also be identified with the limbic system with which the mammalian brain surrounds the inner brain bulb it inherited from the reptiles, that is, with the capacity for emotional feelings. To the reptilian capacity for physical sensations, the mammals bring a capacity for emotions that seems to be tied to the creativity that the diagram tells us is the primary mark of mammalian character. And it tells us yet further things about the nature of the mammals. For like the past-modeled Fa/Fi Sabbath Star, this future-modeled Fi/Sol Sabbath Star also covers and incorporates both the Do hexagram and portions of the Mi Sabbath Star. In the prior instance we said that the Do hexagram embodies the code that could organize quanta into particular molecular structures. In this instance it seems likely that it embodies the code that gives to the higher life forms their unique sense of self, a self distinguished from all others by certain traits of personality. Animal behaviorists who have studied troops of animals over long periods have been able to distinguish such personality differences among the animals so observed—and even more, that different troops seem to have developed some differences in cultural patterning, learned behaviors that were passed on through example and training. For what distinguishes the future-modeled Fi/Sol Sabbath Star from its past-modeled Fa/Fi counterpart is that the Sabbatical configuration of Do-sized hexagrams in that earlier form was internalized, whereas it is externalized in this later form. This suggests that the mammals have a capacity to externalize their individual personalities into new forms of cultural behavior and organization, to give expression to their individual natures and the personal preferences arising from such individuality. But both of these Sabbath Star forms have another similarity in that they cover and may be said to embody aspects of the Mi Sabbath Star signifying the Nefesh soul. If the past-modeled form of the Fi/Sol Sabbath Star may be said to embody an angelic intelligence, this future-modeled form would seem to provide a new body for the incarnation of the Nefesh soul, an animal body in the mammalian form for which it has long waited and in which it can truly be called a Nefesh Chayah.

One can define the Nefesh soul in its mammalian embodiment as that animal soul in which instinctual needs have developed an emotional resonance, but these emotions are still largely in the grip of the reptilian instincts for personal and species survival. For the human mammals that have not grown beyond the Nefesh stage of soul development, instinctual

territoriality has been elevated into a pursuit of status as sexuality has moved beyond reproductive needs to color and transform most emotions into vehicles for its sublimated expression. Though the emotions can be transformed even at the fourth-world stage of development, their true rectification will attend and largely define the soul's growth into Ruach consciousness. Nevertheless, at the Nefesh stage of human development, it is from its mammalian constituents as here defined that human creativity arises. It is the Nefesh emotions that demand the creative expression of their nonverbal experiences that finds its proper outlet in the arts. The human artistic process may, in fact, be modeled by a progressive return to those layers of its inheritance characterized by the signs of creativity. Such a return through the two Sabbath Stars featuring the Sabbatical configuration of Do-sized hexagrams would bring the soul first to that level of mammalian incarnation in which the human emotions are rooted and then to an expansive soul state, the inspiring emotion having been traced to its source and then carried into the enlarged spiritual state that can provide its force with a universalized form, a redemptive art whose triumph over the ravages of time can lift all responsive souls to a higher level of consciousness. But even more important to such growth is that reverse progress through these two particularly creative forms of Sabbath Stars that in chapter 3 were shown to define the Transformative Moment that can prepare for its final evolution of the Nefesh soul to Ruach consciousness.

Though the animals cannot themselves evolve beyond the level of a Nefesh Chayah, they contribute to such evolution precisely in what the mammals bequeath to human nature—individuality. Since they represent the first stage after the cyclical turning point of Fi, one can go further and say that they represent the very first stage of the Tikkun. From this one can further say that the process of Tikkun is by way of the soul's acquisition of personality. It is from this acquisition of selfhood that the mammalian emotions of ego enhancement or threat also arise. But in this emotional development the higher animals reveal as well some sparks of Ruach feeling. The uncritical devotion of a dog to its master can be rivaled by few humans. But it contains no aspect of universality, only offering a functional signpost to man's future spiritual direction. As a dog will sacrifice itself for its master, so does the animal level seem to be an evolutionary sacrifice to the greater Tikkun reserved for the future in which some form of man with little of the animal about him will participate. Whether or not it be believed that man descended from the animals, he certainly does have an animal nature, as he also incorporates the mineral and vegetable aspects of creation, an animal nature that he must learn to transcend in his personal evolution to that enlarged being who will redeem the cosmic process.

THE FOURTH SABBATH STAR OF ASIYAH AND MAN

How mankind alone can fulfill a redemptive cosmic role is paradoxically revealed in the essential feature of its Sol Sabbath Star, the fact that it passes horizontally through the central point of Knowledge (Da'at), literally at cross purposes to the vertical path, earlier traversed by the Fi Sabbath Star, which seems emblematic of the Way. As illustrated in figure 4.9, there are again special markings of its position-defining hexagram, one of its component hexagrams, and the Ri hexagram it covers.

In addition to its horizontal crossing of the Da'at central point, the Sol Sabbath Star is in a state of resonance to the Ri hexagram beyond that of the past-modeled Fa/Fi and Fi/Sol Sabbath Stars that had previously covered it. This greater resonance is due to the analogue between spatial form and musical tonality in the diagram; for, in musical terms, Sol is a major third above Ri and so part of its overtone series of resonance. Because the intermediate Sabbath Stars cannot establish such pure tonal relationships with the hexagrams they cover, the resonant power of the semitone Sabbath Stars exceeds that of the intermediate Sabbath Stars just as these culminating forms on their axes have that greater perfection on which the intermediate variety must model themselves, this form cutting directly through the center of the diagram to provide the unequivocal and perfectly proportioned model for the lesser levels of growth. In its very form, then, the Sol Sabbath Star conveys a heightened power of individuality and freedom beyond anything seen previously.

The Sol Sabbath Star also provides a significant contrast to the Fi Sabbath Star. Even if the Tree of Life Diagram is eliminated from this consideration, it should be clear that the Fi Sabbath Star crosses the central point in a manner that also passes through all the points of the Do hexagram, while the lines of the Sol Sabbath Star that cross the central point miss all six of these points, passing instead through the bars of the Do hexagram. Although the Sol Sabbath Star does touch all of these points, it does not do so in a way that relates them to the center, as is the case with the Fi Sabbath Star. When the Tree of Life Diagram is superadded, however, the meaning of its central column of divine harmony further illuminates the fact that the Fi Sabbath Star overlays it, while the Sol Sabbath Star crosses it at right angles. It suggests that where the plants are perfectly attuned to the divine Way, there is something in man's nature essentially opposed to it.

If the divine Way is a flow that bears all in its path, then the resistance to this deterministic flow can only be the defining characteristic of man, his free will. But if the horizontal crossing of the central point signifies free will, then this is a characteristic that man shares with the pre-incarnate Nefesh soul, whose Mi Sabbath Star also crosses the central point in this manner. In fact, the bases of the ascending component triangles of the Sol Sabbath Star overlay the similar bases of these triangles in the Mi Sabbath Star to complete the covering and incorporation of the Sabbath Star aspects of this Yetziric construction element by the fourth-world Sabbath Stars. All other aspects of the Mi Sabbath Star besides its position-defining hexagram are covered by either the past-modeled Fa/Fi Sabbath Star or the future-modeled Fi/Sol Sabbath Star in concert with the Fa/Fi hexagram, the main feature covered in either case being the Do hexagram. As earlier analyzed, this covering of the Do hexagram may be said to define the coding that distinguishes one physical element from another or the personality by which the uniqueness of each mammal can be similarly distinguished. But the lines

Figure 4.9. The Sol Sabbath Star

passing through the center that signify the capacity for free will were not covered by either of these intermediate Sabbath Stars, the animals not receiving from the Nefesh soul that freedom for which only man could provide the appropriate vessel. Though the animals had developed personality, this sense of selfhood did not by itself confer freedom but rather a still largely compulsive attempt to satisfy the added needs produced by this emergent ego.

The freedom of the Nefesh soul betrays a similar limitation, one that derives from an even more intrinsic characteristic, the permanent identity that most clearly distinguishes a Nefesh soul from the angels, its will being liberated from collective response by its ability to sustain individual identity.

But as we have seen, the freedom of the Nefesh soul seems to be wholly directed toward the acquirement of ever denser bodies of sense in which to function. While devoted to the greater particularization and enhancement of its identity, it thus seems to be more closely related to an instinctual process than to the deliberative process involved in true choice. And all of this accords with the standard definition of the Nefesh as the soul of the instinctive, sense body.

It is only with man, then, that true free will, based upon a choice of direction, becomes possible.* The standard explanation of this is that man

_____

*The following discussion of human free will appeared verbatim in *The Kabbalah of the Soul*, pp. 79–83.

was created with two opposing urges, a good urge, Yetzer ha-Tov, and an evil urge, Yetzer ha-Ra, as well as with the power to choose which of these inclinations to follow. We have seen that the diagram supports this understanding insofar as these Yetziric influences can be associated with the Mi and Fa hexagrams that are all that survive of third-world construction elements at the culmination of the fourth world. But man is endowed with the capacity to counter any such influence through the power of his inherent free will and another power that distinguishes him from the animals, his capacity to name them, to use language. The trouble is that the very power to negate, which gives man the freedom to reverse the trend toward materialization that has thus far characterized the process of divine manifestation, is itself tied to what can and has been called the Sitre Achra, the Other Side. If this supposedly demonic "other side" can, as earlier suggested, be identified with the Fa hexagram, then man may be considered its most significant evolutionary product, since the Fa hexagram provides the necessary foundation for the Sol hexagram of man, exactly a whole tone beyond it. But it is only because he has such a powerful Yetzer ha-Ra to counter and complement his Yetzer ha-Tov that man can become the fit instrument of the Tikkun, his generation from the Fa or demonic side of Yetziric influence providing the creative tension within man's will that is the foundation of the exercise of its freedom.

That man is to be identified with this "other side" can be seen not only from the dependence of the Sol Sabbath Star upon the Fa hexagram, or from its crossing of the center at right angles to the path of the middle pillar of the superimposed Tree of Life Diagram, but also from the fact that its component descending triangles overlay the Ri hexagram. It is this Ri hexagram that provides the hidden support for the first manifestation of apparent evil in the Fa hexagram, which is, itself, the support of the large hexagram of the Sol Sabbath Star. It provides the archetype of ego expansion to which man's nature is in harmonic resonance. Whether we speak of the left side of the Tree of Life Diagram or of the half-step stages of the Sabbath Star Diagram, we are speaking

of the aspect of reality that gradually manifests more and more individuality of form, identity, and will. It is thus interesting to notice that the insertion of the Ri hexagram raises the number of the Fa hexagram to five, the number of the Sefirah Gevurah from whose excesses evil is supposed to emanate.

But Gevurah not only represents severe Judgment; it can also provide a power of just discrimination that can enable the will of man freely to choose the more balanced expression of self that seeks its enhancement in a heightened sense of spiritual communion. Harkening to his angelic rather than demonic impulses, he can start to build his Ruach Tzelem, which can then purify and uplift the Nefesh soul to the more refined and exquisite pleasures that can further rather than retard man's spiritual development. If man is to be considered the goal of creation and the cosmic purpose to lead to greater good, then that "other side" to which he is more native cannot finally be considered to be an independent power of darkness but rather to play an integral part in a larger pattern of good, the balance of contraction and expansion that shines in all the manifest stars and particularly in the great symbol of the hexagram. This is not to deny the power of man's free will to introduce genuine evil into the cosmos. It is to deny that such evil is *caused* rather than *corrected* by the cosmic structure.

By examining that archetype of man's nature figured in the Sol Sabbath Star, we have seen that man is not only endowed with free will but is in a special condition of resonance both to the root of the individualizing tendency (the Ri hexagram) and its first flowering into the Yetzir ha-Ra (the Fa hexagram). This combination would seem to promise such a misinformed exercise of the will as can be correlated with the Fall, though it by no means requires it. But it is precisely this propensity, arising from his cosmically unique freedom, that makes man the true Tzelem, or image, of God. Of all forms of the inverse, this is surely the most startling. For it is the supreme paradox of creation that the being seemingly at cross purposes to the divine harmony should, from this very circumstance, develop that individuality of will through which it alone can truly image its Creator.

In *Derekh ha-Shem*, Moshe Chayyim Luzzatto shows this to be the very purpose of creation:

> God's purpose in creation was to bestow of his Good to another. . . . God's wisdom, however, decreed that for such good to be perfect, the one enjoying it must be its master. He must be one who has earned it for himself, and not associated with it accidentally. In a way, this can be said to partially resemble God's own perfection. . . . This primary, essential creature is man. All other created things, whether above or below man, only exist for his sake. . . .[18]

God's whole purpose in creation, then, was the creation of "another," another being like Himself in the individuality that comes from mastering his own will, a mastery that not only involves freedom but also a perfection of spirit. To this end, God began a deterministic process that would result in the materialization from which man could develop the spiritual Tzelem that would make him the Tzelem of God, a purified but still free individual.

Luzzatto further speaks of this paradoxical inversion that makes for resemblance:

> The world therefore contains two opposite general influences. . . . The deterministic influence is directed downward from on high, while the indeterministic is directed upward from below. This is because the deterministic is the influence that stems from the highest Forces. . . . The indeterministic influence, on the other hand, is the result of man's free will here in the physical world.[19]

Man's free will provides a way of return to the spiritual, or Tikkun, inverse to the deterministic forces that reflect the divine will. But if man's ability to exercise his will free of divine determination is essential to his cosmic contribution, then we can begin to understand the paradox of resemblance through inversion, that man can only become a divine Tzelem through his ability to contend victoriously with the power of the divine will, the very ability enshrined in the name Israel by which such a striver as Jacob can become a Prince of God, the meaning of the name "Israel" given to Jacob after his successful wrestling with the angel who so renamed him.[20] If we can further see man as standing in the pivotal fourth world between the prior worlds of divine determinism and the future worlds of human mastery, then all conditions that keep man within the bounds of such psychic determinism may be viewed as retarding his progress toward the truly free will by which man can become that other whose resemblance to God fulfills "God's purpose in creation." Where such retardation may be associated with the attempt to return to earlier cosmic conditions, that which furthers the liberation of the will may be associated with possibilities arising in the future, with an intuited model of future perfection.

What further illumination the fourth-world diagram can provide will depend upon the prior form of the diagram to which it is added, and this, in turn, will depend upon the form chosen for the animal level of evolution. As we have seen, there are three such forms, though each is presented without discriminating their construction elements: the simple Fi/Sol hexagram of the ideal or unfallen version of the fourth-world diagram shown in figure 3.4, the past-modeled Fi/Sol Sabbath Star of the quasi-fallen version shown in figure 3.6, and the future-modeled Fi/Sol Sabbath Star of the fully fallen version shown in figure 3.7, the latter of which can also be understood as transformative. But if instead of choosing among these versions, we construct a chronological scenario that embraces all three of them, we shall find that they provide models for various stages in the evolution of human consciousness with remarkable correspondence to the remains from the earliest human cultures.

When, in the first instance, the Sol Sabbath Star is added to the ideal form of the diagram, as in figure 3.4, we are given a model of unfallen Adam, that Nefesh Chayah whose consciousness is still hormonally attuned to its solar-regulated environment and in harmony with it.*

The consciousness of such an unfallen man is further developed by R. A. Schwaller de Lubicz in

---

*Much of the material that follows appeared in *The Kabbalah of the Soul*, pp. 83–89.

his study of the significance of the crown of the skull in ancient Egyptian figurations, particularly the fact that the line drawn around the human crown separates the lower brain from the two hemispheres of the cerebrum that are responsible for what he calls "cerebral intelligence."[21] As he goes on to explain:

> If, in the figuration of man, we symbolically separate this *crown of the skull*, it leaves us only the *Divine Man*, Adamic Man (*Kadmon*, the prenatural *Adam* of the Kabbalah) before his fall into Nature. . . . [I]n detaching the crown when the intention so requires, they separate the organ, which is the symbol of the fall from divine, direct Intelligence into transitory nature; and this double brain (right and left) becomes the principle of the sexualization and of the intelligence of the Created World. . . . Thus, "Divine" man (without this part of the brain) represents the Principle or Neter, capable of living and acting, but only as the executant of an impulse that he receives; hence, he plays the role of an intermediary between the abstract impulse, outside of Nature, and its execution in Nature, without actual choice. In this regard, this entity has a primitive, and "prenatural" character.[22]

In this analysis of ancient Egyptian iconography, Schwaller de Lubicz has brought us back to the earliest understanding of precultural or Adamic man as a being acting not on the basis of his double brain but rather through a "direct Intelligence" of the divine received through compelling impulses. In Schwaller's interpretation of this most ancient culture, such impulses are understood to originate not within the primitive neurological structure of the Adamic brain but beyond it, this Adamic lower brain serving as both the receiver and executor of these nonverbal impulses. What is being suggested here is that the past modeling of what can be considered the ideal form of the complete fourth-world diagram provides just such a model of divine man.

In contrast to this model, two further possibilities of fourth-world construction, based on the elaboration of the Fi/Sol hexagram into a past- or future-modeled Sabbath Star, can chart the progress of the human mind away from such unitive intelligence as it moves successively through two main stages in the course of human civilization. Most interesting is the diagram resulting from that elaboration of the Fi/Sol hexagram into a past-modeled Sabbath Star appearing in figure 3.6. If this complete diagram may be said to define the various layers of man's inheritance, then such a Sabbath Star would have further ramifications once it defines not simply the nature of animal consciousness but of this stratum of human consciousness. The most significant feature of this Sabbath Star, shown separately in figure 4.7, is the fact that it covers the Mi hexagram, identified with the angels, a fact that allowed it to be correlated primarily with the colonizing insects, which seem to be ruled by some form of group intelligence. In the case of man, the suggestion of such a component Sabbath Star is of an internalized angelic presence, not simply of an angelic influence capable of being countered by the human will but itself inhabiting that will.

The idea of man as inhabited by an internal angelic presence, which this second form of the complete fourth-world diagram would seem to suggest, is supported by the interesting thesis of Julian Jaynes that man, from approximately 10,000 B.C.E. to 700 B.C.E., was governed by what he calls the "bicameral mind," "that at one time human nature was split into two, an executive part called a god, and a follower part called a man."[23] It is Jaynes's thesis that "bicameral man" was ruled by internal voices, to which he gave divine status and obedience, voices that guided him directly whenever decision making was required. Unlike the mythological ideal defined by Schwaller de Lubicz, the "bicameral man" of Jaynes is a product of the early development of the double brain, and the evidence he has amassed in support of his thesis is most persuasive that a form of human mentality something like what he describes must have existed in the early stages of civilization.

The boldest part of this thesis is the conjecture that at the earliest stage of civilization the portion of the right brain corresponding to the speech area of the left brain had its own form of speech capability:

In ancient times, what corresponds to Wernicke's area on the right hemisphere may have organized admonitory experience and coded it into "voices" which were then "heard" over the anterior commissure by the left or dominant hemisphere. . . . auditory hallucinations exist as such in a linguistic manner because that is the most efficient method of getting complicated cortical processing from one side of the brain to the other. . . . [I]t was excitation in what corresponds to Wernicke's area on the right hemisphere that occasioned the voices of the gods.[24]

Though for Jaynes "the voices of the gods" are simply "auditory hallucinations" produced by the peculiar neurological organization of the early "bicameral" mind, the evidence he presents from early texts shows that such voices were experienced as arising not from within the self but from a higher source both associated with but also beyond that self:

> cuneiform texts state that a man lived in the shadow of his personal god, his *ili*. . . . The evidence from hieratic texts is confusing. Each person has his ka and speaks of it as we might of our will power. Yet when one dies, one goes to one's ka. . . . The Egyptians' attitude toward the ka is entirely passive. Just as in the case of the Greek gods, hearing it is tantamount to obeying it. It empowers what it commands. . . . *elohim* . . . is usually incorrectly translated in the singular as God. "Elohim" is a plural form . . . and better translations of "elohim" might be the great ones. . . . it is clear that elohim is a general term referring to the voice-visions of the bicameral mind.[25]

Jaynes may be right that the divine voices were actually heard as stated in the ancient texts and that they could be associated with the information-processing capabilities of Broca's area on the right hemisphere, that which corresponds to Wernicke's area on the left, a view that is being substantiated by recent neurological studies,[26] but this need not lead to his conclusion that they represent nothing beyond the split psychological functioning of early man. Rather, his

evidence can be used in support of the ancient textual claims of divine auditory experience, seeing the very right hemispheric capacities to which he refers not simply as processors of information originating in the individual but as a receiving mechanism for transpersonal information. Such an interpretation of the evidence is most in accord with the version of the fourth-world diagram now under consideration since this suggests some form of angelic presence in the human mind. And as the stories of Abraham and Jacob show, the angels appear to be interchangeable with Elohim. But as Jaynes has also demonstrated, where such voices are experienced, there is no possibility for the exercise of free will: "volition came as a voice that was in the nature of a neurological command, . . . in which to hear was to obey."[27] Where Schwaller de Lubicz's unfallen man acts upon unspoken impulses derived "by merging with the creative Unity,"[28] the unitive response of the lower brain, with Jaynes' bicameral man the higher cortical functions of the double brain, most significantly its linguistic capacity, have emerged into history but in a dualistic form in which internally heard divine voices are recognized as other than the self and command obedience.

Though the Adamic and bicameral forms of man, which can be correlated with the first two options for the Fi/Sol stage of the complete fourth-world diagram, seem closer to the divine than is the man of modern subjective consciousness, the paradox of what from an "ideal" perspective may be considered the Fall is that it is just this fortunate growth of self-consciousness that liberated the human will and that it is only through such freedom of the will that man can truly become the image of God. The geometric forms are here most expressive, for it is not by modeling himself upon a past condition of divine unity but only upon the model of the future that man can fulfill his divine destiny. In Lurianic cosmology, the repair or Tikkun of the shattered divine vessels is to accomplish a transformation of the original divinity into the Partzufim, the multiple divine personalities, discussed in chapter 2 and to be featured in chapters 6 and 7, and this way of the future is to be a product of man's own spiritual development. It is only by modeling himself upon the future perfection of divine personality that man can accomplish this divine transformation both above and below. In diagram terms, it is not through the past modeling of the Fi/Sol Sabbath Star, with its implied angelic takeover of the human will, that man can make his necessary cosmic contribution, nor through such modern occult forms as trance mediumship that aim at a similar return to the cosmic past. Rather it is through that transformative future modeling which arises only from a fully self-aware ego that man can both model and remodel the divine image.

It is, then, what can finally be considered the transformative rather than fallen form of the fourth-world diagram distinguished by the future-modeled Fi/Sol Sabbath Star that may be said to blaze the way into a future that is to be marked by such externalization of individual creativity as is the special feature of this Sabbath Star. In thus externalizing the cosmic code of the incorporated and Sabbatically reproduced Do hexagram, that process earlier thought to signify the conferral of personality to the animal nature, the future-modeled Fi/Sol Sabbath Star also becomes a proper vessel for the incarnation of the Nefesh soul. In these last two forms of the fourth-world diagram man is given a choice between submitting to an angelic compulsion, which harkens back to the past, and the freedom of the soul urging ever onward into the future. Indeed, it is the futurist orientation of this final animal soul that is the most significant contribution this layer of man's psychic endowment has given to human mentality in its final fourth-world form. What the final layering of the Sol Sabbath Star may be said to contribute is primarily a free will, one biased in favor of the evil inclination but still free and capable of a higher rather than lower enhancement of the animal ego.

The creation story tells us that it is the responsibility of man to establish "dominion" (Gen. 1:28) over all the animals, and this can be taken to include the animal propensities within himself. To fulfill the divine image in which he was created, man is told to follow the way of the plants, to "be fruitful, and multiply," and also to dominate the animal nature. This too is what analysis of the fourth-world Sabbath Stars has seemed to imply. What it further

suggests is that the difference between the right way of the plants and wrong way of the animals is largely a matter of timing, the plants exhibiting a measured ripening process and the animals a restless impatience. Thus if man is to follow the original divine commandments, he must learn the patience of the plants and to control his lower animal nature, its anxiety, impulsiveness, and belligerence. Stabilized in this state, man will become the proper vessel for the higher Ruach and Neshamah dimensions of the soul.*

In the *Midrash ha-Ne'elam* section of the *Zohar*, it is alone the Neshamah level of soul that is thought to achieve immortality.[29] This belief can be paralleled in the system of Gurdjieff and in the ancient Chinese text *The Secret of the Golden Flower*.[30] Both esoteric systems claim that immortality is not universal but that man must, through his own efforts of spiritual discipline, build an immortal spiritual body. The immortal golden flower of the Chinese text, unfolded through a strenuous discipline of meditation, is certainly suggestive of the thousand-petaled lotus of the Hindu crown chakra as that is of the Sefirah Keter, also meaning crown, which can be correlated with the Neshamah soul. In its first movement from the Nefesh to the Ruach soul level, we are also moving, then, from the given spiritual endowment of the fourth world to the potential for further spiritual development, a potential that, though present in the fourth world, can only be fully actualized in the higher immortalizing dimensions of the fifth and later worlds modeled by the Sabbath Star Diagram.[31]

But in being attracted to its own spiritual development, the human will is being affected not by past but future causes. Aristotle had a word for it. He called it the "telos," the Final Cause, which contains "the purpose and the good"[32] for which the three prior causes of form, matter, and the transformative power called the "entelechy" are intended. This concept has had more modern proponents. For Shelley, the future can inspire the most highly

---

*Much of the remainder of this chapter appeared in somewhat different form in the conclusion of chapter 2 of *The Kabbalah of the Soul*, pp. 122–27.

attuned spirits to new modes of being that become models of the new age: "Poets are the hierophants of an unapprehended inspiration; the mirrors of the gigantic shadows which futurity casts upon the present. . . . Poets are the unacknowledged legislators of the world."[33] And central to the more recent thought of Teilhard de Chardin is the evolutionary force exerted by such a future "Omega point": "this kind of attraction . . . linked at its root with the radiations of some ultimate Centre (at once transcendent and immanent) of psychic congregation . . . seems indispensable (the supreme condition of the future!), for the preservation of the *will* to advance, in defiance of the shadow of death, upon an evolutionary path become reflective, conscious of the future. . . ."[34]

To the long tradition stemming from Aristotle that regards the future as exercising an influence over the present, the Sabbath Star Diagram may offer graphic corroboration. Although I have previously focused upon the temporal aspect of the diagram, the order in which the various parts of the diagram were constructed, as significant of cosmic history, its final spatial aspect is equally important. In the final appearance of the diagram, the whole sequence of "temporal" layers is simultaneously present and seen to be interpenetrating. We can now picture ourselves as looking down into a cone of concentric rings of Sabbath Stars, the larger of these containing everything both within and beneath them. This fourth world cross-section of the cone of continuous creation would then appear to contain, not a temporal sequence, but a layering of different levels of spiritual worlds or of consciousness all perceived as simultaneously present. The question of the Fall becomes, then, an illusion, as Eden, with the Tree of Life in its midst, is shown to be perpetually present. The paradox of the future altering the past, which each Sabbath Star may be said to do to the prior elements it covers, is also seen to be an illusion when both are recognized to be simultaneously present. And when in later chapters we contemplate the diagrams of the future worlds, we shall see that these worlds, with their higher soul bodies completed, are already present and just as interpenetrating with the fourth world as are the prior worlds of cosmic emanation.

It is the special genius of such a two-dimensional diagram that it can lift us to a higher dimension where the linear distinctions of time do not exist. But though from the final spatial perspective the two-dimensionality of the Sabbath Star Diagram seems to render time an illusion, it still retains a temporal aspect, and not simply as a metaphor to aid our analytic powers of discrimination. For both aspects of the diagram are true: it was constructed in time though its final appearance is one of simultaneity. It may very well be that the diagram's deepest meanings are revealed not through the analytic but the intuitive understanding as it works on the supraconsciousness through symbolic language. The undifferentiated aesthetic appeal of the diagram may speak more profoundly to the viewer than the volume that has been written about it, lifting him or her with the power of a mandala to a meditative experience of the interpenetration of future and past in a timeless present. Nonetheless, it is imperative that neither the concept of linear time nor that of eternity should so dominate our consciousness of reality as to make the other seem an illusion. Rather, they should both be contained and synthesized in the fuller concept of time that the Sabbath Star Diagram perfectly demonstrates. Viewed in this way, the fourth-world Sabbath Star Diagram, which represents the central moment in the spiral circularity of the cosmic scale that constitutes our present, not only contains all of the past visually present but all of the laws from which the future will evolve.[35] It tells us what we are given and what we must contribute to the ongoing cosmic process. And in its growth processes it encodes the great mystery of human destiny, that the only way to preserve the identity given man with his Nefesh soul is to expand it.

CHAPTER FIVE

The Fifth-World Diagram and the Messianic Age

INTRODUCTION TO THE FIFTH-WORLD DIAGRAM
An Overview of the Fifth World

As chapter 1 provided the theoretical foundation for what is probably the major innovation in this study, the projection of a seven-dimensional cosmos in terms compatible with the Jewish esoteric tradition, we can move directly to the study of what can be considered the fifth world or dimension of this cosmic model. Study of the construction elements of the fifth-world diagram will be the subject of the following full section, and it will show a remarkable correspondence between the forms of these successive elements and the traditional chronology of events within the Messianic Age, one that can provide new illumination as to the nature of this future ideal. The final section will study the stages of Messianic or Ruach consciousness as revealed through analysis of the construction elements, its approach emphasizing the development of such consciousness both individually and in relationship to community, and it will show this relationship to be characteristic of the Ruach soul correlated with this cosmic world as well as the means of its final perfection.

Ruach consciousness has thus far been identified with the consciousness of the chronologically future Messianic Age and so with the future.* But a caveat must be offered before proceeding further with what will be an essentially future-oriented analysis. For the fifth-world diagram can also be correlated with the symbolizing faculty that has been considered definitive of man, that which is a function of true personality and can be considered to occupy a systems level between the *impersonal* realm below and the *transpersonal*, symbolic realm above.[1] Thus in its fifth expansion, the Sabbath Star Diagram seems to be programming the dimension of consciousness that should be normal to man as he passes beyond the state of individual or racial childhood and enters into the

---

*The following paragraphs of this introductory overview appeared in the introduction to chapter 3 of *The Kabbalah of the Soul*, pp. 128–31, and readers familiar with this material may wish to skip ahead to the new material on the fifth-world construction elements ("The Fifth Dimension," page 127).

full powers of his maturity. Indeed, as Chayyim Vital, the foremost interpreter of the thought of Isaac Luria, has said: "as we know, it is the *ruach* that is called 'human.' Understand this well!"[2]

Whether the fifth world of the Sabbath Star diagram is considered to represent a present or a future norm depends, from one interpretative perspective, on whether it is regarded as proceeding directly from the past-modeled form of the fourth-world diagram or from its future-modeled form. Had the passage from the childlike nature of the animal or Adamic Nefesh soul to the higher functioning of the Ruach soul followed the path that the Sabbath Star Diagram may be thought to have ideally programmed for the human soul, all of the higher spiritual powers that shall be unfolded in this chapter would have been the common property of all normal human beings.

But humanity seems to have rather followed the path of development represented by the future modeling of the fourth-world diagram, which, if considered its fallen form, would result in some measure of Ruach power becoming available to man while still locked into the more limited perspective of Nefesh consciousness. And if he used such usurped power only to facilitate his acquisition of worldly power and pleasure, it would have the further effect of blocking the natural development of this power to its full Ruach potential. Thus the mental level available to all men would become the property only of the extraordinary few, those who through special grace or spiritual discipline have been able so to perfect their souls that they could ascend to the purposed level of earthly human functioning. But if the future-modeled form of the fourth-world diagram is understood to model not the fallen condition of man but his proper transformative change from the past to the future orientation necessary to manifest the fifth dimension of consciousness, then it would well model the transitional stage of those few who are better prepared to ascend to the Ruach soul dimension.

It is important to remember, then, that the power of the Ruach Master, which will be defined in the final sections of this chapter and in chapter 9, does not truly belong to an abnormal spiritual state,

rather the state to which man is naturally heir, and that the way now trodden only by the spiritually gifted is the path meant for all. The Ruach dimension can be assigned to the Messianic future only because we still allow ourselves to be victims of the mistakes of our forebears, such mistakes as have been transmitted through the alienating institutions and habits of our society and the neuroses of our equally victimized parents. But though such influences rob each of us of our native Paradise, we have it in our power to regain a greater Paradise, that optimal condition of physical and psychological well-being that represents the full realization of the human potential *on earth*. In chapters 6 and 7 of this part and chapters 10 through 12 of part 3 we shall be considering soul levels that are properly associated with the World(s) to Come and whose appearance in human form *is* abnormal. But the Ruach level represents a spiritual dimension that should be readily available to earthly man and in some measure is present in all symbolic activity. Incorporating the Nefesh soul in its fuller cognitive and emotive scope, it is the Ruach rather than the Nefesh soul that is designed for the most effective and, at the same time, harmonious activity in the bodily state, and its powers are ours to claim, making the future evolution of the race a present reality for ever increasing numbers. Such powers are already present, then, to those who have perfected their Ruach souls, this, indeed, the work we are set on earth to do. The final section should help to chart the steps of the soul work necessary to claim this heritage of spiritual power, and it can be read from the dual perspectives offered by the Sabbath Star Diagram, as a present reality or only as a future possibility, if humanity be deemed to be trapped in the persistent reality of the fourth world.

The Fifth Dimension

If the earlier established coherence between the four cosmic worlds of emanation and the concept of seven worlds derived from Genesis provides for a limited extension of the former, such an extension must also take into consideration the implicit definition of the four cosmic worlds as a series of expanding dimensions.[3] Though nowhere insisted upon, the Pythagorean source or analogue to this kabbalistic concept led to an understanding of these worlds as proceeding through the dimensions of the point, line, plane, and solid, and it seems probable that it was the conceptual difficulty in expanding the dimensions beyond the spatial three of this our solid world that prevented previous attempts to reconcile the two outstanding theories of cosmic history in the Kabbalah.

But the key for an expansion of the dimensions beyond the three of space already existed at the start of the whole kabbalistic tradition, in the *Sefer Yetzirah*. In the fifth paragraph of its first chapter, we are told: "Ten Sefirot of Nothingness: Their measure is ten which have no end. A depth of beginning, a depth of end; a depth of good, a depth of evil; a depth above, a depth below; a depth east, a depth west; a depth north, a depth south. The singular Master, God faithful King, dominates them all from His Holy dwelling until eternity of eternities."[4] In this remarkable passage, we are taken beyond the three dimensions of space to a fourth dimension of time ("a depth of beginning, a depth of end") and from there still further to a fifth moral dimension ("a depth of good, a depth of evil") woven into the fabric of existence that ensures that as we sow so shall we reap, a dimension of purposive causality that can be called Providential. But the passage does not stop there; it gives us yet another dimension, the knowledge that the justice working itself out within the frame of space-time cannot be reduced simply to a mechanism, however marvelous, but is itself controlled by a higher power, a dimension that invests the cosmic mechanism with meaningfulness. And beyond this sixth dimension, itself one of eternity, is the final dimension of Sabbatical rest, the "eternity of eternities" that sums up and contains all these endless measurements.

Confining ourselves at this point just to what the fifth world of the Sabbath Star Diagram can tell us about the fifth dimension so defined, on the level of the fifth-world Sabbath Stars, there are two out of six that, though they appear on different grids with different antecedents, define the exact same moment in the chronology of the fifth world. Both

seem to represent the "curious principle" Jung has termed "synchronicity":

> synchronicity takes the coincidence of events in space and time as meaning something more than mere chance, namely, a peculiar interdependence of objective events among themselves as well as with the subjective (psychic) states of the observer or observers. . . . [C]ausality describes the sequence of events. . . . The synchronistic view on the other hand tries to produce an equally meaningful picture of coincidence . . . [showing that synchronous events] all are the exponents of one and the same momentary situation.[5]

As we proceed further in the analysis of the fifth world, we shall see how it is possible for a Providential order of causality to express itself through the synchronicity of events that may be said to define the fifth dimension.[6]

The Shofar

The ease with which the various features of the Messianic tradition and the fifth-world Sabbath Star Diagram can be coordinated is partly due to the fact that the Messianic Age has been so largely elaborated in biblical and later Judaic mythology. And it may well be that we have more highly developed mythological understanding of the fifth world, as of the third, than of worlds further away from our own just because their proximity results in more information passing into the most sensitive imaginations through what Homer, in *The Odyssey*, called "the Gate of Horn," that through which true visions pass to man. Figure 5.1 gives us our first illustration of the fifth-world diagram with its arresting matrix border, which seems to be an uncanny representation of animal horns.

The surprising likeness of the fifth-world matrix border to horns must turn our attention to the horn that is so central to Jewish ritual, the shofar or ram's horn. In so doing, however, we shall gain our first geometrically derived definition of the fifth world as signifying both the Messianic times and the Ruach dimension of the soul.

Figure 5.1. The Fifth-World Diagram with Its Matrix Border Outlined

In a survey of biblical references to the shofar, I have elsewhere shown that it is consistently viewed as an instrument wherein God reveals his power and trumpets the approach of a Messianic redemption in which knowledge of God will free man from illusion.* As the essence of the Rosh Hashanah service, it retains its ritual symbolism to this day. And what the later ritual of this holiday makes clear to be the major event so commemorated is God's revelation of Himself to the people of Israel on Mount Sinai

amid the sound of the divinely blown shofar (Exod. 19:16).

The ram's horn blown on Mount Sinai can be taken to be that spiral instrumentality of historical process through which the spirit of God makes itself known as an inspiring breath. And the purpose of this divine blasting of the ram's horn is to inspire the faith that will forever confirm the people of Israel in the covenant they have just made. But this covenant is itself placed in the context of redemption, particularly from Egyptian slavery. A similar association of freedom from slavery with the sound of the shofar is made in the commandment concerning the Jubilee: "Then shalt thou cause the trumpet [shofar][7] of the

*See *Renewing the Covenant*, pp. 10–19, for the much fuller survey of biblical references to the shofar from which the following discussion has been drawn.

Jubilee to sound. . . . And ye shall . . . proclaim liberty throughout all the land" (Lev. 25:9–10). It is the association of liberty, particularly the emancipation of slaves, with the sounding of the ram's horn on the Jubilee that leads to the broader association of the Jubilee with the ultimate concept of redemption in the Messianic future, Thus the covenant on Mount Sinai, its ritual commemoration on Rosh Hashanah, and the establishment of the Jubilee can all be variously considered as both preparations for and a foreshadowing of the final Messianic redemption. It is with full consciousness of the singular symbolic role assigned to the ram's horn in the Torah that the prophets attest to a renewed sounding of the "great shofar" heard on Sinai to herald the coming of the Messianic Age, as, for instance, in Isaiah 27:13 and Zechariah 9:14.

For Jeremiah, the human blowing of the shofar becomes a way of answering God's call to a new covenant: "Blow ye the trumpet [shofar] in the land. . . . Behold, the days come, saith the Lord, that I will make a new covenant with the house of Israel. . . . I will put the law in their inward parts, and write it in their hearts; and . . . they shall all *know* me . . ." (Jer., 4:4, 5; 31:31, 33, 34, my emphasis). A nation so filled with Da'at, such inward knowledge of God, would truly be a holy nation, each a sanctified priest permitted to enter the Holy of Holies for direct communication with the spirit of God present above the Ark of the Covenant. But whether blown by God or by His people, the shofar attests to the power of God and of His Presence.

The blowing of the great shofar will herald the day when the holy Presence will animate the whole of a holy nation, each of whose members will be an ark containing the Torah written in their hearts, with the figure of the Messiah among them and personifying the collective holiness of this redeemed nation.

The question we have now to ask is what further meaning may be implied by the sounding of the shofar and its cognates in other traditions. What the function of these horns seems to be is to effect the higher attunement of the auditors they have drawn as a necessary preparation for the next level of their spiritual development soon to take place. The tone of the horn may be said to function ideally as a kind of tuning fork whereby lower and various vibrational levels can be raised into harmony with this one pure tone. What is more, the priests and other functionaries empowered to blow these ceremonial horns are all doing so as divine surrogates, and so this tone may be said to convey the breath of God, the breath that first inspired Adam and whose vibrational level can redeem those descendants whom it spiritually inspires to rise to its level. Thus the breath that causes the horn to sound is always a means of bringing the spirit of God into communion with man. It reveals the power of God and calls man to prepare his vessel for that transmission of power that constitutes true communion.

All the other uses of the shofar may be considered but foreshadowings of its primary revelation as a herald of the Messianic future. And the Sabbath Star Diagram seems to tell us that this too is an age for which the horn can be symbolic. What this means is, first of all, that this age will be filled with the breath of God, with Ruach, and that its defining spiritual element is air. The correlation just made for the fifth-world diagram between the form of the horn and the element of air but confirms what already seemed apparent with regard to the matrix borders for the two forms of the fourth-world diagram.

It will be remembered that the zigzag form of the past-modeled matrix border, appearing in figure 3.4, was shown to be most iconographically significant, such a form having been used to symbolize water in prehistoric cultures throughout the world and one that is still found in the zodiacal sign for Aquarius. Similarly, the plateau shapes of the future-modeled matrix border, appearing in figure 3.7, were thought to be suggestive of land masses. Taken in sequence, the fourth world of Asiyah could be construed to have passed from a more flowing to a more solid state whether this change is understood to signify the Fall or to be transformative to the future orientation of the Tikkun. What is most remarkable about these matrix borders is the uncanny appropriateness of these forms to the worlds in question, in particular their metaphorical suggestiveness of elements and these, in each case, the most appropriate for a specific world or world stage. These correlations of matrix borders with spiritual elements seem to be continued with the correlation just made of the hornlike border of the fifth-world matrix with the element of air, as it will be further reinforced by the sixth-world matrix border shown in figure 6.7, which is suggestive of the fourth spiritual element of fire. With this introduction to some subjects with particular relevance to the fifth world of the Sabbath Star Diagram, we can now turn to its modeling of the Messianic Age.

THE FIFTH-WORLD SABBATH STARS AND THE MESSIANIC AGE

Traditional Messianic Chronology

Recent interpretations of the fossil records have suggested that biological evolution does not proceed gradually but is marked by discrete leaps between species, and quanta are famous for jumping from one discrete energy level to another. Such quantum leaps can also be posited between cosmic worlds. In terms of the Sabbath Star Diagram, the course of evolution that has moved through the four Sabbath Stars of the fourth world does not continue in a regular fashion to the very next Sabbath Star but is reattuned to a new vibrational level from which new laws of nature will arise calling for radical redefinitions.

The most apparent of such redefinitions involves the "tonality" of the diagram. Due to the geometric enlargements that occur from one whole-step progression to the next, as this is correlated with the musical whole tone, the distances between Sabbath Stars on the same grid signify different tonal divisions in different worlds. Thus the three vertical Sabbath Stars of the fifth world, though progressing at the same spatial intervals as the three vertical Sabbath Stars of the fourth world, cannot be characterized as thirds of a tone since this tonal division must be assigned to the three horizontal Sabbath Stars of the fifth world constructed by the whole-step progression from the aforementioned fourth-world Sabbath Stars on the vertical grid, which represented the division of the tone into thirds. Since the third of the fifth-world vertical Sabbath

Stars can be constructed by the whole-step progression from the Fi Sabbath Star of the fourth world, we know that it must be defined by the tonal name of Si, which represents the whole-tone interval above Fi. But since the highest of the fourth-world vertical Sabbath Stars is represented by the tonal name of Sol, and this is just a half tone below Si, this means that the two Sabbath Stars between Sol and Si must represent thirds of a half tone, or sixths of a tone. Though the first of these is only as far above the Sol Sabbath Star as the Fi/Sol Sabbath Star is below it, the latter represents a third of a tone and the former a sixth. Such a new level of tonality is, in fact, a way of identifying the entry into a new cosmic world. For each cosmic world after the given of the first world can be defined by the smallest tonal interval it manifests: the second world ideally by the whole tone; the third world by the half tone; the fourth world by the third of a tone; the fifth world by the sixth of a tone; and the sixth world (discussed in chapter 6) by the ninth of a tone—with further fractionings of the tone still to come.

On the foregoing basis, we can now establish the chronology of the six Sabbath Stars of the fifth world. Referring back to figure 5.1, the first to be manifest is clearly the vertical Sabbath Star that marks the first sixth of the tone. But the next stage is as distinctive of the fifth world as was the first, for it contains that synchronous appearance of two Sabbath Stars referred to in the previous section in defining the fifth dimension. It is simple arithmetic that two-sixths equal one-third; and if the diagram be turned on its side so that the horizontal Sabbath Stars now appear vertical, it will be seen that the Sabbath Stars marking the first third and second sixth of the tone meet at the upper horizontal crossbar of the diagram. This is, in fact, the best perspective from which to view the chronology of the fifth world. As the first sixth comes earlier and the second sixth is synchronous with the first third, so the third sixth lies one half of the distance between the inner hexagon of the La Sabbath Star, which defines the boundary between the fourth and fifth worlds, and the La Sabbath Star's peak, which marks the farthest extension of the fifth world. It thus represents half of the fifth-world whole tone of La, or the half tone of Si, as three-sixths equal one-half. The next stage is marked by the second of the horizontal Sabbath Stars, that representing the second third of the tone, and the last stage by the third of these thirds, signifying the whole tone of the La Sabbath Star. There are, then, only five discrete stages of the fifth world though the six Sabbath Stars that define these stages all appear in the course of them. To summarize these Sabbath Star stages, they are those of the first sixth, the synchronous appearance of the second sixth with the first third, the third sixth or the half, the second third, and the third third or the whole.

Having established this geometric chronology, we now come to the most crucial part of this investigation, the identification of these Sabbath Star stages with the traditional chronology of the Messianic Age. Needless to say, there is no such thing as a hard and fast Messianic chronology in the Hebraic tradition, or of any other hard and fast dogmas, for that matter.* Nonetheless, in the long history of the Messianic idea, from the biblical prophets through the apocalyptic literature to the Talmud and beyond, certain prophesied events did crystallize as essential elements of a generally accepted tradition. Of these, two were clearly of overriding importance, the appearance of a Messianic personality and the subsequent inauguration of the Messianic millennium. Because of their supreme importance and chronological order, their geometric identifications seem obvious, and we can categorically assign them to the two most significant Sabbath Stars in this or any other cosmic world, those defined as the semitones of the Solfeggio scale, which are also the only ones to pass through the center. These assignments would be of the Messiah to the vertical Si Sabbath Star and the Messianic millennium to the horizontal La Sabbath Star.

Without going here into more elaborate geometric analyses, there are a few observations that can be made that will help with the identification of the remaining Sabbath Stars. Most important is the way in which these semitone Sabbath Stars pass through the center, the La Sabbath Star in alignment with

the central column of the superimposed Tree of Life Diagram and the Si Sabbath Star at right angles to it. The path of the Si Sabbath Star through the diagram's center overlays and extends the earlier paths made by the Mi and Sol Sabbath Stars as the La Sabbath Star does that of the Fi Sabbath Star. If the Mi Sabbath Star may be taken to signify Yetziric Adam and the Sol Sabbath Star either fallen or unevolved man, then the Si Sabbath Star, may be said to signify the perfected man who constitutes the Tikkun or reconstitution of man in his originally conceived but never so fully actualized perfection. But however perfected, the individuality of the Messiah seems reflected in the passage of his Sabbath Star through the center in a manner that crosses the central path of the Tree. The La Sabbath Star, on the other hand, in following the garden path of the Fi Sabbath Star, seems in consonance both with the Tree of Life and this most Edenic aspect of the fourth world, that of the vegetable kingdom, which it may be said to raise once more to its former Edenic nature in the changed earth of the millennium. In general, then, the distinction between the vertical and horizontal Sabbath Stars, whose pinnacles here are the Si and La Sabbath Stars, respectively, may be considered that essential distinction between the individual and collective aspects of all existence, with the vertical Sabbath Stars representing the pole of individual development and the horizontal Sabbath Stars its complementary opposite of communal development.[8] Though history should properly balance the records of individual achievement and mass movements, it is the latter that seem most reflective of a Zeitgeist, the defining spirit of an age; the changing epochs of history incorporate it and the individual whose achievements are to be epical, nontragic in their outstanding success, must bring himself into harmony with the age. Thus the horizontal Sabbath Stars will here define the communal aspects of the Messianic Age, the vertical Sabbath Stars those aspects associated with individuality, in general, and with the personality of the Messiah, in particular. How the remaining Sabbath Stars are to be correlated both with these diagram axes and with traditional Messianic stages we are now to see.

---

*The remainder of this subsection appeared in slightly different form in The Kabbalah of the Soul, pp. 132–40.

In his definitive history of the subject, *The Messianic Idea in Israel*, Joseph Klausner concludes his survey of the middle period in the development of the Messianic idea, that of the Apocrypha and Pseudepigrapha, with the following Messianic chronology:

> And thus was forged that *complete* Messianic chain whose separate links are: *the signs of the Messiah, the birth pangs of Messiah, the coming of Elijah, the trumpet of Messiah, the ingathering of the exiles, the reception of proselytes, the war with Gog and Magog, the Days of the Messiah, the renovation of the world, the Day of Judgment, the resurrection of the dead, the World to Come.* Not all the links of this chain are found in every book of the Apocrypha and Pseudepigrapha, or in this order; but *in general* you find it with these links and in the order mentioned. These links are also found in the Talmudic-Midrashic literature, to which the Apocryphal and Pseudepigraphical books serve as a transition from the Bible.[9]

In his following section on the talmudic literature, however, Klausner excludes at least the last three items in this list as belonging to the period after the Messianic Age, that of the World to Come, and so properly to Jewish eschatology, the study of "last things."[10] Excluding items that properly belong to the sixth world, the World to Come, we are left with an extended list of events, some of which can be combined with others. We shall begin by trying to determine what aspect of the prophecies related to communal action can be identified with the first of the horizontal Sabbath Stars, that representative of the first third of the fifth world, and also what synchronous individual action can be identified with the vertical Sabbath Star representative of its second sixth. Of this list, the Messianic event that seems most identifiable with the Sabbath Star signifying the first third of the Messianic Age is the war of Gog and Magog, first prophesied by Ezekiel.

As first developed in Ezekiel, "Gog, the land of Magog" (38:2), shall attempt to conquer Israel only to be defeated by God and left as "a great sacrifice upon the mountains of Israel" (39:17). In its later talmudic development, this great war of the Messianic Age becomes connected with the concept of a second Messiah, not the Messiah ben David who will reign in the Messianic kingdom but the Messiah ben Joseph from the Ten Lost Tribes of Israel who will command the armies of the Lord and fall in battle:

> So *Messiah ben Joseph* became a *Messiah who dies*: he is fated to fall in the war with Gog and Magog, as Bar-Cochbah had fallen in his war against Rome. . . . the Messianic age itself comes after "the wars of the dragons" and after the war with Gog and Magog. The military commander in these great battles can be none other than Messiah ben Joseph. . . . Messiah ben Joseph, the first in time but the second in rank of the two Messiahs, is already present at the time of this war. But the Messianic age reaches its *culmination* only *after* the war with Gog and Magog, when Messiah ben David appears in all his glory.[11]

The great collective event that occurs before the coming of the Messiah ben David and that epitomizes the national woes referred to under the general title of "the birth pangs of Messiah" is, then, that apocalyptic war of Israel with ultimate evil that goes under the name of Gog and Magog and that is synchronous with the personal tragedy of the Messiah ben Joseph, who leads the army of Israel but dies a sacrifice to its victory.

In terms of the Sabbath Star Diagram, it seems clear that this synchronicity of collective and individual events can be associated with the two synchronous Sabbath Stars of the fifth-world diagram, the war of Gog and Magog with that signifying the first third division and the Messiah ben Joseph with that of the second sixth division of the tone, both of which mark the second stage of the Messianic Age. When we come to study these Sabbath Stars more closely, we shall see a further reason for identifying this first third Sabbath Star with the war of Gog and Magog, namely, that this is the first Sabbath Star to cover and thus incorporate into the matrix the Fa hexagram, hitherto associated with the introduction of evil into the world in its various manifestations as the Fall, the *shedim* or demons, and the Yetzer ha-Ra, the evil inclination. As earlier discussed, the continuity of this antithetical force persists from the second half of the third world through the whole of the fourth world to be finally overcome in the first third of the fifth world, the stage just identified with the war of Gog and Magog as it is conveyed by the Sol/Si Sabbath Star.

Having determined that the war with Gog and Magog best defines the great communal action preceding the advent of the Messiah, we have now to determine what should be considered the major action of masses of people to follow the Messiah's appearance. Returning to Klausner's list, this would seem to be the twofold "ingathering of the exiles" and "reception of proselytes." Although the former particularly is featured in many early prophecies as a sign of the Messiah's approaching appearance, the tradition also conceives it as an ongoing process that would vastly accelerate with the coming of the Messiah and the establishment of his kingdom. Klausner shows that "according to the Psalms of Solomon (17:26–28) and the Targum Psuedo-Jonathan (on Deut. 30:4 and Jer. 33:13) the Messiah will bring back the dispersed nation to its own land."[12] And he shows a similar treatment of the subject of proselytes:

> The Messiah will be cordial and gracious to all the peoples. . . . Closely connected with this conception of the Messianic age expressed by R. Jose is the following saying of his contemporary, R. Simeon ben Gamaliel II: "In Jerusalem all nations and all kingdoms are destined to be gathered together, as it is written (Jer. 3:17), 'And all the nations shall be gathered unto it, to the name of the LORD.'". . . The Gentiles will become proselytes of their own accord, without exhortation on the part of the Jews: for they will be irresistibly attracted by the model kingdom where all are priests and all combine to make a holy nation.[13]

The stage in which all Jews and all other nations are gathered together seems the most significant communal response to the presence of the Messiah and the one that should be associated with the second of the horizontal Sabbath Stars that divide the fifth world into thirds, the Si/La Sabbath Star.

The two larger communal expressions of the Messianic Age represented by the horizontal Sol/Si and Si/La Sabbath Stars form an interesting contrast. The former represents a process of exclusion and the latter of inclusion, both of which may tell us something about the Messiah and the development of the consciousness he exemplifies. It would seem that the necessary preliminary to such an advent is a period of sacrificial purification but that, once the vessel has been thus prepared for the influx of a higher level of spirit, this higher spiritual nature will be all-accepting, able to harmonize itself with what had formerly to be excluded in virtue of its own purified vision into the underlying goodness of all. The Messiah will, then, only appear to a people that has defeated the evil in and around itself, and the appearance of such a holy nation will subsequently lead to the conversion of the surrounding nations, formerly a snare but now attracted by its example. With this final ingathering, the stage is set for the culmination of the Messianic Age, the millennium or "Days of the Messiah," exemplifying the "signs of the Messiah," that changed earth of effortless fertility and animal harmony referred to in the Messianic writings that may be identified with the "renovation of the world" listed by Klausner. The three listings just given can all be ascribed to the final stage of the fifth world represented by the horizontal La Sabbath Star, the extended millennium in which man achieves a harmony not only with his fellows and former enemies but with all of nature.

Of Klausner's list only two items are left, "the coming of Elijah" and "the trumpet of Messiah." Elijah was generally considered to be a forerunner of the Messiah, and he was charged with various specific functions, as shown by Klausner:

> as early as the time of Ben-Sira, it was the function of Elijah "to make ready the tribes of Israel." . . . [in the Mishnah passage at the end of Eduyyoth, Elijah] is in the Messianic age transformed into an angel of peace for the whole nation, or even a "refining fire" coming to burn out of the world all unrighteousness and all doubt.

But Elijah has still other functions. He will, in the Messianic age, restore three things to Israel: "The flask of manna, the flask of water for purification, and the flask of oil for anointing. . . ."

"The flask of oil for anointing" is of a very special kind. . . . Elijah, who will restore this marvelous flask to Israel, will of course himself anoint the Messiah with its oil.

. . . Elijah must come one day before the Son of David. Apparently, he will announce the Messiah's coming from the top of Mount Carmel.

. . . Elijah will also appear in the days of Gog and Magog. . . .[14]

The functions of Elijah associated with the three flasks would seem to place him in each of the three stages associated with individual personality, the stages symbolized by the three vertical Sabbath Stars. Through his anointing of the Messiah with the flask of oil, he appears in that of the Si Sabbath Star set apart for the Messiah. But his role as purifier of the nation, associated with the flask of water, will place him also in the previous stage. In alliance with the Messiah ben Joseph, he clearly has a part to play in preparing the tribes of Israel for the warfare that is to "burn out of the world all unrighteousness and all doubt." Can the flask of manna that Elijah also brings be associated in similar manner with the first Sabbath Star of the fifth world, yet to be defined? Before we can answer this question and so properly assess Elijah's relationship to the whole of the fifth-world vertical grid, we must first attempt to define the Sabbath Star that marks this first sixth of the Messianic fifth world.

As the Sabbath Star marking the new vibratory level that distinguishes the fifth world, it is fitting that it should be identified with the last remaining item on Klausner's list, the "trumpet of Messiah." As Klausner explains, this "is not a trumpet blown by the Messiah, but the trumpet of the Messianic age"[15] a concept derived from the biblical prophets: "the prophets speak also of the blowing of a horn (Isa. 27:13; Zech. 9:14) something that gives place afterward to the idea of 'the trumpet of Messiah.'"[16] So we come back again to the great shofar, the significance of which was analyzed at length in the previous section.

As there shown, the great shofar that heralds the Messianic Age is to be blown by God Himself or His surrogate and as such is a means of bringing the divine spirit, the Ruach, into communion with man. Further, this communion brings man into the higher level of attunement that empowers him to participate in the new dimension of Ruach consciousness The "trumpet of Messiah" is, then, the necessary first stage and thus herald of the Messianic Age, the means of effecting a radical reattunement of consciousness. Finally, it is this new attunement that constitutes the new covenant, the law written in the heart. Whether this means an abrogation of the old Torah of Gevurah or, conversely, a new capacity to observe the law in the stricter construction of Shammai (the looser construction of Hillel, in the great talmudic controversies, normally being preferred in the present condition of the world) is not important. For in either case the heart will now be attuned to apprehend the operation of the law in all elements of creation and will naturally conform itself to the Way of God thus manifested.

It is in this last point that we may see a connection between the Messianic shofar and the "flask of manna" Elijah is to restore to Israel in the Messianic Age. As both symbol and demonstration of the power of God working through history, the shofar may be said to represent the Way of God. So too is it with the manna. God tells Moses that the manna is given "that I may prove them, whether they will walk in my law, or no" (Exod. 16:4). The Torah of the manna is a Way, a path, that commands one to gather exactly and only what is needed and that develops an assured trust in divine Providence, the knowledge that God will provide exactly what one requires. Since it was also shown in the previous section that the fifth dimension may be considered the dimension of Providential causality, it is particularly urgent that the "flask of manna," the law originally given in the Exodus, be restored to Israel in this Messianic new world. The manna is, then, as much a direct revelation of the Way of God as is the shofar that conveys the empowering breath of God.

As Elijah is associated with the "flask of manna," so can his function be related to that of the shofar.

Klausner was earlier quoted to the effect that Elijah "will announce the Messiah's coming," and he had shown that such prophets as "Nahum and Deutero-Isaiah also speak of a *herald* (or 'messenger of good news to Zion'), who in later times was confused with *Elijah*."[17] So Elijah becomes the talmudic herald of the Messiah in concert with the shofar, whether or not he is supposed to be the spirit that actually is to sound this horn. But since the Messiah is to be heralded by a shofar and Elijah is the appointed herald, it seems appropriate that it should be he who blows the horn as God's surrogate. Although Elijah animates all three of the Sabbath Stars connected with individuality, it may be possible to associate his name more closely with this first Sabbath Star in which he appears, as the name of the Messiah ben Joseph is associated with the second and that of the Messiah ben David with the third of these vertical Sabbath Stars.

Geometry of the Fifth-World Sabbath Stars

Having correlated the six Sabbath Stars of the fifth-world diagram with elements traditionally included in discussions of Messianic chronology, we are now in a position to give a summary analysis of the geometric implications of these stages. For this purpose individual illustrations will be given for each of these darkened Sabbath Stars that will feature with dashes one of the six component hexagrams within the double outline of the larger composite hexagram and also give a dashed-and-dotted outline of the earlier hexagram that the component hexagram overlays. In the single case of figure 5.3, in which two earlier hexagrams are featured, the smaller of these will be marked by a different dashed-and-dotted outline.

The Sabbath Star signifying the first sixth of the fifth world was previously illustrated in figure 3.13 and discussed in relationship to the fourth world,

Figure 5.2. The First Vertical Sabbath Star

and it was there shown that it represents a future source of attunement with power to effect a rectification of the Nefesh soul. The basis of such a conclusion was that this Sabbath Star contributes the same lines to the fourth-world diagram previously supplied by both the past-modeled form of the Fa/Fi Sabbath Star and the future-modeled form of the Fi/Sol Sabbath Star and so could be said to sanctify this form of the fourth-world diagram as not fallen but transformative, the limbic emotions represented by this Fi/Sol Sabbath Star enabling man to feel and respond to this rectifying future source of attunement.

In the previous subsection we saw that the first of the fifth-world Sabbath Stars, that illustrated in figure 5.2, could be identified with the shofar. And the specific association of the Sabbath Stars it covers, those of the mineral and animal levels in their transformative forms, is also extraordinarily appropriate

from this new fifth-world perspective, for combining them together we get a good specification of an animal horn, namely that of a ram. Though its effect on the matrix of the fourth-world diagram would seem to associate it most closely with the future-modeled Fi/Sol Sabbath Star, which contributes exactly the same matrix elements to this diagram, it may perhaps be even more closely allied with the past-modeled Fa/Fi Sabbath Star, since it covers exactly the same Do and Ri prior hexagrams previously covered by this signifier of the minerals. What this suggests is that the most powerful influence of the higher vibration conveyed by this fifth-world Sabbath Star will be on the physical systems of man and his world, retuning their vibrational level through some form of rhythm entrainment that can bring them to a heightened state of harmony and vitality.

Turning now to the Sabbath Star in figure 5.3,

Figure 5.3. The Second Vertical Sabbath Star

Figure 5.4. The Si Sabbath Star

which represents the second sixth of the fifth world, it can be seen that it covers just the Ri hexagram. As in the fourth-world diagram the individuating Ri hexagram was covered only by the past-modeled Fa/Fi Sabbath Star and by the Sol Sabbath Star, representative, respectively, of the minerals and man, so would the Sabbath Star presently under discussion seem to have an association with earthly man, and this may indicate the tragic conflict precipitated in earthly man by the summons of the shofar in the previous stage. Since this Sabbath Star was earlier identified with the individuality of the Messiah ben Joseph, who dies in the battle with evil, its associated resonance to the earthly man of the fourth

world and the original divisiveness of the Ri hexagram may help to explain this necessarily tragic stage of spiritual development when the old man of the flesh dies so that the new spiritual man may be reborn.

Before proceeding to the next vertical Sabbath Star, we should examine the first horizontal Sabbath Star, the one synchronous with that just discussed and earlier identified with the war of Gog and Magog. Unlike the Sabbath Star for the first third of the fourth world, whose ideal form was thought to be past modeled, that for this phase of the fifth world is correctly future modeled, as are all the intermediate Sabbath Stars for this and all other future worlds.

Figure 5.5. The First Horizontal Sabbath Star

As can be seen in figure 5.5, the two essential features of this Sabbath Star are its initial covering of the Fa hexagram by the bases of its ascending component triangles and the touching of the diagram's center by the points of its descending component triangles. Both would seem indicative of the apocalyptic war with which this stage was earlier identified. Since it is the Fa hexagram that analysis of the diagram has primarily associated with evil, the overcoming of such evil is clearly definitive of such a war. And with regard to the way in which the six component hexagrams meet at the center, this can also be taken to indicate some sort of explosive force. In the earlier analysis of the future-modeled Fa/Fi Sabbath Star,

which takes this same form, it was associated with the "big bang" of material creation, and it can now be associated with apocalyptic war. But the force thus emanating from the center would also seem indicative of a divine source. As it suggests a divine source of even the densely mineralized cosmos, so does it suggest that only a divine power can accomplish the final triumph over evil that can fill the Messianic world with the Knowledge derivable only from the Da'at source of both the cosmos and diagram. And what it further suggests is that this final war will be a wholly spiritual conflict that, though cosmic in its true proportions, will be engaged in entirely on the subtle level of consciousness. Indeed, so subtle is this

Figure 5.6. The Second Horizontal Sabbath Star

true mode of apocalyptic war that, if the world of our planet Earth is not blown up by a false construction of the imperative for war and is allowed to develop beyond that stage of understanding, it will be seen to have left no trace on the future history of the fifth world beyond that signified by the Sol/Si hexagram, itself, which may be considered as a memorial marker of the crucial epoch called "the birth pangs of the Messiah."

Between the first third and the halfway point of the Messianic Age, a glow of possibility would seem to surround the anticipation of the Messiah as, with the final overcoming of the Fa hexagram, the Mi hexagram of prelapsarian Eden is allowed to shine

forth in its former wholeness, inspiring the consciousness with the hope of a new Eden. As figure 5.4 shows, it is precisely the Mi hexagram that the Si Sabbath Star covers and transforms. Covering the Mi hexagram at the proper time, rather than prematurely as with the past-modeled Fi/Sol Sabbath Star, has different implications for this later Si Sabbath Star since the level of the Messiah, which it signifies, is that of the spiritual master. Thus the indwelling angelic presence, which the Mi hexagram was earlier taken to represent, would not be able to control such a master will. That the will of such a Messianic personality may be understood to remain still free is indicated by the way the bases of the ascending

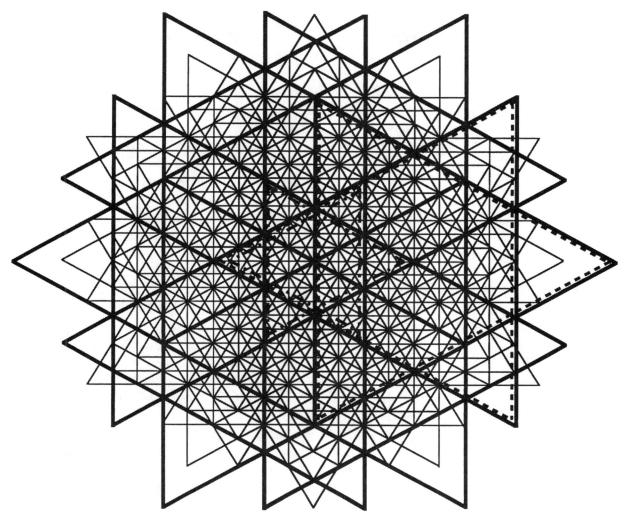

Figure 5.7. The La Sabbath Star

component triangles cross the center in a direction perpendicular to the central column of a superimposed Tree, an aspect that, in the earlier Mi and Sol Sabbath Stars, was understood to represent the freedom of the will. What this suggests is that the angelic presence here represents that prophesied law that would be written in the heart during the Messianic Age. With such an indwelling of the divine law, the purified will would now be able freely to choose the good. Thus with the advent of the Messiah, evil has been overcome both without and within and yet individuality persists, a survival that can also be associated with the concept of an individual Messiah. But whether single or multiple, it is

just this production of purified individuality that seems to be the purpose guiding the whole of material manifestation. With this achievement, the crucial phase of the Tikkun has been reached, and the remaining phases of the fifth through seventh worlds just spell out the further unfolding of redeemed consciousness.

In figure 5.5, we can see that the most significant feature of the next Si/La Sabbath Star is that it covers the Re hexagram with both its ascending and descending component triangles, a hexagram previously covered by the Fi Sabbath Star. Since the Si/La Sabbath Star has been identified with the ingathering of all peoples to form the harmonious

Messianic kingdom, this would seem to imply two things. The first is that these people would now incorporate the spiritual guidance associated with the plants in chapter 4, and so would learn the inner stillness that is the source of true fruitfulness. Secondly, the community that, like the plant kingdom, incorporates the Re hexagram of Beriah (Creation) will also be one able to unfold the creative potential of all its members in a manner transcending the vegetative that is most characteristic of transformed humanity. This creative characteristic of Ruach consciousness is still further underscored by the distinctive nature of this two-thirds Sabbath Star that, like the future-modeled Fi/Sol Sabbath Star a whole step before it, features a unique mode of Sabbatical geometry, a series of six border hexagrams of the same size as the original hexagram the Sabbath Star covers, the Do hexagram for its fourth-world prototype and the Re hexagram for this one. These Sabbath Stars, then, provide a creative bridge to the next world. As the Fi/Sol level of the animals marks the first stage of the cosmic octave after its turning point and thus the beginning of the Tikkun, so the Si/La level marks the first stage after its Messianic fulfillment, a stage whose creative energy will either propel the Tikkun farther into the next world or render it a sterile revelation of no lasting significance. It is the community that must be ready to receive the Messianic energy and transmute it into ever new creative forms, since without the prepared vessel of the holy nation even the true Messiah will have come in vain.

It is this extension of individual revelation into collective experience that is the final prerequisite before the arrival of the millennium, signified by the La Sabbath Star. As we shall soon see, this culminating stage will contain all the accumulated transformations of animal, plant, and human nature that have marked the development of the fifth world but that are only a prelude to the final transformation to be here accomplished of time itself. One of the major concepts related to the millennium is its slowing of time.[18] Whereas each of the two earlier thirds were subdivided into sixths, this last third is one unbroken period double the length of any of the four earlier periods that were fairly evenly divided.

Time, therefore, seems to lengthen, and the millennium becomes an epoch longer in extension than any previous period of the Messianic Age, of the fifth world.

The form of this Sabbath Star, shown in figure 5.7, can provide further illumination of its nature, its characteristics being that the descending component triangles cover the Fa hexagram, previously covered by the Sol/Si Sabbath Star at the first third of this age, and that the bases of the ascending component triangles cross the center in alignment with the central column of the superimposed Tree of Life Diagram, previously covered in this fashion by the Fi Sabbath Star. It is with this final correct alignment of perfected human consciousness that "the earth shall be full of the knowledge [Da'at] of the Lord, as the waters cover the sea" (Isa. 11:9). One aspect of this knowledge will be a new penetration into the meaning of the Fa hexagram. No longer will the necessity of spiritual purification require its exclusion as a source of evil and pollution. The purified consciousness can now forget the former battles and severity of the Sol/Si stage and reembrace this subdued power as a necessary aspect of its enlarged consciousness. With this final stage in the absorption of the Fa hexagram into the matrix, the consciousness can now become a co-determiner of a new dimension of time, the fifth dimension of Providence. It is this new temporal dimension that is the essential characteristic of the millennium, a stage that takes its very name from time. And it marks the final development of Ruach consciousness as it moves from individual awakening to the embrace of collective humanity and from there to a still higher union with the cosmic flow. In this last it again incorporates the spiritual guidance of the plant kingdom and learns the secret of its perfect harmony with nature.

Before concluding our study of Messianic chronology as modeled by the fifth-world Sabbath Stars, it is important to understand the way in which the elements of the fourth and fifth worlds are interrelated in cosmic history. It will be remembered that the fourth-world diagram could be viewed as constituted by its own four construction elements and the Mi and Fa hexagrams of the third world, the presence of such third-world hexagrams indicating the continuing influence of the dual-aspected spiritual dimension they define. Now in the first sixth of the fifth world, this situation remains essentially unchanged since it still features all six of the construction elements of the fourth-world diagram. But to these components it adds a Sabbatical star, named Sol₂/Si in the extended discussion that concludes chapter 3, which infuses the whole with a new and heightened vibration calling all to a new beginning. Not only may it be said to perfect or rectify Nefesh consciousness by its effect on the matrix of either form of the fourth-world diagram, but it also has serious effects on three of its Sabbath Stars. As earlier indicated, it covers all specifically Sabbath Star elements of the past-modeled Fa/Fi and future-modeled Fi/Sol Sabbath Stars and also covers part of the descending component triangles of the Sol Sabbath Star.

Since the Sol₂/Si Sabbath Star only repeats the transformation of either or both forms of the Fa/Fi Sabbath Star already accomplished in the future-modeled fourth-world diagram, its most important effect is on the future-modeled Fi/Sol Sabbath Star. What its original covering of this Sabbath Star may signify is such a transformation of animal nature as that recalled by Isaiah's words: "The wolf also shall dwell with the lamb" (Isa. 11:6). Whether the new attunement, to which the animals will apparently be the most responsive, will immediately lift them above the predator instinct or this final transcendence will be reserved for the last stage of the millennium, there will certainly be an evolution of animal consciousness and a more limited movement of man to overcome his lower instincts. Such an evolution of animal consciousness is already beginning to take place in the animals that man has domesticated, whether for work, study, or companionship. All have learned to respond to verbal signals, some chimps even having been taught to communicate with sophisticated forms of sign language. And can we doubt that, as man cultivates more and more of the earth and segregates the remaining "wild" animals to carefully patrolled parks and zoos aimed at preserving them from extinction, animals largely fed by man will gradually lose the instinct to kill for food. However the

change be defined, the diagram suggests that in this stage animal nature will be so transformed that only its outer shape will remain and that man will begin to undergo a similar change.

To continue the discussion of the effect of fifth-world Sabbath Stars on those of the fourth world, we can now observe the progressive change in the Sol Sabbath Star symbolic of man. The first of the vertical Sabbath Stars had covered about half of the two sides of the descending component triangles, and the second vertical Sabbath Star completely covers these descending triangles. It might be pointed out here that since tonal names are becoming increasingly unwieldy, it seems best, from this point on, to refer to all Sabbath Stars below the level of the third by their fractional equivalents alone. To return to the covering of the Sol Sabbath Star, there remains only the base of the ascending triangles, and this is finally covered by the last of the vertical Sabbath Stars, that named for Si and symbolic of the Messiah. What this seems to imply is that the material orientation of man is completely overcome in the second stage, since this may be associated with the descending component triangle covered by this stage, and that by the third stage man's consciousness has been so transformed that only his outward appearance remains the same.

Of complete fourth-world Sabbath Stars there remains only that of the plant kingdom, Fi, and this undergoes progressive transformation by the first two of the fifth-world horizontal Sabbath Stars. The first of these, Sol/Si, covers the bases of its ascending component triangles and the tops of their descending counterparts, and the second, Si/La, covers the remaining two sides of the descending component triangles, leaving only the sides of the ascending component triangles, which in all the Sabbath Stars form the position-defining hexagram. Since earlier analyses have shown the Fi Sabbath Star of the plants to be the least fallen element of the fourth world, it is fitting that it should survive the longest in its unaltered stage during the Messianic Age. It is, then, not until after the appearance of the Messiah, though before the millennium, that the nature of vegetation will be so transformed that it would seem to approximate such Messianic prophecies as those of Ezekiel, much elaborated upon in the later tradition: "And I will raise up for them a plant of renown, and they shall be no more consumed with hunger in the land. . . . And I will multiply the fruit of the tree, and the increase of the field" (34:29; 36:30). Needless to say, such an increase in agricultural productivity, with the accompanying hope that famine will finally disappear from the earth, is already well under way. Before the millennium arrives, then, plant, animal, and human nature will have been completely transformed. And yet these individual forms of life will still be recognizable as such.

This is not the case, however, with those third-world hexagrams that had survived throughout the fourth world and also through the first sixth of the fifth world. The nature of the fifth world is radically altered by the stage marking its first third with the elimination of the evil conveyed through the Fa hexagram; and with the further elimination of the Mi hexagram, the fifth world becomes, at midpoint, unrecognizable. The third world has now become as integrated into the cosmic structure as the first two worlds; and if the fourth world is still to have a subtle dimension, it can no longer come from the past but only from the future Ruach level of perfected man, of Messianic consciousness.

What all of the preceding discussion means, first and foremost, is that the fourth world continues to be substantially present throughout the whole of the Messianic Age though its nature is being radically transformed from a past to a future orientation, a passage characterized by the transfer of consciousness from the Nefesh to the Ruach level of the soul. But since the fourth world will be as obliterated by the sixth world as the third is by the fifth, the second important implication is that it is essential that we do so evolve from fourth- to fifth-world consciousness if we are to be present in the World to Come.

STAGES OF RUACH CONSCIOUSNESS

In the previous section, the six Sabbath Stars of the fifth world were identified with traditional stages of Messianic chronology, and these stages were then further interpreted on the basis of the form given these Sabbath Stars in the diagram.* The Jewish tradition, both in itself and in the legacy it has bequeathed to the Western world, maintains that the Messianic Age will become an historical reality in the world of the future, and we have seen that its essential phases have a logic that can be supported by the geometry that diagram interpretation best correlates with the next cosmic world. But in addition to its correlation with kabbalistic cosmology, it has been repeatedly stressed that the Sabbath Star Diagram also functions as a model of personal and cosmic consciousness, its "worlds" delineating the successive dimensions of such consciousness. Having defined the stages of the fifth-world diagram in both traditional and geometric terms, we are now in a position to reframe the preceding discussion into an analysis of the stages by which the Ruach dimension of the soul becomes actualized. This mystic internalizing of the Messianic process and personality represents the major approach of the Kabbalah to the prophecies of a Messianic Age, as scholars have recently shown.[19]

The first stage to higher consciousness corresponds to the traditional blowing of the great shofar. It is the deliberate process of attunement to higher spiritual vibrations that forms the heart of all spiritual disciplines. The expanded state resulting from such practices of attunement is such a blissful experience that it inspires a greater commitment to the process of spiritual development and the stricter disciplines by which it can be accelerated.

The movement from the Nefesh to the Ruach level of soul is also one from an orientation dominated by the instinct for personal survival to one dominated by a sense of communal identification. It involves an empathic embrace of the other with an accompanying concern for social justice. The synchronicity of the Sabbath Stars that marks this second stage, while distinguishing it into second sixth and first third aspects, indicates three separate forms that can be taken by the overall stage corresponding to "the birth pangs of the Messiah." Whatever its

---

*The following section is an abbreviated version of the similarly titled section of *The Kabbalah of the Soul*, pp. 141–52.

form, however, this is the one stage in the development of Ruach consciousness that promises to be painful. Taking it in its individualized form, this can reflect the pain caused by the internal war between old attachments and new aspirations as one attempts for the first time the practices that may aid in the development of a new heart. This is normally a product of the prior stage of deliberate spiritual attunement and involves some withdrawal from general society and attachment to a group that will support adherence to a strict discipline penetrating all of the day's activities. The collective form of this stage may or may not be a product of deliberate spiritual attunement. The individual may simply be seized by the Zeitgeist summoning him to an enthusiastic embrace of some social cause that promises to rid the world of evil in one or all of its guises. In addition to those primarily concerned to change the self and those primarily concerned to change the world, the synchronicity of these two modes of change suggests that there may be a third path which synthesizes their polar opposition. In such a path those concerned with personal transformation would also take part in the process of political change while political activists would also devote themselves to spiritual development, the two becoming part of a larger movement of positive transformation that would help protect the spirit from the potential deadening threatened by either polarity in isolation. This fuller mode of the second stage incorporates the two defining characteristics of Ruach consciousness, its purification of the egocentric aspects of spirit and its redirection into social channels.

It is the promise of a humanity purged of its sorrows that is to be fulfilled in the later stages of Messianic or Ruach consciousness and that makes it possible for the aspiring soul to endure the frustrated sufferings of this earlier stage. Such a purgation will come when the soul begins to experience the new empowerment attendant upon its individuality once it has been purified of its limiting egocentricity. But between the bliss of reattunement that attended the first stage and the beginnings of empowerment that will attend the third stage lies the pain of this second stage, and its pain is a symptom of the subtle efficacy of the purifying process as it attacks the egotism to which the Nefesh soul still clings. As the shell must crack to permit the seed to sprout, so all religious traditions agree that there is no spiritual growth without pain. If the sacrifice has been faithfully performed, flesh will be transformed into spirit and a new form of consciousness will be born, that of the master.

Such mastery does not come of itself, except in the sense that it cannot be assured even by the most punctilious observance of a course prescribed to that end, but is the third stage after the awakening of higher aspiration and the diligent practice of a discipline. Taking it first in a purely vocational sense, a master is one who has served an apprenticeship, a course of discipline, in a profession or craft for which he ideally has a vocation, a calling, and can now both guide others to a similar proficiency and use his training creatively. But in another sense the master is the one who gains control, and what he must ultimately control, if his dominion is not to be subject to revolt, is himself.[20] It is to such self-mastery that the skills of spiritual discipline are aimed. But the power to exercise such control comes not from the discipline itself; it comes, rather, from what this discipline releases, the will. What the third stage is devoted to is the further development and exercise of the true controlling will.

It is only by purifying the soul of its egocentricity that it can escape such mechanical conditioning and discover its true individuality, that unique vibration stamped on the fingerprints and the scent which can unerringly select those companions with which it is in vibratory resonance. It is this quality that the master must especially cultivate since it is the necessary foundation of all work with the energies.

Once the master will has developed, it is able to harmonize all aspects of the body, heart, and soul, and this harmonious being will develop a special attunement to deeper cosmic currents that will transform it into a medium of divine revelation. It is only when the individual will and the cosmic will have become thus harmonized that the master can proceed to the fourth stage of true empowerment. The master who has not become one with the community of mankind and thinks to use this power to gain control over the world would, if he could gain such premature access, surely blow himself up in the process, such Providential justice being built into this fifth dimension, but he would also accomplish much evil in the meantime. In the third stage, then, he undergoes a second apprenticeship, working with the higher energies that empower him to be an inspired charismatic leader and teacher able to change the hearts of men and the course of history. It is, in fact, the momentum of his charisma, as it attracts more and more followers, that connects him with the human community and draws him into the fourth stage of his development.

This fourth stage of the fifth world is also the second stage of community development and it reflects a decisive change in its spirit. Whereas the Sol/Si stage was concerned with purifying the vestiges of Nefesh consciousness in the world, the Si/La stage is concerned to give expression to the Ruach soul. Its spiritual communities, therefore, have a different character from that of the earlier phase. No longer needing to raise consciousness through rigid practices and beliefs aimed primarily at exclusion, these communities are so filled with spirit that all their activities are marked by creativity. Both serve necessary functions but the more rigid communities are normally those with long established traditions whereas those filled with creative spirit are normally possessed of a living master or are within only a few generations of that infusion.

Both by example and by direct infusions of his spirit, the communities founded by a master retain the efficacy of his living spirit. But as the community needs such a master to release its spiritual potential, so does the master need the vessel of a community to extend the power of his personal revelation. As the diagram shows us, a master whose primary concern is his own spiritual development will never reach his full potential. It is paradoxically only by moving beyond himself to share his heightened power of understanding that he can receive such a reciprocal infusion of energy as can unify individual with collective consciousness, a unification that is the source of all true magical power.

Between master and community, as between per-

former and audience, a magical entity is created, larger than either in isolation and informing both with its own intelligence. It is only when the master has learned to work with communal human energies that the highest cosmic energies may open up to him and empower him to perform miracles. But what is true of the relationship of master to community is also true of the relationship of each member of the community to the whole. The members must learn to adjust their own energies to those of the community in a manner that not only retains but enhances their creative sensitivity. A community of such members will be alive with joy and its characteristic expression will be laughter.

For the great masters of history, as the diagram shows us, there is no other path of development but that which leads to community. For those whose mastery is less distinguished, though genuine, the path is still the same. It will take them from attunement, through austere personal and social activities aimed at general spiritual improvement, to the first signs of mastery, and this will cause them to reach out to humanity in a new spirit of acceptance and joy. There they may meet others who followed a less arduous path but who are ready to be uplifted through the joint endeavor of communal growth in which each can make a unique contribution.

The diagram shows that there are two paths to reach this point, the simpler two-stage process through the thirds followed by the commonality and the more distinguished four-stage process through the sixths taken by those blessed or cursed by more powerful individuality. At both the two-sixths and four-sixths stages, the individual has a chance to rejoin the collective, temporarily or permanently, and if such reunion at the two-sixths stage is advisable it becomes an absolute necessity at the next opportunity if one's mastery is not to remain at half its potential power. Thus at the two-thirds point the individual becomes integrated with the collective and his future development will grow out of this larger harmony. It is only when he recognizes his membership in this interconnected social whole that he can proceed to the final stage of Ruach consciousness. But just as the diagram distinguishes two paths, so does it indicate the necessity for both. For it is only by maintaining and balancing the influences of the broader and narrower paths that humanity can truly progress.

The path of the individual Ruach Masters, that path divided into the four stages just discussed, is necessary to ensure the highest development of the Ruach community that we meet in the final stage, that stage analogous to the millennium in which time, as we have seen, becomes extended. And it becomes elastic in other ways as well, furthering the properly directed will of the master and bringing its aims to fruition. For in this final stage, the master lifts his community to his own highest recognition of his interconnectedness with all aspects of nature and all the levels of causality determining the shape of natural behavior, the understanding that enables him to perform those wonders completing the development both of the Ruach soul and of Messianic consciousness.

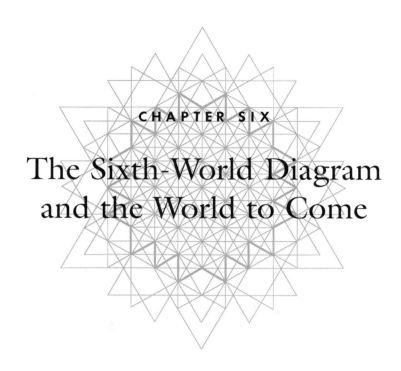

CHAPTER SIX

The Sixth-World Diagram
and the World to Come

A MANUAL FOR SIXTH-WORLD DIAGRAM CONSTRUCTION

Introduction

The sixth world is marked by a new sense of the meaningful through a vision of completed pattern. In this chapter the nature of the sixth dimension of consciousness will be defined through a precise study of the construction elements of the sixth-world diagram, which will not only develop such more theoretical aspects of the Sabbath Star Diagram as its laws of construction and their relation to number theory but also provide a culminating model of the interactions of the Partzufim, the five divine personalities that the Sefirot are sometimes understood to form. We shall begin by offering the reader a "do-it-yourself manual" for constructing this sixth-world diagram in the easiest way possible, not as an expanding diagram but from the outside in, a technique based upon a triangular grid that has special lessons to teach us about the relationship of the sixth world to the fourth.

If the sixth-world diagram may be said to define the dimension of meaningfulness, it does so in most graphic terms. For it is only at this degree of diagram expansion that the intrinsic laws governing correct diagram construction can begin to be determined as well as their implications for at least the past worlds of the diagram. The initial formulation of these laws, a crucial aspect of the diagram analysis presented in this book, will be given in both this section and the next, though it will not be until part 4 that the full diagram program will at last be revealed. The final section of this chapter will be devoted to the now more standard mode of analyzing the diagram construction elements, that involving the naming of the individual elements and the interpretation of their interrelationships, the dominant characteristic of kabbalistic geometry that is here being called the Science of Expressive Form. In this final section, an attempt will be made to correlate the construction elements of the sixth-world diagram with the Partzufim, those divine personalities who may be thought to share with the Neshamah souls the mode of consciousness definitive of the sixth world. And the precise modeling of Partzufim relations in that section will prove to be most reveal-

148

ing not only of the highest levels of consciousness and how these levels can be shared by both Neshamah Masters and the Partzufim but also of human sexuality. The gender association of the construction elements to be developed in the final section, by which the vertical elements are identified with the masculine and the horizontal elements with the feminine, is the subject of the intervening third section, one that continues the concern of the second section with the deep laws of the diagram; and it will finally lead, in part 4, to a reenvisioning of the whole of the Sabbath Star Diagram that will provide the key both to its infinite development and to its deepest cosmic mysteries.

But before we can either make such correlations or derive the initial rules of diagram construction, it will be necessary to construct the sixth-world diagram. And since this one diagram contains all prior worlds, as well as providing the basis for construction of the seventh world, it would be good for the reader, if he or she has not previously been drawing personal diagrams of the various worlds, to attempt at least the construction of this one. As earlier indicated, a new method of construction from outside inward will be employed to facilitate such construction, a method that has various practical and theoretical virtues. This method will enable us to see the earlier worlds, particularly our fourth world, from the perspective of the completed matrix pattern, the Aristotelian Final Cause, and it is through such backward construction that the major rules of diagram construction can finally be learned. Those not attempting such construction, or at least not at this time, can skip the following "do-it-yourself manual" and attend only to the primary analysis of the diagram features in the subsection immediately following figures 6.4 through 6.7.

A Do-It-Yourself Manual

The easiest and most precise way to construct the sixth-world diagram is to use the matrix grid provided in figure 6.1. While generation of the Sabbath Star Diagram from the six radial arc points of an initial circle—the method used in chapter 2—is instructive regarding the process of cosmic expan-sion, unless one is an expert draftsman the attempt to build the further expansions of the diagram in this manner will lead to much distortion as initial imprecisions become progressively enlarged. Use of the matrix grid will not only eliminate this danger but also permit the equally instructive backward method of construction now to be first employed. But such construction is only possible if one has already discovered the correct number of construction elements for a world, a number that can be determined either through regular outward construction from an earlier world or through the unique numerical formula defining the series of these numbers that will be disclosed at the beginning of the second section of this chapter. Since the latter information is not, however, available until after construction of the sixth world has generated the numbers that reveal this formula, it is the outward method that must be initially used. By so constructing the Li and Ti Sabbath Stars in the whole-step progression from the of Si and La Sabbath Stars of the fifth-world diagram, one can determine that the matrix grid will accept exactly nine vertical construction elements and three horizontal elements beyond those of the fifth-world diagram. The following instructions for the use of the matrix grid will be based on this numerical information and the rule of the future modeling of intermediate Sabbath Stars.

Like the matrix grid provided in figure 3.1 to aid such similar construction of the fourth-world diagram, that for the sixth world is bounded by the hexagon that will permit easy construction of the largest hexagrams on both axes, in this being superior to the triangular graph paper available in draftsman's supply stores, which also lacks the interfaced horizontal macrostructure of the full matrix. If turned on its side, the vertical microstructure of the matrix grid can also provide the macrostructure for the next cosmic world, a law of diagram growth that will be considered in the next section. Whether one uses transparencies to trace the diagrams on the grid or makes a copy of the grid and draws directly on it, the grid provided in figure 6.1 with surrounding letters added should prove most useful.

The first step in constructing the sixth-world

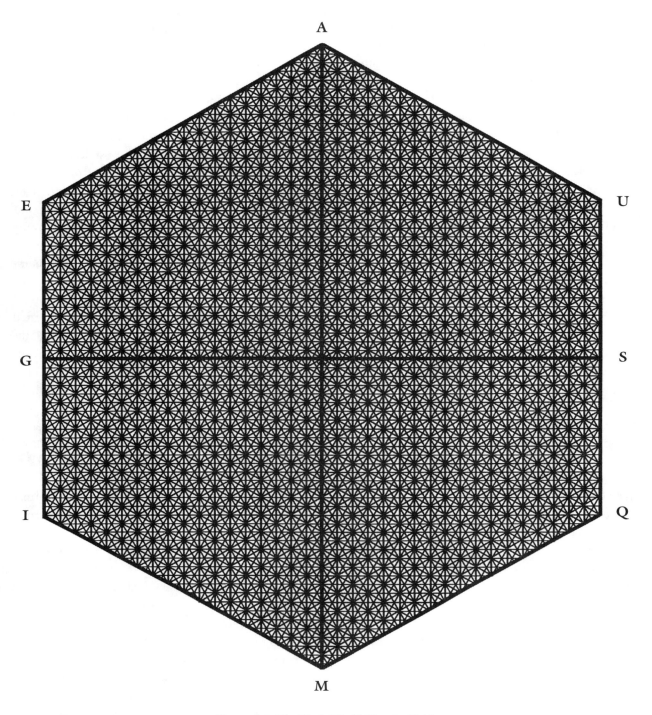

Figure 6.1. The Sixth-World Matrix Grid

diagram is to draft the culminating vertical construction element, the Ti hexagram that can be numbered nine. This is easily done by beginning with the inverted ∨ at the apex of the hexagon marked by the letter *A* and drawing over its

descending diagonal lines until they meet the lower right and left vertices of this boundary hexagon, points *I* and *Q* joining these sides with the baseline *IQ* running between them, the eighteenth such horizontal line below the darkened horizontal axis, line

GS. The crossing triangle is similarly constructed by beginning with the lowest point, marked *M* on the grid, and following the diagonal lines extending from that point until they meet the upper right and left hexagon vertices, points *E* and *U*, between which the upper bar of this triangle, line *EU*, can be seen to lie, the eighteenth up from the darkened horizontal axis *GS*.

This process should be initially repeated three times to complete the upper four hexagrams of the sixth-world vertical grid, shown in their completed Sabbath Star forms in figure 6.2. The eighth hexagram is situated at the next smaller grid lines, beginning with the next lower inverted angle below the letter *A* and the next higher one above the letter *M* (the upper and lower apices of the hexagrams being constructed), with the horizontal lines also coming just within those for the Ti hexagram. Each of the remaining hexagrams should be similarly constructed, one nesting within the other at the next smaller grid lines. One can now construct the upper four vertical Sabbath Stars, beginning with the largest Ti Sabbath Star.

To do this, one should bisect the previously drawn Ti hexagram—the culminating vertical construction element of the sixth-world diagram that is composed of lines *AI, IQ, QA, ME, EU*, and *UM*— at its midpoint with a line going right through the central matrix point. Taking the smaller triangle above this line, which overlays part of line *GS*, to represent the ascending triangle of the component hexagram, one should now cross it with its descending triangle. For this, one should find the descending point of the Sol hexagram, the sixth ∨ below the darkened horizontal axis, line *GS*, and draw ∨-lines upward from it to points on the hexagon sides labeled *D* and *V*, joining these diagonal lines by tracing the grid line that goes between them, line *DV*. Having completed the first of six component hexagrams, one should now repeat this process, first on the other side of the previously drawn bisecting line, that covering part of the darkened line *GS*, and then on the other two axes of the diagram, making the six component hexagrams that together will form the Ti hexagram and the complete Ti Sabbath Star. The Ti Sabbath Star (the first, outermost con-

struction of fig. 6.2) will also have defined the Sol hexagram of the fourth-world diagram.

It is instructive to construct this first Sabbath Star out of its six component hexagrams to understand how it is thus formed. But an easier method of constructing both this and the remaining Sabbath Stars is by following the two sets of continuous lines their component hexagrams also combine to form. Looking ahead to figure 6.2, one can visually trace the first such set by beginning at the upper-left vertex of the Ti component hexagram, point *V*, and following its longer diagonal line to the lower peak at the right of the vertical axis, point *L*, following it next up a shorter diagonal to point *F* on the further right and then across the longer horizontal line to point *T* on the left side of the diagram, then down the shorter diagonal to point *N* on the lower hexagonal border just left of the vertical axis, up the longer diagonal to point *D* on the upper-right hexagonal border, and finally across a shorter horizontal line to one's starting point at point *V*. The second set of continuous lines begins with point *J* on the lower-right hexagonal border and follows it through six continuous lines, first up the longer diagonal to point *X*, just left of the diagram apex, then down the shorter diagonal to point *R* on the left vertical border of the hexagon, across the longer horizontal to point *H* on the right vertical side of the diagram, up the shorter diagonal to point *B* on the upper-right hexagonal border, down the longer diagonal to point *P* at the lower left, and finally across the horizontal line to the second starting point, that at point *J*. Although each Sabbath Star can actually be constructed with the easier method just described, the following instructions will continue to define the component triangles more precisely so that the position-defining hexagrams of the earlier worlds that each Sabbath Star covers can be more clearly specified. As each of the initial hexagrams of the first four worlds will be successively covered in constructing the sixth-world Sabbath Stars, it might be of help to list the order of these hexagrams on the two diagram grids. On the vertical grid, the list from smaller to larger is as follows: Do, Ri, Mi, Fa/Fi, Fi/Sol, and Sol. On the horizontal grid this list is: Re, Fa, Fi.

Once one has constructed the final Sabbath Star of this or any world, it is then easy to draw all the previous hexagrams or Sabbath Stars that the matrix grid of the diagram can accommodate. One simply has to nest them progressively within the final outline already established. Counting the Ti Sabbath Star as the ninth, one begins construction of the eighth Sabbath Star with its upper component trian-

gle, simply drawing its outlines at the next smaller grid lines within the lines forming the upper component triangle of the ninth Sabbath Star and repeating the process within the other five component triangles. To be more precise, the baseline of the ascending component triangle will go through the upper bar of the Do hexagram, on the first horizontal line above the darkened horizontal axis, and

Figure 6.2. The Sixth through Ninth Vertical Sabbath Stars

the lower point of the descending triangle will be fixed at the descending point of the Fi/Sol hexagram, the fifth inverted V below the horizontal axis; and the V-lines emanating from that point will meet a line drawn on the next smaller horizontal grid line. When the eighth vertical Sabbath Star has been fully constructed, it will thus also be found to have produced the Do and Fi/Sol hexagrams and, had the diagram been drawn from the center out, part of the fourth Sabbath Star within the sixth world.

The seventh Sabbath Star is similarly constructed, the baseline of its upper ascending triangle passing through the bars of the Ri hexagram, the second horizontal line above the darkened horizontal axis, and the lower point of its descending triangle originating at the lower point of the Fa/Fi hexagram and ascending in a V to meet the crossing line on the next smaller grid line. Construction of this Sabbath Star will thus also produce the Ri and Fa/Fi hexagrams and cover part of the fifth Sabbath Star of the sixth world, had it been previously drawn.

The sixth is the last of the Sabbath Stars to enter and complete the vertical matrix of the fourth world and the only one to be able to do this whether the diagram is drawn from the center out or from its final form in. To construct it, the base of the ascending triangle within the upper component hexagram is drawn on the grid line midway between the bars and upper point of the Ri hexagram; the base point of the descending triangle is located at the lower point of the Mi hexagram, and the two lines ascending from it in a V meet at the next smaller grid line going between them.

The preceding instructions have taken draftspersons through construction of the upper four Sabbath Stars of the vertical axis, the sixth through ninth, and they can now compare their work with figure 6.2 and correct it if necessary. Construction of the sixth Sabbath Star, the last to complete the manifestation of the first four worlds, whether the diagram is constructed inside out or outside in, not only produces the Mi hexagram at the inner portion of the diagram but six Mi-sized hexagrams in the diagram's outer border, as can later be seen in figure 6.5. This sixth or Li/Ti Sabbath Star is the most

beautiful of the Sabbath Stars of the sixth-world diagram, and its seven Mi-sized hexagrams seem to symbolize creation. As the Ti Sabbath Star defines the final Sabbath Star form to which the smaller Sabbath Stars of its world must conform, so does the Li/Ti Sabbath Star define the form of the border hexagrams within and around which the remaining Sabbath Stars of its world must jointly work to embroider this border with the nested hexagrams defining all the hexagrams of the four worlds of emanation.

Figure 6.2 illustrates just the upper four vertical Sabbath Stars and figure 6.3 the third through sixth vertical Sabbath Stars, the Sabbath Stars of the vertical grid being thus divided for a reason that will shortly become clear. But were they to be constructed successively from the periphery inward, the fifth and fourth Sabbath Stars would be almost completely covered by construction of the seventh and eighth Sabbath Stars. Their surviving elements, however, would combine with them to form the border hexagrams of the same size as those of the inner hexagrams produced or covered by their own independent construction. That is, outward construction of the fourth Sabbath Star produces the Do and Fi/Sol Sabbath Stars just as they are produced by inward construction of the eighth Sabbath Star. But it is only with the cooperation of elements of both of these Sabbath Stars, whether the surviving portion of the fourth Sabbath Star or the added portion of the eighth, depending upon the direction from which the diagram is being constructed, that both the Do- and Fi/Sol-sized border hexagrams become manifest. Similarly the fifth and the seventh Sabbath Stars can each produce the inner Ri and Fa/Fi hexagrams, depending on the direction from which the diagram is being constructed, but can only form border hexagrams of these sizes through their joint cooperation. The final Sol-sized border hexagrams are produced by cooperation between the Ti Sabbath Star and the only surviving element of the third or La/Li Sabbath Star, its hexagram.

Where the third hexagram is the only surviving element of its Sabbath Star, this is not true of the first and second sixth-world hexagrams, which are too small to produce Sabbath Stars in accordance

Figure 6.3. The Third through Sixth Vertical Sabbath Stars

with the needs of the matrix and the defining form of the final Ti Sabbath Star. The smallest Sabbath Star that can be produced so that its six component hexagrams combine to form an enlarged hexagram is one whose descending points meet at the dia-

gram's center, which is the case of the third Sabbath Star in the sixth world and also of the Sabbath Star marking the first third point of the fifth world and the first third of the fourth world when future modeled. It is possible to elaborate the first of the sixth-world hexagrams into such a Sabbath Star and to enlarge around it the remainder of the sixth-world Sabbath Stars up through the eighth. But this progression will not be able to nest within the final definitive form of the Ti Sabbath Star. It will repeat the improper evolution from prior rather than final causes that led to the "Dinosaur Diagram" of the fourth world, figure 3.6, earlier mythologized as a precipitating cause of the subsequent "Fall" in the level of consciousness it symbolized.

To summarize what has thus far been shown about construction of the vertical axis of the sixth-world diagram, this axis is constructed of three hexagrams and six Sabbath Stars, only the upper four of which enter and form the inner portion of the diagram in its completed version. To finish construction of the vertical grid of the diagram through its sixth world, it would now only be necessary to continue to nest the remaining five vertical construction elements of the sixth world within the finished sixth Sabbath Star—these being the surviving Sabbath Star aspects of the fourth and fifth vertical construction elements and the first to third simple vertical hexagrams—as well as the three vertical hexagrams of the fifth world.

The complete vertical axis is composed, then, of six hexagrams and six Sabbath Stars. Figure 6.2 displays *only* the upper four vertical Sabbath Stars so that the manner in which these Sabbath Stars weave the fabric of the fourth-world microstructure may be more clearly highlighted in the space left by the missing six hexagrams. And figure 6.3 features only the third through sixth Sabbath Stars so that this alternate method of weaving the fourth-world microstructure can also be seen. We turn now to construction of the three horizontal Sabbath Stars.

Returning to figure 6.1 and beginning at point G on the darkened horizontal axis, one has only to draw a line following this diagonal grid line until it reaches the opposite upper hexagon border at point W; then draw one following the perpendicular grid line to point O of the lower hexagonal border; and finally return to the starting point of this triangle at point G. This process should now be repeated on the other side of the matrix to complete the Li hexagram, drawing the lines SC, CK, and KS. The two

additional hexagrams needed to complete construction of the sixth-world horizontal grid should now also be drawn, again following the grid lines of the matrix macrostructure, which can be seen to define successively nested triangles within the outlines of the originally constructed horizontal Li hexagram, the vertex of each such hexagram being one diamond apart on the horizontal axis.

It is more difficult to describe the construction of the sixth-world horizontal Sabbath Stars than their vertical counterparts because the twelve shorter peaks of the largest of these Sabbath Stars do not reach the outer hexagonal border where letters can be placed, the point hexagon of the Li Sabbath Star being smaller than that of the Ti Sabbath Star to which the hexagonal grid of figure 6.1 conforms. So those drafting the horizontal Sabbath Stars will have to check the form of the outer two such Sabbath Stars that are featured in figure 6.4 with the upper four vertical Sabbath Stars that earlier appeared in figure 6.2. But to attempt such a construction guide, one again begins the process of horizontal Sabbath Star construction by bisecting its culminating hexagram so that this line goes vertically through the center of the diagram, repeating such bisection on the other two axes of the Li hexagram. Starting with the right component triangle thus produced, one should cross it by locating the left point of the Fi hexagram of the fourth world, three diamonds to the left of the central point on the horizontal axis, that point on the grid of figure 6.1 where the vertical axis bisects the horizontal axis, and drawing V-lines from it to meet a vertical line passing through the right point of the La hexagram, the third diamond in from the outer hexagon, thus also forming the Fi hexagram. One can now easily nest the other two sixth-world horizontal Sabbath Star components successively within the component triangles for the Li Sabbath Star. Taking the larger one first, one should draw V-lines from a point two diamonds to the left of the central point, which is the point of the Fa hexagram, continuing these lines until they meet a vertical line one diamond in at the right from that of the enclosing component triangle of the Li Sabbath Star. The final line that divides the second hexagram into a component triangle is a vertical line originating one diamond to the right of the center, thus forming the Re hexagram. This completes the construction of one component hexagram, a process to be repeated five times to complete this second Sabbath Star, again more easily by drawing two sets of continuous lines, on the model of that given in figure 6.4. This Sabbath Star also covers both the Re and Fa hexagram and most of the first of the sixth-world horizontal Sabbath Stars, had the sixth-world diagram been constructed from the inside out, and it joins with its surviving elements to form the border Re and Fa hexagrams, as illustrated in figure 6.5. When the first of these horizontal Sabbath Stars is completed first, it will be found to cover these same inner Re and Fa hexagrams independently. In this case, the perpendicular of the right triangle within its component hexagram passes through the bars of the Fa hexagram, thus forming it, while the leftmost point of its left triangle is located at that point of the Re hexagram, which the V-lines emanating from this point also form, and these V-lines meet a line going through the vertex of the Si/La hexagram, three and one half diamonds from the center on the horizontal axis.

The outer two horizontal Sabbath Stars of the sixth-world diagram are given in figure 6.4 with the upper four vertical Sabbath Stars of this world, and all three in figure 6.5 with the complete sixth-world vertical axis plus the fifth-world horizontal La Sabbath Star, the latter added to complete the horizontal border hexagrams. Figure 6.5 highlights both the vertical and horizontal border hexagrams, illustrating only a pair of each, those of the vertical construction elements being at the two sides of the horizontal axis and those of the horizontal construction elements at the top and bottom of the vertical axis. In all cases the contributions of Sabbath Star component hexagrams will be highlighted with darkened solid lines and of position-defining hexagrams with darkened dashed lines.

Figure 6.4 is the most arresting illustration of this series, for it shows the fourth world from a completely new perspective, not as self-generated but as the product of sixth-world forces. In this minimal form it is the product of just six sixth-world Sabbath Stars, four vertical, those whose highest and lowest points are along the vertical axis, and two horizontal, those whose widest points are along the horizontal axis, these axes having been darkened in the matrix grid of figure 6.1. As the inner two horizontal Sabbath Stars cover the same earlier constituents, both are not needed and only the outer two are given. It should also be clear that the two needed horizontal Sabbath Stars can combine with either the sixth through ninth vertical Sabbath Stars or the third through sixth such elements to produce the four worlds of emanation, with implications to be further developed in the concluding section of this chapter. Finally we arrive at the complete sixth-world diagram in both figure 6.6 and figure 6.7, the latter of which adds the expressive form of the matrix border.

Implications of the Guide to Sixth-World Diagram Construction

We begin this discussion of the sixth-world diagram at both the culminating point of the previous section and, as we usually do for a diagram world, with a consideration of its matrix border, a feature of each diagram world beginning with the fourth that has seemed particularly expressive. In the two contrasting forms of the fourth-world diagram, the past-modeled matrix border (shown in figure 3.4) was earlier taken to connote the element of water, since its zigzag lines have this iconographic meaning in most primitive cultures, and the plateaulike form of the future-modeled matrix border (shown in figure 3.7) was taken to signify the element of earth. Likewise, the hornlike fifth-world matrix border (shown in figure 5.1) was taken to signify the element of air that could be blown through it. The question now naturally arises as to the sixth-world matrix border. To conform to the pattern just established of the classical elements, it should be suggestive of fire. And to my eye it is. As illustrated in figure 6.7, the sixth-world matrix border not only seems suggestive of fire, but fire of a specific kind, resembling nothing so much as solar flares, a resemblance highlighted in figure 13.5, or perhaps the final prophesied incineration of this world. If the

Figure 6.4. The Upper Four Vertical and Outer Two Horizontal Sabbath Stars

sixth-world matrix is taken to represent the Neshamah soul, then this border may also represent the sacrificial tongues of flame burning away all the gross elements that may have been left in this higher soul level.

But the matrix border appears even more suggestive of the sacred mountain form of Buddhist temple architecture, the stupas and pagodas whose successively recessed stories provide a cosmic map centered on the world axis. Such stepped pyramidal forms also appear in the temple architecture of Central and South American Indian cultures. But wherever they are found, they are variously related to the concept of the sacred mountain, to the sun, or to both, as both may be further related through the element of fire they share, the sacred mountain, as at Sinai, being ideally volcanic, a mountain of the sun. As the classical pagoda plan defines a circle

Figure 6.5. Border Hexagrams of the Sixth-World Diagram

within a square, it signifies just such a mountain, the circle of the sun being contained within the square of earth. Thus the sixth-world matrix border may be taken to signify the sacred character of the world mountain, the transcendent substance of the World to Come also correlated with the sixth-world diagram.

There is a final feature of the sixth-world matrix border to consider. This is the difference between the form generated at the three "vertical" axes and that generated at the three "horizontal" axes. Interestingly, those at the vertical axes seem marked by a sharper and smoother ascent, while those at the horizontal axes seem to pause at each horizontal step in the ascent, a difference that seems consistent with the gender modeling of these axes to be developed later in this chapter. Though the twelve matrix peaks were earlier lumped indifferently together as

Figure 6.6. The Complete Sixth-World Diagram

all expressive of fire, it is also important to distinguish between the different forms produced by the dual orientations of the diagram. In any case, the dual motifs of the sixth-world matrix border provide a remarkably beautifully design.

Turning now to important implications of the method of construction adopted in the prior instructional guide, what figure 6.4 first shows us by its generation of the fourth-world diagram is per-

haps the most important law of diagram construction, that the construction elements of a world should cover the position-defining hexagrams of all worlds culminating with the next to last world before it, the fourth world by such sixth-world construction. Application of this law in chapters 3 and 4 enabled us to distinguish between possible constructions that were "permitted" or "forbidden." A second aspect of this law is that proper diagram

Figure 6.7. The Sixth-World Diagram with Its Matrix Border

construction should also leave the hexagrams of the just-prior worlds intact. Completion of the sixth-world construction elements in figure 6.5 shows that the additional elements add nothing to the generation of the first four worlds. And its ghostlike missing fifth-world elements also suggest the way in which the fifth world might act as a buffer or curtain between the fourth and sixth worlds, shielding the fourth from a more direct perception of its genera-

tion from above. But once these fifth-world elements are added in figure 6.6, the separate identities of these lower worlds become lost in the integrated reality of the sixth-world diagram.

Returning to figure 6.4, another possibly important implication for the fourth world is the specially darkened zigzag matrix border produced by the past modeling of the fourth-world diagram, which is shown to be exactly reproduced by the sixth-world construction elements there given. This would seem to argue strongly for the correctness of this form of the fourth-world diagram and its symbolic representation of an unfallen form of this world, with the further implication that the future-modeled form represents its fallen form, the major question arising in interpretation of the fourth-world diagram. The similar reproduction of the fifth world by the minimal construction of the seventh world required for this, as illustrated in figure 13.1, shows, however, that such backward reproduction does not provide an absolute test of matrix-border correctness, the fifth-world matrix border thus produced not being even close to that produced through outward construction. But the fact that the outward construction of the fifth-world diagram with which it will be compared is future modeled leaves open the question as to the permissibility or even preferability of such past modeling. Thus the identity between the past-modeled fourth-world matrix border and that produced as a by-product of partial sixth-world construction, however suggestive it appears to be of a deeper coherence between these modes of construction, cannot be taken to demonstrate an invariant new regularity in the program for the Sabbath Star Diagram.

Another point involves the question of border hexagrams and how they relate the sixth-world elements to those of the fifth. Returning to figure 6.5, close examination shows that the border Fi-sized hexagrams cannot be formed by its three Sabbath Stars. For such border hexagrams to be formed, the Li Sabbath Star must join with the La hexagram of the fifth-world diagram. This follows a pattern that can be traced as far back as the fourth world. In the fifth-world diagram, the horizontal Sabbath Stars, there marking the thirds, functioned much like the vertical sixth-world Sabbath Stars; the first and third combined to form the Fa-sized border hexagrams while the second alone formed those of Re size. On the vertical grid, however, the first and second combined to form both the Do- and Ri-sized border hexagrams but those of Mi size could only be formed by the combination of the Si Sabbath Star with the Sol hexagram. Thus the Sabbath Stars correlated with the sixths of the tone, the third of

which is equivalent to the half tone, function similarly in both the fifth- and sixth-world diagrams; and in both cases, the semitone Sabbath Stars require the collaboration of the final Sabbath Star of the previous world.

In both of these worlds, this collaboration has significant cognitive implications in terms of the definitions given these stages. The association of the final third of the fifth world with the sixth world is suggestive when we remember that the La hexagram signifies the Messianic millennium, a period in which time itself is to undergo a change in its character, according to kabbalistic tradition. Thus little difference is projected between the millennium and the World to Come. In the fifth world, the collaboration of the Sol hexagram with the Si Sabbath Star to form border hexagrams suggests that the Messiah, identified with the latter, requires the form and participation of man, signified by the former, before he can become manifest. In this linking of worlds, man appears to be as intrinsically capable of participating in the Messianic Age as its final millennium can be considered an earthly Paradise. But this linkage has further implications for the mechanism by which one world evolves into the next. On the one hand, it can be taken to suggest that it is the fortunate discontent of these final world stages with their state of attainment and their pressure to be part of the next world that embodies the evolutionary thrust. Alternatively, the thread of evolution may be said to be pulled from above, the higher worlds of restitution needing the lower and urging on their evolution. This uncertainty will be raised again in the concluding section of this chapter, in which the construction elements will be named and their geometric relationships mythologically interpreted.

A final implication of constructing the diagram from the outside inward may well be its most important, the fact that such construction requires less hexagrams and Sabbath Stars than in the outward method—exactly nine hexagrams and nine Sabbath Stars, eighteen construction elements in all. The vertical grid is constructed from six inner hexagrams, the three of the fifth world and first three of the sixth, and the six outer Sabbath Stars of the sixth world, while the horizontal grid is constructed of the three inner hexagrams of the fifth world and the three outer Sabbath Stars of the sixth. The reason for this should be apparent from consideration of figures 6.2, 6.3, 6.4, and 6.5 as well as the preceding instructions, namely, the fact that the Sabbath Stars of the sixth world produce the position-defining hexagrams of the first four worlds, a diagram feature whose significance will be further considered in the following section.

THE LAWS OF DIAGRAM CONSTRUCTION AND NUMBER THEORY

Although the Tree of Life Diagram was the key through which the working principles for constructing the underlying Sabbath Star Diagram could be unlocked, it is only with construction of the sixth world of this diagram that the logical principles of its construction can be deduced. But in the method of triangular grid construction working from the outside inward, which was adopted in the previous section, it became immediately apparent that such construction depends on prior knowledge of the number of construction elements appropriate to this world, a number that could first be determined only by outward construction, by the whole-step progression of the two semitone hexagrams from those of the previous world and the nesting within them of the number of intermediate hexagrams permitted by the matrix grid. But once this number twelve for the sixth world is so determined and related to the numbers for previous worlds, a pattern emerges that is truly astonishing both in its six-world sum and in the formula it provides for correctly determining the growth pattern for all future worlds.

This formula depends on the construction key provided by the Tree of Life Diagram, which requires only four hexagrams and a Sabbath Star to model the four kabbalistic cosmic worlds with which they were correlated. For reasons explained in chapter 2, the first of these hexagrams was correlated both with the first cosmic world of the Kabbalah, Atzilut, and the Solfeggio tone of Do, and the second with the second world of Beriah and the tone of Re, its double-point construction from the Do

hexagram producing a spatial relationship seen to be equivalent to that of the full tone from Do to Re. The spatial relationships of the third and fourth of these hexagrams were also seen to parallel the tonal relationships of the Mi and Fa tones of the diatonic scale, these tonal relationships being the reason that the Solfeggio names of the diatonic tones were applied to the construction elements of the Elementary Sabbath Star Diagram; and they also were seen to characterize the correlated third world of Yetzirah as so divided into two. Finally the Sabbath Star, being a full step or tone beyond that of Mi, was taken to represent the first half of the fourth world of Asiyah and given the chromatic Solfeggio name of Fi. Now, the first step in self-generating the fourth-world diagram, undertaken in chapter 3, was the addition of the full step Sol Sabbath Star. This produced the hitherto unmanifest hexagram positioned between the vertical Do and Mi hexagrams that, being a half step beyond the Re hexagram, was given the chromatic Solfeggio name of Ri. But the formula that will determine the numbers of all future worlds of the Sabbath Star Diagram requires the omission of the Ri hexagram from the number of second world elements, in this returning to the original key of the Tree of Life Diagram.

Maintaining this esoteric counting of the construction elements of the first three worlds and adding to them the numbers for the remaining three worlds produced through the further self-generation of the diagram, we are confronted with that total earlier described as truly astonishing: $1 + 1 + 2 + 4 + 6 + 12 = 26$! Since 26 is the Gematria number of the Tetragrammaton (Yod = 10, Hey = 5, Vuv = 6, and Hey = 5), there would here seem to be an uncanny union of number with meaning at the very core of the geometry defining the laws of Sabbath Star Diagram expansion, a union whose meaning only becomes revealed with construction of its sixth expansion and world, the world that defines the dimension of meaningfulness and that here seems to be suggesting the divine nature of these six cosmic dimensions, as outwardly constructed. In the opening section of chapter 7, we shall see a second emergence of this most sacred number, the implications of this surprising double manifestation of the Tetragrammaton Gematria number at significant points in the sixth- and seventh-world diagrams being there shown to contain a key to the central gnosis of the Jewish esoteric tradition.

But the numerical ordering within this sum total of 26 (that is, 1 + 1 + 2 + 4 + 6 + 12) also provides a formula for the curious growth pattern of the Sabbath Star Diagram. This formula is additive but in a pattern alternating the addition of first two and then three previous integers after the first sum. Thus the number of the second world is the sum of the number of the previous world, 1 in each case. The number of the third world, 2, is likewise the sum of the previous two worlds or numbers, 1 + 1. And the number of the fourth world, 4, sums up the numbers for the previous three worlds, 1 + 1 + 2. But with the fifth world the alternating pattern begins, for its number 6 is the sum of only the previous two worlds, 2 + 4. Finally, with the sixth world, whose number is 12, we return to the addition of three previous worlds, 2 + 4 + 6. On the basis of the now established pattern, we can proceed beyond the sixth world to chart the seventh, whose number would be the sum of the previous two worlds, 6 + 12 = 18. With construction of the full seventh world in chapter 13, we shall see that this number is validated and that this formula can be used to predict the precise number of construction elements in any future world. Thus an eighth world would again sum the numbers of the previous three worlds, 6 + 12 + 18 = 36, as a ninth world would sum the numbers of the previous two worlds, 18 + 36 = 54, and a tenth would be the sum of the previous three worlds, 18 + 36 + 54 = 108.

This formula, though not previously explored in number theory, is similar to the Fibonacci series of numbers, a series named after a thirteenth-century Italian mathematician that, like the Sabbath Star Diagram series, begins with two ones but then proceeds to add increments through the addition of just the two previous integers: 1, 1, 2, 3, 5, 8, 13, 21, and so on. As the Fibonacci series can be related to the geometry of the pentagram and all fivefold symmetrical expansions,[1] so the series emerging in the successive expansions of the Sabbath Star Diagram is

related to the geometry of the hexagram, which relates the threefold form of the triangle with the two such triangles of its hexagram unification, from which it was derived. Table 6.1 shows the construction elements of this diagram through a possible tenth world, and the geometric derivation of this numerical series reveals further numerical relationships. This table gives both the number of construction elements on each axis as well as the fraction of the space they represent beginning with the fourth world, and it also shows how the sum of such construction elements for each world follows the numerical formula just given.

Table 6.1. Chart of Construction Elements

WORLD	VERTICAL	HORIZONTAL	TOTAL
1	1+	0	= 1
2	(1) +	1	= 1 (+ unmanifest 1)
3	1+	1	= 2 (adds previous 2 totals)
4	3 ($1/3$) +	1 ($1/2$)	= 4 (adds previous 3 totals)
5	3 ($1/6$) +	3 ($1/3$)	= 6 (adds previous 2 totals)
6	9 ($1/9$) +	3 ($1/6$)	= 12 (adds previous 3 totals)
7	9 ($1/18$) +	9 ($1/9$)	= 18 (adds previous 2 totals)
8	27 ($1/27$) +	9 ($1/18$)	= 36 (adds previous 3 totals)
9	27 ($1/54$) +	27 ($1/27$)	= 54 (adds previous 2 totals)
10	81 ($1/81$) +	27 ($1/54$)	= 108 (adds previous 3 totals)

In addition to the numerical series of the totals, what table 6.1 also reveals is that the horizontal elements of one world equal the vertical elements of the previous world while its vertical elements are three times the number of the horizontal elements of that previous world. It is this that allows the vertical grid of the sixth-world diagram, given in figure 6.5, to function also as the horizontal grid of the seventh-world diagram, in which case the number of elements on the sixth-world horizontal grid would have to be tripled, thus creating the full matrix grid of the seventh world.

What is perhaps most interesting about such a shifting of axes to provide the basis of the denser diagram of the next world is that these adjacent worlds would occupy the same space. Though I have actually been mechanically reducing the grids for each world so that the drafted diagrams could fit the same page area, the understanding has previously been that these represented successive expansions of the Sabbath Star Diagram. But we can now see another way of understanding this diagram, not as expanding but as growing ever more complex.

If we were now to construct the diagram not from the outside of a later world inward to cover the smaller, earlier worlds, as in the previous section, but from earlier to later worlds within the same area, it would be best to begin such construction at the same point that regularity emerges in the numerical series, with the third world, its Mi and Fa hexagrams providing the largest elements of the total diagram-to-be. Turning it next from an upright to a sideways position, its vertical grid would have to be tripled and the whole fourth-world diagram constructed with the requisite Sabbath Stars that would also fill in the first and second worlds. At each such turning of the same diagram and tripling of the vertical elements, the diagram would become ever denser though occupying the same space, a space that we shall see in chapter 7 to be partially identified with the space of the Lurianic Tzimtzum, that primordial space left for the creation by the retraction of the infinite essence of Ein Sof.

But whether the diagram of creation be understood to expand from the center to fill this space or to fill the entire space from the beginning and grow ever denser, it is a diagram of ever increasing complexity that follows a strict numerical series of generation. The alternation in this series between a double and triple addition of prior elements can also now be explained as derived from the different densities of the vertical and horizontal grids, the totals for worlds whose culminating element is horizontal being the doubling sum and that for worlds whose culminating element is vertical being the tripling sum.

A final point about both this new numerical series and the mode of construction that increases density rather than space involves the nature of the first two worlds. The fact that such construction is best begun with the third world reinforces the earlier characterization of the first two worlds as defining a progression from the unmanifestable to the unmanifest. Though this was earlier derived from

the status of their potential half-step elements, it would now appear to apply even to their whole-step elements, steady-space construction allowing manifestation only at the third-world degree of complexity. Beginning the numerical progression with the same two ones as begin the Fibonacci series gives the further mathematical support of the Sabbath Star Diagram series for the exclusion of a second numerical stage from the second world in its original conceptualization and construction, an exclusionary principle that we have seen was earlier derived from the construction key of the Tree of Life Diagram and that makes possible the final count of 26 that can identify the sixth-world diagram with the divine Name.

But the rule inherent in this numerical series that would limit the number of permitted construction elements of the second world to 1 has esoteric associations not only with the traditional kabbalistic geometry of the Tree but also with Pythagorean numerology. It gives a geometric support not previously noted to the major Pythagorean distinction between the concept of the monad and the first integer 1, the distinction between the indivisible unity of the monad and the divisibility of the number 1 into fractions. As explained by the second-century Pythagorean mathematician Theon of Smyrna: "The monad is then the principle of numbers; and the *one* the principle of numbered things. That which is one, being tangible, can most assuredly be divided to infinity . . . so that the monad which is intelligible does not admit of division, but that which is one, being tangible, can be divided to infinity."[2] In the Pythagorean system, the distinction between the intelligible and the tangible dimensions of number extends through the range of at least the first four numbers that together comprise the Tetractys, the diagram of ten points in the form of an ascending equilateral triangle, shown in figure 1.1, that was the symbol of the Pythagorean brotherhood. The most important of these numbers are the indivisible monad, the principle of the odd numbers, and the indefinite dyad, the principle of the even numbers. If we can now apply the intelligible qualities of the numbers to the worlds of the Sabbath Star Diagram, then the difference particularly between its first and second worlds can be further clarified. If the first world can thus be considered that of the monad and the second that of the dyad, we can better understand why division of the first world is categorically impossible, whereas that of the second world, while theoretically possible, has the indefinite quality of the unmanifest; for the one construction element of the first world would be representative of the indivisibility of the first monadic world while that of the second world would represent the unmanifest divisibility of the indefinite dyadic world. This distinction between impossible and possible but forbidden modes of construction is a feature of the trivalent logic that was shown at the conclusion of chapter 3 to inform the Sabbath Star Diagram. But we must now return to consideration of the sixth-world diagram and the major law of diagram construction that emerges with particular clarity from the inward mode of construction adopted in the previous section.

In constructing the Sabbath Stars of the sixth world, we saw that these alone appeared to weave the design of the four worlds of emanation as on a loom. This fact is meaningful in itself, for it offers us a new perspective on our fourth world. Where outward construction suggests the self-generation and increasing complexity of the cosmic worlds, inward construction shows these earlier worlds to be the product of worlds yet more advanced and complex than they. Inward construction also provides us with guidelines for the proper construction of the self-generating form of the outwardly constructed diagram, showing us that a world is properly constructed when its Sabbath Stars have the effect of covering the reduced hexagrams of the construction elements of all prior worlds with the exception of the one just preceding it, but that the position-defining hexagrams of the just preceding world must also be left intact.

Having studied both the geometric and numerical features of the sixth-world construction elements, we should now turn to the mythological identifications earlier suggested of these construction elements with the Partzufim, first considering their theoretical implications. For the identifications of the construction elements with the Partzufim will introduce a gender dimension to the geometry and meaning of the Sabbath Star Diagram that will have perhaps the most significant implications for the further development of the diagram.

THE CONSTRUCTION ELEMENTS AND GENDER

The concern of part 2 is to model the "outer" dimension of the cosmic worlds correlated with the expansions of the Sabbath Star Diagram, their chronological or hierarchical stages, by the construction elements of the Sabbath Star Diagram, as their "inner" soul dimensions will be modeled in part 3 by their matrices. Now, if the "outer" dimension of sixth-world consciousness could be equated with the Partzufim, the male and female divine personalities that will be fully defined in the final section of this chapter, then we should be able to trace their features in the main construction elements of the sixth-world diagram. But once this possibility is raised, a solution presents itself of the most far-reaching implications, a solution first based simply upon the size comparison between the longer vertical axis and the shorter horizontal axis. This is the celebrated distinction, which keeps appearing in discussions of the Partzufim, between the size of the male Yesod, the Sefirah identified with the sexual organ, as compared with that of the female. As expressed in the eighteenth-century kabbalistic text, *Sha'arei Gan Eden* (Gates of the Garden of Eden) of Yakof Koppel: "And it happens that the Yesod of the Female is short and wide and the Yesod of the Male is lean and long."[3] The advantage of making this identification of the long axis with the male and the short axis with the female is that the diagram can then be viewed as providing a graphic portrayal of their Yichud, and this coupling of the vertical and horizontal axes can then be seen as symbolic of the processes of cosmic creation and governance.

The sexual correlations just given of the vertical and horizontal axes can be supported on several grounds, and they permit a more comprehensive interpretation of the diagram in gender terms than hitherto possible. On the level of construction elements, this distinction is supported by the fact that the vertical elements cross at right angles to the central column of the superimposed Tree, while those of the horizontal axis are in alignment with it, the former having thus been taken to signify free will and the latter a harmonization with the cosmic flow, qualities that now also seem to convey, respectively, archetypal masculine and feminine characteristics. A second measure of the qualitative difference between these elements is the fact that the vertical elements, and the diagram worlds they define as their culminating constituents, are balanced on a single point, as in figure 6.7, whereas the horizontal elements and the worlds they define have a flat base formed of the five points aligned with the line that could be drawn of the point hexagon of their culminating Sabbath Star, as shown in figure 5.1. The precarious and earned balance of the former is consistent with its previously noted quality of tension, the tension of the perpendicular crossing also defining the danger and elation attending its upward thrust. In contrast, the stability of the latter is consistent with its more collectively determined harmony and horizontal structuring. Finally, the "erect" character of the vertical elements and recumbent character of the horizontal seem further graphic metaphors for the sexual differentiation of the construction elements being here urged as they do define the conditions of readiness for sexual activity appropriate to each of the sexes. The purely geometric differences between the vertical and horizontal construction elements do, indeed, seem to define the differences archetypally attributed to the masculine and feminine characters.

Even the one feature of the diagram that seems to belie these gender correlations can actually be seen to support it. This is the fact that the male-identified construction elements are smaller than the female-identified elements. But at the most essential level of such differentiation, that of the reproductive cell, of the egg and sperm, the gender distinction of the construction elements does hold. As Dorion Sagan has shown: "In many species, including humans, the gametes, or sex cells, of the females became fewer, bigger, and more sedentary while those of the males became smaller, more fast-moving and numerous."[4] The distinction Sagan raises, the

fact that the male gametes are more numerous than the female, is also true of the diagram, as we are soon to see in the numerical comparison of the worlds generated by these gender-defined construction elements.

Consideration of these worlds cannot go further back than the third world because of the irregular nature of the first two worlds in the terms now being defined. For though the first world is defined by a masculine vertical element and the second by a feminine horizontal element, this is only because the truly culminating horizontal element of the first world is unmanifestable, and the truly culminating vertical element of the second world is unmanifest, this in accordance both with the key of the Tree of Life Diagram and the laws of diagram construction established in the previous section. Thus as we there saw, regularity only begins with the third world. Now, the most significant difference in the present context between the feminine third, fifth, and seventh horizontal worlds and the masculine fourth and sixth vertical worlds involves the numbers of their total construction elements, the fact that the feminine worlds feature parity between the numbers of their vertical and horizontal elements while the masculine worlds feature a 3:1 ratio of vertical to horizontal elements.

This is surely a most extraordinary finding in terms of its clear correlation with the differences observed by anthropologists between societies of more matriarchal or patriarchal bent, as well as defining a major distinction between the feminine and masculine personalities. To begin with this latter distinction, the feminine personality generally seeks not to dominate but to achieve equality with the males in her environment, indeed feeling frustrated with both the dominant and submissive roles, whereas the masculine personality generally seeks to dominate the female. A striking example of this can be seen in the reply of Abigail Adams to her husband John after he had laughed at her request that he and the Continental Congress give women the vote: "*7 May, 1776.* I cannot say that I think you are very generous to the ladies; for whilst you are proclaiming peace and good-will to men, emancipating all nations, you insist upon retaining an absolute power over wives."[5] Where patriarchal societies not only establish male domination over women and over nature but domination patterns featuring vertical pyramids of increasingly concentrated power, societies that are more matriarchal, or even feminine organizations within a primitive patriarchal society, honor the male and female roles equally, as they do Mother Nature, and diffuse power through a more horizontal, decentralized structuring of society. The vertical vs. horizontal orientation of such societies is also shown by a more purely spatial aspect they show. The original societies were those of the hunter-gatherer tribes who universally populated the world for some 100,000 years, their chief trait being their journeying around their territories with ever changing camps, what we shall now consider a feminine characteristic. In contrast to such horizontal extension, patriarchal societies tended to settle in one place and build monuments featuring vertical extension. The difference conveyed through the numerical distinction recently defined is also conveyed through their cosmologies, matriarchal societies, both within and outside of patriarchal organization, developing cosmologies that focus equally on masculine and feminine forces or divinities and their generative unification while the cosmologies of purely patriarchal societies largely or totally neglect the feminine cosmic elements and the sexual myth for a unitary or ruling, always male, sky god.[6]

Having seen how closely the geometric features of the vertical and horizontal construction elements can be correlated with the distinctions between the archetypal masculine and feminine personalities, we should now investigate what special intelligence such a gender modeling of evolutionary development by the distinctive worlds of the Sabbath Star Diagram can contribute to an understanding of cosmic development. In charting this archetypal progression, taken through the soon to be defined seventh world, we shall see that it does not display a simple oscillation between eras or dimensions dominated either by masculine or feminine characteristics but more complex patterns both of inversion and synthesis. Table 6.2 lists the purely formal characteristics of these diagram worlds, dividing each into its two halves and correlating each with the gender associations of its construction elements and their numbers:

Table 6.2. Gender Correspondences of the Cosmic Worlds

WORLD PHASE	ORIENTATION OF C.E.	GENDER	NO. OF C.E.
3A	V	M	1V
3B	H	F	1H
4A	H	M/F	1V-1H
4B	V	M	2V
5A	V	F/M	3V-1H
5B	H	F	2H
6A	H	M/F	4V-3H
6B	V	M	5V
7A	V	F/M	9V-4H
7B	H	F	5H

Though each of the worlds is characterized by the orientation of its culminating Sabbath Star, and this in terms of the distinctions earlier cited regarding both their numerical totals and visual appearance, the two halves of each world have markedly different characters. Unlike the changed orientation of the final phase and its uniform character, the first phase maintains the orientation of the previous world and combines both horizontal and vertical construction elements. In this phase, the uniform extremity of the earlier final phase may be said to be brought back into some form of balance before its own waxing nature itself becomes dominant. But the form of balance effected in these synthesizing phases reflects the numerical character of its final Sabbath Star, though in less perfect numerical proportions, horizontal first phases approximating a 1:1 ratio and vertical first phases one closer to 3:1. Indeed, these perfect ratios are exactly maintained in the fourth and fifth worlds, to become less perfect in the more numerous members of the sixth and seventh worlds. Thus at the highest levels of evolutionary development, the former hard and fast distinctions begin to yield to different blendings of masculine and feminine characteristics even within their continuing pattern of such oscillation.

The major pattern of gender oscillation between diagram worlds that we have been considering seems comparable to the yin-yang model of Taoist cosmology, especially with its graphic suggestion that the character of one phase already holds the seed of the next, and such major oscillations of Sabbath Star Diagram construction elements from world to world will be applied to the new gender analysis of human history to be made in appendix D. But there is a difference between such a Taoist view of the complementary necessity of gender-differentiated eras and the more strictly feminist cosmologies within primitive societies earlier considered, namely, that the purpose of complementary gender differentiation is generation, a purpose defeated by simple oscillation.

Such a purpose may perhaps be discerned in the expansion of the Sabbath Star Diagram as in its tabulated growth patterns by viewing them from another perspective. If instead of viewing this progression of gender-correlated states as only composed of the two phases of a world, we consider it to be composed of three phases, those of the second half of one world (A) with the two halves of the world following it (B and C), and further consider these phases to be simultaneous, a perspective suggested at the conclusion of chapter 4, then we may see in table 6.2 the basis of a *generative* understanding of gender cosmology. Such three simultaneous aspects would give us the sharp gender differentiations of the two final world stages, A and C, with the gender mingling of the intervening stage B, which latter might then be viewed as symbolizing the generation of such a child as successively propels cosmic evolution forward with the transformation of each C into the A of a new generative triad. So understood, the Sabbath Star Diagram can provide a model capable of synthesizing the two forms of cosmology that give a central and equal status to the two genders, that which sees them primarily in oscillation and that which sees their purpose as generative.

There is a final aspect of the gender identifications of the two diagram axes to be noted. This involves the further support that table 6.2 can give to the sexual associations soon to be developed for the octave diagram in terms of which the sixth world will be identified with the feminine and the seventh world with the masculine, identifications based on the combined totals of their construction elements, in terms of both inward and outward construction, that will be related to the concept of the unification of the Lord and His Name. Though these identifications would seem to contradict the present correlations of the even worlds with the masculine and the odd worlds with the feminine, we have just seen that the generative multiplication of elements of the sixth world with those of the octave does involve just those phases that do demonstrate the required feminine and masculine characteristics, the horizontal first phase of the sixth world, which maintains the feminine characteristic of the previous world within its gender synthesizing phase, being identified with aspects of the feminine Shekhinah and the vertical first phase of the seventh world, which maintains the masculine orientation of the previous sixth world within its gender synthesis, with the masculine Adam Kadmon. As these gender correlations of the diagram axes will extend into the octave diagram and its analysis, so do they seem consistent with the analyses of the prior worlds. The fifth-world correlations of these axes, the vertical with the individual Messiah and the horizontal with the collective millennium, further reinforce this same distinction, as do the fourth-world correlations with man and vegetation, enabling us now to see gardening Adam as the husband of the fecund Earth.

But the most important consequences of the sexual identifications of these axes with the masculine and feminine is that we can now understand the product of their union, the matrix, as signifying the androgynous cosmic son.[7] This "son" is truly a new conception, for it requires an additional level of discernment to distinguish the matrix border that defines its unique form, a new generation with that self-defining cognitive power also signified by the word "conception" that at each world of the diagram conveys both the soul and the goal of each such cosmic expansion. This new view of the Sabbath Star Diagram as a model of the sexualized generation of the cosmic son may well be the single most important insight into the structural meaning of the diagram in this work, one seminal in the fullest sense of this word.

Such a correlation of the vertical construction elements with the masculine and horizontal construction elements with the feminine is meaningful in itself as well as in the matrix product of their unification. But the most startling as well as most meaningful feature to be encountered in our study of the Sabbath Star Diagram will be the main subject of the crowning final part of this work, that numerical correlation of construction to matrix elements by which the former, indeed, appear to represent the parents of the latter. This is a correlation that could only have emerged from the just suggested gender identifications of the construction elements. For once the vertical elements are identified with the masculine and the horizontal with the feminine, the question naturally arises as to whether the numbers of what can be regarded as these two parental sources could be meaningfully related in terms of the arithmetic process that has been viewed from time immemorial as a metaphor for sexual generation, multiplication. The multiplication of the numbers of vertical and horizontal elements in a diagram world would only yield a significant product, however, if this product could be precisely correlated with a numerical feature of the matrix of that world. And part 4 will develop just such a mathematical function as, in chapter 14, can generate the numbers for an infinite sequence of diagram worlds and, in chapter 15, also the two higher levels of infinite decimal sequences that will then be called the Sabbath Star System, a culminating development whose modeling of the theory of complex systems can also most adequately model the cosmos. Thus the gender identifications of the diagram's axes we are now to consider is something more than fanciful, embodying a key to the deepest structural meaning of its expressive geometry as well as to human history, the subject of appendix D. But it is now time to turn to the first exercise in such sexual interpretation of the Sabbath Star Diagram, the gender identifications of the sixth-world construction elements.

THE CONSTRUCTION ELEMENTS AND THE PARTZUFIM

At the beginning of the previous section, a kabbalistic reason was cited to justify a general identification of the longer vertical axis of the sixth-world diagram with the masculine Partzufim and its shorter horizontal axis with their female counterparts. If we now begin the more specific process of identifying construction elements with the two main composite male Partzufim and consider them in relation to the Sefirot of which they were first formed—Arikh Anpin with the three supernal Sefirot from Keter to Binah and Ze'ir Anpin with the six Sefirot from Chesed to Yesod, nine in all—we can clearly identify all nine members of the vertical axis in terms of both Sefirot and Partzufim, counting them, as in the do-it-yourself manual, in ascending order: the uppermost ninth with Keter or Arikh Anpin (Long Face), the eighth with Chokhmah or Abba (Father), the seventh with Binah or Imma (Mother), and the sixth through first with the lower six Sefirot from Chesed to Yesod that define Ze'ir Anpin (Short Face, the Partzuf of the son).

This leaves the lowest Sefirah of Malkhut to be somehow related to the three Sabbath Stars of the horizontal axis, a requirement not as difficult as might at first appear. For Malkhut has, in fact, three different feminine identifications within the kabbalistic tradition that have heretofore seemed conflicting. These three Behinot or aspects of Malkhut go by the names of the Shekhinah, the Nukvah (Female, the Partzuf of the daughter and sister-bride of Ze'ir Anpin), and Rachel. Assigning these three Behinot of Malkhut to the three horizontal Sabbath Stars, with the Shekhinah equated with the highest and Rachel with the lowest, we not only solve our immediate problem but may help to solve some questions about the relationships among these three "personalities" of Malkhut.

While such an identification of the female horizontal axis with the Sefirah Malkhut reduces the upper female Sefirah of Binah to an intrapsychic aspect of Arikh Anpin, it does emphasize the dominant cosmic role accorded to the unification of

Malkhut with her divine sexual partner, normally associated with the Sefirah Tiferet. This is true whatever names are given to these Sefirot. For each of the female Behinot of Malkhut is matched with a different male Behinah of Tiferet. The one we are most familiar with in discussions of the Partzufim is the relationship of Ze'ir Anpin with that aspect simply called the Nukvah or Female. But Ze'ir Anpin is not ordinarily matched with the Shekhinah, considered the indwelling spirit of God. Rather, the Shekhinah is normally matched with the Holy One, blessed be He. The final coupling is between Rachel and Jacob. This last is, moreover, the purest matching of the simple Sefirot of Malkhut and Tiferet. Although Ze'ir Anpin is sometimes equated with the sub-Partzuf of Jacob, the latter is not normally understood to cover all six of the Sefirot of Ze'ir Anpin but only his central heart Sefirah of Tiferet. As Jacob is the Tiferet of Ze'ir Anpin, so Leah is equated with the Malkhut of Binah and Rachel with the Malkhut of Malkhut.

But to correlate all three of the horizontal Sabbath Stars with the single vertical Sabbath Star identified with Tiferet would not take full advantage of the resources of the diagram to make new connections of mythic material within the guidelines of the kabbalistic tradition. It thus seems desirable to assign alternate Sefirotic mates to the remaining Behinot of the Nukvah and the Shekhinah within these guidelines. Though the main mating of the Shekhinah is with the Holy One, blessed be He, there is a minor tradition that associates Malkhut, as the Shekhinah, with Keter, the end of the cosmic process with its beginning, identified with whatever was conceived to be the primary source of creation, Ein Sof, the Limitless One, or the Or Ein Sof, the Limitless Light. On the model of Malkhut, Keter too may be said to have various Behinot, as the crown Sefirah, as the Partzuf Arikh Anpin, and as the ultimate source, Ein Sof. In the works of Cordovero particularly, the boundary between Ein Sof and Keter tends to get lost.[8] In terms of our present correlations, however, it seems best to identify Keter with Arikh Anpin as the mate of the Shekhinah.

Beginning, then, with the positive identification of Rachel with the Malkhut of Malkhut, and of the Shekhinah as the mate of Keter, it would seem logical to regard the Shekhinah as the Keter of Malkhut. The remaining assignment of the Nukvah to a Sefirah of the "spread out" Malkhut, the full Tree contained somewhat holographically within each Sefirah, is also not too difficult. For the second horizontal Sabbath Star identified with the Nukvah is the only one that has a clear parallel to one of the constituents of Ze'ir Anpin. As shown in the analysis of the fifth-world Sabbath Stars, there is a special simultaneity between the Sabbath Stars marking the first-third and second-sixth phases since these fractions are equal and therefore refer to the same first-third stage. In the case of the lower six constituents of the vertical axis that have been identified with the Sefirot of Ze'ir Anpin, that which corresponds to the second horizontal Sabbath Star of the Nukvah is the third vertical hexagram, and former Sabbath Star, which may be identified with Netzach. It would seem appropriate, therefore, to identify the Nukvah with the Netzach of Malkhut, a correlation that will gain further support and illumination in chapter 10. But as we shall soon see, Netzach cannot be assigned as an appropriate mate to the Nukvah Behinah of Malkhut. Such a mate will emerge from the following discussion of Ze'ir Anpin.

Having analyzed the three Behinot of the lower female Partzuf identified with the Sefirah Malkhut, we can now examine the lower male Partzuf of Ze'ir Anpin from the perspective of his construction elements. What immediately becomes clear is the distinction between the elements identified with his lower three Sefirot and those identified with his upper three Sefirot, for the former are only hexagrams while the latter are full Sabbath Stars. This distinction is similar to a kabbalistic tradition that associates the upper six Sefirot with the divine and the lower four with the human, a tradition that can be surprisingly validated when the Sabbath Star Diagram is interfaced with that of the Tree of Life. As can be seen in such an interface, all six points of the Do hexagram of Atzilut contain or define the upper six Sefirot, two points of the Re hexagram of Beriah define the Sefirot of Netzach and Hod while one point of the Ri hexagram of the virtual second phase of Beriah defines the Sefirah of Yesod. Thus the Sefirot of Ze'ir Anpin are split between an upper Atzilutic triad and a lower Berian triad, the former also signifying an upper divine half and the latter a lower half that is characteristically human.

If this distinction can be further compared to levels of maturation, then there is a remarkable correspondence between these geometric features and the mythological descriptions of Ze'ir Anpin's maturation process in the *Eitz Chayyim*, the most important work of Lurianic cosmology written by Luria's principle follower, Chayyim Vital. As fully analyzed and modeled in chapter 7 of *The Secret Doctrine of the Kabbalah*, this is a three-stage process involving a first pregnancy in the womb of Imma, a second nursing phase outside of her body, and a third phase in which he reenters Imma's womb for her second pregnancy with him prior to his final maturation as a twice-born divine personality. This is summarized in the *Eitz Chayyim* as follows:

> And now we will explain the mystery of the maturation of Ze'ir Anpin. While Ze'ir Anpin was in his first pregnancy, three [Sefirot were] included in three [Sefirot] in the womb of Imma. . . . When Ze'ir Anpin came out to the world . . . His limbs are thin like grasshopper's antennae. . . . [At this stage] they are only called an aspect of [the] six Sefirot, even though he has a small [*katnut*] head. . . . And now we will explain the third stage of the maturation. In order for growth to occur in these small limbs, as small as grasshopper's antennae, it is necessary for the Netzach, Hod, [and] Yesod of Imma to enter into the six Sefirot of Ze'ir Anpin.[9]

To review the three-stage maturation process as here defined, Ze'ir Anpin consisted of only his upper three Sefirot of Chesed, Gevurah, and Tiferet during the first pregnancy, the lower three Sefirot of Netzach, Hod, and Yesod being then still included in the upper three. It is during the nursing phase following his first birth that his three lower Sefirot emerge, those associated with his two lower limbs and genitals, but these are in a most immature state, "thin like grasshopper's antennae."

Let us now see how these Lurianic concepts can be related to the sixth-world diagram, primarily to what they show us about those elements correlated with the Sefirot of Netzach, Hod, and Yesod. As was shown in construction of the sixth-world diagram, the elements related to Yesod and Hod, the first two vertical hexagrams, are incapable of becoming Sabbath Stars, while the third, related to Netzach, has a Sabbath Star phase when the diagram is constructed from inside out, but one that, even then, is completely covered by later phases of the diagram, leaving only the essential form of its stage-defining hexagram. These three hexagrams, the only such construction elements of the sixth world, seem to define the Yesod, Hod, and Netzach of Ze'ir Anpin, and consequently Ze'ir Anpin himself, as essentially immature, as essentially locked into the nursing phase of his maturation.

Such a surprising deduction can be supported from comparison of figures 6.2 and 6.3. If figure 6.3 be first observed, it would appear that Ze'ir Anpin alone is responsible for producing the vertical axis of the fourth world, is its creator, since it does appear to be formed by the third through sixth of his Sabbath Stars, corresponding to Netzach through Chesed. Such a view proves shortsighted, however, upon observation of figure 6.2, for this shows that not only the fourth world but Ze'ir Anpin himself is a product of still higher forces.

It also shows that the fourth world cannot be created, or creatively sustained, without the participation of the highest element of Ze'ir Anpin, the beautiful Sabbath Star identified with Chesed, which has six additional hexagrams in its border the size of the hexagram it covers at the center of the diagram, seven smaller hexagrams in all. It is this symbolic representation of creation that may be said to signify Ze'ir Anpin's rebirth in his mature, twice-born form. As is true of the earlier worlds, so is it also true of Ze'ir Anpin that only the shell of identity can survive from one world into the next. Thus the Sabbath Stars of the fourth world survive into the fifth world only as hexagrams, and the same process is repeated as the fifth world merges into the sixth. The fourth world has now lost even its distinctive hexagrams and of the fifth-world Sabbath

Stars only the hexagrams remain to participate independently in the sixth world. So, too, with Ze'ir Anpin. As the creative capacity of Netzach through Gevurah, the third through fifth vertical elements, becomes a conduit for the highest powers—the ninth Sabbath Star of Arikh Anpin flowing through and empowering the third, the eighth Sabbath Star of Abba flowing similarly through the fourth, as the seventh Sabbath Star of Imma flows through the fifth—Ze'ir Anpin may be said to go through a purification that lifts his consciousness wholly into the loving-kindness of Chesed. He has now left his immature lower hexagrams and once proud lower Sabbath Stars behind and become twice-born in Chesed, to join in this form with Imma, Abba, and Arikh Anpin in the work of creation. It is only this mature form of Ze'ir Anpin, expressed through his Sefirah of Chesed, that can thus provide a fitting mate to the Nukvah, as the second Behinah of Malkhut.

Figures 6.2 and 6.3 present two different views of Ze'ir Anpin, figure 6.3 of his self-important and self-blinded first conception and figure 6.2 of his twice-born role as creative collaborator. Ze'ir Anpin can become a model of human evolution precisely because he, like the fourth world, can be viewed from these dual perspectives. For the fourth world, too, looks quite different when viewed from the perspective of the fourth- or sixth-world diagrams. From the former perspective, the fourth world of material solids seems to be self-created, the product of its own construction; from the latter it seems to have been woven by the Partzufim. But not even the creative collaboration of these four heavenly Partzufim is sufficient to create and sustain this world. In the primarily masculine forms of Arikh Anpin and Ze'ir Anpin, they must also couple with the female personification of the divine as an indwelling spirit. Nothing less than this Yichud of the entire vertical and horizontal axes can produce this result. This can be seen through exploration of the lower couplings.

Before we proceed to the more precise analyses of these unifications, a table of the twelve construction elements of the sixth-world diagram would be useful in summarizing the information earlier given

in the do-it-yourself manual. Table 6.3 gives the number of the construction element on each axis, V or H, counting from outside in, the earlier construction element(s) it may have covered, and the Sefirah/Partzuf with which it may be associated.

Table 6.3. Correlations of Sixth-World Construction Elements

NUMBER	COVERED	ELEMENTS	SEFIROT/PARTZUFIM
9V	Sol	Keter-Arikh Anpin	
8V	Do and Fi/Sol	Chokhmah-Abba	
7V	Ri and Fa/Fi		Binah-Imma
6V	Mi	Chesed of Ze'ir Anpin	
5V	Ri and Fa/Fi	Gevurah of Ze'ir Anpin	
4V	Do and Fi/Sol	Tiferet of Ze'ir Anpin and Jacob	
3V	——	Netzach of Ze'ir Anpin	
2V	——	Hod of Ze'ir Anpin	
1V	——	Yesod of Ze'ir Anpin	
3H	Fi	Keter of Malkhut as Shekhinah	
2H	Fa and Re	Chesed of Malkhut as the Nukvah	
1H	Fa and Re	Malkhut of Malkhut as Rachel	

We have seen that Jacob has been Lurianically identified with the Tiferet of Ze'ir Anpin, and charting his Sabbath Star Yichud with Rachel is simply a matter of highlighting the fourth vertical and first horizontal Sabbath Stars that such a Yichud would involve. As can be seen in figure 6.8, both of these Sabbath Stars produce the smallest versions of the "bow tie" shapes that contribute to the border hexagrams, the Sabbath Star of Jacob contributing the bows of the Do-sized hexagrams and that of Rachel the bows of the Re-sized hexagrams, and these tiny bows seem to package the inner hexagon of the final Ti hexagram with a quality that can only be described as "sweet."

To say this is not to denigrate it, for the apprehension of the sweetness of any experience is one of the great rewards of consciousness. This is all the more true of religious experience. Thus a hymn composed by Rabbi Aharon of Karlin, one of the early hasidic masters, begins: "God—I long for the sweetness of the Sabbath." And on Rosh Hashanah the New Year is blessed that it may be *tova u matukha*, "good and sweet." On a secular level, a Renaissance character says of sexual union: "I thank life for nothing / But that pleasure; it was so sweet to me."[10] And the mad Lear bitterly cries: "Give me an ounce of civet, good apothecary, to sweeten my imagination."[11] Milton also sees in music's "linked sweetness long drawn out" a power capable of "Untwisting all the chains that tie / The hidden soul of harmony."[12] The power of musical sweetness to unchain the soul can also be felt in the music of Mozart and of Dixieland jazz clarinetists, eighteenth-century classicism and the black slave experience providing the perception of a totally enthralling power that can only be managed and transcended through the cultivation of sweetness. When the unchained music of Beethoven and of both rock and progressive-jazz performers replaces the earlier more constricted forms with defiant power, their loss of sweetness is also something to be mourned. Such sweetness arises precisely from that coupling in which the self's imprisoning limitations are transcended without violating the sovereignty of the other, in which the other is embraced as a gift rather than a right. It defines the inner quality of any consummation devoutly wished for, the "linked sweetness long drawn out" of final recognition or victory over one's enemies, of a good meal. It is the sweet dessert of life given to the deserving. Always associated with the sense of taste, it is that which gives to sensual experience its spiritually gratifying quality. It is not surprising, therefore, that it should be graphically depicted in association with the lowest level of cosmic Yichud, the coupling of Jacob and Rachel.

In chapter 5, the vertical axis of the fifth world was associated with three levels of Ruach mastery culminating in the Si Sabbath Star of the Messiah. We may now extend this association to the whole of the fifth-world vertical and sixth-world horizontal axes, those that divide their worlds into three-sixths of the tone, and say that each of these sixths represents a level of either Ruach or Neshamah mastery. It may thus be argued that the three levels of fifth-world mastery defined in chapter 5, all of which were related to the figure of Elijah, derive their pri-

mary power and impetus from the higher sixth-world forces to which they have a clear channel. As the Messianic herald probably responsible for blowing the great shofar, Elijah, at his lowest level of mastery, and other such masters, would be associated with Rachel. This personification would, then, become symbolic of the collective consciousness of all such Neshamah Masters, living and dead.

Such a notion may have been implied in the first allegorization of Rachel, that of Jeremiah:

> Thus saith the Lord; A voice was heard in Ramah, lamentation, and bitter weeping; Rachel weeping for her children refused to be comforted for her children, because they were not. Thus saith the Lord; Refrain thy voice from weeping, and thine eyes from tears: for thy work shall be rewarded, saith the Lord; and they shall come again from the land of the enemy. (Jer. 31:15–16)

In these beautiful verses, Rachel's weeping for her lost children of Israel is regarded as a form of redemptive work, her absorption of Israel's pain as the means of transforming their condition through transformation of her own consciousness. Jeremiah focuses on the Transformative Moment in which the Lord turns Rachel's perception from its uncontrolled grieving for the past to a healing recognition of new future possibility: "And there is hope in thine end, saith the Lord" (Jer. 31:17). It is precisely this absorption and transformation of old sources of pain into joy through the creation of new causal patterns for the future that is the primary work of Neshamah consciousness and of its masters.[13]

If Rachel can be considered as a collective embodiment of human enlightenment, then it may be possible to discern something of its collective work on the higher planes through observing the graphic form of her Yichud with Jacob in figure 6.8. As table 6.2 and figure 6.8 both show, Rachel's Sabbath Star covers or produces the Re and Fa inner hexagrams, while Jacob's does the same for the Do and Fi/Sol hexagrams. Rachel cannot be distinguished from the Nukvah in terms of inner hexagrams covered because both are equally responsible for the same Re and Fa hexagrams. Since Re represents the world of Beriah or Creation and Fa that which brings the power of division into the world of Yetzirah or Formation, both Rachel and the Nukvah seem to have the power to create new forms or patterns and to channel them into existence. What does distinguish them is what they may receive from their mates. And what Jacob brings to his Yichud with Rachel are the inner hexagrams of Do and Fi/Sol, the former signifying a power emanating from the highest world of Atzilut or Emanation, and the latter having something to do with animals. If these two are put together, they would seem to add up to "power animals," something quite familiar to students of the occult. In their benign form they are a main tool of shamanic healing.[14] As "familiars," they can become the destructive tool of witchcraft. They may also be involved in the Egyptian worship of the Neters, the animal-headed divine personifications of various pure functions. This is clearly also the level of much of the "practical" or magical branch of the Kabbalah as of other occult systems.

In associating the fourth vertical Sabbath Star with Tiferet and so with Jacob, we confront another coincidence that appears little less than uncanny; for as this fourth Sabbath Star can be associated with power and animals, so can Jacob, his most astonishing feat of magic being his power over animal reproduction through use of power-charged rods.[15] Despite the biblical celebration of Jacob's animal magic, the use, and more grievous worship, of power animals is probably the most penalized form of occult practice in normative Judaism. Israel's building of a golden calf in the desert is regarded as its greatest sin, and such graven images are specially prohibited in the Second Commandment. Yet power animals reemerge at the very fountainhead of the kabbalistic tradition, in the vision of Ezekiel that forms the foundation of the Merkabah tradition of "chariot" mysticism. For serving as supports of the chariot throne are the four Chayot, each of whom has four faces—the faces of a man, of a lion, of an ox, and of an eagle (Ezek. 1:10)—three of which are of animals.

The Sabbath Star Yichud of Jacob and Rachel was easy to determine since Jacob could only be assigned to the fourth Sabbath Star identified with the Tiferet of Ze'ir Anpin and, as the Malkhut of Malkhut, Rachel could only be assigned to the lowest level of the feminine horizontal axis, its first Sabbath Star. A similar Yichud of Ze'ir Anpin and the Nukvah is more difficult to determine since the diagram offers no clear guidelines as to which or how many of the six constituent elements of Ze'ir Anpin should participate in it. Coupling the second horizontal Sabbath Star of the Nukvah with the first vertical hexagram representing the Yesod of Ze'ir Anpin is impossible since its lack of Sabbath Star elaboration means that it does not enter the inner portion of the diagram. Coupling her single Sabbath Star with all six elements of Ze'ir Anpin seems aesthetically undesirable since it would overload the diagram with vertical elements. And this criterion would also militate against a coupling with the undeveloped third vertical Sabbath Star, signifying Ze'ir Anpin's Netzach, which her Sabbath Star parallels.

As earlier suggested, the most appropriate Yichud of Ze'ir Anpin with the Nukvah would seem to be that which couples her with his sixth and highest Sabbath Star, the creative form identified with Chesed. Not only are these two Sabbath Stars proportionally related as the two-thirds point on each of their axes, but they mingle most significantly in the diagram's core, the Mi hexagram he covers coming between her covered Re and Fa hexagrams. This diagram appears in figure 6.9. That the sixth vertical Sabbath Star should couple most attractively with the second horizontal Sabbath Star tells us only of the aesthetic fitness of this match, but since beauty is ideally a guide to inner harmony, there is clearly added meaning to be found in a beautiful meeting of forms. This particular meaning can be penetrated by remembering that Chesed was earlier identified as the twice-born form of Ze'ir Anpin. Since it is only with this form that Ze'ir Anpin reaches maturity, this is the only form capable of Yichud with the Nukvah. As no such Yichud could take place with limbs "thin like grasshopper's antennae," so no Sabbath Star coupling could occur with Ze'ir Anpin's prior immature Yesod, the first vertical hexagram that is incapable of extension into the center. It is only when he brings his creative power to her as an equal, both containing the whole Tree within one primary Sefirah, that they can engage in the Yichud that creates a Kingdom (Malkhut) of Mercy or Loving-Kindness (Chesed).

Turning now to the power source that the second-degree Neshamah Master might reach through participating in such a union, it seems to be none other than that with which the Mi hexagram has ever been identified, the angels. It will be remembered that in chapters 3 and 4 a distinction was made between the original Mi hexagram and its Sabbath Star development, the former identified with the angels, whose collective consciousness primarily defines the third world of Yetzirah, and the latter with the pre-incarnate Nefesh soul. Now, it is communication with angels that forms the heart of the "practical" or magical Kabbalah. In providing lists of the names and levels of the angelic hierarchy, the "practical" branch of medieval Kabbalah also had great influence on the development of Renaissance esoteric thought and practice. As Frances A. Yates has shown, it was through Pico Della Mirandola's introduction of kabbalistic techniques for the invocation of angels that Christian Kabbalah came to occupy its central role in the Renaissance of esoteric knowledge:

> Pico is basically a mystic, deeply attracted by the hope held out of communicating through Cabala with God and holy spirits. . . . This cosmic-theosophic system is the ladder through which mystical meditation leads the adept into profound intuitions as to the nature of God and the universe. The magical element in it derives from the power of the divine names; with them are associated names of angels. Pico does not actually list these with the Sephiroth, though he refers in other Cabalist Conclusions to invoking Raphael, Gabriel, Michael. The invoking, or conjuring, of angels forms an intrinsic part of the system, difficult to define, on the borderline of religious contemplation and magic.[16]

It was Kabbalah that made Renaissance magic kosher, or "white." And such communication with angels, always a mark of the highest favor and spiritual attainments, is shown to take place throughout the Bible, from Abraham, Hagar, and Jacob to Isaiah.

A final point about the Yichud of Ze'ir Anpin and the Nukvah is that it takes place entirely in the supernal worlds of Creation and Formation, the second and third cosmic worlds that together would seem to be the source of the genesis or creation of forms. In terms of their Sabbath Stars, one can distinguish between the Nukvah and the Shekhinah, shortly to be more fully considered, on the basis of the cosmic worlds they penetrate. Though both inhabit the sixth world, the Nukvah, as we have just seen, can also connect with the consciousness of the worlds of Beriah and Yetzirah, whereas the Shekhinah, through the Fi Sabbath Star she covers or produces, is connected only with the fourth world, the world that contains Earth. Thus it would seem that the Shekhinah is the indwelling spirit not only within man but also his planet, whereas the Nukvah is to be somehow located in the airy realms above it. But since the Nukvah has also been associated with Earth, it may be possible to locate her essence not within but around Earth, as its surrounding body of electromagnetic and other subtle energies. The Shekhinah may similarly be associated with the gravitational fields of Earth. Now, if the Nukvah may be said to represent the energy field surrounding Earth, while Ze'ir Anpin represents the larger energy field of the solar system and galaxy in which Earth is situated, then their Yichud may be understood to mingle and harmonize the information arising from Earth with the structure of probability defined by the synthesis of the surrounding cosmic information. Though the Yichud of Ze'ir Anpin and the Nukvah, by itself, cannot be considered creative of the fourth world, it can thus represent that fine tuning of human with cosmic energies that may be considered the work of Providence.

It is the Yichud of the Shekhinah with Arikh Anpin, shown in figure 6.10, that can be said to create and sustain the world of man. To this union the Shekhinah brings the force of life, the vitalizing force signified by the word *chai*, and the divine name of which it forms a part, which may be similar to what the Hindus call *prana* and the Taoists *chi*. To be thus vitalized by the divine Chai, Arikh Anpin brings the model of the ideal human form as the summit of earthly evolution. But this production of the Fi and Sol inner hexagrams through coupling of the third horizontal Sabbath Star with the ninth vertical Sabbath Star is not sufficient to ensure the survival of man. If his consciousness is not sufficiently developed to be able to exist in the sixth dimension of Neshamah consciousness, he will require a denser world in which to live, solid earth to ground him and air to breathe. For this the cooperation of all twelve constituents of the sixth world is required, six most particularly. Required to complete the four worlds of emanation are the sixth through ninth vertical Sabbath Stars and the second and third horizontal Sabbath Stars, as shown in figure 6.4. In the interaction of these six Sabbath Stars we have a graphic model involving three separate Yichudim, those of Arikh Anpin and the Shekhinah (the ninth vertical and third horizontal Sabbath Stars), of Ze'ir Anpin and the Nukvah (the sixth vertical and second horizontal Sabbath Stars), and of Abba and Imma (the eighth and seventh vertical Sabbath Stars). This latter requires some comment.

The Sabbath Star representation of this Yichud seems to be correlated with an earlier stage of their relationship, that purely mental arousal of Abba and Imma by which Ze'ir Anpin was first conceived. This mental Yichud is described in the following passage from the *Eitz Chayyim*:

> the Yesod of Arikh Anpin, after it was incorporated into the [upper] half of Tiferet, behold, it there gave out a vapor in the midst of Tiferet. And that very vapor divided into two parts. The one on the right side became the brain of Abba and the one on the left side became the brain of Imma. And due to the fact that they have brains, a desire for union develops in Abba and Imma. And this union is without the female waters; it only operates by virtue of kindness [*chesed*], as it says: "I have said the world is built on *chesed*."[17]

It seems appropriate to associate a Yichud "without the female waters" with an overlapping of Sabbath

Stars on the same axis. Thus the vertical axis may be said to represent various stages in the maturation of Ze'ir Anpin. The seventh and eighth Sabbath Stars represent the first mental Yichud of Abba and Imma responsible for Ze'ir Anpin's first birth, the lower six construction elements his immature development during the nursing phase, and the sixth Sabbath Star alone, which engages in Yichud with the second horizontal Sabbath Star of the emergent and mature Nukvah, the form of the twice-born Ze'ir Anpin. As the above passage shows, these first forms of Abba and Imma are themselves only aspects or products of Arikh Anpin's Yesod. As such, they may be considered the aspects of Arikh Anpin that explain his creative potency and can be included as essential constituents of any Yichud between Arikh Anpin and the Shekhinah. In the following discussions of this latter Yichud that of Abba and Imma shall always be understood to be so included.

The need to include the Sabbath Stars of Ze'ir Anpin and the Nukvah, with those of Abba and Imma, in the consummate cosmic Yichud takes us again to a central concept of the *Eitz Chayyim*:

> Just as the souls of the righteous raise the female waters for the purpose of uniting Ze'ir Anpin and the Nukvah, in the same way Ze'ir Anpin and the Nukvah can raise the female waters for the purpose of uniting Abba and Imma. . . . And so it is that the righteous in their death ascend and elevate the holy sparks with them for the purpose of [bringing] female waters to Rachel, which makes possible the union of Ze'ir Anpin and the Nukvah. And this is the same as [it is] with Ze'ir Anpin and the Nukvah when they go up to Abba and Imma. . . .[18]

As the Yichud of Arikh Anpin (containing that of Abba and Imma) with the Shekhinah requires the prior coupling of Ze'ir Anpin with the Nukvah, so that also requires the prior coupling of Jacob and Rachel. But if Jacob is to be so activated, then it would seem that all aspects of the earlier Ze'ir Anpin also need to be brought into play. All twelve creative components of the sixth-world diagram must, therefore, be represented before the Yichud of Arikh Anpin and the Shekhinah can take place to fecundate the good earth. But though each of these twelve components can be separately identified, those of the vertical axis can all be comprehended under the masculine character of Arikh Anpin as those of the horizontal axis can be comprehended under the feminine character of the Shekhinah.

Since the complete diagram of all twelve compo- nents of the sixth world has already been illus- trated in figures 6.6 and 6.7, they need not be repeated and can now be viewed in a new light as containing the composite cosmic Yichud. But graphic portrayals of the three separate levels of cos- mic coupling—which hopefully will satisfy the pruri- ent minded!—will now follow:

Figure 6.8. The Yichud of Jacob and Rachel

Figure 6.9. The Yichud of Ze'ir Anpin and the Nukvah

The cosmic Yichud through which the four worlds of emanation may be said to come into existence consists, then, of three separable levels, all of which are needed to achieve the fullest measure of such creative communion. By viewing these levels from the perspective of its cosmic rather than human participants, we can arrive at a deeper understanding of why the sexual metaphor, if it is a metaphor, has been so strongly emphasized in the most esoteric teachings of the Kabbalah, as also in Hinduism, particularly in Kashmir Shaivism, and Tantric Buddhism. But if we look again at the levels of power or potency that the divine male partners bring to their divine mates, we can also recognize a remarkable similarity between the ascending stages of cosmic Yichud, as just developed, and the highest form of human sexuality.

At the lowest stage, Jacob brings to Rachel what

INNER
TRADITIONS

DESTINY
B O O K S

Park Street
Press

BINDU
BOOKS

BEAR & CO.

BEAR CUB BOOKS

Inner Traditions • Bear & Company

P.O. Box 388

Rochester, VT 05767-0388

U.S.A.

PLEASE SEND US THIS CARD TO RECEIVE OUR LATEST CATALOG.

Book in which this card was found _____

❑ Check here if you would like to receive our catalog via e-mail.

Name_____ Company_____

Address_____ Phone_____

City_____ State_____ Zip_____ Country_____

E-mail address_____

Please check the following area(s) of interest to you:

❑ Health   ❑ Self-help   ❑ Science/Nature   ❑ Shamanism
❑ Ancient Mysteries ❑ New Age/Spirituality ❑ Ethnobotany   ❑ Martial Arts
❑ Spanish Language ❑ Sexuality/Tantra   ❑ Children   ❑ Teen

Please send a catalog to my friend:

Name_____ Company_____

Address_____ Phone_____

City_____ State_____ Zip_____ Country_____

Order at 1-800-246-8648 • Fax (802) 767-3726
E-mail: customerservice@InnerTraditions.com • Web site: www.InnerTraditions.com

Figure 6.10. The Yichud of Arik Anpin and the Shekhinah

we can now appreciate to be an "animal power," the power of sensation, when properly sensitized and heightened, to fill the consciousness with an exquisite sensual ecstasy. With the consummation of this "animal" or sensual passion, the Yichud rises to the level of Ze'ir Anpin and the Nukvah, an emotional passion filled and lifted by a more ethereal angelic power. But even this gripping passion of the purest

and most powerful feelings, the angelic passion of love, is transcended in the final ascension to the Yichud of Arikh Anpin with the Shekhinah. It was earlier shown that this Yichud brought a vitalizing power (the Fi hexagram) into communion with the power of self-aware cognition that may be identified with humanity (the Sol hexagram). This is consistent with what these partners represent: the

Shekhinah, the center of Neshamah consciousness, the knower; and Arikh Anpin, the Final Cause, the final explanatory plan of creation, the known. Thus the Yichud of the knower and the known creates a cognitive passion, the experience of vital knowledge that fills the consciousness with a sense of meaningfulness. And in this experience of meaningfulness, the consciousness becomes focused completely in the moment. The significance of past and future dissolves in the existential wonder of the supremely meaningful here and now, the self-justifying moment of divine consciousness.

It is this conferral of meaningfulness to experience that constitutes the highest level of that cosmic Yichud informing Neshamah consciousness. The three levels of this Yichud can be regarded as sequential or simultaneous, as the instantaneous rush of passion from the sensual through the emotional to the cognitive or as the consummate moment in which these three levels are sensed, felt, and known to constitute one supreme passion.[19] But whether this culmination is understood to be sequential or simultaneous, it is in such Yichud that the transformational work of Neshamah consciousness achieves its crowning reward, the state of meaningfulness, that moment in which the separate self comes into a communion of partnership with the cosmos, which is also the moment in which the purpose of its separate existence and its final direction become clear and fulfilled, meaningful.

Between this all-embracing cosmic Yichud and divine consciousness there is no essential difference, and this because the Shekhinah is both partner in the former and center of the latter. Not only can she be regarded as the "I" of Neshamah consciousness but as that which expresses the highest degree of Neshamah mastery. If the Shekhinah is to be identified with this highest level of Neshamah mastery, paralleling the assignment of Rachel and the Nukvah to its first and second degrees, then we should look again at the nature of the power that Arikh Anpin may be thought to bring to her vitalizing agency.

Unlike the first- and second-degree Neshamah Masters, whose knowledge and power seem to require the mediation of cosmic forces associated with the animal and the angelic, the third-degree or completely realized Neshamah Master would seem to have direct access to knowledge of the Final Cause, that knowledge conveyed through Arikh Anpin's Ti Sabbath Star, but in this knowledge he or she discovers the evolutionary significance of humanity, represented by the Sol hexagram created or covered by this Sabbath Star, the way in which the creation of humankind is ultimately responsible for the development of Neshamah power.

The pivotal role of humanity in the Tikkun is the central concept of the Lurianic Kabbalah, and is equally central to the whole of Jewish, and indeed Western, theology. It is the development of the Partzufim, the divine personalities, that is the goal and purpose that, from the beginning, has driven the process of emanation from its source in the divine unity. And here in this gross earth, it finally found a vessel capable of giving the one ultimate substance individual forms that, unlike those of the angels, could endure through change. But it is not until this matter has itself achieved self-awareness, until man has, after eons, finally emerged to give both eyes and ego to the formerly undifferentiated cosmic consciousness, that the true work of Tikkun can begin. The master work of transformative consciousness is the work of transforming its material vessel into a body of light, a body capable of eternal endurance because its continual moments of rebirth do not annihilate its informing consciousness but give it new vitality for purposive continuity. Without the emergence of human consciousness, with all its flaws of animal appetites, materialism, and egotism, the fields of higher consciousness could not have evolved. The Neshamah Master is one who understands and values the human heritage of his divine personality and seeks to preserve the bubblelike shell of his individuality that is all that separates the light within from the surrounding light.

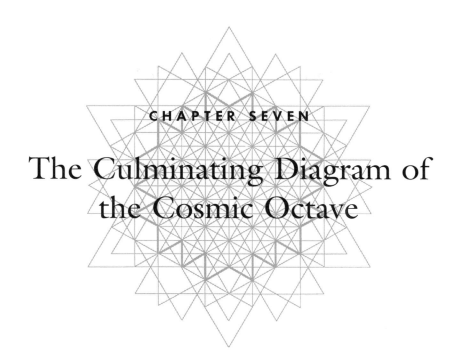

CHAPTER SEVEN
The Culminating Diagram of the Cosmic Octave

CONSTRUCTION ELEMENTS OF THE OCTAVE DIAGRAM

Two considerations urge us on to construction and study of the seventh expansion of the diagram. The first of these is the continuing association of the Jewish esoteric tradition with a Sabbatical cosmology. This begins, of course, in the first chapter of Genesis, whose seven-day creation account can be understood to provide the model for the seven-dimensional cosmos that can best integrate the Lurianic with the Zoharic Kabbalah, as argued in the opening chapter of this work.

But there is a second consideration that not only reinforces the desirability of such seventh-world construction but would give it a special form. This is that analogy of construction elements to tones of the diatonic scale, derived from the initial construction key of the Tree of Life Diagram, developed in chapter 2 and shortly to be rehearsed, which gives special significance to the midpoint of the seventh-world diagram, the significance attaching to the musical octave. If this analogy has any cogency, then the diagram must be expanded at least to that Sabbath Star identified with the upper Do tone, and any construction of the seventh-world diagram must recognize the necessity of discriminating the octave culmination at its midpoint from the complete form of this world of the diagram. Though the whole of the seventh world, which will be analyzed in chapter 13, may be identified with the seventh dimension, and that given its most traditional association of the Sabbath with holiness, its two halves would seem to signify sharply distinguished domains. It is the octave diagram that will be the subject of this chapter, and we shall see that the numbers emerging in this form of the diagram can best be analyzed in terms of the earliest traditions of Jewish mysticism. In this section and the next we shall see how these numbers can first be associated with the Merkabah (Chariot) mystical tradition, founded in Ezekiel's vision of the chariot; for it is the way this Merkabah tradition treats the seventh heaven of Aravot that will provide us with the best definition of this domain. Finally we shall examine the early stream of medieval Jewish mysticism associated with the works of the *Sefer ha-ʾIyyun* (Book of the Speculation) circle. This section will pay most particular attention to the Hebraic significance of the number 13, the number of construction elements of the octave portion of the diagram, and the number 26, the Gematria of the

Tetragrammaton, which reemerges as the sum of the diagram elements needed for construction of the complete octave diagram from its circumference inward.

If the Merkabah tradition can be associated with the octave diagram, than this first half of the seventh world can be identified with that experience of Devekut, communion, which this tradition conceptualizes in terms of the Throne vision it locates in its seventh heaven. The third section of this chapter, "The Working of the Chariot," will not only consider the significance of the two forms of diagram construction that yield the Tetragrammaton number 26, as well as defining the thirteen construction elements of the octave diagram; it will also treat the experience of Devekut, revealing the ultimate meaning and purpose of such spiritual practice and lay the groundwork for further treatments of this central truth of the Jewish esoteric tradition in parts 3 and 4.

Though the Merkabah tradition provides the primary basis for interpreting the octave diagram, there is one concept of the later Lurianic Kabbalah that can help in interpreting the relationship of the two halves of the seventh world, that of the Tzimtzum, the divine retraction that left a circular space for the creation. In the fourth section of this chapter, we shall see grounds for enclosing the octave diagram in just such a circle. Such a conceptual enclosure permits us to identify the construction elements of the cumulative octave diagram with the finite cosmos and the surrounding completion of the seventh-world diagram with the Infinite, with Ein Sof. The seventh world, then, becomes the holy dimension that joins the finite to the infinite in a final divine unification. And study of this culminating cosmic world of the Sabbath Star Diagram will provide the most profound revelation of the ultimate message of Jewish mysticism, the revelation conveyed through the wondrous form of the octave matrix to be illustrated in the fifth section of this chapter.

As a study primarily of the construction elements of the seventh-world diagram, particularly of its octave division, this chapter, like all the previous chapters on the construction elements, will center its analysis on the "outer" aspects of the seventh dimension that can be considered "external" to the individual human soul. Though the octave diagram may be correlated with the Chayah level of the soul and the full seventh-world diagram with its ultimate Yechidah level, this analysis, as that of the sixth world, will concentrate on its definable divine elements. But before such interpretation can begin, we shall have to understand how the half world of the octave diagram is to be constructed.

In chapter 6, when it finally became possible to define the rules of diagram construction, the construction elements of the first six worlds were seen to define a numerical formula through which the number of such seventh-world elements could be properly predicted, and this number proved to be eighteen. In addition to the total number of construction elements that could be determined on the basis of this formula, it was also possible to chart the number of construction elements on each axis of a world of the diagram. As can be seen again in table 6.1, a pattern is established by the third world in which parity between the number of construction elements on each of the axes in odd-numbered worlds alternates with a 3:1 proportion of such vertical to horizontal elements in even numbered worlds. On this basis, one can see that the seventh world will establish parity of number between the nine vertical eighteenths of the tonal division reaching to the upper Do and the nine horizontal ninths reaching to the upper and finally manifest Di, not illustrated until figure 13.2. Indeed, the main analyses of this chapter will be based on information derived from table 6.1, with actual construction of the octave diagram being deferred until its final section.

How such a half world can be constructed may be deduced from the given numbers for the seventh world. For the desired octave diagram should conclude with the Do Sabbath Star marking the halfway or nine-eighteenths point in this world. It would thus be constituted by the nine Sabbath Stars of the vertical axis plus those of the horizontal axis that comprise less than half its length, the first four extending to the four-ninths point. As was shown in terms of the similar ninths of the sixth-world diagram, the first two of these ninths can only form hexagrams. While the third ninth under the normal circumstances of future modeling would find all of its Sabbath Star elements covered by subsequent Sabbath Stars of its world, under these circumstances it will be able to retain its full Sabbath Star form, as will also be true for the Sabbath Star of the fourth ninth. In addition, some earlier elements, which would otherwise have been covered, now have to be retained in their original forms. But first we should consider a fact of major importance, that the sum of construction elements within the octave portion of the seventh-world diagram is exactly 13, the sum of 9 and 4.

Though 13 has traditionally been considered an unlucky number, probably because of its association with the lunar and feminine monthly cycles, 13 of which are contained in the solar year, in the Jewish religious tradition it has ever been held in high esteem, most particularly in association with the concept of the 13 attributes of divine mercy. Indeed, this association of divine mercy with the number 13 would seem to carry some remnant of an earlier cultural association between the feminine character of the number 13 and the concept of mercy.[1] However this may be, it is not only the number 13 that is understood to carry esoteric significance, but also the precise division of 18 into 13 and 5, the division that defines the numbers of construction elements in the first and second phases of the seventh-world diagram. For it is precisely this sequence of 13 and 5 that appears in the very opening paragraph of the most important of kabbalistic texts, the *Zohar*:

> Rabbi Hizkiyah opened, "*Like a rose among thorns, so is my beloved among the maidens* (Song of Songs 2:2). Who is a rose? Assembly of Israel . . . Just as a rose has thirteen petals, so Assembly of Israel has thirteen qualities of compassion surrounding her on every side. Similarly, from the moment אֱלֹהִים (*Elohim*), God is mentioned [in the first verse of Genesis], it generates thirteen words to surround Assembly of Israel and protect Her; then it is mentioned again. Why again? To produce five sturdy leaves surrounding the rose. These five are called Salvations; they are five gates. . . . From the second אֱלֹהִים (*Elohim*) till the third, five words appear."[2]

Most important is the significance here attached to the number of words between repetitions of Elohim in the first three verses of Genesis, a significance that may well represent a continuing tradition of esoteric interpretation going back to the very formulation of these words and enshrining the same revelation of the geometry of creation. As it is only with the seventh world of the Sabbath Star Diagram that the clue is given for unraveling the mysterious significance of the number sequence of 13 and 5, this fact would seem to provide proof that at least the author of the *Zohar* not only knew the geometry of the Sabbath Star Diagram but the particular importance of dividing its Sabbatical world at the point corresponding to the octave.

That the Zoharic reference belongs to a tradition that attached importance to the relationship of the numbers 13 and 5 can be seen in the earlier such reference in what is one of the first texts in the esoteric literature of medieval Judaism, the *Sefer ha-'Iyyun*, a work to be more fully discussed in the next section but that should be introduced in the present context:

> When the thought arose in His mind to bring objects into being, His glory became visible. Then were His Glory and Splendor revealed together.
>
> Knowledge of Him is made explicit through five means: restoration (*tiqqun*), utterance (*ma'amar*), combination (*serruf*), grouping (*mikhal*), and calculation (*heshbon*). Knowledge of these five matters is unique in the branches of the root of change and it increases in the course of the thirteen sorts of transformation (*temurah*).[3]

The number sequence of 5 and 13 appears in the context of the very first stage of emanation, when "His Glory" first became the visible expression of the thought of creation in the divine mind. As we shall see in the next section, the "Glory" was identified with the man on the Throne in the Jewish traditions of Merkabah and medieval German mysticism, and it seems appropriate to identify this Throne vision with the octave portion of the diagram composed of thirteen construction elements. If the reference to the precreative divine mind in the

Sefer ha-'Iyyun can be further related to the kabbalistic concept of Ein Sof and both to the number 5 in this text, the means to "Knowledge of Him," then we would seem to have an exact correspondence between the numbers of construction elements in the two phases of the seventh-world diagram and the cosmological identifications most appropriate to them, as specified in this passage of the *Sefer ha-'Iyyun*. And if the progression in this passage from the limitless divine mind to the particularized Glory can be correlated with its progression from the number 5 to the number 13, then we not only have a means of interpreting the meaning of the two phases of the seventh-world diagram but also the reverse, now using such diagram interpretation to illuminate the geometric basis of this obscure mystical text.

That the *Zohar* also understood the crowning significance of this set of numbers is indicated by its beginning with an explication of them, one based upon a new set of biblical proof texts but like it in its parallel understanding of the number 5, the Zoharic "five . . . called Salvation" and "five gates" being clearly related to the "five means" of "Knowledge of Him," the mystical techniques, of the *Sefer ha-'Iyyun*. Thus the authors of the *Sefer ha-'Iyyun* and the *Zohar* either had direct knowledge of the Sabbath Star Diagram at its seventh level of expansion or were the secondary receivers of a tradition whose numbers derived from such a source of interpreted sacred geometry, a tradition that may well go back to the Genesis text cited by the *Zohar*. But even more important to both texts than the relationship of these two numbers is the paramount importance of the number 13, the number with which the texts of the *Sefer ha-'Iyyun* circle are particularly associated and for which the *Zohar* gives a double derivation.

The double derivation of the number 13 from the repetitions of Elohim in Genesis and the thirteen attributes of mercy based on Exodus 34:6–7 shows that it is this number itself that is more important than anything it might particularly signify. Indeed, the priority of number to significance would also appear to be true of the rabbinical interpretation of Exodus 34:6–7, as J. H. Hertz seems to

suggest: "The Rabbis held that there are thirteen distinct attributes in these two verses; though there are differences as to their precise enumeration."[4] The search for biblical texts to support the significance of the number 13 attests to a prior understanding of this significance deriving from a more esoteric tradition, one that invariably can be found to be based on an understanding of sacred geometry. What study of the sacred geometry of the Sabbath Star Diagram would now seem to reveal is a correspondence between all references to 13 in the Jewish esoteric tradition and the octave form of the diagram, the first half of its seventh world. And this correspondence of the number 13 with the octave diagram will also prove to be true of its matrix constituents, studied in chapter 12. The musical analogue of the same tone at different pitches, the interval of the octave, can also be related to the number 13 since the octave is the thirteenth tone after the twelve semitones of the chromatic scale. This further suggests that the state represented by the harmonic chiming of the musical octave, as of its geometric analogue, should be that of Devekut, communion. What additionally may be symbolized by the octave diagram will become clearer as we turn to the reconstruction of this form of the diagram.

Beginning the reconstruction of the octave diagram with the simpler vertical axis, the half tone of Do adds nine further Sabbath Stars to the nine surviving hexagrams of the sixth world. Counting these seventh-world Sabbath Stars from the bottom up, they each cover one or more of the previous nine hexagrams forming the vertical axis of the first five worlds, as shown in table 7.1. The surviving nine hexagrams of the sixth world complete the count of all vertical elements up to the upper Do. Construction of the vertical axis from the octave conclusion backwards has thus required eighteen elements.

Such construction of the horizontal axis is more peculiar because its seventh-world constituents are cut off after the fourth Sabbath Star. We shall first have to consider its complete seventh-world form before we can appreciate the adjustments that have

Table 7.1. The Seven World Vertical Axis

SEVENTH WORLD NUMBER	ELEMENTS COVERED OF PRIOR WORLDS
9	Si
8	²∕₆ of Si and Do
7	¹∕₆ of Si and Ri
6	Sol
5	Fi/Sol and Fa/Fi
4	Fa/Fi and Fi/Sol
3	Mi
2	Ri and ¹∕₆ of Si
1	Do and ²∕₆ of Si

to be made to complete the Sabbath Star Diagram at the midpoint of the seventh world. Table 7.2 will provide this information for the nine constituents of the seventh world horizontal axis again giving first the number of the seventh-world element and then the names of the prior elements it may cover.

Table 7.2. The Seventh-World Horizontal Axis

SEVENTH WORLD NUMBER	ELEMENTS COVERED OF PRIOR WORLDS
9	La
8	Si/La + Re
7	Sol/Si + Fa
6	Fi
5	Fa + Sol/Si
4	Re + Si/La
3	La
2	
1	

Charting the seventh-world ninths on the basis of their sixth-world predecessors, we see that the lower two members must be simple hexagrams, which can cover no prior elements, that the third Sabbath Star covers the La hexagram, and the fourth and last available horizontal Sabbath Star of the seventh world covers the Re and Si/La hexagrams. This leaves the Fa, Fi, and Sol/Si hexagrams of prior worlds that still need to be covered or retained if the total diagram is to be constructed backward on the

basis of its final elements, normally those of its last two worlds. Now, whereas the normal method of construction by whole worlds would transform the Sabbath Stars of the sixth world into hexagrams, elimination of the upper five Sabbath Stars of the seventh world means that the upper two sixth-world constituents of the horizontal axis will have to retain their Sabbath Star status. For the Li Sabbath Star had previously covered the Fi hexagram as that representing two-sixths of the sixth-world horizontal axis had previously covered the Fa hexagram. Although the Sabbath Stars for both the first and second sixths of the sixth world had covered the Fa hexagram, that for the second sixth is more closely associated with it since, if figure 6.4 be turned on its side, the ascending triangle of the component hexagrams of this second sixth Sabbath Star can be seen to cover two sides of the Fa hexagram, while the upper side of the descending triangle would form the main constituents of the border Fa-sized hexagrams. Since only one of these Sabbath Stars need survive to produce the prior Fa hexagram, it is more economical and appropriate that it only be that for the second sixth. But one more element is necessary to complete the horizontal axis, the Sol/Si hexagram of the fifth world. Since there is no element in the Sabbath Star Diagram that can cover this hexagram prior to the fifth horizontal Sabbath Star of the seventh world, it must obviously retain its own definition into the seventh world, the only element of the fifth world to do so.

The complete horizontal axis of the Sabbath Star Diagram culminating just below the upper Do is composed, then, of the Sol/Si hexagram of the fifth world, the hexagram for the first sixth of the sixth world, the Sabbath Stars for the second and third sixths of the sixth world, the hexagrams for the first and second ninths of the seventh world, and the Sabbath Stars for the third and fourth ninths of the seventh world, eight elements in all. Now, when we add this sum to that of the vertical axis, nine hexagrams and nine Sabbath Stars, we again come to an astonishing sum, for 8 + 18 = 26! This sum is produced even more interestingly when we add hexagrams and Sabbath Stars separately, for adding the four hexagrams spanning three worlds in the horizontal axis to the nine hexagrams of the sixth-world vertical axis, and the four Sabbath Stars from two worlds on the horizontal axis to the nine Sabbath Stars of the seventh-world vertical axis, we find that $13 + 13 = 26$. In chapter 6 we saw that following the formula for outward construction of the diagram through the sixth world also involved exactly twenty-six construction elements. What significance we can draw from these two ways of reaching the Gematria number 26 of the Tetragrammaton, outward through the sixth world and inward from the octave, will be considered in the next section. But first we must consider that figure whose traditional association with the seventh heaven of Aravot will be of central importance in interpreting the thirteen construction elements of the octave diagram.

THE UNIFICATION OF THE NAME

Let us begin by simply referring to Gershom Scholem's summary of the Merkabah tradition: "The Merkabah mystics occupy themselves with all the details of . . . *aravot* (the uppermost of the seven firmaments). . . . But the main purpose of the ascent is the vision of the One Who sits on the Throne, 'a likeness as the appearance of a man upon it above' (Ezek. 1:26). This appearance of the Glory in the form of a supernal man is the content of the most recondite part of this mysticism, called *Shi'ur Komah.* . . ."[5] The realm of the upper Do may thus be identified with "the Glory in the form of supernal man." Though there are more specific identifications of the divine body in the *Shi'ur Komah* and related texts that might be used to define the construction elements of the octave diagram, it seems best to define them in terms of the later development of this concept. In the thirteenth-century Provençal circle linked to the *Sefer ha-'Iyyun*, the *Shi'ur Komah* concept begins to be connected with the name of Adam Kadmon. As Scholem further shows: "Terms like 'the limbs of the King' or 'the limbs of the *Shi'ur Komah*,' the mystical image of God, allude to the symbolism of the supernal man, also called *ha-adam ha-gadol.* . . . The term *ha-*

adam ha-kadmon ("primordial man") occurs for the first time in *Sod Yedi'at ha-Mezi'ut*, a treatise from the *Sefer ha-'Iyyun* circle."[6]

As we have seen, the *Sefer ha-'Iyyun* elevates the number 13 to a prime cosmological position. It represents the number of divine powers unified with the utter transcendence of God: "He, may He be blessed, is united in His powers, yet He remains completely beyond and transcendent to them, elevated endlessly. These are the thirteen powers with which He is united, and each has its own name."[7] Though the following thirteen names are all related to elements of the Throne vision of Ezekiel, in other texts of the *Sefer ha-'Iyyun* circle attempts are made to correlate its "thirteen powers," also associated with the thirteen attributes of divine mercy, with the emerging concept of the ten Sefirot, a correlation originally attributed to a responsa of Hai Gaon[8] and one that chapter 12 will show to be importantly related to the octave matrix. But the "thirteen powers" of the original *Sefer ha-'Iyyun* seem to be related primarily to the symbolism of the Glory, and this is the correlation of this number that will be the focus of the present analysis of the level of Devekut, of such envisioning of the enthroned supernal man as can be correlated with the culmination of the cosmic octave. This number also continues to be of special concern in the next stage of *Shi'ur Komah* symbolism. For the *Idra Rabba* section of the *Zohar* devotes chapters 11 to 23 to a detailed description of the thirteen attributes of mercy contained in the beard of the highest Partzuf, the "Ancient of the Ancients,"[9] a reference to Attika Kaddisha, a higher aspect of Arikh Anpin.

The final development of the *Shi'ur Komah* in relation to the figure of Adam Kadmon occurs in the Lurianic Kabbalah. It is in this metamorphosis that Adam Kadmon becomes the true cosmic anthropos, the figure who is more than the sum of the parts of creation, which he nonetheless contains and temporally surrounds as its beginning and end. Adam Kadmon may be considered the Image or Tzelem of the ultimate force transcending even such limitation, Ein Sof, the Limitless One. As such Adam Kadmon represents the first form of divine emanation and the source of the Shevirah, the Breaking of the Vessels by the light issuing from his various organs. But through the Rectification, Tikkun, of the broken Sefirot into Partzufim, Adam Kadmon himself is reconstituted in a form yet more perfect than that of his original emanation, the multiple forms of the Partzufim.

Scholem sums up the position of Adam Kadmon in the Lurianic system as follows:

> The first form that emanation assumes after the *zimzum* is that of *Adam Kadmon* ("primordial man"), which in the Lurianic system stands for a realm above the four worlds of *azilut, beri'ah, yetzirah,* and *asiyyah* with which pre-Lurianic Kabbalah began. . . . [T]he ten Sefirot first took shape in the *Adam Kadmon.* . . . The promotion of the *Adam Kadmon* to the rank of the first being to emerge after the *zimzum* accounts for the strong anthropomorphic coloring that accompanies all descriptions of the process of emanation in the Lurianic system. The *Adam Kadmon* serves as a kind of intermediary link between Ein-Sof, the light of whose substance continues to be active in him, and the hierarchy of worlds still to come. In comparison with the latter, indeed, the *Adam Kadmon* himself could well be, and sometimes was, called *Ein-Sof.* . . . The breaking of the vessels marks a dramatic turning-point in the relations between the *Adam Kadmon* and all that develops beneath him. All the subsequent processes of creation come about to restore this primal fault. . . . The five principal parzufim of *Arikh Anpin, Abba, Imma, Ze'eir Anpin,* and *Nukba de-Ze'eir* constitute the final figure of the *Adam Kadmon* as it evolves in the first stages of *tikkun*, which is quite different from the figure of *Adam Kadmon* that existed before the breaking of the vessels. . . . certain concluding actions have been reserved for man. These are the ultimate aim of creation, and the completion of *tikkun*, which is synonymous with the redemption, depends on man's performing them. . . . Should the latter perform his task properly, the "female waters" that enable the supernal couplings to take place will be aroused, and the work of the outward *tikkun* will be completed by the supernal lights that have remained concealed in the *parzuf* of *Attika.* . . .[10]

In Scholem's account, "in the first stages of *tikkun*," which we may identify with the sixth world, the reconstitution of the originally emanated Sefirot of Adam Kadmon into the five principle Partzufim is accomplished. The final work seems to involve the continued collaboration of man with aspects of Attika, here apparently used to name a subordinate aspect of Adam Kadmon, which had remained concealed during the reconstitution of the Partzufim. How man can continue to be involved in the Tikkun of the seventh world we shall see in the next section on the "Working of the Chariot," but first we should consider what the analysis thus far can tell us concerning the involvement of the seventh as well as sixth world in the supernal couplings, the analysis of diagram construction.

In the last section we saw that inward construction of the diagram from the octave requires just twenty-six construction elements; and in the previous chapter it was shown that outward construction of the diagram that follows the key of the Tree of Life Diagram, and so omits a possible Ri hexagram in original construction of the second world, is able to complete its sixth world in the same number of twenty-six stages. How these modes of construction can be related to the "Unification of the Name" we will better understand by reviewing the alternate modes of construction in both cases. In the latter case of outward construction, the six worlds of the diagram can be reproduced through inward construction in just eighteen stages. The number 18 is also of great importance in the Jewish tradition. It is associated first and foremost with the concept of "living" since it is the Gematria number of the word meaning this, *chai*, composed of the letters Chet (= 8) and Yod (= 10). The following summary should suggest something of its richness:

> The word *hai* or *chai* means "living" or "alive." . . . Its initial appearance in the Bible is . . . where Adam renamed his companion . . . because "she was the mother of all living" (*em kol-hai*). . . . When Abraham's exiled handmaiden Hagar and

her son Ishmael are rescued in the desert by the miraculous appearance of a well, she names the place *Be'er la-Hai Ro'i*, "Well of the Living One Who Sees Me." . . . The Word *hai* occurs as a motif throughout the Joseph story, seven times. . . . It seems no accident that for the kabbalists the divine emanation (the ninth, Yesod, "Foundation") that is symbolized by Joseph is called by the names *El-Hai* ("the Living God") and *Mekor Mayyim Hayyim* ("Well of Living Waters"). . . . All of these terms reverberate within the ninth divine emanation portrayed by the kabbalists: the point at which God in the upper worlds meets the feminine divine Presence (Shekhinah) dwelling in the lower world. Their point of union is understood sexually.[11]

Chai has a special association with the feminine, with Eve, Hagar, and the Shekhinah; so it is no wonder that this word is used as a neck-adorning amulet primarily by women. And though it is also significantly associated with Joseph, his sexual identity is defined largely by his lack of masculine performance with Potiphar's wife. For the Kabbalists, Joseph is associated with Yesod through the sexual restraint that defines him as a Tzaddik. Needless to say, both *chai* and the supernal females have been associated with "Waters." Most significant of all is the association of *chai* with the divine in the concept of the "Living God." It is this "Living God" that seems to be represented by the first six worlds of the Sabbath Star Diagram, whose outward construction requires twenty-six elements and whose inward construction requires eighteen. And since the number 18 has been shown to have a feminine connotation, the "Living God" responsible for the evolution of these six cosmic worlds from a central point can be identified with that indwelling Presence called the Shekhinah.

If we now consider the numbers for that part of the seventh-world diagram reaching to the upper Do, we can see that it has a primarily masculine character. The sexual association of the Name undergoes an inversion between the sixth and seventh worlds, both of which, as we have seen, feature the Gematria number 26 of the Tetragrammaton as a way of summing up their construction elements. As the Name for the sixth-world diagram was established by outward construction (26), so the Name for the octave portion of the seventh-world diagram is established by inward construction (26). Since the numbers for the octave diagram include and extend beyond the six prior cosmic worlds, it may be said to transcend them, as the Sabbath transcends and completes the six working days of the week. Thus the Name established by inward construction from the octave would signify the transcendent form of God and that established by outward construction from the center through the sixth world the divine immanence. But since the former is associated with the masculine and the latter with the feminine, this suggests a unification of these two forms of the Name, of Adam Kadmon with the Shekhinah, through a coupling of their two worlds, the seventh with the sixth.

Significantly the multiplication of 6 by 7 yields the product of 42, the number that appears at the conclusion of the initial discussion in the *Zohar* of the repetitions of Elohim at the beginning of Genesis: "Just as the image of the covenant is sown in forty-two couplings of that seed, so the engraved explicit name is sown in forty-two letters of the act of Creation."[12] The number 42 has clear associations here with coupling, creation, the covenant, and the Name. And as the Zoharic attention to the numbers 13 and 5 in this same opening paragraph were earlier seen to reflect a continuing tradition originated or mediated by the *Sefer ha-'Iyyun*, so can the number 42 be related to this tradition. In another text of the *Sefer ha-'Iyyun* circle, the number 42 appears in the context of the number characteristic of this circle, 13:

> "God, may He be blessed, is united in the branches of the principle of sound which emerge from the lips of man and extend and strengthen into thirteen sorts of transformations, especially restoration. . . . What is this restoration? . . . the 42 letters . . . Contained therein is the great matter of the unity of God . . . 'And one who . . . makes use of it in holiness . . . inherits two worlds—this world and the world to come.'"

And the Sage said: "I say that these letters—which are forty-two in all—are not one separate word nor one separate name; rather they are gathered letters which indicate the divinity of God, that He is One."[13]

The work of restoration, Tikkun, which would seem to have thirteen gradations, is here identified with a holy and salvific use of human sound with respect to "The forty-two-lettered Name,"[14] a Name understood to indicate "the unity of God." Now, this Name is contained in one of the oldest of prayers, "Ana Bekhoach," each of whose 42 words begins with a letter composing this Name. But what is even more significant is that this prayer features 7 lines of 6 words each. Thus the 42 letters of this Name are understood to signify the multiplication of 6 by 7; and if this Name contains "the great matter of the unity of God," then this "great matter" is none other than the central mystery of the Kabbalah, that *the divine unity is a unification*, Yichud, the unification of the divine immanence, which we have seen can be related to the number 6, with the divine transcendence, similarly related to the number 7, to be effected through prayer.[15] Many of the oldest prayers are composed of either 42 or 13 words, the same numbers that appear in the above passage in which God is understood to be "united in the branches of the principle of sound which emerge from the lips of man."

What we have already seen in this section is the identification that can be made between the number 13 and the octave portion of the seventh world of the Sabbath Star Diagram as well as the two forms of the Tetragrammaton number encoded in the construction of its first six worlds and octave culmination, which were recently related to the divine Yichud of these sixth and seventh worlds. Not only can these construction features help to explicate the mystical purpose of prayer as reflected in its traditional forms, but they can further illuminate the nature of the divine transcendence invoked in such prayer. For the transcendence figured by the octave diagram is not outside of creation but is its culmination. The seventh world can be defined as the dimension that joins the finite

transcendence of the octave, comparable to the numerical category defined by Georg Cantor as the "transfinite,"[16] with the truly infinite transcendence that surrounds the cosmic octave, the former identified with Adam Kadmon and the latter with Ein Sof. With this understanding of the octave diagram, we can now turn to the identification of its construction elements, always the most important stage in analyzing a world of the diagram. In so doing, we shall see how this stage can be related to the Merkabah tradition known as "The Working of the Chariot."

THE WORKING OF THE CHARIOT

In the last section we saw that the octave diagram could be associated with a central mystery of Merkabah mysticism, the Throne vision. We also saw that the prior six worlds and the octave culmination could be suggestively coupled in view of the different ways in which the count of their construction elements could be equated with the Gematria number 26 of the Tetragrammaton, outward through the first six worlds and inward from the octave. We also saw numerical reasons to identify such outward construction with the feminine immanent aspect of the divine and such inward construction with its masculine transcendent aspect. It is in such a sexualized coupling of the divine immanence and transcendence as can be correlated with elements of the sixth and seventh worlds of the Sabbath Star Diagram that this esoteric tradition symbolized the culminating experience of mystical communion, of Devekut. For though we saw that the indwelling power of the Shekhinah does not extend beyond the sixth world, we shall shortly come to understand how it is from this sixth world that the Shekhinah, and the choice spirits who are her highest manifestation, can experience Devekut with the transcendent Glory of Aravot, of "seventh heaven." This is the Ma'aseh Merkabah, the Working of the Chariot. Before this can be done, however, we must first arrive at a more precise identification of the thirteen construction elements of the octave diagram.

In the Merkabah descriptions of what was later to be called Adam Kadmon, we can find a basis for defining the thirteen elements of his seventh heaven. This seventh realm of consciousness must be composed of two main elements, one larger than the other: the supernal man and the Throne. Since Adam Kadmon, as the highest element in his world, should be identified with the Sabbath Star of the upper Do, it seems logical to associate the body of Adam Kadmon with the nine Sabbath Stars of the vertical column. Once this is done, we can follow the kabbalistic tradition of picturing the Sefirot as forming the body of Adam Kadmon. On this basis, we can repeat the Sefirotic identifications of the nine elements of the sixth-world vertical axis for these nine elements of the seventh world. In both cases, the tenth Sefirah of Malkhut would be represented by the sixth-world horizontal axis, most vitally by its surviving middle and upper Sabbath Stars still representing the Nukvah and the Shekhinah, their survival required to cover prior diagram elements that cannot be so covered because of the culmination of the octave diagram at less than half of the seventh world horizontal axis, as earlier explained. It is only by such identifications that the Yichud of Adam Kadmon and the Shekhinah can become a graphic reality. The remaining component of the highest Merkabah heaven is the Throne, and it seems most fitting to identify the four elements of the seventh-world horizontal axis appearing in this portion of the diagram with this Throne. It is the description of this Throne "chariot" (Merkabah) in the vision of Ezekiel that forms the basis of Merkabah mysticism, and it is composed of exactly four parts: the Ofanim or Wheels; the Chayot or Living Creatures; the Firmament; and the Throne. But before proceeding to further analysis of the four horizontal construction elements on this basis, we should return to the interrupted consideration of divine coupling that required the identifications just given of the nine vertical elements of the octave diagram.

We earlier saw, in the discussion of table 7.2, that construction of the half world of the octave diagram requires the retention of the second and third Sabbath Stars of the sixth-world horizontal axis, those identified with the Nukvah and the

Shekhinah, respectively. And once the nine vertical elements of the octave diagram are identified, from top to bottom, with the Sefirot from Keter to Yesod in the body of Adam Kadmon, we can see why it is essential that elements earlier identified with the Sefirah Malkhut retain the main features of their Sabbath Star forms into the seventh world. This is particularly important for that identified with the Shekhinah, her Li Sabbath Star losing only the top bar of the descending triangles of its component hexagrams, which may be said to make her more open to the heavenly influx. For her Yichud with Arikh Anpin in the sixth world was but a prelude to that with Adam Kadmon in the seventh. Looking at these Yichudim from the possible perspective of future causality, the former might be considered the source of man's creation and the latter the source of the Messiah, the former the source of man's mortal condition as the latter is of his immortal life. In the first case, the form of man, the Sol hexagram, was contributed by the Ti Sabbath Star, identified with Arikh Anpin, while its vitality, the Fi hexagram, was contributed by the Li Sabbath Star, identified with the Shekhinah. In the second case, the form of the Messiah, the Si hexagram, is contributed by the upper Do Sabbath Star, identified with Adam Kadmon, while its vitality, again the Fi hexagram, is still a product of the Shekhinah. Though the divine "Father" of the Messiah, of Ruach man, would thus come from a higher dimension than that of Nefesh man, their brotherhood is established by the divine "Mother" they share, the living spirit of the Shekhinah. Incorporating the vital *chai* force of the Fi hexagram, she is that which brings life into earthly flower and also informs cosmic consciousness.

Of the first and second sixth-world horizontal Sabbath Stars, those identified with Rachel and the Nukvah, with the sensual and emotional levels of divine unification, only that of the Nukvah also largely survives into the seventh world, her Sabbath Star retaining the same elements as that of the Shekhinah. This suggests that she, too, has a creative role to play in seventh heaven. If the seventh world Yichudim may be patterned on those of the sixth world, defined in the last section of chapter 6, then the proper mate for the Nukvah would be a personification of the sixth vertical Sabbath Star. At the point two-thirds above Arikh Anpin but not yet at the level of Adam Kadmon, it would seem appropriate to identify this symbolically creative Sabbath Star with Attika Kaddisha, the Holy Ancient One. As figure 7.1 shows that Attika would bring to his Yichud with the Nukvah the same Sol hexagram earlier associated with Arikh Anpin, this Yichud would seem to have something to do with man, though not his full regeneration since, unlike the Ti and upper Do Sabbath Stars associated with the birth and regeneration of man, the intermediate Sabbath Star identified with Attika does not go through the center of the diagram to supply man with the holy spark of creation. As it is the Fa hexagram that the Nukvah contributes, and this was earlier associated with evil, what Attika Kaddisha would seem to contribute to their generative union is rather the sanctification of what had formerly to be rejected as evil. At a later point in this section, we shall see what further role this union may be said to play with regard to the sanctification of the human community. But we must now complete this first discussion of the significance of the surviving sixth-world Sabbath Stars.

The restriction of the seventh-world couplings to those of the Nukvah and the Shekhinah would seem to eliminate from their composite Yichud the sensuous component earlier identified with Rachel, an elimination that seems to signify its total transcendence of the physical world. On the level of Devekut, Yichud is experienced only as the fulfillment of love and understanding. At this transcendent level of consciousness only the divine mind and heart are involved, a characteristic that relates this seventh heaven back to the first world of Atzilut to show a concord between the upper and lower Do of the octave. For as indicated in chapter 6 and illustrated by figure 2.9, when the Tree of Life Diagram is interfaced with the hexagram-worlds of the Sabbath Star Diagram, it can be seen that the elements of the Tree contributed by the first Do hexagram, those identified with Atzilut, are precisely the upper six Sefirot associated with the divine mind and heart, a correlation that will be remarkably substantiated in the matrix modeling of chapter 10. As we also saw in chapter 6, this

geometric conclusion seems to be supported by the Lurianic analysis of Arikh Anpin as first composed of only his upper six Sefirot, the lowest four being contained in his lower heart triad: Netzach in Chesed, Hod in Gevurah, Yesod in Tiferet, and Malkhut in all three. Though the ultimate Yichud of Adam Kadmon and the Shekhinah may thus be said to lack a sensuous dimension, Lurianic analysis suggests that the sensuous has been lifted into the heart dimension, and it is certainly treated most erotically in the literature.

But to understand more fully the inner, mystical aspect of such cosmic coupling, we must now turn our consideration to the Throne vision of Ezekiel and the four horizontal construction elements of the octave diagram with which its four levels were earlier identified. For this purpose the translation of Aryeh Kaplan will here be used:

> I saw, and behold a stormy wind (*ruach*) come from the north, a great cloud and flashing fire, and a Glow (*nogah*) round about, and from its midst a vision of the Speaking Silence (*Chashmal*), in the midst of the fire.
>
> And from its midst was the form of four Chayot (Living Creatures)—this was their form—they had a human form. . . . and they shined like a vision of polished copper. . . . The form of the Chayot had the appearance of burning coals of fire. . . .
>
> The Chayot ran and returned, like a vision of lightning. Then I gazed at the Chayot, and behold there was a single Ophan (Wheel) on the earth near the Chayot. . . .
>
> The appearance of the Ophanim and their actions was like a vision of Topaz. All four had a single form, and their appearance and actions were as if there was an Ophan within an Ophan ["a wheel in the middle of a wheel" in KJV]. . . .
>
> When the Chayot moved, the Ophanim went near them. . . . And when they were lifted from the earth, the Ophanim were lifted beside them, for the *ruach*-spirit of the Chayah were in the Ophanim.
>
> The form above the heads of the Chayah was that of a firmament, looking like a fearsome ice

["terrible crystal" in KJV], spread out above their heads. . . .

Then I heard the sound of their wings, like the sound of many waters, like the voice of the Almighty (*Shaddai*) when they went. The sound of their tumult was like the sound of an armed camp—when they stood still, they let down their wings. And there was a sound from the firmament which was above their heads. . . .

Above the firmament that was over their heads, like a vision of a sapphire, was the form of a Throne, and over the form of the Throne, there was a form like a vision of a Man, on it from above.

And I saw a vision of the Speaking Silence (*Chashmal*) like a vision of fire, as a house for it round about, from the vision of His thighs and above. And from the vision of His thighs and below, I saw a vision like fire, with a Glow (*nogah*) around it. . . . This was the vision of God's Glory. I saw it, and I fell on my face. Then I heard a voice speak. (Ezek. 1:4–28)[17]

Although Kaplan's interpretation of the first of the above verses follows quoted sources from Abarbanel and Vital to the effect that the wind, cloud, and fire there referred to signify impediments to prophetic vision, they would seem, rather, to contain the final vision in a more elemental form. The wind or Ruach is later associated with the lowest level of the Ofanim ("for the *ruach*-spirit of the Chayah was in the Ophanim"), the "flashing fire" with the Chayot (compared to burning coals and lightning), the Nogah with the body of the Glory from the thighs down (which would be equivalent to the level of the Throne), and the Chashmal with the part of the Glory that is above the Throne ("on it from above"). This leaves only one element out of both lists, the "great cloud" of the former and the Firmament of the latter, which would seem to be identifiable. Why the order of the cloud and fire should have changed places is not clear though they can certainly be related since the Chayot were compared to lightning, and lightning is discharged from clouds. In later kabbalistic interpretations, these two levels were further collapsed in the attempt to fit the five levels of Ezekiel's

vision into the cosmology of four worlds: Adam Kadmon identified with Atzilut, the Throne with Beriah, the Firmament and Chayot with Yetzirah, and the Ofanim with Asiyah. But the Merkabah mystics, who developed the mystical implications of Ezekiel's vision most fully, were not concerned with a pattern of four worlds, rather of seven heavens, and with this vision the Sabbath Star Diagram for the cumulative octave portion of the seventh world is most consistent and can be most illuminating.

Looking at the four-level Throne first in terms of its elemental equivalents, the topaz-colored Wheels are touching the earth in the fifth world of Ruach (wind): the copper-colored Chayot are located in the sixth, Neshamah world of fire; at the first third of the seventh world is the great cloud or mist (Arafel) of the crystalline Firmament, which prevents most further vision; and above it are the Nogah of the Throne level on the horizontal axis and the Chashmal on the still higher culmination of the vertical axis, both associated with the sapphire color of the highest consciousness.

The Arafel is first met on Mount Sinai, when the Lord surrounds Himself in it to protect the people while speaking to Moses before them: "And the Lord said unto Moses, Lo, I come unto thee in a thick cloud, that the people may hear when I speak with thee, and believe thee for ever" (Exod. 19:9). But the properly prepared elders are able to see beyond this to the sapphire ground of divine being: "And they saw the God of Israel: and there was under his feet as it were a paved work of a sapphire stone" (Exod. 24:10). The Arafel is a "terrible," a dark, "crystal," through which the Nogah shines to illuminate the worthy few, the Nogah generally signifying the light shining out of darkness. Above the vision of the light radiating from the darkness, glowing as through a mist, and far above the tumultuous sounds of the Chayot and more rarefied sounds in the Firmament, is the final auditory realm of the Chashmal, the "Speaking Silence," the highest source of prophecy. Before considering this height of spiritual mastery, there are other implications to be noted of the identification of the thirteen elements of the seventh world with Ezekiel's vision and the Merkabah tradition.

Perhaps most important, and associated with the question of mastery, is the fact that the Nukvah, and that level of mastery associated with her, cannot penetrate above the level of the Arafel in her Yichud with Attika; for the Firmament, identified with the third ninth of the horizontal Sabbath Stars, and Attika, identified with the sixth eighteenth of the vertical Sabbath Stars, are both on the same first third level. Further comparisons between the horizontal and vertical elements are also interesting. Thus the Ofanim, the wheels within wheels of mechanical functioning, may be associated with the Sefirot of Yesod and Hod that reach to its first ninth level. Similarly the Chayot, informed by the Chai, the vital principle, may be compared to the Sefirot of Netzach and Tiferet, reaching to its second ninth level. The first third level of the Firmament next takes us up through the straits of Gevurah to Chesed, whose personification in Attika becomes the mate of the Nukvah. And beneath, level, and above the fourth ninth level of the Throne are the three supernal Sefirot that represent the highest mental faculties of Adam Kadmon. The Throne level of the Nogah, the light shining out of darkness, can be identified with both Binah and Chokhmah, the left and right hemispheres of the brain at their highest archetypal level, though the left might be more closely associated with the Arafel, the dark cloud, and the right with the light glowing through it. The final level of Keter, of Adam Kadmon and the Do Sabbath Star, could then be identified with the Chashmal, the voice speaking out of the silence.

Another point to be noted is the association of the third horizontal Sabbath Star of the Firmament with the La hexagram of the millennium that it covers, suggesting that even Messianic consciousness will still be too clouded to perceive the true beatific vision. Such limitation also attaches to the first two degrees of Neshamah mastery. It is most severe in the case of the first degree, since this has no potential for entering Aravot, the seventh heaven. Earlier identified with the sensual phase of mystical power, this level would seem to be self-limiting to further growth. Whether associated with the hallucinogenic drugs prized by many sacred traditions and many more less sacred "trippers" or with magical per-

formances, the power thus gained or used creates an addictive attachment to the physical world that blocks any higher spiritual attainments. The more power is expended on sensational miracles, the less is left for the true work of the spirit. But if a genuine Neshamah level has been reached through the combination of such sensual means with truly effective spiritual discipline, the continuing addiction to this level will not prove self-destructive, as in perversions on the Ruach level, but simply self-limiting. As chapter 11 will further show, no one has died from too much nirvana.

On the second level of Neshamah mastery, the problem is less severe. Though the level of the Nukvah is barred the vision of the Throne, her Yichud with Attika is essential to the good of the world. We have seen that the seventh heaven is importantly related to "the thirteen attributes of divine mercy." So if the identification that has been made between the sixth vertical Sabbath Star of the seventh world and both the Sefirah of Chesed in the body of Adam Kadmon and its separate reification as Attika is sound, then it is through this Yichud of Attika with the Nukvah, that the thirteen attributes of the seventh heaven become filtered down to the worlds below, a process that requires their passage through the personification of divine mercy (Chesed). Unlike the Yichud of the Shekhinah with Adam Kadmon, which can be taken to mark an ascending spiritual movement, that of the Nukvah with Attika may be considered to mark a descending flow of divine mercy and grace, for reasons shortly to be developed.

The association of Chesed with Yichud plays a curious role in Lurianic cosmology that may again be pertinent. As we saw in chapter 6, in considering the purely mental first conception of Ze'ir Anpin by Abba and Imma,[18] there seems to be a virtual identification of Yesod with Chesed as the definitive characteristic of this higher mode of nonsensual sexuality, of that heart union in which the highest understanding is rooted.

It is the descent of the thirteen attributes of divine mercy through Attika to the Nukvah that may be said to enable such second-degree Neshamah Masters to move mountains through the power of spiritual love. In the final stages of the Tikkun, it is most important for this power to grow, since it is only this that can counter the disruptive force contained in the surviving Sol/Si hexagram, representative of a surviving belligerence within the Sons of Light toward the vanquished Sons of Darkness of their now past apocalyptic war, a belligerence that reaches all the way up to the Chayot, the sound of whose "tumult was like the sound of an armed camp." We shall return to the question of what survival of this Sol/Si hexagram may further imply at the close of this section, but first we must consider the highest degree of Neshamah Master, the only one to achieve Devekut.

There would seem to be two ways of viewing this higher level of communion, from the point of view of the Shekhinah, as an independent entity performing certain vital cosmic functions, and as a repository of the souls of the highest masters. The former view would be one that related her to the body of Adam Kadmon, in other terms that related her sixth world horizontal Sabbath Star with the whole of the seventh world vertical axis and particularly its crown. The second would be one that related the soul of the Neshamah Master, perched on the third horizontal Sabbath Star of the sixth world, with the four elements of the seventh-world horizontal axis directly above him or her, that is with the four levels of the Throne vision,[19] the "Ma'aseh Merkabah" or "Working of the Chariot."

There is a kabbalistic tradition that at the highest level of mystical ascent the face one sees on the Throne will be one's own. Thus Abraham Abulafia, the great Kabbalah master of meditation, writes: "When an individual completely enters the mystery of prophecy, he suddenly sees his own image standing before him." And he proceeds to support this claim by quoting from a work of Moshe of Narbonne that refers to this earlier tradition: "When the sages teach that the prophets 'liken a form to its Creator,' they mean that they liken the form which is in the prophet's own soul . . . to God. It is thus written, 'Over the form of the Throne there was a form like an image of a Man' (Ezek. 1:26). These forms and images exist in the soul of the prophet. . . ."[20]

This ultimate step of mystical ascent is reflected in the traditions surrounding the central figure of the *Shi'ur Komah*, Metatron, the angelic Prince of the Presence who is called "Youth" (Na'ar). The final development of the Metatron concept is in the work now known as 3 Enoch, which brings the parallel traditions related to Enoch and Metatron into a higher synthesis that clarifies the deepest implications of Merkabah mysticism and of its source in Ezekiel's Throne vision:

[IV] (1) I asked Metatron and said to him: "Why art thou called by the name of thy Creator, by seventy names? Thou art greater than all the princes, higher than all the angels . . . why do they call thee 'Youth' in the high heavens?"

(2) He answered and said to me: "Because I am Enoch, the son of Jared. . . .

[IX] (2) And I was raised and enlarged to the size of the length and width of the world. . . .

[X] (1) All these things the Holy One, blessed be He, made for me: He made me a Throne, similar to the Throne of Glory. . . .

[XII] (5) And He called me THE LESSER YHVH in the presence of all His heavenly household; as it is written (Ex. XXIII. 21): 'For my name is in him.'"[21]

Though subservient to the Holy One, blessed be He, Metatron is yet called "THE LESSER YHVH" and is seated upon a Throne, even though only "similar to the Throne of Glory," where he rules as prince over all the other heavenly hosts. Most significantly, this intermediary between God and the creation, whose size is that of the whole created world, is not simply a supernatural being but the transfigured form of the biblical figure Enoch. Seated on this heavenly Throne, then, is the formerly human body that has become a "lesser" form of the deity.

Scholem summarizes the dual forms of Metatron as follows:

It is already observed in *Shi'ur Komah* that the name Metatron has two forms, "written with six letters and with seven letters.". . . The kabbalists regarded the different forms as signifying two prototypes for Metatron. . . . They identified the seven-lettered Metatron with the Supreme emanation from the *Shekhinah*, dwelling since then in the heavenly world, while the six-lettered Metatron was Enoch, who ascended later to heaven and possesses only some of the splendor and power of the primordial Metatron.[22]

It again seems to be more than a coincidence that a figure having forms associated with the numbers six and seven, the figure of Enoch/Metatron, should also be identified with the Shekhinah, who, as we have seen, is associated with an element of the Sabbath Star Diagram that plays a role in both the sixth and seventh of its worlds.

Enoch is one of the two biblical figures, with Elijah, who become Immortals, in the sense that they are understood to have been translated directly to heaven without having undergone mortality: "And Enoch walked with God: and he was not; for God took him" (Gen. 5:21). The case of Elijah is even more closely bound to the Merkabah: "And it came to pass, when the Lord would take up Elijah into heaven by a whirlwind . . . that, behold there appeared a chariot of fire, and horses of fire . . . and Elijah went up by a whirlwind into heaven" (2 Kings 2:1, 11). Nonetheless, the immortal Elijah came to figure more and more in popular legend and ritual while the immortal Enoch became the central figure in the esoteric tradition. In addition, the *Shi'ur Komah* names Moses as the only human to have seen Metatron in life; so it would appear likely that he also reached the eminent position of Enoch in the World to Come, as Elijah's "chariot of fire" would seem to indicate for him as well. To this special group of three, others whose claim to such mystical vision has been accepted by the tradition are certainly Isaiah—"I saw also the Lord sitting upon a throne" (Isa. 6:1)—Ezekiel, and Rabbi Akiba. These six figures can be considered representative of the highest level of Neshamah Master, and so, of the six-lettered Metatron. From the position of the Shekhinah in the sixth world, they have Devekut with the seven-lettered Metatron seated upon the Throne of the seventh world. Both forms of Metatron are functions of the inwardness, the mys-

tical essence, of the Shekhinah; the six-lettered form can be associated with the outward act of her Yichud with Arikh Anpin in the sixth world and the seven-lettered form with her similar Yichud with Adam Kadmon in the seventh. This brings us to another important aspect of Lurianic cosmology, as analyzed by Scholem:

> Of crucial importance here is the Lurianic distinction between the inward and outward aspects of the supernal lights and the worlds of creation themselves. . . . In the Lurianic system the hierarchical rank of the inward is always lower than that of the outward, but precisely because of this it is within reach of the truly spiritual, inward individual, to some extent at least. Should the latter perform his task properly, the "female waters" that enable the supernal couplings to take place will be aroused, and the work of the outward *tikkun* will be completed. . . .[23]

It is, then, through the Shekhinah's inward contemplation of the Throne, only possible through the realized masters who inform her consciousness with personal identity, that her outward Yichudim can take place to carry the cosmos through the last transformative phases of its evolution. And in this highest vision of the master, consciousness achieves the unification of its lower, humanly derived self, and a higher, divine self, of those aspects characterized as Enoch and Metatron.

Just before the first talmudic reference to Metatron is the famous story of Rabbi Akiba's mystical ascent to the upper Paradise, the Pardes, in the company of three companions, an experience in which only "R. Akiba went up unhurt, and went down unhurt."[24] Judaism, like all great religious traditions, has had both an inward and an outward aspect. And the most secret knowledge communicated in the theophanies of the mystically adept has always been the same. It is the knowledge given on high to Elijah: "And, behold, the Lord passed by, and a great and strong wind rent the mountains . . . but the Lord was not in the wind: and after the wind an earthquake; but the Lord was not in the earthquake: And after the earthquake a fire; but the Lord was not in the fire: and after the fire a still small voice" (1 Kings 19:11–13). One point on which most Jewish and Christian commentators are agreed is that the "still small voice" in which Elijah recognized the godhead was within himself. What distinguishes Elijah and Rabbi Akiba is that their recognition did not lead them into dualism but contained a deeper understanding of the underlying unity between the "inward and outward aspects of the supernal lights," to use Lurianic terminology. From the biblical prophets, through the Merkabah mystics, to the Lurianic Kabbalists, the secret message has always been that man contains within himself the power to become divine and that, in so achieving his own highest development, he is fulfilling the purpose not only of his own creation but of the whole cosmic process, that by which the One, in manifesting Himself in the many, willed His reconstitution as the Partzufim, the multiple personalities of the divine. Thus the master, identified with the Shekhinah, the indwelling divine spirit, which, in turn, is identified with Metatron, can see himself split between his six-lettered human form and seven-lettered form on the Throne and utter praise to the higher power that led him to this vision of the same divinity within and without.

But Rabbi Akiba also came back from this crowning vision. And this is what most distinguishes Jewish from some forms of monastic mysticism, both Eastern and Western. It sees the ascent and descent as two equally important aspects of the individual mystical path, the path of the Tzaddikim that must begin and end in community. The need for such dual movements of the mystical journey can also be correlated with a particular feature of the octave phase of the Sabbath Star Diagram, the fact that the sixth-world Sabbath Stars of both the Shekhinah and the Nukvah have been retained in the octave diagram. For if the Yichud of the Shekhinah can be identified with the upward phase and that of the Nukvah with its downward phase, then this might explain the reason that both are contained in the structure of ultimate vision represented by the octave diagram.

Whether our concern be with the outward Yichud of the Shekhinah with the Keter of Adam Kadmon (the highest element of the vertical axis) or with her inward contemplation, through the flights of her master spirits, of the Throne vision (the highest element of the horizontal axis), this phase of the circular path marks a personal communion with the highest source of knowledge. In the Yichud of the Nukvah with Attika, however, the participating soul is filled with the influx of Chesed, such lovingkindness for those below as can draw the soul back into a willing descent to the world below and the work its new illumination has charted for it there. The returning prophet bears the new form through which Nefesh man can be recreated in the divine image, the image he saw on the Throne and to which he hopes to uplift the generality of men, that they, too, might experience such Devekut in the World to Come.

We come now to the final problem of the Aravot diagram suggested by table 7.2, the fact that its octave bisecting of the seventh world not only requires the retention of the fully creative forms of the Shekhinah and the Nukvah, but also of that stage of the fifth-world representative of apocalyptic war. The survival of the Sol/Si hexagram in the final form it had in the fifth world can be interpreted in various ways. But most important, and defining the nature of the spiritual warfare it represents, is the fact that it was the first element to cover the Fa hexagram, the construction element that earlier analyses variously identified with something like the Fall. This covering of the Fa hexagram by the Sol/Si Sabbath Star was said to mark the first-third stage of the fifth-world Tikkun. But this stage in the lifting of human consciousness was also marked by a militant wariness, by a fierce rejection of all that was deemed less holy than its spiritual warriors. Though the active phase of this belligerence was passed with the coming of the millennium, in which the spirit could now embrace all of creation as holy, this covering of the Sol/Si Sabbath Star by the La Sabbath Star does not seem to have completely effaced, if not the power, then the scars of war. And as the Fa hexagram survived throughout the fourth world and the first third of the fifth, so now it is the Sol/Si hexagram that has not only survived into the sixth world but throughout the first half of the seventh. And, "like the sound of an armed camp," it seems to be carrying something of the disruptive power of the Fa hexagram into the very heart of Aravot.

What, then, is the meaning of this remaining impurity at this transcendent level of consciousness? The first possible answer is that it is precisely from this grain of sand, this remaining trace of the spiritual descent into matter, that the pearl of perfected individual consciousness can be formed. Though spun into a garment of silkiest ether, it is this material remnant that makes possible the Throne vision of the higher consciousness modeled by the octave diagram. The second answer, and it complements rather than contradicts the first, is that it is precisely the irritation of this impurity, with the consequent need to be purged of it, that pushes transcendent consciousness into the second octave. For the only way that seventh heaven can be purged of this impurity is to make the irrevocable move to the very next stage of the seventh world, the fifth horizontal Sabbath Star that, in finally covering the Sol/Si hexagram, converts the upper Do from the conclusion of one octave to the start of another.

This move is irrevocable because movement into the second octave severs the ties of consciousness with life. That same fifth Sabbath Star covering the Sol/Si hexagram also covers the Fa hexagram and so renders the survival of the second of the sixth-world horizontal Sabbath Stars superfluous, that representing the Nukvah and, through her, the returning path of the Neshamah Masters to the world of the living. Although the sixth world can be generally identified with the World to Come, its level is nonetheless reachable by the highest living Tzaddikim. With the movement to the fifth horizontal Sabbath Star of the seventh world, those souls on the highest sixth-world level of the Shekhinah are now truly in the World to Come, from which there is no returning. But these souls still retain their individual identities within the divine consciousness of the Shekhinah. To understand from yet another perspective the essential difference between the octave portion of the Sabbath Star Diagram and any further extension of its con-

struction, the reason that it is only this octave form of the diagram that can be identified with the creation, we shall finally have to turn to the most important analysis of its construction elements to be offered in this chapter.

THE OCTAVE DIAGRAM AND THE TZIMTZUM

The Lurianic concept of the Tzimtzum, the divine contraction that provided the space for a finite cosmos, is clearly described in the following description from the *Eitz Chayyim*:

> Know that before the emanated things were emanated and the created things were created, the pure, divine light filled all existence. . . . Then Eyn Sof contracted Himself into a central point with His light in the middle. He contracted this light and then removed Himself to the sides encircling the point at the center. . . . This contraction, equidistant all around the point at the center, formed a void in such a way that the vacuum was spherical on all sides in equal measure. . . . Then, one stright line descended from the light of Eyn Sof.[25]

Scholem summarizes the further understanding of this line of light in the following terms: "Since the *zimzum* took place equally on all sides, the resulting vacuum was circular or spherical in shape. The light which entered it in a straight line after the *zimzum* has, therefore, two aspects from the start: it arranges itself both in concentric circles and in a unilinear structure, which is the form of Adam Kadmon."[26] The full diagram implied in the *Eitz Chayyim* is not simply of a line of light, representing Adam Kadmon, that penetrates from the circumference of a black circle to its center but of a series of concentric circles within the outer circumference marking the original vacuum of the Tzimtzum, each associated with one of the Sefirot on the line of light. The number of such circles varies in different versions of the diagram from ten, considered either as confined to Atzilut or spread out through the four worlds of Emanation, to forty, ten for each of the four worlds, and even to fifty, in which an additional ten are added for the world of Adam Kadmon, but forty is the most usual number.[27] We are now to see the surprising correspondence that can be made between this traditional circular diagram of the Sefirot and the full octave version of the Sabbath Star Diagram.

As can be inferred from the last section, the total number of *manifest* hexagrams in the octave diagram is precisely forty, a count that adds to the previous figure of thirty-nine (26 + 13) the initially undrawn but later reproduced Ri hexagram. If we now understand each of these forty hexagrams to include or represent the circle that can be circumscribed about its six radial arc points, then the whole of the octave diagram can be viewed as another diagrammatic version of the Tzimtzum. One has only to set aside the previous designations of the forty stage-defining hexagrams and redefine them as the ten Sefirot of the four cosmic worlds, this redefinition of the cosmic octave extending inward from the upper Do, now identified with the Keter of Atzilut, to the lower Do, now identified with the Malkhut of Asiyah. But as table 7.3 shows, it is not so much a matter of setting *aside* the previous definitions of the position-defining hexagrams as setting them *beside* the newer definitions, with implications illuminating for what can be considered the phases of Emanation and of Rectification. But we should first examine some of the theoretical implications of this second method developed in this book of synthesizing the four worlds of the Lurianic Tzimtzum model of kabbalistic cosmology with the seven worlds of the more authentic cosmological model of Jewish mysticism.

It will be remembered that in the "Hexagram of Creation" section of chapter 1, the four worlds of the later Kabbalah were associated with the first four days of the Genesis seven-day creation account, which then became the basis for the seven-world cosmology whose authenticity in this esoteric tradition was further demonstrated in the final section of that chapter, this cosmology being the foundation for all my books and that which my most recent two books have associated with the Lurianic Tzimtzum. In chapter 10 of *The Secret Doctrine of the Kabbalah*, the Tzimtzum model of

kabbalistic cosmology was explained in the scientific terms of quantum cosmology and shown not only to provide a more adequate explanation of the big bang scientific model but also to support a cosmos expanding to seven dimensions. In chapter 1 of *The Kabbalah of the Soul*, the Lurianic Tzimtzum model was synthesized with the differing, purely emanationist, cosmology of the *Zohar* and also shown to support a seven-dimensional cosmos. But neither of these prior attempts to synthesize the Tzimtzum model with a seven-world cosmos treated the four worlds of the Lurianic model as other than the first four worlds of the seven-world model. We shall see that table 7.3 correlates the forty construction elements in its left column with the Lurianic four worlds and in its right column with the seven worlds of the Sabbath Star Diagram. In its left column the Lurianic forty circles are further understood to proceed inward from the circumference of the Tzimtzum-produced finite sphere in the decreasing levels of purity attributed to its four worlds. Similarly, the same forty position-defining hexagrams of the octave diagram are understood, in the right column, to proceed outward from the center in first the decreasing and then increasing levels of purity of its seven worlds, whose transition point is that of the fourth world. But we should first see whether these two different sets of identifications can be meaningfully related, most importantly, whether these two lists can be considered to represent different phases of the cosmic process, whether the four trees on the left of the table, as earlier suggested, represent some original creation and the seven worlds on the right their rectification, their Tikkun.

Such a premise would locate the Shevirah, the Breaking of the Vessels, somewhere in the interval between the Malkhut of Asiyah and the Do hexagram of a reconstituted Atzilut. And it would find such an original manifestation of the Sefirot vessels of all four worlds to have been so essentially flawed that their rectification could not involve a simple repair of the broken vessels, which would result in no cosmic gain, but rather demanded a completely new form of the emanation process, originating from a different source. Let us now see how such a dual-stage cosmic process can be imagined within the terms of kabbalistic cosmology.

To review what has already been shown, prior to the Tzimtzum there was only a pure light that then contracted to a point of light—"[T]he pure, divine light filled all existence. . . . Then Eyn Sof contracted Himself into a central point with His light in the middle." This is followed by the withdrawal of most of the Limitless Light to beyond the finite sphere centered on that point of light and then the reemergence into this sphere of one line of light from the surrounding light. In what is largely the vacuum of finite space, there are, then, two sources of light, distinguished by the process of Tzimtzum, the infinite "inner" light at the center of this space and the infinite light "surrounding" this space that reenters it in the form of a line of light, a line that, in the course of its penetration, also defines a series of concentric rings of light. In my analysis of this process in terms of quantum cosmology, I showed that once the center was defined, the withdrawal of most of the infinite light and its reentry would have been virtually instantaneous.[28] If this be accepted, then we could postulate that the concentric rings of light produced by this line would all have been in place before the infinite light at the center began to expand into this preexistent series of circular lights.

This is similar to an idea of Israel Sarug, an influential follower of Luria. As explained by Scholem, the place that is to become the finite cosmos was originally the locus of Din (also known as Gevurah), the power of contraction, and that one purpose of the Tzimtzum was Ein Sof's desire to be purged of Din.[29] But, in Sarug's version, before this contraction took place, "'primordial points' were 'engraved' in the power of Din, thus becoming the first forms to leave their markings in the essence of Ein Sof . . . and the primordial Torah, the ideal world woven in the substance of Ein Sof itself, came into being."[30] With such an understanding of the ideal Torah woven into the place within Ein Sof that is to become the space of the finite cosmos, we can now identify the Trees of the four worlds of Emanation with this "ideal" version

of creation, an infrastructure woven into the very space-time of the cosmos. But as the similarly "ideal" form of the past-modeled fourth-world diagram can be understood to have suffered something very much like the Fall and to have been replaced by the "real" version of its future-modeled form, so did the four worlds of the Lurianic cosmos suffer a Shevirah. As the line of light producing these forty circles of light derives from the surrounding or transcendent form the Limitless Light, so that originating from the inner light may be associated with its immanent form. It is, then, from the creative powers that can finally be associated with the Shekhinah that a new seven-world cosmos can now be understood to emerge that will restructure the forty previously defined rings according to its own lights and in a form destined to last. But in thus inhabiting this restructured space, it will also gain something from its former inhabitants, as we shall see. With this theoretical synthesis of the two side columns of table 7.3, one that effects such a synthesis of the Lurianic cosmology of the Tzimtzum with the Zoharic cosmology of emanation from a center as that earlier developed in chapter 1 of *The Kabbalah of the Soul*, we can now learn what further illumination this table can afford of the cosmic process.

Table 7.3 of the position-defining hexagrams of the octave diagram, giving their identifications through the four Trees of emanation as well as their prior associations and positions in the cosmic worlds of the Sabbath Star Diagram, should facilitate an understanding of this new way of interpreting the diagram as a model of creation within the circular limits produced in the Tzimtzum, and this correlation will prove illuminating for both. For the following revised scenario of the cosmic process can finally understand the Tikkun as proceeding both on its sevenfold inner path to human perfection while also accomplishing the very fourfold outer path of cosmic reconstruction whose ideal infrastructure has also proven inspirational to its human progress.

Associating the lower ten hexagrams, rather than just the four determined by hexagram expansion, with the fourth world of Asiyah can give us an expanded understanding of the fourth world. From

Table 7.3. The Sabbath Star Diagram within the Tzimtzum

SEFIROT OF THE FOUR WORLDS	HEXAGRAMS	STAGES OF COSMIC EXPANSION
Keter of Atzilut	27V (W. 7)	Keter of Adam Kadmon (Do)
Chokhmah of Atzilut	26V (W. 7)	Chokhmah of A.K.
Binah of Atzilut	13H (W. 7)	Throne
Chesed of Atzilut	25V (W. 7)	Binah of A.K.
Gevurah of Atzilut	24V (W. 7)	Chesed of A.K.
Tiferet of Atzilut	12H (W. 7)	Firmament
Netzach of Atzilut	23V (W. 7)	Gevurah of A.K.
Hod of Atzilut	22V (W. 7)	Tiferet of A.K.
Yesod of Atzilut	11H (W. 7)	Chayot
Malkhut of Atzilut	21V (W. 7)	Netzach of A.K.
Keter of Beriah	20V (W. 7)	Hod of A.K.
Chokhmah of Beriah	10H (W. 7)	Ofanim
Binah of Beriah	19V (W. 7)	Yesod of A.K.
Chesed of Beriah	18V (W. 6)	Keter of Arikh Anpin (Ti)
Gevurah of Beriah	9H (W. 6)	Malkhut as Shekinah (Li)
Tiferet of Beriah	17V (W. 6)	Chokhmah of A.A. (Abba)
Netzach of Beriah	16V (W. 6)	Binah of A.A. (Imma)
Hod of Beriah	8H (W. 6)	Malkhut as Nukvah
Yesod of Beriah	15V (W. 6)	Chesed of A.A. and Ze'ir Anpin
Malkhut of Beriah	14V (W. 6)	Gevurah of A. A. and Z. A.
Keter of Yetzirah	7H (W. 6)	Malkhut as Rachel
Chokhmah of Yetzirah	13V (W. 6)	Tiferet of A.A.+Z.A.+Jacob
Binah of Yetzirah	12V (W. 6)	Netzach of A. A. + Z. A.
Chesed of Yetzirah	6H (W. 5)	Messianic Millennium (La)
Gevurah of Yetzirah	11V (W. 6)	Hod of A. A. + Z. A.
Tiferet of Yetzirah	10V (W. 6)	Yesod of A. A. + Z. A.
Netzach of Yetzirah	5H (W. 5)	Messianic Ingathering
Hod of Yetzirah	9V (W. 5)	Messiah ben David (Si)
Yesod of Yetzirah	8V (W. 5)	Messiah ben Joseph
Malkhut of Yetzirah	4H (W. 5)	War of Gog and Magog
Keter of Assiyah	7V (W. 5)	Trumpet of Messiah
Chokhmah of Assiyah	6V (W. 4)	Man (Sol)
Binahof Assiyah	3H (W. 4)	Life principal in Plants (Fi)
Chesed of Assiyah	5V (W. 4)	Animals
Gevurah of Assiyah	4V (W. 4)	Minerals
Tiferet of Assiyah	2H (W. 3)	Yetziric Fall (Fa)
Netzach of Assiyah	3V (W. 3)	Unfallen Yetzirah (Mi)
Hod of Assiyah	2V (W. 2)	Unmanifest Beriah (Ri)
Yesod Assiyah	1H (W. 2)	Beriah (Re)
Malkhut of Assiyah	1V (W. 1)	Atzilut (Do)

this perspective, the fourth world can be considered to hold the prior three worlds immanently within it and to be open to the call of Ruach consciousness, of the Messianic shofar that calls upon Nefesh humans to "hear" the tone of their higher attunement. It was just such an addition of the first element of the fifth-world diagram to that of the fourth world that was shown, in the next to last section of chapter 3, to accomplish the rectification of what could be considered the fallen form of the fourth-world diagram. And we can now understand it to accomplish as well the rectification of the final world of Emanation, Asiyah.

Moving further into the Tikkun, we can see that the period from the first third of the fifth world to just past the first third of the sixth world has a special relationship to the world of Yetzirah and may be considered its rectification. It includes not only the Messianic Age proper, that which truly begins only after the the Nefesh soul has been lifted beyond the phase of belligerent rectitude into the full Ruach dimension, but also the sensual Yichud of Jacob and Rachel and the immature limbs of Ze'ir Anpin in his first conception, those lower portions of the sixth world still marked by attachment to the material world.

Correlated with the world of Beriah and its reconstitution are the upper two Sefirot of Ze'ir Anpin, which may be considered the arms by which he dispenses Providential justice (Gevurah) and mercy (Chesed); the additional Partzufim of the Nukvah, Imma, Abba, and Arikh Anpin; and the higher Yichudim of Ze'ir Anpin with the Nukvah and of Arikh Anpin with the Shekhinah. In addition to these sixth-world components, three seventh-world components may also be correlated with Beriah: the Yesod of Adam Kadmon, by which he may be said to have Yichud with the Shekhinah; the surviving egotism that may be associated with Hod; and the Ofanim, the Wheels of the heavenly Throne, which were seen by Ezekiel to be set on the earth. Finally we come to the ten highest hexagrams that complete the octave diagram with the upper Do and that alone are to be correlated with Atzilut, the three higher elements of the Throne that rise above the spatial aspect of the multidimensional cosmos

and the seven higher Sefirot of Adam Kadmon that rise above its temporal aspect, those beginning with Eternity (Netzach).

The Tzimtzum version of the Sabbath Star Diagram charted in table 7.3 does not invalidate the earlier identifications based on the equation of cosmic worlds with the whole-step progression of stage-defining hexagrams; rather, it tells us which elements of the worlds of Tikkun are to be correlated with the Lurianic cosmology of the forty Sefirot first emanated on the line of light that penetrated the vacuum of the Tzimtzum to compose the four worlds of emanation. Most fitting is the assigned position of the sixth horizontal hexagram, the fifth-world element connoting the millennium that seems, on the Tzimtzum table, to reach into and be surrounded by the first portion of that sixth world or heaven representing the World to Come.

The Tztimtzum table as a map of the successive stages of rectification can be further illuminated by a concept of the Baal Shem Tov, that of the "free sample" that Rabbi Yitzchok of Kamarna tells us the founder of Hasidism used to explain the process of spiritual development: "The 'free sample' is the Light that a person feels when he first begins to draw close [to God]. Through the taste of this Light, he can subjugate all evil, and return everything to the ultimate Good. This is [a 'free sample'] given to the individual so that he should know the taste of serving God. A mark (*reshimu*) of this remains after [this Light] is withdrawn, in order that he should know what to seek."[31] Applying this hasidic concept to the Tzimtzum table, the reconstitution of the original four worlds of Emanation will be seen at each stage to involve a "free sample" of the next world of Tikkun. Thus the originally emanated world of Asiyah can only be reconstituted by the divine gift to Nefesh man of such a free sample of higher attunement as can aid his development of Ruach consciousness, the free sample of that Sabbatical element conveying the call of the Messianic shofar. Similarly his breakthrough from the Ruach to the Neshamah level will occur when his prayers are answered through such a shared experience of the Yichud of Rachel and Jacob as can accomplish the rectification of Yetzirah. But we should now draw the general cosmological implication of table 7.3 for an understanding of the seventh world of the diagram

We have seen that there are two ways of counting the construction elements of the octave diagram, in terms of the numerical formula for outward construction, in which case the sum is 39, and in terms of the actual number of construction elements manifested through inward construction, the sum in this case being 40. Using the former number, 39, this chapter was earlier able to model the "Unification of the Name," and chapter 12 will show how an understanding of the thirty-nine construction elements of the cumulative octave diagram can model the "Measure of the [divine cosmic] Body," the meaning of the Merkabah text title *Shi'ur Komah*. Similarly, the latter number, 40, makes possible the Tzimtzum model of the diagram and so the positive identification of its forty construction elements with the full extent of the creation.

The difference in the way of counting the construction elements of the octave diagram is not based on the counting of the specifically octave portion of the diagram, which is unequivocally 13. Rather, it is based on the different ways of counting these elements of the first six worlds: that "ideal" way, which eliminates the Ri hexagram from the original counting and results in the number 26; and the "real" way, which includes the delayed manifestation of this second world construction element and thus places this number at 27. Now, there is a kabbalistic tradition involving these two numbers—in which 27 is understood to be the addition of 1 to 26 and so may be construed as the Name in its unity—that may perhaps further validate both countings. This is that their multiplication equals the Gematria for the word Shabbat, composed of the letters Shin = 300, Tav = 400, and Bet = 2, whose total is 702; for 26 × 27 = 702.[32] Thus it is the employment of both countings that may be said to *generate*—the process for which multiplication has ever been the metaphor—the holy dimension of the Sabbath and the seventh expansion of the Sabbath Star Diagram.

What identification of the forty position-defining construction elements of the octave diagram

with the created cosmos can further accomplish is a positive identification of the surrounding second phase of the seventh-world diagram with the infinite substance in which the space of the Tzimtzum was formed, the substance of Ein Sof. Thus the holiness identified with this seventh dimension is seen to consist precisely in the ability of its correlated level of consciousness to unify the finiteness of its first cosmic aspect with its second infinite aspect, the cosmic octave with the infinity beyond.

From this we may further understand the soul level that truly defines the octave division of the seventh world, the Chayah soul level, and how it may be distinguished from the Neshamah souls of the sixth world earlier said to inform the consciousness of the Shekhinah and Nukvah. For the Glory that the Neshamah Masters were able to glimpse on the Throne was still one that they, like Isaiah, could recognize to fill the whole world, that world to which they could yet return. It can, in fact, be identified with the very Chayah soul that truly inhabits the portion of the seventh world within the cosmic circle. Where the Neshamah soul can recognize the glorious Chayah soul it envisions on the ultimate Throne of creation as its higher self, the Chayah soul is engaged in a similar Devekut with its still higher self, that of the Yechidah soul, which is beyond the circle of the Tzimtzum in the infinity of Ein Sof.

It is at this point that all or some of these souls would seem to come to a final threshold that, at a certain level of capacity, they can choose to cross. In so doing, Enoch becomes transfigured into Metatron, the six-lettered name into that of seven letters. The decision must be made at this stage because the next stage of the seventh world, that of the sixth horizontal Sabbath Star, covers the La hexagram of the fifth world, thus rendering unnecessary the survival of the sixth-world Li Sabbath Star equated with the Shekhinah and the highest level of Neshamah Masters. These souls may choose to retain their cosmic consciousnesses, to remain in the first octave enjoying Devekut with its transcendent Glory and serving the world below. Or they may have the possibility, whether by choice or the inexorable push of their own spiritual development, to enter fully and irrevocably into the infinite octaves beyond, into the infinite consciousness of Ein Sof.

What such souls may find there is clouded from our vision by a denser curtain than that which separated the Neshamah Masters from a vision of the Throne, but there are some clues. If Enoch can become transfigured into Metatron, the "lesser YHVH," then the answer does not seem to be a simple dissolution of identity into a primordial divine unity. It seems rather to betoken its divine empowerment. This possibility can also be supported by a musical analogy, one between these expanding octaves and the harmonic series. In the first chapter of this book, we saw how the harmonic series contained the key to the order of creation in the first chapter of Genesis, that the logical order in the Genesis account was based on the harmonic series. In the same way, the harmonic series may provide some clue to the essential nature of the higher possible octaves, particularly the second.

The harmonic series is one of the wonders of creation,[33] its intervals defining a sequence of whole number ratios such as the 2:1 of the octave to its fundamental tone, the 3:2 of the perfect fifth above this first octave to that octave, and the 4:3 of the second octave to the perfect fourth above this fifth. The sequence of the harmonic intervals that emerge through these first two octaves, given with their Solfeggio names, are as follows: Do_1, Do_2, Sol_1, Do_3. What, then, can an association of the first octave with unity, Do-Do, and of the second with division, Do-Sol-Do, tell us? Perhaps that in the first octave the divine power is unified and that in the second it is multiplied. If the first Do hexagram of the diagram can be identified with the Shekhinah and its chiming octave with Adam Kadmon, then the unison heard from the sounding of the lower and upper Do of our octave can be taken to signify that unification of the Shekhinah with her transcendent partner that is the goal of the Lurianic Tikkun. The second octave, however, is essentially divided and, significantly, by the fifth, the tone of Sol, the dominant tone that, in the analysis of the fourth-

world diagram (where the construction elements were correlated with the diatonic scale), was identified with man. It would thus seem that the second octave is somehow connected with that cosmic evolution of man symbolized by the transfiguration of Enoch into Metatron.

Another point to be made about the harmonic series is that it is not until its fifth octave that all the tones of the diatonic scale emerge in this series, an approximate Fa at the twenty-first harmonic and a true La at the twenty-seventh, and this suggests another possibility of interpretation. Since the number five figures most significantly in the Kabbalah with respect to the concept of the Partzufim, it may be that each of these Partzufim can be assigned to one of these evolutionary octaves as its presiding governor. Following through with such a possibility, the first cosmic octave would be associated with the Partzuf of the Nukvah or the Shekhinah, and the four transcendent octaves with the higher four Partzufim, the second octave with Ze'ir Anpin, the third with Imma, the fourth with Abba, and the fifth with Arikh Anpin, a possibility further explored in chapter 15.

Continuing our discussion of the second such possible octave, its association both with man, identified with the Sol Sabbath Star, and Ze'ir Anpin is most suggestive, for we have seen that the evolution of Ze'ir Anpin can be taken as a model of man's spiritual development. As Ze'ir Anpin is associated with six Sefirot, suffers a Fall, and is twice-born,[34] so man suffered a Fall and, twice-born in Metatron, can be associated with six traditional figures: Enoch, Moses, Elijah, Isaiah, Ezekiel, and Rabbi Akiba, all of whom may be related through the concept of Gilgul or reincarnation. Scholem tells us that "the common opinion in the Spanish Kabbalah is that in order to atone for its sins, the soul transmigrates three more times after entering its original body (according to Job 33:29), 'Behold, God does all these things, twice, three times, with a man.'"[35] But the quotation from Job on which the Spanish Kabbalists based their opinion could be read differently, not as twice or three times but as twice three times, or six times, this being the precise meaning of the Hebrew words *pa'amayim shalosh*. Both Ze'ir

Anpin and Metatron can be associated with the number six, a number that, though signifying perfection, is nonetheless multiple. In moving from his six-lettered form (Mem, Tuf, Tuf, Raysh, Vuv, Nun) to his seven-lettered form (Mem, Yod, Tuf, Tuf, Raysh, Vuv, Nun), Metatron moves from his first-octave identification with the Shekhinah to his second-octave identification with Ze'ir Anpin, and, in so doing, lifts Enoch and his later avatars from the cosmic to the infinite realms. Thus if Enoch and the Yechidah souls may be said to become governors of the second-octave worlds, then the premature offer of the Edenic snake would finally seem to become realized. Redeemed from the Fall through the spiritual process of the Tikkun, and "knowing good and evil" through Devekut with the Crown of Wisdom, man will become "as gods."

THE ANGELS OF ARAVOT

Even if one does not project an evolutionary future through five octaves, it can still be said that man has the capacity to make a quantum leap from the lower level of the World to Come associated with the sixth world-dimension-heaven to the yet more transcendent level identified with the seventh heaven. Such transcendence is graphically portrayed by the matrix borders of both the sixth-world diagram, shown in figure 6.7 and the portion of the seventh world that can be associated with the higher Do and the seventh heaven of Aravot, the amazing emergence in figure 7.1. For as the primary story of the sixth-world matrix border is one of incineration, that of the matrix form added by the first half of the seventh world is one expressive of transfiguration, of the phoenix rising from the flames, of Metatron spreading his wings. Figure 7.1 displays the remarkable matrix addition of the Aravot diagram. It is only this winged form that the half world of Aravot adds, the matrix border of the sixth world not being otherwise altered since it is only with the seventh horizontal Sabbath Star of the seventh world that the matrix specifically contributed by the horizontal axis will begin to be formed.

The angels of Aravot have a particular feature that associates them still more closely with the Chayot seen by Ezekiel in his Throne vision: "every one had four wings. . . . Their wings were joined one to another. . . . their wings were stretched upward" (Ezek. 1:6, 9, 11). Though not exactly fitting the description of Ezekiel in some of its more difficult anatomical aspects, figure 7.1 does provide its own vision of such four-winged angels or, more properly, Cherubim. For Ezekiel finally recognizes that it was Cherubim he saw in his original vision of the Throne: "This is the living creature that I saw under the God of Israel by the river of Chebar; and I knew that they were the cherubims" (Ezek. 10:20). In this model, which visualizes the Cherubim from behind with hidden faces, we can imagine the fully displayed back wings and partially displayed front wings as moving in an opposite synchronization; when the back wings are extended outward, the front wings are extended upward, and the reverse. The peculiar shape of the octave matrix border permits us to see these two extreme wing positions, the largely hidden front wings having been outlined more lightly. A final feature of figure 7.1 to be noted are the spanning arches produced by the third and fourth horizontal Sabbath Stars, forms separated from the rest of the diagram because of the missing fifth through ninth horizontal Sabbath Stars.

The imagery of the four-winged Cherubim appears variously in the Bible and represents man's condition at the beginning and end of his spiritual evolution. Its first appearance is in the Garden of Eden after the Fall: "So he drove out the man; and he placed at the east of the Garden of Eden Cherubims, and a flaming sword which turned every way, to keep the way of the tree of life" (Gen. 3:24). Fallen man, driven out of the Garden, will one day in mystical vision again behold the Cherubim, whose holiness is represented by the cubic Holy of Holies in the earthly Temple that houses their images, "the chariot of the cherubims, that spread out their wings, and covered the ark of the covenant of the Lord" (1 Chron. 28:16). And as we have seen, it is these Cherubim that Ezekiel finally recognizes that he saw in his original Throne vision.

If the winged forms contributed to the matrix by

Figure 7.1. The Angels of Aravot

the vertical Sabbath Stars of the seventh-world diagram can, indeed, be equated with the Cherubim, then we would seem to have an astonishing explanation for the reason that only this form was exempted from the prohibition contained in the Second Commandment: "Thou shalt not make unto thee any graven image, or any likeness of any thing that is in heaven above . . ." (Exod. 20:4). God makes this specific exemption when he commands Moses:

And thou shalt make two cherubims of gold, of beaten work shalt thou make them, in the two ends of the mercy seat. . . . And the cherubims shall stretch forth their wings on high, covering the mercy seat with their wings, and their faces shall look one to another; toward the mercy seat shall the faces of the cherubims be. . . . And there I will meet with thee, and I will commune with thee from above the mercy seat, from between the two cherubims which are upon the ark of the testimony. . . . (Exod. 25:18, 20, 22)

In the later tradition, the space between the Cherubim in the Temple was understood to be the source of prophecy. Meditating on the Cherubs revealed in the octave unfolding of the Sabbath Star Diagram would also seem to provide a source for prophetic understanding. And it may not be too much to say that it is their uncanny appearance in the octave form of this diagram, through processes discoverable but yet inexplicable to human reason, that is somehow involved with the unique position accorded the Cherubim in Jewish iconography.

The most continuously surprising aspect of the Sabbath Star Diagram is that the appearance of its matrix borders through the octave diagram cannot be precisely predicted in the way that the numerical ordering of its Sabbath Stars is predictable, and it is the invariable fitness of its appearance to the world being defined that is most awe-inspiring, defining as they do the elements associated with the various worlds with extraordinary appropriateness. But it is also true of another aspect of the octave diagram with which we are now concerned. For the two horizontal Sabbath Stars of Aravot span the directions of the diagram in a most expressive form. Indeed, their physical appearance and meaning are remarkably close, the space between them being identifiable with the Firmament or Curtain separating the lower spiritual orders from sight of the Throne and its heavenly King. Throughout biblical and kabbalistic writing, great emphasis is placed on the Cloud, Garment, Firmament, or Curtain that surrounds the divine essence and prevents our direct perception of it. In previous analyses of the seventh-world Sabbath Stars, we have seen that the third on the horizontal axis could be identified with the Arafel, the cloudy Firmament, and the fourth with the Nogah, the Glow of the Throne coming

through the Arafel. For the fourth on up to the culminating Do Sabbath Star are constituents representing the forms of divine sovereignty, the Throne of the fourth horizontal Sabbath Star, the Crown of the ninth vertical Sabbath Star, and the Wisdom of the eighth vertical Sabbath Star just under the Crown. Interestingly, the two Sefirot of Keter (Crown) and Chokhmah (Wisdom), appearing above and level with the Throne, are the ones normally identified with the Yod of the vertical Tetragrammaton, the same Yod that transforms the six-lettered Metatron into the seven-lettered Angel of the Presence. Between the third and fourth horizontal Sabbath Stars is the precise space, then, of the separating Firmament. Omitted from the earlier quotation of Ezekiel's vision is a striking image that seems particularly relevant to the appearance of these two spanning Sabbath Stars: "And from the vision of His thighs and below, I saw a vision like fire, with a Glow (*nogah*) around it. Like a vision of the rainbow in the clouds on a rainy day, so was the vision of the Glow around."[36] The fourth Sabbath Star identified with this Glow does seem to suggest the form of a rainbow, significant because the rainbow is the sign of God's covenant of salvation to all humanity.

It is as the signifier of the Throne, however, that this Sabbath Star is most expressive, particularly in its association with the winged form. This image seems closely related to one feature of the revelation given in *Shi'ur Komah*: "When Metatron enters before the Holy One, blessed be He, under the Throne of Glory, he holds [the Throne] with a multitude of wings."[37] The translators' bracketed insertion seems consistent with the image given in figure 7.1, one that can now be interpreted as Metatron upholding the Throne with his wings. The dual nature of Metatron may also be glimpsed in this image, for in addition to the right and left lines descending to Metatron's shoulders from the Throne Sabbath Star, there is also the central line descending still further to his heart from the third horizontal Sabbath Star of the Firmament. This would suggest that though the Angel Metatron provides support to the Throne through the power of his wings, in his heart he retains the character of the Youth Enoch, one whose very personality serves to cloud his ultimate vision. But it also suggests that the heart of the prophet has wings that can soar above his human limitations to behold the Throne of God. If these three lines are further associated with the three pillars of the Tree of Life Diagram, which they do seem to suggest, then the middle line could also be taken to signify the force of mediation, with the final significance that the Throne vision must be mediated to the living Neshamah Master through the enclosing curtain of the Firmament.

But figure 7.1 takes us beyond the *Shi'ur Komah* to Ezekiel's original vision of the Chayot with outstretched wings beneath the Firmament, both the Chayot-Cherubs and Metatron being comprehended in this same winged form. Not only can we find visual counterparts for the Throne, Firmament, and Chayot of Ezekiel's vision but even for the fourth element of this vision, the Ofanim or Wheels. This was earlier equated with the first horizontal hexagram, and it seems reasonable to illustrate it by the inner hexagon of this hexagram. Though Ezekiel later indicates that he saw four wheels—"one wheel by one cherub, and another wheel by another cherub" (Ezek. 10:9)— his first impression was of "one wheel upon the earth" (Ezek.1:15), and it is this first vision that it seems best to illustrate in figure 7.1. As all of the Wheels have the same appearance, of a wheel within a wheel, the design also includes a second smaller hexagon, one enclosing the continuous matrix. Illustrating the Wheels in this fashion also reveals the way in which the Wheels and Chayot are connected, "for the spirit of the living creature was in the wheels" (Ezek. 1:20); and it provides as well a visual center that can focus the vision of a meditator. Since the space bounded by this "one wheel upon the earth" is also the place between the Cherubs that has traditionally been understood to be the source of prophetic vision, this space can be seen to provide an opening into the higher dimensions. If one further views figure 7.1 as providing the underside of Ezekiel's Throne vision, with the glow of the Throne radiating just beyond the extent of the Firmament, as the elements of the

fourth horizontal Sabbath Star extend just beyond those of the third, then the Throne, itself, may be considered to occupy the other side of this two-dimensional representation. Only in this case it would not be the Throne side but our side that could be denoted by the kabbalistic concept of the Sitra Achra, the "Other Side." In this view, the ground of our side of this representation would be equated to the Firmament, with the Cherubs and wheels within wheels superimposed upon it. Through meditation on the bounded space between the Cherubs, it would become possible, however, to break through the obstruction of the Firmament to an unclouded vision of the divine side, to Ezekiel's vision of the Man on the Throne. Figure 7.1 can thus be regarded as the Sabbath Star Diagram version of Ezekiel's vision in the form of a two-dimensional mandala. The difference between the two is that, unlike mystic vision, physical representation of the divine must always be confined to this side of the Firmament, must, in fact, be no other than a delineation of the Firmament.

If figure 7.1 is suggestive of the Firmament in two-dimensional form, this suggestion becomes overwhelming when this form is further projected into three dimensions. Once the outer hexagonal form highlighted in figure 7.1 is reconceptualized as the cube of figure 7.2, not only the Cherubs but the whole nature and relationship of the fourth through seventh dimensions becomes brilliantly clarified. As can be seen in this illustration, the visible Cherubs are situated at the exact center of each of the visible cube's faces, and these Cherubs also mark the exact spots at which the points of an enclosed octahedron can be located. As an outer cube can be formed from the given point-hexagon of the Ti Sabbath Star, so the points of its dualing octahedron can be located at the tip of the Si Sabbath Star, and that of its inner cube at the points of the Sol Sabbath Star. In terms of the identifications originally given to these construction elements, the inner Sol cube would be identifiable with created Adam and the Nefesh soul body, the mediating Si octahedron with the Messiah and the Ruach soul body, and the outer Ti cube with both the inner boundary of the body of Adam

Kadmon and the outer boundary of the Neshamah soul body. These wondrous forms may be seen in figure 7.2.

Most interesting in this context is the definition of the creation of man that the *Zohar* makes in terms of a cube modeled on a supernal cube:

> South displayed the power of the light inherited from the head and was empowered by the East.

East empowered North; North aroused and expanded, calling potently to the West to draw near, to join him. . . . Then East draws near West, and West abides in joy, inviting them all: *Let us make a human being in our image, according to our likeness* (Genesis 1:26), resembling this in four directions, above and below. East cleaved to West, generating him, and so we have learned: "Adam emerged from the site of the Temple."

Figure 7.2. The Cube of Creation

*Let us make a human being in our image,
according to our likeness* (ibid., 26), embracing six
aspects comprising all, as above, with smooth
members arrayed fittingly in the mystery of wisdom, an entirely supernal array. Let us make a
human being—mystery of male and female,
entirely in supernal, holy wisdom.[38]

The cubic form that defines created man's spiritual
essence also defines the holy center of the Temple;
and if the "holy wisdom" that created man in its
likeness can be identified with the upper two
Sefirot of Adam Kadmon, Keter and Chokhmah,
that the Sabbath Star Diagram represents by elements rising above the level of the Firmament they
define, then we can recognize the outer cube of
figure 7.2 as formed by the body of Adam
Kadmon, in whose likeness the inner cube of
Edenic Adam was modeled. The representation of
the median octahedron is geometrically significant
because the easiest way to enlarge or condense a
cube is through the intervening octahedron, and in
chapter 7 of *The Secret Doctrine of the Kabbalah* I
showed that such a construction can solve the geometric enigma of the *Sefer Yetzirah*. When the
dimensions of the inner and outer cubes of figure
7.2 are compared, they will be seen to be exactly
mediated by the intervening octahedron. What this
diagram would thus seem to show is that the only
way for man to develop to the point of Devekut
with his "likeness" on the Throne is through the
pyramid shape of the intervening octahedron representing his evolution to Messianic consciousness.
In Egypt and Mexico the pyramid became the
highest representation of Temple structure, that
sacred space in or through which man could be initiated into the mysteries of divine transformation.
At Sinai, man was instructed in the form that
focuses the power of the pyramid, the Holy of
Holies' inner cube containing the graven Cherubs
upon the Ark of the Covenant, and told to build
the surrounding pyramid of his Messianic spiritual
body through adherence to the Commandments
contained therein.

If we look closely at the Cherubs on the outer
cube, they would appear to be portrayed from

above, only the backs of their wings being visible,
their heads facing downward toward the parallel face
of the inner cube, as in the biblical quotation: "their
faces shall look one to another; toward the mercy
seat shall the faces of the cherubims be." Though
the golden Cherubs on earth may have faced each
other over the Ark cover, those on high face each
other from opposite ends of the cosmos and from all
three of the spatial dimensions, their gaze focused
on the Holy of Holies housing the written word of
God and their power transmitting to this most
sacred of all Temple spaces the prophetic messages
of God's continuing revelation.

Most significantly, the Cherubs appear to be
sealing the highest development of Messianic consciousness to the transcendental dimension granting
eternal life, empowering it with the Holy Spirit and
granting it a glimpse of the Nogah, the glow of the
celestial Throne through the dense covering of the
Arafel. For it is this that the outer cube ultimately
represents, and understanding the meaning of the
Firmament, we can arrive at a deeper understanding
of the final implications of the diagram given in figure 7.2. As the function of the Firmament created in
the second day was to divide the upper from the
lower waters and hide the heavenly light now identified only with the upper waters, so may it be said
to serve the same function in the transition between
the first and second octaves. If we may identify the
multidimensional hypercube containing the creation
with the Firmament, then all that surrounds it may
be identified with the Limitless Light, the Or Ein
Sof, personified in Adam Kadmon. Thus this hypercube can be understood as defining the point where
the divine body of Limitless Light meets and
encloses the cosmic octave. In so doing, it defines
both the outer form of the Chayah soul body and
that lowest extension of the Garment of Limitless
Light called the Arafel, the cloud or mist equated by
Ezekiel with the Firmament.

But if the Limitless Light may be understood to
extend in all directions from this hypercube of creation, it could be pictured as "heading" in all directions to infinity. We might thus be able to correlate
this cube with those "back parts" of God's Glory
revealed to Moses in his crowning vision:

And he [Moses] said, I beseech thee, show me thy glory. And he [God] said, I will make all my goodness pass before thee, and I will proclaim the name of the Lord before thee; and I will be gracious to whom I will be gracious, and will show mercy on whom I will show mercy. . . . And it shall come to pass, while my glory passeth by, that I will put thee in a cleft of the rock, and will cover thee with my hand while I pass by: And I will take away mine hand, and thou shalt see my back parts: but my face shall not be seen. (Exod. 33: 18–23)

The first thing that God proclaims is the unfathomable nature of His goodness, the undisclosed reason why to some he mitigates His justice with mercy while to still others he bequeaths an unmerited special grace. God then demonstrates His goodness by shielding Moses' perception from the infinite vision that would destroy his particularity. He lifts Moses to a crevice in the rock of material existence through which Moses can see, not God's face, but his "back parts," the completed plan of cosmic creation. But if this plan is being presented to him in the form of the Sabbath Star cube, then it may answer his questions experientially, showing him that it is only the free gift of God's goodness that can explain the beautiful gift package of creation, the cosmic cube sealed with Cherubic kisses. For Moses to see the cosmic cube from the aerial perspective pictured in figure 7.2, he must already have entered the Limitless Light, have become, for at least the transfiguring moment of this mystic vision, a centering point of that Light. The cube he would thus see is transparent to his gaze, revealing the same holiness within and without, the inner cube of man corresponding to the outer body of Glory. But he also sees that knowledge of the Arafel, the dense mist surrounding and giving shape to the divine essence, is all that man can see and live, the permitted vision of God through observation of the wonders of creation.

Figure 7.2 highlights the two outstanding features of the diagram of Aravot, the elements of the third and fourth horizontal Sabbath Stars that can be perceived as a cube and the matrix addition that resembles a winged form. It is now time to try to relate the comparative placements of these two pic-

torial forms, to determine whether the winged form should be pictured as within or on top of the cube. It was earlier argued that the whole space between the bars formed by the horizontal Sabbath Stars should be counted as constituting the layer of the Firmament, the Throne rising above the top of the Firmament, at the level of the fourth of these Sabbath Stars, and the creation descending below its lower boundary, the level of the third of these Sabbath Stars at which the Firmament begins. But if the Firmament is equated with the densest form of the divine body, then this "body" may be said to meet and form the Chayah soul body at the lower level of the Firmament.

Now, if the winged matrix form is to be identified with the Cherubim, there is no question as to where it should be placed: below the Firmament. We remember that Ezekiel recognized the Cherubim he later saw to be the same as the Chayot of his earlier vision, at which earlier time he had said: "The form above the heads of the Chayah was that of a firmament." Thus the Cherubs may be understood to represent the lowest manifestation of the divine being and the means of its communication with the creation; they seal the transcendent Yechidah soul body and the cosmic body of the Chayah soul together. And they do this at precisely the point in the Firmament that permits a threefold union of these two supernal levels with the person of the Messiah. This is particularly interesting in view of an association earlier made between production of the Messiah and the Yichud of Adam Kadmon with the Shekhinah. However such "parenting" of the Messiah is to be understood, what does seem clear is that the highest development of Messianic or Ruach consciousness provides the crevice through the rock of ordinary perception that permits the channeling of prophetic messages and that the Cherubs are that crevice, the nearest place from which the divine may be apprehended within the creation.

The winged matrix form may be differently interpreted, however, not as the Chayot of the Throne vision but as the angel Metatron, the bearer of the Name of God who "enters before the Holy One, blessed be He, under the Throne of Glory" and who "brings the deafening fire and puts it in the ears of the Hayoth, that they hear not the voice of the glory of the Holy One, blessed be He."[39] As the quotations from the *Shi'ur Komah* indicate, Metatron can perceive what the Chayot are forbidden to see and hear. Though "under the Throne," he is yet above the level of the Firmament, above the level of the third horizontal Sabbath Star that forms the transparent floor of heaven. The Chayot-Cherubim are, conversely, below the level of the third horizontal Sabbath Star that forms the translucent ceiling of the created cosmos. Yet both may be equally represented by the same winged form, now perceived as below the Firmament and now as above it. As Cherub, this form represents the lowest descent of the divine. As Metatron it represents the highest ascent of man, the transfigured form of Enoch. In this one form, then, we may read the same lesson contained in the fundamental symbol of creation, the hexagram, whose intersecting triangles also represent the modes of divine descent and human ascent. What is more, the two main features of the Aravot diagram, the cubic and winged forms, reveal as well the central message of the diagram's numerological association with the Gematria of the Holy Name. For the Firmament bonding transcendent floor to cosmic ceiling, in the Sabbatical heaven made holy by just this bonding, also brings us to that day, prophesied in Zechariah 14:9 and repeated thrice-daily in the prayer services, when "the Lord shall be One, and his name One."[40] So, too, does the winged matrix form unite the lowest descent of the transcendent Lord, in the Cherub, with the highest ascent of transcending man, Enoch transformed into the angelic Metatron who bears the Name of God, the divine Cherub descending to grace man with revelations of ultimate meaningfulness as spiritually developed man ascends to the heavenly Throne, spreading his angelic wings and flying through the rainbow to his place in the Limitless Light.

PART THREE

A New Model for Kabbalistic Soul Psychology

CHAPTER EIGHT

The Fourth-World Matrix
Model of the Nefesh Soul

UNDERSTANDING THE HEXAGRAM MATRIX

Introduction

There are two ways of viewing the Sabbath Star Diagram: the chronological order of its construction provides a temporal perspective on the diagram, and its two-dimensional appearance provides a spatial perspective through which the viewer can be lifted to a realm beyond the linearity of time, one in which all segments that before had appeared chronological in sequence now appear to be simultaneous and interpenetrating. In part 2, the construction elements were studied for what they could tell of the sequence of cosmic evolution. But understanding of the final simultaneous appearance of those elements can best be gained through study of the matrix that first properly emerges as a product of the construction of the fourth cosmic world, the subject of this chapter. As part 3 will now demonstrate, the matrices of the successive diagram worlds, particularly as comprehensively treated in terms of the remarkable revelations of chapter 10, provide a most precise and revealing model for the multidimensional soul psychology of the Kabbalah. The matrix comes properly into being at the precise generative center of the octave spiral, immediately covering the first three worlds and being thenceforth associated with the Tikkun. In the folds of this spiritual garment and its wondrous colors all the mysteries of cosmic functioning and purpose lie encoded.

In part 2, the matrix was studied largely in terms of its defining borders; for the two forms of the fourth-world diagram studied in chapter 3 this was in terms of its zigzag and plateaulike borders and for the fifth world studied in chapter 5 in terms of its hornlike border. In chapter 3 the earlier stages of the fourth-world diagram were also studied in terms of the pattern of seven loose-packed or close-packed hexagons. It was in chapter 6 that the gender associations of the vertical axis with the masculine Partzufim and of the horizontal axis with their feminine counterparts allowed us to see these construction elements in a further way, as the "parents" of a matrix "son," a correlation whose full meaning will only become clear in part 4. But before we can use the matrix to model the soul levels of such a "son," we must understand its structure. We shall begin this analysis of matrix structure with its simpler triangle level and then move to the more complex hexagram level that will finally provide us with a precise model of the soul.

What distinguishes the macrostructure from the microstructure of the hexagram matrix at its simplest level is the structural difference between its triangular components. The macrotriangles, those of the size constituting the six points of the Re hexagram, feature lines defining all three of their lines of symmetry, the line perpendicular to the base that can be dropped from each of its apices, while the microtriangles, those of Do hexagram size, feature lines defining only one of their lines of symmetry, the lines of symmetry in the microtriangles also constituting the outlines of the interfaced macrotriangles. Translating this difference into three dimensions and understanding the macrotriangular outlines to represent rods on which the material planes of the microtriangles are strung, we can begin to understand something of their qualitative difference. For such trisection of the macrotriangles by their three symmetry lines would hold the macrotriangles firmly in place, while the bisection of the microtriangles would leave them free to spin on their single line of symmetry. The interfacing of these two triangular levels can well model the distinction made in general systems theory of dual-leveled systems in which the upper level represents the level of deterministic rules and the lower level the indeterministic freedom of the individual components of the system,[1] the systemic union of the two seeming to result in the probability functioning throughout the cosmos. More generally, they can be taken to represent the interface of form and force.[2] As I have elsewhere analyzed the triangle matrix more fully,[3] it need not detain us further here, and we can move directly to analysis of the higher-level hexagram matrix it forms and the further definitions that can be given to its structure. Redefinition of the matrix in terms of hexagrams will reveal a complex series of macrocircuits interfacing with microcircuits.

The Matrix Macrostructure

The first step toward a true understanding of the matrix structure is to see the matrix as a repeating pattern of interfacing Do- and Re-sized hexagrams. But in analyzing the hexagram matrix, we shall first give separate consideration to its macrostructure and its microstructure before considering their interface. In all cases what was and can be considered the "ideal" form of the fourth-world diagram will be used, with the zigzag matrix border defined by its ruling macrostructure, this form chosen because its fewer fourth-world constituents allow for a simpler initial definition of matrix elements. Because the diagrams that define these matrix elements will be distinguishing four to twelve categories of these elements, the clearest way to distinguish these elements will be by color. The reader is thus referred to the insert of color plates to illuminate the detailed analyses that follow. In plates 7 and 8, the highest degree of total completion in the fourth world is that indicated by the filling in of the six constituent triangles of those hexagrams that lie wholly within the zigzag matrix border. The median degree is indicated by the simple outlining of the hexagrams completed in the fourth-world diagram but not wholly within this matrix border and so deficient in the number of lines of symmetry in some of their constituent triangles. The lowest degree is indicated by the broken lines outlining the constituent triangles of those hexagrams incomplete in the fourth world that nonetheless contribute some finished macrotriangles to its matrix. This matrix macrostructure can be seen in plate 1 of the color insert.

Plate 1 shows the way in which the matrix can be decomposed into a pattern of repeating Re-sized hexagrams in various stages of completion. But before we proceed to analyze this growth pattern, we must first refine our understanding of the matrix through a further decomposition of the matrix macrostructure into the independent systems of which it is composed, systems defined by the point-to-point meeting of hexagrams that are each given a different one of the four colors used in this diagram.[4] If we look at plate 1, we can see that the hexagram matrix is composed of two basic systems, which can be defined as *central* and *lateral*. The central system is composed of the central Re hexagram of the original Sabbath Star Diagram and the additional six broken-lined hexagrams that meet the points of the Re hexagram and are arrayed in all directions around it. In contrast to the centered position of the central system in the diagram are the three lateral systems, each composed of a pair of completed hexagrams oriented along one of the three axes of the matrix macrostructure that pass through the original Re and Fa hexagram points. Although the descending points of these lateral matrix hexagrams paradoxically meet at the center, the complete hexagrams are off the central balance that, as a group, they laterally surround.

It is these lateral hexagrams that contain the close-packed hexagons that were identified with the fallen Nefesh soul body in chapter 3. What is further interesting in this regard is that on this macroscopic level the loose-packed hexagons identified with the unfallen Nefesh soul body have no such definition in terms of an enclosing macrohexagram; they have simply become imperceptible. Now, if the Re-hexagram size can be identified with form, as was earlier suggested with respect to its component macrotriangles, we can say at the least that whatever was represented by the loose-packed hexagons does not exist within the *forms* of the fourth world, a point to be later clarified.

We can finish this primary description of the past-modeled fourth-world matrix by noting that, as the single completed central hexagram meets six incomplete central hexagrams with which it forms an independent network, so in each third of the lateral system each of the two completed hexagrams meets two half-completed hexagrams for a total of six half-completed hexagrams for the whole lateral system. Since both the half-completed lateral hexagrams and the largely incomplete central hexagrams are completed in the fifth world and are thus really fifth-world entities, their spectral appearance in the fourth-world matrix enables us to learn something of the fifth-world matrix, at least as much as the fourth world can disclose, as well as giving us a clearer picture of the differences between the central and lateral systems and of their patterns of development.

In this definition of the fourth-world macrostructure, we can observe two differences between the forms taken by its central and lateral systems. There is first the contrast between the one central hexagram and the three pairs of lateral hexagrams. Where unity is a characteristic of the fourth world's central macrohexagram, its lateral system demonstrates multiplicity. The second contrast derives from the fact that the central macrohexagram would seem to be the collective source of all six of the central macrohexagrams of the fifth world, that it has, as it were, a collective nature, whereas the lateral macrohexagrams show the greater individuation that can be associated with their color differentiation along the three axes of the diagram. Thus the central system may be associated with the collective form of unity that seems characteristic of the cosmic past while the lateral system seems equally related to the individuating multiplicity that is to become characteristic of the cosmic future.

The central system may be said, then, both to represent and to provide access to a collective unity identifiable with the source of the cosmos; and such access may be associated with another aspect of the numerical relationship between the central and lateral macrohexagrams of the fourth world, the fact that the central macrohexagram appears in a configuration of seven and so may be identified with the grace of the Sabbath. In its interpenetration of the surrounding six work-a-day lateral macrohexagrams, the central macrohexagram may be said to bring them into contact with the transcendent unity of the Sabbath. And yet it is the fourth-world lateral macrohexagrams that may be viewed as even more closely in touch with this source. For it is they, and not the central macrohexagram, that touch the Da'at center of Knowledge, which in the overlaid Tree of Life Diagram is at the center of the Sabbath Star Diagram.

The Matrix Microstructure

Having thus extensively examined the matrix macrostructure, we should now turn to a similar examination of the complementary matrix microstructure featured in plate 2, its components defined by the same four colors and the same method of indicating the three main types of microhexagrams as in the macrostructure.

In plate 2 of the matrix microstructure those hexagrams completed in the fourth world have been filled in, those completed in the fourth world but not within its matrix border, and so really fifth-world elements, have been outlined, and those fifth-world hexagrams that are incomplete in the fourth world have been outlined with broken lines. What should be most clearly visible in this figure are the seven green microhexagrams of the central system completed in the fourth world, each of the points of the central Do hexagram meeting the point of another microhexagram, the basis on which matrix hexagrams can be understood to form a similarly colored circuit. The lateral elements of the fourth-world microstructure are somewhat more difficult to discern. But if the central microhexagon within the Do hexagram is observed, it can be seen that it contains three differently colored pairs of point-to-point microtriangles, each such triangle being a member of a microhexagram. In addition to the pair of microhexagrams that meet at the diagram's central point, and so may be considered "inner" microhexagrams, each lateral circuit also contains two "outer" microhexagrams, each touching the inner microhexagrams of its circuit with two of its points. In contrast to the single inner and six outer microhexagrams of the central system, the three combined circuits of the lateral system contain six inner and six outer microhexagrams for a total of twelve. To compare the microstructure further with the macrostructure, it can be seen by these numbers that the microstructure is, as it were, a cosmic world ahead of the macrostructure, a fact that will be utilized in constructing the much later eighth-world diagram in chapter 13. Whereas seven macrohexagrams defined the completed fourth-world macrohexagrams and twelve the macrostructure of the fifth world, the completed fourth-world microstructure contains seven inner microhexagrams and twelve outer microhexagrams, each category combining members from both the central and lateral systems. The microstructure can thus be said to contain its quickest, most advanced elements.

If one looks again at the seven green microhexagrams of the central system and tries to visualize the point-hexagons surrounding these hexagrams, it can be seen that they are identical with the loose-packed hexagonal matrix earlier identified with the unfallen form of the Nefesh soul body. If one now visualizes the point hexagons around each of the six lateral outer microhexagrams, it can be seen that they are close-packed around the central hexagon and thus can now be equated with the close-packed hexagonal matrix earlier identified with the fallen form of this soul body. Thus what was earlier correlated with the unfallen state can now be seen to be largely central in character, while that which was earlier correlated with the fallen state is now revealed to be largely lateral. They are not exclusively one or the other since the close-packed hexagonal matrix surrounds a central microhexagram in its innermost hexagon, and both forms of hexagonal matrices contain the inner lateral microhexagrams that the earlier hexagonal analysis of the matrix was too gross to be able to discern. We shall be able to give a still finer analysis of these earlier matrix configurations after we have interfaced the two levels of the matrix to achieve a clearer understanding of its nature.

The Interfaced Lateral System

Having decomposed the matrix into its macrostructure and microstructure, and seen how both of these structures contain central and lateral systems of hexagrams, it is now time to take the next important step, the interfacing of the macrostructure by the microstructure through which the internal lines of symmetry are produced that truly define the matrix. But to clarify the component parts of this interfaced matrix, it will be necessary to give different diagrams for the lateral and central systems. There are, in fact, four different circuits, corresponding to the four colors used thus far to define the separate macrostructure and microstructure, that can individually fill the entire matrix with no overlapping from the other circuits when the microstructure and macrostructure are interfaced in a single diagram. It is because of the possibility of such independent displays that the circuit analogy has been used in describing the matrix, for its different structures and systems can be selected out for independent display, as with electrical circuits monitored by a computerized switchboard.

Plate 3 gives us one-third of the lateral system, the other two-thirds of this system being identical except for their differing axes. In addition to this, and as a further aid to perception, the two symmetrical halves of this one-third of the lateral system are further distinguished by color into two subsystems. The red circuit was chosen to represent the lateral system both because its orientation along the horizontal axis in the microstructure and macrostructure provides the most balanced appearance and for another reason that will become clearer in the last subdivision of this section and in the following section. The two colors into which this circuit is further discriminated, scarlet and turquoise, were chosen to conform to the full-color model of the matrix that will be introduced in the next subsection. This further color discrimination will not only prevent the confusion in distinguishing the lateral microhexagrams of plate 2, but will introduce the third significant step in analyzing the structure of the matrix, after its decomposition into a macrostructure and microstructure and into central and lateral systems, that interfacing seen in plate 3.

In color-discriminating the former red circuit into its symmetrical parts, the fourth-world macrohexagram on the right was given the scarlet color and that which its point touches at the center the color turquoise. But as soon as one of the half-completed fifth-world macrohexagrams had to be assigned one of these colors, it immediately became apparent that this would initiate a swirl pattern. For reasons that will later become clear, the counterclockwise direction was chosen for this swirl, the upper macrohexagram being colored scarlet and the lower one turquoise. The same process had now to be undertaken for the microstructure. Of the two inner microhexagrams that meet at the center, one had to be colored scarlet and the other turquoise, and these had further to be connected to the two outer microhexagrams in a way that would coordinate their movement with the macrohexagrams of their color. It soon becomes apparent that the way this can be accomplished is to color the lower inner and right outer microhexagrams scarlet, their sym-

metrical mates being assigned the turquoise color. Completing this direction of color movement with the remaining fifth-world microhexagrams by color, it becomes clear that by further distinguishing the three-color lateral matrix into six colors (of which only the two along one axis are here involved), what had before assumed a static pattern has now developed a most significant spiral pattern.

As the spiral is the most significant of all movement patterns in the cosmos, defining all flowing movement from that of water to that of the galaxy, its discovery in the growth pattern of the matrix is most important. The reason for the omnipresence of the spiral is that this is the form imposed upon circular movement by time. This is particularly true of flowing movement. It is the nature of water to attempt to achieve circularity, as any drop of water can show. When a force such as gravity is applied to water, its flow will always assume a spiral form, as will all the organs and organisms formed by water.[5] As water forms downward spiral vortices, so its opposite, fire, forms upward spiral vortices, this being the reason they are symbolized in alchemy by the inverted triangles of the hexagram. Needless to say, there are nebulae that also assume the form of spirals. This essential feature of flowing movement in time can now be illustrated in the Sabbath Star Diagram. It is, in fact, because the spiral is a natural form whose shape is influenced by time that the counterclockwise direction of the matrix spiral was chosen. If we imagine the diagram as rotating in the clockwise direction signifying the forward movement of time, then the matrix spirals can be viewed as a form of "time streaming."

If we look at the macrohexagrams in plate 3, it can be seen that each one contains a microhexagram of its own color. There are, however, two different forms of microhexagrams, those that are contained within macrohexagrams of their own color and those not so contained within an independent or singly colored macrohexagram. In the interfaced diagram, the enclosing of the first category of microhexagrams within macrohexagrams of their own color gives them a new dimension of definition in terms of these larger forms. In appendix A we shall consider the scientific implications of this feature of the matrix more fully. But for the moment it is sufficient to point out that the interfaced macro-hexagrams seem to be lifting certain microhexa-grams from the more general force field that can be equated with the independent microstructure into the greater particularity provided by the forms of the macrostructure. This same distinction between those microhexagrams that have a particular chim-ing resonance with macrohexagrams of their own color frequency and those that do not will be shown to be of utmost importance in the full discussion of Nefesh psychology to which the second and third sections of this chapter will be devoted. At this point all that shall be noted is the further refinement this matrix interface provides for understanding the ear-lier cosmic manifestation of the close-packed hexag-onal matrix, that it is the lateral microhexagrams within these hexagons that will develop the greatest individuated power within the fully defined fourth-world matrix, the added resonance given them by the color chiming of their enclosing macrohexa-grams. In concluding this preliminary analysis of the interfaced lateral system, it should also be noted that there are six such differently colored lateral spirals in the matrix.

The Interfaced Central System

It is not only the lateral system that can be decom-posed into six color spirals. This is also a property of the central system; and through this process we can learn far more about both of these systems and their interrelationship within the matrix. Since we will, from this point on, be dealing with a twelve color system, it seems useful to adopt a parallel system that has been used extensively in color healing. This is the "Twelve Color Spectro-Chrome System" of Dinshah Ghadiali,[6] an Indian physician who used the hexagram as a model for the distribution of the colors he used in healing. Dinshah assigned six of these colors to the points of the hexagram and the other six to the vertices of its inner hexagon. A revised version of Dinshah's diagram, which assigns the latter six colors not to the vertices but to the six triangles contained within this inner hexagon, can be seen in plate 4, the six colors defined by the

hexagram points being clearly correlated with the central system of the Sabbath Star Diagram as those of the inner hexagon can be related to the lateral system.

Plate 4 will be the basis of all further discussion of the color identifications of matrix spirals, its twelve triangles being identical in their arrangement to the twelve microtriangles of the Do hexagram and its inner hexagon, from which the twelve spirals of the matrix can be seen to originate. But we must first complete the initial description of the color-decomposed central system.

In plate 5 we may see the complete central sys-tem decomposed into the six Dinshah colors of magenta, red, yellow, green, blue, and violet. It illustrates this complete central system for both the fourth and fifth worlds as well as a portion of the sixth-world blue spiral sufficient to indicate the dif-ferent character of the central color spiral. In plate 5, the fourth-world elements are completely filled in, the fifth-world elements outlined with dashed lines, and the sixth-world element suggested with dashed-and-dotted lines.

What we can see most immediately is the startling difference between the color-individuated elements of the fourth- and fifth-world central system. Beyond the central collective unit composed of the original Do and Re hexagrams, there are in the fourth world only unrestricted color-individuated microhexa-grams. In contrast, the fifth-world contains only complete macrohexagram units, those with the microhexagrams of their own color that they always contain within the matrix border of a world, and there are no unrestricted microhexagrams.

Considering the implications of this distinction for the fourth world first, we can now see that the fourth-world individuated central microhexagrams lack the resonant power of those of their lateral counterparts contained within a color-coordinated macrohexagram. Thus the main polarity in the fourth world is between the collective nature of the central system and the individuated nature of the lateral system, the color-individuated central micro-hexagrams being in a recessive relationship to the more dominant individuation of the lateral system. It will be remembered that these unrestricted central microhexagrams were earlier identified with the loose-packed hexagonal matrix that had seemed to define the unfallen form of the pre-incarnate Nefesh soul body. We can now see that this aspect of the prehistory of cosmic evolution is still contained within the matrix of the fourth world, but in a recessive form. It is only in the fifth world that the individuated form of the central system can achieve the stability and resonant power given to its microhexagram forces by their enclosure within the forms of the macrostructure as well as a numerical parity with the macrostructural forms of the lateral system. But unlike the six unrestricted lateral microhexagrams that accompany its single macrohexagram unit in the ideal form of the fifth world, there are no unrestricted central microhexagrams in this world. For the central system, then, there would seem to be a kind of quantum leap between the manifestation of its color-individuated forms in the fourth and fifth worlds, from that only of unrestricted force to that only of force restricted by form. This is obviously an important distinction and its some of its implications will be discussed in appendix A.

The final point that should be noted at this time concerns the shape of the color-individuated central spirals. We have seen that the fourth-world diagram contains enough elements of the fifth-world matrix to enable us to gain some understanding of its constituents, but of the nature of the sixth-world matrix it can give no glimpse beyond the form given to the central spirals by the addition of its macrohexagram. As will be shown in chapter 10, arguably the most important chapter in this work, each central spiral has just one macrohexagram in the sixth-world matrix, whose position can be deduced from that of the fifth-world central macrohexagram. Although nothing further of the sixth-world central matrix system can be deduced from the fourth-world diagram, the addition of the sixth-world macrohexagram to a single central spiral, the blue macrohexagram shown at the top of plate 5, gives to the blue spiral of the central system a different character from the color spirals of the lateral system. Unlike the gyrating spirals of the lateral system, this would seem to cut a one-sixth spiral swath through the enclosing cosmic circle. The total

matrix, then, may be said to interweave a moving shuttle of the lateral woof through the central warp to make the beautiful fabric of divine reality. And in this wonderful technicolored twelvefold spiral matrix, not one triangular particle of color overlaps another.

Having studied the matrix in its separate macrostructure and microstructure and in its separate lateral and central interfacing systems, we should now be ready to observe the complete chromatic matrix in which each of the twelve color spirals can be seen to interpenetrate the others without losing its distinctness. In plate 6 all aspects of the matrix may be studied and mastered. Because of its complexity, the fourth-world macrohexagrams will be defined by continuous lines, the fourth-world microhexagrams will be filled in, and all the fifth-world macrohexagrams and microhexagrams will be defined by dashed lines, whatever their degree of completion in the fourth world. The macrostructure is complete for both the fourth and fifth worlds as is the central system of the microstructure, but the lateral system of the microstructure features only five microhexagrams, two for the fourth world and three for the fifth, two less than in plate 3 and four less than that actually contained in the cumulative fifth-world microstructure but a number that should be sufficient to show the character of the lateral spiral. Plate 6 is the culminating diagram of this introduction to the matrix.

THE DUAL SPIRAL MATRIX IN ITS UNFALLEN AND FALLEN FORMS

In the previous section, a preliminary analysis of the complex structure of the matrix was given in terms of the twelve colored spirals that could be discriminated in this structure. The intelligence of the diagram, if so it can be called, does not give any indication, at the level of the fourth-world matrix, of the desirability of further simplification of its structure. It is only at the level of the sixth-world diagram that a most meaningful pattern emerges in the cumulative matrix, as chapter 6 had shown was the case as well for the cumulative construction elements, thus reinforcing the definition of the sixth world as the dimension of meaningfulness. As will be seen in chapter 10, this most meaningful pattern in the matrix is one based on a dual spiral composed of central and lateral elements in a specific spatial relationship. Though the final analysis of the seventh-world matrix will again integrate this single developmental strand into the fuller sixfold structure of the matrix, the interim analyses of the matrices of the fourth through sixth worlds as of their correlated soul levels will, from this point on, focus on a single lateral spiral and the central spiral with which it is united in any particular world.

The lateral spiral that we shall be following in its long journey through the cosmic worlds will be the turquoise spiral, whose position in the matrix is the most outstanding. But in addition to its position, this color can also be associated with the developmental level identified with the Sol Sabbath Star of humanity if the Dinshah Ghadiali "Twelve Color Spectro-Chrome System," defined in the previous section, is correlated with the twelve-tone scale and its "chromatic" Solfeggio names.[7] The position of the turquoise lateral spiral is most appropriate for our analysis because its inner microhexagram appears at the highest centered point in the lateral microstructure of the fourth world, and in the sixth world it again achieves the highest centered position in the matrix. Though its movement in the fourth and fifth worlds will appear to be in a downward direction, a feature that will later prove to be most significant, the total pattern of the turquoise spiral will finally lift this human spiral to the heights that are its ultimate goal. Such an upward movement can already be seen in the last two fifth-world microhexagrams of this spiral sketched in at the right of plate 3.

The central spiral with which the turquoise lateral spiral will be associated in the fourth world is that of the red color. Though the full implications of the double spiral and of the fourth-world union of the turquoise with the red spiral will not become clear until chapter 10, when the spectacular final pattern will stand revealed in the sixth-world matrix, the geometric relationships of their fourth-world elements, as interpreted through the methodology

of the Science of Expressive Form, will reveal much about the functional nature of the consciousness that can be associated with this world. We shall consider, then, only the turquoise spiral and its intersection first with the red and then with the blue central spirals in this and the following three chapters, which will chart the soul's progress through the three main kabbalistic levels of the soul—the Nefesh, Ruach, and Neshamah soul levels—and we shall not be considering the twelve-spiral matrix again until chapter 12.

As in the case of the construction elements, the patterns that determine the proper form of earlier elements only become clear at the sixth dimension of meaningfulness. But what the sixth-world diagram cannot define is the matrix borders of the earlier worlds, and it is only through knowledge of these borders that an accurate modeling of the various dimensions of consciousness can be achieved. Thus the matrix of each world of the diagram has its own lessons to teach and its study can be rewarding even without the final illumination that will be provided in chapters 10 and 11 on the sixth-world matrix. The following study of the fourth-world matrix is complicated, however, by the fact that it has two forms: a past-modeled form with its zigzag matrix border and a future-modeled form with its plateaulike matrix border, the former border suggestive of the less structured medium of water as the latter is of the solidity of earth, and these expressive forms are further suggestive of the distinction between an unfallen and fallen condition that they will largely be considered to symbolize in this chapter.

We have seen that it is at the fifth-world level that man is ideally programmed by the diagram to develop the higher symbolic functions that fully distinguish him from the animals. Thus the simpler structure of the past-modeled fourth-world matrix is sufficient to model the "vital soul," here taken to represent the proper functioning of the Nefesh soul in its ideally intended incorporation within the larger structure of Ruach consciousness. But it is the more complex structure of the future-modeled fourth-world matrix that can more adequately define the actual functioning of humans who have not undergone the spiritual development that, following upon such a Fall as can be attributed to the sequence of these two forms of the fourth-world diagram, is now needed to achieve the Ruach level. This section will analyze the elements within the matrix borders of these two diagram forms and the next section will analyze the elements beyond these matrix borders, elements that are always taken to symbolize dangers to proper spiritual development. Plates 7 and 8 signify what can be considered the unfallen and fallen forms, respectively, of the fourth-world matrix. In plates 7 and 8 the macrohexagrams within the matrix border are represented in bold, the microtriangles composing the microhexagrams within this border being filled in, and all elements beyond the border appearing with dashes, however incomplete. In the versions of these illustrations shown in figures 8.1 and 8.2, however, the constituent triangles of both the macrohexagrams and microhexagrams within the matrix border are filled in, the constituent triangles of the central elements being filled with black, and such triangles of the lateral elements being filled with gray. Since these central and lateral matrix elements overlap each other, figure 8.1 will feature the central elements overlaying the lateral and figure 8.2 the lateral elements overlaying the central; and these figures should be compared to better understand the arrangement of these elements not only in the fourth world but in those to come. It should be noted that because of the increasing density of representing the expanded diagrams of the later worlds in the fixed space of the same page size, lighter shades of gray and finally white will be used the better to set off the lateral elements. But this can also be taken symbolically to signify the increasing enlightenment of the originally "muddy vesture"[8] of the lateral system. Finally, all lateral elements beyond the matrix border will be outlined with dashes and all such central elements with dashes and dots.

As can be seen in plate 7 and figure 8.1, the unfallen form of the fourth-world matrix at the minimum level of the dual spiral consists of four elements, two macrohexagrams containing restricted microhexagrams and two unrestricted microhexagrams, one of each category being central and the other lateral. Since all macrohexagrams within the matrix border of a world contain microhexagrams of their own color, all future references to macrohexagrams will be understood to contain such microhexagrams unless further qualified, and all references of microhexagrams will be similarly understood to be to the unrestricted variety. Each system, then, has one macrohexagram and one microhexagram in symmetrically overlapping configurations, the most obvious difference being between the nature of these macrohexagrams.

In the previous section, it was shown that the one central macrohexagram of the fourth-world matrix has a unique character. It is the collective source of all six central spirals. Thus the central macrohexagram has both a unitive and collective character. In contrast, the lateral macrohexagram is one of a multiplicity of such macrohexagrams, and it is marked by an individualized color.* If we can consider the macrohexagrams to represent centers of consciousness in a matrix modeling of the various levels of such consciousness, then we may say that the Nefesh level of the psyche is marked by the existence of two such centers with opposing characteristics. There is, on the one hand, a collective center associated with a condition of unity and, on the other, an individualized center associated with the state of multiplicity.

This double-aspecting can be related to the Zoharic understanding of the soul; and so it would be well, at this point, to review some aspects of the kabbalistic understanding of the soul, particularly of its main three levels, known by their acronym Naran. The Nefesh is the lowest level and represents the birthright animal or vital soul that cannot by itself survive the decomposition of the body. The higher two levels are personal achievements of soul growth that can survive the disintegration of the body after death and even prevent the disintegration of the vital soul. Where the Neshamah is the divine element in the human soul, the Ruach represents the fully realized human level on which mankind

---

*The remainder of this section repeats the analysis of Nefesh consciousness that appeared in *The Kabbalah of the Soul*, pp. 3–4, 90–94.

Figure 8.1. The Fourth-World Matrix Model of the Unfallen Nefesh Soul

should be functioning. But the Neshamah is deemed necessary both to complete the human soul, fulfilling the potential of its lower levels, and also to illuminate the higher realms.

To understand the distinction made here between the Neshamah and the lower levels of the soul as well as the structure of these Nefesh and Ruach levels, we should turn to the treatment of the soul in the *Midrash ha-Ne'lam on Ruth*, thought to be in the earliest stratum of the *Zohar*:[9]

> The Holy One, blessed be He, gave two fine crowns to man, for him to use in this world, namely, *nefesh* and *ruah*. . . . the *nefesh* cannot

Figure 8.2. The Fourth-World Matrix Model of the Fallen Nefesh Soul

survive in the body without being stimulated by the *ruah,* which rests above it.

When man begins to serve and worship his Creator with these two, he is stimulated by a holy stimulus from above, which rests upon man and surrounds him on every side. . . . And what is its name? *Neshamah.* The *neshamah* is a higher power than that which is called *ruah,* because the *ruah* was provided by the Holy One, blessed be He, for service in this world, while the *neshamah* always acts as a stimulus for service in the upper realms. . . .

Just as there is a *ruah* and a *nefesh* on the right-hand side, on the side of the good inclination, so there is a *ruah* and a *nefesh* on the left-hand side, on the side of the evil inclination.[10]

The vital Nefesh soul is meant in man to function as part of a conjoined Nefesh/Ruach soul "for service in this world," and when such human activity is intended as a form of divine "service," it draws down the holy Neshamah soul "for service in the upper realms."

In the first treatment in this passage, the dual forms of "service" by the human and divine elements of the multileveled soul are both recognized to be good, however opposing in orientation. But in the final treatment there is a reversion to the talmudic understanding of the soul as subject to the opposing influences of the Yetzer ha-Tov (the good inclination) and the Yetzer ha-Ra (the evil inclination), an understanding the *Zohar* synthesizes with its new view of the soul as so divided at each of its levels. This is not the simpler understanding of the conflict in the soul as one between its divine and so good element, the Neshamah, and its animal and so bad element, the Nefesh, an understanding whose vitality has persisted well into the hasidic period.[11] It is rather one that recognizes each of the earth-oriented soul levels as being essentially double-aspected, a double nature that may subject the soul to such temptation as has been symbolized by the myth of the Fall but is necessary for the soul's final perfection.

Returning now to the matrix representation of this double-aspecting, there are various further ways in which the central and lateral systems may be interpreted. One way would be to identify the lateral individualized center with conscious awareness and the central collective center with the subconscious. The former could further be associated with the waking Nefesh consciousness and the latter with the Nefesh consciousness during sleep. The collective central macrohexagram would seem, in fact, to be a perfect model for Jung's concept of the "collective unconscious," and the dream state in which this form of consciousness is most structured does use an archetypal visual language consistent with Jung's concept of the collective nature of such consciousness. But the dream reality of such central consciousness, though characterized by psychic powers not normally avail-

able to the waking state, lacks the coherence and continuity of the waking state that largely obscures its existence. Since the normal state of Nefesh consciousness contains traces of subconscious activity, the waking state will, however, have some intimation of another order of reality. But in the dream state of central consciousness there is no suspicion of a lateral realm of greater fixity and contraction.

If we now look at all four components of the unfallen matrix, they appear to define a circuit that can be identified with the normal functioning of the Nefesh soul. The lateral microhexagram emerging at the top from the central macrohexagram can be considered a centrifugal force, moving away from the original stability of collective consciousness to the new stability of individual consciousness represented by the lateral macrohexagram at the left. And the central microhexagram emerging at the bottom left from the lateral macrohexagram may similarly be viewed as a centripetal force, moving back from such stabilized individuality to its original state of collective consciousness.

These dual movements are representative of the daily functioning of the vital soul, the outgoing contraction of consciousness representing the awakening and fully awake Nefesh soul and the ingoing expansion its sleeping state, going from the dream state to that of deep sleep. Both movements of consciousness are clearly necessary for the healthy functioning of the Nefesh soul, daily recharging it both with vitalizing energy and the inner assurance of its ultimate wholeness. In this circuit of lateral and central elements we may also read the biological round of anabolic and catabolic functions as well as the further dynamics of the biophysical world, in which life forces build up higher forms of informational order to counter the physical effects of entropy. In the central and lateral macrohexagrams we can see the basic polarities of this world, that between collective and individual consciousness, the potential and the manifest. And we can also see in the lateral and central microhexagrams the centrifugal and centripetal forces that bind this functional polarity into a regenerating whole whose oscillation creates the rhythmic processes that inform all things.

Thus the elements given in the matrix of the

past-modeled fourth-world diagram are precisely those needed to maintain the vital functioning of the body at the lower level of consciousness that may be equated with the animal state, the state of the Nefesh Chayah, or living soul, that characterized both Adam and the animals brought before him for naming. It was earlier indicated that in its modeling of the psyche, the macrohexagrams represent centers of consciousness. We can now further expand the identification of matrix elements by identifying the microhexagrams with faculties in the service of such centers. The two psychic faculties that can be most closely correlated with the level of the vital soul are instinct and intuition, and it would seem appropriate to identify instinct with the lateral microhexagram and intuition with the central microhexagram. Instinct may be said to have a lateral character insofar as it defines a pattern of behaviors that is rational to the extent that it has proven survival value for the individual or species. Intuition, which serves as an emergency adjunct to such normal instinctual functioning, has a central character, however, since it arrives at its knowledge through nonrational paths. But what is most interesting about the matrix modeling of these faculties is the way they overlap the centers of the opposite system. Thus instinct would seem to be derived or in touch with the very center of collective consciousness while intuition is equally in touch with the center of individual consciousness. This cross-connecting of the systems seems exactly what is required to explain animal functioning since instinct defines a collective mode of behavior suitable for the general case while intuition allows for the unexpected through which the general can be individually adapted to fit the unusual case.

The simple model given in plate 7 and figure 8.1 may be said to define the functioning of the animals, of man at his most primitive level of tribal development, and of the animal level of man at a higher level of his spiritual development. Plate 8 and figure 8.2 model the more complex psyche that may be taken to signify the fallen Nefesh soul, one where greater sophistication has been achieved without the spiritual development necessary for its proper use. What figure 8.2 adds within its matrix border are the two lateral microhexagrams at the bottom, which were already fully present in figure 8.1 but beyond the limits set by its zigzag matrix border. To continue the specific identifications of the lateral microhexagrams, that at the left, which overlaps the central microhexagram and touches the microhexagram within the lateral macrohexagram, may be identified with the faculty of the emotions; and that at the right, which is separated from its lateral spiral by the incomplete macrohexagram beyond the matrix border and so not really able to maintain the continuity of this spiral, may be identified with the faculty of intellect.

These added faculties complete the natural endowment of what may be considered the fallen state of man. In this first way of interpreting the future-modeled form of the fourth-world diagram, their development is considered forbidden to the Nefesh soul because they are ideally supposed to function in collaboration with the higher centers of Ruach consciousness. The effect of drafting the fourth-world diagram in this future-modeled form can be interpreted, then, as causing the "fall" of the higher faculties of emotion and intellect from the fifth- to the fourth-world level of functioning, though it by no means demands it. Rather than serving the higher social purposes of Messianic society through the Ruach lateral center that they would ideally serve were the fifth-world diagram added to the unfallen form of the fourth-world diagram, they can be understood to have now become the exclusive adjuncts of a lower lateral center of consciousness still essentially at the reptilian level of the inner brain. Their greater sophistication is thus only serving an animal level of consciousness at its initial point of ego development, of its assertion of territorial rights and willingness to fight for their protection and extension. The faculties of feeling and thought have become dominated, indeed contaminated, by the impulses deriving from the primary lateral faculty of the Nefesh soul, the instincts of self-preservation and sex. In only serving the lowest center of lateral consciousness, the faculties of emotion and intellect have become molded into conformity with the mode designed to serve this center, that of instinctual gratification, and now employ all their talents to enhancing both the quantity and quality of such lower gratification.

The matrix modeling of the fallen faculties is as suggestive as that for the unfallen faculties previously considered. With regard to the second lateral microhexagram identified with the emotions, its overlapping of the central microhexagram gives support to the intimate relationship that seems to exist between the feelings and intuition, for intuitions are felt before they are rationally articulated. But the problem with this fourth-world development of the emotions is that they are directed downward to the lateral center of Nefesh consciousness rather than upward to this center of Ruach consciousness. Since the fifth world, whose elements appear at the bottom of the matrix diagram, represents a higher dimension of consciousness than the fourth, we can better appreciate the misdirection of the second lateral microhexagram by visualizing plate 8 in a reversed, upside-down position. We would then have a more coherent model for the way the fallen emotions, rather than lifting the instincts and intuition up to the Ruach center of consciousness, are themselves dragged down to add their color to Nefesh experience.

The disconnected state of the third lateral microhexagram gives even more expressive form to the state of alienation that most characterizes the fallen intellect. The simple round of healthy physical functioning that had marked the matrix of the unfallen Nefesh soul, that which went out with the lateral and back with the central, has been extended by the added lateral microhexagrams so that no simple return to the center is now possible. Though an enlarged cycle of return will once again becomes possible at the fully developed Ruach level, the development of these faculties at the level of the Nefesh soul may be thought to have distorted the natural functioning of the vital soul so that it reflects a state of disease rather than of health, the unintegrated higher faculties interfering with the proper functioning of the lower soul as well as losing all sense of their own proper direction.

One way in which this sense of direction can finally be restored and these elements transformed is through reconceiving the future-modeled fourth-world diagram not as fallen but as transformative

from a past to the necessary future orientation that can enable the process of Tikkun and the fulfillment of the cosmic purpose. The fourth-world diagram may be understood to model such a transformation of orientation if its first intermediate construction element, that coming just before the turning point of cosmic time, is past modeled, while the second intermediate construction element, that coming just after the cosmic turning point, is future modeled. Though this latter construction element covers the Sabbath Star modeling of the former, it can still be understood to be virtually present and the future-modeled diagram to be thus transformative.

Another way is by adding to its past-modeled construction just the first vertical Sabbath Star of the fifth world that adds precisely the matrix elements produced by its future modeling. Both of these alternatives to construing the future-modeled form of the fourth world as fallen were developed in chapter 3. Adding this fifth-world construction element to the six prior construction elements of the fourth-world diagram, the four of the fourth world and the two of the third world that must also be included, can be considered, then, to lift this world into a state of Sabbath consciousness. Such a Sabbatical form of the diagram may be viewed either as the proper first stage in the evolution of the unfallen Nefesh soul to the Ruach level or as the rectification of the fallen Nefesh soul and prelude to its now proper road to higher development.

We have seen that the matrix elements in figure 8.2 could be subject to different interpretations depending on whether they were seen as the product of the fallen form of the fourth-world diagram or either of its transformative or extended Sabbatical forms. So too can the Fall be modeled in two different ways by the matrix. We have thus far been interpreting the fallen nature of Nefesh consciousness from the perspective of the future-modeled form of fourth-world diagram construction identified with it, the matrix elements added by such construction being understood to signify fallen characteristics. But it is also possible to study the fallen Nefesh soul in terms of the unfallen form of the fourth-world diagram, by analyzing the elements beyond its matrix border. Thus in addition to the rules that distinguish between permitted and forbidden construction, there is also the primary rule of matrix definition and interpretation, that it is the border defined by the matrix macrostructure at its furthest continuous extent that distinguishes between the permitted and forbidden elements of the matrix, that can be considered its Torah.

The most expressive forms beyond the unfallen matrix border can be interpreted as signifying the pathways taken by fallen Nefesh consciousness. But to do so, the matrix elements representing the unfallen Nefesh soul must be given a more human construction than previously, when they were meant to be contrasted with the fuller constituents of the fallen matrix. As with unfallen Adam who named the animals, the model of the unfallen Nefesh soul must now be understood to involve a perfect balancing of a conscious center containing some measure of individual thought and feeling with a subconscious collective center, their own cyclic rhythm merging into the larger rhythm of the cosmic flow as does a natural part to a whole. The elements beyond this matrix border will not now be understood to represent centers and faculties of consciousness, although comparison with their previous identifications in the fallen matrix can give added richness to their new associations, but they will be understood to model the false pursuits that define the condition of fallen man. Indeed, the extended analysis to follow will show these border elements to provide an archetypal model of the various alternative pathways whose false allure has tempted man to transgress the limits of his Garden state for a life of exile.

TEMPTATIONS BEYOND THE MATRIX BORDER

Introduction to the Temptations of a Fallen Culture

In interpreting the symbolic meaning of the extraborder elements in the fourth-world matrices, it will be most helpful to use the particularly relevant terminology appearing in the second sentence of Genesis that defines a state of chaos: "And the earth was without form [Tohu] and void [Bohu]."* These Hebrew terms for formlessness and emptiness are most appropriate to discussion of the extraborder elements. What can immediately be seen in contemplating the three expressive forms beyond the matrix border of the unfallen fourth-world diagram, in plate 7 and figure 8.1, is that the fifth-world lateral macrohexagram, complete at least in outline beyond this border, appears without the interior microhexagram counterpart that all macrohexagrams feature when properly within the matrix border of their cosmic world. Using the biblical terminology from the second sentence of Genesis, this would seem to represent a pure Bohu, a formal entity devoid of content. When we later study the elements beyond the fallen matrix border of plate 8 and figure 8.2, we shall see that the fifth-world central microhexagram appearing beyond this border also has the character of a pure Tohu, since it is still lacking the surrounding central macrohexagram that can give the required form to its content. Though the two extraborder microhexagrams of the unfallen diagram are thus not true "Tohus," they do represent a type of chaos since the missing microhexagram of the Bohu between them breaks the lateral spiral that should connect them both to each other and to the larger field of the microstructure, thus leaving the one farthest out totally disconnected. What can be seen beyond the unfallen matrix border, then, is a representation of chaos, paths that lead nowhere and experiences of form without meaningful content. Although the initial analysis in this section will be of the elements beyond the unfallen matrix border, in the final discussion of the contrasting elements beyond the fallen border, we shall be able to chart a yet deeper form of the Fall, one that has moved from the defining quality of Bohu, of meaninglessness, to that of Tohu, total psychic disintegration.

At the growing edge of each cosmic world, then, there is a border that separates the order within from the chaos without, each successive world pushing the surrounding chaos further away and increas-

---

*Most of this section appeared in *The Kabbalah of the Soul*, pp. 95–115.

ing the island of order within.[12] What distinguishes the path of Tikkun from that of Tohu is that in the former the elements of higher consciousness are achieved, as in the Sabbatical diagram, by such spiritual discipline as may be compared with the actual work of constructing a further world of the diagram; in the latter, the attempt to achieve higher powers is not only made without such discipline but with a further violation of the law of limitation that can be compared with violation of the matrix border. Though the growth necessary for the Tikkun always carries the danger of following a false path into Tohu, what primarily differentiates the path of Tikkun from that of Tohu is the recognition that there is a border of law that distinguishes the permissible from the forbidden and that it is only in the former that the divine order is expressed.

Beyond the Unfallen Matrix Border: Particular Dangers to the Nefesh Lateral Personality

In plate 8 and figure 8.2 we are given a graphic representation of the proper place in which the Nefesh individuality should abide: it is within the lateral macrohexagram of the completed fourth-world matrix. It is only within the form of this larger structure that the individualized Nefesh consciousness can achieve the stability necessary for it to play its proper role in the Tikkun, the role of a part conscious of its participation in a larger enveloping and supporting whole and so at peace with its position in the cosmic scheme. On the Nefesh level of soul development, such peace is only possible for that stabilized lateral consciousness which feels at home in a world of physical solids it recognizes as divine and with whose limitations its individuality is in harmony.

If such individualized consciousness has not learned to abide within the world sanctified by observance of the divine laws of limitation, it can follow the unhallowed paths represented in the diagram by the two lateral border microhexagrams. The more accessible of these paths is that with which the stabilized lateral microhexagram is immediately in contact. We may consider this left border microhexagram to represent such narcissistic inflation of the ego as recog-

nizes no operative restraints to the pursuit of its own self-aggrandizement. Having lost the sacramental sense of life, it can only worship the false idols of secular society, power and pleasure.

On the more benign level of general mankind, this may mean no more than the pursuit of a prestigious position in society, one embracing the right job, spouse, and possessions by which society measures success and that are advertised to bring happiness. When the goal of a lifetime's striving has been achieved, however, when one arrives at the place of social success, it will be found empty of all true contentment, as the border macrohexagram toward which such energy was directed is empty. It is normally only at such moments of consummation that the hollowness of a life directed primarily to personal success is revealed. Though such individuals may be model citizens and even formally committed to their religion, their real belief is only in themselves and in taking whatever they may safely get away with. But the self whose never-satisfied needs they serve is as hollow as the success they may finally win. The utopia to which the materialism of the modern world beckons the self-enfranchised individual turns out to be the "no place" that Thomas More signified by his neologism. For the empty macrohexagram that, like the microhexagram leading to it, extends beyond the matrix border is "no place" for a Nefesh soul to abide. Its utopia turns out to be a chaos of Tohu and Bohu in which the soul can find no meaning that can integrate its elements and restore it to its proper place of peaceful stability.

On the more malignant level of unrestrained individuality, this same path to "no place" is that taken by the great villains of history and literature. This is particularly the path of the Shakespearean villain, of Iago, who says, "Virtue! a fig! 'tis in ourselves that we are thus or thus" (1.3.322), and of Macbeth, who similarly says, "For mine own good, / All causes shall give way" (3.4.35–36). But neither villain is as much the master of causality as he believes, and both are left empty and defeated by the fulfillment of their destructive pursuit of ego satisfaction, Iago concluding "From this time forth I never will speak word" (5.2.304), and Macbeth expressing a similar emptiness: "I 'gin to be aweary of the sun, / And wish th' estate o' th' world were now undone" (5.5.49–50). The ultimate punishment for all those who have followed the path that leads individualized consciousness away from the sacred space in which it experiences its harmony with the whole is not the just defeat or death that may overtake it but the emptiness to which that individual must inevitably arrive who cuts himself off from all sense of cosmic or social connection. Though originally motivated by a spiritually undeveloped egocentricity, there was yet about this course a certain buoyant self-confidence that promised the soul much good through fulfillment of its worldly aims. Marlowe's Tamburlaine shows such innocent enthusiasm when he asks: "Is it not passing brave to be a king, / And ride in triumph through Persepolis?" (2.5.53–54). It is only when the soul experiences the failure of this expectation in the finally empty consummation of its wishes that it may then experience the inverse side of its disconnected individuality, the anguished perception of its alienation and the meaninglessness of existence. Thus Macbeth, in a dramatic world filled with signs of supernatural power and purpose, can only find life to be "a tale / Told by an idiot, full of sound and fury, / Signifying nothing" (5.5.26–28).

If the left-border microhexagram represents the unrestrained individuality that mistakenly seeks its bliss in ego enhancement, the right-border microhexagram would seem to represent the alienated individuality whose consciousness of being imprisoned in a disconnected psyche is filled with existential despair. This right-border microhexagram completes the lateral spiral through the forbidden territory that lies just beyond the matrix border and thus defines the logical last step in the lateral path of an individuality that, by knowing no bounds, is brought to emptiness and final alienation. The dream of worldly success, which cut it off from its deeper roots, turns into a nightmare of bitterness with the frustration of its expectations and loss of faith in the false gods it had substituted for the true. Having cut itself off from all limiting connections with a bold impunity, it now finds itself in an alienated state of self-created isolation from which there is no exit, the disconnected lateral microhexagram

proving a fit emblem for such a hell. But this final hellish state of alienated individuality is not only approached through the successive steps of the lateral spiral; it seems directly available to some few spirits that have apprehended only the isolating effects of their individuality with no appreciation of the bonds to community and cosmos without which it could have no being. The archetypal form of such consciousness is that of Melville's Bartleby, the gentle scrivener whose negative assertion of individuality—"I would prefer not to"—leaves him "alone, absolutely alone in the universe. A bit of wreck in the mid-Atlantic."[13] The negative states to which the lateral elements within the Nefesh soul are prey when not abiding in the Sabbath consciousness of their proper cosmic place would seem to be fully comprehended by the forbidden portion of the lateral spiral beyond the matrix border.

Particular Dangers to the Nefesh Central Personality

The proper functioning of the Nefesh soul is not only endangered by the lateral attempt to enhance its individuality through a disconnecting breach of its limitations. It can also leave the stability of the lateral macrohexagram by entering too fully into the unitive consciousness of the central microhexagram or by never having sufficiently emerged from this consciousness into the stable lateral acceptance of physical limitation and multiplicity. For the Nefesh level of soul development is structured to give a necessary dominance to its lateral elements, without which dominance it cannot function in the physical world. As the unfallen fourth-world matrix contains no individuated central macrohexagrams, whether completed in the fourth-world matrix or just appearing beyond its matrix border, the central microhexagram can achieve no stable fulfillment in the physical world and should remain recessive.

There are, however, many individuals and even societies and historical periods in which the recessive central elements in consciousness have achieved a premature Nefesh development. One such literary portrayal is that of the Reverend Arthur Dimmesdale in Hawthorne's *The Scarlet Letter*: "Notwithstanding his high native gifts and scholar-like attainments, there was an air about this young minister,—an apprehensive, a startled, a half-frightened look,—as of a being who felt himself quite astray and at a loss in the pathway of human existence, and could only be at ease in some seclusion of his own. . . . Coming forth, when occasion was, with a freshness, and fragrance and dewy purity of thought, which, as many people said, affected them like the speech of an angel."[14] Dimmesdale is one who has not fully emerged from the central consciousness of unfallen Yetzirah, where the pre-incarnate Nefesh soul is hardly to be distinguished from the collective consciousness of the angels. "Quite astray and at a loss in the pathway of human existence," he cannot deal with the moral ambiguities inherent in the human condition, atoning so extremely for what he conceives to be his fall into sin that, like the proverbial good, he dies young. Though monastic forms of religion and martyrdom provide one mode of escape for such angelic personalities from the complex demands of human existence, the primary cultural modes of commitment to the absolute have been romantic or "courtly" love and honor. Both demand a fidelity to absolute values that, in a world of often dishonorable contingencies, can lead, as with Romeo, to making "a dateless bargain to engrossing death" (5.3.115). To prefer death before dishonor in an imperfect world is to win a spiritual victory over mortal limitation by a paradoxical choosing of its ultimate form, which is death.

This choosing of death for honor is everywhere displayed in Homer's *The Iliad*, but its best representative is probably Sarpedon, who stirs others to battle with the argument: "Ah, my friend, if after living through this war we could be sure of ageless immortality, I should neither take my place in the front line nor send you out to win honour in the field. But things are not like that. Death has a thousand pitfalls for our feet; and nobody can save himself and cheat him. So in we go, whether we yield the glory to some other man or win it for ourselves."[15] It is precisely because of the power and permanence of death that man's honor resides in that pursuit of glory which will bring death the sooner upon himself. And in Sarpedon's own death "he breathed defiance, like some proud tawny bull who is brought down among

the shambling cows by a lion that has attacked the herd, and bellows as the lion's jaws destroy him."[16] The hero's victory over death consists in just this defiant bellowing "as the lion's jaws destroy him." For the ultimate hero, Achilles, the choice is also clear. Recognizing that "you cannot steal or buy back a man's life, when once the breath has left his lips," he continues: "My divine Mother, Thetis of the Silver Feet, says that Destiny has left two courses open to me on my journey to the grave. If I stay here and play my part in the siege of Troy, there is no homecoming for me, though I shall win undying fame. But if I go home to my country, my good name will be lost, though I shall have long life, and shall be spared an early death."[17] Since the choice between long life and early death is placed in this context of shame or undying fame, Achilles' Hellenic destiny is determined. As his mother had said, he is "doomed to an early death."[18]

This same structure of values informs the courtly love tragedy of *Romeo and Juliet*,[19] "The fearful passage of their death-mark'd love" (prologue, 9). Like Achilles, Romeo is faced with the choice: "I must be gone and live, or stay and die" (3.5.11). He had earlier said to the Friar: "Do thou but close our hands with holy words, / Then love-devouring death do what he dare" (2.6.7–8). Thinking her dead, his absolute fidelity demands that he join her in a defiant love-death, triumphing over detestable death through bringing it upon himself:[20]

Thou detestable maw, thou womb of death,
Gorg'd with the dearest morsel of the earth,
Thus I enforce they rotten jaws to open,
And, in despite, I'll cram thee with more food!
(5.3.45–48)

Thus does the romantic idealist Romeo "shake the yoke of inauspicious stars / From this world-wearied flesh" (5.3.111–12). None of these devotees to absolute love or honor chooses a death he believes will be a gateway to personal immortality but rather the reverse, a death that will annihilate his personality. They are "world-wearied" and want no more of individuality, with all its compromising limitations.

The reason that central consciousness on the

Nefesh soul level develops what might be called, with Freud, a "death wish" may perhaps be explained by a reexamination of plate 7 and figure 8.1. Since this fourth-world diagram manifests no central elements of future worlds, there is only one direction in which the outer central microhexagram can move, and that is back to the inner central macrohexagram at the diagram's center. But this source of the twelve rays of individuated consciousness is itself still in a state of collective consciousness. Thus a premature return to this source, before the individuated central consciousness has become stabilized at the Ruach soul level, can only mean the permanent loss of individual personality with its total reabsorption into collective consciousness. From the lateral perspective, whose consciousness is enjoying its incarnation in physical matter, such a death of individual consciousness appears to be a tragic waste. As Milton's Belial says:

> To be no more; sad cure; for who would lose
> Though full of pain, this intellectual being,
> Those thoughts that wander through eternity,
> To perish rather, swallowed up and lost.
> (*PARADISE LOST*, 2.146–49)

And however desirable this return to a state of collective consciousness may appear to that minority of Nefesh souls in which the central system is more strongly marked than the lateral, it certainly does signify a short-circuiting of the process and, it would seem, purpose of cosmic manifestation. For these forms of individual consciousness are now forever lost, as is their contribution, to the process of cosmic evolution and perfection.

There has always been that spiritual minority, more cursed than blessed, in which the central system has achieved dominance before the soul has developed sufficiently to harmonize its higher sensitivities with the limitations that alone permit individuality. As Blake put it in "Auguries of Innocence," "Some are Born to sweet delight. / Some are Born to Endless Night" (ll. 123–24). And the two major forms of Nefesh religion develop from these two polarities of personality,[21] as Blake further shows in the conclusion to this poem:

> *God Appears & God is Light*
> *To those poor Souls who dwell in Night,*
> *But does a Human Form Display*
> *To those who Dwell in Realms of Day.*
> (LL. 129–32)

Though those "Born to Endless Night" may perceive a higher image of God than the happier inhabitants of the lateral day world, they are nonetheless "poor Souls," ill equipped to survive in a world of imperfect contingencies whose demands soon make them world-weary and anxious for such annihilation of individual consciousness as that expressed by Keats, when transported by the nightingale's song: "Now more than ever seems it rich to die /. . . . Still wouldst thou sing, and I have ears in vain— / To thy high requiem become a sod" (ll. 55, 59–60).

The suffering artist is a cultural stereotype because so many artists, especially when young, have a markedly central character without the soul development necessary to give proper perspective to their visions. Though their heightened attunement to the source of being may endow them with enormous creative power, their vision of life is largely that of the young and, though he knew it not yet, shortly to die Keats, one "Where but to think is to be full of sorrow" (l. 27).

But though the beauty with which such tragic visions have been expressed has given the artist's agony a power to move and uplift that can redeem both the artist's suffering and that which it has aroused in a sympathetic heart, there is another kind of art that, though no greater, yet springs from a higher source of inspiration. From Bach to Wagner, from Michelangelo to Rodin, and from Milton to Tolstoy, there have been commanding artists who have reached a sublime level of art beyond tragedy, an epic art illuminated with a sense of cosmic purpose in which the enduring human will is allowed to play a meaningful role. This Ruach inspired art, though ever aware of the sufferings of the human condition, yet places these sufferings in an affirmative cosmic perspective that finally transmutes them into joy. This is the highest art, for the creative utterances of Neshamah souls do not cloth themselves in imaginative fictions but become the prophetic foundations of civilizations.

It is epic endurance that is especially required of those marked for the central path. Though it makes possible an accelerated spiritual development for those who have committed themselves to such development, it is not until the Ruach soul level has been attained that central consciousness can rise above the pain of its mortality that drives it to suicidal modes of behavior, preferring to "become a sod" than longer to endure the pain of thought. To strengthen this capacity of the undeveloped central consciousness to endure, to resist the centripetal pull back to collective consciousness that spells the death of personality and to stay firmly on the path to a saving spiritual development, the safest course may well be that of strict, even monastic, forms of organized religion. Because such religious practices transmit a spiritual energy accumulated through the millennia of devotional observance, they can greatly enhance the power of individual devotions as well as guiding it along a safe path of spiritual evolution.[22]

This religious form of life—which sacramentalizes all permissible activities through spiritual devotions that, by bringing the divine dimension into everyday consciousness, educates the Nefesh soul as to its true spiritual direction—provides a well-tried way of conforming to that culminating commandment with which Moses concludes and contains the whole of the law: "See, I have set before thee this day life and good, and death and evil. . . . therefore choose life, that both thou and thy seed may live: That thou mayest love the Lord thy God, and that thou mayest obey his voice, and that thou mayest cleave unto him: for he is thy life, and the length of thy days . . ." (Deut., 30:15, 19–20). Against Achilles' Hellenic choice of death, the Hebraic tradition commands one to "choose life." Not recognizing the validity of that pursuit of personal honor and glory for whose realization death may be chosen, it can only condemn such a choice of death as evil and a fit punishment for those who would arrogate to themselves the glory belonging only to God. But the life one is commanded to choose is to be one not so forgetful of its origins as to say, "My power and the might of mine hand hath gotten me this wealth" (Deut, 8:17). Rather, it is the choice of a life that recognizes its dependence upon a greater, divine whole and willingly abides within its limitations to realize its true nature: "For he is thy life, and the length of thy days."

Beyond the Fallen Matrix Border

In this study of the elements beyond the unfallen matrix border, we have seen that they can provide an archetypal model of the main paths away from the sacred space bounded by divine law that identifies life with limitation. But before closing this subject, we should examine the more extreme dangers to further spiritual growth represented by the equally expressive forms of the elements beyond the fallen matrix border of plate 8 and figure 8.2 There are two such elements: the central microhexagram that, lacking its ultimate enclosure by a central macrohexagram, was earlier shown to represent a true state of Tohu or chaotic formlessness; and the lateral macrohexagram, now containing the outlines of its still incomplete interior microhexagram. Because we have just been considering the sad character of premature central dominance at the Nefesh level of development, it seems best to continue with the further plight to which such centrally dominant Nefesh souls are prone.

In analyzing the unfallen matrix, we saw that there was no place for a central consciousness individualized at the level of the fourth-world microhexagram to go except back to the central macrohexagram of collective consciousness. In the last section such a returning central movement was shown to be as necessary as the outgoing lateral movement for optimal functioning in the material world. The problem only arises when the Sabbath is so extended that no food is gathered, when the dream state is confused with consensus reality, when the meditative breath is held too long. Then the forces meant for periodic regeneration of life prove its death. This is the suicidal malaise that we understood to afflict the prematurely developed central type of Nefesh soul in the immediately prior discussion. But though such centrally dominated Nefesh souls may eventually commit suicide after a most melancholy life, they are yet more fortunate than those whom a completely unbalanced central development has blighted almost from the beginning of their physical embodiment. Those who have somehow been born to the fallen condition, as defined by plate 8 and figure 8.2, would seem almost immediately to stray past its matrix border to inhabit a Tohu of fifth-world centrality, a psyche of such complete chaos as characterizes psychosis, primarily schizophrenia but perhaps also the extreme form of infantile autism. For the difference between the central predicament in the unfallen and fallen forms of the matrix is that the fallen form does now provide a forward position to which individualized central consciousness can progress. Rather than being drawn back to the central stability at the center, it can now be caught by a not yet stabilized form of Ruach central consciousness. Such schizophrenics may well display some of the higher psychic powers that characterize the Ruach soul, particularly in its central aspect, but in a nonfunctional form.

In the first section we saw that there was a kind of quantum leap between the manifestations of the individualized central spirals in the fourth and fifth worlds. In the fourth world such central individuality appears only as an unrestricted microhexagram while in the fifth world it appears only as a macrohexagram with its enclosed microhexagram. What this suggests is that its manifestation in the fourth world is as a subtle form of energy, whose activities seem to contradict the normal perceptions of lateral consciousness and so are largely dismissed as coincidental, whereas its appearance in the fifth world is in the form of commanding visions. The central system appears here only in the form of discrete structures, of immediately embodied thought, a circumstance that may explain many features of what is called the astral plane. The indications of entry into the central system of Ruach consciousness would thus appear to be quite pronounced, almost like a light switch that dispels the darkness of disturbing paranormal hints on the Nefesh level with the certainty of meaningful visions, an astral realm as real as the physical but following different laws that must be learned for successful navigation. As will be shown in chapter 9 analyzing the fifth-world matrix, it is as important at the fifth-world level as at the fourth for the central

system to remain under the unremitting control of the lateral. The reason for this can be seen in the position of the Ruach elements at the bottom of the diagram. Though the Ruach soul represents a higher level of consciousness than that of the Nefesh, it operates on a dimension that may be compared with the shamanic concept of the lower world, not a hell but a spiritual realm characterized by a fluid form of consciousness and such a sense of descent as that the Merkabah tradition ascribed to those engaged in "chariot" mysticism. But the central spiral of Ruach as of Nefesh consciousness represents a danger to the soul's ultimate form of spiritual development because it is, in truth, going in a different direction than that of the lateral spiral that defines its abiding personality, to the bottom rather than the top of the diagram. It would lead man away from his development of the purified personality that can finally direct the highest of cosmic powers to their purposed end, leading him to the destruction rather than empowerment of personality.

From the foregoing, it should be apparent why a premature entry into the unstabilized form of the Ruach central system present beyond the fallen fourth-world matrix border would be characterized by the cacophony of commanding visions definitive of schizophrenia. For the visions meant to enlighten Ruach consciousness as to the proper direction of its higher energies have here no such larger context of individual and social spiritual development. Lacking both the stability of vision represented by the missing central macrohexagram enclosure and the control of this visionary center by a still inactive lateral center, it can only torment the psychotic consciousness with a confusion of visionary states masquerading as reality and commanding the individual to perform either impossible or destructive acts.

Turning now to the lateral element beyond the fallen matrix border, we see that the former lateral Bohu has here been filled with at least the outline of its interior microhexagram. What this means is that the power promised by this lateral temptation will no longer be empty but real. This is essentially the distinction between worldly and spiritual power. The previous discussion of transgression beyond the unfallen matrix border was concerned with just such worldly power, whether in its physical or social forms. For whether man has harnessed the power of the atom or of empire, such power has not fulfilled its promise of conferring meaning to his life, its very achievement revealing the spiritual emptiness of worldly power. At the less developed stage represented by plate 7 and figure 8.1, the lure of Ruach power glimpsed by the fallen Nefesh soul was only that outer form that it sensed it needed but only knew how to fill with the selfish, physical counters of its own Nefesh level of understanding. But at the more advanced stage represented by plate 8 and figure 8.2, the fallen Nefesh soul has, indeed, forced its entry into a source of genuine spiritual power. The lateral macrohexagram of the fifth-world matrix is, in fact, the powerhouse of the whole double spiral completed in the sixth world. There are ideally six fifth-world lateral microhexagrams that may be said to serve this one lateral macrohexagram, more than are attached to any other macrohexagram in the completed spiral pattern. Though the acceptance of the validity of the future-modeled fourth-world diagram would reduce the number of fifth-world lateral microhexagrams to four, this is still much higher number than that commanded by all other lateral macrohexagrams and all but one central macrohexagram. In chapter 10 we shall see further correlations of this macrohexagram with the psychic center identified with power in both kabbalistic and yogic psychology. Thus even a forced entry into this center will endow an individual with certain psychic powers, the powers of the black magician. In chapter 9 this completed center with all its associated microhexagram powers will be analyzed in terms of the true powers available to such a white magician as can be called a Ruach Master. The difference between the holy and unholy uses of this power center is not simply the greater power of the spiritual master but also the self-defeating nature of all such occult power as has been perverted to lower ends. For a sorcerer who, through the use of black arts, has gained access to sources of power beyond his Nefesh level of development, can only pervert such power to the Nefesh end of ego aggrandizement. Its effects will be as self-defeating as was Jepthah's victory, purchased with divine power at what proved to be the price of his only child (Judg. 11).

Without a properly prepared spiritual vessel, the invocation of such supernatural powers by a central personality can only produce a psychic overload leading to just such a derangement as that represented by the central Tohu. In a laterally dominated individual, however, the union of this unenclosed central microhexagram with the almost completed lateral macrohexagram unit can be a formidable combination, its further access to central power leading to the derangement not of schizophrenia but megalomania. But perhaps the most serious though less drastic effect of such misbegotten and misdirected spiritual power is that its counterfeit of spiritual mastery is believed by the self and so prevents all further true spiritual development. Though the very violence of such enlargement of consciousness may have some success in reaching that part of the self whose resistance to participation in the cosmic harmony can best be overcome through the proof of just such an experience of expanded consciousness, it is an unsure way. For whatever psychic power has thus been acquired has been at the price of short-circuiting the further spiritual development that alone could yield the lasting satisfaction to the self that results from the perfect coherence of the individual will with benefit to the whole. There will be more said about the false spiritual direction of the magician in the final discussion of elements across the matrix borders to which chapter 11 is devoted, which will reexamine what has been said in this section from the further perspective of the whole pattern.

We shall there see that in every cosmic world there are conditions and limitations that must be discovered and obeyed if spiritual experience of such higher states is to be the path of Tikkun rather than of Tohu. For what distinguishes the spiritual master from a false guru is that true observance of the Torah of cosmic limitation that enables one to find his or her proper "place" in the cosmic scheme, the place of a dependent part that, through grateful acknowledgment of this dependence, can grow in consciousness until it can become aware of its participation in the power of the whole, such growth as we shall be exploring in this new multidimensional model for "transpersonal psychology."

CHAPTER NINE

The Fifth-World
Matrix Model of the Ruach Soul

PRIMARY DEFINITION OF THE FIFTH-WORLD MATRIX

The Sabbath Star Diagram offers various approaches to psychological modeling. The most important contribution of part 2 was its development of a therapeutic model on the basis of a peculiar possibility of fourth-world construction, the fact that this diagram world[could uniquely be constructed with the past modeling of the first intermediate Sabbath Star and the future modeling of the second. This circumstance permitted such a form of the fourth-world diagram to model a "Transformative Moment" of insight into the failure of past patterning that can permit the projection of a new possibility of future behavior. In this part we have already seen how the fourth-world matrix can provide an even richer model of the Nefesh level of the soul. In this chapter we shall see how the cumulative matrix can provide a model of Ruach consciousness that also defines the dynamics of the meditative state, a model centered on a similar moment of transformational insight.

In developing this model, we shall continue to follow the turquoise lateral spiral earlier identified with man[1] in its association with a central spiral, here as in the fourth world that of the red spiral. In the fourth and fifth worlds of the diagram, these conjoined spirals describe a downward curve through the matrix, one that would graphically seem to belie the conception of the fifth world as a sphere higher than that of the fourth world from which certain powers could "fall," unless the diagram center be viewed as representing something like a gravitational source. The graphic position of the main features of the fifth-world matrix at the bottom of the diagram, at a position lower than that of the fourth world, seems consistent, however, with the Merkabah conception of mystic experience as a "descent to the chariot"[2] as well as the shamanic conception of a "lower world" that is also a higher state of consciousness. And as the spiral of man continues its passage through the matrix, it will arrive at the top of the diagram in the sixth world, its dimension of consciousness again being consistent with the shamanic concept of an "upper world."[3] Though we will not understand the reason for the selection of these spirals until we do reach the "upper world" of Neshamah consciousness, we can still learn much from the specific matrix features that define the "lower world" of Ruach consciousness as they appear together with the fourth-world matrix elements in both plate 9 and figure 9.1. In figure 9.1 the triangular elements filled in with black signify the elements of the red central spiral and those filled in with gray the elements of the turquoise lateral spiral, here in a lighter shade of gray to signify their growing "enlightenment."

A most significant point regarding the fifth-world matrix involves the number of its constituents, a number that depends upon the form of the fourth-world diagram from which it is expanded. If it is added to the past-modeled fourth-world diagram, taken to represent its unfallen con-dition, its lateral microhexagrams would number six. If it is added to the future-modeled form, whose inclusion of the two lateral microhexagrams beyond the past-modeled matrix border can be taken to characterize this fourth-world model as fallen, it would add only four such lateral microhexagrams. In either case, the cumulative fifth-world matrix would have a total of seven lateral microhexagrams. If we continue the scenario of the Fall largely developed in the previous chapter, then its full fifth-world manifestation can be taken to restore to the fifth-world matrix the two lateral microhexagrams that may thus be said to have "fallen" from their proper

Figure 9.1. The Fifth-World Matrix Model of the Ruach Soul

fifth-world position. Chapter 3 has shown, however, that the future-modeled form could be understood to be "transformative" rather than fallen, enabling that transformation from the past to the future orientation that can lift the soul into its Ruach dimension and so begin the process of Tikkun. But whether the future-modeled fourth-world diagram be understood to be fallen or transformative, movement into the Ruach dimension modeled by the fifth-world diagram lifts the soul to the redemptive plane of humanity's optimal functioning on earth that leaves the question of a fourth-world Fall far behind. Thus it is best simply to use the cumulative counting of lateral microhexagrams from one to seven without concern for which ones are exclusively the product of the fourth world or the fifth. While not forgetting the earlier considered resonances of these elements, this more neutral view of matrix elements will be the approach largely adopted in this chapter.

Before defining the matrix elements completed by the fifth-world Sabbath Stars, it would be helpful to review the elements of the fourth-world matrix and conventions for discussing such elements. It should be remembered that since matrix macrohexagrams always enclose microhexagrams of their color, they are understood to do so, unless otherwise qualified, when referred to simply as macrohexagrams. Similarly, references to microhexagrams are understood to refer only to those that are unenclosed by color-coordinated macrohexagrams. The major distinction between the macrohexagrams and the microhexagrams so defined is that the former are taken to represent centers of consciousness and the latter powers associated with these centers.*

In the case of the Nefesh soul, the central macrohexagram represents the collective form of consciousness, which normally functions only when the rest of the system is "unconscious," whereas the lateral macrohexagram represents self-consciousness and is associated with the ego. The power that aids the Nefesh ego in determining its responses to chal-

lenges from its environment is that of the instincts identified with the lateral microhexagram, the first on the lateral spiral and one that not only overlaps the central macrohexagram but touches the source of all Knowledge (Da'at) at the diagram's center. The primary organ of the collective aspect of the Nefesh soul is that identified with the central microhexagram; and it represents an area as uncharted by modern brain research as the collective consciousness of the central macrohexagram to which it is directly connected, the power of intuition. It is through this power of paranormal knowledge that the collective consciousness can inform the self-consciousness of urgent matters, particularly regarding imminent threats to its survival.

The future-modeled form of the fourth-world diagram adds two additional lateral microhexagrams, that occupying the second position on the lateral spiral being identified with the emotions and that in its third position with the reason. Significantly, this third lateral microhexagram, identified with the analytic intelligence, is totally disconnected from its spiral, a disconnected condition that the spiritually uninformed reason could, indeed, conclude its cosmic position to be. When we look at the fifth-world diagram, however, we see that these disassociated aspects of Nefesh consciousness have all become hooked up to a larger system in which they evidently have important roles to play. To understand how all the fifth-world matrix elements operate, we shall first have to determine the functions of its macrohexagrams.

The lateral center of Ruach consciousness can be identified with the essential lateral quality that can be associated with the Ruach Master, the truly free will, particularly as defined by Gurdjieff:

> Instead of the discordant and often contradictory activity of different desires, there is *one single* I, whole, indivisible, and permanent; there is *individuality*, dominating the physical body and its desires and able to overcome both its reluctance and its resistance. Instead of the mechanical process of thinking there is *consciousness*. And there is *will*, that is, a power, not merely composed of various often contradictory desires

---

*The material in the remainder of this chapter has already appeared, largely verbatim, in chapter 3 of *The Kabbalah of the Soul*.

belonging to different "I"s, but issuing from consciousness and governed by individuality or a single and permanent I. Only such a will can be called "free," for it is independent of accident and cannot be altered or directed from without.[4]

The will of the master can be self-directed rather than directed by external influences, a cause rather than a result, because it is one with the true individuality of that self. The Nefesh soul, in its primary desire for personal success and security, had submitted to the social conditioning that promised to satisfy these desires as well as secondary needs it had instigated. The result is that the soul developed a mechanical, mass-produced personality that could no longer distinguish its true nature and affinities. It is in the lateral Ruach center that the higher "I" of Ruach consciousness resides, and when the whole psychic entity moves either permanently or temporarily from a Nefesh to a Ruach state of consciousness, the transfer of identity from the lower to the higher ego that then takes place is from the earlier lateral center of Nefesh self-awareness to this new center. The difference between these two levels of self-awareness can be largely attributed to the quality of the wills they express, the lower will being overly determined by external forces while the higher will is a true expression of genuine individuality. Perhaps the still primitive level of Nefesh individuation is being influenced subconsciously, to rejoin a state of collective consciousness.

For the most part, the detribalized man of the last five thousand years is not truly civilized, insofar as truly valuing his independent voice, and seeks in mass conformity a return to a sense of tribal belonging. It may well be that Nefesh consciousness is best described as tribal, and that the mechanization of the will that Gurdjieff described results from the unsatisfactory way in which human beings, thrust prematurely into a higher civilization for which they are spiritually unprepared, attempt to recreate the lost tribe of their dreams. Few are the truly civilized who, valuing their hard-won capacity for individual creative thought, can answer the invitation of tribal howling as does Conrad's Marlow in *Heart of Darkness*: "An appeal to me in this fiendish row is

there? Very well; I hear; I admit, but I have a voice, too, and for good or evil mine is the speech that cannot be silenced."[5]

If the voice of the truly individual will can be associated with the lateral macrohexagram, the central macrohexagram can be associated with a faculty just as essential to Ruach consciousness, that of the imagination. The best definition of the imagination is still that given by Coleridge in his discussion of the ideal poet:

> He diffuses a tone and spirit of unity, that blends, and (as it were) *fuses*, each into each, by that synthetic and magical power, to which we have exclusively appropriated the name of imagination. This power, first put in action by the will and understanding, and retained under their irremissive, though gentle and unnoticed, control (*laxis effertur habenis*) reveals itself in the balance or reconciliation of opposite or discordant qualities: of sameness, with difference; of the general, with the concrete; the idea with the image; the individual, with the representative; the sense of novelty and freshness, with old and familiar objects; a more than usual state of emotion, with more than usual order. . . .[6]

The higher imagination of which Coleridge speaks is a "synthetic and magical power." It is in truth the faculty most necessary for producing those effects that shall be here unabashedly referred to as magic. And this faculty is closely dependent upon the power for which it was named, the power of imaging, of visualization. But it is also a "synthetic" power, and that which it synthesizes first and foremost is "the idea with the image." It provides an individual and concrete form for a general truth or idea, thus lifting its images to the level of symbols. Such symbolic forms express in the language of imagery the truths perceived by that inner vision known as insight, and the source of its insights is a heightened state of emotional sensitivity, of empathy, of seeing into the heart of the other. Beyond all this, it is a power that seeks to balance, reconcile, or fuse all "opposite or discordant qualities," that "diffuses a tone and spirit of unity."

Many of the above qualities will sound like the familiar, popular descriptions of the "right side of the brain." For the current theory based on split-brain research divides all mental processes into those of the analytic left brain and the synthetic right brain, and one goal of popular psychology has been to develop the power of the normally recessive right brain in the belief that a more "holistic" person will thereby emerge. But what is being asked of the poor, mute, image-processing faculty of the right brain is impossible without further spiritual development, and is, indeed, a description of higher consciousness. The right hemisphere of the neocortex corresponds to what Coleridge calls the "primary imagination," the "prime Agent of all human Perception."[7] It processes the perceptions of the physical eye for interpretation by other portions of the brain. The "secondary imagination," earlier discussed, is a higher faculty which "dissolves, diffuses, dissipates, in order to re-create."[8]

If the distinction between the functions ascribed to the right and left sides of the brain has any validity, it is on the higher level of Ruach consciousness and may be associated with the central and lateral macrohexagrams currently under discussion. But the relationship of these two centers of higher consciousness must still be as Coleridge defined them, for the imagination should be activated and ever under the control of the will. When we later study the complete sixth world matrix, we will come to understand why the central system poses such a danger to psychic survival in the fourth and fifth worlds. We have seen that the central pursuit of the ideal on the Nefesh level can lead to various forms of suicidal behavior. So too, the Ruach imagination, if allowed unfettered expression of its visionary power, can lead to psychosis. Its power of astral projection can threaten the body or the mind and even in milder forms can unleash a power of the irrational that can make a virtue of vice

All of these aspects of the imagination are brought together at the conclusion of Coleridge's great poem on the irrational, "Kubla Khan." Composed in a drug-induced state, the symbolic images of the poem first describe the "stately pleasure-dome" that Kubla Khan had built beside under-ground caverns, and then the imagery switches to a vision of a damsel singing, concluding:

> *Could I revive within me*
> *Her symphony and song,*
> *To such a deep delight 'twould win me,*
> *That with music loud and long,*
> *I would build that dome in air,*
> *That sunny dome! those caves of ice!*
> *And all who heard should see them there,*
> *And all should cry, Beware! Beware!*
> *His flashing eyes, his floating hair!*
> *Weave a circle round him thrice,*
> *And close your eyes with holy dread,*
> *For he on honey-dew hath fed,*
> *And drunk the milk of Paradise.*
>
> (LL. 42–54)

The truly creative imagination depends on a special state of attunement, of higher harmony, but such a magical power of creation, though fed by Paradise, is threatening to the normal consciousness of auditors and seer alike. For magical effects that inspire rather than threaten, the imagination must be under the "irremissive" control of the will.

A similar distinction between correct and improper uses of the imagination was earlier voiced by the thirteenth-century master of kabbalistic meditation Abraham Abulafia. Warning against its improper use, he writes: "The power of your imagination will overwhelm you, making you imagine many utterly useless fantasies. Your imaginative faculty will grow stronger, weakening your intellect, until your reveries cast you into a great sea. You will not have the wisdom ever to escape from it, and will therefore drown."[9] Elsewhere he shows us what can be accomplished through the proper control of the imagination by the will: "if his mind can control its fantasies, then he can ride [his mind] like a horse. He can control it as he desires, spurring it on to go forward, or reining it to stop where he pleases. At all times, his imagination remains subject to his will, not straying from its authority, even by a hair-breadth."[10]

The primary definitions of the Ruach macrohexagrams just given were determined by the larger consideration of this chapter, the development of a matrix model for the functioning of higher consciousness, particularly in the meditative state. But there is a more general way of defining them that can be integrated with the identifications already made. As earlier suggested, the way the distinction between right and left brain functioning is often put could be better applied to the two aspects of Ruach consciousness, those associated with the central and lateral systems, respectively. We can go further and identify the Ruach central system with the higher Ruach heart and its lateral system with the higher Ruach mind, understanding the imagination and the will to be lodged in the Ruach heart and mind thus defined. Such an association of the imagination with the heart is reflected in the biblical phrase "the imagination of man's heart" (Gen. 8:12).

But the identification of the central macrohexagram with the Ruach heart is also most revealing in graphic terms, though again these are not terms that can be appreciated at the level of the fifth-world diagram. In chapter 8, it was suggested that a circle could be drawn through the matrix that went out with the lateral and back with the central, a circle that appeared to define the healthy functioning of the unfallen Nefesh soul; and in chapter 12, we shall see that the line drawn in this fashion through the involuted form of the full sixth-world matrix spirals and their doubles, as illustrated in plate 15, seems to define two conjoined soul bodies, one of whose remarkable features is that the Ruach central macrohexagram of one set of spirals appears to be in the body otherwise delineated by the other, complementary set. The implication that the Science of Expressive Form can draw from this feature of the matrix is that the Ruach heart is, in some sense, in the "body" of the Other, and that it is from this very circumstance that it gains its imaginative grasp of meanings that are beyond the mind's rational powers.

On the basis of this expressive form, we can assign to the Ruach heart the characteristic quality of empathy[11] and understand from this how its emotions are to be distinguished from those of the Nefesh soul. For as the Nefesh heart or emotional system can be considered to be selfish, so can its Ruach counterpart be considered selfless. Its identification with the needs of the Other represents the highest quality of the Ruach soul and is the very quality that can make the coming of the Messianic Kingdom possible. When we come to our final understanding of the matrix spirals in the next chapter, we shall see that the fifth world central macrohexagram does occupy a higher spiritual position than its lateral counterpart. But as its very selflessness can constitute a danger to personal survival at the Ruach level and so short-circuit the higher development of the soul to the Neshamah level, the imaginative Ruach heart must remain ever subject to the will of the Ruach mind, "not straying from its authority," in Abulafia's words, "even by a hairbreadth."

The reason that the Ruach mind can exert such authority can be explained by another, earlier-discussed feature of the matrix, the fact that the fifth-world lateral macrohexagram can ideally be considered to be attended by six fifth-world lateral microhexagrams, which would give it the largest number of any macrohexagram in the complete sixth-world matrix. If, as earlier suggested, the microhexagrams of a particular world can be considered as "powers" of the faculties represented by the macrohexagrams of its spiral, then this would make the Ruach lateral macrohexagram the most powerful faculty in the complete model of soul development. But even if the fourth world is accepted as properly future modeled and the Ruach lateral macrohexagram is accordingly only allowed four microhexagrams, this is still a high number, second only to the sixth world's central macrohexagram with five attendant central microhexagrams and the highest of all the lateral macrohexagrams. In either case, the implication that can be drawn from this expressive form is that the Ruach mind and will, represented by this lateral macrohexagram, can be characterized by power, not only in the fact of its power but in its concern for the enhancement and employment of such power; it is the reason that the individual at this level of soul development is driven to become a spiritual master. For it is only such an exercise of Ruach power, consistent with the desires of the Ruach heart for communal sharing, that is ultimately rewarding, perversions of this power to private ends proving to be equally self-defeating because of that built-in fifth dimension of Providential justice operating precisely through this spiritual power.

In the later-to-be-established order of the macrohexagrams, the first is, as it should be, the collective central macrohexagram at the center of the fourth-world diagram, the second the fourth-world lateral macrohexagram, the third the fifth-world lateral macrohexagram, and the fourth the fifth-world central macrohexagram. Now, as can be seen in plate 9 and figure 9.1, this hierarchical order, for which sound grounds will be established in chapter 10, contradicts the natural order of the conjoined matrix spirals, in which the central macrohexagram precedes the lateral. But if the rule be applied by which the movement goes out with the lateral and back with the central, we can discern a subsidiary reason to equate the fifth-world lateral macrohexagram with the third hierarchical position and its central macrohexagram with the fourth.

It will be remembered that this rule was first formulated in terms of the four elements of the unfallen fourth-world matrix, the cycle thus established going out through the lateral microhexagram to the lateral macrohexagram and back through the central microhexagram to the central macrohexagram. But in applying it to the more complex matrices of the expanded diagrams, it becomes necessary to restrict the cycle only to the macrohexagrams. As the matrix border is defined by the matrix macrostructure, so would the movement cycle appear to be defined by the macrostructure through each matrix of the diagram worlds, this macrostructure having earlier been appropriately identified with the dimension of form. Indeed, once this rule is thus qualified, it can be applied even to the fourth-world matrix, the line going out to the lateral macrohexagram and back to the central not really requiring the use of the intermediary microhexagrams. As already noted, the forms that emerge through application of this rule to the fourth- and sixth-world matrices are most metaphorically suggestive, but the most expressive form of all is that which emerges in the fifth-world matrix, as illustrated in figure 9.1, which depicts only its labeled macroelements.

The remarkable form that emerges in figure 9.2

is none other than that which has been accepted as the symbol of infinity. Though this figure-8 curve seems to have first appeared only in the seventeenth century,[12] the rapidity with which it spread from an obscure mathematical treatise into a universally accepted symbol of infinity indicates that its originator, John Wallis, had hit upon an archetypal form for this concept, one that, though long hidden in the collective unconscious, could be immediately recognized both by Wallis and all who followed as the right symbol. Its appropriateness is further underscored by its appearance in the fifth-world matrix, due to the reversed positions the fifth-world central and lateral macrohexagrams take with respect to those of the fourth world. For when the movement rule is applied, to return with the central system, after having moved from the fourth-world lateral macrohexagram out to that of the fifth, the line must double back in the classic infinity curve.

The implication of this would seem to be that it is only at the Ruach level that the human soul gains a guarantee of infinite continuity, of eternity. This is consistent with the Jewish esoteric tradition that, like some other such traditions, does not regard man's birthright animal soul to be immortal but believes such immortality to be a personal acquisition dependent upon spiritual development. Now we see an uncanny graphic indication that it is at the fifth dimension of the Ruach soul that man first acquires a soul body capable of eternal endurance. The association of the highest Ruach macrohexagram with the concept of eternity, and so that of the whole Ruach soul level, is doubly underscored by the redefinition of this macrohexagram that will become possible in chapter 10 upon recognition of the whole sixth-world matrix pattern. As can be seen, all of these various analytic approaches are mutually reinforcing and enable us further to appreciate the Sabbath Star Diagram as a vast structure in whose graphic hieroglyphics one can read the nature and development of multidimensional reality. And what it now tells us is that, as the first of the future worlds, the fifth world is also the first to be attached to infinity.

With this further justification of the order of the macrohexagrams provided by the infinity curve of

Figure 9.2. The Movement Line through the Fifth-World Matrix

the movement line, we can now consider a significant correlation that can be made between these macro-hexagrams, taken as psychospiritual centers, and another esoteric system of such centers, that of the yogic concept of chakras. This correlation is most evident at the Ruach level, which is the reason it has not been previously considered. For the identification of the third chakra with the power center and of the fourth chakra with the expanded and compassionate heart can clearly be related to the geometric characteristics of the Ruach macrohexagrams just considered. The six or even four microhexagrams attached to the lateral third macrohexagram give it a configuration of power suggestive of an

association of this macrohexagram, representative of the Ruach mind, with just such power. Similarly, the position of the central fourth macrohexagram in the earlier considered double forms comprising a full third of the sixth-world matrix, one that makes it appear to be in the body of the Other, gives to the Ruach heart it represents the quality of empathy. The third and fourth macrohexagrams of the conjoined spiral have characteristics, then, that closely resemble those assigned to the third and fourth chakras, the centers of spiritual power and selfless love. Given the impressive correlations of the third and fourth macrohexagrams and chakras, it is tempting to extend this effort at correlation to the first and second macrohexagrams. And in the next chapter, we shall see further grounds for such a correlation as well as possible additional correlations of sixth-world matrix macrohexagrams to the remaining three chakras.[13] But of all these correlations, it is those with which we began that are the most striking, the power reservoir of the third and the other-body position of the fourth giving a graphic basis to these chakra-correlated macrohexagrams that can further our appreciation of these Ruach centers as expressive of "will power" and the selfless heart.

For it is only when we come to the Ruach level that the mind and heart functions can express their true natures rather than the shaping influence of the animal instincts upon the Nefesh soul. This is in accord with the depiction in chapter 5 of the Ruach soul as the level proper for optimal human functioning on earth. What we can thus far understand of this ideal condition is that it is one in which the mind, with its extraordinary level of will power, in concert with the heart, whose equally extraordinary quality is its capacity for imaginative projection into the state of another recognized to be one with the self, will work to lift that self and all else on the planet to a level of heightened empowerment and harmony that can only be called Messianic. But it is because this Promised Land remains only our potential heritage that it must here be treated not as our normal condition but rather as a mode of higher consciousness, one that can be both apprehended and achieved through such spiritual practices as meditation. Central to the meditative experience are the two centers of consciousness identified with the two Ruach macrohexagrams whose characteristics have just been defined. But functioning importantly with them are those elements of feeling and thought identified with the second and third lateral microhexagrams, whether or not they are considered to have formerly been fallen. What contribution they have to make at the expanded level of Ruach consciousness we shall now consider.

In "Kubla Khan" Coleridge had shown, through its absence, that the first step to the properly controlled exercise of the imagination must be one of attunement to higher harmony, that the magic of creativity could only arise from the "deep delight" experienced in such attunement. Abulafia describes a similar state resulting from use of his meditative techniques: "You will then feel as if an additional spirit is within you, arousing you and strengthening you, passing through your entire body and giving you pleasure. It will seem as if you have been anointed with perfumed oil, from head to foot."[14] The power of such attunement as can lift normal consciousness into the expanded dimension of the Ruach soul would seem to be lodged in the emotional-limbic system, most probably in the hippocampal circuit of this system that is noted for its emissions of theta frequencies,[15] the frequencies associated with the meditative state. It is this system that can be identified with the second lateral microhexagram, and its relationship to meditation is graphically reinforced by the position of this microhexagram in the diagram. Examination of its position in figure 9.1 reveals that it is practically drowned and largely obscured by the central system of the matrix, which interpenetrates it from both the fourth and fifth worlds. It would also appear to be as much of a bridge between the Nefesh and Ruach forms of the central system as it is between the Nefesh and Ruach lateral macrohexagrams. Its descending point enters the center of the Nefesh central microhexagram and its ascending point enters the corresponding center of the Ruach central macrohexagram. Thus the power of attunement by which the identity can be enlarged from the Nefesh to the Ruach soul is lodged in the emotional system, which has been identified with the one lateral element of the complete Nefesh-Ruach soul matrix that interpenetrates the central system; and it would seem to function like a membrane permeable to central influences as well as to the passage of lateral energies between the fourth and fifth worlds. It would also seem that its attuning power can be activated either by the Nefesh lateral macrohexagram or the Nefesh central microhexagram, that is, either by the Nefesh will to higher consciousness or by some spontaneous experience of central harmony, as sunset over still waters or the satisfied silence of a congenial group. This state of meditative attunement is the highest experience of Nefesh consciousness. But it can go beyond this, achieving the goal of such spiritual discipline in the activation of higher spiritual powers.

In chapter 8 we observed some of the dangers to which the Nefesh emotional system is prone. Now we can see that its highest extension and probably its truest purpose lies in hooking up to and activating the Ruach level of the soul, that it functions like an electrical circuit that, when switched on (or, in the more evocative vernacular, "turned on"), passes an energy current through it that powers the whole mechanism of Ruach consciousness. The same may be said for the third microhexagram of the lateral spiral, earlier identified with the analytic functioning of the Nefesh mind. In the fourth world diagram, its disconnectedness from the lateral spiral conveyed a potential for intellectual alienation. In the fifth-world diagram, however, we can discover the higher purposes of this analytic function. Hooked up to the mechanism of the Ruach soul, it becomes an essential factor in all its higher spiritual work. In the meditative process, for which the fifth-world matrix will be shown to provide a model, it is the analytic power associated with this microhexagram that supplies the initial instructions given by the will to the imagination and that then interprets the images summoned by the imagination in obedience to the will. If the higher function of the second lateral microhexagram is its power to attune the soul to the higher vibrational level of the Ruach dimension, that of the third lateral microhexagram is its capacity to define the focus of concentration and to diagnose its initial condition, an activity that distinguishes the meditative practice of the true master from that which is no more than a mode of relaxation. We have thus far defined the meditative functions of the Ruach macrohexagrams and of the second and third microhexagrams of the lateral spiral. The specifically meditative functions of the remaining four elements of the Nefesh soul should now be defined with one additional Ruach element.

Simplest is the first lateral microhexagram, associated with the reptilian bulb of the inner brain and the Nefesh animal instincts, whose function would seem to be to maintain and monitor the bodily functions during the exalted states of meditation and particularly during any out-of-body experience. Should any internal or external danger to the body arise, this first lateral microhexagram would activate the dormant lateral macrohexagram so that it can bring the soul down and safely ground it. But this Nefesh macrohexagram can sometimes improperly interfere with Ruach functioning, responding with fear to unfamiliar Ruach experiences and calling the soul back prematurely. When such an identity shift suddenly occurs during high Ruach states, it is due to the arousal of Nefesh self-consciousness suddenly aware that its identity is truly imperiled and, like Augustine, saying: "God make me chaste—but not yet." It is because Nefesh self-consciousness can provide such an impediment to higher spiritual work that all the practices of spiritual discipline are necessary; for these are geared to purifying the Nefesh soul prior to engaging in such high meditative states so that it will not be resistant to the soul's higher development and play its correct role of preserving the body as the vessel of the soul.

There are two remaining central elements of the Nefesh soul that have not yet been mentioned, the macrohexagram at the matrix center and the microhexagram that connects it to the Ruach central macrohexagram. And the function of these two elements in this model would seem to be that suggested by such a connection. That is, when the Ruach imagination is asked to supply an image of a condition, to "show what it looks like," it may be thought to send such a message through the circuitry of the central system, the connecting link of the central microhexagram, to the macrohexagram at the diagram's center representing the collective unconscious. This collective unconscious contains the Knowledge (Da'at) of all that is presently existent, on both the gross and subtle levels, together with the chain of causality linking past to present to probable future, and it files this information under various archetypal symbols. When so called upon, it would select the appropriate image storing the precise information requested and send it back through the central microhexagram to the Ruach central macrohexagram, where it would finally appear on the screen of the imagination for interpretation by the third lateral microhexagram, now the analytic faculty of the Ruach mind.

The last element necessary for normal Ruach functioning in this model is the fourth lateral microhexagram appearing right below the third lateral microhexagram in the fifth-world matrix diagram. As can be seen, this exclusively fifth-world microhexagram has direct contact with the lateral macrohexagram representing the Ruach mind and so would seem to be a mental power. Like the disconnected final microhexagram at the upper right corner of plate 9 and figure 9.1, the microhexagram presently under discussion is positioned wholly beyond the matrix border of the fourth-world diagram, the future manifestation of these two microhexagrams not even being hinted at in that diagram. As both of these microhexagrams are the only Ruach elements that are wholly beyond the fourth world, they would seem to represent the quality most distinctive of the fifth world and to define the highest flowering of this level of consciousness, creativity. But whereas the creative power represented by the final Ruach microhexagram can only be unlocked by a Neshamah Master operating at the Ruach level in order to communicate with humanity, that of its twin at the bottom of the diagram is the most readily available of the four microhexagrams completed by the fifth-world matrix.

Having identified this microhexagram with mental creativity, it would seem to be the element necessary for a meditative joining of the lower mind with a higher source of knowledge. For if this lowermost microhexagram does not directly represent the divine mind, it would seem to be the conduit through which messages from this highest mind enter the higher mind of Ruach consciousness and to define the distinctively Ruach nature of this mind. The Ruach mind, as figured by the lateral macrohexagram, has, then, two major faculties of thought, a lower analytic and a higher creative faculty, though the former is actually higher in the diagram and the latter lower; and it is the joining of the two that results in Ruach sagacity. As the lower analytic faculty connects the Ruach and Nefesh levels of consciousness, so it would seem that the higher creative faculty joins the Ruach level of consciousness to that of the Neshamah. Though not itself of the sixth world, as one of the highest of fifth-world elements,

and one wholly uninfluenced by fourth-world legacies, it is in the best position to receive and transmit the purity of the highest messages, and its authentic voice, when not joined to that of the lower analytic function, may be considered prophetic, a power it shares in lesser degree with its matrix counterpart, the final Ruach microhexagram. But however inspired, creative, and synthetic, it cannot be associated with the right brain since its principle tool of thought is language. As earlier insisted upon, it represents, rather, the distinctive characteristics of the higher Ruach mind. Before concluding this initial definition of the Ruach matrix, a final word should be said about the disconnected nature not only of the final fifth-world lateral microhexagram but also its similar form in the fourth world.

The disconnectedness of the highest powers in the fallen fourth- and rectified fifth-world soul bodies may, indeed, be a source of restless dissatisfaction that goads the soul on to its higher development, a concept well understood by Goethe's Faust and by George Herbert in *The Pulley*, whose God withholds rest from his gifts to man in the belief that such "repining restlessness . . . may toss him to my breast" (ll. 17, 20). Just as this last Ruach power can only be utilized by a Neshamah Master, so it may well be that the full powers of the entire Ruach system can only be activated by such a Neshamah Master. It would nonetheless appear that the miraculous effects of such a master are performed through the mechanism of the fifth world rather than that of the sixth. He must come down again, revisualizing the desired effect with the Ruach imagination. But the mechanism of Ruach consciousness we are now to explore does not demand this higher development and is sufficient to powerfully manifest the will of a Ruach Master. Having defined all of the elements of normal Ruach consciousness, we should now consider its relationship to kabbalistic meditation.

In *Renewing the Covenant* I devoted chapter 2 to kabbalistic meditation, including an attunement process derived from the *Sefer Yetzirah* and a guided Master Meditation, and that earlier work provides an important base for the present discussion, just as the matrix model of kabbalistic meditation that will here be offered can provide an understanding of the psychic mechanism of guided meditation that should further validate that earlier treatment. Also included in that earlier treatment was an extended survey of classic kabbalistic texts on meditation, two of which were reprised in chapter 3 of *The Kabbalah of the Soul*. Since interested readers can check back for a study of these kabbalistic texts that directly support the following modeling of the meditative process, we can proceed directly to this application of the fifth-world matrix.

THE RUACH MATRIX MODEL OF MEDITATION

We shall now see how the matrix model can in general define the meditative process, beginning with an attempt to use this matrix model to demonstrate the nature of psychic healing, perhaps the simplest and most accessible of all "magical" processes. This is not to say that all such healing, and other transformative processes with which it can be allied, follow the same step-by-step procedure that shall be outlined. For many adepts or those of natural talent, the process may be both spontaneous and instantaneous. Nonetheless, it is possible to analyze even such a natural process into the following steps, and they can certainly be consciously practiced with increasing effectiveness.

We begin, then, with the process of attunement that was earlier identified with the second lateral microhexagram of the emotions. For some this process can be no more than a conscious focusing on the subject at hand and a dissociation from mundane matters and tensions, a redirection of the consciousness to a higher level of concentration. For most, however, this redirection can be facilitated by one or more of the meditative techniques taught in the kabbalistic or other traditions. Most effective is the silent repetition of a divine name, known in the yoga tradition as a mantra, accompanied by a conscious regulation of the breath. I would suggest use of the "mantra" I have decoded in the *Sefer Yetzirah*, the name of the first Sefirah in this text, "Ruach Elohim Chayyim" (Breath of the Living God), breathing in to Ruach, holding the breath for

the divine name Elohim, and exhaling to Chayyim, repeating this twenty-six times, the number correlated with the Gematria number of the Tetragrammaton.[16] By this stage in the meditative process, a experience of higher spirituality can be felt, in the words of Abulafia, "passing through your entire body and giving you pleasure." For many, this experience is sufficient. It relaxes the stress of the mind and the body that, in itself, can promote both healing and happiness. But its spiritual effects can be still greater; for it can open a channel through which the highest spiritual forces can work on an unconscious level, developing and perfecting the soul even to its attainment of Ruach ha-Kodesh, the Holy Spirit, the highest state of spiritual enlightenment. Because the effects of meditation consistently practiced can be so great, many traditions are content simply to teach the various simple techniques by which it can be stimulated. But the primary thrust of the kabbalistic tradition of meditation has been on those conscious and directed processes by which the powers of a spiritual master can be both developed and manifested. It is to the techniques of such Master Meditation that we now turn, with particular emphasis on healing.

When the properly activated and attuned higher will wishes to heal the self or another, it will direct the visual center to provide an image of either the healer's body or that of another, absent or present, which will reveal any condition, physical or spiritual, that requires treatment. The image that the "heart imagines" will now be presented to the lower analytic function of the mind for diagnosis. To translate the process thus far to the Ruach matrix, we can say that its lateral macrohexagram directs its central macrohexagram to provide a symbolic image of a condition, which the latter accomplishes by going to the depths of the central system, the collective macrohexagram contacted through the central microhexagram. The image that can be thought to appear on the screen of the individuated Ruach central macrohexagram is now subject to interpretation by the third lateral microhexagram at the direction of the Ruach lateral macrohexagram. This lower mental faculty has the capacity, when enlisted in such higher Ruach processes, of interpreting psychological and spiritual causes and probable effects as well as purely physical causes and effects, but its capacity is limited to deterministic analysis. It can diagnose, often brilliantly, the causes and course of a condition and prescribe any known treatments for this condition. But it cannot discover any new solution or cure.

This is a function of the higher creative faculty of the mind, represented in the matrix by the lateral microhexagram appearing just below that defining the analytic faculty. When the conscious will has received the diagnosis of the analytic faculty, it then calls upon its creative power to prescribe a cure. The source of this remedy will not be from the accumulated record of the past, represented by the collective macrohexagram at the diagram's center, but from the still unmanifest future, the World to Come or Olam ha-Ba, for which this Ruach creative faculty serves as a channel. If we look again at figure 9.1, we can see that of the four microhexagrams completed only in the fifth world, the first and the fourth appearing in the spiral are located higher in the horns of the matrix border than are the second and third of these microhexagrams. Since the disconnected fourth microhexagram is not normally available for use at this level of development, this means that it is only the first of these microhexagrams that has effective contact with the horn area of the matrix border. It will be remembered that in the extended discussion of the horn in chapter 5 it was shown that it is through the horn that the breath of God, Ruach Elohim Chayyim, can inspire man, lifting him through the power of the Holy Spirit that it transmits to higher levels of prophetic revelation. It is, then, in the state of higher consciousness initiated by silent repetition of the divine name Ruach Elohim Chayyim that the breath of God can communicate to the highest readily available faculty of man, inspiring his understanding with a new vision of possibility. This new cognitive vision is then transmitted through the higher will to the imagination for translation into visual form. This is the most important step in the process. The imagination, which had before projected an image of a diseased condition, is now asked to revisualize the same subject in terms not only of its cure but of its highest perfection that can be imagined in a form coherent with the present personality. With this image before

the visual center, the verbal center should now express the higher will with an affirmation of its purpose that this image be translated into manifest reality.[17]

This is the technique but the extent of its effectiveness will depend on the development of the consciousness, a development that, in the matrix model, can be gauged by the number of the Ruach microhexagrams that can be activated by the Ruach will. We have thus far examined the workings of Ruach consciousness when only the first of its exclusively fifth-world microhexagrams has become empowered, whether through spiritual practices or some spontaneous spiritual development, and we have not yet finished our exploration of this level of consciousness. In terms of healing, this minimal model of Ruach consciousness, which contains all of the Nefesh and Ruach matrix elements up to and including this fourth lateral microhexagram but excludes the remaining three Ruach microhexagrams, is most effective for self-healing and problem solving. If one understands the causes and nature of one's illnesses or problems and, rather than resting indulgently with such knowledge, then projects a positive image to the self of its health and prospects, it is clear that this positive mental outlook will go far, in and of itself, to cure the disease that has attacked the body and spirit as well as marring all of the self's social and professional relationships. But this positive attitude is most effective when it does not rely wholly on the will, though even this can ensure significant results, but is also informed by new insight into the causes of a negative condition and a creative approach to remedying it. For such insights can encourage the normal rational consciousness to believe that change is possible and then to decide to take such steps as will bring this change about. Though all of this may sound quite normal and even sensible, it nonetheless contains unexplained or magical elements, but elements so usual in our experience that we do not generally stop to wonder at them. The influence of spirit on matter by which negative attitudes can produce disease and positive attitudes cures is so accepted in medical practice today that the spiritual implications of such psychosomatic effects is not even remarked upon. And all our normal functioning is so dependent upon our capacity for insight and creative solutions that we rarely question how it is possible to arrive at such insight.

But it is not only in healing that these features of Ruach consciousness are present. They are present in all modes of creative thought and expression and their effects are just as magical. When one listens to Beethoven's Ninth Symphony or one of his late quartets, who does not find such creations miraculous, even were Beethoven not deaf at the time of composition? So too with Einstein's revisioning of all of modern physics in the single equation $E = mc^2$. For such commanding acts of creative thought as can transform the nature of an art or science, there is no adequate explanation provided through physiology and the laws of cause and effect. The imagination of such a creative being is, as Coleridge said, a "magical power," and its mode of operation is that of all magic: "it dissolves, diffuses, dissipates, in order to re-create."

The lowest level of Ruach magical power is, then, a very high level, indeed. It accounts for all the creative thought and expression that informs the various arts, sciences, and social movements. But though such creativity always springs from inspired moments of insight, moments that must be prepared for but that cannot be determined, it is accepted as a normal mode of human functioning. In fact, it is the normal mode of Ruach functioning and already implies a development of consciousness beyond the requirements for animal survival and satisfaction. Whether employed to write a symphony, solve the problem of pollution, or heal an ulcer, its results will always be considered natural and within the higher limits of normalcy. But in the process of arriving at these results, a certain restructuring of the consciousness will ordinarily occur that will facilitate the development of the next level of Ruach power, that represented by the fifth lateral microhexagram.

THE LEVELS OF RUACH MASTER POWER

The process of creative revisioning, which has here defined the normal functioning of Ruach conscious-

ness, depends on the adoption of a positive approach to the possibility of change.* Rather than remaining a prisoner to the treadmill of mechanical responses, a condition that when recognized without an accompanying hope of correction can lead to an ever increasing negativity of spirit, the persons who can creatively refashion their lives through a positive belief in its possibility will find their positiveness reinforced in theory and strengthened in power by the very success of their endeavors to free themselves from a life of unproductive limitation. And as their spirits become increasingly positive, increasingly relaxed and joyous, so will the circumstances of their lives become increasingly easy. Their health will improve, as will their social relationships, and all their projects will prosper. Doors will suddenly open and opportunities arise just when they is ready to make use of them.

Of course, all such effects will be put down by the disbeliever as the product of chance and coincidence, at best as the natural result of such a person's increased charm and charisma. But note those words, the former associated with magic as the latter is with miraculous spiritual power. The very language has enshrined the belief that a certain kind of personality can influence events in its favor. The subject is normally dismissed by considering such a person as lucky. But rather than closing the subject, the existence of people who are consistently lucky poses a mystery.

The mysterious power to win against the odds of mechanically determined chance is one experienced intermittently in all successful gambling and the secret of its appeal. Gamblers strive for that state of altered consciousness in which they feel "hot," in which they know the dice or the cards will turn up in accordance with their wishes, clearly a feeling of godlike power. The concept of sacred lots, cast by the early Hebrew priests as also the priests in other religious traditions, implies that the outcome of such lots will not be determined by chance but by a divine force, that spiritual power can manipulate the

---

*Much of what follows appeared in *The Kabbalah of the Soul*, pp. 179–201.

instruments of mechanical chance to influence the outcome. Beneath the more modern concept of luck as chance lies the older belief in Fortune or destiny as an overriding force determining the shape of one's life. To be fortunate was to be in the grace of God or the gods. The biblical belief that the reward of goodness is prosperity and long life also reflects this understanding that to the person living in the Way of God all health and riches will flow.

It is this power to influence the complex strands of causality so that two such lines meet just when one, a person moving "in the spirit," has need of what the other has to offer that I am identifying with the fifth lateral microhexagram. It operates through what Jung has called "synchronicity,"[18] and always assumes the appearance of chance. Most who are favored by this power have no idea what they are doing to cause such desirable effects. A book will come to their attention or be published just when they have need of that information and they may even open it exactly to the right page. They will start to meet the people needed for their personal or professional development, according to the old saying: "When the student is ready, the teacher appears." They will start remarking that they always seem to find parking spaces just when they arrive. At most, such people will recognize that at such times and at more and more of the time they are feeling "in the flow," that they are feeling a flow of heightened, exhilarating energy through their beings and also that they are moving in harmony with a larger, surrounding flow of events, with a cosmic energy.

Since the feeling is so fulfilling, they will start to do all they consciously can to enhance it, monitoring themselves with a kind of natural biofeedback that tells them when the "vibes" are good or bad and so increasing those experiences and associations that produce the former while eliminating those with negative results. And as their vibrational level becomes higher and purer, so will its influence on external events seem to increase. The breaks will all fall their way and, as the doors of opportunity open, so will they gain increasing command of their faculties, always knowing exactly what to say and do. They will have enormous charm and seem to live a charmed life. For this is the level on which what is normally called magic does operate.

Such fortunate people are natural magicians, working with the higher energies without conscious awareness of what they are doing. Some will go beyond such natural magic to apply the techniques of creative revisualization for practical results. It will work to some extent, for these techniques do have magical power, but their full power can only be released by a highly developed spirit who will use them for purposes higher than his own needs.

It is only such a person who will be able to consciously command the power manifested in synchronicity. Such a person will be able to heal others as well as himself, though the former will be put down to coincidence as the latter was to nature. The master can, of course, use his power to meet human needs that must be satisfied for him to continue his higher work, but he will ordinarily prefer that these needs be met by natural means and not pervert higher powers to lower purposes. The apprentice who uses these techniques only for personal gain may become surprised that the indices of personal success seem less favorable than when he was just starting spiritual training and that, if the techniques do work and he gets what he asked for, he will discover that he did not understand what to ask for and is being punished by getting what he ignorantly wanted. Nonetheless, if a person is in the flow, is motivated by the Ruach desires to help others and fulfill the Highest Will, then he can increase the natural magic that will strew his path with good fortune by conscious techniques of visualization and affirmation.

But the true master of synchronicity will do more than this. He will have perfected his willpower so that it can be applied precisely as required to accomplish its purpose. Such perfecting of the will, which is the task and test of the master, is achieved through a process similar to that of the natural biofeedback earlier discussed and is, in fact, the same process on a higher and more conscious level. It involves an attunement of the master's will to the vibrational level of the event to be influenced and then a transmission of directed energy on that wavelength such that all on its frequency will resonate to that influence and be pulled into the orbit of its purpose. The technique will be similar to that earlier defined for the minimal Ruach system except that the visualizations will not be on the object but vibrational level and will be concerned not with static images but processes. It is as though the focus of attention is not on the aspect of reality as particle but as wave, and the wave pattern is not so much visualized as felt imaginatively. The master will project himself imaginatively into a given situation and feel the quality of its vibration. From this he will be able to understand analytically the factors that are at play in it. He will then arrive at a creative understanding of how that situation should be altered to bring it into conformity with his intention and then translate his revisualization of this situation into a retuning of the original vibration within the limits of its affinities. Finally, he will transmit this retuned vibration through the power of his will to the situation at issue with such directed force that it will be pulled into resonance with his will. It will then begin so to evolve that when the time comes for him to enter this situation it will be ready to embrace his purpose. What seems coincidental when it occurs will have been carefully prepared for on the subtler planes of reality. Even when the process is not this conscious, a high and pure will attracts to its purposes all those latent possibilities within circumstances that have an affinity for them and empowers these latencies to become actualized. The master's will and the potentialities within historical process are mutually reinforcing and their mutual powers arrive at a future convergence.

We have thus far spoken of such manifestations under the term *synchronicity*, for this is how such events may appear in the present instant, but an older and truer name for it is Providence. As I have often stated, the fifth dimension is the dimension of Providence, and the true Ruach Master is the one for whom this dimension is as palpable as time and space, who apprehends its operations in all the mundane events of human experience. While its general direction is set and monitored by the spiritual hierarchy of the sixth world, the Ruach Master can fine-tune its processes in the particular space-time frame in which he is located. It is true that all great events occur through the meeting of the man with the moment, neither being sufficient without the other. So it can be said that the force of Providence requires the vessel of a living master to achieve its larger historical purposes. But their alliance is operative even in smaller matters. Just as Einstein tells us that matter bends space, so the power of a master bends the Providential dimension of reality to support and effect his will, and he does this not alone through techniques of conscious focusing but simply through being. He is both a master and agent of Providence.

As the master develops his power to influence the operations of Providence, so will he develop still higher powers that can no longer be explained away as coincidence but must be considered miraculous. Such is the power represented by the sixth lateral microhexagram, the highest power attainable exclusively through the fifth world though most often exercised by masters whose souls have already developed to the Neshamah level of the sixth world. It would seem, indeed, that the master who has learned to operate through the Providential dimension begins to move into the sixth world while still perfecting the Ruach powers through which he can directly influence and communicate with the world of ordinary humanity. Once he begins to operate successfully with the higher energies, his development will accelerate and become multifaceted. At this next level, the master of Providence also becomes the master of transformation, this the defining characteristic of the power conveyed through the sixth lateral microhexagram.

While it is true that all Ruach spirituality is transformative, that the same technique of creative revisualization with verbal affirmation can be employed on all its levels, the scope of this transformative power expands with each level of development. Though all the effects of the first level of Ruach power can be put down to nature and of the second level to coincidence, when we arrive at the third level of Ruach power, the secret is out. The master must become public, for there is no explanation for his powers other than that they are miraculous. No longer confined to the temporal processes of history, he can now directly effect and transform material substance.

What changes as one after another of the fifth-world microhexagrams becomes activated is the depth of visualization. At the lowest degree of Ruach power, the imagination can visualize and revisualize images only of objects in space. At the next degree of power, the imagination can now visualize such spatial entities as particular vibrations, as events not only in space but also of time. But the vibrational attunement is still to particulars, to the macrostructural distinctions of this man, that group event. At the third degree of power to which we now come, the Ruach imagination has achieved a degree of magnification by which it can focus on the microstructure of objects, people, or events, a level at which all individual distinctions disappear and the ground of all performs its quantum dance. Once such a level of consciousness is reached, it is fairly easy to see how it can be employed in transformative magic. Of the swamis noted for such extraordinary powers, perhaps the most celebrated of our time is Satya Sai Baba. It is alleged that Satya Sai Baba can pass his hand through sand and transform it into a ruby, motion pictures having been made that purport to demonstrate this miraculous power of transformation.

If we are to accept this or other accounts of magical transformation, the mechanism would seem to be explicable through the process of master meditation being defined. A master must visualize the all-pervasive microstructure in and around the object on which his concentration is focused, sand or lead as the case may be, while also attuning himself to the vibrational frequency of its particular molecular structure. He must then reattune himself to the vibration of the imaginatively transformed object, ruby or gold, while directing his will to the quanta within the original physical object. If his will is of such a pure energy that it can be accepted by the quanta as their own, they will begin to resonate to it and will then respond by mimicking any morphic changes communicated within the field of vibratory sympathy they share with the master. Thus the quanta within a piece of lead, accepting the master's vibration as their own, will rearrange themselves to define the characteristics of gold when the master transmits both the new vibrational frequency of gold

and the influence of his more powerful will. The power of this new frequency can be said, then, to produce a rhythm entrainment of the weaker or slower frequency of the quanta, forcing it to operate at the new frequency of gold rather than the old vibratory pattern of lead.[19] Whether or not the influence of mind over matter be explained by the physics of rhythm entrainment, that subtle process by which one frequency can force others that are close to oscillate in phase with it, there is evidence to suggest that the proper direction of mental frequencies can develop a power capable of effecting matter.

More subtle and yet more significant than such alchemical magic is the most celebrated instance of magical transformation in Western history, Jesus' transubstantiation of the bread and wine of his last Passover feast into his body and blood without any visible sign of such a change. It is more significant because the Christian sacrament of the Eucharist, which Jesus thus instituted with a verbal declaration, continues to exert its power to communicate the spirit of the master to the devout communicant to this day. Here we see the true power of ritual, which is to conserve and convey the living spirit of its founding master and, through this, the divine spirit and source of all. All religions are structures designed to conserve and perpetuate the divine fire manifested through a master spirit and transferred by him into specific rituals, a communion facilitated by an ordained priesthood empowered to perform the ritual transubstantiation of matter into a vehicle for spiritual experience.

As Jesus is credited with having transformed the nature of bread and wine so that, under certain specified conditions, they could contain and transmit his spirit, so does the yoga tradition claim a similar mode of spirit transmission through the power of mantra. As Baba Muktananda explains this power: "Truly speaking, the divine name is the mantra obtained from the Guru. Repetition of the name activates the inner Shakti with full vigor. . . . A mantra charged with the potency of Parashiva, the highest Guru, is not merely an inert pattern of sounds. The supremely glorious, universal, divine power is hidden within it. In such a mantra,

Parashiva and the Guru are united. Therefore, it is endowed with consciousness."[20] Baba Muktananda tells us that the reason a particular pattern of sounds has the power to transform an individual has nothing to do with natural human physiology, endorphins and the like, but is the result of a spiritual process by which an "inert pattern of sounds" has, itself, become transformed into a carrier of Shakti, that of the guru who gives it and of the deity by which he gives it. When a meditator takes such a divinely charged mantra into his consciousness, what is working within him is the real spirit of his guru, his guru's lineage, and the deity whose name appears in the mantra, Shiva in the case of Baba Muktananda's mantra "Om Namah Shivaya."

Most religious traditions treat certain phrases with a special reverence. For Muslims it is the *zikr*, which translated means "There is no God but God." For Jews the most highly charged phrases are the Mosaic Sh'ma, normally translated "Hear, oh Israel, the Lord your God, the Lord is one,"[21] and the Kedushah of Isaiah: "Holy, Holy, Holy is the Lord of Hosts. The whole earth is filled with His Glory" (6:1). Greater than these and felt to be so highly charged that it could not be pronounced by any but the high priest and only on the Day of Atonement is the Tetragrammaton. The transubstantiation of matter through the power of blessing is also a feature of Jewish ritual, of the Sabbath wine, challah and, perhaps most powerfully, in the lighting of the Sabbath candles.

Of course, the effects on Christian communicants of taking the wafer, on yoga meditators of repeating the mantra, and on Jewish women of lighting the Sabbath candles can and have been explained in terms of natural, if abnormal, psychology and physiology. What I am doing here is looking seriously at the claims of Christian, Hindu, and Jewish theologians and practitioners that miraculous transformations of ordinary foods, words, and candles do occur, when properly charged, that make them the transmitters of higher spiritual energies. But though masters in all spiritual traditions are capable both of initiating such rituals of transformative magic and of empowering their successors to reenact them with undiminished potency for as long

as their traditions persist, the true concern of spiritual masters is not with material transformations but with the transformations of persons. When we speak of a charismatic master, it is not simply in a figurative sense that such charisma or spirit should be understood. For the power to attract and influence large groups of people *is* a spiritual power. In the yoga tradition it is precisely defined as Shaktipat, the direct transmission of spiritual energy, normally by touch. Through his speech, thought, and look, as well as touch, the charismatic master enters and transforms his disciples. It is this power, far more than the miracles of material transformations, that constitutes the highest expression of the third degree of Ruach power.

There is one final degree of Ruach power, represented by the disconnected seventh lateral microhexagram, that is available only to Neshamah Masters and normally not utilized even by them, who prefer to interact with humanity through the second and third degrees of Ruach power. If the defining characteristic of the third degree of this power is transformative, that of this fourth degree can be considered truly creative, not simply the creation of art from thought as with the first degree of Ruach power, but of some thing from nothing. And the reason for this is that at this level of power the Ruach imagination is no longer operative. To be able to perceive the source of that which materializes out of "nothing," the master would have to place his consciousness in the Neshamah imagination, which we will see in chapter 10 to be represented by the central macrohexagram of the sixth world. But if he does this, he will not be able to function in the fifth dimension, the bridge between the highest consciousness and the space-time bounded consciousness of ordinary humanity. To be able to use the seventh lateral microhexagram of the fifth world, he needs to traverse the missing lateral macrohexagram of the first phase of the sixth world.

As we shall see in this next chapter, the sixth world has two distinct phases defined by the directions their elements take in the diagram. But since the first phase at the right of the Neshamah diagram is exclusively lateral and it is not until the second phase at this diagram's top that central elements do appear, the experience of this first phase will be one of darkness, void, nothingness. The first phase of the sixth world is beyond the power of the Ruach imagination and it has not yet arrived at the omniscient center of the Neshamah imagination. The result is that spiritual work involving this first half of the sixth world would register as a blank on the Ruach imagination. That a state variously called the void or *ayin*[22] exists in spiritual experience is well attested to in a variety of traditions, particularly Buddhism, and normally it is not considered to be the final stage of realization but the penultimate stage. The facts of the sixth-world matrix just considered would seem to encode the explanation for this spiritual phenomenon, as also that yoga maintenance of waking consciousness during deep sleep called the *tandra* state. For the first Neshamah phase features a similar experience that cannot be visualized except as a black nothingness.

The ability to materialize something out of nothing is the most spectacular of magical effects, whether true or contrived, and the very fact that stage magicians regularly feature such magic tricks as the high point of their shows merely underscores the preeminent position stories of such powers hold in the annals of all spiritual traditions of holy men. Since the production of something out of nothing is a feat that directly corresponds to the divine creation of the universe, it is only possible through the participation of elements from the sixth world, the realm of the divine. If we look again at figure 9.1, it can be seen that between the sixth and seventh of the lateral microhexagrams lies a connecting microhexagram incomplete in the fifth world. For the highest Ruach microhexagram to be empowered, then, it would seem that the Neshamah elements would have to be already in place, the divine working through the level of perfected Ruach consciousness.

In the Jewish tradition, the most remarkable legends involving this highest level of power are centered on the divine ability to imbue a clay figure with life, an ability seeming to be attributed by the *Sefer Yetzirah* to the patriarch Abraham, by the Talmud to various sages, and in the later legends of the golem primarily to Rabbi Loew of Prague. The

Sefer Yetzirah reference and the many medieval commentaries upon it all derive from the biblical verse "And Abram took Sarai his wife . . . and the souls that they had gotten in Haran" (Gen. 12:5). Thus to Abraham, above all other figures in Jewish history and legend, was attributed the divine ability to create souls. Less spectacular but more largely reported was the legendary ability of the prophet Elisha who, like Jesus, was able to restore the dead to life (2 Kings 4:32–6). Nonetheless, it is said of Moses and only of him: "And there arose not a prophet since in Israel like unto Moses, whom the Lord knew face to face" (Deut. 34:10–11). The mighty power of Moses derives from the face to face knowledge of Himself that God granted only to Moses. In this mystical union of Da'at, some portion of the divine spirit was imparted to him that could be seen and that endowed him with a special holiness: "And it came to pass, when Moses came down from mount Sinai with the two tables of testimony . . . that Moses wist not that the skin of his face shone" (Exod. 34:29). If "there arose not a prophet since in Israel like unto Moses," it was not because of "all the signs and the wonders . . . which Moses showed in the sight of all Israel" (Deut. 34:12) but because he established the basis for creating a holy nation. It is in such creation that the higher souls can truly be begotten that testify to the supreme manifestation of the Ruach spirit on earth, the Ruach ha-Kodesh. And it is only through the descent of this Holy Spirit that one can experience a reality that seems to "come down" (Num. 11:17) from nothing, *ayin*. Moses' great teaching is of the sacramental nature of the divine commandments, that when properly empowered the ritual commandments can become the transmitters of that holiness constituting the Presence of God: "If ye walk in my statutes, and keep my commandments, and do them; Then . . . I will walk among you" (Lev. 26: 3, 12).

Of all the commandments that which is considered by the rabbinical tradition to be so holy that its performance alone can be regarded as fulfilling the entire covenant is the Sabbath. It is the only ritual observance to be included in the Ten Commandments and the only one of these commandments to be designated as holy: "Remember the sabbath day, to keep it holy" (Exod. 20: 8). The concept of hallowing time involves an understanding of the central concept with which all discussion of the fifth world has been concerned, that time has a fifth dimension of spiritual power and purpose and that the Ruach Master is he who can so attune himself to this dimension that he can enhance in his own being and empower for others the special spirituality conveyed through observance of its rhythms. It is the ritual empowerment of the apparent nothingness of time so that its divinely invested spirituality can be apprehended that constitutes the highest development of the Jewish revelation and the source of its strength. It is the holy jewel of the Mosaic legacy. There are many Jews today as in the past who observe the Sabbath because of the trait that God so often bemoaned, a stiff-necked refusal to let secular time reduce the Jewish people to oblivion, a stiff-necked commitment simply to endure, to triumph over the millennia that have consumed so many empires. But the true triumph over the nothingness of time that the Sabbath can provide is the holiness that its ritual observance can instill in all those who participate in its spirit. Nor is this holiness to be understood as a metaphor for a purely subjective affect. The Torah meaning can best be appreciated by taking it seriously, that is, literally, by understanding that it is a real spiritual entity that comes from beyond the individual to rest on him, to infuse and engulf him, in its performance of certain prescribed rituals. As Abraham J. Heschel has said of such performance: "They confer holiness upon us."[23] In his uniquely meaningful book on the Sabbath, Heschel further explores the manner in which it serves to sanctify

time: "its spirit is a reality we meet rather than an empty span of time which we choose to set aside for comfort or recuperation. . . . The Sabbath is the presence of God in the world, open to the soul of man."[24] In the Sabbath, then, Moses transmitted to Israel and the world the highest degree of spiritual holiness. And the wonder of this highest degree of Ruach power, the Ruach ha-Kodesh, is that it is available to every man, woman, and child who takes the time to receive it, who has learned to sanctify the Sabbath.[25]

With this brief tribute to the Sabbath, we bring to a close the analysis of the fifth-world matrix, that precise model both of the faculties of Ruach spirituality and of its four degrees of power. And it seems not coincidental that the holiness of the Sabbath should emerge as the highest expression of the degree of power represented by the seventh lateral microhexagram. We earlier saw that the first construction element of the fifth-world diagram could also be viewed as the seventh such element of the fourth world, and its identification with the "trumpet of the Messiah," the great shofar, also gave it an attributed capacity to effect the higher level of spiritual attunement that can be associated with the Sabbath. The periodicity of the seventh seems to carry a special spiritual quality or meaning in all sorts of circumstances, and this is particularly true of its various manifestations in the Sabbath Star Diagram, a diagram whose cosmic coding is embodied in the form and expansions of that unique sevenfold geometric figure fittingly named the Sabbath Star. But we have yet to embark on the truly otherworldly dimensions of the cosmos as of its geometric model and the wonders they have yet to reveal.

CHAPTER 10

The Sixth-World Matrix Model of the Neshamah Soul

THE COMPLETED PATTERN OF THE SPIRAL TREE

We come to the long-awaited matrix of the sixth-world diagram that will reveal the most spectacular correlation of the Sabbath Star Diagram with the Kabbalah. The sixth-world matrix is of particular importance because it is only at this degree of complexity that a meaningful pattern emerges through which the matrices of all the diagram worlds can be coherently defined and interpreted. This is similar to the laws of diagram construction that emerged in the earlier treatment of the construction elements of this same sixth-world diagram, given in chapter 6, both of these chapters together attesting to the significance of the sixth world as the dimension of meaningfulness.

This chapter will deal with various significant aspects of this matrix pattern that will serve to introduce the necessarily extended analyses of this pattern in this chapter and the next, the first dealing with the matrix elements within the sixth-world matrix border and the second with those elements beyond this border as well as beyond the matrix borders of the fourth- and fifth-world diagrams. After revealing the nature of this extraordinary matrix in the present section, the following three sections will explore three fundamentally important subjects related to this final pattern. We shall first turn to a subject closely associated with the material of chapter 6, that of the Partzufim, and, through their matrix modeling, see startling proof of the coherence of the Sabbath Star Diagram matrix with a formerly inexplicable aspect of Lurianic cosmology. This will lead to further introductory background on the purpose of spiritual development that is necessary for the following comprehensive matrix modeling of the Nefesh to Neshamah levels of the soul. Finally, chapter 11 will close with a new method of counting matrix elements that will provide both a provisional understanding of how the earlier worlds should be constructed and the basis of the culminating extrapolation of the Sabbath Star Diagram to infinity undertaken in part 4.

In analyzing the matrices of the fourth and fifth worlds, a lateral spiral and a central spiral were associated without explanation. No such explanation was then possible because it depended on an understanding of the sixth-world matrix that could not be previously presented. Let us return, then, to the first states of matrix analysis, those that distinguished the central and lateral systems but did not attempt to relate them, and carry one lateral and one central spiral forward through the sixth world. As can be seen in plate 10, in which the featured lateral spiral is colored turquoise and its central spiral green, and in figure 10.1, in which the lateral spiral is white and the central spiral black, these distinguished spirals produce a most expressive form when taken together, the lateral spiral appear-

ing serpentine and the central spiral appearing to endow that serpent with wings. The implications of such a winged serpent will be considered in chapter 12, on which basis we can now see in this flying serpent a symbol of the divinized human intellect.

But even more significant than its appearance are the numbers that constitute this double spiral. Before considering these numbers it should be further

Figure 10.1. The Separate Central and Lateral Spirals

pointed out that in figure 10.1 the inner hexagons of the unenclosed microhexagrams of both the lateral and central spirals will be filled in with their respective colors, white for the lateral spiral and black for the central spiral, this to more easily distinguish the macrohexagram units from these unenclosed microhexagrams. Turning now to their cumulative numbers, the lateral spiral is composed of seven macrohexagrams and sixteen microhexagrams while the central spiral is composed of three macrohexagrams and six microhexagrams. This gives us a sum of ten for the macrohexagrams and of twenty-two for the microhexagrams! These numbers are truly astonishing, for they are identical with those of the Tree of Life Diagram, that from which the Sabbath Star Diagram was originally derived and which has exactly ten Sefirot and twenty-two connecting paths. What makes this result most remarkable is that these Tree numbers—containing, as they do, the primary numbers of the base-10 counting system and the number of letters in the Hebrew alphabet—should emerge from such a different geometric construction.

That the sixth-world diagram should produce a matrix whose numbers can be correlated with those of the Tree of Life Diagram indicates, first of all, that the method of constructing the Sabbath Star Diagram at this level of expansion must be considered correct, correct in the sense that it unlocks the very same cosmological code that appears in the central diagram of the Kabbalah. This fact can give further support to the thesis that the kabbalistic Tree was geometrically derived from the Sabbath Star Diagram and serves as a hidden key to its reconstruction. What it indicates secondarily is that the Sabbath Star Diagram up through its sixth world can be identified with the structure of the Tree of Life Diagram and the living cosmos it represents. And what it may finally indicate is that there is a geometric basis to the numbering and the alphabets of the ancient world that might somehow have its archetypal source in the sixth-world matrix of the Sabbath Star Diagram.

But though the numbers comprising the flying serpent add up to those of the Tree of Life Diagram, its form does not parallel the structure of the Sefirotic Tree. To make the macrohexagrams of the matrix assume an order parallel to that of the Sefirot, it is necessary to restructure the relationship of the central and lateral spirals so that they interpenetrate rather than diverge. But the only way this can be done is to have one lateral spiral interpenetrate first one central spiral and then its inverse. This most illuminating manner of relating the central and lateral spirals so that they form a matrix Tree can be seen in the colored forms of plate 11 and their black-and-white counterparts in figure 10.2, given in the same format as that of figure 10.1, though this time with the central black elements overlaying the lateral white elements. In figure 10.2 the black elements at the bottom signify the red central spiral and the black elements at the top signify the blue central spiral. Figure 10.3 then identifies all the matrix elements of the Spiral Tree, assigning numbers to the microhexagrams that correspond to the paths with which they may be correlated, at least the initial letters of the Sefirot identifications of the macrohexagrams, and indicating elements of the central system by diamond shapes and those of the lateral system by squares.

In the Spiral Tree of the completed sixth-world matrix shown in plate 11 and figures 10.2 and 10.3, the macrohexagram Sefirot can best be defined by changing the direction of observation. If one begins situated beside the collective central macrohexagram and facing westward or left toward it, one will then see a lateral macrohexagram above this central macrohexagram, both produced by the fourth-world diagram. If the collective central macrohexagram, from which the spiral of creation originates, can be identified with the Sefirah Malkhut, then the one above it can be identified with Yesod. Turning now to the south or the bottom of the diagram and the macrohexagrams produced by the fifth-world diagram, the central macrohexagram to the right would be identified with Netzach, while the lateral macrohexagram to the left would be identified with Hod. Turning next to the east or the right, one sees the three lateral macrohexagrams produced in the first phase of the matrix of the sixth world, the one to the right identifiable with Chesed, that to the left with Gevurah, and that in the center with Tiferet.

Figure 10.2. The Spiral Tree

Turning finally to the north and top of the diagram, one sees the three macrohexagrams associated with the second phase of the sixth-world matrix, two lateral macrohexagrams flanking and interpenetrating a central macrohexagram from the central spiral inverse to that earlier encountered. The lateral macrohexagram to the right can be identified with Chokhmah, the lateral macrohexagram to the left with Binah, and the central macrohexagram between them with Keter. Since such an arrangement of the central and lateral spirals permits an exact correspondence of their macrohexagrams with the Sefirot of the Tree of Life Diagram, this would seem to represent the most illuminating method of

Figure 10.3. The Sefirot and Paths of the Spiral Tree

structuring the matrix, and it was therefore adopted in defining the matrices of the fourth and fifth worlds. Now that we can recognize the correspondence between the earlier analyzed macrohexagrams and the Sefirot, we can begin to understand them from an entirely different perspective.

The above identification of macrohexagrams with Sefirot is based upon the initial equation of the collective macrohexagram at the diagram's center with Malkhut, an equation that distinguishes the Spiral Tree from that of the traditional Tree of Life Diagram. For whereas the traditional Tree is understood to progress from Keter to Malkhut, the Spiral Tree reverses the direction of divine activity and proceeds from Malkhut to Keter, thus apparently signifying the Spiral Tree as the Tree of the Tikkun. What is most interesting about the relationship of the Tree of Life and Sabbath Star Diagrams in these two cosmic phases of Emanation and Tikkun is that the apportionment of Sefirot to cosmic worlds remains coherent, the two phases appearing as mirror images of each other. For when the Tree of Life Diagram is interfaced with the Elementary Sabbath Star Diagram, as in figure 2.9, which labels all the elements of both, a pattern of Sefirot emanation emerges that locates the upper six Sefirot in the first world of Atzilut modeled by the Do hexagram, the Sefirot of Netzach and Hod in the second world of Beriah modeled by the Re hexagram, and the Sefirot of Yesod and Malkhut in the third world of Yetzirah, modeled in reverse order by the Mi and Fa hexagrams, though Yesod is more technically produced by the still unmanifest Ri hexagram. Malkhut, normally associated with the fourth world, also touches the turning point in the octave progression of hexagrams, the Fi hexagram of that tonal Sabbath Star formation defining the first half of the fourth world of Asiyah. But despite these qualifications regarding Yesod and Malkhut, they can still be primarily associated with Yetzirah. In the complete six-world matrix, however, a reverse pattern emerges that locates Malkhut and Yesod in the fourth world associated with the Nefesh soul, Hod and Netzach in the fifth world of the Ruach soul, and the upper six Sefirot in the sixth world of the Neshamah soul. From the perspective of the Sabbath Star Diagram, then, the traditional Tree becomes a key to the process of Sefirot emanation in the first three worlds, while the Spiral Tree produced by the matrices of the fourth through sixth worlds defines the corresponding process of the Tikkun, that process through which both fallen man and broken Sefirot can be recreated in closer conformity to the divine image. In a later section we shall see how the Spiral Tree can provide a most significant key to the proper progress of the soul. But we must first see what further understanding it can provide of the laws of the Sabbath Star Diagram.

As previously indicated, it is the spectacular emergence of the precise counterparts of the Tree in the sixth-world matrix that was accepted as defining the proper form of the diagram, everything that determined such an emergence being regarded as correct and anything that would alter the precise number of the constituents of the Spiral Tree being marked as incorrect. In terms of the matrix itself, what this settled once and for all is the fact that the matrix border for a world is to be defined by the macrostructure. The reason for this is that in the sixth world, as in those previous to it, there are always some fully defined microhexagrams extending beyond the continuous border formed of macrotriangles. Until the exclusion of just such microhexagrams of the sixth-world matrix was required in order to reach the number corresponding to the paths of the traditional Tree that would result from this exclusion, there was no way of knowing whether the matrix border should be defined by the macrostructure or the microstructure. Though chapter 13 will reveal another role for the matrix whose border is defined by the microstructure, this does not change the primary identification of the matrix of a world with its macrostructure. But once such extraborder microhexagrams are excluded from the correct matrix of a world, it becomes possible to make a definitive analysis of the constituents of this matrix, given the proper construction of the world of the diagram. But that "given" is another matter still difficult to determine on the basis of the sixth-world matrix.

The two factors that permitted the emergence of the Spiral Tree were the exclusion of extraborder microhexagrams from the sixth-world matrix and the construction of the sixth world of the diagram in terms of future-modeled intermediate Sabbath Stars. This would seem to imply that such future modeling is to be the law for intermediate Sabbath Star construction. And so it has proven to be for all worlds of the diagram containing such intermediate Sabbath Stars with the important possible exception of the fourth world, for reasons we shall consider in the closing section of chapter 11. But now we must see how the Spiral Tree can provide a modeling for the Partzufim. Not only will this add considerably to the understanding of the Partzufim gained through earlier study of the sixth-world Sabbath Stars in chapter 6 but also provide startling evidence for the association of the Spiral Tree, and so the Sabbath Star Diagram through its sixth world, with Lurianic cosmology.

THE MATRIX PARTZUFIM

Observation of the sixth-world macrohexagrams reveals a counterpoint of three against two among the lateral macrohexagrams, three of which appear in the first phase of the sixth world and two in the second, these latter two being further integrated with the single central macrohexagram appearing in the second phase. Correlating these macrohexagrams now not simply with the Sefirot but with their reconstitution as Partzufim, we may observe another counterpoint of three against two, of the upper three Partzufim against the lower two. It is in this last counterpoint that we can best understand the function of this distribution of Partzufim, why the supernal Partzufim of Arikh Anpin, Abba, and Imma should be associated with the ultimate powers of creation while the lower Partzufim of Ze'ir Anpin and the Nukvah should be associated with the fine tuning of cosmic processes through the operation of Providence. A rationale for this distinction of function can be found in their numerological definition. Three is the number of harmony, in esoteric terms of the balancing of expansion and contraction that represents the immutable triadic law of creation symbolized by the hexagram, while two is the number symbolizing duality and so can be associated with freedom. So their functions seem implicit in their conjoined numbers, the upper Partzufim being three and the lower Partzufim two, the upper thus associated with immutable harmony and the lower with the mutable, with shifting harmonies. But before considering what the Spiral Tree shows about Partzufim relationships, we should observe what it reveals about Ze'ir Anpin's six Sefirot. For we can now see that as his upper triad is a product of the sixth world, so is his lower triad a product of the fourth and fifth worlds. Thus Ze'ir Anpin combines in his own nature the very union of the divine and earthly that man is to emulate.

If we now observe the upper Partzufim on the Spiral Tree—the central macrohexagram identified with Arikh Anpin, the right lateral macrohexagram with Abba, and the left lateral macrohexagram with Imma—we get the clearest graphic illustration of their relationship. We can now understand why the Yichud of Abba and Imma did not need to be distinguished from that of Arikh Anpin and the Shekhinah in the encoding of the sixth-world Sabbath Stars analyzed in chapter 6. The reason that here becomes clear is that they are, in fact, inseparable, Arikh Anpin interpenetrating and being interpenetrated by Abba and Imma. The Yichud of Abba and Imma in and with Arikh Anpin becomes understandable in the light of the appearance of these Partzufim on the Spiral Tree. And their association with divine mentality is also supported by their position in what can be considered the "head" of the serpentine spiral.

But if the upper Partzufim occupy the head of the serpent, it is the lower Partzufim who are spread out in its long, coiled body, and it is the exact positions of their components in its spiral length that will provide the most startling feature of the Sabbath Star Diagram. If the Spiral Tree is observed in terms of the directions taken by the turquoise spiral in plate 11 and the white spiral in figure 10.2, the directions of the lower seven Sefirot that constitute these Partzufim can be charted from a vantage point just east of Malkhut as follows:

Gevurah	North
Tiferet	East
Chesed	South
Netzach	South
Hod	South
Yesod	West
Malkhut	**West**

What is startling about these associations is that, with some qualifications regarding the positions of Netzach and Hod later to be considered, these Sefirot directions also appear in the tradition of the Lurianic Kabbalah, and this although these directions have no such perfect counterparts in the Sefirot arrangement of the traditional Tree of Life Diagram.

The text from which these traditional Lurianic associations are derived is the *Pri Eitz Chayyim* (Fruit of the Tree of Life) of Chayyim Vital, in a section from chapter 3 of the gate on the Lulav, one of the four species of fruit ritually associated with the festival of Sukkot, a section that correlates the spatial directions in the ritual waving of these species during Sukkot with a Kavanah (a mental intention) involving Ze'ir Anpin and the Nukvah:

So too with the order of the shaking movements: one must begin from the South, which is Chesed, and then go to the North, which is Gevurah, then to the East, which is Tiferet, and then upwards, which is Netzach, then downwards, which is Hod. . . .

The head of the Lulav always has to be upright, after which it is shaken towards the West, which is Yesod, where all the lights are intermingled. Behold, the Lulav represents Yesod, and it draws down the drop from Da'at through the spinal column. Therefore, the Lulav needs to be longer than the Hadas and the Arava. . . .

And the 'Etrog represents the Malkhut in him, and being in the state of the Nukvah, even though [she is] included in him [Ze'ir Anpin], [she] is not tied to him with the other three species; and it [the 'Etrog] is the corona of Yesod in it, meaning the Malkhut in it, and this is what the Rabbis, of blessed memory, said, "the 'Etrog, that is the Holy One, Blessed be He . . ." that is to say, all the species, even the 'Etrog, are in him; so we shake the Lulav towards him and we bring it back to the breast, for there, against the breast in the back, the head of the Nukvah emerges. For the entire Kavanah is to activate light to Rachel. . . .

The secret of the Lulav, 'Etrog, Hadas, and Arava [the four species], their Kavanot, is to bring down the aspect . . . to Da'at of Ze'ir Anpin, himself, and thereby light up from them the Nukvah, as mentioned.[1]

Chesed is positioned to the south, Gevurah to the north, Tiferet to the east, and Yesod, which is connected with Malkhut, to the west, as in the Spiral Tree. To understand better how these directions of the Sefirot comprising Ze'ir Anpin and the Nukvah can be related to the sexual positioning and activation of these Partzufim, the stated purpose of the above Lurianic Kavanah, we must be acquainted with the further ramifications of these Sefirot directions in the Lurianic tradition. References to this traditional understanding appear in Aryeh Kaplan's commentary to his translation of the *Bahir*; and though somewhat unclear divorced from the *Bahir* passages being discussed, they are invaluable:

The author states that the Chet in the word *Ruach* alludes to the three directions or winds— *Ruch-ot* in Hebrew—which are closed. These closed directions are south, east and west, corresponding respectively to the Sefirot of Chesed-Love, Tiferet-Beauty, and Yesod-Foundation. The only open direction is the north, which corresponds to Gevurah-Strength . . . which, as mentioned above, is both north and evil. . . . In Kabbalistic teachings, "Judgment" is Zer Anpin itself. . . . Here it is evident that the primary purpose of the seven Sefirot of Zer Anpin and the Female is to control providence. They act as a feedback mechanism, dealing with man according to his deeds. . . . the head of the Female is opposite the heart of Zer Anpin, which is the Sefirah of Tiferet-Beauty . . . it [the Female] is also to the "West" of Zer Anpin, opposite Yesod-Foundation. . . . When we speak of the Personification of Zer Anpin, it is usually pictured facing downward with its head to the east and its feet to the west, bestowing spiritual sustenance to the world. The Female, Malkhut-Kingship, which is opposite Tiferet-Beauty, is therefore also to the east. The "seed of Israel" travels down the spinal cord from the brain, and therefore comes from the east. Malkhut-Kingship, the Bride, is also seen as lying with her head to the east. Therefore, her womb is to the west, and it is in this womb that all seed is "mixed together." Malkhut-Kingship is therefore called Aravot, which has the double connotation of "west" and "mixture." . . . Souls are born through the union of Yesod-Foundation and Malkhut-Kingship. . . . Yesod-Foundation only functions to create souls when it is in conjunction with Malkhut-Kingship. Therefore, the main day in which it functions is the Sabbath. . . . Here we see Malkhut-Kingship as the source of all the other Sefirot. . . . Netzach-Victory and Hod-Splendor correspond to the feet of Zer Anpin, and the feet are the lowest part of the body, even below the sexual organ. The usual picture of Zer Anpin presents this Personification in a lying down position with his head to the east. The right foot, corresponding to Netzach-Victory is raised upward, while the left foot, corresponding to Hod-Splendor, is lowered downward. Hence, Netzach-Victory and Hod-Splendor, are said to represent the up-down directions. . . . Since the head of Zer Anpin is to the east, his feet are to the west. . . . Netzach-Victory and Hod-Splendor are the lowest Sefirot, touching the "ground."[2]

From this detailed description, we should be able to recognize in the Spiral Tree the outlines of the bodies of Ze'ir Anpin and the Nukvah as they are traditionally imagined. Tiferet to the east represents the area of both the heart of the upper body of Ze'ir Anpin and the head of the lower body of the Nukvah. To the west is the sexual organ with which the Nukvah is primarily identified as the Partzuf of Malkhut, located in close contact with the Yesod of Ze'ir Anpin. Beneath their conjoined sexual organs are the knees of Ze'ir Anpin, the parts of the lower limbs traditionally represented by Netzach and Hod. Netzach and Hod thus share the western direction with Yesod and Malkhut but beneath them, to their south. The contradiction between the directions for Netzach and Hod given in the *Pri Eitz Chayyim* and the Spiral Tree can be resolved through the Kaplan understanding of these Sefirot as representing the positions of the feet of a prone Ze'ir Anpin, the right foot raised and the left foot lowered, a position only possible if the knees of both these limbs are "grounded." The suggested position, then, has Ze'ir Anpin resting on his knees, the left knee slightly forward of the right knee since in the Spiral Tree, when viewed from below, Hod appears to the right or east of Netzach, with the right foot raised upward and the left foot dangling over the edge of Cloud Nine, or wherever. His but-

tocks are, however, raised above the knees on which he is resting, with the Nukvah's lower torso lifted up and her legs crossed over his lower back to facilitate coital contact.

This traditional picture portrays the positions of the macrohexagrams identified with Tiferet, Netzach, Hod, Yesod, and Malkhut as they appear in the Spiral Tree. Not yet accounted for are the bodily positions of Gevurah and Chesed. Given the traditional understanding of the Yichud of Ze'ir Anpin and the Nukvah as involving a facing, prone position, he above her, it would seem that the northern Sefirah of Gevurah must be identified with his back and the southern Sefirah of Chesed with hers. The former accords with Kaplan's understanding of "Judgment" as identified both with Ze'ir Anpin and "Gevurah-Strength, which is the source of judgment."[3] Passed over in silence is the necessary, correlative identification of Chesed with the Nukvah if this couple is to be pictured as making, in the words of Shakespeare's Iago, "the beast with two backs"(1.1.117). With this identification, we can see that the only parts of this pair that touch their resting place are her back and his knees, the three macrohexagram-Sefirot that occupy the southern positions in the Spiral Tree.

Before considering the implications of this final identification of Chesed with the back of the Nukvah, we should pause to examine a pictorial representation of the Unification of Ze'ir Anpin and the Nukvah, drawn as are the constellations over the stars of the lower seven macrohexagrams on the Spiral Tree so that they reveal the bodily forms and positions accorded them in the Lurianic tradition. Such an artist's rendering can be seen in figure 10.4.

To say that figure 10.4 gives a "graphic" representation of the Yichud of Ze'ir Anpin and the Nukvah is, for once, not to use this term humorously. But it is important so to represent it because it reveals perhaps the most hidden doctrine of the Kabbalah, the cosmic mysteries pertaining to sex and the feminine presence. "It is declared everywhere, but everywhere also it is concealed,"[4] says A. E. Waite, who variously shows that "the Supreme Wisdom is a Mystery of Sex . . . from the union of male and female—meaning, of course, in the tran-

Figure 10.4. The Unification of Ze'ir Anpin and the Nukvah

scendence—come all souls which animate men . . . which union is the source of all other Mysteries."[5]

The identification of the Nukvah with Chesed on the Spiral Tree helps us to appreciate the little recognized truth also enunciated by Waite "that Shekinah is on both sides of the Tree."[6] In the form of the supernal mother, Binah or Imma, the Shekhinah dominates the process of Emanation through the left side of the traditional Tree with which she is identified, and in the form of the daughter or bride in Malkhut, the Nukvah, she dominates the process of Return through the right side of the Tree. As figure 10.4 demonstrates, she returns in her lesser aspect as the Nukvah via the

Sefirah of Chesed on the right pillar controlled by this Sefirah. Though Abba and Ze'ir Anpin may be assigned to the alternate pillars during these phases—we have seen the complementary association of Ze'ir Anpin with Gevurah in figure 10.4 and Lurianic mythology—the generative power in both phases seems to derive from the feminine sides. Concentrating on the Tikkun, the creative power of the Nukvah is revealed through the two Sefirot identified with her in the Spiral Tree, Malkhut signifying the womb of primary generation as Chesed does the power of regeneration. But it is the form of the Spiral Tree that best reveals its informing feminine presence, beginning as it does with Malkhut and ending with Binah.

The Sefirot associations of Ze'ir Anpin and the Nukvah, arrived at through combining the traditional Lurianic way of picturing their union with their placement on the Spiral Tree, provide as well a new understanding of the nature of the divine heart, that aspect of Neshamah consciousness manifested in the first spatial phase of the sixth-world matrix. For they identify the judgmental aspect of the divine heart, its Gevurah, with the masculine, the merciful aspect, its Chesed, with the feminine, and the balancing faculty, its Tiferet, with androgyny, Tiferet clearly symbolizing the "understanding heart" insofar as it combines the heart of Ze'ir Anpin with the head of the Nukvah.[7] Envisioning the "Mystery of Sex" within the Spiral Tree enables us not only to understand the generation of souls but also the heart of their future bliss.

Not only does the Spiral Tree provide "graphic" illustration of the threefold Yichud of Abba and Imma with Arikh Anpin and the twofold Yichud of Ze'r Anpin and the Nukvah that unifies the heart of Neshamah consciousness, but it reinforces the three types of mating by Malkhut earlier treated in the analysis of the sixth-world Sabbath Stars in chapter 6. In the traditional Tree, Malkhut is only in proximity to Yesod, with Yesod blocking its passage to Tiferet and Keter. In the Spiral Tree, however, it can be seen that, from the position of the collective central macrohexagram at the center of the diagram identified with Malkhut, she can engage in a sexual mating with Yesod to her west, an emotional mating

with Tiferet to her east, and a mental mating with Keter to her north, having a clear access to each.[8] The unobstructed vertical union between Malkhut and Keter has never before been seen so clearly despite much kabbalistic commentary on this point. Kaplan reflects this general understanding when he says: "In the Soul dimension, Malkhut-Kingship is precisely opposite Keter-Crown."[9] But the traditional Tree cannot demonstrate this precise relationship. If the emergence of a matrix Tree in the sixth-world form of this diagram seemed uncanny, its ability to display with precision the most arcane aspects of Partzufim mating, down to the curious arrangement of Sefirot during the coupling of Ze'ir Anpin and the Nukvah, seems more than coincidental; and it becomes possible to argue that the Spiral Tree, rather than the traditional version of the Tree, was, in fact, the basis of the original kabbalistic descriptions by Luria and others of the processes and personalities of the Tikkun, and it certainly can provide the model for a modern Kabbalah.

In revealing the path of Tikkun, the Spiral Tree becomes, then, a precise model for the development of the divine personalities that fulfill the purpose of creation. Since this development of multiple personalities is represented in Lurianic cosmology as the ultimate point of divine history, the implication would seem to be that Ein Sof entered the process of creation precisely to achieve this multiple individuation of the divine essence. The *Eitz Chayyim* tells us at its very beginning that one reason for creation involved God's desire to achieve multiple forms of His divinity: "When it arose in His will, blessed be His name, to create the world in order to be good to those He created, and that they should be able to recognize His greatness and merit being a chariot for the Divine, to be attached to Him, the Blessed One, He emanated one point, which included ten (and they are the ten Sefirot of the points [*akudim*] that were in one vessel), and they were invisible."[10] Bound up with the manifestation of the ten Sefirot out of the primal form of divine unity, with all the soon to be related drama of Shevirah and Tikkun this necessitated, was the divine desire to create creatures who would "merit being a chariot of the divine." Man, too, was to become a chariot of the divine, a mystical vessel and manifestation of the divine essence.

Thus not only was the divine unity to be rectified into the five Partzufim who would serve as the cosmic manifestation of the divine will, but into the divine personalities of those creatures who could embody and cleave to the divine—Abraham, Isaac, Rachel, and perhaps even Leonora. For the names of the first three and others are also affixed to the Sefirot, also give these divine attributes personality. It is here that we may find the hidden meaning of the Lurianic Kabbalah and the source of its abiding power. For its message is that the divine personalities to be produced through the Tikkun will be the work of human beings and manifest not only a transformation of the divine essence but a transformed humanity. In the next section we shall consider some further aspects of the Spiral Tree that are most suggestive with respect to man's proper path of spiritual development.

THE SEFIROT AND THE PATH OF THE SOUL

If we look again at the depiction of the Spiral Tree in plate 11 and figures 10.2 and 10.3, perhaps its most surprising aspect involves the passage of its component lateral spiral through two different and opposite central spirals. The red central spiral that the turquoise lateral spiral first intercepts is thus not its safest guide since it is moving in a direction opposite to that which is the ultimate goal of its development. It was for this reason that earlier analyses of the central system stressed the dangers presented by the color-individuated fourth-world central microhexagram and fifth-world central macrohexagram, the dangers of the paranormal at these early stages of spiritual development and the need to keep the central system under the firm control of the lateral system until Neshamah consciousness has been reached. The colors of the Spiral Tree, adopted from the system of Dinshah Ghadiali as explained in chapter 8, are particularly interesting in view of their cultural symbolism. For red can be associated with the fires both of desire and of eternal punishment. As the primary color component of

the earth, soil, it is also significantly opposed to the blue color to which the turquoise lateral spiral finally ascends, the color of the sky, these colors symbolizing the opposition of the earth and heaven. The red central spiral, on the other hand, finally joins the scarlet lateral spiral of what can be considered the Shadow Tree, to use Jungian terminology. And scarlet has long been the color symbolizing whoredom, as both a venal sin and a symbol of spiritual infidelity. Thus the red spiral to which the turquoise spiral of man is first joined is headed toward a dangerous union with the scarlet spiral of spiritual whoredom, and something radical must occur to turn the turquoise spiral around from a downward to an upward direction.

The difference between the routes taken by the central red and lateral turquoise spirals may well be related to an essential difference between the yogic chakra and kabbalistic Sefirah systems.[11] For if we follow the more direct route of the central red spiral, we can see that it is associated with exactly seven macrohexagrams, the four that it shares with its original turquoise partner and the final three that it shares with its ultimate scarlet partner, exactly the number of the chakras. In contrast, the longer lateral path, shared first with a red and then a blue central partner, is associated with the ten macrohexagrams that can be correlated with the Sefirot of the kabbalistic Tree of Life Diagram and the Spiral Tree. The system of yoga would seem, then, to be primarily related to the central spiral of the Sabbath Star Diagram matrix and the kabbalistic system to the lateral spiral. What the central spiral lacks is precisely those missing three elements of the divine heart that may be associated with the concept of grace. Yogic meditation is a self-willed practice that places little reliance on a petitioning for a divine grace beyond its control and whose goal is nirvana, that blissful state in which personality is annihilated. The highest form of kabbalistic practice, on the other hand, is the performance of the ritual prayers with the Kavanah or mystical intention of unifying the transcendent and immanent forms of the divine both with themselves and with the praying soul. It is only through such prayer that the heart can be truly opened to receive that divine love through which the Neshamah soul is generated and with it the goal of kabbalistic practice, the achievement of divine personality. Where the path of yoga ideally leads to the annihilation of personality in some final return to the source, the path of mystical Jewish practice is rather toward that state of Devekut or communion in which the personality is preserved while becoming one of the multiple forms clothing the divine. That there are exceptions and overlappings between these two major categories of mystical theory and practice does not invalidate the force of this generalization, of a major difference between Eastern and Western mysticism that can be well modeled by the difference between the central and lateral spirals of the Sabbath Star Diagram. But if the matrix can thus model both forms of spiritual practice, the distinction it reveals between them is also significant. For the more direct central path is seen to be both more limited than the circuitous lateral path and also oriented in an opposite direction, down rather than up and suggestive of a return to the cosmic past rather than a progression to a future cosmic goal. While allowing for both, the matrix would seem, then, to be prescribing the longer and more inclusive lateral path leading to divine personality and associated with the future-oriented process of the Tikkun.[12]

This correlation of the lateral spiral with the future and of the central spiral with the past, which can be related to the earlier defined circuit of matrix elements understood to go out with the lateral and back with the central, can be seen even more clearly by examining the relationship of the lateral turquoise spiral to the central green spiral, shown in plate 10 and its black-and-white version, figure 10.1. For it is not alone from the red spiral of earth that the turquoise spiral of man must turn. Let us look again at these first illustrations of the matrix, which show the complete and separated lateral and central spirals of the turquoise (or white) and green (or black) colors. These colors were intimately associated at the start of cosmic manifestation, in what can now be regarded as the womb of Malkhut, the green triangle filling the upper triangle of the Do hexagram and the turquoise triangle that facing it from the divided hexagon produced within the Do

hexagram with the manifestation of the matrix. Now what is most interesting about the subsequent development of these original mates is that they diverge never again to meet. Though the turquoise spiral passes through all the other five central spirals and joins with two of them to form the Spiral Tree, it carefully avoids the green spiral. The implication of the avoidance of the green spiral by the turquoise would seem to be none other than that old adage, "You can't go home again." What this means in terms of cosmology is that we cannot return to the Garden, cannot retrace the cosmic steps back to the point of origin but must proceed forward, following the path of Tikkun to a greater perfection than that with which we started, the path from the green originating life principle to the heavenly blue higher consciousness of divine personality, the passage from Malkhut to Keter that the Shekhinah takes with man and that the Spiral Tree so unerringly traces.

This brings us to a final point about the central system, not what happens if we follow one central spiral through its mating with two opposite lateral spirals but what emerges from examining the succession of central elements on the Spiral Tree. Let us begin by considering the significant fact that the matrix Tree begins with Malkhut, significant because it defines the process of the Tikkun as proceeding from the feminine, immanent aspect of the divine, in its lower Behinot or aspects known by the names of Rachel and the Nukvah and in its highest aspect as the Shekhinah. In chapter 6, also on the sixth-world diagram, we saw geometric and kabbalistic reasons for defining these three Behinot as the Malkhut of Malkhut, the Netzach of Malkhut, and the Keter of Malkhut. If we now look at the labeled Spiral Tree in figure 10.3, we can see that it is precisely the Sefirot of Malkhut, Netzach, and Keter that represent its central system and would thus seem to ally this system most closely with the feminine aspect of divine and human consciousness represented by Malkhut.

The final feature of the Spiral Tree that bears on the question of man's spiritual path involves the first of its lateral heart elements, Chesed, whose form in the matrix is most significant. For the macrohexagram identified with Chesed is the only one after that identified with Malkhut to be surrounded by six microhexagrams, six surrounding a seventh always being a symbol of creation. But where the six central microhexagrams surrounding the macrohexagram of Malkhut mark the beginnings of all six central spirals, the six microhexagrams surrounding the macrohexagram of Chesed are all of its own color. Where the first creation may be said to bring a newborn into the collective family of humanity, with its legacy of all the earlier stages of cosmic and vital evolution, the spiritual movement into Chesed not only makes such a human twice-born but may be said to confer the true individuality of a master. It is surely remarkable that the two geometric forms associated with Chesed should so differently convey the same symbolism of creation. It will be remembered from chapter 6 that the sixth vertical Sabbath Star of the sixth-world diagram, identified with the Chesed of Ze'ir Anpin, was the only Sabbath Star of its world to feature six complete border hexagrams surrounding a similarly sized central hexagram; and now again that feature of the matrix that alone produces an individual configuration of six around a central seventh has, through the impenetrable intelligence of the diagram and the logic of its matrix, required identification with Chesed. The diagram would thus seem to be encoding through these two linked forms a central factor of spiritual life, that to reach the highest point of salvation one must be reborn in loving-kindness, in Chesed. But if it is only in Chesed that one's true individuality is born, then the ego identified with the lower self must represent a false identity, none other than one's human nature, and the spiritual path that which leads to rebirth as a divine personality. As the matrix modeling of the Partzufim displays their Sefirot in positions cited in the Lurianic tradition but impossible in terms of the Tree of Life Diagram, and thus gives support to this aspect of the Lurianic tradition, so does it again make clear that the Sabbath Star Diagram is no ordinary geometric construction but one in which the whole of both the Jewish esoteric tradition and the history of the cosmos it has so unerringly defined are somehow encoded.

THE SPIRAL TREE AS PSYCHOLOGICAL MODEL

We come now to the most important treatment of the matrix in this work, that in which its elements are reinterpreted in terms of the amazing emergence of a Spiral Tree in the matrices of the fourth through sixth worlds of the Sabbath Star Diagram. It is with this new correlation to the kabbalistic terminology of the Tree that it now becomes possible to model the various levels of what, with a current school of therapy, can be called "transpersonal psychology" and in a manner that fully integrates such an approach with the esoteric psychology of the Kabbalah. The Spiral Tree not only makes clear the relationship of soul levels to the Sefirot, thus adding to our understanding of kabbalistic psychology, but its precise modeling of these levels in terms both of matrix geometry and Sefirotic connotations should provide a useful guide both for psychological theory and therapy, providing a new ability to diagnose soul levels and the factor of central or lateral dominance.

This latter distinction, a product of matrix analysis, may or may not be related to that between the right and left hemispheres of the brain, but it can certainly be related to kabbalistic psychology, particularly to the more recent version developed by the founder of Habad Hasidism and expounded by his son, Dov Baer of Lubavitch. In his tract *On Ecstasy*, Dov Baer defines each of the five soul levels as composed of two different souls, called natural and divine, the former characterized by a sense of separateness from the divine and the latter of unity with it, the former also exhibiting freedom and the latter an involuntary quality. Although focused on the question of ecstasy, his following account clearly has more general application:

> With regard to the natural soul it is all in the category of an ecstasy that is separate from the divine essence. Whereas the ecstasy of the divine soul is an essential ecstasy, the result of the divine itself that is rooted in her and implanted in her as if it were her actual nature.
>
> Now the divine soul is also composed of *nefesh*, *ruah*, *neshamah*, *hayyah* and *yehidah* and she is clothed by the *nefesh*, *ruah*, *neshamah*, *hayyah* and

yehidah of the natural soul. . . . Such an ecstasy comes of its own accord, involuntarily, without any choice, will or effort whatsoever. It is caused solely by the essence of the divine soul when she is moved to ecstasy. . . . Even though the ecstasy is sensed greatly in the heart this state cannot be termed self-awareness. On the contrary, there is a total lack of self awareness. . . .[13]

Though the normal kabbalistic distinction between the natural and divine souls is one of levels, the divine soul beginning with the Neshamah and the natural with the levels below it, primarily that of the Nefesh, the distinction here made by Dov Baer is clearly comparable to the matrix distinction between central and lateral elements at each soul level. However it may be related to brain structure, it does seem to model the complex functioning of consciousness. How it can model the psychic functioning of the three major soul levels we are now to see.

THE FOURTH- AND FIFTH-WORLD MATRIX MODELS OF THE NEFESH AND RUACH SOULS

The macrohexagrams of the fourth- and fifth-world matrices were earlier analyzed only in terms of the central and lateral systems for two reasons: to demonstrate the geometric logic of the matrix and its applicability to human concerns on its own terms, apart from the kabbalistic structure of the Tree; and to provide this added dimension to the later discussion of these macrohexagrams when their precise correspondence to the Sefirot could be established, a correspondence that should be illuminating to both. To aid the reader's comprehension of the following summary of these prior analyses, figure 9.2 should be consulted, as well as plate 7 with figure 8.1, providing the past-modeled or unfallen fourth-world diagram, plate 8 with figure 8.2, the future-modeled or fallen fourth-world diagram, and plate 9 with figure 9.1, the cumulative fifth-world diagram, that whose elimination of any interior fourth-world matrix border renders the question of a fourth-world Fall forever moot.

Before beginning the analysis of these matrix diagrams, mention should be made of one feature of the earlier analyses, the association of the first four macrohexagrams with the corresponding psychic centers of the chakra system. This association was made in terms of the expressive natures of these hexagrams with no reference to the further correlation now before us of these matrix elements with the Sefirot. But once this further correlation is made, it is clear that there is also a direct correlation to be made between these Sefirot and chakras. In the following analysis I will briefly call attention to the obvious correspondences between the lower and upper three sets of Sefirot and chakras.

In chapter 5 of *The Secret Doctrine of the Kabbalah*, I showed how these two esoteric systems could be identified despite the problem of different numeration, the fact that there are ten Sefirot and only seven chakras. My solution involved a modification of the Jewish understanding of the "double heart," traditionally understood to refer to the good and evil inclinations of the heart, the Yetzer ha-Tov and the Yetzer ha-Ra. In my modified use, the double heart was taken to refer to the union of the Ruach and Neshamah hearts, the former identified in my model with Netzach, also correlated with the central macrohexagram of the fifth-world diagram, and the latter with the three Sefirot of Tiferet, Gevurah, and Chesed, now correlated with the three lateral macrohexagrams in the first phase of the sixth-world diagram. This permitted an equation between the fourth chakra identified in the Indian yogic system with the heart, whose hexagram emblem is suggestive of a similar unification of higher and lower halves, and the fourth through seventh of the upwardly counted Sefirot, which in turn permits a full correspondence of Sefirot with chakras. But though these two esoteric psychological systems can be so correlated, the numerical distinction between them is still important in pointing to the essential difference in spiritual direction of these systems just treated. The correlation of chakras and Sefirot is, nonetheless, still important.

In analyzing the fourth-world matrix as a diagram of the Nefesh soul, the collective central macrohexagram was associated with the Jungian collective unconscious and the lateral macrohexagram with individual self-consciousness, one still largely motivated by the reptilian level of brain evolution. Identifying them now with the Sefirot of Malkhut and Yesod, respectively, we can understand the prior identifications in a new light. The association of Yesod, the sexual Sefirah, with the first lateral macrohexagram gives support to the Freudian view that human consciousness is dominated by the libido in both its direct and sublimated forms, but it should be added that this is only true of its Nefesh level of consciousness. The association of Malkhut with the first central macrohexagram is also appropriate since Malkhut is the receptacle in which all the higher spiritual energies are collected, and this macrohexagram can also be considered to be collective. It thus can be thought to provide unconscious access to the accumulated experience of the whole cosmic process. As the second of these Sefirot (the ninth on the Tree) may clearly be associated with the second chakra since both are centers of sexuality, so may the first Sefirah of the Tikkun, Malkhut, be associated with the first chakra, identified with both the instinct for survival and the Kundalini energy. Thus the Nefesh or animal soul is primarily concerned with personal survival and the perpetuation of the species, aims that cannot be faulted as long as they do not contaminate the higher powers of the soul.

The higher powers of the Ruach soul are controlled by the fifth-world lateral macrohexagram, now identified with Hod, in association with its fifth-world central counterpart, now identified with Netzach. Correlating these Sefirot with the third and fourth chakras is again most illuminating. The third chakra has generally been viewed as the source of spiritual power. Located in the solar plexus, it is the place where the spiritual being can be centered and is called the *hara* in Buddhist psychophysiology. But the third chakra is also the place that can be associated with perversions of the power principle, with the Nietzschean (and Adlerian) will to power. This contamination of the third chakra can be more readily understood by examining its macrohexagram-Sefirah counterpart in both its fourth- and fifth-world forms. It will be remembered that in the

fourth-world diagram this macrohexagram was already present but beyond either of its matrix borders. Thus the Nefesh soul, which had moved beyond survival and reproduction to the pursuit of personal power, was entering Hod prematurely with a now contaminated animal consciousness. In the fifth-world diagram, however, it is this lateral macrohexagram identified with Hod that becomes the source of spiritual power, its four levels associated with the four lateral microhexagrams completed by the fifth-world diagram. Thus the manipulative person, who seeks to control others for personal aggrandizement, is by this very means cutting himself off from his true source of power, the Glory (one meaning of Hod) attained through Hod when the self is properly controlled so that it can become an instrument of higher powers. It was earlier shown that the highest power of the Ruach soul, that represented by its last lateral microhexagram, could only be effectuated by the master who had already reached the Neshamah level of development and so was able to connect it with the missing link on its spiral. If we now observe the full matrix of the Spiral Tree in figure 10.3, we can see that this missing link is the Sefirah of Gevurah and thus that it is only through the control of a divine judgment that this highest level of creative spiritual power can be released into human history.

But the turning of the power of Hod into an instrument of the highest will requires the collaboration of Netzach, the Sefirah now identified with the Ruach central macrohexagram. This macrohexagram is, in many ways, the most interesting of all. Its correlation with the Ruach portion of the fourth chakra will be better understood in chapter 12 when we trace the involution of the matrix spiral back to the center and then further to include its opposite in the Double Spiral Tree. It will then be seen that this macrohexagram actually belongs in the spiritual body of the "Other," the Shadow being that can be correlated with an expanded sense of the self, with the beloved, or with the whole cosmos. It is because the lateral macrohexagram representing the higher will cannot function without the imaginative faculty represented by this central macrohexagram, and it in turn is vitally connected with the Other, that the enormous power of Hod will only be released for the good of the whole.

We can also now understand the factor that distinguishes the higher heart of Netzach from that emotional power associated with the Nefesh ego and represented by the lateral second microhexagram of the fourth-world diagram in its future-modeled form. When that form of the fourth-world diagram is considered to model the process of transformation, this emotional power can be understood to represent an organ of attunement to higher consciousness. But when it is considered as a model of the Fall, this emotional power is understood to be or became a function of the lower ego residing in the first lateral macrohexagram, that identified with the Sefirah Yesod. The sexualized and egocentric lower heart is then primarily concerned with its own gratification, is mainly directed toward the sexual partners and children who will minister to its self-esteem, and is easily hurt by any criticism or rejection that would threaten such self-esteem. The Ruach heart, on the other hand, is primarily concerned with ministering to the Other. Indeed, it is so identified with the Other that it is ready to sacrifice all to it. It feels rewarded by the happiness or relief it can bring to others and is deeply pained by the misery of the world. And it is precisely because it is truly identified with the Other that it has such an intimate, intuitive knowledge of conditions other than its own as can open the Ruach mind to the imaginative understanding of those unseen depths beyond the self that can properly channel its power into cosmic service.

Thus Netzach and Hod, the fifth-world central and lateral macrohexagrams, must work together if the Ruach soul is both to survive and serve. As the Ruach soul can only serve if Hod, the Ruach mind, is properly directed by the imaginative heart of Netzach, so can it only survive if the merging tendencies of Netzach are properly controlled by the higher but still individual will vested in Hod. For there are further dangers to the soul's proper development arising from Netzach's primary attachment to the central spiral other than that to which the soul must ultimately travel. This will become clear in chapter 11 when we consider the dangers at each

soul level posed by those matrix elements beyond the matrix borders of the various worlds.

But though Netzach poses some danger to the survival of Ruach consciousness in its earthly form, it is entrance into the sphere of a properly controlled Netzach that seems to be necessary to ensure the survival of the soul after death. Netzach signifies Eternity, and the meaning of this on the human level would seem to be its power to confer immortality to any soul that enters in the orbit of its power even to the slightest degree. A similar view appears in the yoga tradition that associates the fourth chakra with the attainment of immortality. What is necessary to begin this opening of the fourth chakra, this movement of the soul into Netzach, is the pure experience of caring for another. For most, this is achieved through parenting. However egocentric parents may be, however their love for a child may be predicated on its meeting their own expectations, there will be moments when most normal parents will feel real joy at the happiness of a child and distress at its pain, will want to nourish its development for the child's own sake. If not with children, then certainly with pets, and even plants, a pure experience of caring for the life and well-being of something beyond the self can arise that can begin the higher development of the soul necessary for ensuring its permanence. And in so caring for something beyond the self, the self becomes rewarded, not only with the well-being experienced through expansion of the heart, but with power. New intuitive capacities develop that can lead to all the spiritual powers of the Ruach Master. It is through giving up or forgetting the jealous concern for personal power over others that the self becomes truly empowered, moves from the instinctual responses of the animal Nefesh level into the truly free will of the Ruach soul.

Having reinterpreted the previously analyzed fourth- and fifth-world matrices in the light of the sixth-world matrix Tree, let us now see what this Tree can add to our understanding of Neshamah consciousness as a unified psychic structure. Neshamah consciousness parallels the lower two levels of consciousness in being composed of two parts, but it differs from them in that these parts are not to be as strictly divided between the central and lateral systems. We have seen that the major distinction within the Nefesh soul was between the largely subconscious, paranormal central Sefirah of Malkhut, and the self-consciousness of the lateral Sefirah of Yesod that represents its "normal" state of functioning. On the Ruach level, the paranormal becomes fully conscious in the central Sefirah of Netzach, which like Malkhut may be credited with the power to form astral space into imaginative structures, the Nefesh central system doing so primarily in sleeping dreams while the Ruach central system does so in the "waking dreams" of meditation, visions, and out-of-body experiences. But the consciousness of self still resides in the lateral system, Hod representing the higher "I" as Yesod does the lower ego. Whereas the instinctual, emotional, and mental functions of the Nefesh soul were all in the service of the libidinous ego lodged in the lateral macrohexagram of Yesod, in the Ruach soul the mental and emotional functions become fully empowered psychic centers in their own right, lodged in Hod and Netzach, respectively, with Yesod restored to the natural instinctive functioning for which it was intended, both sexually and as a regulator of the body during the soul's higher experiences.

The Neshamah soul parallels the Ruach soul in distinguishing between its heart and mind functions, but it reverses their order. Though the Ruach heart may need to be controlled by its mind, it represents the highest development of its soul level and defines its essential nature. In the case of the Neshamah soul, it is the mind that preeminently defines its highest nature with the heart serving as both its outer covering and connection to the lower soul levels. The Neshamah heart and mind are not so much distinguished through the central and lateral systems as through the phases of the diagram. Where the Sefirot of the Nefesh soul were positioned toward the left or west side of the matrix spiral, and those of the Ruach soul were positioned toward its bottom or south side, the Sefirot of the Neshamah soul are divided into two groups, the first facing toward the right or east side and the second toward the top or north side of the diagram. Those to the east are, in their matrix order, Chesed,

Tiferet, and Gevurah, while those to the north are Chokhmah, Keter, and Binah. Since the first group has traditionally been associated in the Kabbalah with the heart and the second group with the mind, it seems advisable to preserve these identifications. But the distinction between the central and lateral systems remains significant on the Neshamah level, and it is in understanding the relationship of these systems to the two phases of the Neshamah soul that we can best define their natures.

As figure 10.3 has shown, the Neshamah soul is composed of five lateral macrohexagrams and one central macrohexagram, the arrangement of the lateral elements being that three of its macrohexagrams are located in the first phase and two in the second, while the sole central macrohexagram appears in the second phase. Since central macrohexagrams, by the measurement of "light units" that will be developed at the close of chapter 11, can be considered to be far more powerful than lateral, the appearance of the central Neshamah macrohexagram in the second, mental phase indicates the central domination of the Neshamah mind. The Neshamah heart, just as surprisingly, is exclusively lateral. The Neshamah soul is thus just as much the reverse of the Ruach soul in structure as it is in spiritual direction. As the Ruach soul is oriented in a downward earthly direction, with lateral mental functions and central feelings, so the upward heavenly orientation of the Neshamah soul would somehow seem to require a reversal of functions by which its heart becomes lateral and its mind essentially central. To understand why this is so is to understand the definition of Neshamah consciousness encoded in the matrix of the Sabbath Star Diagram.

THE SIXTH-WORLD MATRIX MODEL OF THE NESHAMAH HEART

If we begin by examining the three Sefirot normally associated with the divine heart, we can see that the heart they compose must be radically different from those on the lower two levels of the soul. We have seen that the Nefesh heart was essentially selfish and the Ruach heart essentially selfless. In contrast to these two extremes of feeling, the Neshamah heart involves a balancing of the polarities of expansion and contraction. This is, indeed, how the heart triad of the Tree of Life Diagram has been traditionally interpreted. The task of the Neshamah heart is, then, to balance the mercy of Chesed, that quality which most allies it to the Ruach heart, with the just discrimination of Gevurah, a quality of contraction lifted by its justice above the self-serving of the Nefesh heart; and these complementary requirements of a responsible heart are given their proper weight in the balance of Tiferet. The distinction between soft and hard love, often made with regard to parents, also applies to the difference between the Ruach and Neshamah hearts. It is the difference between Rachel weeping uncontrollably for her children and Jacob giving each the just blessing he deserves. This difference is also appropriate to the distinction between Ruach and Neshamah Masters, the former serving a flock and the latter primarily serving as agents of just Providence.

Throughout the analysis of the matrix as a model of the psyche, the macrohexagrams have been interpreted as centers of consciousness and the microhexagrams as powers of these psychic centers. It has not been necessary to discuss the first eight microhexagrams of the spiral because the identifications previously given them in chapters 8 and 9 have only to be applied to the new understanding of the earlier considered macrohexagrams as Sefirot. But though these will be listed in table 11.1 and may be consulted now, it will help the following analysis of the sixth-world matrix to summarize this listing here. Thus in the past-modeled, more strictly animal form of the fourth-world matrix, the central first microhexagram is identified with intuition and the lateral second microhexagram with the instincts. To this the future-modeled, more human form of the fourth-world matrix adds the lateral third and fourth microhexagrams, the former identified with the emotions and the latter with the intellect, the former also interpenetrating the central microhexagram identified with intuition and the latter disconnected from its spiral. In the fifth-world matrix there are no additional central microhexagrams, but there are four additional lateral microhexagrams, that

numbered fifth being identified with creative thought and the remainder with three levels of Ruach Masters, the sixth with the Master of Synchronicity, the seventh with the Master of Transformation, and the eighth, also disconnected from its spiral, with the Master of Creation, both the first and fourth of these microhexagrams, those identified with creation, appearing higher in the horns of the matrix border than those of the intermediate levels. We come next to the six microhexagrams associated with the first phase of the sixth-world diagram, and these should now be considered, thus enlarging our understanding of its three macrohexagrams and the functioning of the Neshamah heart as an organ of Providence.

As will be shown in the first section of chapter 11, in reviewing the matrix rings, the six microhexagrams of the first phase of the Neshamah matrix, which appear to form one bordering ring, are actually members of two matrix rings. Thus the microhexagrams to the right and left of the macrohexagram signifying Tiferet are actually members of the matrix ring that includes the first and fourth of the microhexagrams completed in the fifth-world matrix, those that represent its most creative powers. The pairs of sixth-world microhexagrams most closely associated with the macrohexagrams identified with Chesed and Gevurah belong, conversely, to the next and later-completed matrix ring. What this means is that the microhexagrams representing the full powers of Tiferet are in place before those of Chesed and Gevurah and that, therefore, these latter centers are empowered only after the achievement of the psychic balance represented by Tiferet.[14] This feature of the matrix also brings this aspect of the Spiral Tree more closely into harmony with the traditional Tree of Life Diagram. Where the traditional Tree places Tiferet below Chesed and Gevurah, the Spiral Tree seems to differ in placing it above them. But understanding of the order of microhexagram manifestation resolves this apparent discrepancy by revealing the prior activation of Tiferet and so its functionally lower position.

Each of the three macrohexagrams representing centers of the Neshamah heart is associated, then, with two microhexagrams, one to its right and one to its left. If we can associate the microhexagrams to the right with the definitive Sefirah of the right column of the Tree and those to the left with the Sefirah similarly definitive of its left column, the former identified with the expansive mercy of Chesed and the latter with the restrictive judgment of Gevurah, then it seems appropriate to identify these microhexagrams first with these qualities. Thus when one is positioned at the center of the diagram facing eastward, the lowest or southernmost microhexagram could be identified as the Chesed of Chesed, that to its left as the Gevurah of Chesed, the next to the right of Tiferet as the Chesed of Tiferet, that to its left as the Gevurah of Tiferet, the next as the Chesed of Gevurah and the final topmost microhexagram to its left as the Gevurah of Gevurah.

Although the spiral order of this triad of Sefirot is the opposite of that on the traditional Tree, it is most illuminating with regard to the soul directions defined by the Spiral Tree. For the Chesed of Chesed, its essential nature, points in the same downward direction as do the Ruach soul and the central spiral to which the macrohexagram of Netzach belongs, that heart of the Ruach soul with which the Chesed of the Neshamah heart is most closely allied. And the Gevurah of Gevurah points in the same upward direction as that of the Neshamah mind and thus indicates the mental orientation of that faculty of judgment it contributes to the Neshamah heart. The whole of the Spiral Tree through Chesed may be correlated with the lower direction and that beginning with Gevurah with the upper direction, with Tiferet at its heart of hearts to balance these two directions and orchestrate the turning of the spiral upward.

But as earlier noted, these soul directions also have interesting parallels with shamanic cosmology. If the Nefesh soul can be associated with the earth, then the fifth world of the Ruach soul is, indeed, a lower world with regard to the earth, located below it in the matrix, and the sixth world of the Neshamah soul, particularly in its purely mental aspect, is an upper world, located as it is above the earth equivalent in the matrix. The matrix gives us,

then, the most graphic equivalents between the worlds of kabbalistic and shamanic cosmology as both may be derived from an initial hexagram model of creation.[15]

Let us return now to consideration of these microhexagrams as powers of the macrohexagrams and see how their above identifications with the qualities of Chesed and Gevurah can be related to an understanding of their functions. In the Adam Kadmon Tree, these two Sefirot are associated with the right and left arms and hands. If the right hand of Chesed can now be pictured in the expansive form expressive of its nature, that is, as open, and the left hand of Gevurah in the contracted form that expresses its nature, as a closed fist, then we can begin to understand the functioning of these microhexagram powers. The closed position of the hand has two primary functions, to hold and to strike, the open position to give and to stroke. From this we may ascribe two functions to each of these microhexagrams. The three left-hand members of these pairs can be viewed both as its receptive organ and its more severe aspect, the three right-hand members as both its dispensing organ and its more lenient aspect.

Let us now define these six microhexagrams more exactly and then see how they can function both as organs of intake and outflow and as stages of Providential justice. Beginning with Chesed, we can say that its rightmost microhexagram, previously identified as the Chesed of Chesed, may be considered to represent the quality of unmerited grace, and that to its left, the Gevurah of Chesed, the forgiving mercy that mitigates or suspends justice. This distinction may be seen in the two aspects of the divine goodness that God distinguished to Moses: "I will be gracious to whom I will be gracious, and will shew mercy on whom I will shew mercy" (Exod. 33:19).

The microhexagram to the right of Tiferet, its Chesed, would best be represented by the power of harmony, as that to its left, its Gevurah, may be associated with that of proportion. If Tiferet, itself, is to be identified with balance, then harmony and proportion would be two powers by which it could effect such balance. Harmony and proportion, understood in their broader senses, are metaphors derived from music and geometry, respectively, and the distinction between them can be traced to this derivation. Though both bring all elements in a composition together and make them work as one, the former does this through blending and the latter through distinguishing. The former unites the parts, the latter allows them to be seen as related but still distinguished parts of a larger whole. The power to harmonize diverse elements or to see them in proportion is, then, necessary to achieve balance among them, but their affective qualities differ in degree. Harmony is to be associated with Chesed, the lenient or gracious aspect of experience, in the reconciliation and peace it conveys. Proportion may similarly be associated with Gevurah in that both are informed by restraint, by measure. Tiferet means Beauty, and as the beauty of harmony is sweet, so is that of proportion more severe.

Arriving finally at Gevurah, its two aspects of justice or judgment may be distinguished as discernment and rigor, the former associated with its right or Chesed aspect as the latter is with its left or Gevurah aspect. Though both words are used synonymously with judgment, discernment allows for a possibility of leniency lacking to rigor. Discernment should also be associated with the loving-kindness of Chesed if its goodness is not to be wasted. And though the Kabbalah traditionally derives evil from an excess of Gevurah, that aspect of Gevurah of which we now speak, it is through rigor alone that a spiritual master may be perfected.

The Spiral Tree defines the three stages in the first phase of Neshamah development in an order different from that of the traditional Tree but one that seems appropriate to this penultimate phase of the Tikkun. It begins with the heart expansion of Chesed, moves to the centering of Tiferet, and ends finally with those severe forms of discipline—retreats, fasting, forty days in the desert or on a mountaintop—that seem to be necessary for the final stages of spiritual purification. What this process and these three Sefirot are most associated with is character. The Sefirot define it and the process builds it. The qualities of Chesed, Gevurah, and Tiferet are those of temperament. We have not met them before on the Tree and it is for this reason that only at this Neshamah phase may such true personality as is divine be said to be formed. For this is the phase that marks the completion of the divine personality of Ze'ir Anpin, the central Partzuf concerned with the Providential government of this world It is also at this phase that the Neshamah Master develops the force of personality that can endure eternally. It was earlier said that the soul achieves immortality upon entrance into Netzach, but it may well be that the immortality of the Ruach soul is confined to Gilgul, Reincarnation. At the Neshamah level, however, the soul has mastered the power to preserve its individual identity without conscious lapse through all eternity, a mastery that, as just indicated, requires a final discipline of the utmost rigor. We shall later trace more closely the six steps to this last stage when we further subdivide the three stages just defined in terms of Sefirot into their microhexagram counterparts. But first we should see how these microhexagrams may also operate as organs of intake and outflow, for in so doing we shall better understand the transformative process by which the enduring character of a Neshamah Master will be built. Though these later discussions will define these microhexagrams in terms of their Chesed or Gevurah, right or left, position in the matrix, their more precise identifications should also be borne in mind. These are, in summary: Chesed of Chesed = Grace; Gevurah of Chesed = Mercy; Chesed of Tiferet = Harmony; Gevurah of Tiferet = Proportion; Chesed of Gevurah = Discernment; and Gevurah of Gevurah = Rigor.

If the three macrohexagram-Sefirot of the Neshamah heart may be said to have such organs of taking in and giving out as we have attributed to their left (Gevurah) and right (Chesed) microhexagram powers, then these two powers must be essential to the functioning of the Neshamah heart. For what each of these centers of the Neshamah heart would seem to be devoted to is none other than the transformation of that which is taken in into the distinctive product of its nature.[16] This can be better understood by taking the work of each of these centers separately.

The primary function of Chesed is the dispensing of divine grace, either directly through the psychic field identifiable with Ze'ir Anpin or through the blessing of a Neshamah Master. In the case of the latter, with which we shall now be primarily concerned, the Neshamah Master will, through his left receptive power, take into his heart all the divine goodness that he everywhere perceives being bestowed upon him. His special empowerment is certainly a sign of his own condition of grace, but he sees such grace as well in every drop of dew, in every breath he breathes. He will exude a grace of movement and graciousness of manner that will attract love and all the gifts that flow from it. But his primary concern will be to direct the cosmic grace he receives into the particular channels where it will do most good. While the Ruach Master is concerned to succor the needy, though their need will be just as great on the next day, the Neshamah Master expands the capacities of the needy so that they can become both self-providing and self-determining. He is, indeed, the dispensing arm of divine grace. His very presence is uplifting, and where he blesses all flourishes.

If the primary function of Chesed is to dispense grace, that of Gevurah is to be the dispensing arm of a just Providence. Again the Neshamah Master will take into his heart, through the left receptive power of Gevurah, all the injustice and persecution to which the world in general is subject and he in particular. Beginning first with those injustices he must personally bear, he will strive to transform them into lessons or challenges. He will seek to discover a pattern of personal responsibility for the adversities he has encountered and, if none can be discovered, yet to bear them with fortitude, thus converting adversity into dignity. His firmness under pressure will become a source of strength to all those similarly afflicted, and he will make their cause his own, fixing the responsibility for all such misery where it is due. Because his wrath is never personal and his bearing noble, his judgments will awaken conscience, and where he curses all will wither.

The Neshamah Master is, then, the dispenser of both divine grace and Providential justice, but which he does and to what degree of severity and effectiveness will depend upon the authority he

derives from Tiferet. Only if he, himself, is balanced in Tiferet can he avoid the pitfalls to which the extremes of his nature make him prone, the evil that good men do either through too much mercy or rigor. With the left receptive power of Tiferet, he must weigh the intake of both extremes, all the cosmic and personal good and evil he has experienced and transform them into an appropriate response, dispensing with its right power a justice or mercy that will normally be tempered with its opposite and in due measure. There will be times when the extreme convictions of Chesed or Gevurah will triumph over the balance of Tiferet and produce an extreme response, times that demand such a response. But the effectiveness of even such extreme responses still depends on the degree to which he remains centered in Tiferet rather than being personally drawn into the grief or wrath that might cloud the understanding of his heart.

The Providence that brings about unexpected good or marvelous justice is the work of the three Sefirot of Tiferet, Gevurah and Chesed, and it may be said to have six degrees, comparable to the six microhexagrams of this first Neshamah phase, ranging from the extreme of Chesed at the bottom of the matrix to that of Gevurah at its top. It may clarify these distinctions to observe some of the biblical workings of Providence. Perhaps the best example of a personality blessed by the Chesed of Chesed would be David. Gifted beyond all others—poet, religious ecstatic, warrior, king, lover—he seemed to lead a charmed life, his dangers easily overcome, his sins all forgiven him. An example of one blessed by the Gevurah of Chesed would be Joseph. Also talented and ultimately successful, his triumphs all came with great difficulty. Interestingly, these two characters are kabbalistically associated with the two lowest Sefirot, David with Malkhut and Joseph with Yesod.

The next two or three Sefirotic characters would also seem to be comparable to the next two Tiferet classifications. Aaron is identified with Hod and Moses with Netzach and both seem to fall under the category of the Chesed of Tiferet. To define the justice of Tiferet a little more clearly, we may say that this is the justice experienced by most, one in which the individual is responsible for what he suffers but the suffering is not excessive. Its two degrees reflect different balances between responsibility and the severity of punishment. Where Gevurah dominates, the individual may say, with King Lear, "I am a man / More sinned against than sinning" (3.2.59–60), and where Chesed dominates the proportions are the opposite. As examples of Chesed of Tiferet justice, both Moses and Aaron are punished for their imperfect behavior at the water of Meribah, the punishment being that they shall not enter the promised land (Num. 20:12), but both have had long lives specially graced by God, do not question or appear to suffer from their punishment, and Moses is personally shown a vision of the promised land before his death and divine burial. Exemplifying Gevurah of Tiferet justice would be the character normally associated with Tiferet, Jacob. The insight that came to Jacob through the Providential consequences of his sins[17] seems to have burdened as much as it recreated his spirit, for in summing up his life to Pharaoh, he says: "few and evil have the days of the years of my life been" (Gen. 47:9).

The two most severe forms of Providential justice may also be associated with the personified forms of the Sefirot, Isaac being the kabbalistic personification of Gevurah as Abraham is of Chesed. In the last-moment staying of Isaac's sacrifice and the refining awe with which it fills Isaac's later life, we may see a positive example of Chesed of Gevurah justice, just as the testing of Abraham, which he meets unflinchingly to that very last moment, may be considered to exemplify both the Gevurah of Gevurah justice of God in its positive, perfecting mode and the Gevurah of Gevurah nature of the Tzaddik. If Abraham and Isaac, the prime Tzaddikim of the Bible,[18] may be so associated with this strictest form of Providential governance, then we may better appreciate the high position awarded to Gevurah by the matrix. We have seen that it is only through mastery of Gevurah that the highest of Ruach power can be released to the Ruach Master, and now again we see that the highest of Neshamah Masters, Abraham and Isaac, have had to pass through the severity of Gevurah to achieve their spiritual perfection. In the reversal of Sefirot order between Chesed and Gevurah manifest in the Spiral Tree, we may read a new way of understanding the process of the Tikkun. This new way of the Tikkun would associate entrance into Neshamah consciousness with being twice-born in Chesed, the rebirth signified by its Sabbatical conformation, and entrance into its inner, mental essence with the final discipline of Gevurah.

But there are also negative forms of Gevurah justice associated with genuine tragedy. Examples of such Chesed of Gevurah justice would be Jephthah and Samson, from the Book of Judges, who came to tragedy through the Providential workings of their own character, reaping as they sowed though still accomplishing the divine purpose. Finally, with the Gevurah of Gevurah justice we come to the great examples of divine wrath, Sodom and Gomorrah and the Flood.

Why one degree or another of Providential justice is meted out in any individual case cannot be determined alone from that case since the sources of the decree go beyond the individual to embrace and shape the whole of the historical process. Sometimes the combination of an individual's contribution with the needs of the whole will necessitate a stricter and sometimes a milder form of justice. But whatever the fate of the individual, whether tragic as with Samson or triumphant as with Joseph, it is the larger good and divine will that is always being served. Ranging from the most forgiving to the most punishing, as the totality of information is sifted and weighed by the imperatives of mercy, severity, and balance, the divine heart makes its determinations of Providential justice for the good of the whole.

Returning to the curious parallels between the biblical personifications of the Sefirot and the six degrees of Providential justice understood as stages in the process of Tikkun, we would seem to be able to make further correspondences on this basis between the personified forms of justice and the cosmic worlds. If Chesed justice is to be associated with David-Malkhut and Joseph-Yesod, then it would seem most characteristic of the fourth world, particularly in its postdiluvian phase, as indicated in God's resolve: "I will not again curse the ground anymore for man's sake; for the imagination of man's heart is evil from his youth" (Gen. 8:21). The daily continuance of a habitable world in the light of man's persistent sinfulness can surely be considered a proof of the overriding dominance of the divine mercy in the government of the world. The fifth world, containing Aaron-Hod and Moses-Netzach, would then be associated with the milder form of Tiferet justice, one in which the Providential law of cause and effect is beginning to be understood and the punishing effects of sin are beginning to be accepted as a school for spiritual development. The Ruach Master is learning the secret of Tiferet, that balance between the self and the larger whole that can open the self to the flow of cosmic empowerment. In the further path of spiritual development, the first phase of the sixth world may be considered a graduate school marked by the increasing rigor of Gevurah. In Jacob-Tiferet, Isaac-Gevurah, and Abraham-Chesed we encounter the three most severe stages of discipline, those associated with the Gevurah of Tiferet, the Chesed of Gevurah, and the Gevurah of Gevurah. Only by passing a final Abraham-like testing can one be admitted into the mind of God.

Before entering this inner sanctum, we must consider the question posed when first beginning analysis of the sixth-world matrix, the significance of the exclusively lateral composition of the Neshamah heart. This significance would seem to be associated, first and foremost, with the self-conscious individuality that has always been identified with the lateral system of the matrix. The Neshamah or divine heart retains, then, the principles of multiplicity and individuality earned at such high cost through the processes of Tzimtzum, Shevirah, and Tikkun, but it retains them in a spiritually developed or mature form. This is implied by the threefold nature of its components, a triadic structure that not only ensures but is defined by its balance. On the Ruach level, the opposition of lateral mind and central heart required that the lateral mind both restrain and yet attune itself to the central heart, a practice through which it could learn the principles of cosmic attunement. It is this education of the lateral system that enables it to emerge purified and

matured into the Neshamah level of consciousness. On its lower heart level, the triad of lateral macrohexagrams permits the Neshamah heart to manifest a balance that was impossible to the dualism of the Ruach heart, yoked to an individual self alien to its true nature. The judgment it can thus show is most appropriate to the essentially mental nature of the Neshamah soul. For its primary concern is not compassion but harmony, not the relief of individuals but the smooth functioning of the whole that can sometimes require the hard decision to terminate a source of dissonance. Its task as Providential judge is ever to make the appropriate response, mitigating justice with mercy where it can but ready to be more severe or unexpectedly gracious where required by the larger picture. In fulfilling this task, it works in counterpoint with the lateral elements of the Neshamah mind, the counterpoint of two against three best modeled by the triangular matrix, whose interface of trisected macrotriangles with bisected microtriangles was earlier taken to indicate the interface of freedom with determinism resulting in probability.[19]

As we shall now see, however, the dualism of lateral elements in the second phase of the sixth-world matrix is, itself, harmonized by the central macrohexagram they interpenetrate. Where the sixth-world lateral system counterpoints the upper two mental macrohexagrams against the lower three macrohexagrams of the just emotions, the two phases of the sixth world each contain a triadic structure. To the lower lateral triad the upper phase synthesizes lateral duality with central unity.

THE SIXTH-WORLD MATRIX MODEL OF THE NESHAMAH MIND

We now come to the culminating phase of the matrix spiral, its three macrohexagrams representing the supernal triad of the Spiral Tree, the lateral Sefirah of Chokhmah to the right, the lateral Sefirah of Binah to the left, and between and interpenetrating both the central Sefirah of Keter. Most significant is the crowning Sefirah of Keter, for its central macrohexagram not only marks the first appearance of the central system since Netzach and the first contact with the upward lateral spiral of this system, but it is also the only central macrohexagram of the sixth-world matrix. Since it is only the central system that seems to have direct knowledge of the total plan, it is only through this crowning macrohexagram that the Neshamah soul can have access to this knowledge.

On each level of the central system, its macrohexagrams function as sources of vision. On the Nefesh level, such vision is presented largely through dream images whose realism always provides a symbolic or mythic structure of meaning that relates these images to the larger system of knowledge contained in or transmitted through the subconscious. On the Ruach level, such vision, consciously directed and received, has a different quality of realism, not the symbolic allegories produced by the subconscious but actualities perceived so that their subtle natures and connections are made apparent.

A similar distinction may be found in the poetry that Coleridge and Wordsworth contributed to their joint volume of poetry entitled *Lyrical Ballads.* As Coleridge describes their plan:

> In this idea originated the plan of the *Lyrical Ballads*; in which it was agreed, that my endeavors should be directed to persons and characters supernatural, or at least romantic; yet so to transfer from our inward nature a human interest and a semblance of truth sufficient to procure for these shadows of imagination that willing suspension of disbelief for the moment, which constitutes poetic faith. Mr. Wordsworth, on the other hand, was to propose to himself as his object, to give the charm of novelty to things of everyday, and to excite a feeling analogous to the supernatural. . . .[20]

In fulfillment of this joint project, Coleridge wrote "The Rime of the Ancient Mariner" and Wordsworth "Tintern Abbey," among other poems by both, the first of which may be compared to the definition here given of the Nefesh imagination and the second to that of the Ruach imagination. Not

that either of these two masterpieces are poetically inferior to the other but that the image of the ancient mariner with the albatross hung from his neck is closely associated to the "willing suspension of disbelief" occurring during dreams, whereas the scene at Tintern Abbey impresses the mind with the subtle dimensions of the real, "Of something far more deeply interfused" (l. 96), in a manner similar to that of meditative contemplation, the principle mode of the Ruach imagination. Nefesh imagination is always fictional and mythic, Ruach imagination always focused on the network of subtle connections and implications surrounding the real, on whatever level of organization it is being contemplated.

Unlike the lower modes of the imagination that, however associated with supernatural or paranormal aspects of experience, are always focused on particulars, the Neshamah imagination takes in and is ever contemplating the plan of the whole. And it does so not in images that, whether fictional or not, are based on combinations of the real, but in images of geometric form. As Kepler said, "God forever geometrizes." The mind of God, that represented by the second phase of the sixth-world matrix, originates in mathematical reasoning, and it encodes its laws of numerical and proportional relationships primarily through geometric models. If the present study has any validity, then it would not be going too far to say that in the mind of God is the image of the Sabbath Star Diagram, not alone, perhaps, but there. But whether the Sabbath Star Diagram contains the whole code of creation or is just one small aspect, one angle of vision, of a much vaster and more complex plan, it is some such geometric abstraction that both engages and constitutes the mind of God, and in its central macrohexagram-Sefirah is focused the identity of Neshamah consciousness.

It is in this that Neshamah consciousness is most to be distinguished from the lower modes. Where the "I" of Nefesh consciousness is located in the lateral macrohexagram identified with Yesod and that of Ruach consciousness in the lateral macrohexagram identified with Hod, the highest consciousness is central in nature, located in that central macrohexagram identified with Keter. It is because the Keter of the central blue spiral alone knows the correct plan of development for the lateral turquoise spiral, is alone associated with its final stage of perfection, that it can form the identity of its highest soul level. The intermediate component of the central system, that central macrohexagram equated with Netzach, is a member of the central red spiral, a spiral that can inform the Ruach soul of conditions in the Other precisely because it *is* going in the other direction. As such, it cannot serve as the identity of the Ruach soul without fatal danger to its development. The first component of the central system also cannot serve as the identity of the Nefesh soul since its collective nature would prevent that individuation for which souls were created. It is thus only the individualized second macrohexagram of the central blue spiral that can serve as the soul identity for that composite soul level it finally shares with the lateral turquoise spiral.

The nature of this soul identity is also different from that of the lower two levels, particularly as it is experienced on the lower levels. If one views one's consciousness as functioning generally on the Ruach level, one will certainly be aware of the lower Nefesh identity pulling one down from one's high resolves and more flowing experiences with its insistent demands for ego satisfaction. But there are times of particular harmony and stillness when one will also become aware of another consciousness surrounding, as it were, one's normal perception of self and witnessing its innermost experience. It is this "Witness Consciousness," as it is sometimes called, that can be identified with the self of the Neshamah soul, and it represents one's highest self, that aspect of the divine mind that has become individualized as one's highest, one's divine, personality. To be in Neshamah consciousness is to become one with this witnessing self, which not only knows one totally, since it has been there from the beginning, but also knows all things, the whole plan and one's individual place within it. It is because of this knowledge of the whole that it has been able to feed the lower self with vital information when necessary. And the Ruach self can reverse this direction by asking its higher self for whatever information is needed.

It is in moving from the contemplative seizure of the whole plan to the unfolding of a particular implication or consequence that the central system of the divine mind needs its two lateral adjuncts, the macrohexagrams identified with Chokhmah and Binah and so with the right and left hemispheres of the brain, respectively, as they are identified in the anthropomorphic form of the Tree of Life Diagram identified with Adam Kadmon. It is they that not only draw out the implications of the total plan for any particular individual or situation but, more importantly, the laws by which any aspect of creation is to function so that it may conform to the law intrinsically informing the cosmos and its geometric model. It is the articulation of this Torah of the divine self that is the primary work of the macrohexagram equivalents of Chokhmah and Binah and one that requires their conjoined labors.

If the function of Chokhmah and Binah may be defined as such an articulation of the implications of a geometric model, then it may be considered the archetype and prime example of the Science of Expressive Form, the mode of interpretative understanding here used to explicate the Sabbath Star Diagram, which is as much an art as a science. The model is scientific insofar as it is built on self-generating laws that can be explicated. But the interpretation of these laws is an art.

The joining of such implications and explications to form meaning involves the complete integration of Chokhmah and Binah both with each other and with the object of their scrutiny. They must become cognitively one, as they are represented to be in the matrix, Chokhmah and Binah interpenetrating Keter as it interpenetrates them. In defining the method of his poetic imagination, Coleridge said that he had need to be "still and patient, all I can; / And haply by abstruse research to steal / From my own nature all the natural man."[21] It is similar with the divine mind, most particularly with Chokhmah who, through stillness, can come to the intuitive knowledge of the universal laws contained in the self. If the cosmos can be considered to be a product of the divine mind, then it must operate by the same laws that define that mind and give it its characteristic nature. The cosmos will betray the signature of its Creator in every aspect of its being just as a poem or painting will reveal the idiosyncratic nature of its creator. This cosmos is the way it is because it is the product of a certain set of characteristics, and given that original set it can be no other. The intuitive part of the divine mind must, then, delve deeply into itself to draw forth the intrinsic laws of its nature, which can then be formulated more objectively by its more analytic aspect. But such formulation is as inspired an act of rationality as the logically prior act of intuition since Binah must be able grasp what Chokhmah holds, the mystery of comprehension. Through Chokhmah and Binah, then, the abstract laws governing the cosmos are articulated into the lateral forms that can be transmitted to the arms of cosmic government operating through the divine heart. There the abstract laws given it can be fitted to the particulars arising from multiplicity and freedom, issuing from thence as Providence.

Having defined the psychic centers of the Neshamah mind, we should now explore the powers associated with these centers and represented by their associated microhexagrams. In this final phase of the matrix, there are eight microhexagrams. As clearly distinguished in figure 10.3, five of them are central and three lateral. Beginning with the central microhexagrams, there is one such microhexagram directly below the central macrohexagram, and two to each of its sides, one above the other. Exemplifying the art of interpreting expressive form, we may say that five adjuncts of a center representing psychic knowledge would seem to signify the five senses, understood here in their highest, inner forms, as the hidden sources of the physical senses. If we can draw such a conclusion, then we can identify the upper right microhexagram with inner sight, that to the upper left with inner hearing, that to the lower right with inner smelling, that to the lower left with inner tasting, and that at the lowest central point with inner touching.

The significance of the upper two is clear enough; they represent clairvoyance and clairaudience. But the reason why these identifications have been given to the upper right and upper left microhexagrams derives from the meanings of the macrohexagrams with which they are associated. The

association of inner sight with Chokhmah and of inner hearing with Binah relates to the earlier suggested correlation of Sefirot with chakras, for the fifth chakra is identified with the throat and its power of articulation while the sixth chakra is identified with the visionary power of the "third eye." Since there are clear correlations between the conceptualizations of Binah and the fifth chakra and of Chokhmah and the sixth chakra, as these psychic centers have been separately defined by the kabbalistic and yogic traditions, it seems appropriate to expand our conceptions of these Sefirot by further identifying Binah with the understanding of sound signals, signals transported as waves through time, and Chokhmah with that of visual signals, signals transported as particles or particulars in space. Once these macrohexagram-Sefirot are so understood, the definitions of the left and right microhexagrams adjacent to them can be better appreciated, that near Binah identified with inner hearing or clairaudience and that near Chokhmah with inner sight or clairvoyance.

As for the correlation of the seventh "crown" chakra with the Sefirah Keter, meaning Crown, the only thing that matrix analysis has thus far added to this obvious equation is the central character of this highest Sefirah. But as we now return to consideration of the five central microhexagrams that serve this central macrohexagram of Keter, those just identified with the five inner senses, the understanding of Keter will be further expanded, as should also be that of the Crown chakra. The upper two inner senses have just been considered, but the remaining three will require further analysis.

The sense of smell is the most underrated in considerations of paranormal or "psychic" powers, especially surprising in view of its more subtle functions. From biology we can discover that each organism has its own distinctive smell, the mark of its individuality as expressed through its immune system.[22] It is through the subtle inner form of this sense that we not only can know the distinguishing characteristic of each living being but also its value, whether it is appealing or stinks. It is, therefore, the sense by which we either do or do not allow something to enter our system, most notably food but by extension also experiences and people. The subtle sense of taste provides another means of discrimination, not that of discriminating between the wholesome or putrid nature of something external to the self but of expressing one's own distinctive nature. Of taste there is no disputing; it is the signature of our personality. And it is through the subtle sense of taste that one can discover affinities, know whom to accept not simply as an acquaintance but as an intimate. Perhaps most important is the subtle sense of touch. It is through this that we can be spiritually touched, gripped, seized, and so touch others. It is the power of charisma, the sum total of spiritual empowerment. Furthermore, its position in the matrix is significantly at the lowest portion of its culminating phase, the finger of God just a synapse away from the finger of Adam uplifted to it, and passing between them the spirit of the living God.

It is through these five subtle senses, most notably through clairvoyance and clairaudience, that the Neshamah mind can most fully function. As they permit the divine Chokhmah and Binah to read the hidden depths of the divine Keter, so are they the principal modes of supersensory knowledge available to the Neshamah Master. For as the divine mind can use its subtle sight to design and perceive the geometric forms by which it is manifested in space, and its subtle hearing to design and perceive the harmonic resonances by which it may similarly be manifested in time, so can the Neshamah Master, thereby altering the components of space and time in accordance with the high design of creation. And he can as well use these subtle senses as channels for receiving divine commandments or other urgent cosmic messages requiring his attention. In addition to the visions and voices experienced by a master, these subtle senses are also the sources of those arts that most exemplify expressive form, the visual arts expressing through their forms the creative potential of inner sight as music does for inner hearing and as dance does for both, setting spatial forms to music. Shelley says of these arts, as of poetry: "men dance and sing and imitate natural objects, observing in these actions, as in all others, a certain rhythm or order. . . . [T]hose who imagine and express this indestructible order . . . [participate] in the eternal,

the infinite, and the one. . . . Poetry redeems from decay the visitations of the divinity in man."[23] Of the verbal arts we shall shortly speak, but first we should appreciate that the arts whose meanings are expressed exclusively through form derive their knowledge of such nonverbal languages from the same subtle senses of sight and hearing that are the sources of prophecy. Indeed, Shelley considers "prophecy an attribute of poetry."[24]

To understand the position of language as a cognitive power of the Neshamah mind we must now turn to the lateral microhexagrams. Of these three, one is above the macrohexagram of Chokhmah, one above the macrohexagram of Binah and one below and interpenetrating the macrohexagram of Keter. The first, coming just above and interpenetrating the central microhexagram representative of inner sight, would seem to involve geometric thought. The second, having the same relationship to the central microhexagrams representative of inner hearing would seem to involve some form of harmonically related understanding. But the last, coming between and interpenetrating both the macrohexagram of Keter and the microhexagram earlier identified with inner touch and the transmission of spirit, requires further analysis before it can be fully defined.

As that which comes between and would thus seem to mediate between the understanding of geometric form and harmonic resonance, this lowest and centered lateral microhexagram can first be most appropriately identified with the capacity for numbering. As I have developed at large in chapter 3 of *The Secret Doctrine of the Kabbalah*, harmonic and geometric proportions are reciprocals mediated by number, this being the deepest insight of Pythagorean thought. But as also there shown, in the sacred science of the *Sefer Yetzirah* these three elements of Pythagorean science are understood to be contained in a still more comprehensive cognitive capacity, that of language. The subject of language is one that was also extensively explored in chapters 4 and 5 of *The Secret Doctrine of the Kabbalah* as well as being the subject of appendix C of the present book, and it is not possible here to do more than hint at the richness of these analyses. But these hints will here enable us to establish on the basis of matrix modeling what cannot otherwise be as precisely demonstrated, the close association of the three more mathematical sciences of geometry, harmonics, and especially number (arithmetic) with language.

The most important hint comes from the field of semiotics, a linguistic science founded by Ferdinand de Saussure, which I have discussed at some length in appendix C. As there shown, Saussure defined the linguistic sign as a compound of a signifier and a signified, the former identified with a sound slice and the latter with a concept. However, I have agreed with a long line of thinkers from Aristotle, through Wittgenstein, to Ricoeur, that the primary element of what Saussure has called the signified is not a concept but an image. If the signifier can thus be identified with a sound slice and the signified with an image, it is clear that these two components of the sign or word can be modeled by the same microhexagrams as define the harmonics of sound, that at the upper left above the macrohexagram identified with Binah in the Spiral Tree, and geometric form, that at the upper right above the macrohexagram so identified with Chokhmah. The question now arises as to how their synthesis in the linguistic sign can be identified with that also defining the microhexagram between them, number.

But once the question is raised of the possible equation of language with number, the answer emerges from the very resources of language, the associations enshrined in its roots. The equation of narrative with number appears in the English word *tell*, which comprehends both the meanings of "tale" and "tally." It is derived from the Indo-European root *del*, which, in addition to its meanings as "counting" and "recounting," words to which we shall shortly return, also carried the meaning of "cutting," a meaning to be further considered in relation to the similar Semitic root. From the words *counting* and *recounting*, it seems clear that narration, storytelling, was understood to somehow involve a linguistic translation of numerically encoded information. Both meanings are further contained in the word *account*, which can refer indifferently to either a numerical sum or a story. But this second group of words also adds a third

dimension of value to the previous equation of tale and tally. To stand up and be counted, to be accountable, somehow equates moral responsibility with the concept of "one's number," what one "amounts" to. This association of value with that which can be counted, or counted on, would seem to be derived from its Indo-European root of *peue* that, in addition to "cutting," also has the primary meaning of "purifying" and "cleansing," a connection that may be rooted in the concept of religious sacrifice, such a devotion of one's sheep and heart to a higher power ensuring one's moral accountability.

Turning now to Hebrew, the triliteral root that comprehends much of these same meanings is that of Samach, Pey, and Raysh. Both *sapare* and *sipare* variously connote the same triple association of counting, recounting, and cutting, the latter also associated with shearing. Since the ancient Hebrews were shepherds, it may well be that it was at shearing time that the capacity for counting first developed, a count from which we may assume that some sheep would have been sacrificed in thanksgiving, a count also from which any losses would have to have been explained. It is in justifying the numerical count (tally) that a verbal account (tale) would also have to have been rendered. But whether or not this triple association developed out of a sheep-rearing culture, the understanding of counting as a cutting has a deeper significance. Though it can be explained simply in terms of the precise meaning of "tally," as a stick on which notches are cut to keep a count generally in a series of five, it would also seem to imply a conceptual cutting of an item out of a continuum for selective attention, an attention that permits it to be both counted and described.

Finally, there is the kabbalistic science of Gematria in which each letter of the Hebrew alphabet is assigned a special number, and through the sum of these numbers in a particular word this word can be conceptually associated with other words having the same number. The technique of Gematria assumes, then, such a deeper connection of language with numbers as we have just been exploring, its name further implying the association of both with the Greek word for geometry from which it appears to have been derived. In the first verse of the *Sefer Yetzirah*, moreover, the association of language with sound, form, and number is further defined in terms of three variants of the same triliteral root of Samach, Pey, and Raysh just discussed, that which is also the root of *Sefirah*, a term that comprehends a number, a name, and a shape.[25]

The present analysis provides a matrix model that not only can show the Pythagorean relationship of number to both harmonics and geometry and the semiotic relationship of the sign to both the signifier and the signified, but their mutual relationships, most importantly that between number and the word. If geometry and harmonics, by occupying the highest positions on the Spiral Tree, may be said to model the inner workings of the divine mind, its interrelating of the finite particle nature of forms in space and the infinite wave nature of sound or vibrations in time, it is through a numerically informed language that the laws of proportion and harmony may be translated from an ideal model into the creations of spirit. In the beginning God spoke and there was light.

The biblical account of creation through the spoken word reflects the creative function of language to specify the accidents that can transform an archetype into an actuality. A sentence fixes reality like doom. Its deep syntactical structures reveal an inner logic as mysterious and as rooted in the cosmic source of thought as are harmonics and geometry. For its syntax similarly connects Being (nouns) to Becoming (verbs). Language is thus able to provide the mythic forms through which the numerical abstractions of the logics of sound and form can be interpretatively specified. It is through mythological images and narratives that the higher mind normally feeds the mathematical laws of the cosmos to the lower understanding; and the extent to which such mythology provides a true map to the more subtle dimensions of reality is the extent to which it is based on the frozen music of a geometric model. As I said in the opening part, "mythology recapitulates geometry."

Myths represent a more developed form of the metaphoric power of language, its power of naming in accordance with the true nature, its numerically unique vibration, of that which is named. As the

deep syntactical structures of language reveal the laws of the cosmos, so its vocabulary points to the subtle connections of that aspect of the whole specified as separate entity by a name. The creative power of language to manifest particulars in accordance with a model of their natures is shown not only by God in the creation but in the first divinely appointed task of unfallen Adam, his naming of the animals: "out of the ground the Lord God formed every beast of the field, and every fowl of the air; and brought them unto Adam to see what he would call them: and whatsoever Adam called every living creature, that was the name thereof" (Gen. 2:19). Out of that same ground of being from which Adam was earlier formed, God formed other beings with which Adam can relate through intrinsic knowledge, a knowledge revealed in his apprehension of the appropriate name for each. In the notes to his biblical translation, J. H. Hertz comments on this passage: "Man alone has language, and can give birth to languages. In giving names to earth's creatures, he would establish dominion over them (I, 26, 28). The name would also reflect the impression produced on his mind by each creature."[26] Hertz well connects man's required dominion over the animals with the power of language he commands, a power by which he becomes a cocreator in the specification of the particularity of an entity within the larger vibrational field that connects it to the whole. In designing man as a cocreator and so a master of language, God recognized that man would thus need to live in a world of other particulars, that "It is not good that the man should be alone" (Gen. 2:18). But though Adam creates conceptual entities from vibrational fields through the process of naming them, it is through their vibrations that he can fix on them those linguistic metaphors that reveal their more subtle natures, metaphoric names that also reveal the response of his own nature to them. The further development of this concept in Lurianic thought is described by Scholem: "Every constellation of light has its particular linguistic expression, though the latter is not directed toward the lower worlds but rather inward toward its own hidden being. These lights combine to form 'names' whose concealed potencies become active. . . ."[27] Every constellation of light, every vibrational pattern of energy, has a subtle sound form, a name through which it can know itself and has the power to become known.

Human language would seem to develop through those more elevated of its members who can still hear the vibrational name through which a pattern becomes known to the divine mind and can translate it into the approximations permitted by the vocal and linguistic capabilities of a particular culture.[28] Because only the words that are somehow appropriate to their subject survive, this felt appropriateness attesting to the sensitivity of those who first articulated them, a perception of language that revivifies the dead metaphors embodied in words and can connect cognate words together and to their roots can trace the contours of the whole subtle dimension of reality as it has always been apprehended at the deepest level of human culture. This can be exemplified by just reiterating those words recently used in this analysis whose metaphoric content was thus revived: stink, taste, touch, account, and sentence. If metaphor is the prime characteristic of poetic language, then those first and even contemporary creators of language must be accounted poets, for as Shelley said, "A poet participates in the eternal, the infinite, and the one." As shown by their matrix counterparts, the power of artistic representation in painting or music is largely central in origin, deriving from the microhexagrams associated with inner sight and inner hearing, whereas that of poetry is lateral. In its reliance on language, it derives from the primary source of mental specificity. But its lateral microhexagram counterpart is placed in the closest proximity to the central system, closer to the ultimate source of knowledge and the power to touch than the other arts because it interpenetrates both the central macrohexagram of Keter and the central microhexagram signifying subtle touch, and combines as well the modalities of Chokhmah and Binah that it joins.

With this return to the diagram, we come to the best example of the distinction between the ideal model of geometry and language. For though the diagram itself may be said to contain all the elements and processes of creation, it is only through the cor-

rect naming of its matrix or construction elements that the implications of that element can be comprehended. Once it has been named, it can then be interpreted through the larger narrative structure of myth. The totality of its visual impact can only be unfolded and clarified through such interpretative myths. There is only one Sabbath Star Diagram but many possible interpretations, and the extent to which a naming and interpretation of one element can make another more comprehensible is the extent to which its myth reveals the true structure of its higher model. Language can thus take a geometric model like the Sabbath Star Diagram and, by interpreting one of its aspects, bring that aspect to light, as in the beginning.

It is because the divine mind of the cosmos, which is also the higher mind of man, delights in remembering what it knows that it enters the creative aspect of thought. To comprehend its own geometrically encoded knowledge, it must bring one aspect up to the surface of its consciousness, unfolding its particular implications from the universal laws implicitly contained in the enfolded whole of its knowledge. Such explication is creative because its exact nature is fashioned in the very process by which it draws out and specifies one possible application of a law as well as defining its universal character. Prior to such specification, the mind did not know it had such knowledge, and when this newly formalized knowledge sinks back to the depths of consciousness it does so with new contours that can attract, through some form of "morphic resonance,"[29] other similar forms into a network of subtle associations. When the same form is next recalled, it will come to surface consciousness with a far more comprehensible structure and greater depth of resonance. Thus language tells the mind what it knows in a manner that increasingly enriches both its self-knowledge and potency. Once an idea is named it can be given material or social form, and once so formed it can be used. It is, finally, through such use that the intrinsic laws limiting and defining its nature can be recognized and the circle of cognition completed. It was to achieve such enlightenment that the divine mind entered the creative process of linguistic specification, and it is to enhance this process that it remains attached to the lower worlds and the feedback it can receive from their myriad strands of specificity. In this spiral process of cognition, the word inspired by the model and the model made increasingly compre- hensible through the word, the evolution of consciousness is accomplished, whether in the cosmos, the Neshamah soul, or in our comprehension of the Sabbath Star Diagram.

CHAPTER 11

Forbidden Crossings and the Illusion of Knowledge

INTRODUCTION: TOHU OR TIKKUN?

In this chapter we shall be considering a unique feature of the Sabbath Star Diagram, the fact that it permits various forms of freedom in both the construction and interpretation of the diagram. The focus of this chapter will be upon the matrix elements appearing beyond the matrix borders of the fourth through sixth worlds. These have been taken to represent violations of the Law or Torah of the diagram that limits proper development only to expansion within the matrix borders of these worlds. As such they have been understood to symbolize temptations to the various levels of the soul on its cosmic journey. But before proceeding to such voyaging into the realm of evil on the Sitra Achra, the "Other Side," a review would be advisable of the meaning of this matrix border.

"And the earth was without form [Tohu] and void [Bohu]" (Gen. 1:2) is the description given of the dark waters whose chaos is to be organized by the divine light in the first day of creation. In the Sabbath Star Diagram, that which divides creation from chaos at each dimension or world of the cosmos is the matrix border defined by the macrostructure of that world. But at every level of geometric expansion there will be some fully formed microhexagrams, with all their hexagram outlines and lines of symmetry, that appear beyond the limits of this matrix border. That they are forbidden elements despite being fully present within the fourth through sixth worlds is proven by two circumstances of the sixth-world diagram; their exclusion makes possible the perfect count of the paths on the Spiral Tree and the suggestive count of the "light units" in the sixth-world matrix, the latter of which will be the concluding subject of this chapter. In addition to such fully formed unenclosed microhexagrams across the various matrix borders, the sixth world also features some complete "Tohus" and a "Bohu," while all three of the fourth to sixth worlds contain incomplete "Tohus" and "Bohus." It seems appropriate to apply these precise biblical terms for chaos to the various forms of macrohexagrams appearing beyond the matrix borders, Tohu to a microhexagram that should be enclosed by a macrohexagram of its color and so is "without form," and Bohu to a macrohexagram appearing without its normal complement of an enclosed microhexagram of its color and so is "void." Since there are such complete or incomplete Tohus or Bohus across each of the concerned matrix borders, we seem here to have another example of expressive forms, of forms that exactly express the state conceptualized as being "without form and void." It is this coherence of form with conceptual content that is the basis of the earlier identification of these matrix elements with a condition like that of chaos.

Beyond the matrix borders of the fourth through sixth worlds, then, there are both complete and incomplete elements. A complete microhexagram is one in which all six of its component microtriangles contain all of their exterior lines and each expresses just its single line of symmetry. A complete macrohexagram is one in which all six of its macrotriangles contain all of their exterior lines and each has all three of its lines of symmetry. Incomplete microhexagrams and macrohexagrams will only be considered if they have all six of their exterior lines and are missing only some of their interior lines of symmetry. Between the complete and incomplete elements so defined, it is the complete elements that clearly represent a more present and powerful danger than the incomplete elements. For the elements beyond the matrix borders can be viewed as representing the principal dangers and temptations to which the soul is prone at each stage in its path of evolution, the path of Tikkun. Thus at each stage the soul is confronted with the need to choose between Tohu and Tikkun, between the return to a state void of individualizing content and form or the progress toward a state of perfected individuality, of divine personality. To facilitate this analysis a table of all the microhexagrams defined in chapter 10 would be helpful. Table 11.1 gives the number of the microhexagram (the number used when referring to such an element whether it is within the border or extraborder) and the power it represents (boldface if central), its world, and its matrix ring (a diagram feature to be later considered).

BEYOND THE FOURTH-WORLD MATRIX BORDERS

Analysis of the fourth-world matrix border is complicated by the fact that there are two such borders in this world, that defining the limits of the past-

Table 11.1. The Microhexagrams Defined in Chapter 10

NUMBER	WORLD	RING	POWER
1	4	1	Instinct
2	4	2	Intuition
3	4 or 5	3	Emotion
4	4 or 5	3	Cognition
5	5	5	Creative Thought
6	5	4	Synchronicity
7	5	4	Transformation
8	5	5	Creation
9	6A	6	Grace
10	6A	6	Mercy
11	6A	5	Harmony
12	6A	5	Proportion
13	6A	6	Discernment
14	6A	6	Rigor
15	6B	5	Inner Touch
16	6B	6	Inner Smell
17	6B	6	Language & Number
18	6B	6	Inner Taste
19	6B	7	Inner Sight
20	6B	7	Inner Hearing
21	6B	8	Geometry
22	6B	8	Harmonics

modeled Nefesh soul and that expanded border beyond which lie new dangers to tempt its future-modeled counterpart. The elements beyond both of these borders were extensively discussed in chapter 8, those beyond the border of the former being viewed as temptations to the unfallen Nefesh soul and those beyond the latter border as temptations to the fallen Nefesh soul, the former, in particular, being given a major analysis that comprehended such cultural patterns as worldly aspiration, courtly love, and honor. The present treatment will briefly review the conclusions of that earlier analysis, though without its full richness, and add to it the new illumination provided both by the subsequent analysis of the fifth-world matrix and the sixth-world emergence of the Spiral Tree with its new Sefirot identifications.

Comparison of the two matrix borders in figure 11.1 and 11.2 shows that it is the elements beyond the unfallen border that pose the gravest danger to the Nefesh soul, fallen or unfallen, because it is only among them that we can find fully complete matrix elements. These are the microhexagrams numbered three and four on the Spiral Tree, elements previously considered as, in fact, constituting the Fall. Analysis of these and other matrix elements will thus not only focus on the Sefirot identified with the macrohexagrams but on the numbers that can be assigned to the microhexagrams on the Spiral Tree. An illustration of the Spiral Tree so numbered and lettered was given in figure 10.3, and table 11.1 correlated these numbered microhexagram-paths to the names previously given to them. But it would also help the following analyses to compare this important illustration of the labeled Spiral Tree first with figures 8.1 and 8.2 on the fourth-world matrices and then with the following figures 11.1 and 11.2, which only show those elements beyond the matrix borders of these diagrams, and which may be considered, respectively, to signify the unfallen and fallen forms of the Nefesh soul. In the black-and-white figures of extraborder elements in this chapter we shall continue, with some modifications, to follow the protocols previously used for the black-and-white diagramming of matrix elements: central elements will be signified by black matrix triangles and lateral elements by the hue of gray correlated with their world; but incomplete micro- or macrohexagrams (those with all their exterior lines but missing some of their lines of symmetry) will only have their triangles filled in with black or gray while complete elements (those with all their exterior and interior lines) will also fill in their inner hexagons with these black or gray colors; finally, Tohus will have their outer hexagons outlined.

Comparison of figures 11.1 and 11.2 shows a progression from Bohu to Tohu, for the unfilled lateral macrohexagram of figure 11.1, that which can now be identified as a component of Hod, becomes filled, in figure 11.2, only to be replaced by the unenclosed central microhexagram, which we can now identify as a component of Netzach, emptiness yielding to formlessness. But the Tohu and Bohu beyond the matrix borders of the fourth world represent only a lesser form of chaos, for they are actu-

ally within the precincts of what will become the Spiral Tree, the evolutionary order carved out of the original chaos of the Tzimtzum. If the Spiral Tree can be said to represent the growing edge of created order, then the area beyond the Spiral Tree but within the unfinished matrix area may be considered to be still more chaotic. But if the Nefesh soul is not as endangered by the encroachment of chaos as are the more empowered higher levels of the soul, it nonetheless can experience these states in a more figurative sense.

In the earlier discussion of the fourth-world matrix border, the Bohu form was associated with the literal meaning of Thomas More's Utopia, "no place," with the implication that the false utopia of secular materialism and freedom is "no place" for a Nefesh soul to abide. In that discussion, its proper place, associated with the "place" of sacred consciousness one is commanded not to leave during the Sabbath (Exod. 16:29), was deemed to be the individuated lateral macrohexagram, now identified with the instinctual responses of Yesod. Though the unfallen Nefesh soul had a greater range of emotional and intellectual power available to it, represented by the third and fourth extraborder microhexagrams, it was commanded by the Law of the Matrix Border not to develop these powers prematurely, before it had reached the Sabbatical level of Ruach consciousness. In pursuing these forbidden lateral powers, the emotions, identified with the left extraborder microhexagram, become filled with the desire for personal power in the belief that only such validation of individual existence can bring true happiness. But the pursuit of such power only leads to the emptiness represented by the illusory Bohu form, illusory because, unlike the completed microhexagrams representative of the developed emotions and intellect, it is not yet present in this world. Where their proper use as a part of the conjoined Nefesh/Ruach soul will lead to spiritual empowerment and fulfillment, their perversion to lower uses leaves the soul empty and wasted. This is particularly true for the fourth extraborder microhexagram identified with higher mental power, whose disconnection from its lateral spiral well illustrates the condition of the modern alienated intellect. But,

Figure 11.1. Elements beyond the Matrix Border of the Past-Modeled Fourth-World Diagram

occurring within the limits of the Spiral Tree, it represents a loss still capable of Tikkun.

The greatest danger to the soul at both its Nefesh and Ruach levels arises not from its lateral but its central system, a system that, because it points in directions other than that which must be the goal of the lateral spiral, can lead the soul away from its true path of Tikkun. As presented in the earlier discussion of the fourth-world extraborder elements in chapter 8, the danger posed by excessive development of the central system at the unfallen Nefesh stage is due precisely to the lack of any individuated central macrohexagrams either within the

fourth-world matrix or beyond its border. Faced with no source of worldly stability, the individuated central microhexagram, that numbered two in the Spiral Tree, is drawn backward to the collective central macrohexagram from which it had emanated. The danger of central dominance at the undeveloped Nefesh level is that such a soul cannot cope with its very individuality and can be driven to seek a return to the collective state through suicide. The death orientation of such cultural forms as romantic love and the honor code attests to the alliance of the most pure and idealistic souls with behavior models leading to and validating suicide. In terms of the

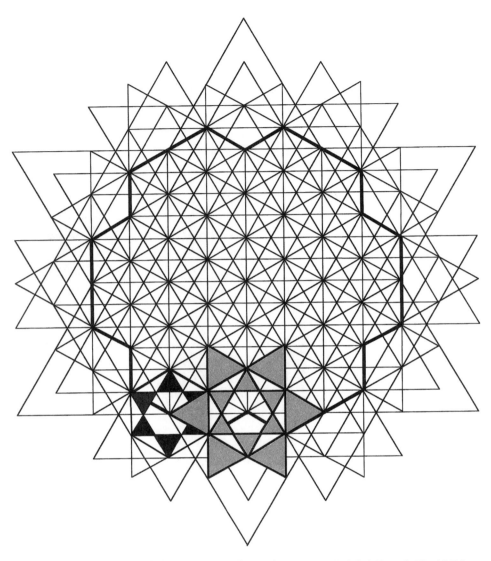

Figure 11.2. Elements beyond the Matrix Border of the Future-Modeled Fourth-World Diagram

diagram such a premature return to the source short-circuits the cosmic process and spells the death of the individual soul, the very consummation for which it devoutly wished.

Insofar as the state of undifferentiated being to which these centrally dominated souls return is one without individual form, it can be considered a type of chaos. Compared to this ultimate destruction of the individual soul, the Tohu to which the fallen central element may be drawn is not as serious. In the illustration of this matrix border in figure 11.2, we see a new manifestation of the central system in the form of the incomplete microhexagram compo-

nent of Netzach without its enclosing macrohexagram. Since Netzach has been identified with the Ruach imagination, the appearance of just its inner microhexagram would seem suggestive of an unstable, uncontrolled imagination. The equation of such an imagination with a form expressive of formlessness, of the chaos to which Tohu literally refers, tells us further of the chaotic nature of the imagination to which a fallen, centrally dominated Nefesh soul is prone. And since this Tohu is incomplete, it can be viewed as delusional rather than a manifestation of present reality. A chaotic imagination out of touch with reality would be a good description of schizophrenia; and this would seem to represent the gravest danger to a centrally dominated Nefesh soul that had managed to avoid suicide, while still in its purest state, only to "fall" into a condition of inner pollution through commerce with this world. From the horror of such a condition, schizophrenia may provide the only escape. Such psychosis may be considered less serious then suicide to the extent that the continuance of life provides hope of some effective therapy, and there are more successful forms of treating schizophrenia today than ever before, treatments and practices that can cure the soul of its sickness and bring it back onto its proper path.

Again with the lateral system, the danger to which the fallen laterally dominated Nefesh soul may be prone is less severe than the fact of the Fall, itself, the corruption of the emotional and rational faculties of man, and the reduced power of such temptation is again indicated by the incomplete nature of the lateral, as of the central, elements beyond the fallen matrix border of the fourth world. But Hod, though still incomplete, is no longer a Bohu, for it now contains both its macrohexagram and microhexagram elements. A further development is that the fallen Nefesh soul has gained command of the full range of emotional and rational powers available to undeveloped man, those represented by the third and fourth numbered microhexagrams now within the fallen matrix border. But in self-enfranchising himself, fallen man has come to believe himself to be more empowered than he actually is, that his dominion has no limits. Deluded by the seeming availability of such power for the taking, of Hod already present and offering him the source of that spiritual power devoted to interaction with and command over nature, he makes an assault upon domains beyond his real power, both secular and sacred. Perhaps the best examples of his deluded attempt to control nature are the literal power plants that exploit the earth for its natural resources and replace them with the polluted by-products of their operations. But the impunity with which man has reared the artificially powered towers of his modern Babel has belied the facts of his true powerlessness against the consequences of his deeds, which now threaten mankind both through the pollution of its earthly habitat and through nuclear destruction.

As fallen man seeks to tap the reservoir of power controlled by Hod in the secular realm, so does he attempt to tap it for direct spiritual power, its proper domain. But where the former attempt is a perversion of sacred power to alien secular ends, the latter exploits it within its own realm. Thus man may become, or attempt to become, a magician. Whether or not his tricks exhibit any real paranormal powers, he will, in any case, be using them for the wrong reasons, for entertainment and money. If they are completely spurious, consciously manipulated delusions, the punishing effects of such travesties of the miraculous will lie in the reinforcement they provide for the alienation of those who perpetrate them, an alienation from the very spiritual realm that continues to fascinate them despite their denials of its reality. But even more grievous are those who do have some small portion of paranormal abilities, whether natively or developed, while still functioning at a Nefesh level of development. The trouble with such premature acquisition of paranormal power without the control of a broader spiritual development is that it cannot help but be exploited for the debased ends of fame and fortune. Such exemplars of the occult arts prey on the unwary even if their arts are genuine, since their spiritual power is being transmitted with poor discernment as to its best use and with negative energy. The punishing effects of such an incursion into the realm of sacred power will be far graver than for those who just mimicked this power, not only preventing the true acquisition of all these and greater powers through proper progress to the Ruach dimension but producing an overload to the psychic and physical systems that can lead to physical deterioration and psychic derangement. Many of these true magicians will, in fact, be centrally dominated Nefesh personalities who turn to the occult as the only arena in which they can function in this world and whose brief success in exploiting their special powers provides but an interlude before a final descent into schizophrenia. In such individuals, the entire forbidden realm beyond the fallen matrix border may be experienced, with all its delusive hopes and sorry consequences. For all these elements are incomplete, delusions whose promise of power does not ultimately exalt but snares the heedless in a net of confusion.

Though the effects of movement beyond the fallen matrix border seem punishing, indeed, since delusions followed can lead one into quicksand as easily as real but ill-intentioned guides, they are yet less absolute than movement beyond the unfallen matrix border. The self-defeating nature of exploitive power can show one the way to a new reverence for the larger order in which one is placed and the limits it imposes. Moral and psychological illness is curable, but suicide and fallen faculties are absolute. From the first there is no recourse. It is the gravest of sins, the choice of "death and evil" (Deut. 30:15). From the second the only recourse is the patient and difficult process of spiritual discipline by which these fallen faculties can be purified and raised to their intended functions as adjuncts of higher spiritual centers, the path of Tikkun leading from Nefesh to Ruach consciousness. But once the soul arrives at the Ruach dimension, new temptations await it beyond the fifth-world matrix border, temptations more dangerous than any it may have encountered on the Nefesh level.

BEYOND THE FIFTH-WORLD MATRIX BORDER

Movement beyond the fifth-world matrix border is more serious, especially respecting the central system, than anything yet encountered in the fourth world because it can take one beyond the Spiral Tree and into a true condition of chaos. Analysis of these fifth-world extraborder elements was delayed until this point precisely to make use of the emergence of the Spiral Tree that can further illuminate them. As plate 12 and figure 11.3 show, the greatest danger arises from the central system both because it contains the only complete elements beyond the matrix border and because these can take the Ruach soul beyond the Spiral Tree. Due to the greater complexity of border elements beyond the fifth- and sixth-world matrix borders, in plates 12 and 13, respectively, incomplete macrohexagrams will appear in continuous outline, incomplete microhexagrams

with filled-in microtriangles, complete macrohexagrams with filled-in macrotriangles, complete microhexagrams with the additional filling of their inner hexagons, and all microhexagrams that are also Tohus with the additional outlining of their outer hexagons. The only difference between the black-and-white and color versions of these figures is that in the black-and-white versions all extraborder macrohexagrams will also have filled in macrotriangles.

The only completed elements beyond the fifth-world matrix border, as they are shown in plate 12, are the three central microhexagrams of the red spiral at the bottom of the diagram and the blue spiral at its top. The following discussion will distinguish between these blue and red central elements, understanding the black elements in figure 11.3 that are at the top to represent the blue central spiral and those at the bottom to represent the red central spiral, the completed microhexagrams in this figure again being completely filled in. To define these central microhexagrams more precisely, those at the top, going from right to left, represent the sixteenth, fifteenth, and eighteenth microhexagram-paths of the Spiral Tree and those at the bottom the mirror images of these paths, proceeding from left to right through these same sixteenth, fifteenth, and eighteenth numbered paths. But the crucial difference between these microhexagrams of the red and blue spirals is that those of the red spiral are powers of the Other and lead directly to the incomplete Bohu of its Keter, whereas the incomplete Bohu of the blue Keter, while premature at this stage, represents the true crown of the Spiral Tree and so a lesser danger to the Ruach soul. If the desire for magical powers poses the gravest spiritual danger to the fallen Nefesh soul, the greatest spiritual danger to the errant Ruach soul is that of Satanism, the worship of evil for its own sake. The Ruach soul that cultivates the forbidden central powers available to it on the red spiral becomes drawn at last to assume an alien and empty crown, to assert with Milton's Satan: "Evil be thou my Good" (*Paradise Lost*, 4.110). For at this stage of spiritual development, the crowning Other can only be perceived as manifesting the antithesis of that ultimate good whose more difficult pursuit has been renounced.

Figure 11.3. Elements beyond the Fifth-World Matrix Border

To define these available but forbidden red powers more closely, that below the macrohexagram of Netzach on the left would represent the power of spiritual scent, that below and interpenetrating the macrohexagram of Hod the power of spiritual touch, and that below and interpenetrating the fifth microhexagram-path of creative thought the power of spiritual taste. If we view the blue versions of these paths at the top of this figure as those coming from the correct direction or "right side," it can be seen that they represent powers of the supernal Sefirot. In the normal progression, these powers would be filtered down to Netzach and Hod through the intervening Sefirot and paths of Chesed, Gevurah, and Tiferet. Thus the direct

movement to the red paths beyond the matrix border at the bottom of the fifth-world diagram involves the bypassing of the balancing faculty of Tiferet and of the whole spiritual disciplining of the Neshamah soul in the first phase of the sixth world needed to prepare the soul to be a proper vessel for these higher powers.

Coming as they do from an opposing direction, these microhexagram-paths provide a graphic representation of the kabbalistic concept of the Sitra Achra, the Other Side of the Tree associated with evil. They are, indeed, elements of what might be termed the Negative Spiral Tree, that followed by the lateral scarlet spiral through first the blue and then the red central spirals in mirror opposition to the "positive" path of the Spiral Tree followed by the lateral turquoise spiral. Though we shall consider another approach to the Negative Spiral Tree in the discussion of plate 15 in chapter 12, at this point it is clear that these completed red elements beyond the matrix border provide a second and more punishing testing ground for the soul. As the fourth-world completed extraborder elements were identified with the Fall, so these first-encountered completed extraborder elements of the fifth world constitute the still graver threat of a fall from the redemptive path of Tikkun into the consuming power of evil, from the path of increasing psychic organization to one leading to chaos.

We can understand this negative progression better by considering the role played by each of these inverse microhexagrams, beginning with the rightmost extraborder microhexagram of figure 11.3, which can be pictured as appearing under the microhexagram numbered fifth in the Spiral Tree, as earlier shown in figure 10.3, that representing creative thought.

The association of this rightmost extra microhexagram signifying subtle taste with that microhexagram within the matrix border numbered fifth and signifying creative thought is most interesting, for it suggests that such thought as can creatively unfold some never before manifested aspect of the enfolded order is somehow a function of developed and expressive personality, that truth can only be expressed through and with some personal bias. Since the subtle dimension of taste is precisely such an expression of personality, the danger of its premature employment in the revelation of divine truth is that the insufficiently developed soul can mistake its own constructs of uninspired thought for ultimate revelation. As earlier shown, true prophecy is the function of the eighth microhexagram, under the control of Gevurah and implying development to the Neshamah level of soul, rather than of the fifth microhexagram. But those who have activated the inverse of the eighteenth microhexagram will come to regard every manifestation of their personality as expressive of divine truth. This is the beginning of those proclamations of salvific truth made by false Messiahs, the fifth world providing the spiritual

environment that encourages such false Messianic development as well as the true.

In order for a false Messiah to develop a following, he not only needs such an inflated appreciation of his personal understanding but an unerring ability to discern the nature and needs of those whose discipleship he covets, an ability derived from the subtle dimension of the sense of smell. This inverse sixteenth microhexagram is again appropriately associated with the macrohexagram directly above it, that of Netzach. It was earlier shown that the Ruach faculty of the imagination associated with this macrohexagram-Sefirah had a capacity for insight into conditions beyond the self precisely because it was of the red spiral and so belonged in the body of the Other. But this permitted and necessary level of insight can be greatly expanded when allied to the further red extraborder microhexagram signifying a higher level of discrimination regarding the Other, the ability to "scent" that which is approaching from without, such as danger. The precise imagining of such "scents" made possible through this heightened empowering of the Ruach imagination tells the false Messiah exactly what he needs to know about the personalities and circumstances he is confronting so that he can present himself and his self-generated doctrines in the most favorable light, one that will seem to fulfill and validate the suppressed fantasy hopes of his listeners.

But neither subtle taste nor subtle smell are sufficient to produce the true phenomenon of a false Messiah without the third of the subtle senses forbidden but available to the errant Ruach soul, that of touch, the power of charisma. Believing his own Messianic delusions and sensitive to the secret desires of the multitude for a deliverance in unholy alliance with vengeance on its persecutors, the would-be Messiah would still fail of his purpose without the charismatic ability to touch the spirits of the many with hope and belief. Again it is most appropriate that this power of spiritual touch should appear just beneath and interpenetrating the lateral macrohexagram identified with Hod, the locus of spiritual power. We have just examined the perversions of the spiritual power of Hod by the fallen Nefesh soul, but these are nothing compared to the perversions possible on the Ruach level. For only the delusion of such power was available to the Nefesh soul whereas the Ruach soul not only has command of at least the lowest level of the power of Hod but can also command the forbidden power of personal charisma. When such charisma is perverted to enhance the genuine spiritual power of a Ruach Master and captivate the thronging hopefuls into worshipful obedience to his will, the worst of human evils is possible—Hitler, Jim Jones, Sabbatai Tz'vi.

The danger of such figures can be explained through the diagram as the result of combining the lowest level of Ruach mastery, that reaching no higher than the fifth microhexagram representative of creative thought, with the three forbidden sixth-world microhexagrams fully complete and beckoning the Ruach soul from beyond the fifth-world border just at the point where this border encloses the macrohexagrams of Netzach and Hod and the microhexagram of creative thought. It is the association of precisely these three permitted and three forbidden elements that spells the greatest danger to the individual soul and to the world.

In their appointed positions on the Spiral Tree, the fifteenth microhexagram of spiritual touch is beneath Keter, the sixteenth of spiritual smell beneath Chokhmah, and the eighteenth of spiritual taste beneath Binah. Thus the expression of Law through the bias of personality, of taste, is a property of Binah, the heightening of insight through the power of subtle scenting is a property of Chokhmah, and the power of spiritual touch is a property of the crowning macrohexagram-Sefirah of Keter. Interestingly, the eighth microhexagram that endows the Ruach Master with the highest power of true prophecy is positioned adjacent to the upper blue form of the fifteenth microhexagram of spiritual touch and overlaps the upper blue form of the sixteenth microhexagram of spiritual smell, while having no contact with the upper blue form of the eighteenth microhexagram of spiritual taste. This suggests that the prophet is not projecting his own personality and taste as truth but rather that coming to him from the Sefirot of Gevurah, Chokhmah, and Keter, all of whose macrohexagrams the eighth microhexagram touches. In addition to touching the microhexagrams representative of subtle smell and touch, it is also in contact with the fourteenth turquoise microhexagram of rigor and the seventeenth turquoise microhexagram of language. Thus the true prophet is gifted with the power of discerning the moral stench of society and of expressing the spiritual call to reform with charismatic language.

The false prophet, in contrast, working only from the level of the fifth turquoise microhexagram of creative thought, is being tempted by the hidden faculties of the demonic mind, by the scarlet Chokhmah and Binah and the red Keter, whose powers of subtle smell, taste, and touch he is seduced into accepting as his own. Abandoning the turquoise for the scarlet spiral, the arduous and circuitous path of the former for the immediate gratification of the latter, the false prophet can become a false Messiah, leading first himself and then others into a delusive salvation from the discipline of Law, into a self-intoxicated dance across the matrix border whose destination can only be the incomplete Bohu of an empty crown.

The short-circuiting of the discipline characterizing the true path of Tikkun for the brief exaltation of a spurious divinity is thus graphically portrayed by the various figures we have examined of the fifth- and sixth-world diagrams. They show us how the turquoise spiral, in harkening to those paranormal powers it should control, can be led by its alliance with the red spiral to forget its true nature and assume the identity of the scarlet spiral as it races to its final communion with the red Keter, a downward spiral beyond the power of that grace vested in the turquoise Chesed to arrest and turn upward to its true heavenly goal. When Netzach takes control of the Ruach soul away from Hod and leads it to embrace the forbidden powers represented by the red extraborder microhexagrams, it does so to bring about a premature consummation of its own path, because of its own central impatience for divine consummation. Had it been able to wait until the sixth world, it would have achieved that consummation in concert with the scarlet spiral after the latter had completed its own circuitous path through what for it are the pitfalls of the blue spiral. Now it becomes trapped with the turquoise spiral in the forbidden portion of the fifth world, in powers that can lead only to emptiness. The incomplete Bohu that has attracted the fallen Ruach soul becomes a source of lasting punishment to it, ever reminding it of the failure of its hopes. If the central elements of this soul are tormented by the emptiness to which their delusions have brought them, the lateral elements are more severely tormented by its alien nature, framed to meet every desire with its opposite. To the lateral self-consciousness of the Ruach soul, this constant meeting with opposition may begin to appear as a conspiracy of persecution, its hell the constant reenactment of paranoid delusions.

Compared to the real and lasting dangers to the Ruach soul posed by these central extraborder elements, those posed by the lateral such elements are minor. They are minor both because these elements are incomplete and because they are within the sixth-world boundaries of the Spiral Tree. As there were two borders to be considered in the fourth world, so is there a sequence of at least two border areas to be considered in the fifth world, the earlier southern border containing the complete extraborder elements of the central system we have just examined and the later eastern border containing only incomplete border elements, these exclusively of the lateral system. Thus having circumvented the more serious central temptations to its integrity, the Ruach soul is now confronted with some final lateral delusions associated with the exta-border appearance of elements of the sixth-world macrohexagram-Sefirot of Chesed, Tiferet, and Gevurah. All are in incomplete form, therefore delusional like the red Keter earlier encountered, but those of Chesed and Gevurah are also Bohus, as was the red Keter. This suggests that, whatever the nature of the delusions represented by these extraborder elements, association with Tiferet will be more satisfying than the guaranteed emptiness associated with the extremes of Chesed and Gevurah.

The fact that Tiferet is in a more finished form than Chesed and Gevurah at this stage in the diagram's development points again to the inner coherence between the Spiral and traditional Trees regarding Tiferet. The fact that it, as well as all the microhexagrams surrounding it, is finished earlier in the development of the diagram than are Chesed, Gevurah, and their associated microhexagrams argues for an equation between its earlier manifestation on the Spiral Tree and its lower position on the traditional Tree. This greater wholeness of Tiferet will again be apparent when we consider the temptations to which it and its companion Sefirot are subject from beyond their own sixth-world matrix border. In both the fifth and sixth worlds, the more balanced Sefirah of Tiferet would seem to pose less of a danger and be posed by lesser danger than the more extreme Sefirot to its sides.

Whether being analyzed in their own nature or as extraborder elements, the archetypal significance of these three Sefirot would seem to be most important in determining their specific significance, Chesed representing merciful expansiveness, Gevurah representing judgmental constriction, and Tiferet the balance between these extremes. What they may more specifically signify was earlier suggested in chapter 5 on the chronological stages of the Messianic Age. In discussing the stage marked by the War of Gog and Magog, it was suggested that a misconstruing of the essentially spiritual nature of apocalyptic war could lead to a social activism that might leave its adherents spiritually empty and embittered if not accompanied by personal spiritual work, and this despite the social good it may achieve. It was then said that all such devotion to the good of society implies some degree of Ruach consciousness, a level of consciousness marked by just this redirection of psychic energy from the needs of the self to those of the community of which it now feels a part. If we can make this association between a dedication to social welfare as the greatest of goods and these three extraborder macrohexagrams, then we may be able to determine more precisely the varieties of spiritual danger they may pose, the evil that good men do.

Once this equation is made, it would seem most logical to identify the Bohu of Chesed with the goal of social revolution, the Bohu of Gevurah with the goal of strict law and order, and the incomplete ideal of Tiferet with the centrist political machinery of the state, the first with the revolutionary, the second with the policeman, and the third with the politician.

Taking the last first, the politician does do some good, does keep the machinery of the state functioning to provide a measure of safety and community for its members; but the compromises he is forced to make to these ends must corrupt the ideals with which he entered public service. But if the society he serves is less than ideal in its primary concern for consensus, it is yet less damaging to the community than the more extreme forms of purgation through revolution or the police state, both of which can lead to a similar brutalization of the spirit far worse than the shallowness and venality attendant on centrist politics. The revolutionary terrorist who throws bombs into public places to publicize his Utopian cause is no less devoid of true feeling for the sufferings of individuals than is the torturing policeman. Like the revolutionary he tortures for information or punishment, the policeman believes he is serving an ideal more important than his selfish comfort and will daily risk his safety to that end. But the ideals both serve are equally Bohus, first because the revolutionary is willing to risk not only his own safety but also that of his whole society and because the policeman is willing to sacrifice to such safety the higher ends of society, the inner development of its members and their freedom to share their best creative efforts. The second reason these ideals prove equally empty and that even the accomplishments of centrist politics finally must seem less than sufficient is that all are delusions, social goods masquerading as final ends. Social welfare has become the god of an essentially godless politics, is being asked to provide a sense of meaningfulness to human existence beyond its power and all the worldly power society can bestow. So although social service is a high pursuit that does much good, it can lead to spiritual damage if it becomes an end rather than a means. Only then will social progress reveal its delusional character and the successes of social extremists prove empty to those who have sacrificed a lifetime of private happiness on its behalf. Theirs is not the evil of the charismatic Satanist or his hell, rather that which attends the substitution of a lesser for a greater good, the loss of that greater good and a growing bitterness toward the god that failed.[1]

We have thus far been considering these lateral border elements without reference to the fifth-world elements most susceptible to them, the first three microhexagrams completed in the fifth world and particularly the third of these, that numbered seventh and signifying Transformation. The danger to the Ruach soul is that, as it acquires the capacity for creative thought, the synchronous power of being in the right place at the right time, and the ability to transform its new conceptions into reality, it will apply these spiritual powers not to the inner dimensions but to the outer, will attempt to transform not the self or a spiritual community but the whole of secular society, and that in terms of only its material and social good. As with these powers of Hod, so Hod itself may become perverted into seeking power in society for its own sake, not through the forbidden central powers earlier examined but the misapplication of its permitted and developed powers to false or inadequate goods.

There is one final danger to the Ruach soul that afflicts the highest of Ruach powers, the power of prophecy lodged in the eighth microhexagram. We earlier saw how this microhexagram was in touch with a variety of sixth-world macrohexagrams and microhexagrams but now must point out that some of these are already present to it as extraborder elements in the fifth world. Not only is the Bohu of an incomplete Gevurah available to it but also the blue central elements paralleling the red ones earlier discussed, the fifteenth, sixteenth, and eighteenth microhexagrams in complete extraborder form and the Bohu of the incomplete blue Keter. Thus the prophet is ever in doubt whether he is operating from a genuine Neshamah level that truly invests him with these powers or only from the Ruach level at which these powers are forbidden and whose use might therefore become a snare to his soul as well as that of his people. Even if he does not fall thereby into the primary danger of premature prophecies of doom, he must be ever careful to discriminate between his higher Neshamah level of inspiration and his less mature Ruach intimations and ever prone to self-doubt. Since the prophet normally operates in a condition of defeat, this additional burden of doubt can only lead him to recurring bouts of depression and despair, with the final danger of making his personal pain and vindication seem more important than God's message of salvation, as with Jonah.

At every level of the Ruach soul there is spiritual danger threatening to intercept or stall its progress, and it must constantly be wary of these dangers and choose to remain on the path of Tikkun defined by the Law of the Matrix Border. Yet as the Ruach soul succeeds in overcoming one after another of these temptations, the dangers it encounters, though ever more subtle in their character, become increasingly less severe. Thus the gravest danger is posed by the red extraborder elements of what, in this context, might be called the Enemy since they can lead the soul completely off the Spiral Tree of its salvation and into a hell of emptiness and confusion. Less severe are the turquoise extraborder elements of what will be the first phase of the sixth world, which can simply stall its progress through a mistaking of means for ends since these lead at worst to excesses in the name of a lesser good rather than to the embrace of evil. Finally we come to the least damaging danger to the further progress of the soul from the Ruach to the Neshamah level since it does not prevents its progress. This is the soul sickness that may afflict not the false but the premature and indiscriminate prophet and which he must ever strive to overcome that he may continually mature in his punishing calling as the true instrument of divine revelation. As the dangers to the soul lessen at each stage of the fifth-world spiral, so do they lessen between the Ruach and Neshamah dimensions. Yet difficulties and the need for spiritual discipline remain.

BEYOND THE SIXTH-WORLD MATRIX BORDER

Interpreting the elements beyond the sixth-world matrix border is more difficult than for the comparable elements beyond the matrix borders of the fourth and fifth worlds because we no longer have the key of the Spiral Tree to guide us. To clarify the large assortment of extraborder elements in plate 13 and figure 11.4, the complete microhexagrams will continue to have filled-in inner hexagons, those which are also Tohus being further outlined by their

point-hexagons, as will the incomplete Tohus, and the one complete macrohexagram will have filled in macrotriangles. The vast chaotic mass shown in plate 13 and figure 11.4 represents the partial constituents of the full seventh-world matrix. But of its thirty-one complete and incomplete elements, only four will be contained within the extended matrix of the octave portion of the seventh-world diagram. The remaining twenty-seven elements will only become incorporated into the matrix with the completion of the seventh world. It seems logical to identify them as constituents of Ein Sof itself. Thus these extraborder elements can be associated both with chaos and Ein Sof.

The elements beyond this final matrix border can no longer be defined by their future positions on either the positive or negative Spiral Trees. They exist in an "outer space" susceptible to the alternative interpretations already suggested. On the one hand they represent the true condition of chaos since for the first time they manifest completed forms of Tohu and Bohu. To be more specific, of the ten completed elements beyond the sixth-world matrix border, there are nine lateral microhexagrams, two of which are also Tohus, and one central Bohu, the later formed by the semidetached border elements. In addition to these, there are also eleven incomplete lateral microhexagrams, three of which are also Tohus, five incomplete central microhexagrams, one of which is also a Tohu, three incomplete lateral Bohus, and two incomplete central Bohus. Because of the complexity of these extraborder elements, it will be necessary to confine our attention primarily to the completed elements, of which the most significant are the Tohus and the Bohu. Of these elements it is only the nine completed lateral microhexagrams that have their inner hexagons filled in with their white color, as was true for such black microhexagrams in figure 11.3, while the Tohus are again represented by an outer hexagon enclosing such microhexagrams of both the central and lateral spirals.

Viewing these elements in the counterclockwise direction of the Spiral Tree, we come first to a disconnected group comprising two complete and one incomplete lateral microhexagrams, second to a

Figure 11.4. Elements beyond the Sixth-World Matrix Border

larger disconnected group composed of nine elements, and third to another disconnected group exactly paralleling the first, although its overlapping of central elements associated with the second phase of the sixth world makes it more difficult to discern the three members of this third group as well as their disassociation from the three additional, vertically aligned lateral microhexagrams, which parallel the similar three to the far left top of the diagram and are properly extensions of the second phase of the sixth-world diagram. We will begin by examining the parallel members of the first and third groups in this first phase of the sixth-world diagram.

In the first group, whose members can all be clearly distinguished, the most important is the uppermost of its two completed microhexagrams. For this is a genuine Tohu, the inner microhexagram of a missing macrohexagram that would be touching that of Chesed, and it is also in touch with both the ninth microhexagram of grace and the tenth of mercy. The real dangers facing both grace and mercy and so Chesed itself are signified by these two completed microhexagrams, but since the closest of them is a Tohu it is inescapable and there is little need to identify the lesser degrees of real or delusive danger arising from it, those represented by the attached complete or incomplete microhexagrams, respectively. If the form of a Tohu may be associated with extreme psychic disorganization, with psychic chaos, then we may ask what extreme manifestation of Chesed may lead to such mental breakdown. Perhaps the one biblical instance of mental illness, that of Saul, may be associated with such an excess of Chesed. Because Saul did not utterly destroy the Amalekites but took their king Agag prisoner and spared the best of the cattle, Samuel tore Saul's mantle, symbolizing the Lord's rejection of Saul, and then "hewed Agag in pieces" despite Agag's touching appeal: "Surely the bitterness of death is past" (1 Sam. 15:32–33). Recognizing that Samuel's fierceness rather than his own pitiful weakness was what God required of him, and unable to overcome the repeated examples of his softness under pressure, Saul goes into a state of acute depression: "an evil spirit from the Lord troubled him" (1 Sam. 16:14). Though we tend today to sympathize with Saul rather than Samuel, the prophet's reply to Saul's excuse that the Amalekite cattle had been spared for sacrifice defines the central moral understanding of the prophets: "Hath the Lord as great delight in burnt offerings and sacrifices, as in obeying the voice of the Lord? Behold, to obey is better than sacrifice" (1 Sam. 15:22). As the specially chosen and anointed of the Lord has a greater obligation to obey God's commandments, however troubling, violation of the Law of the Matrix Border, even out of excessive mercy, will cast the Neshamah Master into a similar state of confusion. Another example, out of Germanic legend and Wagnerian opera, of divine punishment for excessive mercy is the case of Brunhilde, who brought about both her own mortality and that of the gods through the loving-kindness she showed to Siegmund and Sieglinda despite Wotan's express command that these children of his be shown no mercy. There can be no greater source of psychic distress to the willing servants of the divine than to be faced with higher counsels that contravene their impulses to charity.

Turning now to the third group, which has a parallel association with Gevurah and its powers of discernment and rigor, we may again look to the Bible for an extreme example of Gevurah leading to total disaster. If the need to inflict judgment on wicked oppressors arises from Gevurah, then an excess of Gevurah leading to confusion would be a need so great as to cause an individual to sacrifice his life for such vengeance, as in the case of Samson: "And Samson called unto the Lord, and said, O Lord God, remember me, I pray thee, and strengthen me, I pray thee, only this once, O God, that I may be at once avenged of the Philistines for my two eyes. . . . And Samson said, Let me die with the Philistines" (Judges 16:28, 30). Though it is through Samson's very spiritual limitations that the divine will is spectacularly fulfilled, such fulfillment would not have required his life had he been able to abide within the law, particularly the law of the Nazarite that forbade the cutting of his hair, whose breach led to the loss of his eyes and his suicidal prayer for revenge.

Like Saul, Samson was divinely chosen and empowered and failed similarly to use his divine power within the limits of divine commandment. Failure at such a high level can only result in self-punishment, the divine aspect of personality punishing itself for its remaining human frailties. The Tohu, chaos, into which the Neshamah Master can fall through violating the proper boundaries of Chesed and Gevurah is thus a part of divine consciousness, of that highest consciousness of Ein Sof that reveals the laws of necessity and the true position of freedom, such freedom as is only possible within bounds and must, of necessity, be lost with the violation of those boundaries. As with freedom, so is individual consciousness lost through violating the boundaries that permit its existence, that separate the divine personality of the Neshamah Master from the divine unity of infinite consciousness, of Ein Sof. Saul and Samson are able to peer into the chaos produced by their disobedience and to accept the punishing disintegration of their personalities.

Compared to the real dangers of psychosis and suicide, the delusive dangers attached to excessive grace or rigor are insignificant. Thus a Neshamah soul may fear that too much charity may render it the poorer or too much rigor the less popular. These are delusive fears it must learn to transcend, the products of a still powerful ego attachment to Nefesh values of self-aggrandizement. It must learn to trust to the divine manna for its sustenance and to be satisfied and fulfilled by the inner knowledge of behavior meriting divine approval. Such delusive fears represent temptations to restrict the proper expression of grace or rigor for improper reasons, and entering into the power of such delusions can only lead to the impairment of these Neshamah powers. Saul's lack of sufficient rigor derives from this fear, "Because I saw that the people were scattered from me" (1 Sam. 13:11), and leads finally to the loss of his kingdom and his suicide (1 Sam. 31:5). The fear was a delusion he should not have heeded, the excess of Chesed a reality revealing the failure of his leadership to fuse Israel into a proper instrument of the divine will.

The complete Tohus just discussed to which excesses of Chesed or Gevurah may lead are surrounded by only two or three border elements, respectively, plus two more within the matrix border, while the three incomplete Tohus at the top of the diagram are surrounded by only two to four. The incomplete Tohu with which Tiferet is associated, on the other hand, is surrounded by six microhexagrams, all beyond the matrix border. Since this configuration of six surrounding a seventh has been taken to signify creation or re-creation, it would again seem to betoken some form of rebirth, only here such possibility of rebirth would have to be considered a delusion. Although four of these microhexagrams are complete, it is the configuration of the seven that seems most significant and the incomplete form of its central element its most telling aspect. Not only is Tiferet confronted by an incomplete Tohu surrounded by six complete and incomplete microhexagrams but also by two framing incomplete Bohus. But though endangered by both Tohu and Bohu, these dangers are yet less serious than those confronting Chesed and Gevurah, whose Tohus are complete.

What, then, is this promised rebirth that must prove a delusion to the Neshamah soul guilty of an excess of Tiferet, and what may such an excess of Tiferet signify? One danger posed by Tiferet would seem to lie in its very capacity for harmony. The desire for greater and greater harmony may become so powerful that the Neshamah Master may seek for a final integration with the infinite harmony of Ein Sof. Believing that such integration would represent a second rebirth, not simply as with Chesed into divine personality, but into actual unification with the Infinite, the Neshamah Master may now take the drastic step of crossing the line dividing his personality from the infinite bliss he thinks to lie beyond. Filled with partial bliss and yearning for a state of constant beatitude, he may now prick the bubble of his personality only to find that the promised rebirth in divinity was a delusion and that his consciousness has become a Tohu, without form. The Neshamah Master who is thus impatient for divine union forfeits the chance to enter the divine realm in a transfigured form, maintaining that thinnest bubblelike shell of individuality that can render him a centering point of the Limitless Light. His union with the divine is, instead, with the loss of his individuality, something that is the goal of many spiritual traditions. He becomes part of the divine emotion of bliss.

His impatience to achieve such a state of eternal bliss at this stage of his development is understandable in view of its emotional character and becomes even more understandable when viewed in connection with the impatient Partzuf whose position on the Spiral Tree he shares, that of Ze'ir Anpin, the Short Face or Short Tempered or Impatient One. The anthropomorphic portrayal of Ze'ir Anpin in figure 10.4 shows that when the traditional position of Ze'ir Anpin is placed on the Spiral Tree his head could be associated with the location of the seven extraborder microhexagrams with which we are now concerned.[2] The part of Ze'ir Anpin that is within the matrix border comes just up to his neck. He is the divine heart, the head of which is properly to be found higher up on the Spiral Tree, in the mental Partzufim of Arikh Anpin, Abba, and Imma. But figure 10.4 suggests that Ze'ir Anpin, too, may want his own head, that, like a reined horse, he may want to be "given his head," allowed to follow his own lead. In fact, the *Eitz Chayyim*, drawing upon the *Zohar*, tells us that Ze'ir Anpin "becomes a fetus again in [the womb of] Imma, a second gestation, in order to acquire consciousness for himself, even though he had already completed for himself a whole Partzuf of six Sefirot in the days of his nursing."[3] Now what can be more like the bliss of submersion in a larger whole, which would seem to be betokened by the Sabbatical configuration before us, than such a return to the womb as has been ascribed to Ze'ir Anpin? The problem in following such a desire, even for Ze'ir Anpin, is that he can thus be led to think that the bliss of expressing his own mind, a second meaning here of the Tohu confronting Tiferet, is the sole purpose and only function of his consciousness. For the brains he needs to acquire is not that illusion of independent will beckoning him from beyond the matrix border but precisely that which he can only gain through collaboration with the higher mental Partzufim.

The fact that the Neshamah soul of man and the divine personality of Ze'ir Anpin can both be modeled by same features of the sixth world diagram, as they may here be thought to be vulnerable to the same temptation modeled by its extraborder elements, has broader implications. It suggests such a complementarity of the evolutionary levels of both man and his God as would seem to be the central message of the Lurianic Kabbalah. The new theory of "co-evolution" argues that animals and the plants necessary to feed them evolved together and symbiotically, and so may it be that man and God are both in need of the other for their own perfect and converging development.

In Lurianic terms, the Shevirah, or Breakage, of the divine Sefirotic vessels led to the need for their Rectification, that Tikkun through which the originally unconnected Sefirot are to be reconstituted as the Partzufim; and this Rectification is deemed to be possible only through the spiritual devotions of man. Thus as Abraham Joshua Heschel has consistently argued, God is as much in need of man as is man of God:

> *God is in need of man for the attainment of His*
> *ends, and religion, as Jewish tradition understands*
> *it, is a way of serving these ends, of which we are in*
> *need, even though we may not be aware of them,*
> *ends which we must learn to feel the need of. . . .*

God is now in need of man, because He freely made him a partner in His enterprise, "a partner in the work of creation." "From the first day of creation the Holy One, blessed be He, longed to enter into *partnership* with the terrestrial world," to dwell with His creatures within the terrestrial world. (*Numbers Rabbah*, ch. 13, 6; compare *Genesis Rabbah*, ch. 3, 9). . . . "When Israel performs the will of the Omnipresent, they add strength to the heavenly power; as it is said: 'To God we render strength'" (Psalms 60:14). . . . (*Pesikta*, ed. Buber, XXVI, 166b). . . . "the righteous are the support of God" (*Genesis Rabbah* ch. 69, 3). . . . [Judaism] teaches us that every man is in need of God because God is in need of man. Our need of Him is but an echo of His need of us.[4]

With much talmudic quotation, Heschel shows that the understanding of God's partnership with man in the continuing work of creation is at the heart of the Jewish religious tradition. From the Bible, through the Talmud, to Luria there has been a continuous understanding that the purpose of creation involves an interdependent evolution of both God and man. As man's prayers are understood to produce the progressive Tikkun of the Partzufim, so does the returning energy from these more personalized divine forms enhance man's own spiritual development, the inner Tikkun of man proceeding only to the same extent as does the outer Tikkun of the Partzufim.

But both man and Ze'ir Anpin seem to have tarried overly long at the incomplete stage of the Tikkun that may well be represented by such an immature form of this Partzuf as this border configuration of forbidden elements would seem to model. And if such impatience with higher authority on the part of Ze'ir Anpin can endanger the whole process of cosmic evolution, its consequences for the Neshamah Master are still more grave, ending his further evolution and the contribution it might have made to the ongoing cosmic process.

The Tohu or chaos to which the soul is prone in the first phase of the sixth world differs significantly from the earlier forms of chaos encountered beyond the borders of the fourth and fifth worlds, and this because its chaos is largely a sixth-world delusion. Viewed from the later perspective of the completed seventh-world diagram, it will be seen to represent the infinite order of Ein Sof, one that can only appear chaotic from the sixth-world perspective because it is being viewed through the lens of individuality that is a property of master consciousness. Once this lens is broken through the premature entry into the seventh world, the soul will be reabsorbed into the divine matrix from which it had emerged, informing it with all the information that soul had accrued while itself becoming an undifferentiated part of its knowledge, power, and bliss. But this is only true for that Neshamah Master exhibiting an excess of Tiferet. For those guilty of excesses of Chesed and Gevurah, the chaos awaiting them is more real, a disintegration of personality not into bliss but pain. Such knots of pain are a product of the purifying self-punishment by which divine personalities attempt to purge themselves and the divine unity in which they are rooted of the taint of their guilt. But since these knottings of the Limitless Light into nodes of pain are also irritants disturbing the infinite bliss, the consciousness of Ein Sof will seek to rid itself of such irritants, working to untie these knots and restore both its contents and the divine unity of which they are a part to a state of perfect harmony. Gershom Scholem has interpreted Lurianic cosmology as originating in "the daring suggestion that the whole process of *simsum* and emanation was set in motion in order to eliminate the forces of *din*, like a sort of waste product, from the essence of the Godhead. The whole process would thus have to be conceived as a kind of divine catharsis."[5] It is precisely these divine forces of Din or Gevurah, Judgment, with which we are now concerned. It is within the matrix boundaries that graphically depict the nature of the cosmic law that the forces of Din, of Providential Judgment, are meant to function. Thus violations of the limits set even on such Providential Judgment, through excesses of Chesed or Gevurah, recharge the divine essence with exactly those forces of self-punishing constriction that the cosmic process was intended to eliminate. It is therefore more incumbent on

Neshamah Masters than on lower masters not to yield to impatience and to continue their cosmic journeys. For though the pain of those guilty of excesses of Chesed or Gevurah is purgatorial and will end with their restoration to bliss, it delays the Tikkun. Failures at the Neshamah level, though having more serious repercussions for the whole of the cosmic process, are finally less injurious for the soul that has developed to this point than failures at lower levels since it has already attained a state of divine permanence. But it may have to suffer a severer purgatorial process than had it not been so guilty or become nonfunctional through excessive addiction to bliss, in either case losing its defining individuality and returning to an undifferentiated state of divine unity.

It may be possible to associate the Tohus and Bohu surrounding the sixth-world matrix border with another Lurianic concept related to the Tzimtzum, a subject crucial to the interpretation of the seventh-world diagram. This is the concept of the Reshimu. Scholem explains that, after the Tzimtzum, "Only a faint vestige or residue of the divine fullness and light, the *reshimu*, remained in the primordial vacuum thus created,"[6] and that this Reshimu was both an "inchoate mixture"[7] and a "receptive substratum."[8] It is, then, the Reshimu that is to be identified in the Lurianic system with the Tohu and Bohu of Genesis, that residue left within the finite sphere produced through the withdrawal of the Limitless Light. If we can so identify the matrix elements beyond the Sixfold Spiral Tree with the Reshimu, we can gain further understanding from this Lurianic perspective of how they may be identified both with chaos and Ein Sof.[9] These matrix elements would thus represent the last vestiges of the original chaos lying beyond the sixth-world matrix border of creation and signify as well the final dangers in the path of its perfection. But when the Tikkun will have been completed, these chaotic elements will find their proper place within the seventh-world matrix, its second half beyond the sphere of the Tzimtzum also serving to define the consciousness of Ein Sof.

Before turning to the extraborder elements associated with the second phase of the sixth world, we should review the eight completed elements associated with the first phase, since in considering the second phase we shall only be concerned with its two complete elements. The difference between the completed elements associated with Chesed and Gevurah and those associated with Tiferet is that, in the first case, the first completed elements encountered are Tohus while, in the second, they are simple microhexagrams. The first thus represent unformed centers of consciousness and the second powers of such psychic centers. Since the Tohus are encountered before the powers touching them, there would seem to be no way for the chaotic soul to utilize these powers. But perhaps they may be considered the source of those strange powers possessed by divine simpletons and mad prophets of doom that, though they cannot profit these poor creatures, may yet affect others with healing or remorse. The case with Tiferet is different because the soul is here confronted with real available powers. Since there is no way of determining what these may be, it seems best to consider them as "powers" per se, that is as the higher powers of harmony, to the right, and of proportion, to the left. Thus the pair closer to Tiferet, taken together, might represent the power of harmonic proportions squared and the further pair the power of harmonic proportions cubed. But where the Neshamah Master is able to contain the simple power of such harmonic proportions, when they are squared and cubed they may simply burn out his containing consciousness, electrocute him, as it were. Moving into the lower of these powers may, however, prove so exhilarating and seem to promise such orgasmic heights that he will be unable to restrain himself from the final excess of the second pair, feeling, like Othello, "If it were now to die, / 'Twere now to be most happy" (2.1.187–88). Without even entering the delusion of divine rebirth represented by the incomplete Tohu at the center of this Sabbatical configuration, he will have burnt himself out in ecstasy.

Unlike the eight completed elements beyond the first phase of the sixth-world matrix border, which could be defined in terms of the elements of the Spiral Tree within that border, further specification of the consciousness of Ein Sof is lacking in the kab-

balistic tradition to facilitate such definitions of the extraborder elements associated with the second phase with the exception of two complete such elements, the last extraborder elements of figure 11.4 we shall be considering. Beginning with the lateral microhexagram rising out of Keter and linked to both Chokhmah and Binah, it seems possible to attempt its definition because we already know precisely what it is rising into, the Cherubic form, illustrated in figures 7.1, 7.2, and 12.1, completed with the octave portion of the seventh-world matrix that seems expressive of spiritual flight.

Though figure 11.4 shows us that such flights are still empty fantasies, the Cherubic forms manifest at this stage only as the three Bohus at the top of this figure, the one complete border microhexagram we are now considering does provide Chokhmah and Binah with a real additional but still forbidden power. If this power can be associated with spiritual flight, then it would seem to betoken some power of levitation, some power of astral travel beyond the purely psychic phenomenon possible at the Ruach level of the imagination. The power of which we here speak might involve the capacity to appear in seeming corporal form in one place though one's actual body, physical or spiritual if coming from the world beyond, is elsewhere. At its highest level, such power has been reported of Jesus and of Yogananda's guru, Babaji, both of whom are said to have appeared to a few of their disciples at different places after their deaths. This is not to say that such figures had not attained the proper use of this power, had not reached the level of seventh heaven and Devekut at which this power becomes natural, but that this power would seem to be dangerous if used thus prematurely. The danger, as always, is that it prevents further growth, that playing with this godlike power of multi- or omnipresence prevents the true consummation of Devekut. At this level, however, even failure is largely rewarding, and when the true emptiness of this reward is perceived by the delay in achieving divine communion consequent upon the premature use of this power, the almost perfected Neshamah Master has only to pull back from such still forbidden power and perfect his spiritual discipline.

We come now to the final and most fascinating border element, the one complete Bohu to be manifested by the Sabbath Star Diagram beyond the sixth-world matrix border, a central Bohu that must be associated with Keter. To understand the possible meaning of this Bohu, we should review the nature of the matrix rings, a review that will be summarized in table 11.2 and is facilitated by study of the sixth-world border elements but that must also refer ahead to the discussion of the seventh-world matrix in the next two chapters. If we begin with the collective central macrohexagram of Malkhut, which serves and connects all six of the Spiral Trees, the first matrix ring surrounding it can be seen to contain six lateral macrohexagrams, the Yesods of each of the Spiral Trees. The second ring, similarly, contains twelve macrohexagrams, the six central macrohexagrams of Netzach and the six lateral macrohexagrams of Hod. The third ring contains eighteen lateral macrohexagrams, the six of Chesed, the six of Tiferet, and the six of Gevurah. The fourth ring with which we are now concerned appears, however, to break the order of numerical accretions by six since its three macrohexagram-Sefirot—the lateral Chokhmah, central Keter, and lateral Binah—when multiplied by six totals only eighteen. But our sixth-world central Bohu is actually a member of this fourth matrix ring, one that lies beyond the matrix border because of the incomplete state of its enclosed microhexagram. As the fourth ring thus has twenty-four potential members, twelve lateral and twelve central, so the fifth ring can be seen to have thirty potential members, five for each Spiral Tree, all lateral. These are five of the lateral Tohus and Bohus across the sixth-world matrix border: the complete Tohu associated with Chesed, the incomplete lower Bohu, Tohu, and upper Bohu associated with Tiferet, and the complete Tohu associated with Gevurah. The last complete ring to be manifested by the seventh-world matrix is the next ring of thirty-six, eighteen central and eighteen lateral, three of these being turquoise and three blue in adjacent, alternating positions. The second to fourth of these appear in the three Bohus above the Spiral Tree at the top of the sixth-world diagram, which will be completed in connection with the matrix of the

octave diagram, the first, fifth, and sixth in the adjacent incomplete Tohus to be completed by the second half of the seventh-world diagram. As can be seen in figure 13.3, the seventh-world matrix border cuts severely into the next three rings, leaving only twenty-four of the ring of forty-two, and twelve each of the rings of forty-eight and fifty-four. In table 11.2, the matrix order through the rings is given for only one Spiral Tree, and the numbers for its macrohexagrams should be multiplied by six to account for the whole matrix of each world.

Table 11.2. Rings of Matrix Macrohexagrams

RING	MACROHEXAGRAMS	TYPE
1	1	Lateral
2	2	Central and Lateral
3	3	Lateral
4	4	Central and Lateral
5	5	Lateral
6	6	Central and Lateral

It is with the fourth ring that we are now concerned, that which completes the Spiral Tree with the three supernal Sefirot and which has one additional but forbidden extraborder macrohexagram whose inner element is not completed until the second half of the seventh world. Though lower in the matrix than any other sixth-world extraborder element, it is not completed until after the octave, not until the third of the five horizontal Sabbath Stars beyond the upper Do of the octave diagram to be generated with construction of the full seventh-world diagram in chapter 13. What is particularly interesting about this macrohexagram is that it is positioned to the right of that for Chokhmah and directly above that for Gevurah and, were it to be included in the Spiral Tree, could thus be said to come between them. Now what comes between Chokhmah and Gevurah on the traditional Tree is the non-Sefirah, sometimes considered an eleventh quasi-Sefirah, of Da'at. Here we confront again one of those uncanny coincidences that seems to confer an intelligence to the Sabbath Star Diagram beyond human comprehension. For we are, indeed, given a quasi-Sefirah, a Bohu, exactly where we might expect an eleventh Sefirah on the Spiral Tree as on the traditional Tree, were both not strictly limited to exactly ten Sefirot, the latter by convention and the former by the Law of the Matrix Border.

As the *Sefer Yetzirah* clearly states: "Ten Sefirot of Nothingness: Ten and not nine; ten and not eleven. Understand with Wisdom, and be wise with Understanding. Examine with them and probe from them, make a thing stand on its essence, and make the Creator sit on His base."[10] If we are to "Understand with Wisdom [Chokhmah] and be wise with Understanding [Binah]," each of these faculties must not only contain the other but also recognize that they do not represent the height of comprehension, which can be identified with "ten and not nine." Even more important, they are not to confuse ten with eleven. What is to be understood is that the Tree lifts up the creation so that it can serve as the Throne of the Creator, can "make the Creator sit on His base." It is the Creator, Ein Sof, in whom the eleventh "Sefirah," that source of ultimate Knowledge, resides in a plane ever above and beyond the Tree.

The Sabbath Star Diagram provides two different explanations of the special ontological position of Da'at, Knowledge, one related to the traditional Tree and one to the Spiral Tree. In the first case it shows Da'at to be the center of the underlying Sabbath Star Diagram and so to be associated with its source rather than, as with the ten Sefirot, one of its manifestations. In the case of the Spiral Tree, it unerringly eliminates the possible inclusion of the remaining macrohexagram on the fourth matrix ring by the strange excision of a rectangle from the matrix just where the inner microhexagram of this macrohexagram is located. This excision can be discerned more clearly by observing a parallel location on figure 11.4. If, for instance, the innermost perpendicular line at the middle left of this matrix border is chosen, it can be seen that two microtriangles of the microhexagram it bisects are without their symmetry lines, whereas all other elements of this microhexagram and its surrounding macrohexagram are complete, including the single matrix macrotriangle to their left that serves to complete the Bohu

of Da'at. The diagram thus gives to the element that can be identified with Da'at the peculiar form named a Bohu that seems perfectly to convey its ambiguous status, both in and out of the Tree. But what the inclusion of this Bohu in the Spiral Tree can tell us is that any presumption to ultimate Knowledge on the part of the creation is empty, that such knowledge is not even within the provenance of Keter, which must be considered the Crown of *cosmic* knowledge. Between these two central macrohexagrams, that within the matrix border, Keter, would seem to contain the laws of cosmic creation, of the finite, and that beyond the matrix border, Da'at, the laws of the Infinite.

How true this is will be remarkably confirmed by the later exploration of the seventh and still higher worlds in chapter 13. For these are the worlds that may be considered to go beyond the circle of the Tzimtzum defining the finite cosmos that chapter 7 showed could be correlated with the forty construction elements of the cumulative octave diagram; and what the further study of chapter 13 will show is that it is only in this realm of the infinite that full regularity reigns. Thus it is appropriately in the second half of the seventh world, which marks the beginning of this infinite regularity, that the signifier of such knowledge of the infinite appears, a knowledge for which the irregularity of the finite-correlated worlds can provide no clue. This is surely the most extraordinary of the inexplicable coincidences that the Sabbath Star Diagram is ever manifesting and that seem to reveal it, indeed, to be somehow informed by Da'at. The placement of the macrohexagram signifier of Da'at beyond that limit of the finite cosmos to be defined by the octave diagram also indicates that such knowledge is beyond both the Partzufim and the Neshamah Master, beyond even the hosts who minister before the Throne and experience Devekut. It is Ein Sof's alone.

LIGHT UNITS AND THE ILLUSION OF KNOWLEDGE

The sixth dimension has been understood to be that which confers meaningfulness to existence by revealing the patterns that underlie it. But the previous section concluded with the attribution of true Knowledge (Da'at) only to the sphere of Ein Sof beyond the cosmic circle. It is certainly with the sixth-world diagram that major patterns of the Sabbath Star Diagram begin to be made clear, not only the unquestionable importance of the Spiral Tree but also the numerical progression of the construction elements. The third such pattern to emerge in the sixth-world diagram, that of matrix "light units," has implications that will, however, be proved uncertain with the full disclosure of the seventh world. But though the following three chapters will continue to use, question, and refine the concept of "light units" in the matrix, its value will finally be assured by the basis only it can provide for the final extrapolation to infinity, in the culminating chapter of this work, of the most vital surviving function of the Sabbath Star Diagram in the realm of the infinite.

"Light units" is the term that has here been adopted for the degrees of power that may be assigned to the various matrix elements. Since in making such assignments a meaningful pattern arises where none was apparent before, it is a significant aspect worthy of further investigation, and such investigation will bear surprising fruit. Let us begin by again reviewing the numbers that emerge in the sixth-world matrix. In the central system there is the *one* macrohexagram identified with Keter and the *five* microhexagrams that serve it and have been identified with the five inner senses. In the lateral system there are *five* macrohexagrams and *nine* microhexagrams, the three macrohexagrams of the heart Sefirot—Chesed, Gevurah, and Tiferet—with the two microhexagrams each that serve them and the two mental Sefirot of Chokhmah and Binah with their total of three adjunct microhexagrams. If we assign 3 light units to a central macrohexagram, 1 light unit to a central microhexagram, 1 light unit to a lateral macrohexagram and $1/3$ unit to a lateral microhexagram, we can achieve a parity between the central and lateral systems of eight light units each. The one central macrohexagram is worth three units and the five central microhexagrams are worth five units, for a total of eight units, while the five lateral

macrohexagrams are worth five units and the nine lateral microhexagrams are worth three units, again for a total of eight, sixteen for the whole of the sixth-world portion of the Spiral Tree.

As one of the alternative ways of constructing the fourth-world diagram can allow a similar parity to be achieved in both the fourth and fifth worlds as well, this would seem to be a desirable feature of the diagram and to make light-unit parity an aim of diagram construction. Before noting the problems of such a conclusion, we should see how such light-unit parity can be effected in these earlier worlds. This requires the selection of the past-modeled form of the fourth-world diagram, figures 3.4 and 8.1, as, indeed, its ideal form, a conclusion further supported by the fact that its border is shown in figure 6.6 to be precisely that produced by backward construction of the sixth-world diagram. Turning first to the fifth-world matrix spiral, if we understand figure 9.1 to signify its ideal form, that in which we imagine the fifth-world diagram to be added directly to the past-modeled fourth-world diagram and that thus gives to it the third and fourth numbered microhexagrams of the Spiral Tree otherwise produced by the future modeling of the fourth-world diagram, we again achieve parity with this system of light units. To the 3 light units of its one central macrohexagram, the lateral system can show 1 unit for its one lateral macrohexagram and 2 units for its six lateral microhexagrams, totaling 3 units for the lateral as for the central system and six units for the fifth world portion of the Spiral Tree

The fourth world, as always, creates a problem, but in the past-modeled form of figure 8.1 one easily capable of resolution. Leaving the collective central macrohexagram out of the counting for the moment, the remaining central microhexagram is worth 1 unit while the lateral macrohexagram is worth 1 unit and the lateral microhexagram $1/3$ unit, for a lateral total of $1\frac{1}{3}$. To achieve parity between the central and lateral systems in the fourth as in the higher worlds, we would have to assign to the red portion of the collective central macrohexagram $1/3$ light unit, bringing the fourth-world central portion of the Spiral Tree to a total of $1\frac{1}{3}$ equaling that of this lateral portion, with the grand total for this fourth-world spiral amounting to 2⅔. To now bring the fourth-world total up to what would seem to be a preferable whole number, that of three, we would have to draw another ⅓ unit from the collective macrohexagram that, though itself central, is the source of all twelve individual spirals. Such an additional ⅓ unit could be considered the gift of the collective macrohexagram to each of the six Spiral Trees, the combined six Trees composing the full matrix that we will be meeting in the final section of chapter 12. As a gift of the matrix source, the divine womb, to the individuated manifestations of her cosmic creativity, it seems appropriate to identify it with the holy spark with which each soul is thought to come into being. The first surprising result of counting light units has been this location of the holy sparks in the Sabbath Star Diagram. An additional result is its apparent support of the past-modeled form of the fourth-world diagram as, indeed, its ideal model.

But the greater perfection with which it appears to endow the future worlds of the Spiral Tree is at great cost to the fourth-world diagram, giving it a form so idiosyncratic as virtually to guarantee the initial errors of construction that seem so analogous to the concept of the Fall. Indeed, this concept seems to serve very much the same function in theological thought, ensuring the theoretical perfection of the divine through the attribution of evil to man. But when we come to analysis of the full seventh-world diagram in chapter 13, we shall see that a truly predictable form of matrix regularity only begins with the seventh world, with those worlds of the diagram beyond the circle representative of the finite cosmos that chapter 7 had suggested can be drawn around the Sabbath Star of the upper Do at the midpoint of the seventh world. But this very new regularity will lead to further questioning of the basis on which light-unit parity is here being established, though the present analysis will also provide the key for establishing what will prove to be the most significant regularity of all, that which it will take much of part 4 fully to explore. Thus we have another measure of the limitation of vision to which each world of the diagram is subject with respect to the greater complexity of those surrounding it. As

no rules for construction of the fourth-world diagram coherent with the further expansion of the diagram could be discovered at that level, so even at the sixth-world level, at which all the rules of diagram construction seem finally to have been revealed, we will find its intelligence to extend only to the finite, though increasingly spiritual, worlds of the Spiral Tree and to reflect only a relative truth. But though the analyses of chapter 13, will cause a necessary reframing of the laws of diagram construction as originally based first on the seemingly arbitrary configuration of the Tree of Life Diagram and then on the emergent form of the Spiral Tree, it will not invalidate these prior bases of the experimental geometry that, in bringing us as far as the sixth world, has also brought us to our first understanding of the intrinsic laws informing the evolving Sabbath Star Diagram.

Though accepting the rule of light-unit parity in all the worlds can provide one way of determining the matrix border of the fourth-world diagram and the construction elements needed to produce it, an even more startling result can arise from counting up the totals thus far arrived at for both the Spiral Tree and the collective macrohexagram at its start. In the first case, the addition of light units for the three worlds of the Spiral Tree comes to a suggestive number: $16 + 6 + 3 = 25$. And in the case of the collective macrohexagram, the ⅓ unit given to each central spiral plus the ⅓ given to each Spiral Tree, when multiplied by six such Trees, leads to the following sum: $2 (⅓ × 6) = 4$. Now, both of these totals seem to fall short of a more appropriate number and in complementary fashion. The number 25 for the Spiral Tree is conspicuously lacking just one unit to reach the divine number 26, which is the Gematria of the Tetragrammaton. Chapter 6 has already shown us that the number of drawn hexagrams needed to complete the sixth-world diagram in outward construction is also 26: 1 for the first world, 1 for the second (since the later manifested Ri hexagram is disallowed by the key of the Tree of Life Diagram), 2 for the third, 4 for the fourth, 6 for the fifth, and 12 for the sixth; thus $1 + 1 + 2 + 4 + 6 + 12 = 26$. And chapter 7 revealed that inward construction from the octave also required just 26 construction elements, numbers that suggested that these two forms of construction were accomplishing their own unifications both of the sixth and seventh worlds and of the Name. It would seem appropriate, therefore, for the uncanny intelligence informing the Sabbath Star Diagram to designate 26 as the number of light units for the Spiral Tree. But if we accept this as its proper number, then the only place where the Spiral Tree can get this extra light unit would be through a spiral involution to the source, to the collective macrohexagram. The addition of 6 such extra light units, one for each of the Spiral Trees, to the 4 units already ascribed to this macro-hexagram, would bring its total to 10 light units, just what we should expect from this originating cosmic source. At the beginning of the *Eitz Chayyim*, Chayyim Vital says of this source: "He emanated one point, which included ten (and they are the ten Sefirot of the points that were in one vessel)."[11] The collective macrohexagram of the Sabbath Star Diagram, which we have here just deduced should have 10 light units ascribed to it, gives graphic demonstration of this central principle of kabbalistic cosmology. But as will be shown in chapter 14, further light units will be required from this matrix source at later cosmic stages that will bring its final radiance to 20 light units, the number of the Trees of the two cosmic worlds denoted by the Do and Re construction hexagrams that comprise this central collective macrohexagram.

Another important principle of both talmudic and kabbalistic cosmology that would seem to be demonstrated by the involution of the spiral from the height of the Spiral Tree to this matrix source for the acquisition of a final portion of light is the principle that there is such a portion of light stored up for the righteous. Commenting on the biblical statement, "Light is sown for the righteous" (Psalm 97:11), the Midrash (*Shemos Rabbah* 35:1) explains that "this verse refers to the original light which illuminated the world at the time of Creation. With this light, a man could see from one end of the world to the other. But God realized that wicked men might someday use this light for corrupt purposes. Therefore, God hid this light in the Garden of Eden, where it is reserved as a reward for the right-

eous."[12] This concept of reserved light will be discussed more fully in chapter 12.

It can be further related to the earlier developed principle of a directional line of matrix movement. In analyzing the fourth-world matrix in chapter 8, we saw that a circuit could be established on the principle of going out from the center with the lateral system and back to the center with the central system. This same principle was also shown in chapter 9 to be operative in the matrix of the fifth world, and it will also be demonstrated for the sixth world in chapter 12. The solution just provided for bringing the sixth-world light-unit total up to the Gematria number of the Tetragrammaton, that of a return to the center for a portion of reserved light, can also be applied, however, to the fifth world, and it would permit light-unit parity to be achieved as well by the form resulting from the future modeling of the fourth-world diagram. Such a possibility can be further supported both by matrix modeling and esoteric cosmology. It was just observed that the line of outgoing and returning matrix movement could also be applied to the fifth-world matrix, and it should be further noted that at this level the movement line, illustrated in figure 9.2, forms an infinity curve. Since this form results from the reversed positions of the macrohexagrams now identified with Hod and Netzach, and the latter means "eternity," the matrix explanation of the way that the Ruach soul can achieve the immortality that can thus be ascribed to its soul level would be for it to follow the infinity curve back to the center. Though the return to the center at the sixth-world Neshamah level can be located wholly in the World to Come also identified with this diagram world, such a return at the Ruach level is best correlated with the kabbalistic belief in Gilgul or reincarnation, a subject to be considered more fully in the next chapter. The traditional interpretation of Job 33:29, "Behold God does all these things, twice, three times, with a man,"[13] as implying three incarnations of the soul can well be identified with the Ruach soul. In terms of such Gilgul, we could interpret its windings through the fifth-world matrix as involving two returns to the center for the added portions of $\frac{1}{3}$ light unit at each reincarnation that would bring its lateral system total of $2\frac{1}{3}$ up to parity with the 3 of its central system. But if we want to hold to the number 26 as the total for the Spiral Tree, this would leave the light unit total for the future-modeled fourth world matrix in an irregular state without parity. For if the total number of light units attributed to the collective macrohexagram is, at least at this stage, also to remain at 10, with the fifth-world matrix now drawing 4 total units and the sixth-world matrix 6, then there would be no further units available for the fourth-world matrix, whose 2 lateral units per Spiral Tree would not be matched by the 1 central unit of its color-individuated microhexagram. And it would also lose that extra $\frac{1}{3}$ unit previously identified with the holy spark. In chapter 13 we shall see, however, that it is precisely the light unit totals originally arrived at for the lower levels of each Spiral Tree—3 for its fourth world level and 6 for its fifth—that will provide the primary key for the most important of diagram regularities. And we now see that they can be arrived at through either the past or future modeling of the fourth-world diagram, both of which can be justified in terms of kabbalistic concepts. But since either way of establishing light-unit parity for the fifth-world matrix produces irregularity at the fourth-world level, we arrive at the fact, later to be absolutely established, of the basic irregularity of the fourth-world diagram however it is constructed, with the unique freedom of choice this offers. At the sixth-world level, it would seem, nonetheless, to be the idiosyncratic past modeling of the fourth-world diagram that should be chosen because it can establish parity throughout the Spiral Tree.

But if we accept the competing regularity estab-lished by the sixth-world diagram, that of future modeling, and continue to count light units in the matrix, then a new view of the matrix becomes a possibility, the fact that the parity so demonstrated by the sixth-world matrix is not the rule for all of the worlds. Because of the unique nature of the collective central macrohexagram of the fourth world, it is still possible to achieve parity through it in the fourth world. Its three lateral microhexagrams would equal 1 unit and its one lateral macrohexagram 1 unit for a total of 2 lateral units, while its one central microhexagram would equal 1 unit and 1 unit could be drawn from the central macrohexagram for the parity number of 2 central light units. The fifth world would now not feature light-unit parity, its lateral macrohexagram's 1 light unit and four lateral microhexagram's worth of $1\frac{1}{3}$ units equaling only $2\frac{1}{3}$ units and not matching the 3 light units of the central macrohexagram. The totals of 4 units for the fourth world, $5\frac{1}{3}$ units for the fifth world, and 16 units for the sixth world equal $25\frac{1}{3}$ light units, $\frac{2}{3}$ light unit below the preferred number of twenty-six. But since the collective central macrohexagram of the fourth world would still be understood to equal 10 light units, the returning paths of the soul could still garner these extra fractional units either just on the Neshamah level, earning $\frac{2}{3}$ unit, or on both the Ruach and Neshamah levels, earning $\frac{1}{3}$ unit on each return. It could be, then, that light-unit parity is, indeed, a matrix rule but only for the even-numbered worlds, while the odd-numbered worlds would not feature such parity. Which of these possibilities is correct will have to wait for further intelligence from the infinite worlds to which we now turn.

CHAPTER 12

The Octave Matrix of the Chayah Soul

CHERUBS AND TREES

This part culminates as did part 2 with that seventh heaven of Aravot, as it was known in the Merkabah tradition, which can be correlated with such half construction of the seventh world of the Sabbath Star Diagram as will bring us to the higher octave of the original hexagram of creation, the prior study focusing on its construction elements as this part does on its matrix. How the musical code of the octave instructs us to divide the seventh-world diagram into two chronological parts at that midpoint marked by the Sabbath Star of the upper Do was explained first in chapter 2 and then in chapter 7; so it need not detain us here. But this octave portion of the seventh-world diagram is a level both connected with that of the sixth world and yet transcending it. The remarkable matrix addition of the Aravot diagram, the cherubic form outlined by its matrix border that will shortly be viewed in figure 12.1 and plate 14, was the subject of much of the analysis of chapter 7 on the octave diagram, and as there explained, it is only this winged form that the half world of Aravot adds, the matrix border of the sixth world not being otherwise altered since it is only with the seventh horizontal Sabbath Star of the seventh world that the matrix specially contributed by the horizontal axis begins to be formed. But what could not be there revealed is the spectacular further identification of these culminating winged forms with the serpentine matrix Tree, this the most astonishing graphic emergence in the whole development of the Sabbath Star Diagram.

We shall soon consider the iconographic significance of such a winged form atop the Spiral Tree, but before we begin the more precise analyses of the angels of Aravot we should note something of the analyses to follow it. These will take us from the simple Spiral Tree, the main subject of chapter 10, first to the Double Cherub-Tree and finally to the Sixfold Cherub-Tree, the former associated primarily with the Chayah soul as the latter primarily is with the Yechidah soul. Not only may these two highest levels of the soul be identified with two such incremental passages through these Trees but also with the two phases of the seventh-world diagram, the Chayah soul level with the octave diagram, the subject of this chapter, and the Yechidah soul level with the full seventh-world diagram, the first subject of chapter 13. But the Cherubs with which the Chayah soul may be most narrowly identified must be understood to be the culminating stage of a process that includes the Double Spiral Tree beneath them. And the Sixfold Spiral Tree must also be comprehended in

313

the still further extension of the full seventh-world matrix that defines the Yechidah soul.

Analysis of the Double Cherub-Tree will be aided by consideration of Sabbatian theory, particularly the concept of redemption through the Other Side, a concept with affinities to the Jungian category of the Shadow and of its need for integration with the conscious self. But it will also provide a corrective to the excesses of Sabbatian theory and practice. So too will the analysis of the Sixfold Cherub Tree provide a solution to the geometric enigma of the Merkabah text *Shi'ur Komah*, the Measure of the Body. But first we must turn to the analysis of the octave matrix, which will bring us to the kabbalistic concept of the Tzachtzachot, the three "Splendors" added to the Sefirot in the *Sefer ha-'Iyyun* and other texts. Thus the explication of the geometric features to be soon encountered will provide illumination of some of the most mysterious aspects of the Kabbalah.

When we first viewed the sixth-world matrix in plate 10 and figure 10.1, we saw that the separation of its lateral and central constituents produced the striking image of a winged or plumed serpent. And though we seemed to lose this plumed shape in moving to the more serpentine form of the integrated Spiral Tree in plate 11 and figure 10.2, we now can see how this snake becomes transformed into a winged bird or angelic form at the culminating stage of the octave matrix to reveal the meaning of its Cherub-Tree.

The imagery of the winged serpent has been traced as far back as the Upper Paleolithic period and appears to have been universal. Its main expressions, however, have been in the religious iconography and myths of Egypt, Greece, and Mexico. The most famous of these images derives from the latter two cultures, in the myths of the phoenix and of Quetzalcoatl. William Irwin Thompson has analyzed the implications of the iconography appearing in these two myths:

the myth of the phoenix presents many striking similarities with the myth of the plumed serpent. The quetzal bird is said to make its nest only on the top of trees in the full light of the sun. The serpent that has turned into a bird thus has to make its way up the trunk of the tree to move out of the dark into the light. And so it is with the phoenix, for it is said to have once been a lowly worm that fed in the dirt, but then as it slowly made its way up the trunk of the tree, it began to become transformed into a bird. . . . Here in its nest it created its own funeral pyre and was transformed into flames; from the ashes left behind, another phoenix was born. . . . The religious iconography of bird-tree-snake is almost universal. . . . The snake is the earth, and the bird is the sun; the feathered serpent is the world in harmony with heaven, and earth sculpted into a "Pyramid of the Sun." The snake is the fallen human race; the bird is the bodhisattvic race; and the feathered serpent is the human race in the condition of enlightenment. . . . the religious initiate who has consciously moved from physical to spiritual evolution.[1]

Peter Tompkins quotes an earlier scholar to similar effect: "To Sejourné, Teotihaucan was the place where the serpent learned miraculously to fly, that is 'where the individual, through inner growth, attained the category of a celestial being.'"[2] The iconography of bird-tree-snake that appears so widely in initiatic civilizations and symbolizes its most esoteric knowledge is also the highest truth revealed in the octave unfolding of the Sabbath Star Diagram. It demonstrates the mythic association of serpent with tree in its reconfiguration of the Sefirot and paths of the Tree of Life Diagram into the form of a snake, and it shows how the winged shape that is the divinized form of this snake nests precisely in the upper branches of this Spiral Tree. Though we cannot here go into the extensive background earlier presented in relation to the octave Cherubs, one aspect of this earlier discussion should be again rehearsed, the various biblical treatments of these figures that seem to be the direct analogues to our matrix birds.

The iconographic association of snake and tree appears in the Bible as well as in the myths earlier discussed and represents man's condition at the beginning and end of his spiritual evolution. Its first appearance is, of course, in the Garden of Eden, where the snake and a winged form are not only radically separated but associated with different trees, the snake with the Tree of Knowledge and the winged Cherubim with the Tree of Life: "So he drove out the man; and he placed at the east of the Garden of Eden Cherubims, and a flaming sword which turned every way, to keep the way of the tree of life" (Gen. 3:24). Fallen man, driven out of the Garden in a condition that identifies him with the snake, must now climb the Tree of Life internally, through the initiatic practices of kabbalistic meditation. When he has reached the crown of that Tree of Sefirot, he will come to the "chariot" vision of the Cherubim, whose holiness is represented in the cubic Holy of Holies of the earthly Temple, in "the chariot of the cherubims, that spread out their wings, and covered the ark of the covenant of the Lord" (1 Chron. 28:16). It is such Cherubim that Ezekiel finally recognizes that he saw in his original vision of the Throne: "This is the living creature that I saw under the God of Israel by the river of Chebar; and I knew that they were the cherubims" (Ezek. 10:20).

If the winged forms contributed to the matrix by the vertical Sabbath Stars of the seventh-world diagram can, indeed, be equated with the Cherubim, then we would seem to have an astonishing explanation for the reason that only this form was exempted from the prohibition contained in the Second Commandment: "Thou shalt not make unto thee any graven image, or any likeness of any thing that is in heaven above. . ." (Exod. 20:4). God makes this specific exemption when he commands Moses: "And thou shalt make two cherubims of gold. . . . And the cherubims shall stretch forth their wings on high . . . and their faces shall look one to another" (Exod. 25:18, 20).

There is a particular matrix feature that associates our angels of Aravot most closely with the Chayot-Cherubim seen by Ezekiel in his Throne vision: "every one had four wings. . . . Their wings were joined one to another. . . . their wings were stretched upward" (Ezek. 1:6, 9, 11). In observing figure 12.1 (and plate 14), one should view one pair of wings as originating from the upper back and the other, largely hidden, from the upper chest, with those at the right and left somehow joined and working in a synchronized opposition, such oscillating wing positions as were suggested in figure 7.1 and were the subject of descriptive comment there

The twelve-colored version of the octave matrix in plate 14 not only defines the matrix components of the Cherubs identified with the Double Cherub-Tree but also those of the remaining four Cherubs that, together with them, are further associated with the more fully developed Sixfold Cherub-Tree. These six Cherubs are further divided into two groups distinguished by their relationship to the sixth-world matrix border. The Cherubs at the top and right side of the plate 14 are featured with those matrix elements wholly contained within their Cherubic forms, while those at the bottom and left side feature only the matrix elements that connect the octave addition to the full sixth-world matrix. Figure 12.1 simplifies this diagram by featuring only the matrix elements of the top and bottom Cherubs, central elements again being signified by black and lateral elements by white. In figure 12.1 the central elements on the top Cherub signify the blue spiral and those on the bottom Cherub the red spiral, while the lateral elements on the top signify the turquoise spiral and those on the bottom the scarlet spiral.

Beginning the analysis with the single individuated Cherub at the top of figure 12.1, we can see that the most outstanding feature of this form is the lateral macrohexagram that covers or comprises the main bodily portion of the Cherub. Covering its heart area, it may be said to define the identity of the Cherub. In addition to its defining lateral macrohexagram, this Cherub also contains three central microhexagrams, two in its upper wings and one at its base, in what might be considered its tail feathers. If the lateral macrohexagram gives the Cherub its individual character, the central microhexagrams would seem to give it the power of transcendent flight.

Turning now to the lower Cherub of figure 12.1, we can see that it is the two central macrohexagrams that connect the Cherub to the Spiral Tree as an undifferentiated aspect of the larger

Figure 12.1. The Octave Matrix

octave matrix. This distinction between the central and lateral macrohexagrams appears to signify the individuating thrust of the lateral system and the central system's pull toward collectivity. In addition to the two central macrohexagrams that overlay the matrix borders of the sixth world and of the octave Cherubs, there are also three lateral microhexagrams that serve to ground the Cherubs. This reflects another distinction between the central and lateral systems; for if the triad of central microhexagrams within the Cherubic form at the top may be associated with the power of ascension, of spiritual flight, the triad of lateral microhexagrams at the bottom, overlaying the sixth-world matrix border may be associated with the reciprocal capacity for grounding. Thus the central system can be associated with collectivity at the macrostructural level and with ascension at the level of the microstructure, while the lateral system can be associated with individuality in the macrostructure and groundedness in the microstructure. These matrix associations are most appropriate to what we know of these systems from prior analysis and endow the two versions of the Cherubs with a special status as archetypes of the matrix. In these culminating forms of the octave matrix, the essential meaning of the matrix would seem to be both clarified and realized, that perfect and necessary union of the central and lateral systems that gives to the upper Cherub its capacity for spiritual ascent without loss of individuality and to the lower form its capacity to return to the state of collectivity that can refertilize the ground of being with new creative potential.

Though the octave matrix does not itself distinguish the individual Cherubs from its extension of the sixth-world matrix border but endows all six of its matrix additions with both those elements within the individual Cherubic forms and those within the larger octave matrix border, the distinction made in plate 14 and figure 12.1, as with all particular matrix displays, does provide a new way of understanding the forms thus displayed, a new way in which not only the Cherubs identified with the turquoise and scarlet lateral macrohexagrams that largely define them, but the Chayah soul and Double Spiral Tree can be understood. On its basis we can posit that the turquoise Cherub above the positive pole of the Double Spiral Tree would feature its powers of individuality and ascension while the scarlet Cherub beneath its negative pole would feature its powers of collectivity and groundedness. In the later analyses of the Double and Sixfold Cherub-Trees we shall see reason to associate the positive Trees with consciousness and the negative Trees with the unconscious, and these associations can be imported into the present interpretation of all six matrix additions of the octave diagram, the turquoise, indigo, and purple additions, those on the top, upper right and lower right, featuring the distinctive Cherubic forms while the scarlet, orange, and lemon additions, those on the bottom, lower left, and upper left, do not distinguish these forms but merge them into the main body of the sixth-world matrix. Viewed in this manner, the Double Spiral Trees, whether considered individually or tripled into three such Trees, can be thought to culminate in two distinguishable Cherubic forms, one emphasizing its individuality and the other its collective nature. But, in fact, the two are simply different faces of the same spiritual entity that, like the soul itself, has both the individual and collective aspects of its lateral and central systems. If we now choose to view each of the Cherubs as such composites, as both outlined and merged, each featuring all of its matrix constituents, particularly its three macrohexagrams, we can discover in this a new relationship to another aspect of kabbalistic theory.

If the octave matrix is simply added to the Spiral Tree below it to form one undifferentiated Tree-Bird, one flying serpent, the nature of these three macrohexagrams can be reinterpreted in the light of the earlier ten macrohexagrams of its Spiral Tree component. Since these earlier ten macrohexagrams were equated with the ten Sefirot of the Tree of Life Diagram, it would follow that these additional three macrohexagrams should also be considered Sefirot; and such a postulation of a thirteen–Sefirot Tree has, indeed, an honored place in the Kabbalah. From the thirteenth-century Provençal texts of the *Sefer ha-'Iyyun* circle, and a famous responsa of that time, to the sixteenth-century work of Cordovero in Safed, the possibility of thirteen such Sefirot remained an important cosmological issue, as Scholem has shown:

> of the writings attributable to the circle of the *Sefer ha-Iyyun* . . . One group of texts interprets the 13 attributes of divine mercy as the sum of the powers which fill the world of emanation, some authors adding three powers to the end of the list of *Sefirot*, while in other texts the three powers are added to the top, or are considered to be intellectual lights shining within the first *Sefirah*. This view, which stimulated many speculations as the development of the Kabbalah continued, occurs in the responsa attributed to Hai Gaon on the relationship of the ten *Sefirot* to the 13 attributes. . . . There it is stated that, above all emanated powers, there exist in "the root of all roots" three hidden lights which have no beginning, "for they are the name and essence of the root of all roots and are beyond the grasp of thought". . . . It is stressed that these three lights constitute one essence and one root which is "infinitely hidden"

(*ne'lam ad le-ein sof*), forming a kind of kabbalistic trinity that precedes the emanation of the ten *Sefirot*. However, it is not sufficiently clear whether the reference is to three lights between the Emanator and the first emanation, or to three lights irradiating one another within the substance of the Emanator itself—both possibilities can be supported. In the terminology of the Kabbalah these three lights are called *zahzahot* ("splendors"), and they are thought of as the roots of the three upper *Sefirot* which emanate from them (see Cordovero, *Pardes Rimmonim*, ch. 11). The need to posit this strange trinity is explained by the urge to make the ten Sefirot conform with the 13 attributes predicated of God. . . . Cordovero interprets the three *zahzahot* mentioned above as the three hidden *behinot* of *Keter* in *Ein-Sof*.[3]

The need to posit the trinity of Tzachtzachot as either three Sefirot above the ten or as the supernal roots of the upper three Sefirot or of just the first Sefirah, the various theories involving the Three Splendors, need not be explained, however, as Scholem does in terms of an "urge to make the ten Sefirot conform with the 13 attributes predicated of God." Rather, it can be explained on the basis of the geometry underlying kabbalistic cosmology, a geometry that was probably filtered through the mystic revelations of influential figures of the Merkabah and later kabbalistic traditions, but may have derived from their own geometric practice, and, in any case, is fully displayed in the Sabbath Star Diagram, in particular in its octave culmination.

It was shown in chapter 7, also on the octave diagram, that the number thirteen is related to the octave diagram insofar as it is the product of just thirteen added construction elements. The significance of this number in the texts of the *Sefer ha-'Iyyun* circle seemed particularly relevant to the emergence of this number in the construction of the octave diagram. Now again in the more detailed study of the octave matrix, we see how its three added macrohexagrams can be taken as signifying three added Sefirot beyond Keter, thus raising the number of such Sefirot to the thirteen postulated by some members of the *Sefer ha-'Iyyun* circle and later

developed into the concept of the Three Splendors beyond but related to the Tree of Sefirot.

We can also see why the various theorists concerned with this question were at pains both to associate their hidden lights with the upper Tree and yet to distinguish them as more closely involved with the very substance of Ein Sof. For as the diagram shows, these three macrohexagrams are, indeed, both above the upper portion of the Tree and yet a part of the seventh world of Ein Sof. They are, in fact, the part of the full seventh-world macrostructure that alone can be viewed from the two possibilities suggested by the Hai Gaon responsa, that is, both as "three lights between the Emanator and the first emanation, or . . . three lights irradiating one another within the substance of the Emanator itself." Viewed from the perspective of the octave diagram, they appear between the Emanator and the first emanation; but viewed from the perspective of the complete seventh-world diagram, they merge indistinguishably with the substance of Ein Sof that its fuller matrix can be said to signify. It is the double character given to these three macrohexagrams by their appearance in both the more delimited octave diagram and the full diagram of the seventh world that, while making them infinitely more hidden then the macrohexagram-Sefirot of the sixth-world diagram, yet makes them thus far apprehensible by thought that they can be named. They are still constituents of the cosmic octave, which the surrounding substance of Ein Sof is not.

Association of the three matrix macrohexagrams of the octave with the Tzachtzachot, as with the association of the lowest macrohexagram beyond the octave circle of the Tzimtzum with Da'at in chapter 11, has been made possible because their proximity to the Spiral Tree permits the transfer of such kabbalistic designations as are appropriate to their precise locations. But beyond these lowest definable elements, the terminology of the traditional Tree ceases to be relevant to the seventh-world matrix. Indeed, the whole of the seventh-world diagram, its construction as well as matrix elements, no longer seems expressive of this central model of the classical Kabbalah. Where the Tree provided the primary interpretive key to the first six worlds of the diagram, its seventh world would seem to place this kabbalistic focus within the context of a larger tradition of Jewish esoteric thought. In this and the following chapter, the forms and numbers generated by the geometry of the seventh-world diagram seem related primarily to a cosmology rooted in the central events and principles of the Bible, particularly of Genesis and Ezekiel, a priestly cosmology that took clear shape in the biblical and intertestamental apocalyptic works whose core meaning has continued to inform the mystical heart of Judaism in all its forms, the understanding that the purpose of cosmic evolution is just such a generation of the divine son as is hinted at in the Gematria of the son (Ben = 52) that emerges in consideration of the Double Spiral Tree, one that the remaining sections of this chapter as well as the next will strongly confirm to be the final revelation of this work.

THE DOUBLE SPIRAL TREE: REDEMPTION THROUGH THE OTHER SIDE

It is the talmudic-kabbalistic concept of the light reserved for the righteous that will provide our entry into an understanding of the Double Spiral Tree. The talmudic concept of the light treasured up for the righteous was traced from its biblical source (Psalm 97:11) to its Midrashic explication (*Shemos Rabbah* 35:1) in the final section of chapter 11, in connection with the original analysis of matrix light units. As will be remembered, it was through this concept that the soul, which had completed its ascension through the Spiral Tree and earned 25 light units, could be associated with the Gematria number 26 of the Tetragrammaton, an association that could further relate this fully realized Neshamah soul to such an angelic being as Metatron, the transfigured form of the formerly human Enoch, to whom the biblical statement "My Name is in Him"[4] was applied in the *Shi'ur Komah*. This earlier discussion showed that there are two ways in which this number of light units could be gained by the soul that had completed its progress through the Spiral Tree, depending on whether the fourth world was past or future modeled.[5] But in either case, it would involve an involution to the matrix center, its collective macrohexagram being further understood to be worth the 10 light units that could be associated with the original source of the Sefirot. Since this matrix center can be associated with the beginning of creation, at least of its expansive phase, the geometry of the diagram would seem to be coherent with the midrashic myth that the light reserved for the righteous was the original light from the time of creation, hidden since then from the wicked, and this myth can be used reciprocally to interpret the diagram, guided by the further development of this concept in the Zohar.

To its quotations from Psalms and the Midrash, the *Zohar* adds a new theoretical twist in interpreting the concept of the light treasured up for the righteous:

> Rabbi Yitshἰak said, "The light created by the blessed Holy One in the act of Creation flared from one end of the universe to the other, and was hidden away. Why was it hidden away? So the wicked of the world would not enjoy it, nor the worlds enjoy it because of them. It is preserved for the righteous—for the righteous, precisely, as it is written: *Light is sown for the righteous, joy for the upright in heart* (Psalms 97:11). Then the worlds will be fragrant and all will be one. But until the day when the world that is coming arrives, it is preserved, treasured away.
>
> "That light radiated from the midst of darkness hewn by truncheons of the Concealed of All, until a single secret path was carved by the hidden light, leading to darkness below, where light dwells. Who is darkness below? The one called *Night*, of whom is written: *And the darkness He called Night* (Genesis 1:5). So we have learned: *Revealing depths out of darkness* (Job 12:22).[6]

Though the primordial light treasured up for the righteous is only good, it is from this stored up light that "a single secret path was carved by the hidden light, leading to darkness below, where light dwells" If we can interpret this understanding of light in darkness as meaning that the "secret path" to the "darkness below, where light dwells" is through the portion of light that the righteous will come to inherit in "the world that is coming," then we can begin to chart the further journey of the righteous soul after it has gained the reward of this light. In terms of the Sabbath Star Diagram matrix, the reward that comes through involution to the source of the collective macrohexagram also opens a door to the Other Side, to the side of the red-scarlet Spiral Tree that contains its own profound meanings, "*Revealing depths out of darkness.*" And it opens the door as well to the kabbalistic concept of the Kelipot.

A central concern of the Lurianic Kabbalah is the redemption of the holy sparks that have fallen into the power of the Kelipot as a result of the Shevirah, another way of referring to the Zoharic light residing in the darkness of the lower world. As Vital presents this doctrine: "Know that through Adam's sin all souls fell into the depths of the *qelippoth*. . . . Therefore the Shekhinah . . . descended among them in order to gather in the soul-sparks, . . . to sift them [from the *qelippoth*], to raise them to the sphere of holiness, and to renew them."[7] The need to raise the sparks from the Kelipot, a necessary condition for the fulfillment of the Lurianic Tikkun, resulted in two opposing approaches among later Messianic Kabbalists, particularly among the followers of Sabbatai Tz'vi. As the Sabbatian Nehemiah Hayon explained: "It is supposed among those versed in esoteric lore that the redemption can be brought about in either one of two ways: either Israel will have the power to withdraw all the sparks of holiness from [the realm of] the *kelipah* so that the *kelipah* will wither into nothing, or else the *kelipah* will become so filled with holiness that because of this repletion it must be spewn forth."[8] Both approaches can be demonstrated by the Sabbath Star Diagram.

On the one hand, we can postulate that the soul that has successfully overcome all the temptations in its path and reached the height of Keter has now only to be transfigured into the Cherub and fly aloft to communion with the divine. This can, indeed, be taken as one definition offered by the Sabbath Star Diagram for the level of soul above the Neshamah level of the Spiral Tree, that of the Chayah soul. It is particularly appropriate so to identify it since this is the level of the Chayot, the Living Creatures of

Ezekiel's Throne vision that provide one definition of the Cherubic forms manifested by the octave matrix. But to make this simple passage the end of the spiritual journey is to deny the relevance of the opposite path of involution to the Other Side that we shall now see to provide the most satisfying version of the Tikkun offered by the diagram.

Before turning to study of the Double Spiral Tree, it will be necessary to trace some further ramifications of Sabbatian theory, since it comes closest to illuminating this aspect of the diagram.* This is not to say that the Sabbatians or Sabbatai himself fulfilled or properly understood this theory. Indeed, Sabbatai is an exemplar of the false Messiah who crosses prematurely to the Other Side in the fifth world rather than after completion of the sixth. As expounded by Sabbatai and his leading exponents, Nathan of Gaza and Abraham Cardozo, the Sabbatian doctrine of redemption introduces a new element into the Jewish concept of the Messiah. In Scholem's summary, as long as the divine sparks have not been released from the Kelipot.

> the process of redemption is incomplete. It is therefore left to the Redeemer, the holiest of men, to accomplish what not even the most righteous souls in the past have been able to do: to descend through the gates of impurity into the realm of the *kelipot* and to rescue the divine sparks still imprisoned there. As soon as this task is performed the Kingdom of Evil will collapse of itself, for its existence is made possible only by the divine sparks in its midst.[9]

The apostasy of Sabbatai to Islam, and later of Jacob Frank to Catholicism, which this doctrine can so well explain, is not, however, crucial to the understanding of a Messiah whose primary task it is to enter the Other Side and rescue the souls imprisoned there. Indeed, Nathan of Gaza had developed

---

*Much of the first half of this section, covering the topics of Sabbatian and Jungian theory as well as the treatment of Jacob and Esau in the context of the kabbalistic concept of the "Other Side," appeared earlier in *The Kabbalah of the Soul*, pp. 275–86.

its main tenets in a significant work of Sabbatian theology written before the apostasy, the *Treatise on the Dragons*, part of which is summarized as follows by Scholem:

> When the light substance of *En-Sof* entered the *tehiru* in a straight line . . . not the whole *tehiru* was affected by the irruption of the ray of light from En-Sof. The "straight line" penetrated only the upper half of the primordial space (which should be pictured as a sphere), and there built the world of its "thought"; it did not reach the lower half, described by Nathan as "the deep of the great abyss." The great work of cosmic *tiqqun*, which Israel has to accomplish through the strength of the Law and the divine commandments, relates to the upper part of the *tehiru* only. The lower part persists in its unformed and chaotic condition (*golem*), dominated by the *qelippah* until the advent of the messiah, who alone can perfect it. As a matter of fact, the thought-less lights too built worlds unto themselves, to wit the demonic worlds of the *qelippah*, whose sole intent is to destroy the worlds of the thought-some light. . . . In the context of this doctrine, the Zoharic designation of the sphere of evil . . . refers to the "other side" of *En-Sof* itself, that is, to that half of it which resists the process of differentiation and organization, and which, by its very resistance to the dramatic process of creation, becomes actually Satanic.[10]

Nathan's cosmology comes closest to being a description of the Double Spiral Tree, shown in plate 15, whose turquoise spiral may be associated with the thought-some light of creative evolution and its scarlet spiral with the thought-less light that resists the creative process.

The first thing that can be said upon viewing the Double Spiral Tree in its full-colored form is that it is this form of the matrix Tree that has the greatest meaning and beauty, the perfect symmetry of its ovoid form revealing the central truth of sacred science, the necessity of integrating complementary opposites into a balanced whole. It follows that if this Double Spiral Tree is to be identified with the Chayah level of the soul, then this soul level must be vitally concerned with the Other Side of its spiritual development. For Nathan of Gaza's principle point is that the Tikkun cannot be completed through the positive path of spiritual discipline alone, that the perfected soul must then enter the "gates of impurity" both to complete its own development and to redeem the weaker souls imprisoned there. Nathan of Gaza's "thought-some" and "thought-less" light may perhaps be related to the modern psychological categories of the conscious and the unconscious self, and these to the turquoise and scarlet sides, respectively, of the Double Spiral Tree. The identification of the scarlet side with the unconscious portion of the psyche can be extended to include the Jungian concept of the Shadow. Jung defines this concept in his discussion of the psychic opposition between archetype and instinct:

> But, just as between all opposites there obtains so close a bond that no position can be established or even thought of without its corresponding negation, so in this case also "les extrêmes se touchent." They belong together as correspondences. . . . True opposites are never incommensurables; if they were they could never unite. . . . These counter-positions . . . form the twin poles of that psychic one-sidedness which is typical of the normal man of today. . . . but the one-sidedness . . . can be removed by what I have called the "realization of the shadow.". . . the growing awareness of the inferior part of the personality, which should not be twisted into an intellectual activity, for it has far more the meaning of a suffering and a passion that implicate the whole man. The essence of that which has to be realized and assimilated has been expressed so trenchantly and so plastically in poetic language by the word "shadow" that it would be almost presumptuous not to avail oneself of this linguistic heritage. . . . The "man without a shadow" is statistically the commonest human type, one who imagines he actually *is* only what he cares to know about himself.[11]

For Jung, the development of the "whole man" requires his "realization of the shadow," that part of him he had not previously cared to know about himself and therefore repressed, with grave consequences to his psychic health and spiritual evolution. At some point, due either to psychological distress or spiritual stagnation, the individual will need to confront this Shadow if he is to progress to a greater sense of wholeness, both with himself and with the cosmos. Some such confrontation and working through this repressed material is desirable at various stages in the process of maturation, but since the witness of the diagram is that this Negative Tree continues its hidden growth in pace with the flourishing Tree above, what the diagram seems now to be telling us through the short count of the light-unit values, the need of the Neshamah soul to return to its point of origin to gain the reward of the hidden light, is that the point at which this confrontation becomes imperative is exactly at the crowning point of the Spiral Tree.

The soul of man, having followed the turquoise lateral spiral to the top of its Spiral Tree, may now be considered to be carried aloft by the Cherub atop this Tree. Here another aspect of the Jewish esoteric tradition, though again in a talmudic formulation, becomes relevant. This is the concept of the "Kaf ha-Kela," the sling or catapult, that appears in *Tractate Shabbath* (152b):

> It was taught, R. Eliezer said: The souls of the righteous are hidden under the Throne of Glory, as it is said, *yet the soul of my lord shall be bound up in the bundle of life* [I Sam. 25:29]. But those of the wicked continue to be imprisoned, while one angel stands at one end of the world and a second stands at the other end, and they sling their souls to each other, for it is said, *and the souls of thine enemies, them shall he sling out, as from the hollow of a sling* [I Sam. 25:29].[12]

This concept of the Kaf ha-Kela, of two angels standing at opposite ends of the world to sling the soul between them, has obvious relevance to the Cherubic diagram before us, particularly as interpreted by Rabbi Zalman Schachter-Shalomi to refer not necessarily to the wicked but rather to the insufficiently purified soul:

> All the sounds that a person has heard during his life continue to vibrate within his soul following his death. . . . He is, thus, unable to . . . receive the angelic or heavenly voices. . . . In order to rid the soul of this "dust," it is shaken in the *Kaf ha-Kela*, the Catapult. The sages say that "two angels stand at each end of the world and toss the soul from one to the other." It is almost as if the angels try to rid the soul of its accumulated psychic dust by putting it through a cosmic centrifuge until only pure soul remains. Were this treatment not administered to the soul, however, it would be unable to silence all the sense images and noises that were carried with it from this world and would have to wander in the world of Tohu . . . for ages.[13]

When we are told by the talmudic sages of the two angels at opposite ends of the world who sling the soul back and forth, it is hard to believe they have not been contemplating the Sabbath Star Diagram. For there in figure 12.1, atop the branches of the Double Cherub-Tree, we may project a vision of those two angels standing at each end of the world, with the turquoise Cherub ready to toss the just crowned Neshamah soul to the scarlet Cherub a world away. We may even discern the path of this catapulted soul. Having risen to Keter via the turquoise lateral spiral, it would now take the more direct returning route through the blue central spiral to Malkhut, where its stored up portion of light awaits it, and from there on through the red spiral to the arms of the scarlet Cherub. So powerful is the catapult by which the turquoise Cherub may be thought to send the soul flying that it can appear to make no stay at Malkhut, passing more brightly lit through its revolving doorway to the Other Side, a divine representative from whose twenty-six light units the holy Name shines forth.

It is here that Sabbatian theory falters in its understanding of the redemptive role to be played on the Other Side and that the Sabbath Star Diagram can provide a corrective. For to continue its progress through the path of the scarlet lateral spiral, the soul must now proceed *backward* from Keter to Malkhut, gently placed there, we may suppose, by the scarlet Cherub who caught it, after first carrying it at least to what is now the depth of the Sabbath Star for the upper Do. Though this backward path is opposite to that taken by the turquoise spiral, this does not mean that the soul's behavior must be opposite to that commanded in its earlier positive path, that "the old rabbinic concept of *mitzvah ha-ba'ah ba-averah*, literally, 'a commandment which is fulfilled by means of a transgression,'"[14] need be interpreted, with the Sabbatians, as commanding such transgression. The backward path would rather seem to involve the *undoing* of whatever was inscribed in the forward passage of this scarlet spiral. If we can consider the Negative Spiral Tree to be the Shadow of its positive mate, and to contain a living record of whatever was repressed by the soul in its upward spiritual journey, then the forward passage through the scarlet spiral occurred as a mirror reflection of the soul's similar passage through the turquoise spiral.

But this mirror was more like the picture kept by Dorian Grey in his closet, which Oscar Wilde imagined as visually recording all of Dorian's corruption. All such hidden corruption or repressed desires retain their potency as long as they are not confronted, and they exercise a power to tie the soul to the earth as with knots. Before the soul can be released from such "sense images and noises," as Rabbi Schachter-Shalomi puts it, it must untie each of these knots. It was for this reason that, in the language of the diagram, the redeemed soul that had earned its spiritual crown had to be catapulted from the upper to the lower world, from what was open to the light of consciousness to what was hidden in the unconscious, that it could undo all that still captivated the soul and release itself from its Tohu of unresolved confusion. For from the point of view of the soul, only the turquoise spiral has been made manifest, the scarlet remaining in the realm of Tohu in which it had earlier been encountered in the fifth world. Not only must the crowned Neshamah soul redeem itself from the knots of unresolved conflict that have lain dormant there but also those other Ruach souls that passed there beyond the fifth-world matrix border and have since been imprisoned among the Kelipot of the chaotic Other Side.

It is these ensnared souls that the perfected Neshamah soul can redeem insofar as they may be considered parts of its larger identity, its soul root. An important element in the kabbalistic doctrine of the soul, as Scholem has shown, is that "there is an inner bond, a kind of sympathy of souls, linking all sparks deriving from the same root, and they—and they only—can help one another and influence one another for their mutual *tiqqun*."[15] It is not enough, then, for the perfected Neshamah soul to fly to Devekut. It must also return to the lowest depths of the fallen world and play a redemptive role in the general Tikkun, one that its special affinities uniquely fit it to perform. This movement to the role of Redeemer occurs on the purely spiritual dimension of the World to Come and marks the progression of the soul to its Chayah level. Thus by helping those weaker souls who gave in to rather than resisting the impulses of the Shadow self, the redeeming soul expands its own capacities and furthers its own Tikkun.

But the movement to the Other Side is not solely a work of grace. It is also necessary to perfect the Chayah soul through the further spiritual work of self-redemption. And it is only the perfected Neshamah soul that can safely engage in this work in view of that development of character that is the hallmark of this soul level, the level of the true master soul. With such strength of character and crowning wisdom, the soul can begin what Jung has called "the realization of the shadow," realization, one may suppose, in its double senses of growing awareness and emerging reality. For as the soul grows in its awareness of its own implication in the Other Side, its Shadow life begins to be exchanged for the true vitality that characterizes the Chayah soul, the full vitality only possible to the whole self. Thus in making the return journey through the scarlet spiral, the Chayah soul also redeems this path from Tohu and brings it to manifestation as a necessary part of what now becomes the Double Spiral Tree.

The journey through the reverse Spiral Tree, which culminates the path of the Chayah soul, begins at just the point that completed the path of the Neshamah soul, at its blue crown, from which it is catapulted to the Shadow crown of the red Keter.

There the repressed presumption to infinite knowledge, earlier identified with the final blue Bohu beyond the sixth-world matrix border, is exposed to the light of Chayah consciousness and its lingering hold on the soul released. Beginning with the most recent and retracing its path to its earliest contributions to the shadow side, the Chayah soul relives all the conscious and unconscious distress it suffered in its earlier conformity to the difficult Abrahamic path demanded of the *tzaddik* by God: "walk before me, and be thou perfect" (Gen. 17:1). But it does it now not with the ignorance of the outward journey, rather with the wisdom born of seeing the completed pattern. For as the Neshamah soul is traditionally associated with Binah, so is the Chayah soul associated with Chokhmah, Wisdom.

These traditional associations are most appropriate to the implications of the Double Spiral Tree. For Binah, the articulating rational side of consciousness, is appropriately associated with what can be considered the "solar" upward spiral and Chokhmah, the intuitive irrational side, with the "lunar" downward spiral, and this despite their apparent inversion of gender connotations. These dual Spiral Trees can also be associated with the figures of Jacob and Esau,[16] biblical archetypes of polar opposition for which the talmudic sages foresaw an ultimate reconciliation. Though the brothers were reconciled in the Bible, the failure of Jacob to fulfill his promise to Esau that he would "come unto my lord unto Seir" (Gen. 33:14) became a source of Messianic allegory in the later tradition. As J. H. Hertz notes: "There is no record that Jacob went to Seir to see his brother. But, add the Rabbis, Jacob will yet visit Esau in the day of the Messiah when the reconciliation between Israel and Edom will be complete."[17] For if Jacob waxes in biblical time, the time of this world, Esau's true value will only become apparent at that future perfection projected by both prophet and sage. At that time, what formerly had to be rigidly rejected as dangerous to proper growth and so evil can be reembraced as a necessary part of the higher good.[18]

As the Chayah soul completes the lower spiral back to the collective source, it can view all its formerly repressed desires and resentments in the light of that hard won wisdom whose present state of ease and fulfillment can make all such past bitterness seem foolishly trivial and so lose its force. It has not only achieved the liberation of those soul sparks of its own root that had been trapped in a purgatory of blasted delusions but of those parts of its own identity also held hostage there until they could be exposed to the light, and it experiences a greater and greater sense of its liberation in this process of expanding awareness. This process may be compared with the *tandra* state of which yogis speak, the state in which the unconscious, even in deep sleep, is opened to and experienced with full conscious awareness. In the Chayah soul, what was formerly lost in an unconscious Tohu, a "thought-less light" insofar as thought is equated with consciousness, has been redeemed to conscious thought and redeemed through a process that heals its pain. Since whatever Jacob gained through his aggressive attachment to the upward thrust of his evolution was at the cost of his twin brother's suffering, his upward spiral cannot proceed further until he can recognize his functional identity with his brother, that every wrong done another is also a wrong done oneself since it builds an immediate Providential or karmic liability that will eventually have to be discharged. Thus the suffering Esau is the true soul twin or Shadow self of Jacob, and Jacob can only proceed higher by finally involuting, by taking the downward path that can now release Esau, his Shadow self, to take the upward reverse path through his scarlet spiral.

From this perspective, then, there is nothing on the Other Side but the passion of passively suffering the sins of the world, and one moves to the Other Side not to do sin, since this can only increase this suffering, but to undo it, to undo its inhibiting effects on further soul growth. But in undoing the negative effects of sin, the soul also benefits from the suffering it caused, gaining heightened sensitivity and increased capacity to exist in the purely spiritual realm. For the shadow side of conscious awareness does exist on a plane free from all the limitations of the space-time coordinates of material existence. It functions in the realm of pure, nonlinguistic imagination with perfect ease and considerable power, something the conscious self can do far less effectively. And this capacity is one it must acquire if it is to continue effective existence on the "other side" of material reality. But if Jacob needs Esau to teach him the pathways to spiritual power, Esau needs Jacob even more. The Shadow side, while not losing its superior spiritual technology, needs to be raised to conscious self-control, to be enlightened.

The Double Spiral Tree can be read on two levels, on that of the higher soul dimensions of the World to Come and on the dimension of ordinary human psychology. Clearly, there are implications for human psychology in what has just been developed, implications Jung and other psychoanalysts have already explored quite fully. But what the present analysis can contribute to an understanding of such therapeutic probings of the hidden side of consciousness is a note of caution. Bringing repressed materials up to an undeveloped consciousness is inviting exactly the same misapplication of such information as was historically expressed through the Sabbatians. This is the false belief that only harm can come from repression and that every desire or feeling must be given an overt outlet. While harm does come from all forms of repression, this harm may be outweighed by the good deriving from it, the space it gives for other more slowly developing fruits to be nurtured and for the social agents necessary for such husbandry. But when that fruit has ripened and the soul developed sufficient strength and wisdom, then the reconciliation with the negated self must be made and its silent suffering ended. So it is wise to delay the reconciliation with the Shadow self until all aspects of the self have matured. Jacob did not visit Esau in Seir when it seemed so close, just over the fifth-world matrix border. He went "according as the cattle that goeth before me and the children be able to endure" (Gen. 33:14), at the slower pace of the upward lateral spiral that would allow for a more natural purification of the animal nature and outgrowing of the inner child.

Though there are some mature individuals who can profit from such an exploration and embrace of the Other Side in this life, for whom it can ease the various rites of passage, this process remains a necessity for the purely otherworldly work of the soul and is its primary rite of passage from the sixth to the seventh world, from the Neshamah to the Chayah dimension of the soul.

Just as a partial "realization of the shadow" can take place in this life, unblocking the system for the further growth of self-realization, so it might be thought to take place between lifetimes at lower soul levels, as shall later be discussed; but it is only when the Neshamah crown has been earned that the soul can complete the entire journey through the Double Spiral Tree and be doubly rewarded, receiving first the portion of light stored up for the turquoise-blue spiral and then that stored up for the scarlet-red spiral, as it arrives at last, but also again, at the storehouse of Malkhut's plenty.

In achieving its second reward after having passed through another Spiral Tree, the soul may now be thought to have doubled its earlier count of light units from 26 to 52. This is again a significant number in kabbalistic numerology; for it is the number of one of the four expansions of the Tetragrammaton—named Ab, Sag, Mah, and Ben—which Luria understood to be the higher source of the individual letters of the Tetragrammaton and of the four worlds and Partzufim with which these letters have been correlated. What distinguishes these four expansions of the Tetragrammaton is the way in which its four letters are spelled out as words, Ab being expanded with Yods, Sag with a combination of Yods and Aleph, Mah with Alephs, and Ben with Heys. It is the Gematria totals of these expansions that are given the names of the letters that signify these numerical sums. The first is called Ab because its numerical equivalent, 72, is signified by the letter-numbers Ayin (= 70) and Bet (= 2). Similarly Sag (= 63) is compounded of Samakh (= 60) and Gimel (= 3), Mah (= 45) of Mem (= 40) and Hey (= 5), and Ben (= 52) of Bet (= 2) and Nun (= 50). It is this last with which we are now particularly concerned.

As can be seen, the Tetragrammaton expansion called Ben does not follow the regular sequence of the upper three expansions; it is out of the numerical sequence, being a higher number than that of

Mah just above it, and it reverses the order of the units and tens followed in those upper expansions, all of which are also multiples of 9. This would suggest that the equation Ben = 52 had a different source from the orderly progression of the upper three expansions and subsequently became associated with them when the theoretical need arose for such a fourth expansion.[19] At the moment it is only the verbal meaning of Ben that is of interest, this being the Hebrew word for "son."

The equation of the number 52 with the verbal connotation of its signifying letter-numbers, son, is important to the present analysis because this number has appeared here for the first time in the interpretation of the Sabbath Star Diagram and in a context that has associations with the secret doctrine of the son I developed in an earlier book.[20] As we have just seen, the count of light units for the Double Spiral Tree is 52, and this form of the matrix Tree is equated with the Chayah soul as that is with the octave portion of the seventh-world diagram. But as we shall see in chapter 13, this number and the concept of the son reappears in yet another way to become the final revelation of the seventh-world diagram.

In my earlier extended analysis of the Gematria equation Ben = 52, this number was shown to have an astronomical connotation of particular significance for its present consideration in terms of the geometry of the seventh world of the Sabbath Star Diagram. To summarize that earlier analysis, what was shown is that the concept of the son is related to the ability to count the fifty-two Sabbaticals of the solar year. It is again a sign of the uncanny intelligence of this diagram that the number 52 should be a feature only of its Sabbatical world, and this not only with respect to the light unit count for the Double Spiral Tree of the Chayah soul but also for another counting of light units related to the Yechidah soul in chapter 13. In fact, the equation of Ben = 52 will prove to be the most significant key to an understanding of the seventh world, enabling us to recognize both the Chayah and Yechidah souls as exemplars of such sons of the World to Come as hold the key to the *Shi'ur Komah*.[21] But from what has just been developed, we can say that the per-

fected Chayah soul, which has completed the Double Spiral Tree and earned precisely 52 light units by passing twice through Malkhut, thus achieves a second generation and can truly be called a "Ben Adam," son of man, a son of Adam Kadmon of the World to Come. What its nature may be we are now to learn through further examination of the geometry of the Double Spiral Tree.

In contrast to the Neshamah soul, which can be identified with only a single Spiral Tree, the Chayah soul comprehends both halves of the Double Spiral Tree, not just the Negative Tree. It both includes and understands itself as a whole made up of inverse but complementary halves. It understands that each action has an equal and opposite reaction and that both must be embraced as authentic aspects of any whole, especially of its own self. Thus after it has brought to light the desires and resentments it had previously repressed in its upward spiritual quest, and liberated the whole soul from the knots of guilt and pain that had silently afflicted it and impeded its further progress, the perfected Chayah soul is now able to recognize the just claims of the Other Side and give them some form of temperate expression. The Chayah soul recognizes that impulses from the Other Side are also God-sent, and that, since it is from the Other Side of God that they are ultimately derived, they cannot be evil. The Tikkun of the Other Side has accomplished its restoration to divine goodness.

Since the limited perspective of the lower soul levels could see only evil in such impulses and rightly so, as their very naturalness sought to chain the soul to the Nefesh level of the animal soul, it could only exaggerate the baneful effects of indulgence and by so doing pervert nature into sin. Once nature had been so perverted, the claims of the natural self could only be satisfied at much greater spiritual cost, warping the soul whether through indulgence or abstinence. But when the soul has finally reached the state where it can begin what Jung calls the "realization of the shadow," it can perceive nature as a divine garment, can feel, in the words of Vaughan, "through all this fleshly dress / Bright *shoots* of everlastingness."[22] Animated by such a constant sense of divine influx, the Law becomes internalized and all its impulses can only be holy. This is not simply a semantic license to sin, as the Sabbatians would have had it, but involves a rectification of the impulses so that they will not desire what is injurious either to the self or to others. But such rectification can only be accomplished through confronting the Other Side and redeeming it from a false dualism. By being able to discern what is truly evil and what actually good on that side, one can redeem the sparks of spirit that have become trapped in the Kelipot of a soulless materialism, dissolving this evil and leaving only holiness to the Other Side.

That the Double Spiral Tree is holy in all its parts is a conclusion one can draw by observing it again with the path of its spiral involution drawn upon it, a geometric process that here, as previously, yields a most expressive form. To recapitulate the earlier discussions of such movement lines, we have seen that for the fourth-world matrix an expressive form emerges if the soul's path is defined as moving out through the lateral system and back through the central system; its expressive form is that of a circle of simple return to the source. The even more startling soul path formed by this method in the fifth world is that figure 8 which, in its horizontal form, has been accepted as the sign of infinity. This is particularly significant since the highest point of Ruach development is marked by the Sefirah Netzach whose meaning is Eternity. The graphic expression of temporal eternity is thus spatial infinity, and this emergence of the infinity sign at the soul level associated with Netzach encodes the essential truth about the Ruach soul, in what would seem to be another uncanny example of the oracular power of the diagram, that it contains the guarantee of soul survival, of Eternity. But perhaps the most expressive form of all is that produced by this method in the Double Spiral Tree, a seamless line that unites the two halves in a soul embrace.

Though connected, the spiral line drawn through the two halves of the Double Spiral Tree in figure 12.2 seems to define two separate soul bodies or Tzelemim. For the same figure that defines one complete Chayah soul may also be considered to comprise two complementary Neshamah souls. It is on the Neshamah level, then, that true soul mating

can occur, and when true soul mates embrace—even at the Nefesh or Ruach stages of their developments—it seems likely that their Neshamah Yetirot, "additional souls," are aroused to participate in a higher soul mating. Such a mating is threefold, the lateral spiral weaving around the Yesodot of the two partners, each interpenetrating the same central Malkhut in their midst, with its suggestively similar yin-yang form of cosmic harmonizing. It is of such a mating that the Bible says: "a threefold cord is not quickly broken" (Eccles. 4:12).

As each Yesod-defining curve also seems to be penetrating its mate's body, so is the position of Netzach in each of these soul bodies equally telling; for in each case Netzach is *in* the soul body of the Other. If figure 12.2 is compared with plate 15, it can be seen that the red Netzach allied with the Positive Tree becomes part of the Tzelem of the Negative Tree and the blue Netzach allied with the Negative Tree becomes incorporated as well in the Positive Tzelem It was to this feature of the involuting double spiral that reference was earlier made in defining the Ruach heart, signified by Netzach, as in the body of the Other. And it is a most telling detail of the matrix geometry, serving to explain the intuitive sympathy, the understanding of the Ruach heart. It is this intimate heart knowledge of the Other through sympathetic inhabiting of the partner's soul body that creates the higher Ruach joining of a couple through love. To this threefold physical joining on the Nefesh level and mutual inhabiting of the other on the level of Ruach love, the Neshamah soul adds an overarching presence, the grace-bestowing power of the very soul level that connects the individual with the divine.

But what are two connected soul bodies on the Neshamah level, connected in their physical bodies, their hearts, and souls, become, on the Chayah level, a new soul, the soul of the relationship created by true soul mating. It is to achieve this ecstatic higher unity that soul mates seek each other out, for only when the two souls are so joined can the complementary energies flow and recharge in a manner mutually empowering that brings each half to its highest level of potentiality and fulfills the purpose of their relationship, the generation of the Chayah

Figure 12.2. The Movement Line through the Double Spiral Tree

soul that joins them. And as the Chayah soul is that which ultimately binds two lovers, so is it at this level that the individual soul can embrace its own inner opposite and achieve its perfection.

In terms of sacred geometry, the Spiral Tree defines only part of the cosmic spiritual process, a process that can only be completed through the double spiral formed by reentry into the vortex. Jill Purce has developed this concept at length:

In so far as the archetypal flow and growth form assumed by the mushroom, the embryo and the brain embody a forward impulse which turns back on itself, they demonstrate the forming of a vortex ring. . . .It is from the involution of the unformed waters that the egg crystallizes by the turning in on itself of energy. . . . But the right way back to the beginning is by going on. . . . The universal spherical vortex can be seen as that which issues from the point, and contains it. . . .

328   A NEW MODEL FOR KABBALISTIC SOUL PSYCHOLOGY

The opposing solar and lunar currents symbolized by the serpents [on the caduceus] are the alternating forces of expansion and contraction, manifested in the two halves of the Yin Yang symbol or the two halves of the double spiral or the world egg, and constituting, when joined, the spherical vortex. . . . one of our foremost cosmologists, J. A. Wheeler, describes how the very structure of our universe is none other than the vortex ring—a manifestation of the universal spherical vortex.[23]

Purce speaks repeatedly of the egg form in relation to spiral involution, and the Double Spiral Tree is indeed ovoid in shape, an emblem, of the "world egg." So too does the lateral spiral, in turning in to Keter and then down to Malkhut, "embody a forward impulse which turns back on itself . . . forming . . . a vortex ring." Though it can be associated both with the new physics of Wheeler and the old Taoism of the yin-yang symbol, the continuous double-spiral path of the Chayah soul has yet a distinctive shape and beauty, meeting yet still diverging and each half turning around to observe the "back parts" of the other with what appears to be a benign grace, almost a maternal devotion.

The Double Spiral Tree illustrated in figure 12.2 with its movement line is meaningful in itself, equally defining the self's union with its Shadow, its soul mate, and its cosmic habitat. But it is an incomplete depiction of the cumulative octave matrix since it lacks its remaining Cherub-Trees that we are now to consider in relation to one of the great mysteries of the Jewish esoteric tradition, the Measure of the Body.

THE SIXFOLD CHERUB TREE AND THE MEASURE OF THE BODY

We come now to the crowning analysis of the matrix as a kabbalistic model for the "Measure of the Body," a phrase signified by the title of an important Merkabah text we are shortly to explore, the *Shi'ur Komah*. This text asserts that it is precisely this measurement of the divine body filling the cosmos that can "assure" the spiritual aspirant of being "a

son of the world to come."[24] Again, and for the second time, we see how the seventh-world diagram can be correlated with what I have called "the secret doctrine of the son," the doctrine I have shown to be at the heart of the Jewish esoteric tradition and that becomes the ultimate revelation of the Sabbath Star Diagram. And we have yet to encounter a third and most important such correlation in chapter 13.

Let us begin our study of the Measure of the Body by seeing how the *Shi'ur Komah* associates the solution of this mystery with what I have defined as the secret doctrine of the son:

> Rabbi Yishmael said: Metatron the Great Lord said to me: I bear this testimony on behalf of YHVH, Elohim of Israel . . . that . . . His total height [is] 236 ten thousand thousands parasangs. . . . It is said that he who knows this mystery, is assured of his portion in the world to come (is assured to be a son of the world to come). . . . Rabbi Yishmael said to me in the presence of his pupils. I and Rabbi Aquiba vouch for this, that whoever knows this measure of our Creator, and the praise of the Holy One, blessed be He, he will surely be a son of the world to come, provided he learns it regularly every day. . . .[25]

Though the translators here indicate the equation of the phrase "son of the world to come" with the concept of the portion reserved for and to be inherited by the righteous in the World to Come, and this connotation has been substituted for the more literal rendering "son of the world to come" in some translations, the phrase "*ben ha-olam ha-ba*" does appear in almost all of the known manuscripts of the *Shi'ur Komah*.[26] And it is precisely those light units identified with the reserved portion of light that we have seen to bring the sum of light units earned by the Chayah soul in its progress through the Double Spiral Tree to the number 52, a number whose Gematria equivalent of "son" would seem to define the prerequisite for its further status upon completion of the Measure of the Body, that of a "son of the world to come."

To "surely be a son of the world to come," two activities are required of the spiritual aspirant, gnosis and praxis, knowledge of "this measure of our Creator" and "praise of the Holy One, blessed be He," both presumably involving a recitation of the *Shi'ur Komah* "regularly every day." It is this angelic activity of praise that, in the *Shi'ur Komah* and other apocalyptic-Hekhalot texts, enables the similarly engaged devout soul to share the communion experience definitive of Aravot. And it is in this that the "son of the world to come" and Metatron, the highest angel of this tradition, are most truly united. As I have represented much of the pertinent material on Metatron in chapter 7 that had earlier appeared more fully in my last two books, I need not repeat this material here and can now turn directly to a closer examination of how the Sabbath Star Diagram can provide a solution to the enigmatic number 236 of the divine measure.

We can begin with Scholem's useful summary of this tradition:

> The Merkabah mystics occupy themselves with all the details of . . . *aravot* (the uppermost of the seven firmaments). . . . But the main purpose of the ascent is the vision of the One Who sits on the Throne, "a likeness as the appearance of a man upon it above" (Ezek. 1:26). This appearance of the Glory in the form of a supernal man is the content of the most recondite part of this mysticism, called *Shi'ur Komah* ("measure of the body").
>
> The teaching on the "measure of the body" of the Creator constitutes a great enigma. . . . However, the verse which holds the key to the enumeration is Psalm 147:5: "Great is Our Lord, and mighty in power," which is taken to mean that the extent of the body or of the measurement of "Our Lord" is alluded to in the words *ve-rav ko'ah* ("and mighty in power") which in *gematria* amount to 236. This number (236 × 10,000 leagues, and, moreover, not terrestrial but celestial leagues) is the basic measurement on which all the calculations are based. . . . the *Shi'ur Komah* was an early and genuine part of the mystic teaching in the days of the *tannaim*.[27]

The "great enigma" of how the number 236 can be related to the divine measurement is one that I shall

now attempt to solve not through the traditional Gematria explanation Scholem offers but through a further possibility of geometric derivation. For that measurement of the cosmic man whose traditional key number is 236 provides a most important means of interpreting the Sixfold Spiral Cherub-Tree of the Sabbath Star Diagram ultimately traversed by the Yechidah soul. The solution of this mystery begins with a division of 236 by the hexagonal number 6, a division that leads to the quotient 39 ⅓. Once we have solved this part of the problem, the further questions that arise are: (1) What is the significance of the number 39? (2) What is the significance of that final ⅓? And (3), why must this number be reached by six increments of 39 ⅓?

The number 39 can be readily explained in terms of the number of construction elements needed to encompass the octave division of the seventh-world diagram. There are actually two ways of figuring this number and both are importantly related to an understanding of the octave diagram. There is no question of the number of elements needed to construct the half world of the octave; it is thirteen, the nine eighteenths of the vertical column culminating in the Sabbath Star of the upper Do and the four ninths of the horizontal column that reach just under this halfway mark. But there are two ways of figuring the number for the first six worlds. On the basis of the numerical formula for such construction increments, developed in chapter 6, the number through the first six worlds of the diagram is 26: 1 + 1 + 2 + 4 + 6 + 12 = 26. This formula proceeds through the addition of first two prior numbers and then three. That which makes this series perfect is the double ones at the beginning derived from the original construction of the elementary diagram from the code of the Tree of Life Diagram. These double ones also appear at the beginning of the Fibonacci series, which has been related to all fivefold symmetrical expansions and which grows through the addition of just two previous numbers: 1, 1, 2, 3, 5, 8, 13, 21, and so on. And it can also be related to the Pythagorean distinction between the "monad" and the number one, the former not admitting of division and the later permitting such division.[28] Adding the number 26 to the prior number given for the octave, 13, gives us the 39 we are seeking.

But in terms of actual construction the unity of the second world is subsequently divided by the Ri hexagram later added to the second world through the construction of fourth-world vertical Sabbath Stars. And so the actual number of construction elements finally manifested through the sixth world is 27, which added to the 13 of the octave gives us 40. It was this number that, in chapter 7, provided the geometric justification for placing the circle of the Tzimtzum around the Sabbath Star of the upper Do that divided the seventh world into the finite and infinite halves so important for an understanding of the seventh dimension of holiness. For in the Lurianic tradition, the finite area provided by the Tzimtzum was understood to be occupied by the forty concentric circles that define the individual Trees of emanation of the four cosmic worlds. But if the actual numbers of construction elements filling the diagram grid is 40, the number 39, conforming to the more esoteric numerology of Pythagoras, to the analogous Fibonacci series whose spiral is found throughout nature, and to the original construction code provided by the kabbalistic Tree of Life Diagram can now be seen to play an equally important role in interpreting the highest diagram level of the cosmos, showing how it can enable the diagram to model the Measure of the Body. It might even be said that the divine number 26 of the Tetragrammaton (YHVH: Yod = 10, Hey = 5, Vuv = 6, and Hey = 5) defines the ideal number and 27 the actual, as with the two models of the fourth-world diagram.

Another way of viewing these two numbers is to understand the Gematria of 27 to be YHVH-A. Though this will be taken in chapter 13 to signify the unity of God, Aleph being equated with the number one, there is another traditional way to understand the letter Aleph (א). As can be seen, the Aleph can be deconstructed into a diagonal Vuv (= 6) and two Yods (= 2 × 10). Thus the Aleph has long been understood to be numerically equated with the Tetragrammaton. If we now add the 26 esoterically equated with the Aleph to the 26 of the Tetragrammaton, then we can understand the number 27 to be equal to the 52 that is the Gematria of the son. Thus these two ways of counting the construction

elements of the first six worlds would tell us that in these cosmic worlds both God and the son are journeying together.

There is another kabbalistic tradition, earlier noted in chapter 7, involving these two numbers that is again illuminating here, the fact that their multiplication equals the Gematria for the word Shabbat. This word is composed of the letters Shin = 300, Tav = 400, and Bet = 2, whose sum total is 702; and this is equal to the multiplication of our two numbers, for 26 × 27 = 702.[29] Thus it is the multiplication of both countings that were found in chapter 7 to be particularly appropriate to the conception of the world of the Sabbath, multiplying having ever been the metaphor for generation. And it suggests that the holiness that characterizes both the Sabbath and its world is the product of creatively combining both the "ideal" and "real" ways of progressing through the first six worlds.

At any rate, it is to the ideally 39-numbered construction elements of the octave diagram, which combine the counting of 26 for the first six worlds with the 13 reaching to the Sabbath Star of the upper Do, that the fraction $\frac{1}{3}$ must be added. Turning now to that final $\frac{1}{3}$, this can as readily be derived from the concept of light units applied to the constituents of the matrix, in this case most precisely to a lateral microhexagram, whose value is that $\frac{1}{3}$ in question. It is only with the definition of the ninth-world matrix border in chapter 13 that the best rationale for this crucial microhexagram could be discovered, that darkened macrotriangle representing a microhexagram just beyond the micromatrix border displayed in figure 13.7, which marks the lowest point of the tenth-world matrix. Rising into this area of the future tenth-world matrix, the Cherubs could be thought to go up with the vertical construction elements to touch that lowest point in the tenth-world matrix and then down with the horizontal before catapulting the soul back to the center. Indeed, their movement up, back down, and forward is just that of a pitcher's windup before such a pitch as may be related to the angelic slingshot of the Talmud recently applied to the mythology of the octave diagram.

If the number 39 can be identified with the more

esoteric method of counting construction elements through the octave diagram and the additional ⅓ with a particular lateral microhexagram of the tenth-world diagram to which the soul could be lifted by the Cherub atop a Spiral Tree, then the fact that there are actually six such Cherub-Trees in the octave diagram can explain the final numerical question earlier posed, why the number 39 ⅓ must be multiplied by 6 to reach the final number 236 of the Measure of the Body. Though the image of the Double Cherub-Tree is complete onto itself, it is clear that passage through it neither defines the full sixth-world matrix nor the Measure of the Body. To reach the required number 236 of the divine Measure, the Yechidah soul must further voyage through the remaining two Double Cherub-Trees, in each case being lifted by a Cherub through the remaining ideal 39 steps of the octave diagram to and beyond the precise position of that added lowest lateral micro-hexagram, whose light unit value is ⅓, which will only become manifest as part of the matrix of the tenth world. In the Measure of the Body, as in the reconstruction of the four worlds of emanation summarized in table 7.3, the soul would thus seem to be given a "free sample" of a state far beyond its own level of development to aid it in its process of spiritual evolution. It is now that the soul that had measured six increments of 39 ⅓ and so completed the Measure of the Body would finally become a "son of the world to come." Significantly, it is only at this final incremental level of the Measure that the soul that began its development with the turquoise lateral spiral of man is strong enough to encounter the green central spiral from which it was parted by the temporal centrifuge of the fourth world. It can now meet its beginning without fear of being sucked back into undifferentiated unity as it returns a sixth time to Malkhut for its final portion of reserved light.

As that equated with the octave division of the seventh-world diagram and so of all six Cherubs defined by its matrix, the Chayah soul is also to be associated with the remaining two Double Cherub-Trees as well as the first that properly defines its character. These latter two levels may be viewed as representing the higher states of the Chayah soul level contained in the fuller Yechidah soul. This is similar to an earlier such merging that we saw in relationship to the highest two microhexagrams completed by the fifth-world diagram that were understood to represent both higher levels of Ruach power and levels at which the Neshamah soul was increasingly operating in order to effect the fifth world. Thus though these same second and third Double Cherub-Trees may be associated with distinctive aspects of the Yechidah soul, it is possible to synthesize these two approaches to the Double Cherub-Trees in question by finally viewing them as representing those higher levels of the Chayah soul through which the Yechidah soul can function within the limits of the cosmic octave.

But if the soul's windings through the second and third Cherub-Trees may, like any repetitive process, be thought to become easier with each successive repetition, then it would be possible to offer a yet more detailed overview of such further windings that would have the additional value of bringing this geometric interpretation of the Measure into coherence with two other aspects of kabbalistic theory. This most coherent scheme would involve a speedier entrance into the Ruach level of the second Double Cherub-Tree and a still more rapid rise into the Neshamah level of the third Double Cherub-Tree. Thus the soul that had entered upon its original turquoise Spiral Tree with a starting Nefesh level might be considered to enter its second indigo Spiral Tree directly at the fifth-world Ruach level and its third purple Spiral Tree directly at the sixth-world Neshamah level, the colors representing the Cherubs that can be imagined above these Positive Trees in plate 14. In all three cases the progress through these successive Spiral Trees would be followed with a complementary passage through the parallel portions of each of their Shadow Trees, the first through all three soul levels, the second only through the upper two levels and the third only through the upper third, the earlier such portions being instantaneously traversed.

Now, if each of these Double Cherub-Trees may be thus defined by its starting level, the first with the Nefesh, the second with the Ruach, and the third with the Neshamah, then this model can be related to the most important Zoharic definition of the soul: "Three names has the soul of man: *nefesh, ruah, neshamah.* They are all comprised one within the other, yet they have three distinct abodes. . . . for all three are one, forming one whole, united in a mystical bond, according to the prototype above, in which *nefesh, ruah,* and *neshamah* constitute together one totality."[30] The Zoharic doubling of the three primary soul levels into a lower triad and an upper "prototype" of these same three levels can be related to the present interpretation of the Measure if the upper triad can be identified with the three positive Cherub-Trees, understood to embody the "thought-some" forms of these soul levels, and the lower triad with the three negative Cherub-Trees, understood to embody their "thought-less" forms, to again use the terminology of the Sabbatian Nathan of Gaza.

But this model is also suggestive in terms of the kabbalistic concept of Gilgul, the multiple reincarnations of a soul at successively higher spiritual stages. Rather than understanding the whole process of the Measure to be occurring in the World to Come, the soul's further progress through the second and third Double Cherub-Trees might be understood to involve an earthly reincarnation at each new ascent of a positive Spiral Tree. The concept of reincarnation or Gilgul, though opposed by normative Judaism, is a generally accepted principle of the Kabbalah, as Scholem has shown:

> [T]ransmigration is taken for granted in the Kabbalah. . . . the term *gilgul* became prevalent . . . its singular purpose was always the purification of the soul and the opportunity, in a new trial, to improve its deeds. . . . the common opinion in the Spanish Kabbalah is that in order to atone for its sins, the soul transmigrates three more times after entering its original body (according to Job 33:29, "Behold, God does all these things, twice, three times, with a man"). However, the righteous transmigrate endlessly for the benefit of the universe, not for their own benefit.[31]

But the statement from Job might be interpreted as implying not four incarnations but six, reading "twice three times" without punctuation as the mul-

tiplication of three by two, which is, indeed, what the Hebrew *pa'amayim shalosh* of the Job text literally means. And it would seem to apply directly to the three Double Spiral Trees if each be accorded its special incarnation. But it seems best to view the soul more traditionally as incarnating only three times, first on the Nefesh level associated with the turquoise Spiral Tree, then on the Ruach level associated with the indigo Spiral Tree, and finally on the Neshamah level, associated with the purple Spiral Tree, the intervening periods on the "other side" being spent in the Shadow Trees of each, which may be thought to act as an unconscious reservoir of all unfinished spiritual business and to hold the soul hostage until it can bring this material to consciousness and discharge its debts.

Such a possibility can account for the higher spiritual level that some children demonstrate almost from birth. A notable case in point is that of Samuel, whose birth seems to have been negotiated between his mother Hannah and the Lord. The barren Hannah prayed for this son in a state of high spiritual ecstasy, promising that were she to be given a son she would dedicate him to God's service, "And the child grew before the Lord. . . . and was in favour both with the Lord, and also with men" (1 Sam. 2:21, 26). Though there is no evidence of any such negotiation on the part of David's parents, he is another notable example of a highly spiritual youth: "Behold, I have seen a son of Jesse the Bethlehemite, that is cunning in playing, and a mighty valiant man, and a man of war, and prudent in matters, and a comely person, and the Lord is with him" (1 Sam. 16:18). If Samuel and David may be said to begin their spiritual development on a natural Ruach level, we may suppose that the great founders of religions began theirs on the Neshamah level, such figures as Moses, Lao-tzu, Buddha, Zoroaster, Jesus, and Muhammad.

"Tradition has it," as Jill Purce notes, "that the evolution of the soul takes three lifetimes,"[32] a tradition with which the Spanish Kabbalah is in conformity and for which the Measure of the Body through the three Double Cherub-Trees can provide a model. But whether or not this evolution of the soul is accomplished in part through reincarnation or wholly in the World to Come, it is only with the completion of the Measure that the highest Yechidah level of the soul may be considered to ascend from Malkhut through all six of its Spiral Trees to inhabit the very Cherubic forms that declare it to be a "son of the world to come." Such a sixfold ascent would accomplish a final review of the soul's earlier experiences in the light of its total voyage, a review that may be instantaneous, as the complete life is said to flash before our eyes in the last moment before death to yield a final sense of pattern and meaning. So it may be that, in the words of T. S. Eliot, "the end of all our exploring / Will be to arrive where we started / And know the place for the first time."[33] Rising upward through the landscape of its former existence, the soul, which had grown from the initial condition of divine sonship earned through completing its first Double Spiral Tree to its final status as a "son of the world to come" upon completing the three such Trees of the divine Measure, may finally be thought to enter the winged forms of Aravot with yet another youthful identity, that of the ascending Metatron. For in addition to providing the number of the Measure and the equation of such knowledge with the status of a "son of the world to come," the *Shi'ur Komah* also provides an important definition of the figure of Metatron in terms of the dual spelling of his name: "The name of the Lad is like his Master's, as it is written, '. . . for my name is in him.' The name of the Holy One, blessed be He, has seventy-two letters, and the name of the Lad has seventy-one letters, [both] when he ascends with six letters and when he descends with seven letters."[34] Though not exactly equated with the Holy One, blessed be He, the Lad Metatron is made almost equivalent to the divine name of seventy-two letters.

This concluding section of the *Shi'ur Komah* also provides an explanation of the meaning of the two spellings of the name Metatron, with or without the letter Yod. If the six-letter spelling, without the Yod of the Tetragrammaton, is to be identified with the ascent and that of the seven letters including the Yod with the descent, then Metatron may be said to ascend as Enoch,[35] perfected man, and descend as that with which he has also been identified in this quote, the divine Presence, it being the angel of the Presence, of whom it is said in Exodus 23:21, "for my name is in him." The *Shi'ur Komah* further tells us that "the Shekhinah is on the throne of glory,"[36] and, as Scholem says of the later Kabbalists who followed the *Sh'ur Komah* tradition: "They identified the seven-lettered Metatron with the Supreme emanation from the *Shekhinah* dwelling since then in the heavenly world."[37] It is the Shekhinah who sits on the Throne of Glory and, as earlier shown,[38] there is a tradition that the face one sees in a Throne vision will be one's own, the face of one's highest possible realization, Metatron. We may conclude this discussion of Metatron by observing a final aspect of him, his cosmic size. "His own body," as Martin Samuel Cohen shows, is "called appropriately, *qomah . . . qomato male'ha olam*, 'his body fills the universe.'"[39] Thus the Measure of the Body, which the soul takes in its journey first at both the Chayah and Yechidah levels through the three Double Cherub-Trees and then exclusively at the Yechidah level through the final Sixfold Cherub-Tree,[40] can be identified with the body of Metatron, which is also its own, a body finally coextensive with the cosmos.

The cosmic Metatron, whose measurement defines the highest realization of the Chayah soul, would seem, then, to be that form identified with the six-letter spelling of his name, the form we may further identify with ascent from the Spiral Trees of the sixth world. Similarly, the name spelled with seven letters may be identified with the form of Metatron who descends into the cosmically individuated Cherubs from the infinite expanse of the full seventh world, the dimension of the Yechidah soul, finally to be united with the Chayah soul in the communion experience of Devekut that defines the seventh heaven of Aravot and its octave diagram model. So also, as the Chayah soul meets its Yechidah higher self in accomplishing the Measure of the Body that certifies it as a son of the World to Come, it takes from its higher Yechidah self a taste of what can only be called the tenth heaven. But this is not the end of its journey, for the final part of this book will uncover the ever richer patterning of infinity that is the soul's true inheritance.

PART FOUR

A New Model for the Infinite

CHAPTER THIRTEEN

Exploring the Geometry of the Infinite beyond the Cosmic Circle

THE SEVENTH WORLD

The analysis of the seventh-world diagram up until this point has been based only on construction of the first half of this diagram, with its Cherubically defined matrix, and on the numbers of its further construction elements determined through a predictable numerical sequence. But to define the full seventh-world matrix, the full seventh-world diagram must be constructed. This is what up to this point has most distinguished the Sabbath Star Diagram as a system, that the numbers and forms of the construction elements for each world or expansion of the diagram can be predicted while those of the emergent matrix cannot. In terms of the new "sciences of complexity," the matrices of the first seven worlds can be said to have an "unsimulatable complexity."[1] As with some "cellular automata," number sequences run on computers with specific rules called "algorithms,"[2] there are no rules that can tell us the precise makeup and border of these early matrices, and the only way to discover these is to construct the diagram.

The association of this diagram with the computer has thus far been tangential; only its graphics capability has been utilized to ensure the greater accuracy of the higher worlds of the diagram as well as the beauty of all the illustrations. A computer program has not yet been developed that can generate the evolution of the diagram through all its expansions, though such a program is well within the power of computer science and would, through internal scanning, permit a precise exploration of worlds so complex that to print them on regular-sized computer paper would result in no more than a large blob. It is, indeed, such blobs that have resulted from the attempt to fully construct the eighth-world diagram, it being only through "cheating" the diagram, as it were, that any information on the matrices of the eighth and ninth worlds will be forthcoming later in this chapter. But as we are to see, this will be enough to reveal all the secrets of the diagram without the need for such computer generation or calculation of unconstructible diagrams as was just considered a possibility. Because of the great complexity that this diagram can generate from its few simple rules and initial components, that which can allow this diagram to be categorized as a complex system, the seventh world is, in fact, the last that can be constructed with visual clarity even with the aid of ordinary computer graphics, a fact that has particular significance in terms of the esoteric cosmology it has thus far been modeling. In the following analysis, we shall see how this modeling has implications for two broad areas: the cosmological implications that can be drawn from its strictly mathematical characteristics, and the esoteric cosmology it can further model.

What follows are six illustrations of the highest world of the Sabbath Star Diagram that can be fully constructed. Figure 13.1 shows the incomplete seventh-world diagram that leaves out the sixth-world hexagrams to reveal the fifth-world matrix border produced by such inward construction. Figure 13.2 shows the complete seventh-world diagram, the last to be so fully constructed. Figure 13.3 shows the seventh-world diagram with just its matrix border outlined. Plate 16 is of its matrix central system, not alone of the red and blue spirals, which were the components of the primary Spiral Tree, but of all six components of the central system. The complete central system has been presented both for its aesthetic value and to demonstrate the exact components of each of its six spirals without the possibility of error, the counting of each element being of utmost importance in terms of both the systems and cosmological implications of the diagram. To facilitate such counting, the macrohexagrams in this and the following plates, numbered 17 and 18, will feature fully colored inner microhexagrams, and the unenclosed microhexagrams will feature a lighter shade of their shared coloring. Plate 17 shows the matrix lateral system, here only of the seventh-world extensions of the two spirals that were components of the Double Spiral Tree, those of turquoise and scarlet, again both for beauty and to demonstrate that there has been no overlapping of matrix elements. Finally, in plate 18, we shall see the interface of just the blue and turquoise spirals of the original Spiral Tree. To best utilize the space available on the page, this horizontal world is being presented vertically, and all of its illustrations should be turned sideways to view.

As previously noted, the first point to be considered when approaching the matrix of a world is the visual impression conveyed by its border, a form not produced through the construction elements alone but involving, as it were, a second generation, an artifact of the geometer added to highlight the demarcation between the matrix and the surrounding area. This distinction may be related to the new view of the matrix, advanced in chapter 6, as the "son" of gender-differentiated construction elements. For if such a view can be entertained, then the "second generation" of the matrix border might further be viewed as signifying such a son's independent act of self-definition. If we can regard the geometric drafting of the Sabbath Star Diagram as no more than an imitation of an inherent geometry governing cosmic evolution, then this distinction of generations could be given an ontological status. We could regard the sexually differentiated forces or principles of cosmic creation as generating both the "body" and "soul" of the cosmic dimensions and that soul as achieving the further generation of evolving self-consciousness through which it can finally become identified as the twice-born son, the evolved soul through which the cosmos can comprehend its own purpose. We shall return later to the association of the matrix borders with the concept of the cosmic son, especially as related through the numbers of the seventh-world matrix, but first we should try to determine what character this border is giving to the seventh-world diagram.

It will be remembered that the matrix borders of the fourth through sixth worlds were thought to signify the "element" characteristic of each world. The past-modeled zigzag border of the fourth-world diagram was thought to be expressive of the fluid character of water, the plateaulike border of its future-modeled form to be expressive of the solid earth, the hornlike forms of the fifth-world border to be expressive of the air, breath, or spirit blown through such a shofar, and the flamelike border of the sixth-world diagram to be expressive of fire. To maintain consistency with these suggestions of symbolically interpreted "elements," the matrix border of the seventh-world diagram should be expressive of the final esoteric element beyond fire, that of the ether, the element thought to pervade the space beyond the earth's atmosphere, the space of the celestial spheres.

Figure 13.1. The Incomplete Seventh-World Diagram with the Fifth-World Matrix Border It Produces.
Note: Turn sideways to the right to view.

If we now look at figure 13.3, the correspondence of the form suggested by the matrix border with the locale of the heavens is as startling as the form itself. It appears to be none other than a twelve-pointed star. The almost equidistant twelve points of this star, and the way they flare up from their bases as high as those bases are from the center, are both suggestive of the unity and starlike appearance of this border, the sharp indentations on the edges of these twelve pointed forms being fur-

ther suggestive, as with the similar indentations along the sixth-world matrix border, of fire, that of starlight or of solar flares. Though this later association is even stronger for the sixth world, it is the twelve points of the seventh-world star that continue the association of this evolving matrix form with the sun, for twelve is a number that in the earlier cultures appears to be indicative of a solar-oriented cosmology.[3] From the twelve tribes of Israel to the twelve hides of Glastonbury,[4] the number twelve

Figure 13.2. The Complete Seventh-World Diagram

may be taken to indicate an astrological framework involving the movement of the sun through the twelve signs of the Zodiac, a framework going back to Neolithic times,[5] which also seems to be the source of the use of this number to define the main measures of space and time, the twelve inches of the foot and both the twelve hours of the day and twelve months of the (solar) year, as well as such commercial uses as the dozen for packaging and the twelve-based monetary system, as in twelve shillings to the English pound. The implications of the star formation of the seventh-world matrix border, as well as the differences of this border from that of the sixth world, will be considered at various later points in this chapter. But there are other important aspects of this diagram that must first be considered.

It will be remembered from chapter 6 that construction of the sixth-world diagram from the outside in disclosed that its construction elements alone produced the diagrams of the first four worlds. The

Figure 13.3. The Seventh-World Diagram with Its Matrix Border Outlined.
Note: Turn sideways to the right to view.

exclusion of the fifth-world hexagrams not only clarified this relationship but seemed to provide further
support for the past-modeled form of the fourth-
world diagram since the matrix border that could be
added to the fourth-world diagram so produced was
precisely that zigzag line, traditionally suggestive of
water, which defined the matrix border of the past-
modeled fourth-world diagram. To test whether
such backward construction could be a sure indicator of the correct matrix border for the diagram two
worlds before it, the same procedure was initially

followed in constructing the seventh-world diagram, stopping construction after completion of just
the seventh-world construction elements and without those of the sixth world necessary to complete
this diagram. As figure 13.1 should show, such construction does produce the first five worlds but not
the hornlike matrix border of the future-modeled
fifth-world diagram constructed from inside out.
Such future modeling of all the "future" worlds of
the diagram has become standard for two main reasons: it produces a more coherent and beautiful dia-

gram than that produced by past modeling and, at the sixth-world level, it also produces the precise number of matrix elements that allows the cumulative matrix to be reconceptualized as a Spiral Tree, an emergence of the utmost significance for its modeling of kabbalistic soul psychology and an apparent proof of the correctness of such construction. Thus this form of incomplete construction seems to have relevance only for such backward emergence of the fourth-world diagram in its idiosyncratic past-modeled form. But whether this "proves" the past-modeled form to be correct or "ideal" or whether it can be set down simply to coincidence, however extraordinary, there is no way to know. We shall soon see further bases of support for such an idiosyncratic form of the fourth-world diagram also called into question, the proofs that seemed so sure at the sixth-world level collapsing under the weight of the new evidence coming from that seventh dimension that chapter 11 has shown to be the true domain of Da'at, Knowledge.

But the most important and also problematical aspect of the seventh-world diagram that should be considered before turning to the all-important count of its matrix elements is the design decision regarding the placement of the turquoise and blue spirals. As can be seen most clearly in plate 18, these were placed at the right side and top of the diagram, respectively, just beyond the similar placement of these spirals in the sixth-world matrix, rather than at the opposite sides of the diagram that would continue the forward motion of these spirals. There were two reasons for this decision. In the first place, it was desirable to assign the top of the diagram to the turquoise and blue spirals because of those elements in them that could be related to the Spiral Tree: the elements within the Cherubic matrix of the octave diagram correlated, in chapter 12, with the three Splendors, Tzachtzachot, which were kabbalistically regarded as the roots of the upper three Sefirot and so most appropriately placed just above them; and the lowest macrohexagram within the post-octave matrix identified, in chapter 11, with the quasi-Sefirah Da'at in view of its position between the macrohexagrams identified with the Sefirot of Gevurah and Chokhmah in the Spiral

Tree, the same position it occupies in the traditional Tree. Though one could have maintained the top position for these spirals and then continued the lateral turquoise spiral to the left side, this would have already confused the issue. For the most logical continuation would be for the turquoise spiral to proceed forward to the left side and bottom for reunion with the red spiral, which would mean that it could no longer contribute to the octave Cherub just above its Spiral Tree, an undesirable option. If, on the other hand, it stayed with the blue spiral in the seventh world to rejoin the red spiral in the eighth and then proceeded to occupy the right side, there would be a clear interruption in the rhythm of the spiral progression. But if the spiraling motion were to continue forward, there would also be the question as to whether the blue spiral should not proceed to the upper two peaks or rays on the left side, thus leaving the Cherubic and Da'at macrohexagrams to new color spirals, again an undesirable option. The best way to maintain both the turquoise and blue spirals at the top of the diagram most coherent with the kabbalistic identifications of their elements is, then, to stop the spiraling motion of the seventh-world matrix. But this would not be a sufficient reason in itself were there no other aspect of this matrix arguing in its favor. And there is.

This second reason arises from the very form of the matrix border, with its deep inward slopes that interrupt the continuity of the spirals. In the earlier worlds, all of the main matrix elements were within the portion of the diagram that could be circumscribed by a circle. Even in the fifth world the first and fourth microhexagrams completed by this diagram did not enter into the upper horn portion of the border, though the fourth such microhexagram, like the third of the future-modeled fourth-world matrix, was disconnected from its spiral. And in the sixth world only two microhexagrams entered into the flamelike extensions of the border, those identified with geometric and harmonic comprehension. In the fourth through sixth worlds of the Spiral Tree, then, all of the macrohexagrams, at least, were parts of a connected spiral within the main body of the matrix. In the seventh-world matrix, however, the situation is entirely different. Here macrohexagrams of both the central and lateral spirals, as well as many microhexagrams of both spirals, rise high into the separated star points. Rather than being connected with each other across the intervening space, they seem to be occupying and giving form to a premanifest field of their own color. When we see the shapes of the eighth- and ninth-world matrix borders later in this chapter, it will become still clearer that, from the seventh world on, the matrix is assuming a shape of uniform outward extension rather than of forward spiraling motion. Though maintaining the forward spirals would allow for a clearer color discrimination between the matrices of adjacent worlds, this would also seem to be introducing a false distinction, that there is a continuous forward motion rather than the obvious merging of the seventh matrix into the eighth and the eighth into the ninth. Thus though it is a design decision to give a permanent matrix position to the color spirals from the seventh world on, the position formerly occupied by the true spirals of these colors in the sixth-world matrix, it is one that seems to be supported by the best evidence available. But once this decision has been made, it is clear that it has major cosmological significance.

It is significant that the area occupied by a particular spiral pair in the seventh and later matrices is the same as that first occupied by this pair in the sixth-world matrix, significant in terms of the original correlation of the sixth world with the World to Come, for it suggests that all of these later worlds can be considered to be higher layers of the World to Come, higher "heavens." But there is yet this difference between the matrices of the sixth and of the later worlds, that the sixth-world matrix is part of a true spiral beginning with the fourth-world matrix while the seventh and later matrices appear to simply extend outward in space. This would seem to define the main difference between the sixth and later worlds, the difference between the finite and the infinite, which is also the difference between time and eternity. As shown in chapter 7, an important correlation can be made between the circle of the Tzimtzum, of the finite creation, and the octave diagram. In these Lurianic terms, the seventh-world diagram has been understood to be split into two parts, its first half culminating in the cosmic octave and its second half beginning the infinite realm of Ein Sof. And one of the chief characteristics of the finite is the presence in it of temporal process. It seems not far-fetched to regard the spiral form as a metaphor for time since calendar time is routinely described in terms of such a spiral, being viewed not as a circular return to the time of origin but a return at a higher spiral turning, the same date a year later. Now, if we can make such a metaphoric correlation, then it is clear that the spiral form of the fourth-through sixth-world matrices can be taken as a graphic indicator of the temporal character of these worlds. Similarly, the potentially infinite outward extension of the seventh and later matrices would be descriptive of the infinite transformation of time into eternity. Indeed, the star form of the seventh-world matrix border is indicative of a changed concept of time, one that identifies it with space, with straight-lined spatial extension. For astronomical distances *are* measured in terms of "light years," Vega, for instance, being twenty-six million light years from Earth, again that special number 26. Thus the temporal distinction between what can be regarded as Earth-centered time and astronomical or stellar time, that graphically indicated by the distinction between the spiral and the straight line, would also seem to be true of the difference of the sixth and earlier worlds from the seventh and later worlds, the former matrices characterized by the form of the spiral and the latter by that of the straight line. Now whether this be understood to signify the distinction between the finite and infinite or that between Earth and the heavens, two sets of terms that can clearly be related, at least mythologically, such a distinction has long been recognized, and it can now be seen to be graphically indicated by the Sabbath Star Diagram. This diagram distinction also seems to give geometric support to Plato's description of time in the *Timaeus* as "a moving likeness of eternity."[6]

Before we arrive at the final implications that can be drawn from these circumstances, we must consider the actual constituents of the matrix and the total of their "light units," a consideration that will be illuminating in its own terms and problematical in terms of the diagram as a whole, raising a problem that can only finally be resolved through the further determination of the eighth- and ninth-world matrices. Because of the importance of the seventh-world count of matrix elements, I will take the readers slowly through each such element in the preceding plates, but they can, if they wish, jump ahead three paragraphs to the discussion that follows the description of the process of counting matrix elements.

Let us begin the more precise study of the seventh-world matrix by turning to plate 16 and observing the constituents of the blue matrix elements at the top of the diagram. The lowest macrohexagram of this, as of the other five central color divisions, is the macrohexagram previously identified with Da'at. Above it, there is a row of three blue macrohexagrams, the two surrounding the vertical axis being those that formerly were seen to connect the octave Cherubic matrix with the sixth-world matrix and the third being a new element. This third can be placed at either side of the other two, but it seems more suitable to place it at the right, where it can fill out the area including the macrohexagram of Da'at. At the next higher row are two final macrohexagrams extending into the points of the star. The count is, then, of six central macrohexagram per central color, for a total of 18 light units per color.

Turning now to the blue microhexagrams in plate 16, it can be seen that there are nine of them. In the vertical line up from the Da'at macrohexagram, there are two, one on top of another, and a third above the highest macrohexagram, these three being paralleled on the other side, and there is another pair, one to the left of the highest macrohexagram on the right and the other to the right of the highest macrohexagram on the left. Finally there is an odd microhexagram exactly at the center, that which rose directly above the sixth-world central macrohexagram identified with Keter on the Spiral Tree. These nine microhexagrams are worth 9 light units, which give us the following seventh-world central light-unit value per color: $18 + 9 = 27$.

Turning to the much more complicated turquoise lateral color division shown in plate 17, we should first try to observe its fourteen macro-

hexagrams. Starting from the top and then moving backward down the right side, we should first note the three macrohexagrams at the top, the central one of which had earlier defined the body of the octave Cherub, next the two in diagonal lines in both the highest and lowest of the star points on the right, and finally the seven in the middle two points on the right, three each in horizontal rows and one in the center between them. The light-unit count of these fourteen is also 14. We come now to the crucial count of lateral microhexagrams. Looking first at the two points at the top, it can be seen that each has six, for a total of twelve, with a further thirteenth at the center, this odd microhexagram having previously emerged from the center of the macrohexagram of Keter to join the sixth-world and Cherubic matrices. Of the six on each side, five of them surround the macrohexagram on their side and the sixth is directly above the one on the top. Turning now to the upper and lower points on the right, it can be seen that each has five microhexagrams, two directly above the macrohexagram in that point, two to its side, and one joining the outer points to the middle points, the total of these ten plus the previous thirteen now reaching twenty-three. Finally, there are the fourteen microhexagrams in the middle two points on the right, three each on the highest and lowest rows, another two along the inner rim of the matrix border, and six surrounding the odd macrohexagram at the center of this middle configuration, bringing us to the following significant count: $13 + 10 + 14 = 37$. What is significant about this count is its light-unit value: $37 \times \frac{1}{3} = 12 \frac{1}{3}$. For adding this amount to the light units of the lateral macrohexagrams gives us the following final lateral total: $14 + 12 \frac{1}{3} = 26 \frac{1}{3}$.

We now come to the startling fact that the seventh-world matrix does not show light-unit parity, that $26 \frac{1}{3}$ does not equal 27! The lack of light-unit parity in the seventh-world matrix must lead us to question the previous assumption of such parity in the matrices of all the worlds, an assumption based on this parity in the sixth-world matrix that also resulted in the possible allowance of an idiosyncratic mode of constructing the fourth-world diagram to avoid the lack of parity in the fifth world that would develop from the future modeling of the fourth. But the appearance of nonparity in the seventh-world matrix suggests that a different view be taken of the whole question of matrix parity. It suggests that there is in this, as in other aspects of these worlds, an oscillation between vertical and horizontal worlds, that the vertical worlds might show such parity while the horizontal worlds would not, the fourth and sixth worlds being vertical and the fifth and seventh horizontal. Were such oscillation to prove to be the rule, then it would seem to be the future modeling of the fourth-world diagram that would have to be accepted as correct, its interpretation as a fallen world qualified, and the whole analysis of the fourth and fifth worlds viewed from a different perspective, though one that has repeatedly been suggested as a possibility. This is obviously an issue of the gravest importance for this work and one that demands a resolution not possible at the seventh-world level.

All that we can *know* at the seventh-world level, the ostensible level of Knowledge, Da'at, is that we can no longer be sure of what had seemed at the sixth-world level to be a virtual certainty. The masculine sixth world is the level of the highest mental soul, the Neshamah soul, and can be considered the source of all systematic philosophy and theology that seems to convey a commanding insight into cosmic truth. The truth conveyed through the sixth world diagram was one consistent with its masculine nature, a vision of steady progress to ever greater heights within a structure characterized by regularity. But the regularity of the higher cosmic worlds of the Spiral Tree was a construct that depended on the correlative premise of an ideal form of the fourth-world diagram so idiosyncratic as to make errors of construction probable, a probability taken to be symbolic of a fallen material world. Without this premise there would neither be the general light-unit parity that was deduced, in the concluding section of chapter 11, from its appearance in the sixth-world matrix. The development of this rigorous interpretation of the diagram through the sixth world seems to exemplify the same process of reasoning that appears in most systematic theologies, the complementarity of the beliefs in supernal perfection and in a human imperfection responsible for the evil in this world, this being the preferred method of freeing the divine from all blame for earthly evil. But when, at the seventh-world level, we examine this rational construct *sub specie aeternatatis*, all such certainty fades and we learn, with Socrates, that all we can know is the limitation of our knowledge.

At this level there are two equal possibilities, that the matrices of the finite worlds do show parity and that nonparity only enters into the diagram with the infinite worlds or that there is oscillation between the even vertical worlds of parity and the odd horizontal worlds of nonparity. The former view of at least finite uniform progression reflects the more masculine perspective of the even sixth world as the latter does the more feminine perspective of the odd seventh world.[7] The only way of resolving this issue is again to go to higher levels. Only by determining the precise constituents of the eighth- and ninth-world matrix can this major cosmological question of the Sabbath Star Diagram be resolved. But before we turn to the resolution of this issue, we should see what else we can learn from the matrix numbers of the seventh world.

In the seventh-world matrix the light-unit value of the lateral component is $26\frac{1}{3}$ and that of the central component is 27, the sum of the two being $53\frac{1}{3}$. Whatever the outcome will prove to be of the larger question raised by this lack of parity, these particular numbers are extraordinarily expressive of meaning. All are precisely related to important Gematria numbers, to the two numbers that have kept emerging in analysis of the geometry of the seventh-world diagram, the number 26 of the Tetragrammaton (Yod = 10; Hey = 5; Vuv = 6; and Hey = 5) and the number 52 of the son, Ben (Bet = 2 and Nun = 50). Now what is particularly significant about the numbers of the seventh-world matrix is not only their closeness to these numbers but also their precise differences from them. If we can view 26 as the basic number of the separate components of this one-sixth of the seventh-world matrix and 52 as their combined number, then the lateral elements may be viewed as equivalent to $26 + \frac{1}{3}$, the central elements as $26 + 1$, and the composite as $52 + 1 + \frac{1}{3}$. What can this mean?

Since 26 is the Gematria of the Holy Name, YHVH, what this suggests is that both the central and lateral components of this matrix pair are equally divine. But though they can both be identified with the Tetragrammaton, it is with this difference, that the central would seem to signify the divine in its aspect of unity and the lateral the divine in its fractional aspect of multiplicity. In the case of the central, its correlation with the divine unity would seem to be signified by the addition of the unit to the number of the Tetragrammaton, an addition that can be represented by the letter-numbers YHVH-A and that would also seem to be related to the final reference to the Name in the Sh'ma, "YHVH echod [one]." In the case of the lateral, its correlation with the divine multiplicity seems equally signified by the addition of a fraction to the Tetragrammaton number. If we can accept this identification, then as 26 + 1 may be taken to signify the divine in its transcendent unity, so may 26 + ⅓ be taken to signify the divine as immanent in multiplicity, particularly in the human soul and even more so in such developed souls as may be said to constitute the supernal Community of Israel. As 26 + 1 may be related to the "YHVH echod" of the Sh'ma, so may 26 + ⅓ be related to the earlier reference to the Name in the Sh'ma "YHVH Elohaynu," the latter word being a plural form that also specifically relates the divine to man, its meaning being "our God."[8]

We come now to the further significance of the composite light-unit value of this matrix pair, 52 + 1 + ⅓. The linguistic equations of these numbers seem obvious and the total number to refer not only to the divine son but to the further definition of this son (52) as he who combines in his own nature the divine unity (1) with the divine fractioning of this unity into multiplicity (⅓). The definition could not be more exact and seems to convey the final message of the seventh-world diagram and so of the whole Sabbath Star Diagram, that the purpose of the cosmos is the birthing of just such a son as is finally realized in the Yechidah soul, that highest soul level identified with the full seventh-world matrix that unites a finite lower half still contained within the cosmic circle with the infinite higher half enclosing this circle in its Limitless Light.[9]

That the light-unit value for this matrix pair should so perfectly signify the character of this matrix derived from other considerations is perhaps the most uncanny evidence for the cosmological significance of this diagram, that this is a geometric construct expressive of meaning, and that it is only the use of such expressive numerical meaning that can fully unlock or decipher its cosmic coding. Before commenting further on the larger implications of this composite light unit value, it should be noted that we not only can break this number down into its conceptually significant components, 52 + 1 + ⅓, but precisely identify the particular microhexagrams signified by its last two numbers. For there is only one odd or unmatched central microhexagram (= 1) and one such lateral microhexagram (= ⅓) in this whole portion of the seventh-world matrix. As noted in the counting of matrix elements appearing in plates 16 and 17 above, these are the two rising out of the sixth-world central macrohexagram identified with the Sefirah Keter, the lateral microhexagram touching its exact center and the central microhexagram rising just above it. And they can both be further characterized by their relation to the Cherubic matrix just above the crown of the Spiral Tree, the central being fully within the Cherubic form, in what can be considered its tail feathers, while the lateral is half in the Tree and half in the Cherub, tying them both together into one form. If the central microhexagram may thus be associated with flight and the lateral with grounding, as suggested in chapter 12, then it may be possible to associate the number (1) of this central element even more closely with flight, seeing it as signifying a flight to transcendent unity, and associate the number (⅓) of this lateral element with the soul's clinging to the finite world of multiplicity. The characteristics of these specific odd microhexagrams are thus fully coherent with the cognitive significance of the numbers they add to the remainder of the matrix whose light unit value is 52, the number of the son, and they define this son as he who combines the divine unity with the divine multiplicity.

This is the first time the Yechidah soul could be precisely correlated with the Gematria of the son, a correlation that the previous chapter made in different terms with the Chayah soul level. To recapitulate the earlier correlation of the Chayah soul with the Gematria number of the son, this was based on the light-unit value of the Double Spiral Tree, $26 \times 2 = 52$, most specifically identified with this soul level. Since the Chayah soul was further identified with the octave portion of the seventh-world diagram, this was our first intimation of the significance of this concept to the cosmology of the Sabbath Star Diagram and particularly to its seventh dimension. But we can now see that this correlation is even truer of the Yechidah soul identified with the whole of the seventh-world matrix. For where the prior correlation with the Chayah soul was based upon some questionable though suggestive mathematics, particularly the original raising of the count of light units in the Spiral Tree from 25 to 26, the light-unit count for the seventh-world matrix is an exact measure, every aspect of which is expressive of the precise nature of the son being defined by this matrix. This is not to denigrate the esoteric considerations that entered into the earlier Chayah correlation, but simply to point out the unquestionable fact that the light-unit value for the matrix pair of the full seventh-world diagram is precisely $53 \frac{1}{3}$, a number whose combination of $52 + 1 + \frac{1}{3}$ seems to encode the final mystery of the Sabbath Star Diagram, the secret doctrine of the son, a son who has achieved the still higher level of divine sonship in which the finite and infinite become unified.

The holiness of the Sabbath, the Presence that descends from the seventh dimension of divine consciousness, is that divine child to which the cosmos has given birth and for which it was created. All parts of the Jewish esoteric tradition develop this same mythological explanation of the cosmic process as a birthing of the divine son through the agency of earthly man, not that this son was incarnated in man but that his development either derived from man, as Metatron evolved from Enoch, or is facilitated by man, as in the later Zoharic-Lurianic Kabbalah. Though this esoteric doctrine of the divine child is played down in most Jewish discussions of the Kabbalah because of its supposed similarity to Christianity, in its Danielic and Enochian form it predates Christianity and in its later sexualized form is markedly dissimilar.

THE EIGHTH WORLD

Though the biblical model of creation is essentially Sabbatical, the Bible also pays particular attention to the number that follows the Sabbath and thus can be considered beyond all temporal reckoning. An understanding of this biblical conception may help us to understand something of the eighth world of the Sabbath Star Diagram. For as the Bible identifies six with the work of creation and seven with the dimension of holiness, so does it set the eighth day apart as one of special consecration to the divine. This is the day of covenantal circumcision, of priestly ordination, of the leper's final cleansing and atonement, and of the final holiday in the Mosaic liturgical year, the eighth day of Sukkot known as Shemini Atzeret, the meaning of Shemini being the "eighth." The number 8 is, then, associated with the infinite realm of the divine beyond the holy, beyond the Sabbath, and its biblical usage suggests that man can be connected with this realm through a special act of covenantal consecration, that it is, in fact, the nature of the covenant to promise such a connection. For the Sabbath Star Diagram, the concept of Shemini further suggests that through man's covenant with the Infinite the divinized human soul may be able to progress even beyond the world of the Sabbath to that of Shemini, both the eighth world and the symbol of the infinite octaves that lie ahead.

But to construct this eighth world poses a major problem since even the best computer graphics program[10] cannot provide sufficient clarity for a diagram as complex as that of the eighth world, given the space limitations of the printer to an $8 \frac{1}{2}$-by-11-inch page. The growth rate of construction elements was given in table 6.1, a rate that becomes critical for computer printers with the eighth world of the diagram. The eighth world has nine horizontal elements, which can occupy the same positions as the similar number of horizontal-appearing vertical elements of the seventh-world diagram, drafted on their side to make best use of the rectangular printer page. But in place of the nine horizontal-appearing vertical elements of the seventh world, the eighth world has three times this amount, twenty-seven, an amount leading to such density, when fully constructed, as will not permit the constituents of the matrix to be clearly perceived, becoming blobs that only grow when the whole diagram is enlarged. And this printer limit reinforces the cosmological considerations that had earlier placed a Sabbatical limit on the expansion of the Sabbath Star Diagram. Thus while the computer can aid the draftsman in constructing the difficult addition to the octave diagram that can complete the diagram of the seventh world, this is the last world that, even with computer aid, can be fully constructed with visual clarity.

But though the eighth-world diagram is too complex to permit full construction, it is still possible to accurately determine the nature of its matrix. The reason for this is that the matrix border and the location of all the matrix elements can be accurately determined by another method than that by which they have hitherto been determined, that more proper method in which the macrostructure determines the matrix border and the relationship of matrix elements. But as was pointed out in the initial analysis of the matrix in chapter 8, the microstructure is numerically a world ahead of the macrostructure. And as analyses of the construction elements in chapter 6 have further shown, the vertical construction elements, those productive of the matrix microstructure, are numerically equivalent to the horizontal construction elements of the next world, those productive of the matrix macrostructure. Thus if the diagram for one world is turned on its side, its microstructure will be equivalent to the macrostructure of the next world and it will be possible to determine all the matrix elements on its basis. In this case the reoriented microhexagrams would stand for the macrohexagrams of this next world and the remaining microhexagons, each containing just one macrotriangle, would stand for the microhexagrams of this next world. To determine the precise numbers of these redefined elements, however, it is also necessary to properly define the matrix border of this next world. This can be done by using the outer matrix microtriangles to define the border resulting from the same originating point as determines the matrix macroborder. This is the point produced by the crossing of the Sabbath Stars that culminate the vertical and horizontal axes of a diagram world; following the macrotriangles from this crossing point produces the macroborder of this world and following the microtriangles from this same point produces its microborder, the equivalent of the macroborder of the next world.

Before using the seventh-world diagram in this fashion to define the eighth-world matrix, this new regularity should be demonstrated in terms of the prior worlds. Significantly, it is the future-modeled fourth-world diagram whose microstructure can reproduce the macroborder of the fifth-world diagram. In terms of future projection, then, the regular construction method of future modeling must be used. But though the seventh-world diagram had undermined the original basis on which an idiosyncratic form of the fourth-world diagram was considered to be ideal, that of light-unit parity, we shall see further reasons in the remainder of this chapter for still allowing this idiosyncratic form to be considered a legitimate form of this diagram world. What follows in plates 19–21, then, will be versions of the future-modeled fourth- through sixth-world diagrams, which will feature a darkened micromatrix border and the fifth- to seventh-world matrices, the macrohexagrams represented by microhexagrams and the unenclosed microhexagrams by macrotriangles.

What is even more significant about plates 19, 20, and 21 than the fact that they can validate the new method of determining the eighth-world matrix soon to be employed is what they disclose about the dual-aspected nature of all the worlds. This is the fact that their matrix elements are subject to dual interpretations. When any of the even vertical worlds is viewed vertically, its macrohexagrams will signify its matrix macroelements and its microhexagrams its matrix microelements. However, if it is viewed horizontally, its microhexagrams will signify macroelements and its macrohexagrams, in terms of their dismembered macrotriangles, microelements. And though odd horizontal worlds, which are meant to be viewed horizontally, maintain the normal definition of macro and microelements, they can still represent the next world with the new definition of these elements.

It could thus be said that in these dual-aspected

worlds, the macromatrix contains forms derived from the energetic pattern of the previous world's micromatrix and its micromatrix provides the energetic pattern for the forms of the next world's macromatrix, a breathing pattern, as it were, in which what is "exhaled" by a previous world is "inhaled" or otherwise taken in by the next, microelements being transformed into macroelements as the system further enlarges into the infinite. The metaphoric associations of the matrix macrostructure with form and of its microstructure with force, associations that have been maintained since the matrix was first defined in chapter 8 and that will be further developed in appendix A, can be further related to the earlier gender associations of the microelements with the masculine and the macroelements with the feminine. And if these associations can continue to seem appropriate, then we can go further to say that, as with an organism, so the worlds of the Sabbath Star Diagram seem to be functionally giving off free energy and forming substance of what they take in, holding the past within it as form and the future within it as energy. Psychologically as well this changed perspective on the diagram worlds can offer new understanding and promise. If we seem stuck in particular forms, a refocusing on deeper energy patterns can reveal the forms of the future that we should now be shaping just as it can help us to understand the past sources of our present forms—and distress.

In the effort to determine the nature of the eighth-world matrix without the necessity of drafting this far too complex world of the diagram, a whole new understanding of the deep structure of the diagram has emerged. We have seen that as the numbers of vertical construction elements are repeated in the horizontal construction elements of the next world, so the matrix microstructure of one world can model the matrix macrostructure of the next when it is viewed horizontally and defined by a new matrix microborder. And in restructuring these borders we have been able to perceive a new regularity emerging in the form of the matrix border. Where the borders of the fourth through sixth worlds had seemed expressive of sharply different elemental archetypes, we now see that from the sixth

world on a pattern emerges that will reappear in all future worlds in versions ever more stretched.

The major difference between the sixth- and seventh-world matrix borders that can be clearly seen in figures 13.6 and 13.7 is the proportion between the border area and the inner matrix, that of the seventh cutting far more deeply into the core matrix area and so transforming the flamelike form of the sixth-world matrix border into one more recognizably star shaped. Thus though the star formation of the seventh-world matrix border has been prefigured by the similar but shorter patterning of the sixth-world matrix border, its deep indentations can also be said to set it off from that earlier form and establish the final form of the enlarging star formation of the infinite diagram worlds to come. Though we cannot yet predict the numbers of the various classes of matrix elements for these future worlds, there is one element of the matrix that appears to have finally become predictable, the matrix border. In observing the matrix borders of the sixth and seventh worlds, we can already see that the same vertical and horizontal border patterns will be repeated in ever elongated form and with alternating axes, the design at the vertical axes featuring a sharper declination while that at the horizontal axes features the retrogression to the horizontal at each step of its downward progress that gives it its greater jaggedness. One final thing we have now learned about the matrix borders, and it is something that will enable a still further determination of the ninth-world matrix border, is the fact that the apex of each of the twelve border peaks is a point defined by the crossing of just the final vertical and horizontal Sabbath Stars of a world. Thus the new understanding we have just gained of the relationship of the microstructure of one world to the macrostructure of the next and the positioning of the matrix borders will enable us to extend our geometric exploration of the Sabbath Star Diagram to the two extracosmic worlds that will finally reveal all the cosmological secrets encoded in this diagram.

Turning finally to the reconceptualization of the seventh-world diagram as the simulacrum of the eighth, the eighth-world matrix border will first be viewed in figure 13.4 just the blue portion of the eighth-world central system in plate 22, and just the turquoise portion of this matrix lateral system in plate 23, the interfacing of these systems being eliminated to allow for the clearer definition of the four matrix categories. And it will be remembered that the seventh-world microhexagrams represent the eighth-world macrohexagrams and the seventh-world macrotriangles represent the eighth-world microhexagrams. Also included will be an outline of the earlier seventh-world matrix border.

Turning first to the visual appearance of the eighth-world matrix border, it can be seen that it again resembles a twelve-pointed star. But with the sixth- to eighth-world matrix borders now before us, and with the special highlighting of the lowest points of these borders made possible through the inscribed circles of figures 13.5, 13.6, and 13.7, it finally becomes possible to chart a new emerging pattern of relationship between these worlds. This primarily involves the varying relationship between the different designs associated with the vertical and horizontal axes and an inner circle whose central

Figure 13.4. The Eighth-World Matrix Border

Figure 13.5. The Sixth-World Matrix Border with an Inscribed Circle

point is the center of the diagram and whose radius is the lowest point of the matrix border. If the sixth-world matrix border is observed in figure 13.5 with such an inscribed circle, it can be seen that the lowest point of both the vertical and horizontal designs touch its circumference. It is the large circle that can be so inscribed within the sixth-world matrix border and the equal rises of the foreshortened twelve ascending peaks of this border that give it the close resemblance it has to solar flares. If we now turn to

the seventh-world matrix border similarly shown in figure 13.6, it can be seen that it is the vertical design that now defines the radius of such an inner circle and that the lowest point of the horizontal design is far above it. Turning finally to the eighth-world matrix border, shown with a similarly inscribed inner circle in figure 13.7, we can see that the lowest point of the horizontal design now provides the radius of such a circle and that the similar point of the vertical design is now above its circumference. It would thus

Figure 13.6. The Seventh-World Matrix Border with an Inscribed Circle

appear that the sixth-world matrix border provides the base from which an oscillating pattern in the borders of the further worlds will emerge, the seventh horizontal world showing a deeper declination of its border at the vertical axes and the eighth vertical world a deeper border declination at its horizontal axes. Such an inverse pulsation is also exhibited in the spread between the peaks of the two border designs, the peaks at the horizontal-appearing vertical axes of the horizontal seventh world being slightly farther

apart than those at its horizontal axes and the peaks at the horizontal axes of the vertical eighth world being just as slightly farther apart than those at its vertical axes. It is, then, with the seventh and eighth worlds that a pulsation begins between the vertical and horizontal portions of the matrix border design that can be said to give a particular character to the twelve-pointed star these borders are defining, that of a pulsating star, a pulsar. But it is not alone in its pulsation that the star formations of the seventh- and

Figure 13.7. The Eighth-World Matrix Border with an Inscribed Circle

eighth-world matrix borders differ from that of the sixth world. It is also in their comparatively greater height. For the sixth-world matrix border, with its short peaks surrounding a large inner circle, does not convey the symbolic meaning of a star universally accorded to the graphic design with five or more deeply defined radiating points. Rather it more resembles the solar flares seen most distinctly when the sun is in eclipse, flares mythologized as the long locks of the sun god Apollo, the "god unshorn."[11]

At the sixth-world level the size of these border designs makes it possible to observe their beauty more clearly, how they form a repeating dual pattern that is both graphically pleasing and further sugges- tive of primitive design motifs, most particularly of the many-storied sacred mountain, also reflected in the design of the Buddhist pagodas and stupas, which were understood to contain the divine fire, an inner sun. If the sixth-world matrix border can be associated with the sun, those ever denser and smaller border lines of the seventh- and eighth-world matrix borders seem to signify an astral body at ever greater removes from the observer, not our warming home star called the sun but that which is truly called a star. If these separate borders are understood to signify the evolution of a single, ever more complex and pulsating star, and if such a pulsation can be projected as continuing in all the further worlds that can theoretically be constructed, then it becomes important to determine at least the shape of the ninth-world matrix border as well, to see if it continues this pulsation or reverts to the equal declination of the sixth-world matrix border. Though the original reason of trying to draft the eighth-world diagram was to see if the central and lateral matrix systems would come back into light-unit parity, the form of the eighth-world matrix border, similar in its starlike twelve points and yet different in the positions and depths of these points, now makes it seem just as imperative to continue, as best one can, to determine the shape of the ninth-world matrix border, to see if there is some other way to cheat the diagram and gain access to more of the secrets hidden in the vastness of its increasing complexity. But before turning to what the ninth-world matrix can reveal, we should try to determine the numbers of the eighth-world matrix elements.

I will not, as I did with the seventh-world matrix, trouble the gentle reader with the rigors of counting each such matrix element in turn, being content simply to give the totals for each category, totals that can be verified at leisure from the given illustrations. These counts are as follows: 15 central macrohexagrams, 39 central microhexagrams, 51 lateral macrohexagrams, and 99 lateral microhexagrams. Translating them into light units will answer our original question regarding parity, an answer with profound implications for the proper modeling of the fourth-world diagram:

CENTRAL	LATERAL
15 x 3 = 45	51 x 1 = 51
39 x 1 = 39	99 ÷ 3 = 33
84	84

As can be seen, our first question has been answered; there *is* light-unit parity between the central and lateral systems of the eighth-world matrix. What this means, of course, is that there is a regular oscillation between such parity in vertical worlds and nonparity in horizontal worlds as had seemed possible at the seventh-world level and is similar to the oscillating form of these worlds' matrix borders. And what this means for the matrix elements is that the fifth-world matrix should *not* show light-unit parity, a condition that requires the future modeling of the fourth-world diagram. The matter would thus seem to be settled once and for all—except for one circumstance to be considered in chapter 14. But first we must conclude our geometric investigation by turning to the final constructible matrix, that of the ninth world.

THE NINTH WORLD

Because of the need to construct some valid form of the ninth-world matrix, a way was found, one that turned out to be rather simple. It involved first copying the vertical seventh-world simulation of the eighth-world diagram on a much larger sheet of paper, manually constructing the culminating vertical and horizontal Sabbath Stars of the ninth-world diagram and then transferring the twelve points made by the intersection of these two elements back onto the computer version of this simulated form of the eighth-world diagram. But once this had been done, it also became possible to construct a wholly artificial ninth-world matrix by extension of the lines of the eighth-world matrix grid. Thus without constructing all of the cumulative fifty-four horizontal and eighty-one vertical construction elements of the ninth-world diagram, it has become possible to determine the components of the ninth-world matrix as accurately as those of the eighth. But this seems to be the limit of such subterfuges since any such artificially constructed tenth-world matrix would take us off the procrustean page that is being accepted as the natural limit for diagram exploration. Indeed, even the middle two points on the sides of the ninth-world matrix have had to be manually extended beyond the computer side margin through scissors and paste.

We come now to the ultimate limit of my present powers to explore the geometry of the Sabbath Star Diagram, with the artificially derived matrix border of the ninth world and its artificially filled-in matrix. Figure 13.8 offers a preliminary form of the ninth-world matrix that more clearly shows how its lines fit into the peaks of earlier Sabbath Stars, and it also features the darkening of the lowest macrotriangles appearing just beyond the ninth-world matrix border, *macrotriangles* that in this continuing micromatrix represent the lowest lateral *microhexa-*

grams of the potential tenth-world matrix, this chapter's closing subject. Figure 13.9 will then show the completely filled-in matrix, plate 24 just the ninth-world central system, and plate 25 just its lateral system.

Let us turn directly to the count of matrix elements in plates 24 and 25: 54 central macrohexagrams, 99 central microhexagrams, 150 lateral macrohexagrams, and 327 lateral microhexagrams. Translating this into light units, the 54 central macrohexagrams = 162 light units, and the 99 cen-

Figure 13.8. The Preliminary Ninth-World Matrix Border

Figure 13.9. The Complete Ninth-World Matrix

tral microhexagrams = 99 light units, for a total of 261 central light units; while the 150 lateral macro-hexagrams = 150 light units, and the 327 lateral microhexagrams = 109, for a total of 259 lateral light units. The ninth-world matrix thus demonstrates the expected lack of parity between these systems. This answers our most important question about the ninth-world diagram. The second question is about the shape of its matrix border and whether this will continue the pulsation of the twelve-pointed star defined by the seventh- and eighth-world matrices, and we are now in a position to answer this question.

As can be seen in figures 13.8 and 13.9, it is now again the vertical border portions that decline more deeply toward the center than do their horizontal counterparts, thus continuing the pulsation begun in the seventh world and enabling us to project such a continuing pattern of oscillation with certainty. By this it can be seen that a new regularity has emerged in the hitherto most unpredictable aspect of the Sabbath Star Diagram, the form of the matrix border, and we can now accurately predict the form of all further matrix borders in the potentially infinite expansions of the Sabbath Star Diagram. All will continue to feature the form of a twelve-pointed star but its shape will oscillate between the deeper plunge of its vertical design elements in the horizontal worlds and of its horizontal design elements in the vertical worlds. Perhaps the first point to consider about this new regularity is that as the Sabbath Star Diagram becomes more complex, it also becomes more regular. This bears some comparison to statistical probability, where the fewer the numbers the more unpredictable the behavior and predictability is understood to be a function of the law of large numbers. So the overall development of the diagram is *not* toward chaos, the only alternative to parity earlier considered, but toward greater regularity, a pattern that we shall see to characterize the new model for complexity that will be developed in the final chapter.

Having established the pulsating nature of this infinitely expanding matrix star, we can now finally turn to an equally remarkable aspect of this evolving form and the reason this fuller consideration of its implications was deferred until after the matrix borders of the eighth and ninth worlds could also be determined. When the seventh-world diagram was first discussed, reasons were given for discontinuing the forward spirals of the various color components and replacing that spiraling motion with a simple outward expansion of the twelve-color components of the matrix. And since the seventh-world diagram represents the first world to expand beyond the cosmic circle into the realm of the Infinite, of Ein Sof, this difference was also said to convey the distinction between time and eternity that could also be attributed to these different realms. Now that we see it is not just the seventh-world matrix that takes the form of a star but the matrices of all the infinitely expanding worlds of the diagram, we can draw a still finer distinction between these two realms. For as all the matrices of the realm of Ein Sof can be considered to compose a single expanding form, so can the matrices of the worlds within the cosmic circle.

What is most remarkable about the fact of these two contrasting multiworld matrix forms is the nature of these forms, that as the realm of the eternal is symbolized by a star, so is that of time by the spiral form of a tree. It is remarkable because of the way it connects the beginning of the Sabbath Star Diagram to its end, a connection that seems to convey a special truth about the relationship of the infinite to the finite, of the star to the tree. It will be remembered that the Sabbath Star Diagram emerged from the systematic union of the six-pointed star form of the hexagram with the Tree of Life Diagram. But what we find at this ultimate point of diagram expansion are these same originating forms imprinted over the two main divisions of the diagram matrix, the Spiral Cherub-Tree and the Pulsating Star, the former the symbol of finite as the latter is of infinite life. As the Cherub-Tree represents the inner aspect of the matrix, its constituents, and the Pulsating Star its outer aspect, its border, so may these multidimensional forms be related to the Lurianic distinction between the inner light and the surrounding light, the distinction as well between the finite cosmos and the surrounding infinity. This is surely the most fitting and most inexplicable climax to our study of the Sabbath Star Diagram.

But these answers are just the beginning of the revelations afforded by this last matrix capable of any graphic reconstruction. For in chapter 14 the ninth-world matrix will be shown to reveal a pattern of regular matrix expansion by which it will be possible to predict the matrix constituents of all possible future worlds. Although the necessary development of the preliminary formulae for determining this precise matrix growth will be largely mathematical, and thus may tax the more literary reader, I assure such a reader that the mathematics is really within his or her capacity and should be attempted at some point. The next chapter begins the final numerical extrapolation of the Sabbath Star Diagram to infinite worlds, the first stage in what will come to be called the Sabbath Star System, with its infinitely varied patterning, to be explored in chapter 15.

In this chapter we have continued our exploration of the Sabbath Star Diagram by taking it into the realm of the Infinite beyond the cosmic circle. It is the artificial extension of the diagram to define the ninth-world matrix that not only answers all our questions but will permit the extrapolation of the Sabbath Star Diagram to infinite dimensions on the basis of a numerical simplification that also has profound cosmological implications. It is the final geometric expression of the two symbolic forms with which we began, the star and the tree. And between the form of the Tree, culminating with the sixth-world matrix, and that of the star, which begins with the seventh, is the expressive form of the winged creature through which the soul of man can make the transit from time to eternity.

As we take our leave of the visual beauty and expressive meaning of this geometry, we should contemplate the implication of the remarkable convergence in the final fully constructible diagram of the form of the star with the concept of the cosmic son as the evolved form of the human soul. For this is an association that was made in the earliest strata of human culture and has continued to inform even recent esoteric doctrine. From still existing aboriginal culture, through Greek and Roman civilization with its influence upon all later Western culture, even to the Kabbalah, the belief has persisted that the eternal abode of the soul of at least the remarkable or evolved human being, of the hero or saint, is in the regular sphere of the fixed stars. Scholem has spoken of this association in the Jewish esoteric tradition:

> A man's personal angel is equated with his lucky star, *kokhab massalo*. The Merkabah literature already speaks of a celestial curtain before the throne into which all beings are woven: cf., for example, in the third Book of Enoch, chap. 45. In the *Alphabet of Rabbi Akiba*, a work composed

from the same Merkabah materials, Moses sees "the star [*mazzal*] of R. Akiba in the celestial curtain"; cf. ed. Wertheimer (Jerusalem, 1914), 50. The same idea also dominates the psychological theories of Eleazar of Worms, who treats it at length in his *Hokhmath ha-Nefesh* (Lemberg, 1876), fols. 18, 23, and 28. According to him, the archetype, *demuth*, of a man is his "angel" as well as his "star." This relationship between angel and star is already found in a familiar dictum of *Bereshith Rabba*, section 10: "There is no blade of grass that does not have its star in heaven which strikes it and says to it: grow." Similar ideas are also found frequently in *Sefer Hasidim* . . . ed. Wistinezky, section 1514.[12]

Whether the appearance of such a soul-identified star in the highest worlds of the Sabbath Star Diagram attests to the truth of such a belief or that this belief results from a mythologizing of intimations derived from such an archetypal geometry is impossible to say. But we can at least view this archetypal geometry as constituting a clue as to the highest visualizable state of both the cosmos and the members of its collective soul. And viewing this matrix star with an understanding of its significance, we can hope that it bodes some such future state for our souls as that once addressed to a superior departed soul:

> *Look up and see thy spirit made a star;*
> *Join flames with Hercules, and when thou sett'st*
> *Thy radiant forehead in the firmament,*
> *Make the vast crystal crack with thy receipt;*
> *Spread to a world of fire; and the aged sky*
> *Cheer with new sparks of old humanity.*[13]

CHAPTER 14

Charting the Infinite Future

EXTRAPOLATING THE MATRIX TO INFINITY

Chapter 13 closed with the image of an infinitely expanding and pulsating star as the embodiment of the evolving soul of man. But before we consider the infinitely expanding final form of this cosmic child in chapter 15, we must first develop the fact of a numerical function relating construction to matrix elements on which that final extrapolation builds, a function that derives from the gender association of the construction elements earlier suggested in chapter 6. And before we can develop that numerical function we must discover the finally developing regularity in the matrix from the sixth through ninth worlds that the numbers developed in chapter 13 will reveal. The explorations of the present chapter will thus serve as a bridge between the geometric evolution of the Sabbath Star Diagram through its ninth incomplete expansion, undertaken in chapter 13, which gives us the numbers of matrix elements necessary for this extrapolation, and the algebraic simplification of this transitional exploration in chapter 15 that will lead to the two higher levels of what will there be called the Sabbath Star System, a crowning culmination that not only will provide a new modeling of the infinite but a new mathematical model for complexity theory. As the explorations of this chapter are not only transitional to the more important development to follow but largely numerical, there are some readers who might want to postpone their present study of this transitional phase and move directly ahead to the higher phases of the Sabbath Star System in chapter 15, a new modeling of infinity remarkable both in its wealth of patterning and its correlations with the Kabbalah. Those readers will, however, have to accept my reduction of the seventh through ninth diagram worlds to the single fraction for each of these worlds with which chapter 15 begins without the proofs provided in the present chapter, proofs within the capacity of even the most mathematically challenged, and will miss the intriguing process of discovery they entail, particularly in the second section. But they will find the more important implications of the present study italicized for their convenience.

The regular pattern of matrix elements we are now to discover only fully begins with the numbers for the sixth world, and so table 14.1 will begin with this world, thus temporarily also avoiding the problematics of the fourth- and fifth-world matrices. Table 14.1 lists the world and the four matrix categories, giving each a further letter heading (A, B, C, or D), and the total sixfold light units XLU).

With the full numbers for all the matrix categories through the ninth world now before us, it

Table 14.1. The Matrix Elements

WORLD	C MAC (A)	C MIC (B)	L MAC (C)	L MIC (D)	XLU
6	1	5	5	9	96
7	6	9	14	37	320
8	15	39	51	99	1,008
9	54	99	150	327	3,120

becomes possible for the first time to see if the increasing regularity of various other aspects of the diagram is also true for the one aspect of the diagram that has thus far largely resisted such analysis, the matrix. Indeed, *the one previous appearance of matrix regularity, that of uniform light-unit parity, has now been disproven, though a new regularity has been demonstrated of oscillation between such parity in even worlds and nonparity in odd worlds.* But these light-unit figures, though they will prove to be of the utmost importance in the final numerical extrapolation of the diagram at ever higher orders of abstraction, do not provide a key to predicting the precise levels of matrix enlargement. Rather, it is from the raw figures now before us that organizing principles for the interrelationships among the four categories of matrix elements can be discerned that will permit us to predict the further expansion of the Sabbath Star Diagram without the necessity for further construction. It is only with the ninth-world matrix figures that such principles can be discerned because this gives us a pair of both vertical and horizontal worlds, enough to trace any patterns that may emerge through what has been established as the central process of oscillation between worlds.

In the following discussion, as in table 14.1 the central macrohexagrams will be identified by the letter A, the central microhexagrams by B, the lateral macrohexagrams by C, and the lateral microhexagrams by D. *Study of this table reveals that there are precise formulae for determining the numbers of each of the four matrix categories beginning with the given figures for the sixth world, formulae by which the numbers for the matrix can now be accurately projected for all future worlds* of the Sabbath Star Diagram. The following rules can thus be considered the algorithm of the Sabbath Star Set for the matrix:

1. Beginning with the numbers 1 at 6A, 5 at 6B, 5 at 6C, and 9 at 6D, and using p to refer to one of these four-letter categories of a previous level or world,
2. Derive As by one of two formulae:
   A) $A = pA + pB$, or
   B) $A = pC + 1$ for two worlds and then a progression through the multiples of 3 of additions to pC in pairs of worlds;
3. Derive Bs by one of two formulae, each distinguished into further even and odd categories:
   A) For odd Bs either repeat pD ($B = pD$) or double A and subtract a number in a progression of the multiples of 3 beginning with 3 at the seventh world ($B = 2A + 3$);
   B) For even Bs either repeat pD and add a number in a tripling progression beginning with 2 at the eighth world ($B = pD + 2$) or double A and add a number in a tripling progression beginning with 9 at the eighth world ($B = 2A + 9$);
4. Derive Cs by the formula: $C = pC + pD$;
5. Derive Ds by doubling Cs and adding or subtracting a number in a tripling progression differing for even and odd, beginning at the sixth world with $D = 2C - 1$ and at the seventh with $D = 2C + 9$.

These formulae will be better appreciated by study of table 14.2, which lists the fourth through thirteenth worlds, adds the light-unit values, and distinguishes the central (C) and lateral (L) figures, their difference (−) and sum (+), as well as denotes with an asterisk the irregularities of number or formula application, irregularities whose importance with respect to the fourth-world diagram will shortly be considered.

Table 14.2: Double-Octave Extrapolation of Matrix Elements

W	A	B	C	D	LU	
4	0*	1	1	2*	C:	1 + ?
					L:	1 + ?
	(2A + 1)			(2C − 0)	—:	?
					+:	?
5	1	0	1	4	C:	3
					L:	2 1/3
	(pA + pB)	(2A − 1)*	(pC + pD)*	(2C + 3)*	—:	2/3
	(pC + 0)(pD)*				+:	5 1/3
6	1	5	5	9	C:	8
					L:	8
	(pA + pB)	(2A + 3)	(pC + pD)	(2C − 1)	—:	0
	(pC + 0)	(pD + 1)			+:	16
7	6	9	14	37	C:	27
					L:	26 1/3
	(pA + pB)	(2A - 3)	(pC + pD)	(2C + 9)	—:	2/3
	(pC + 1)	(pD)			+:	53 1/3
8	15	39	51	99	C:	84
					L:	84
	(pA + pB)	(2A + 9)	(pC + pD)	(2C − 3)	—:	0
	(pC + 1)	(pD + 2)			+:	168
9	54	99	150	327	C:	261
					L:	259
	(pA + pB)	(2A - 9)	(pC + pD)	(2C + 27)	—:	2
	(pC + 3)	(pD)			+:	520
10	153	333	477	945	C:	792
					L:	792
	(pA + pB)	(2A + 27)	(pC + pD)	(2C − 9)	—:	0
	(pC + 3)	(pD + 6)			+:	1,584
11	486	945	1,422	2,925	C:	2,403
					L:	2,397
	(pA + pB)	(2A - 27)	(pC + pD)	(2C + 81)	—:	6
	(pC + 9)	(pD)			+:	4,800
12	1,431	2,943	4,347	8,667	C:	7,236
					L:	7,236
	(pA + pB)	(2A + 81)	(pC + pD)	(2C − 27)	—:	0
	(pC + 9)	(pD + 18)			+:	14,472
13	4,374	8,667	13,014	26,271	C:	1,789
					L:	21,771
	(pA + pB)	(2A − 81)	(pC + pD)	(2C + 243)	—:	18
	(pC + 27)	(pD)			+:	43,560

*Denotes irregularities of number or formula application

The full table reveals the perfect formulaic consistency of matrix elements from the actually constructed sixth- through ninth-world matrices that, with the formula for the equally regular progression of construction elements for all future worlds, can permit the extrapolation of the Sabbath Star Diagram to infinite worlds. This table can also explain why the previously given algorithm was said to begin with the figures for the sixth world; for these both form the basis of the formula applications of the seventh world and are themselves wholly consistent with these formulae—but only when the fifth world's figures are those resulting from the future modeling of the fourth world. Such sixth-world formulaic consistency also involves an acceptance of the tripling progressions based on 3 as going back first to 1 and then to 0, as seen in the various progressions for categories A and D, as well as the alternate for B. Though the light-unit evidence would seem to argue against this for such progressions beginning with 2, if we consider 1 to be the base of both even and odd numbers, as in Pythagorean arithmetic, then we can have full formulaic consistency.

As just indicated, the formula applications to the sixth world would seem to validate the numbers produced by the fifth-world matrix when that of the fourth is also future modeled. For the numbers 1, 0, 1, 4 of the fifth-world matrix give us the formula sums for 6A and 6C, the two categories based on previous-world categories, as well as for the 6D derived from 6C. This would seem to validate the future-modeled version of the fourth-world diagram as, indeed, the correct one, and this even through there are major problems with the formula applications to the fifth-world categories, only 5A being formula correct and even that with qualification. The categories 5B and 5D, based upon same-world formulae, do not properly correlate formulae with construction figures: in the case of 5B, $2(1) - 1 = 1$, not the 0 determined by actual construction; for 5D, $2(1) + 3 = 5$, not again the 4 produced by construction. And since the formula for B is dependent upon A, as that for D is upon C, this also serves to question the figures for A and C. What is further at issue are the formula applications for A, C, and the alternate for B, since these depend on previous-world categories. To resolve this question, we must finally turn to the most problematical case of all, that of the fourth world.

As the numbers for the A and C categories of the fourth world cannot be initially established since they depend on those of a previous-world matrix, which is here nonexistent, we can begin with the B and D figures and formulae. Here backward extrapolation can give us relatively certain formulae. Since the 6B formula is $2A + 3$, that for 4B has to be $2A + 1$. But the only way this could fit the fourth-world possibilities would be to assign 0 to 4A and 1 to 4B. Such assignments would also allow 5A to be formula regular. But what this would mean is that the collective central macrohexagram is not to be counted as part of the fourth-world matrix or of its light-unit figures though it certainly appears in the fourth-world matrix. And since it was finally granted that even with its past modeling there was no way of determining the light-unit value of this unique collective element, the present evidence would seem to verify that this element is not to be counted as an exclusive member of the fourth-world diagram.

When we turn to the lateral categories, however, an even greater problem arises. Here there is no question that the formula for 4D should be $2C - 0$. Since that for 6D is $2C - 1$ and for 8D is $2C - 3$, and since the second formula for category A also follows a sequence from 0 to 1 to 3, the formula for 4D must be considered to be absolutely correct. But though this would allow the number 1 to 4C, there is no number at 4D that could fit this formula, since the number 2 resulting from applying this formula ($2 \times 1 = 2 - 0 = 2$) is a number that cannot be produced by any method of constructing the fourth-world diagram but is exactly between the 1 resulting from the past modeling of the fourth-world diagram and the 3 resulting from its future modeling. The number 2 for 4D is thus most irregular, and for two reasons. First, to conform to the formulae for 5C and the alternate for 5B a zero would be required. But even more significantly, the 2 for 4D and the 4 for 5D consistent with the formulae for both cannot add up to the 7 lateral microhexagrams for the combined fourth- and fifth-world matrices produced by actual construction. So what we are left with are fourth-world matrix figures inconsistent with the future modeling of the fourth-world diagram and fifth-world matrix figures demanding such future modeling of this same fourth-world diagram, a conflict incapable of resolution in terms of formulae and even more so in terms of the evidence of actual construction. *The only conclusion that can be drawn from these circumstances is a recognition of the fundamental irregularity of the fourth-world diagram*, with perhaps some tribute to the intelligence informing the program of this geometric construction in its attempt to work out a compromise solution!

What the recent investigations have made especially clear is the paradox of regularity emerging from initial irregularity. Though the numbers of construction elements are to become regular by the third world and the future modeling of intermediate construction elements to become standard by the fifth world, if not the fourth, this whole structure of increasing regularity is erected upon a base of required initial irregularity, the irregular orientation of the first two hexagrams. So, too, with the matrix, whose first introduction into the fourth-world diagram is in a form whose numbers cannot be made coherent with the formulae emerging from the later sequence of matrices but that yet provide the base from which matrix regularity will be progressively built, the figures for the fifth world being consistent with sixth-world formulae and those from the sixth world on being fully regular with their own and future formulae applications. But it is only at the ninth world that full numerical regularity in the matrix becomes clearly observable. That the Sabbath Star Diagram should increase in regularity as it grows in complexity confutes some of our expectations about complex systems and can lead to the new model for complexity theory to be presented in chapter 15 on the basis of the matrix figures just now developed, a theory whose definition of a complex system is precisely one that gains in regularity as it grows in complexity.

If we are now to move beyond construction data to numerical extrapolation in charting the tenth and further worlds of the Sabbath Star Diagram, this will mark a new and most radical phase shift in the development of this system, one from the two-dimensional realm of plane geometry to the linear dimension of the graph, the visual form in which the final regularities arising from the shift from two-dimensional geometric construction to numerical computation can be translated back into geometry. It is just such a linear graph that we shall see to emerge from the final investigation of this chapter into the Sabbath Star Diagram, one that will finally develop the functional relationship between construction and matrix elements able to carry its seed into that remarkable flower of infinite patterning to which the next chapter will be devoted.

THE RELATIONSHIP OF CONSTRUCTION AND MATRIX ELEMENTS

The most important implication of chapter 13 may well be its identification of the seventh-world matrix with the concept of the son, and it brings us back to the earlier such conception of the son presented in chapter 6, a conception developing from the gender identification of the construction elements of the sixth and octave diagrams with the Partzufim, the divine personalities that were considered to represent the "outer" aspects of these diagram layers. It was numerical circumstances that determined the assignment of the masculine Partzufim to the vertical elements and the feminine Partzufim to the horizontal. But once these assignments were made, it became clear that they represented a deeper truth about the Sabbath Star Diagram, for it is the interaction of these vertical and horizontal construction elements that does, in fact, produce the matrix, an interaction for which the sexual metaphor seems apt and that allows us to view the matrix as their offspring, their "son." Before we proceed to develop this functional relationship, however, we should give fuller attention to the parental sources of this new generation, to that correlation of the vertical construction elements with the masculine and horizontal construction elements with the feminine meaningful both in itself and in the matrix product of their unification.

As just indicated, the correlation between construction elements and gender was theoretically developed in chapter 6, where various geometric and mythological characteristics of the diagram were offered in its support that need not be again rehearsed. Thus we can now turn to what may well be the most startling as well as meaningful feature yet encountered in our study of the Sabbath Star Diagram, the numerical correlation of construction to matrix elements by which the former, indeed, appear to represent the parents of the latter. This is a correlation that could only have emerged from the gender identifications of the construction elements. For once the vertical elements are identified with the masculine and the horizontal with the feminine, the question naturally arises as to whether the numbers of what could be regarded as these two parental sources could be meaningfully related in terms of the arithmetic process that has immemorially been viewed as a metaphor for sexual generation, multiplication. The multiplication of the numbers of vertical and horizontal elements in a diagram world would only yield a significant product, however, if this product could be precisely correlated with a numerical feature of the matrix of that world. And such an equation does emerge from the count of light units in the matrix when two qualifications are met, that the complete or sixfold matrix be counted and that the fourth-world diagram be constructed in the form previously deduced to be "ideal," that is, with an irregular past modeling, a circumstance that again seems to validate its idiosyncratic form. Though this latter will not prove to be an absolute necessity, it was on its basis that this most important new regularity was first discovered, and this preliminary exposition will be made in its terms.

It will be remembered from the original study of matrix light units, in the final section of chapter 11, that parity could be established between the central and lateral systems of the sixth-world matrix if its constituents were given the following "light-unit" values: 1 central macrohexagram = 3 light units, 1 central microhexagram = 1 light unit, 1 lateral macrohexagram = 1 light unit, and 1 lateral microhexagram = $\frac{1}{3}$ light unit. On this basis the sixth-world central system was shown to have 8 light units and the lateral system 8 light units for a total of 16 light units. Such parity also could be shown for the

fourth and fifth worlds if the fourth world were irregularly constructed with the past modeling of its first intermediate Sabbath Star and no Sabbath Star development of its second intermediate construction element. With such construction, the fifth world could also show a parity of 3 light units each for the central and lateral systems, for a total of 6 light units. As the fourth-world diagram has the unique collective macrohexagram that can be assigned any light-unit value, parity could be established for it whether it was constructed in its past- or future-modeled forms. The former, reconfirmed in its identification with the ideal because it also allowed for what we saw in the previous chapter to be the now dubious proposition of fifth-world light-unit parity, provided 3 light units for its fourth-world portion of the Spiral Tree, a figure reached by assigning 4 light units to the collective macrohexagram, $\frac{2}{3}$ to each Spiral Tree. Adding together just the 3 light units of the fourth-world Tree to the 6 light units of the fifth-world Tree and the 16 light units of the sixth-world Tree gave a total of 25 light units for a single Spiral Tree. To this an extra light unit was originally granted each Spiral Tree through involution to the center for the portion of "reserved light" that would bring its total to the 26 that is the Gematria number of the Tetragrammaton, a possibility that became the basis of the analysis of the Double Spiral Tree in chapter 12.

It is important to understand the original logic on the basis of which the concept of light units was first developed and the irregular construction of the fourth-world diagram was preferred, important because it is precisely this determination that now appears to be unexpectedly validated by the present consideration of the construction elements as the sexually differentiated "parents" of a matrix "child." But to get an exact equation between the product of construction elements and the light units in the matrix, certain protocols must be observed. The first is that all construction elements manifested by the fourth-world diagram should henceforth be counted. What this involves is a rejection, in this circumstance, of the numerical formula for construction elements that eliminates the Ri hexagram from the counting because of its "unmanifest" status in the second world, an esoteric counting of construction elements that was previously used to establish the Gematria number 26 as the count of outwardly constructed elements through the sixth world. Instead, the Ri hexagram, whether considered to be a permitted member of the second world or to be only manifested by a fourth-world Sabbath Star, is now to be counted. The second rule is that it is not only the matrix constituents of a single Spiral Tree that are to be counted but those of the entire matrix, the previously given number of light units for a world as multiplied by six.

Both of these new rules for counting are perfectly legitimate though they have never previously been required. The Ri hexagram does appear in the later worlds of the diagram and can only be eliminated from the count on esoteric grounds that are not uniformly applicable and that mar another numerical regularity its inclusion permits, that which brings the cumulative octave number of construction elements to the forty that can model the four Trees within the Lurianic cosmic circle, as chapter 7 has shown. And it is not one but six Spiral Trees that are actually developing through the expansions of the Sabbath Star Diagram. The equations we are now to observe are based, then, on the most complete countings possible of both construction and matrix elements, equations that reveal a correlation of these elements expressive of the ultimate truth conveyed through this diagram: that cosmic evolution is at all of its stages a product of the generative unification of forces having distinguishable masculine and feminine characteristics and that this generation is twofold, of what can be considered the "body" of each cosmic world and of its "soul," the cosmic son.

Before charting the results of these most cosmologically significant counts of diagram elements, it would be helpful first to run through the numbers for the fourth and fifth worlds as "ideally" constructed The fourth world has six cumulative vertical construction elements, and three cumulative horizontal elements. Multiplying these numbers gives us the following equation: $6 \times 3 = 18$. This is the same figure arrived at by multiplying the 3 light units of the past-modeled fourth-world portion of

one Spiral Tree by the 6 such Tree portions appearing in this diagram. The fifth world adds 3 vertical and 3 horizontal elements to the 6 and 3 of the fourth-world diagram, giving us totals of 9 and 6, respectively, which, when multiplied, yields the following result: $9 \times 6 = 54$. Again this is the same figure arrived at by adding the 6 light units of the fifth-world matrix to the 3 light units of the fourth-world matrix and multiplying the total by 6: $6 + 3 = 9 \times 6 = 54$. It is these exact correspondences between the construction and matrix elements of the fourth- and fifth-world diagrams that seem to provide further validation of the earlier preference for the construction of the fourth-world diagram in the form considered to be "ideal" that was so explanatory of the likely "Fall" of this world. And it also enables us to see a new regularity that, with some modifications, will prove to be of the utmost importance in understanding the structural regularity of the seventh and later worlds.

It might be helpful to chart at this time the figures for the fourth through sixth worlds, completing the necessary figures for the sixth world and giving the following items: world (W); central light units (CLU); lateral light units (LLU); added cumulative light units times six (XLU); vertical construction elements (V); horizontal construction elements (H); multiplied cumulative construction elements (XCE); and the difference between XCE and XLU given in numbers (# D) and decimals (DD):

As can be seen, we seem to encounter a problem when we come to the sixth world. For this world adds 9 vertical elements to the previous 9 for a total of 18 and 3 horizontal elements to the previous 6 for a total of 9. When multiplied, these numbers yield the following product: $18 \times 9 = 162$. The number of light units we would like to see in the cumulative matrix for the Sixfold Spiral Tree would thus be 162. But adding the 16 light units of the sixth world to the 6 light units of the fifth-world portion and 3 light units of the fourth brings us to a total of 25 light units, which multiplied by 6 yields the following product: $25 \times 6 = 150$. This is 12 light units short of the number we need to get a perfect equation.

In the earlier development of the idea of light

Table 14.3. Comparison of Construction and Matrix Elements

W	CLU	LLU	XLU	V	H	XCE	# Dif	DD
4	$1 + \frac{1}{3}$* =	$1\frac{1}{3}$	$1\frac{1}{3} + 1\frac{1}{3} = 2\frac{2}{3}$ $2\frac{2}{3} + \frac{1}{3}$* = 3 3 x 6 = **18**	6	x 3 =	18	0	0
5	3 =	3	3 + 3 = 6 x 6 = 6 x 6 = 36 36 + 18 = **54**	9	x 6 =	54	0	0
6	8 =	8	8 + 8 = 16 x 6 = 16 x 6 = 96 96 + 54 = **150**	18	x 9 =	162	−12	−.074074

*Items contributed by the collective central macrohexagram

units, in both chapters 11 and 12, the number 25 was increased to 26 for esoteric reasons by the expedient of a return to the center for a portion of "reserved light," a talmudic concept that is accepted throughout the Kabbalah. Not only did such a return to the center seem reciprocally to support this talmudic concept as well as another involving an angelic slingshot, but it enabled the initial increase in the light-unit value of a single Spiral Tree from 25 to the divine number 26. On the basis of the present analysis, however, this number must now be raised still higher to 27; for an extra 12, rather than 6, must be raised over the figure of 25. But as we have seen in chapters 12 and 13, the number 27 can also be understood as the sum of 26 + 1, which can be translated by Gematria into the letters YHVH-A and understood to signify the Tetragrammaton in its aspect of unity. If some further mythological explanation is desired, this is not far to seek.

We have seen that the collective central macrohexagram contributed 4 light units to the fourth-world matrix in its past-modeled form. Even though the rule of future modeling has gained priority over light-unit parity in the further matrix modeling of the seventh world, the lower worlds would still need to draw 4 light units from the central source, if balance is still desired between the number of fifth-world light units that would give it the same parity with the multiplied construction elements of this world. But the fourth world would also need to draw another 6 light units from this source to balance its own light units, light units that could be

regarded as that same hidden portion reserved for the righteous in the World to Come, a reward the Neshamah soul could still involute to the center to pick up on its passage through the Double Spiral Tree. So the central element must still contribute 4 light units to either the fourth- or fifth-world matrix (the former if the fourth world is past modeled and the latter if it is future modeled) and 6 light units to the fourth- or sixth-world matrix (again either directly after completion of the sixth-world Spiral Tree, if the fourth world is past modeled, or directly to the future-modeled fourth-world diagram but kept hidden until the soul has completed the Spiral Tree). In the latter case, these 6 light units would have to be counted with the sixth-world matrix and the fourth world considered not to be awarded any light unit value from the central macrohexagram, a feature of the fourth-world matrix defined in table 14.3. In either case, the total number of light units for the Spiral Tree would be 26, with 10 for the central macrohexagram of Malkhut, as previously determined.

We now see, however, that the sixth world requires another 6 light units, and we shall soon learn that the seventh world will require another 4 light units. This brings the total required number to 20 light units. And as the first 10 light units were correlated with the ten Sefirot of the Tree of Life Diagram, so may the second 10 light units be correlated with another such Tree, a requirement easily met by the Sabbath Star Diagram. For the Lurianic Kabbalah maintains that each of the original four worlds contained its own Tree, and in the Sabbath Star Diagram the collective central microhexagram is actually composed of the elements defining two such worlds, the Do and Re hexagrams, each of which may be thought to contain the 10 light units identified with its Tree. As we shall later see that no further deficits need be made up by this central element, we can accept the demand now being made of it by the sixth-world matrix.

But we are faced with the paradox that the sixth-world matrix is at the same time the only matrix with a clear claim to light-unit parity, a parity that led to the whole development of the concept of light units, and the one whose undoctored total is the furthest away from parity with the multiplied product of its construction elements. And yet it was from the attempt to establish the matrix regularity of light-unit parity that the resultant matrices of the fourth and fifth worlds achieved the number of light units that would now seem to be establishing a far more significant regularity, that relating matrix to construction elements. But the fact that the cumulative totals of light units and of multiplied construction elements come close to parity once more with the seventh-world diagram, given the 12 light units added to the sixth-world matrix totals, indicates two things, that this is a major structural regularity and that 12 light units must be added to the sixth-world matrix. Thus the mythological explanation given for the addition of these 12 light units is as likely a story as any in view of the fact that these 12 light units must be added and that the place from which they can most logically come would seem, at this level of analysis, to be the unique collective macrohexagram at the diagram center.

But this raises another problem. For this unique macrohexagram cannot simply be given these full 20 light units from the beginning, for then the light-unit totals for the fourth world would be off and the basic equations between their construction and matrix elements would be impossible. No, the diagram would seem to demand a progressive generation of the light units that can balance each of the worlds, with a return to the center at the fifth, sixth, and even seventh world for such extra light units as have traditionally been understood to be reserved

for the righteous from the original light of the creation and treasured up for them in the World to Come. And if the number of light units apportioned to the central macrohexagram is to remain at the mythologically justified number of 20, and all of the 12 light units required by the sixth-world matrix—not now to balance the central and lateral light units but the multiplied construction elements—must all be awarded only to the sixth-world matrix, then this means that the central macrohexagram could give no light units to the fourth-world matrix and render it completely irregular. This is a possibility we have seen to be supported by the backward extrapolation undertaken in the first section for all the matrix figures developed through the ninth world.

But since the purpose of this return to the center is to balance the number of multiplied cumulative light units with those of the multiplied cumulative construction elements, we can get unquestioned results by simply adding the absolute number of such construction elements to the number of light units at each world as if they were representing the cumulative light units of the prior worlds, thus effecting a rebalancing of the figures for the prior world retroactively. Thus whether the 12 light units in which the sixth-world matrix is deficient is thought to be made up from the collective macrohexagram or by the rebalancing technique of counting light units that makes possible a coherent method of computation applicable to all possible worlds of the diagram, the Sabbath Star Diagram does exhibit a deep structural function by which its construction and matrix elements can be related.

We have seen that the metaphor of the son can be doubly applied to all of the matrices, first insofar as they can be considered the visual product of the graphic interaction of the vertical and horizontal construction elements and then as related to the numerical product of the multiplication of the numbers of these differently oriented elements, such multiplication going beyond ordinary metaphor to integrate geometry with an arithmetic process equally expressive of linguistic meaning, of a sexualized generation whose product can a fortiori be called a son. But of all the matrices, it is that of the complete seventh-world diagram whose numbers we have seen to be most strongly associated with the Hebraic secret doctrine of the son.

To complete the study of the seventh-world matrix and diagram, we must finally consider the correlation of its construction and matrix elements, a correlation that is remarkably close. The figure for the multiplied construction elements is: $27 \times 18 = 486$. The figure for the sixfold seventh-world matrix is: $53 \frac{1}{3} \times 6 = 320$. If we now add to this number that previously arrived at for the rebalanced cumulative sixth-world matrix, we get the following close total: $320 + 162 = 482$. To be only 4 units less than such a large number as 486 is itself remarkable and could be simply accepted as a close approximation.

As recently suggested, there is a mythological way in which this equation can become exact. This is to draw the 4 extra units from that ever fertile source, the collective macrohexagram that had already given 4 units either to the fourth-world six-fold matrix or to that of the fifth world as well as twelve to the sixth world. The appropriateness of this final contribution from the maternal cosmic source to the world containing the cosmic octave, one reflective of the resonant connection between the original Do hexagram and its octave double, is further supported by other numerical and geometric cosmological features of the diagram. As earlier shown, the addition of these 4 extra units to the earlier 16 drawn from this source would bring the total to 20, a number uniquely fitting to the macrohexagram of Malkhut, composed of the original Do and Re hexagrams identified with the cosmic worlds of Atzilut and Beriah, each of which may be said to contain its own Tree, a traditional concept, whose combined Sefirot number would be twenty. But it seems advisable from this point on rather to accept the rebalancing technique of relating construction and matrix elements that eliminates the need for such mythological explanations and sees this correspondence not as one of equality but of differences. The decimal difference in the case of the seventh world, while still negative, comes closer to zero: $^{-4}/_{486} = -.008230452$.

Though this new functional relationship between construction and matrix elements first

seemed to be demonstrated by the numbers deriving from the past modeling of the fourth-world diagram, if we are to accept the new rule of oscillating light-unit parity, this would identify the odd fifth-world matrix with nonparity, a condition resulting from the future modeling of the fourth-world diagram. Let us now see what numbers result from comparing these alternate light-unit values with the fifth-world construction elements.

The total for one-sixth of such a fifth-world matrix is $5 \frac{1}{3}$ light units and its sixfold measure is 32, but to compare this with the cumulative multiplied construction element total of 54 we have to add to the fifth-world light-unit total that of the fourth. To avoid the problematics of such a count, let us simply add the previously arrived at parity figure for the fourth world of 18, the number of its multiplied construction elements, to the 32 of the light units multiplied by 6. This would bring the cumulative fifth-world light-unit total to 50 ($32 + 18 = 50$), 4 short of the parity figure of 54. Using the same method of determining the decimal difference previously utilized for the sixth world, we arrive at the following surprising figures: $^{-4}/_{54} = -.074074074$. This is surprising because it is the same negative decimal that emerged at the sixth-world level and was earlier considered to be far from the mark. The reason is that both $^{4}/_{54}$ and $^{12}/_{162}$ reduce to the same fraction of $^{2}/_{27}$, both this reduced fraction and its decimal expression being numbers whose significance will be a major subject of chapter 15. We also saw that the decimal difference for the seventh-world diagram, while still negative, comes closer to zero: $-.008230452$. Thus what originally seemed to be a relationship of equality appears now to define a sequence of related differences.

Though this relationship of matrix to construction elements is not likely to have been discovered without the past modeling of the fourth-world diagram that first disclosed their apparent numerical parity, we see that it can be sustained at the fifth-world level even with the future modeling of the fourth once it is reconceptualized as a relationship of differences. For what the earlier mythological explanations accomplished numerically was a bringing up of the light-unit values to parity with the multiplied construction elements, a rebalancing at each world level that could thus serve as a base for the next cumulative sums. Thus whatever the raw figure for the fourth-world matrix may be, its rebalanced number is eighteen, the parity figure of the multiplied construction elements of this world, and a firm base can be supplied by it for the structure of decimal differences, beginning with the fifth world, that is to provide the final cosmological model of the larger Sabbath Star System, that numerical extrapolation of the diagram to infinity with which this work culminates.

But though the future modeling of the fourth-world diagram can regularize the contribution of the fifth to the larger oscillating structure of the expanding diagram, it has an opposite effect upon its own relationship to this structure. We have seen that diagram oscillation would correlate the even fourth world with such light-unit parity as is also demonstrated by the even sixth and eighth worlds. But since the future-modeled form of this world has 2 light units for the lateral system (1 macrohexagram = 1 light unit; 3 microhexagrams = 1 light unit) and its one color-individuated central microhexagram is also worth 1 light unit, a matching single light unit would have to be drawn from the collective central macrohexagram to bring each one-sixth of the fourth-world matrix up to parity, each thus having 4 light units with the total sixfold number being 24, 6 *more* than the parity figure of 18. If, however, no extra light units are drawn for the future-modeled fourth-world matrix, we would have an exact equality between the matrix and construction numbers, which could serve as a base for all further deviations, but no central-lateral matrix parity as should be featured by an even world. *So one way or another, a future-modeled fourth-world diagram would produce irregularity in its own domain.*

On the other hand, the past modeling of the fourth-world diagram would produce an irregular parity of central and lateral light units in the fifth-world matrix, however desirable the dual zero bases for the sequence of decimal differences would also be. But even the four light units earlier considered to have been drawn for the past-modeled fourth-world matrix to bring it up both to matrix parity and

a whole number cannot be validated by any other aspect of the diagram since there is no way of determining the light-unit value of the collective central macrohexagram. It is the very fact of its indeterminate value that precludes any rational method of determining the total number of fourth-world light units and so renders this world fundamentally irregular. But our present survey of fourth-world possibilities, rather than ruling out the earlier concept of light units, has only succeeded in reestablishing it on a new basis. And the concept of light units, shorn of mythological interpretation, will prove most fruitful in providing the basis of the final extrapolation of the diagram to infinite worlds when further related to the gender modeling of construction elements here first essayed. It may be useful to partially extend table 14.1, using the nonparity fifth-world figures.

The correlation between construction elements and gender, developed theoretically in chapter 6, was just developed into a mathematical function relating construction elements with matrix elements up through the seventh world. We are now to see how this function can be further extrapolated to infinity, finally remaining the only aspect of the diagram productive of further unpredictable change. For we have a final truth to learn from the eighth-world matrix, one deriving from the new relationship of construction to matrix elements as applied to this world.

The numbers of cumulative construction elements for the eighth-world diagram are 54 vertical and 27 horizontal elements, which multiplied yields the following product: $54 \times 27 = 1,458$. Turning now to the matrix elements, we saw that the light-unit value for the central components is 84 as it is also for the lateral. If we now add them together and multiply them by the 6 for the full matrix, we reach the following product: $84 + 84 = 168 \times 6 = 1,008$. Taking the figures for the seventh world in table 14.3 and adding its total previous accumulation of rebalanced light units, 486, brings us to the following sum: $1,008 + 486 = 1,494$. This sum is again quite close to the eighth-world product of multiplied construction elements, 1,458, just 36 units above this target figure. If we exclude the irregular

Table 14.4: Comparison of Construction and Matrix Elements

W	CLU	LLU	XLU	V	H		XCE	# DIF	DD
4				6	x	3	=	18		
5	3	2 1/3	3 + 2 1/3 = 5 1/3 5 1/3 x 6 = 32 32 + 18 = 50	9	x	6 = 54		−4	−.074074
6	8	8	8 + 8 = 16 16 x 6 = 96 96 + 54 = 150	18	x	9 = 162		−12	−.074074
7	27	26 1/3	27 + 26 1/3 = 53 1/3 53 1/3 x 6 = 320 320 + 162 = 482	27	x	18 = 486		−4	−.008230

fourth world, this is the first time the difference, however small, is a surplus rather than deficit, the positive decimal of .024591358. And this may be another indicator of a basic distinction between the worlds related to cosmic limitation and those wholly identified with the realm of the infinite. The eighth is the first such world, and we shall see if it sets a pattern to be followed by the ninth. But whatever the case may be, it is surely remarkable that, even with the earlier attributed additions from the collective matrix source that brought the seventh-world light-unit total to the parity figure of 486, the addition of the eighth-world sum of 1,008 should result in an approximation at such large numbers that is as close as 1,494:1,458. This indicates beyond a doubt that the light-unit measure of matrix elements and multiplied product of construction elements are somehow related.

If the change to a positive difference seen at the eighth-world level is to be followed by the infinite sequence of all the later worlds that can collectively be called Shemini, the "eighth" domain, then this change from the negative differences of the fifth through seventh worlds to the positive differences of all worlds beginning with the eighth would be a remarkable confirmation of the earlier mythological correlations of the Sabbatical worlds with the bounded finite cosmos and the worlds of Shemini with the infinite extension of Ein Sof, the Limitless One. It is appropriate that such a change should begin with the eighth world wholly identified with the infinite rather than with the seventh, whose halves are split between the realms of the finite and of the infinite. The seventh world follows the sixth in exemplifying such a transitional nature. As the sixth was connected to the earlier worlds in the Spiral Tree it shared with them and also to the further Worlds to Come in establishing both the form of the future matrix borders and the portion of the expanding diagrams to be defined by its colors, so is the seventh world connected to the earlier finite worlds in its negative difference and to the following worlds in the star shape first fully defined by its matrix border. But with the eighth world, a decisive change, a phase shift, would seem to be occurring in the Sabbath Star Diagram, one from an earlier stage in which the cumulative light units were fractionally less than the cumulative multiplied construction elements to one in which they are fractionally more, a difference that, if sustained, can obviously make an important contribution to the cosmological implications of the diagram.

Though these surpluses can be as easily balanced mythologically by the divine transcendence as the deficits were by the divine immanence, the former understood simply to be absorbed by the very infinity of its expanding structure, there is no longer a need for such mythological explanations now that we have moved to the rebalancing method of purely numerical computation. But if we are to continue this computational method of rebalancing the differences between the actual count of light units in a world with the multiplied cumulative counts of its vertical and horizontal construction elements, then we would be adding another "mythological" element to the absolute realm of geometry, the theory that there is a homeostatic mechanism at work in the deep structure of the diagram that rebalances the differences between the counts of matrix and construction elements at each new world level rather than letting these differences float freely. The computational difference is that in the rebalancing method the light-unit counts for a world would be added to the cumulative product of regular construction elements for the previous world, the assumed parity figure for the light units of that world, whereas in the free-floating method the light-unit count would be added to the unrebalanced cumulative light-unit count of the previous world. But as we shall see still more clearly in what follows, it is only the rebalancing method that can provide valid results for any further extrapolation of our knowledge of the Sabbath Star Diagram beyond the ninth world. The reason for this is the true irregularity of matrix components in the fourth world, an irregularity from which a firm base cannot be provided for any later computation of free-floating differences. A final reason to retain the method of rebalancing is that it has led to the recognition of an important phase shift from negative to positive numbers at the eighth world, which is a major teaching of this diagram level. For whereas in the seventh world the difference between the infinite and finite worlds was graphically conveyed through the contrasting multiworld matrix forms of the star and the tree, at the eighth world this difference would seem to be reflected in the shift from negative differences to a positive difference, from deficits to a surplus.

We must now conclude our geometric investigation of the relationship of such sexually defined construction elements to their matrix child by turning directly to the results of the final constructible matrix, that of the ninth world. The total for both systems is 520, and multiplying this final sum by 6 for the complete matrix and adding the cumulative light units of the eighth-world matrix by the rebalancing method, we arrive at the final ninth-world

sum: $520 \times 6 = 3{,}120$; $3{,}120 + 1{,}458 = 4{,}578$. The next step is to compare this figure with that of the multiplied cumulative construction elements for the ninth world, the multiplication of its 81 vertical elements by its 54 horizontal elements that yields the product of 4,374. As this is lower than the light unit totals, the difference between multiplied construction elements and cumulative light units is again a sequentially related positive decimal: $4{,}578 - 4{,}374 = 204$; $204 \div 4{,}374 = .04663923$. The major question raised by the eighth-world shift from negative to positive differences was whether this would continue, and we see that it not only does continue this positive direction but increases the difference. It would thus appear that this shift at the eighth-world level is not an anomaly but the beginning of a new sequence of expanding positive differences of major cosmological significance, signifying no less than the shift from the bounded finite realm to the unbounded realm of the infinite.

By the ninth world, all aspects of the expanding Sabbath Star Diagram have become regular and the most significant still evolving element of the Sabbath Star Diagram is that of the decimal differences between the construction and matrix figures when calculated in accordance with special rules. Since table 14.2 showed the expansion of the matrix to be governed by regularities as predictable as those for the construction elements, there is nothing further to be learned by such numerical extrapolation. But the sequence of decimal differences still has secrets to reveal.

To generate this sequence from the various formulae thus far developed for calculating the increases of matrix and construction elements, a further procedure or algorithm must be followed:

1. To derive the figure for the multiplied construction elements, multiply the previous such number by 3 beginning with 18 at the fourth-world level.
2. To derive the rebalanced light-unit count:
   (A) First derive the light unit counts for the individual categories in the following manner: $(A \times 3) + B + C + (D \div 3)$;
   (B) Then multiply the light unit product thus derived by 6;

(C) Finally, add the multiplied light units thus derived to the number for the multiplied construction elements of the previous world.

3. To derive the decimal difference between no. 1 and no. 2, subtract the rebalanced light units (RLU) from the multiplied construction elements (XCE) of the same world and divide the difference by this same XCE.

In table 14.5, this complicated procedure will be followed only through the thirteenth world, that which concludes the second octave of the musical analogue to the diagram. This table has seven columns: the world (W); the final light-unit totals taken from table 14.3 (LU); these light-unit totals multiplied by 6 (XLU); the rebalanced light units (RLU), which add to the XLU figures those of the previous world's multiplied construction elements; the multiplied construction elements (XCE); the numerical difference between the RLU and XCE figures (#D), and the final all-important decimal difference between the #D and XCE figures (DD):

What can already be seen through the numerical extrapolation of the diagram to its thirteenth world is that the decimal differences derived through complicated algorithmic procedures do, indeed, form a sequence. It is a sequence that switches permanently from the negative to the positive at the eighth world

and then undergoes a rapid inflation that can be simply graphed. The further features of this infinite decimal sequence will be developed in chapter 15, a treatment that brings the experimental mathematics of this study to a stunning close with the development of a new infinite model for cosmic complexity, and there is no need to continue the exploration of this sequence here. But there are a few final points to be considered about the initial extrapolation of the diagram to the thirteenth level of expansion that will complete its mythological interpretation.

The first is the meaning of the functional difference between the XCEs and RLUs, that is, between the multiplied construction elements and the rebalanced matrix light units; for the decimal differences between them are defining a mathematical "function," a rule of correspondence between two sets. And since this function is based upon a multiplication of complementary construction elements generative of a matrix product, the whole procedure may be regarded as a mathematical metaphor or analogue for sexual generation, as providing an abstract archetype that at a lower level of correspondence is reflected in just such reproduction. If, therefore, the construction elements may be regarded as the parents and the matrix as their offspring, then what this function is defining may be said quite literally to be the "generation gap." What is most interesting about this generation gap is what

Table 14.5. Double-Octave Decimal Differences

W	LU	XLU	RLU	XCE	#D	DD
4				18		
5	5⅓	32	50	54	−4	−.074074074
6	16	96	150	162	−12	−.074074074
7	53⅓	320	482	486	−4	−.008230452
8	168	1,008	1,494	1,458	+36	+.024691358
9	520	3,120	4,578	4,374	+204	+.046639231
10	1,584	9,504	13,878	13,122	+756	+.057613168
11	4,800	28,800	41,922	39,366	+2,556	+.064929126
12	14,472	86,832	126,198	118,098	+8,100	+.068587105
13	43,560	261,360	379,458	354,294	+25,164	+.071025758

it shows about the difference of this relationship in the first and second octaves, that in the first octave the parents are dominant while in the second the son achieves ascendancy. This can be derived from the distinction between the negative differences in the worlds associated with the finite, the fifth through seventh worlds, and the positive differences in the worlds wholly associated with the infinite, those beginning with the eighth world. Translating this still further in terms of mythological interpretation, we may say that in the fifth to seventh worlds the soul is still subject to the constraints of material creation while from the eighth world on it becomes ever more dominant over them.

We can understand this better by appreciating the nature of these spiritual dimensions, particularly those that can be identified with the World to Come. The dimension of the sixth world can be identified as the transpersonal force that may be thought to work through the conditions of man and his earth, informing natural law, particularly probability, the tides of history, and social relationships, an identification more fully developed in appendix B. That of the seventh world can be more distinguished from nature, revealing itself in the experience of the holy as an apprehensible Presence. Both are high dimensions, and may be further considered to define those lowest levels of the World to Come whose recognizable earthly features have entered into the fables of an afterlife cherished by most religious traditions. But whether correlated with recognized categories of spiritual phenomena in this world or the next, they are still bound to the experiences and constraints of this world of matter. What the change to positive differences in the second octave suggests, however, is that from the world of Shemini onwards, the soul of man will evolve into dimensions relatively free of such constraints.

Though we have now left the experimental geometry of the Sabbath Star Diagram for that of abstract number, let us remember that the major impression of its final diagrams taken in sequence was that of a pulsating star. Since the matrix can, in general, be identified with the concept of the son, that of the seventh world particularly so in view of its suggestive count of light units involving the Gematria of the son, Ben, the conclusion to which we seem drawn is that the form of the ascendant androgynous cosmic child will be that of a star pulsing with eternal life. We can go even further on the basis of previously interpreted geometric evidence, in the final section of chapter 12, and say that, at least as far as the tenth world, the eternal life with which this star is pulsating is the higher evolved form of earth-born man.

Interestingly, the tonal analogue to the culminating element of the tenth world is the upper Sol Sabbath Star, the octave of the Sabbath Star identified most closely with man. In terms of the diatonic octaves, the first culminates at the midpoint of the seventh world while the second culminates at the midpoint of the thirteenth. But in terms of the harmonic octaves, the second octave is broken only by the Sol harmonic, the series to this point being Do^1, Do^2, Sol^1, Do^3. Thus whether we speak in terms of diatonic or harmonic octaves, the midpoint of the second such octave is that of Sol, a tone that we can identify either with the higher resonance of man (diatonic) or his higher emergence (harmonic). And this point marking the octave of man in the double octave diatonic scale can be correlated with the tenth world of the Sabbath Star Diagram, the highest from which we can derive any visual clues. If it is such visual evidence that is the criterion for the continued geometric expansion of this diagram, then the fact that the tenth world is the highest into which we can peer may also bring the Sabbath Star Diagram into coherence with the ten dimensions of superstring theory.

But as we take our leave of this geometry and its harmonic correspondences, there is one final conclusion that I would like to draw from the very process of bringing the construction of the Sabbath Star Diagram to this ultimate point. For the difficult process of moving this geometric voyage of discovery ever further, of figuring out ways to map the matrices of first the eighth and then the seemingly impossible ninth world, a process that finally revealed all of its secrets, has also provided me with the most important teaching of all: that if you go as far as you possibly can, you will get where you need to be.

CHAPTER 15

The Final Model of Infinity: The Sabbath Star System

THE PERIODIC DECIMAL SEQUENCE

Chapters 13 and 14 may well be the most significant thus far on the laws both of diagram construction and complexity, serving to qualify and extend earlier conclusions as well as conquering ever further realms of complexity through the logical clarity of geometric modeling and numerical extrapolation. Chapter 13 gives us our only geometric intelligence regarding the infinite realms beyond the finite circle of the Lurianic Tzimtzum, that identified with the midpoint of the seventh-world diagram and analogous to the musical octave. After regularities in the growth of the matrix were discovered in chapter 13, chapter 14 first takes the matrix numbers so developed and numerically extrapolates them further. It then relates these numbers to the gender distinction of the construction elements earlier defined in chapter 6, which distinguishes a "masculine" vertical grid from a "feminine" horizontal grid and explores the generative purpose of such gender difference. For the matrix produced by the intersection of the horizontal and vertical construction grids can be regarded as the product or "son" of such parentally defined construction elements. That these definitions were somehow more than just metaphoric, or metaphor itself to have a more rigorous basis, emerged when the biblical metaphor of multiplication was applied literally to that interaction of horizontal and vertical construction elements now being associated with generation. It was the multiplied sum of the horizontal and vertical construction elements within a world that proved to have a functional relationship to a particular method of counting light-unit values in the matrix, the parental elements being functionally related through arithmetic multiplication to a special value of their matrix offspring.

This understanding of the matrix provided the most significant interpretative clue to the final destiny of that with which it was now identified, the androgynous son born of the cosmos but transcending its finitude in the pulsating form of an infinitely expanding star. It was with the ninth-world matrix that the regularities beginning with the full seventh-world matrix became clear and an algorithm could be written for the numerical extrapolation of the diagram to infinite worlds. But what seemed at the end of chapter 14 to be the final and culminating point to which analysis of the Sabbath Star Diagram could be taken will now be seen to be a limit true only of its geometric aspects. In this chapter we shall investigate the higher levels of numerical abstraction to which the larger Sabbath Star System can be taken, beginning where the previous chapter left off to chart a new model for complexity theory based not upon infinite geometric expansion but the expansion of the infinite decimal sequences derived from the finally most significant functional relationship of construction to matrix elements in the later worlds of the Sabbath Star Diagram.

What is most remarkable about the incomplete construction of the eighth and ninth diagram worlds recently attempted is that it was possible to push such geometric exploration just far enough for it to yield a new level of numerical abstraction, one in which all the components of each further world could be calculated without the need for actual geometric construction. While it would be possible to continue the geometric exploration of the diagram through a shift to more powerful computer technologies, the information resulting from what would finally be the numerical product of internal computer scanning would still be of a lower order than that which we shall see to result from the process of numerical abstraction just begun. Thus the progression from geometric construction to numerical calculation can be viewed as marking a phase shift in the development of the larger Sabbath Star System, a shift much like that of a substance from the solid to the liquid state.

But the complicated procedures outlined in the previous chapter for determining the abstract numerical expansion of the diagram, that which finally yielded the decimal difference of the all-important functional relationship between their construction and matrix elements, is only a transitional stage in the shift to a truly higher order of numerical abstraction. As an end in itself, it only provides a more convenient tallying of the numerical aspects of the diagram. It is not the attempt to simplify the data of the diagram to just its numerical terms that can bring us to a level of abstraction more meaningful than continued geometric expansion; rather, it is the shift of attention from the now com-

pletely regular aspects of the diagram to the one aspect it retains still capable of generating change, that of the decimal differences. For the phase shift from study of all aspects of a two-dimensional diagram to study of just one linear function of that originating numerical source gives us a means of studying the structure of what we can now call the Sabbath Star System at the simplified linear dimension from which its expansion can be carried to infinity. But this is not only the shift from two dimensions to one. What is even more important is that the decimal sequence can become entirely independent of the geometric categories of the diagram, can become no longer a function of the relationship of two regular sets of numbers but self-generating. And though such a study could be pursued through the more cumbersome method previously outlined, the move to self-generation marks a truly radical phase shift in the system.

By carrying this decimal sequence through further extrapolated worlds of the diagram a pattern could be discerned in its development that can be reduced to a simple formula: $D = (B - A)/3 + C$. We shall now proceed directly to the instructions for the initial uses of this formula,[1] which becomes regular with the seventh world.

The fact that the decimal difference for the seventh world is a negative means that it has to be added rather than subtracted from the eighth-world decimal, in accordance with normal arithmetic rules. For all the later decimals, however, the regular formula should be used. Since the full study of this decimal sequence will require the use of ever larger decimal places, if one is using a computer it is important that the first A, B, and C values fed into it be the original fractions, not any limited decimal expansion. These original fractions can be determined on the basis of table 14.4 in chapter 14, the numerator being the difference (#D) between the rebalanced light units (RLU) and multiplied construction elements (XCE) figures for a world and the denominator just its XCE figure. For the seventh through the eleventh worlds, these fractions and their expansions to eight precise digits, precise in that the final rounding digit has been left off, are found in table 15.1.

Table 15.1. The First Formula-Derived Decimal Differences

WORLD	FRACTION #	DECIMAL
7	−4/486	−.00823045
8	36/1,458	+.02469135
9	204/4,374	+.04663923
10	756/13,122	+.05761316
11	2,556/39,366	+.06492912

In verifying this formula with a simple calculator, it is better to first derive the decimal expansions of each of the three fractions involved and then apply the formula to the decimals. If the first A is that of the seventh world, the formula, applied as $(B + A)/3 + C$, would work out as follows: $(.02469135 + .00823045)/3 + .04663923 = .05761316$. If A begins with the eighth world of positive decimals, the formula, applied as $(B - A)/3 + C$, would work out similarly: $(.04663923 - .02469135)/3 + .05761316 = .06492912$.

The decimal sequence was earlier taken only through the thirteenth-world level, but if we now take it as far forward as the thirty-third world and as far back as the sixth, a remarkable structure will begin to emerge. There are a few reasons why it seems best to begin table 15.2 with the sixth world. The first is the still unresolved conflict between the two ways of modeling the fourth-world diagram that can give the differing light-unit totals for both the fourth- and fifth- world matrices seen in tables 14.3 and 14.4. Though the regularities later developing in the matrix would seem to give greater support to the fifth-world figures appearing in table 14.4, which result from the future modeling of the fourth-world diagram, they also show the imperfect coherence between these later derived rules and the numbers for the fourth- and fifth-world matrices. Thus we are only on certain ground with the numbers for the sixth-world matrix. Indeed, even if the decimal difference for the fifth world is allowed that makes it the same as that for the sixth world, a consistent progression of the decimal sequence can still only begin with the sixth, a circumstance that may

be said to unite the identical decimals of the fifth and sixth worlds into a single functional unit. But the final reason is most decisive, that it will give a more meaningful form to the sequence extending from it to the thirty-third world. In table 15.2, the world number will first appear, followed by the number of the decimal in the formula-derived sequence, and finally the decimal itself, taken to only seven precise places except for the thirty-first and thirty-second worlds, where an eighth place will be added in parenthesis.

There are a few extraordinary facts about this sequence, perhaps the most immediately striking being that it begins and ends with the same repeated numbers, .0740740. This is all the more striking inasmuch as the initial negative form of this decimal is not part of the formula-derived sequence but a product of what had originally appeared to be a wild irregularity, the sixth-world deficit of 12 light units with respect to the figure of 162 for its multiplied construction elements. Even more interesting is the fact that the fraction $^{-12}/_{162}$, as also the fraction $^{-4}/_{54}$ of the fifth world, reduces to that of $^{-2}/_{27}$, this being the lowest fractional equivalent of the decimal expansion .074074074. . . . Whether positively or negatively, then, the periodic decimal expansion with which we are concerned is the equivalent of the fraction $^2/_{27}$ or its closest approximation. The latter is the case with the negative sixth-world form, which is already an infinitely expanding periodic decimal. In the case of the positive decimals, however, it takes many iterations of the formula to go from one repetition of the numbers 074 to the next, and there is always some remainder. Whether this remainder will finally be resolved at infinity or continue to be generated is a question that cannot be answered. But what we can say is that the infinite expansion of the periodic decimal −.074 is already fully contained in its sixth-world fractional equivalent while it will take at least to infinity to arrive through the formulaic process at its positive counterpart. What is more, the fraction $^2/_{27}$ seems to contain a key to the most immediate meaning of this sequence. For as indicated by the list of formula numbers, there are exactly twenty-seven stages between the decimals of the sixth and thirty-third worlds, two of which are

Table 15.2. The Sabbath Star Periodic Decimal Sequence

WORLD	FORMULA#	DECIMAL
6	0	−.0740740
7	1	−.0082304
8	2	+.0246913
9	3	+.0466392
10	4	+.0576131
11	5	+.0649291
12	6	+.0685871
13	7	+.0710257
14	8	+.0722450
15	9	+.0730579
16	10	+.0734644
17	11	+.0737353
18	12	+.0738708
19	13	+.0739611
20	14	+.0740063
21	15	+.0740364
22	16	+.0740514
23	17	+.0740615
24	18	+.0740665
25	19	+.0740698
26	20	+.0740715
27	21	+.0740726
28	22	+.0740732
29	23	+.0740736
30	24	+.0740737
31	25	+.0740739(1)
32	26	+.0740739(8)
33	27	+.0740740

different from the others in terms of being negatives. As these two negative decimals represent $^2/_{27}$ of this sequence, so would they seem to epitomize the meaning of the whole.

This meaning can be apprehended more clearly by reviewing the earlier definitions of these worlds. As developed in the previous chapter, the shift from negative to positive decimals corresponds to the distinction otherwise made between the finite and infinite worlds, the finite division culminating within the seventh world and the infinite fully beginning with the eighth, the number biblically associated with a realm beyond time, beyond even the Sabbath. If, therefore, the positive elements of this decimal sequence define the ever expanding realm of the infinite and the negative elements not only define the bounded finite realm but also epitomize the whole sequence, then we can say that the sixth and seventh worlds, the lowest of the spiritual dimensions, are a true mirror of the infinite, in this conforming to the Hermetic dictum: "As above, so below." Like the concept of the holy that its dimension signifies, the seventh world unites the finite with the infinite, a characteristic seen again in this sequence insofar as it is united with the finite through its negative number and with the infinite in being the first decimal to conform to the formula for further decimal iteration. But it is the sixth world that was earlier identified with the dimension of meaningfulness, and its uncanny intelligence is again confirmed by the key it provides for the whole infinite sequence of positive decimal expansion. As its precise number of matrix components had earlier made it possible to discern a Spiral Tree in its cumulative matrix, so now what had appeared to be a light-unit count most irregular in its correlation with the multiplied construction elements of its world proves to contain the key to a higher level of numerical abstraction, the linear system going from the negative to the positive form of the periodic decimal .074.

If it is the sixth- and seventh-world diagrams that can be said to epitomize the whole infinite expansion of this decimal sequence, then what these two twenty-sevenths of the initial sequence are particularly mirroring is precisely the relationship of the finite to the infinite given such expressive form by their distinctive matrices, that of the sixth world completing the finite tree and that of the seventh beginning the infinite star. When we have completed the full analysis of this decimal sequence and the still higher level of abstraction to which it can finally be taken, we shall be able to recognize in the sixth and seventh worlds an even more precise mirroring of the whole structure of the infinite. We shall be able to see the same distinction between the mythological correlations that had earlier characterized the sixth- and seventh-world diagrams emerge again as most characteristic of the distinction between the two levels of numerical abstraction to which this chapter will be devoted, that in terms of which the sixth world was associated with the cosmological level of the Partzufim, the divine personalities, and the seventh world with Ein Sof, the Limitless One. But we should now look more closely at the first twenty-seven stages of this lower-level decimal sequence.

Such observation will reveal four clearly distinguished major phases. The first comprises the sixth and seventh worlds and is characterized by both the negative nature of its decimals and their extremely rapid deflation from −.0740740 to just below zero. The second comprises the eighth through thirteenth worlds and is characterized by both the shift to positive decimals and their rapid inflation from .02 to .07. As the seventh world is variously transitional, so is the thirteenth, the third phase beginning with it and extending to the twenty-first, a period in which the high positive curve of the preceding phase begins to flatten out, going in eight stages from .0710 to a high point of only .0740. With the next twelve steps of the final fourth phase, the infinitely repeating nature of this decimal becomes manifest with its first repetition, .0740740. The four phases are, then, those of the negative and, after the shift to the positive, of vertical inflation, of horizontal flattening, and of repetition. What such phases can further symbolize may perhaps be gleaned from the one identification already made for the decimals of the second phase at the end of chapter 14.

It was there suggested that the second octave, most specifically the six worlds from the eighth through the thirteenth, could be associated with the concept of the son insofar as the decimal function of the relationship of matrix son to parental construction elements indicated an ascendancy of the elements of the son over those of the parents. In terms of the geometry of the diagram, the construction

elements will always be correlated with the sexually distinguished parents of a matrix offspring and the decimal sequence will define the functional relationship of parents to child. But once this sequence becomes self-generating it can be interpreted apart from any such geometric correlations. It can become an independent model of the dimensions of the infinite. For where the seven fully constructed worlds of the Sabbath Star Diagram were finally seen to provide a geometric model of the generation of the cosmic son, the four phases of the linear sequence can place this son in a larger context, that of the Partzufim. We have already seen that the first octave can also be associated with the concept of the Shekhinah, this in view of the fact that the collective central macrohexagram of Malkhut, the Sefirah traditionally identified with the Shekhinah or its Partzuf correlate of the Nukvah, was considered to provide a reservoir for light-unit rebalancing through the seventh world. Thus we come to the linear model with suggestive identifications of its first two phases derived from its two-dimensional source, the negative decimals being identified with the Partzuf of the daughter and the rapid vertical inflation of the positive decimals with the Partzuf of the son. Once these lower phases have been so defined, there seems reason to identify the upper two phases with the parental Partzufim. This is particularly strong for the third phase, which begins as the second ended with the thirteenth world and changes the shape of the linear graph from an ascending curve to a virtually horizontal line. With the background of the last two chapters, we should be able to recognize a masculine character in the sharply vertical rise of the second phase and a feminine character in the horizontality of the third phase. Added to this is the fact that the number thirteen with which it begins has been culturally linked to the feminine in view of the thirteen feminine cycles within the solar year. The features of the third phase are suggestive, then, of its identification with the Partzuf of the mother, Imma, and there is reason to identify the fourth phase with the Partzuf of the father, Abba. We have already seen that there is more than one way to number the successive stages of the decimal sequence. And as the decimal sequence can be numbered either in accord with the worlds of the Sabbath Star Diagram or the beginning of the formula-derived sequence, so can it be numbered beginning with the first of the positive decimals, changing 8 now not to 2 but to 1. If this last numbering system is adopted, the thirty-third stage will prove, in the positive sequence, to be the kabbalistically significant number 26, the Gematria equivalent of the Tetragrammaton. It is the Tetragrammaton that provides the most meaningful correlation not only with the culminating phase of the decimal sequence but with its larger four-stage structure.

The twenty-sixth numbered stage of the positive decimal sequence does not mark the end of the sequence, only of the period that defines its character, the periodic reappearance of the numbers 074 that will continue at various iterations to emerge with the infinite applications of the formula ($B - A)/3 + C = D$. It is a miniature version of this infinitely extensible sequence. This double character accords well with the Tetragrammaton model of the five Partzufim. In this model the upper two, Arikh Anpin and Abba, also identified with the Sefirot of Keter and Chokhmah, respectively, are correlated with the single letter of the Yod (= 10); the third Partzuf Imma, also identified with the Sefirah Binah, is correlated with the upper Hey (= 5); the fourth Ze'ir Anpin, also identified with the six Sefirot from Chesed to Yesod, is correlated with the Vuv (= 6); and the fifth of the Nukvah, also identified with the Sefirah Malkhut, is correlated with the lower Hey (= 5). In their vertical arrangement the four letters of the Tetragrammaton are also thought to signify the all-containing figure of the cosmic anthropos Adam Kadmon, the Yod signifying his head, the upper Hey his shoulders and arms, the Vuv his torso, and the lower Hey his pelvis and legs, as should be apparent in the following illustration.

Thus the four major stages of the decimal sequence may be said to signify the same structure of the divine as that conveyed through the vertical Tetragrammaton model, whose four letters, when taken together, symbolize that divine figure of Adam Kadmon in whose image man was created and, when separated, the five divine personalities

derived from this anthropocosm. To complete this model of a four-stage cosmology, these four letters have also been correlated with the four worlds of emanation, the Yod with Atzilut, the upper Hey with Beriah, the Vuv with Yetzirah, and the lower Hey with Asiyah. In the Lurianic Kabbalah these worlds were regarded as originally supernal, but the catastrophic Shevirah was thought to lower each so that Asiyah was finally reduced to the material realm of the Kelipot, the shards of the Sefirotic vessels that had broken in the Shevirah. In terms of our decimal sequence, the effects of such a Shevirah may perhaps be discerned in the negative decimals identifiable with the lower Hey, Malkhut, and Asiyah. To continue this numerological exegesis, if the seventh world, which attaches the finite to the infinite, is now regarded as the lowest stage of the formula-derived sequence, and its number of stages is given in the earlier developed Gematria terms of YHVH-A by which the number 27 can be taken to signify the unity of God, then we may view the twenty-seven stages of the formula-derived sequence as signifying the reunification of the world of matter, Asiyah, with the upper three transcendent worlds allied to the Tetragrammaton in its more restricted identification with the positive spiritual realm.

But whether or not the number 26 of the positive sequence is related to the Tetragrammaton, it is clear that the four stages of the decimal sequence can be so related, the negative numbers with the lower Hey, the vertical inflation of the positive with the Vuv, its horizontal leveling with the upper Hey, and its repetitive round with the Yod, a correlation that also extends to the Partzufim and worlds associated with them. As we have seen, the lower two of these stages can be significantly correlated with the cosmology deriving from the Sabbath Star Diagram, its seven cosmic worlds having been associated with the lower feminine Partzuf of the Shekhinah or Nukvah and promising the ascendancy in the following stage of the son, both the perfected spiritual form of humanity and the Partzuf of Ze'ir Anpin. But this is as far as the geometry of the diagram can take us. It is rather the visualizable shape of the derivative decimal sequence as a linear graph that can enable us to place these prior personifications

Figure 15.1. The Vertical Tetragrammaton

into a larger cosmological context. We can now see that the era or level of the son is not the highest stratum of the divine supernal structure but comprised of only six of its stages, a number that is most significant, however, since the number 6, as both the Gematria of the Vuv and the number of Sefirot from Chesed to Yesod, has always been associated with the son Partzuf of Ze'ir Anpin. Beyond this is the longer horizontal phase of the divine mother and beyond that the still longer phase of the divine father in which the meaning of this cosmological decimal first becomes evident, that periodicity whose endless further repetitions may be identified with the realm of the still higher and androgynous Arikh Anpin but which is first manifest with the stage variously numbered as 33, 27, or 26.

Before we turn to further exploration of the realm of Arikh Anpin, there is a final point to be made about the numbers of the decimal as it emerges at this stage, .0740740. This is its remarkable association of the numbers 7 and 4, the two rival numbers of Jewish esoteric cosmology. We have just seen the way in which the number 4 figures in classical kabbalistic cosmology, but the earlier biblical and Merkabah cosmology was centered on the number 7, the days of creation and levels of heaven.

In the prior analysis of the Sabbath Star Diagram, an attempt was made to integrate these rival cosmologies into a larger structure of seven worlds, the four worlds of emanation of the classical Kabbalah and three further worlds of rectification, with the fourth world of Asiyah serving as the turning point between the worlds of the past and the future. But this inclusion of the four supernal worlds can now be viewed as another way in which the seven cosmic worlds mirror the infinite realm of the divine transcendence. For we now can see that the seven worlds of the two-dimensional model can be contained within a higher order of simplification reducible to a linear graph, a higher order in which these seven worlds are included as the lowest of four phases. Thus as the seven contain the four, so reciprocally do the four contain the seven. In the two-dimensional model, the first three worlds are primitive, the matrix only properly emerging with the fourth and gaining in complexity until it finally achieves full regularity in the seventh. In the one-dimensional model, the first seven worlds are primitive, the positive decimals only emerging with the eighth and gaining in value until the thirty-third when their regularity first becomes apparent. Thus the higher order of simplification to which we have moved is not the same as that at which we began. If the four major stages of the linear graph can, indeed, be identified with the concept of four supernal worlds, then these mark a new level of evolution of far greater range than the original hexagram elements of the Sabbath Star Diagram.

The most comprehensive cosmological model that can thus far be derived from the Sabbath Star System would seem to be that contained in the first four digits of the Sabbath Star periodical decimal sequence: .0740. Beginning with nothing, or more properly the nondimensional point, the Sabbath Star Diagram developed through seven two-dimensional stages, at which point it began to go through a phase shift to a linear equation, whose repeated iterations were marked by four major one-dimensional stages. How this total evolution may finally arrive at another nondimensional point, a point not the same as the first, we shall see as the Sabbath Star System undergoes a final phase shift to a still higher order of simplification. But to sum up what the intervening numbers of this cosmological decimal sequence have thus far shown us, it would appear that the seven-based cosmology of the two-dimensional diagram can be associated with the evolution of a finite cosmos, a cosmos informed by the immanence of spirit, the four-based cosmology of the linear sequence with the infinite structure of the divine as it largely transcends the finite cosmos, and that at certain stages in the evolution of complexity phase shifts occur that bring this system to ever higher orders of simplification.

THE CONVERGING DECIMAL SEQUENCE

Exploring the Data

In the previous section we have seen a radical shift occurring in what can now be called the Sabbath Star System from the plane geometry of the Sabbath Star Diagram to a linear formula for the independent generation of a periodic decimal sequence. And we have seen how the seven finite worlds of the Sabbath Star Diagram are transformed through a phase shift into the lowest level of a four-tiered linear system that can model with rare precision the

kabbalistic concept of the four supernal worlds and of their relationship to the finite cosmos. But our understanding of the structure of the infinite need not stop with the twenty-sixth positive decimal that shows this sequence to be periodic. We can also study the intervals of its periodicity to see what further we can learn of its structure, a study that may be said to lift us from the realm of Arikh Anpin, which is still at the lower level of the Partzufim, to that of Ein Sof. The difference between these realms is that the infinitely extended realm of the highest Partzuf is still generated by a formula derived from a Sabbath Star Diagram function while that of Ein Sof will involve a still higher level of abstraction, a new decimal sequence generated by the functional relationship in the primary sequence of world level to incidents of repetition. In the process a unique mode of experimental mathematics will be charted that, with the lower two levels of the Sabbath Star System, will provide the comprehensive model for a new theory of complex systems. This subsection will explore the data of this metasequence and the following subsection its implications for kabbalistic cosmology.

In this subsection, then, the formula generating the periodic decimal sequence will be taken by stages to a final 6,300 iterations at 1,500 decimal places[2] and the data reduced to a new set of decimal-expansible fractions, the numerators defining the number of the 074 repetition in the primary sequence and the denominators the world at which this repetition number appears in the reiteration of the formula. Interestingly, in charting the numbers of this sequence all three possibilities for numbering the first positive decimal were initially tried and that consistent with the worlds of the Sabbath Star Diagram proved to be the most trustworthy insofar as it yielded the most regular decimal sequence when so expanded. This would seem to indicate the larger coherence of all three levels of the Sabbath Star System, and in the following tables the numbers of the denominators will be those of the diagram worlds, the first positive decimal being identified with the eighth world. Table 15.3 gives just the principal points of decimal increase so that the major direction of the sequence can be gleaned.

Table 15.3. The Overall Metasequence

FRACTIONS	DECIMALS
1/20	.05
20/259	.07722007
32/410	.07804878
90/1,139	.07901668
109/1,378	.07910014
147/1,858	.07920258
213/2,686	.07930007
387/4,874	.07940090
500/6,295	.07942811

Unlike the periodic decimal sequence emerging from iterations of the diagram-derived formula ($B - A$)/3 + $C = D$, that emerging from a comparison of the number of 074 repetitions in this periodic sequence (the numerators) to the number of iterations of the formula necessary to reach such repetitions (the denominators) yields a different form of sequence when these fractions are expressed in their decimal equivalents. It is a sequence that appears to be increasing toward an asymptotic limit at infinity. There are three major stages of this increase: 0–20, which brings it through rapid inflation up to .077; 20–90, which brings it though a leveling of the curve to .079; and the final stage from just beyond 90 to infinity, which by 500 has only risen from .0790 to .0794. As will later be shown, the slowing of the sequence after 90 is matched by the increasingly small differences between each regular advance in the sequence. As these differences become increasingly infinitesimal, it seems clear that the sequence will converge at its asymptotic limit only at infinity. It would also seem that this limit point will be .08.

The first major implication of the decimal sequence defining the highest level of the Sabbath Star System is most appropriate in terms of the Jewish esoteric tradition. For from its biblical beginnings, the number 8 has always signified that highest cosmic stage beyond even the temporal periodicity of the Sabbath, a final stage that well accords with the personality hitherto ascribed to this metasequence, that of Ein Sof, the Limitless One. As the primary decimal

sequence combined the two most significant cosmological numbers of this tradition, seven and four, so does the metasequence derived from it bring us to the last cosmologically significant number of this tradition, eight. Curiously, the Arabic shape of this numeral is allied to the still more recently invented shape of the symbol of infinity, which itself brings us back to the esoteric meaning of the number 8 in the Hebrew Bible. As earlier shown in introducing the subject of the eighth-world diagram, the eighth day is one of special covenantal dedication, the day of circumcision, of the anointing of the priests, and of the last holiday of the Mosaic sacred year, Shemini Atzeret, the eighth day of Succot. The biblical sacred calendar moves from the seven days of Passover in the spring to the eight days of Succot in the fall, a progression paralleled by that from the Sabbatical model of the Sabbath Star Diagram to the modeling of the infinite by the two tiers of decimal sequences that begin and end with the realm of Shemini, of the eighth day.

The diagram plus the primary and metadecimal sequences derived from it form a system in which each higher order of simplification may also be said to represent an altered return through the same geometric dimensions through which the diagram originally emerged. As was shown in the introductory chapters of this work, construction of the first hexagram of the Sabbath Star Diagram requires three prior geometric steps that are also a model for the first acts of creation: the fixing of an initial point, the linear extension from that point, most easily by the movable foot of a compass, and the drawing of a circle around that fixed radius. But as within the seven worlds of the diagram the process of return was not from the fourth world back to the first, that signified by the original or Do hexagram, but forward to the seventh world of the octave, to the hexagram of the upper Do, so within the larger system, the return through the dimensions is accomplished through a forward progress. From the two-dimensionality of the Sabbath Star Diagram, the first order of numerical simplification led to a linear numerical formula whose reiterations produced a periodic decimal sequence. The second order of such simplification, involving study of the rate of periodic repetition in the primary sequence, resulted in a different form of decimal sequence, one converging to an asymptotic limit. Where the first will continue its .074074074 repetitions infinitely, the second will arrive at .08 at the point of infinity. The first would thus seem to represent an infinitely extending line and the second an infinite point.[3] And what they suggest is that after seven cosmic stages and four supracosmic phases, there will be a final movement of the whole toward convergence.

I earlier suggested that all of both Sabbath Star and kabbalistic cosmology could be summed up in the first four numbers of the primary decimal sequence, .0740, that these zeros could be equated not with nothing but with the nondimensional point, and that the second point was not the same as the first. In Zoharic cosmology creation begins with the fixing of an initial point and in Lurianic cosmology this point is further defined as centered in the finite space produced through the Tzimtzum, the circular retraction of the infinite substance of Ein Sof that left this finite space. In Sabbath Star cosmology, this finite space was fully occupied by the midpoint of the seventh world and the further development of the diagram system, first geometrically and then numerically, marks a progressive, four-stage movement into the very substance of Ein Sof. On the level of the primary decimal sequence, the finite worlds of the Sabbath Star Diagram were identified with the lowest level of a four-tiered system that could also be correlated with the five Partzufim, the first seven worlds with the Shekhinah, the next six worlds with the son Partzuf of Ze'ir Anpin, the next eight worlds going from thirteen to twenty-one with the maternal Partzuf and the following twelve to the thirty-third, which is also the twenty-sixth of the positive decimal sequence, with the paternal Partzuf. It was at this twenty-sixth positive stage that the periodic nature of the sequence first emerged and all subsequent repetitions of each periodic element were identified with the realm of the all-containing Partzuf of Arikh Anpin. It is not on the level of the Partzufim that convergence takes place, however, but on that of Ein Sof, of the metasequence that can be derived by tabulating the incidents of periodic repetition in the primary diagram-derived sequence. And this metasequence also has a structure of four phases.

The portion of the converging Ein Sof sequence to be examined in tables 15.4 through 15.8 has four major phases, the first of which can also be considered introductory, the next two as intermediate, and the fourth as final. The first introductory period may be considered to go from 0 to 17, the two intermediate phases from 18 to 83 and from 84 to 295, and the final phase from 296 to 5,005. In the last three phases of the system there are certain repetitions that advance the decimal sequence toward convergence and others that retard it, and tables 15.4 through 15.8 will be divided between them, the retarding decimals to the left and the advancing ones to the right. Various other regularities will also be charted. Following the initial fraction to the left, that in which the numerator defines the number of the 074 repetition in the primary sequence and the denominator the world at which iteration of the formula produced this particular 074 repetition, there will be a listing of the number of formula iterations or steps between such repetitions, that is, the difference between one denominator and that immediately preceding it, the list concluding with the decimal expansion of the original fraction taken to nine places. In table 15.4, the sequence will be taken only through the seventeenth world that concludes the first phase.

Table 15.4 of the introductory phase shows it to be marked by two characteristics, rapid inflation and a particular rate of formula iterations to 074 repetitions. This rate is one that varies between twelve or thirteen steps in a particular Sabbatical pattern that properly begins with the double thirteens: 13, 13, 12, 13, 12, 13, 12. Though there is nothing in this introductory phase to indicate that this pattern should begin with the thirteen of the fourth periodic repetition rather than the twelve of the first, later developments will confirm this to be the basic structural unit of the decimal sequence. As we shall soon also see, this basic pattern will be interspersed with another shorter unit of only five members in the following order: 13, 13, 12, 13, 12. But from this point on both these "weeks" and "subweeks" will display further patterning with respect to the increasing rate of sequence retardation. In the second phase (table 15.5), all of the twelve-step decimals

Table 15.4. The Converging Sequence—Phase I

FRACTION	STEPS	DECIMAL	FRACTION	STEPS	DECIMAL
	Sequence Retarding			Sequence Advancing	
			0/8	0	.0
			1/20	12	.05
			2/33	13	.060606060
			3/45	12	.066666666
			4/58	13	.068965517
			5/71	13	.070422535
			6/83	12	.072289156
			7/96	13	.072916666
			8/108	12	.074074074
			9/121	13	.074380165
			10/133	12	.075187969
			11/146	13	.075342465
			12/159	13	.075471698
			13/171	12	.076023391
			14/184	13	.076086956
			15/196	12	.076530612
			16/209	13	.076555023
			17/221	12	.076923076

Table 15.5. The Converging Sequence—Beginning of Phase 2

FRACTION	STEPS	DECIMAL	FRACTION	STEPS	DECIMAL
	Sequence Retarding			Sequence Advancing	
18/234	13	.076923076			
19/247	13	.076923076			
			20/259	12	.077220077
21/272	13	.077205882			
			22/284	12	.077464788
23/297	13	.077441077			
24/310	13	.077419354			
			25/322	12	.077639751
26/335	13	.07761194			
			27/347	12	.077809798
28/360	13	.077777777			
			29/372	12	.077956989
30/385	13	.077922077			
31/398	13	.077889447			
			32/410	12	.07804878
33/423	13	.078014184			
			34/435	12	.078160919
35/448	13	.078125			
			36/460	12	.078260869

Table 15.6. The Converging Sequence: Transition to Phase 3

Sequence Retarding			Sequence Advancing		
FRACTION	STEPS	DECIMAL	FRACTION	STEPS	DECIMAL
77/976	13	.078893442			
78/989	13	.078867542			
			79/1,001	12	.078921078
80/1,014	13	.078895463			
			81/1,026	12	.078947368
82/1,039	13	.078922040			
			83/1,051	12	.078972407
84/1,064	13	.078947368			
85/1,077	13	.078922934			
86/1,089	12	.078971533			
87/1,102	13	.07894368			
			88/1,114	12	.078994614
89/1,127	13	.078970718			
			90/1,139	12	.079016681
91/1,152	13	.078993055			
92/1,165	13	.078969957			
93/1,177	12	.079014443			
94/1,190	13	.078991596			
			95/1,202	12	.079034941
96/1,215	13	.079012345			
97/1,228	13	.078990228			
98/1,240	12	.079032258			
99/1,253	13	.079013750			
			100/1,265	12	.079051383
101/1,278	13	.079029733			
			102/1,290	12	.079069767

will be sequence advancing and all of the thirteen-step decimals sequence retarding. Though this second phase extends from 18 to 83, only its first three units will be shown in table 15.5 to illustrate its controlling patterns.

The first break in the introductory pattern of rapid inflation is hardly a break at all since the first two decimals of phase 2 neither advance the sequence nor pull it further back. But since any lack of advance retards the sequence, they may be considered sequence retarding. As we shall later see,

such overlapping between phases will mark the transition points of all the phases. What table 15.5 illustrates are one subweek and two weeks of the sequence-advancing and -retarding pattern of phase 2. The whole of phase 2 is composed of the following units, the first figures signifying the number of units and the second the number of their constituent members, five or seven: 1-5, 3-7, 1-5, 5-7. Table 15.6 picks up the sequence with the last week of phase 2 and the first three units of phase 3.

As can be seen, the clean division between the

twelve steps of the advancing decimals and thirteen of the retarding decimals is beginning to be altered as the first of the three advancing decimals of a seven-member unit goes over to the retarding column. In phase 3 the seven-member units now have only two advancing decimals and the five-member units only one. The larger tabulation of units for phase 3 is as follows: 1-7, 1-5, 2-7, 1-5, 7-7, 1-5, 2-7, 1-5, 7-7, 1-5, 2-7, 1-5, 5-7. The main divisions are into sets of two or seven weeks with a subweek between each set of weeks. In table 15.7 we shall see what happens when the second of the original twelve-step advancing decimals goes over, as it eventually must, to the retarding column. Table 15.7 begins with the last unit of phase 3 and the first four units of phase 4.

In the progressive pattern of retardation that marks this as any converging decimal sequence, the portion occupied by phase 3 is vast, almost 600 decimal places reaching to just under 900 such places at its close with the fraction $^{295}/_{3,717}$. But that of phase 4 promises to be still vaster. For the little more than 600 decimal places still remaining to the 1,500-decimal-place computer printout of this formula program just enables us to enter its portals. It is with this fourth and probably last phase of the converging sequence that we can properly appreciate the Sabbatical nature of its progress. For it is only now that the seven-member pattern of retreating and advancing decimals form themselves into a recognizable week, with six work-a-day retreating decimals and a finally advancing Sabbath. Deferring further consideration of the remarkable emergence of such a Sabbatical pattern until the close of this discussion, it should next be noted that the subweeks have now ceased to participate in the forward advance, can, in fact, be joined to the following week to make a larger twelve-member unit with only a single advancing decimal. But maintaining the formal division between such a subweek and the following week will help us to see the larger structure of sequence organization. Tabulating the units of phase 4 as far as the 1,500-decimal-place computation takes us yields the following pattern: 2-7, 1-5, 2-7, 1-5, 6-7, 1-5, 2-7, 1-5, 7-7, 1-5, 2-7, 1-5, 4-7, inc.

It is the apparently anomalous 6-7 set that actually provides the key to a far vaster megacycle that can be seen to be operating in the total sequence if the last weekly set of one phase is added to the first of the next. As will become clear in table 15.8, this would allow the first set of phase 4, 2-7, to merge with the last set of phase 3, 5-7, to form one larger regular set of 7-7. Even more significantly, the earlier merger of the closing 5-7 set of phase 2 with the opening 1-7 set of phase 3 would give us a similar 6-7 to that which has just emerged in phase 4. As the smaller units of weeks and subweeks begin with a distinctive double thirteen, so would it seem that the larger cycling of these units begins with a distinctive 6-7 set. As each set of weeks is preceded by a subweek, so may we consider the megacycle to begin with the subweek preceding the first 6-7 set, at $^{44}/_{561}$, and to close precisely where table 15.7 does, at $^{328}/_{4,132}$. Table 15.8 provides the full list of these units with other pertinent information.

In table 15.8 the solid lines indicate the phase changes and the broken lines the megacycle changes, and it can be seen that the larger cyclic changes pay no attention to the shifting patterns of advancing and retarding decimals that define the phases, but form sets that bridge the phase boundaries. It would thus appear that the only fully defined megacycle begins with the 44th repetition of 074 in the periodic sequence and ends with its 328th repetition, covering a total of 285 such repetitions at 3,584 formula iterations, the total number of steps per cycle. Recognizing that there is a 1-5 set before every set of weeks and so eliminating it from a simplified counting of the cycle units, the remaining cycle would consist of the following pattern of units: 6-7, 2-7, 7-7, 2-7, 7-7, 2-7, 7-7, 2-7. As can be seen, a new cycle begins at 329 and completes about two-thirds of this second cycle before it must stop because of inadequate decimal places for further propagation of the metasequence. But up to this stopping point, the pattern of repetition is exact: 6-7, 2-7, 7-7, 2-7, 4-7+. The pattern stops just in the middle of the second 7-7 set. It actually stops just before the final figures given in the chart, at the retarding fraction $^{499}/_{6,283}$, the last experimental advancing figures being those for the previous week of $^{493}/_{6,207} = .079426454$. But I have extrapolated the data from the final fraction

Table 15.7. The Converging Sequence—Transition to Phase 4

Sequence Retarding			Sequence Advancing		
FRACTION	STEPS	DECIMAL	FRACTION	STEPS	DECIMAL
289/3,642	13	.079352004			
290/3,655	13	.079343365			
291/3,667	12	.079356422			
292/3,680	13	.079347826			
293/3,692	12	.07936078			
294/3,705	13	.079352226			
			295/3,717	12	.079365079
296/3,730	13	.079356568			
297/3,743	13	.079348116			
298/3,755	12	.079360852			
299/3,768	13	.079365079			
300/3,780	12	.079365079			
301/3,793	13	.079356709			
			302/3,805	12	.07936925
303/3,818	13	.079360921			
304/3,831	13	.079352649			
305/3,843	12	.079365079			
306/3,856	13	.079356846			
307/3,868	12	.079369183			
308/3,881	13	.079360989			
			309/3,893	12	.079373234
310/3,906	13	.079365079			
311/3,919	13	.079365079			
312/3,931	12	.079369117			
313/3,944	13	.079361054			
314/3,956	12	.079373104			
315/3,956	13	.079365079			
316/3,982	13	.079357106			
317/3,994	12	.079369053			
318/4,007	13	.079361118			
319/4,019	12	.079372978			
320/4,032	13	.079365079			
			321/4,044	12	.079376854
322/4,057	13	.079368991			
323/4,070	13	.079361179			
324/4,082	12	.079372856			
325/4,095	13	.079365079			
326/4,107	12	.079376673			
327/4,120	13	.079368932			
			328/4,132	12	.079380445

Table 15.8. The Converging Sequence—Megacycles

PHASE	SETS	STEPS	OPENING FRACTION	FINAL FRACTION	FINAL ADVANCING DECIMAL
1	1–3*	37	1/20	3/45	.066666666
	2–7	176	4/58	17/221	.076923076
2	1–5	631	8/234	22/284	.077464788
	3–7*	264	23/297	43/548	.078467153
	1–5	63	44/561	48/611	.078559738
	(5–7*)	440	49/624	(83/1,051)	.078972407
3	(+1–7*)	88	(84/1,064)		
	6–7			90/1,139	.079016681
	1–5	63	91/1,152	95/1,202	.079034941
	2–7	176	96/1,215	109/1,378	.079100145
	1–5	63	110/1,391	114/1,441	.07911727
	7–7	616	115/1,454	163/2,057	.079241614
	1–5	63	164/2,070	168/2,120	.079245283
	2–7	176	169/2,133	182/2,296	.079268292
	1–5	63	183/2,309	187/2,359	.079270877
	7–7	616	188/2,372	236/2,975	.079327731
	1–5	63	237/2,988	241/3,038	.079328505
	2–7	176	242/3,051	255/3,214	.079340385
	1–5	63	256/3,227	260/3,277	.07934086
	(5–7*)	440	261/3,290	(295/3,717)	
4	(+2–7*)	176	(296/3,730)		
	7–7			309/3,893	.079373234
	1–5	63	310/3,906	314/3,956	
	2–7	176	315/3,969	328/4,132	.079380445
	1–5	63	329/4,145	333/4,195	
	6–7	528	334/4,208	375/4,723	.079398687
	1–5	63	376/4,736	380/4,786	
	2–7	176	381/4,799	394/4,962	.079403466
	1–5	63	395/4,975	399/5,025	
	7–7	616	400/5,038	448/5,641	.079418542
	1–5	63	449/5,654	453/5,704	
	2–7	176	454/5,717	467/5,880	.079421768
	1–5	63	468/5,893	472/5,943	
	4–7*	352	473/5,956	500/6,295*	.079428117

by adding another repetition at twelve steps to reach the round figure of $^{500}/_{6,295}$. What further can be learned from table 15.8 about both the beginning and end of this higher order infinite decimal sequence we are now to consider.

About its beginnings we see the same feature of irregularity that also characterized the evolution of the Sabbath Star Diagram from which it was ultimately derived, an initial irregularity yielding to final regularity as the system grows to sufficient complexity.

This can be seen in the initial subweek of only three members and the second set of weeks whose number is also an irregular and deficient three. A second point to be observed about the opening of the metasequence is that it resolves the issue of whether the primary sequence should be thought to begin with the seventh or eighth world, the former being the first case of formula applicability and the latter the first positive decimal. We have seen that the number of steps can only be twelve or thirteen, and since the first appearance of .074 in the primary sequence is at $1/20$, twelve steps would fix the originating point of the metasequence at the eighth world and thirteen at the seventh. Looking again at table 15.8, we can see that replacing the initial twelve steps there given by thirteen would produce a still more irregular set. As given, we have the 12, 13, 12 that always comes before the 13, 13 start of a new set, these latter being the number of steps that begin the first full week at the fourth and fifth repetitions, and we can extrapolate backward to an unmanifestable double thirteen at the beginning of its subweek. But beginning this first set with 13, 13, 12, and then going to 13, 13, 12, 13, 12, 13, 12, would mean that a necessary 13, 12 addition to this first subweek set has unaccountably been eliminated, a greater irregularity. This would seem to prove that the sequence should not be considered to begin with the negative decimal of the seventh world that, though it is consistent with the formula, would bring the interval of steps to a double thirteen abnormal for this position in the sequence. Having completed our experimental exploration of the converging decimal sequence, we should now turn to its implications.

Exploring the Implications

The converging sequence identified with Ein Sof and the infinite is most properly begun with the eighth world of Shemini that also signifies the realm of the infinite. And the further implication of this for the primary periodic sequence is that such counting of the eighth world as its first decimal gives a special importance to the number that defines the emergence of its periodicity, the number 26 that, as the Gematria of the Tetragrammaton, identifies this sequence with the Holy Name. What is even more remarkable is that a decimal function that entered its positive phase at the eighth world of an expanding geometric diagram should be taken to another order of abstraction in a decimal sequence converging to an asymptotic limit of .08. Thus from beginning to end, our exploration of the higher levels of numerical abstraction to which the Sabbath Star Diagram could be taken has been a modeling of Shemini, of that eighth day that can also be considered the infinite realm of Ein Sof.

"Had we but world enough and time,"[4] it would be interesting to continue the experimental investigation of this converging sequence. But beyond absorbing the operations of a university main frame computer and taking more than a lifetime, little further would be learned in terms of structural principles. I believe that at 1,500 decimal places the basic structure of the final phase of this decimal sequence and of the existence of larger megacycles has been discovered and what remains to be learned are only the more trivial details of the correct numbers for each cyclic period and the number of weeks in each set. For at even 1,500 places there is no way of predicting how long the cycle will persist and what cycling might follow. Before venturing some guesses about the sequence's final pattern of convergence, we should consider what reason there might be for considering its fourth phase to be its final one.

Although it is hazardous to draw any final conclusions about an infinite decimal sequence from a finite portion of it, it is the pattern of retardation to which we have now arrived that makes it appear that the fourth must be the final phase of this sequence. For this pattern cannot suffer any further retardation within its basic seven-member set without losing its distinctive character, a character that this final phase most clearly defines by its proportion of six retarding to one advancing decimal. Thus what most characterizes this last, eternally extending phase is the Sabbatical character by which it advances. After six weekday-like stages, which move back and forth without advancing at all, the seventh stage arrives by which alone the sequence can progress to its final infinite convergence. This feature of the sequence would seem to have significant nonmathematical implications, telling us that on earth as well the real spiritual work connecting one to eternity is that done on the Sabbath. The association of the eternal hereafter with the Sabbath is also a traditional Hebraic-Christian concept, perhaps nowhere better expressed than in Spenser's final, fervent hope that "thence-forth all shall rest eternally / With Him that is the God of Sabbaoth hight: O that great Sabbaoth God, graunt me that Sabbaoths sight."[5]

It is through the holy Sabbatical portion of time that we can progress beyond time to the eternal realm of Shemini. And this definition of eternity is marked by Sabbatical periods that would also seem to contain the final message of this infinite decimal sequence, that the process it is modeling is not so much a passage from time to eternity as the progressive eternalizing of time. This can be further understood by more closely examining the mechanism of this sequence's infinite progress, its patterned alternations between twelve and thirteen steps. For as the just considered numbers seven and eight of the sequence have cosmological significance, so do the numbers twelve and thirteen, numbers that for millennia have been associated with gender. Twelve is the number of masculine, solar reckoning and thirteen of feminine, lunar reckoning, and such gender associations of their correlated decimals will be seen to be consistent with the similar associations given to the worlds of the Sabbath Star Diagram. This would associate the horizontal, odd worlds with the feminine and the vertical, even worlds with the masculine, the feminine worlds conveying the grounded quality of their horizontal orientation and the masculine worlds the aspiration conveyed through their verticality. If now we look at the metasequence from this new perspective, we can see that the number thirteen correlated with the feminine is marked primarily as the mechanism of sequence retardation while the number twelve correlated with the masculine is the primary mechanism of sequence advancement, a distinction definitively manifested in phase 2. Thus if the direction of this sequence is toward convergence at infinity, and this can also be equated with eternity, then the force of

retardation is one pulling toward the finite and time while that of advancement is toward the infinite and eternal. These forces would also seem to reflect the gender distinction that can be made with respect to the divine, the feminine associated with the divine as immanent within the finite and the masculine with the divine transcendence and the infinite. If these traditional associations can be made, then we may also see operating within this converging sequence the same forces as inform the cosmos, the divine feminine principle retarding the sequence toward the finite and time, the divine masculine principle attempting to advance it toward the infinite and eternal. For though at the beginning they both collaborate to ensure its rapid inflation, their basic tendencies begin to separate out in the second phase, and from that point on the feminine seems to be gaining over the masculine, drawing ever more power from it to slow its advance. As this retardation continues, so may we imagine that first one and then the second of the two-week sets will go over to the column of retardation, leaving just the 6-7, 7-7, 7-7, 7-7 sets to advance each megacycle until they also are further reduced and the cycle itself undergoes still further change. But it is precisely this adjustment that is necessary to ensure the infinite progress of this decimal sequence. Without such functioning of both the masculine and feminine forces, "time, that takes survey of all the world, / Must have a stop."[6] Where the cessation of the masculine force would end the sequence and time at a finite point, the cessation of the feminine would bring eternity upon us too soon. Thus the lesson of an infinite converging decimal sequence is that both the forces of advancement and retardation are necessary to extend the process infinitely, that the true infinity is not only at the point of convergence but also in the process toward it. It is through the fine adjustment of these two forces both toward each other and toward the end of their progress that each new set and cycle is generated, such generation always being the result of an archetypal distinction and relationship of the sexes. So also has such a process been found to account for cell division, the union of one enduring and one mutable protein; and we are told that "when the proteins clasp together they take on the vitality of young lovers, galvanizing a cascade of changes in the cell that culminates in division."[7] From the replication of cells to the highest levels of spiritual rebirth, all forms of cosmic generation seem to be informed by the same interaction of complementary opposites as can be modeled by the highest level of the Sabbath Star System. For this infinite converging sequence but gives new form to the final cosmological message of the Sabbath Star Diagram, that same birthing of the cosmic child that it shows to be a product of the very union of time and eternity that also eternalizes time.

This is a lesson that any converging decimal sequence can teach, but it is the unique set of numbers emerging in this sequence, as in the primary sequence from which it was derived, that gives it special force as an archetypal cosmic model, numbers ultimately deriving from the even greater mystery of the Sabbath Star Diagram. That a mathematical model deriving from the hidden geometric tradition of the Kabbalah should carry special cosmological meaning but confirms the special access this tradition has to knowledge of ultimate principles. And yet one cannot help but be surprised at the complex encoding of this knowledge revealed by every aspect of the Sabbath Star System capable of experimental exploration. We have seen that the Sabbath Star Diagram may be said to model a seven-dimensional cosmos both because this is the furthest expansion of the diagram capable of ordinary construction and because the numerical and graphic features of this seventh expansion can be closely correlated with various aspects of the Jewish esoteric tradition. But nothing in this diagram can explain why a second-order simplification of a numerical function of this diagram should result in a Sabbatical pattern of decimal increase, why also the whole of this infinite decimal sequence should move to a convergence point at the very number eight that, for this tradition, symbolizes the transcendence of even such divinely informed time as is represented by the Sabbath, or why this movement should be mediated by the numbers twelve and thirteen expressive of the generative interaction of sexually associated forces that is the central mystery of this tradition. A mystery just as great is the complex patterning we have seen to emerge from the reiterative application of a simple formula to just three original fractions. Before seeing what final esoteric implications can be drawn from the successively higher orders of the Sabbath Star System, we should first examine their implications for complexity theory.

CONVERGENCE AND THE LAW OF COMPLEX MAGNITUDES

As a model for complexity theory, the Sabbath Star System may be said to be composed of four basic levels: the two-dimensional geometry of the Sabbath Star Diagram taken with complete construction through its seventh expansion or world and with incomplete construction through its ninth world; the first numerical phase in which the various aspects of the seventh through ninth worlds of the diagram are reduced to formulae for computing both their components and the functional relationship of their matrix to construction elements, and the worlds of the diagram are then taken by numerical extrapolation to the thirteenth world; the second numerical phase in which this geometric function, expressed through a decimal sequence, becomes independently generated by a formula and goes through four phases until the emergence of its periodicity at the thirty-third world; and the third numerical and second decimal phase that, at a higher order of abstraction, generates a new decimal sequence derived from the major functional relationship in the primary sequence taken to 1,500 decimal places in 6,300 iterations, a converging sequence that also has four major phases.

These four levels may be compared to astronomical levels: the first centered on Earth and its relationship to the Sun and Moon, the second on the solar planetary system containing Earth, the third on the Milky Way galaxy containing the Sun, and the fourth on intergalactic space. On this last, the news from outer space is no less than a discovery of "evenly distributed clumps of galaxies stretching across vast expanses of the heavens, suggesting a structure to the universe so regular and immense that it defies current theories of cosmic creation and evolution."[8] It is a similar movement toward immense regularity that the Sabbath Star System reveals.

On the lowest level of the Sabbath Star Diagram this system first showed itself to be one that gains in regularity as it grows in complexity. It moves from a first stage of irregular construction extending to the complete fourth world, through a period of regular construction and irregular matrices culminating with the sixth world, to a final period of regularity absolute for both its construction and matrix elements, one beginning with the seventh world but apparent only at the ninth. It is at this final glimpse into the increasingly regular structure of the diagram that it finally becomes too complex for continuing construction, but the regularity it has attained now also permits a further extrapolation of its growth. From this extrapolation a formula emerges that can continue the evolution of just the main functional relationship discovered in the geometric diagram, that of construction to matrix elements, now on the new numerically abstract level of a decimal sequence. This sequence also goes through various stages until it achieves a periodic regularity. But what is even more significant is the fact that though all the ingredients for generation of this independent decimal sequence are regular and the sequence itself exhibits the regularity of its periodicity, it yet develops a new level of functional unpredictability, that defining the relationship of the number of formula iterations needed to arrive at a new repetition of the three-digit unit of this periodic decimal, 074. Nonetheless, when the primary sequence is taken to 1,500 decimal places, and the functional relationship of repetition to reiteration is expressed in a higher level or metadecimal sequence, this higher sequence also moves through four phases to achieve a complex final mode of regularity.

At every scale of the system the same basic pattern of evolution is to be found. Each level begins with a few simple ingredients, a particular set of hexagrams or fractions and the procedures for their reiterative expansion. The first phases of each level have various irregular features that at a certain level of complexity become more regular only to drive the system to the new higher order of abstraction, which is also one of simplification, that again begins with greater irregularity and moves to greater regularity as it grows in complexity, a process that theoretically can be endlessly continued at ever larger scales. But in addition to those elements that are conserved from scale to scale, each level at each of its phases is characterized by a unique generation of patterning. The Sabbath Star System would seem to offer a new model for the theory of complex systems, one in which the growth is toward greater overall regularity rather than entropy. It is this theory that provides the best paradigm for the various forms of the experimental mathematics exploring dynamic systems that have emerged and the one in fullest accord with the evolution of the Sabbath Star System.

The nature and implications of complexity theory are well summarized by Jeremy Campbell:

> Complexity is not just a matter of a system having a lot of parts which are related to one another in nonsimple ways. Instead, it turns out to be a special property in its own right, and it makes complex systems different in kind from simple ones, enabling them to do things and be things we might not have expected. . . . Complexity is a decisive property. Below the critical level, the power of synthesis decays, giving rise to ever simpler systems. Above that level, however, the synthesis of more elaborate systems, under the right conditions, becomes explosive. . . . The power of a small number of fixed rules to produce an unpredictable amount of complexity is very striking. . . . A modest number of rules applied again and again to a limited collection of objects leads to variety, novelty, and surprise. . . . [W]ithout a code, a system is useless. . . . It is unable to become complex. . . . [C]hoice and constraint . . . coexist as partners, enabling a system, be it a living organism, a language, or a society, to follow the arrow not of entropy but of history. This is the arrow which distinguishes past from future, by moving away from the simple, the uniform and the random, and toward the genuinely new, the endlessly complex products of nature and of mind.[9]

The "decisive property" of complexity involves a particular coding of component behavior within a system generative of new complex forms of patterning. But in addition to this established principle of the theory, the evidence of the Sabbath Star System can contribute a new and still more decisive property of complexity, the evolution of a complex system to greater *regularity* as it grows in complexity. Now that the geometry of the diagram has been taken to still higher levels of experimental linear mathematics, we can see that the distinction between freedom and determinism, or between the irregular and regular, applies to the evolution of each major phase of the system as well as of the system as a whole.

In the three larger phases of the Sabbath Star System, that of the diagram achieves general regularity by the seventh world, of the periodic decimal sequence by the 21st world, and of the converging decimal sequence by the 561st world, the first decimal of one complete megacycle. The two-tiered decimal sequences also go through initial phases of rapid inflation, the periodic sequence ending with the same 21st world and the converging sequence with the 221st world. Taking the system as a whole, and simplifying it to the propagation of just the functional relationship of construction to matrix elements expressed as decimals, it can be said that the system begins with the absolute irregularity of the fourth world, at which this decimally expressed function first emerges, and the relative irregularity of the next two worlds, then goes through a period of rapid inflation, extending at the highest systems level through the 221st world, finally to develop a proliferation of deterministic but unpredictable large-scale patterning. In the context of recently noted astronomical discoveries, this model has some surprising implications.

If the Sabbath Star System is first taken as a model for the expanding universe, then it shows some similarity to what has been called the "chaotic inflationary model." In terms of the Sabbath Star System model, the evolution of the universe could be understood to begin with the absolutely irregular "singularity" of the big bang, go through a period of rapid inflation, move through stages of relative irregularity from the earliest phases of quantum radiation to the galactic level of organization, and finally achieve the regularity currently thought to be exhibited by the still vaster level of intergalactic structure. Whether or not the inflationary feature is introduced into this model of evolution, the movement it depicts from "chaotic boundary conditions" to conditions like the present state of the observable universe is one that has posed a problem for some theorists. As Stephen Hawking has stated: "It is difficult to see how such chaotic initial conditions could have given rise to a universe that is so smooth and regular on a large scale as ours is today."[10] But the Sabbath Star System provides just such a mathematical model, a model that also clearly contradicts the prevailing view of a universal progression to entropy.

There is an even more interesting way to understand this model, however, with its originating point not taken to define that infinite condensation of matter and space attributed to the big bang but rather the originating location of any observer in the expanding universe. It has been generally accepted on the basis of Alexander Friedmann's interpretation of the general theory of relativity that the universe appears to be expanding in all directions from every point within it. But if this is true, then what this model would seem to be defining is the paradoxical situation that while every individual constituent point of the universe demonstrates the capacity for irregularity, for "singularity," it is embedded in a cosmic whole marked by immense regularities. Nor can such universal large scale regularity be shown to derive from the irregularity of its constituent parts, a condition by which it could and has been argued that the universe is "self-organizing."[11] For rather than deriving from its individual constituents, it contains them, with implications shortly to be examined. A further implication, and possibly the most important, of this model of increasing regularity radiating out from each point of origination is that freedom is thus not lost for these individual constituents despite the evolution of the system as a whole to regularity. It is the unity within a system of the dual levels of microindeterminacy and macrodeterminacy that can not only explain the rule of probability operating throughout the universe but, when applied to the universal system, can best explain the coherence of chaotic originating conditions in the infinitesimal with the regularity of the infinitely large scale. Conversely, it can explain why the attempt to combine the theories of quantum mechanics and of general relativity, appropriate to the different scales of these realms, into a unified explanation that disregards this difference, as most recently in string theory, is doomed to fail.

That different theories of physics can best explain the operations within these scales—quantum mechanics for the subatomic level, relativity for the astronomical, and Newtonian physics for the middle realm between these extremes—is a circumstance whose lesson would seem to be that there are different laws operating within these progressively larger domains, a process whose workings would also seem to be better demonstrated by experiments with computer programs rather than with cyclotrons. The model of the Sabbath Star System can thus not only provide new ways of viewing the expanding universe, but also a way of synthesizing the distinctive features of general with complex dynamical systems theory and of such reformulated systems theory with scientific cosmology. What further it can contribute both to the new astronomy and to the theory of complex systems, we are now to see.

If the Sabbath Star System is a valid model for the theory of complex systems, then the first implication of this model is that any system whose final phase features general irregularity is either not truly complex or has not been taken far enough to exhibit its final evolution to regularity. In the former case, this is a criticism that can be made of Stephen Wolfram's monumental attempt to model an irregular universe on the basis of a fairly unique cellular automaton that exhibits such total irregularity.[12] His exploration does, however, establish the capacity of simple computer programs, applied reiteratively to a few simple initial components, to model such a generation of complex patterning as is also demonstrated by the Sabbath Star System.

A truly complex system would be defined as one whose originating organization is such that some element capable of continuing generation will survive through various phase shifts in its evolution to enable the formation of new levels of organization. An organism would clearly conform to this definition, a storm system or house of cards not. Both of these latter types would more properly belong to the category of simple systems, those unstable systems that can only reach a certain level of complexity before they collapse into disorder. It has been argued that such catastrophic disorder is the necessary prerequisite for the establishment of a new level of organization, but this is only true when it occurs in the phase shifts of a complex system, as we have seen with the converging decimal sequence. When a house of cards collapses or a drop of ink permeates a fluid, no new organization of cards or ink can develop; the movement is simply to entropy. Even the emergence of convection cells in a boiling liquid cannot lead to a truly stable new level of organization. However interesting the study of instabilities may be, it cannot be extrapolated into a general theory of the whole, and the only instabilities that have such relevance are those that either originate or only punctuate the evolution to new, more highly organized states of equilibrium in a complex system, the disorder caused by the collision between its older and newer patterns.

That growth in viable complexity should be accompanied by an equal growth in regularity need cause no surprise if one considers the most normal state of affairs in which one is engaged. In terms of society, the smaller the independent groups of people, the less regulation is required, but at certain stages of membership growth this freer organization will either collapse into disorder and return to smaller units or develop a higher level of regularity. In the first case the groups do not possess the essentials for complex evolution, a higher level of guidance with or without access to a more compelling new ideology or technology, and in the second case the groups have such leadership as can both mobilize the resources and regulate the interactions of its larger population. In a fully complex society, the larger the administrative level the more it must regulate its activities and those in its power if it is both to maintain order and to keep track of all in its domain. The same is true for one's personal finances or social life; the smaller they are the less effort and organization is required to manage them; the larger they are the more they require records, regulation, and subordinate personnel. It is SIZE that would seem to be the determining factor in driving an expanding complex system to new levels of organization, size that has its own threshold for how much complexity its level of organization can handle.

Thus complex systems may be said to be controlled by what I shall call the Law of Complex Magnitudes. A "complex magnitude" can be recognized by the emergence at its start of a new mode of regulating its members, and it is of two kinds, similar to those posed in the Gould-Eldredge evolutionary theory of "punctuated equilibria":

> Evolution proceeds in two major modes; in the first, phyletic transformation, an entire population changes from one state to another. . . . The second mode [is] speciation. . . . New species branch off from a persisting parental stock. . . . Eldredge and I refer to this scheme as the model of *punctuated equilibria*. Lineages change little during most of their history, but events of rapid speciation occasionally punctuate this tranquility.[13]

These modes are analogous to stages of the Sabbath Star Diagram, those within a world being comparable to speciation and those between worlds to "phyletic transformation." Such a distinction between species and phyla would also seem to be true for the two decimal sequences that form the upper levels of the Sabbath Star System, the former corresponding to the immediate succession of decimals in the sequence and the latter to the larger changes in patterning. Taking the system as a whole, the phyletic changes would now be identified with the radical shifts between the modes of generating expansion—the Sabbath Star Diagram, the periodic decimal sequence and the converging decimal sequence—and the species changes those that mark new phases within these modes.

We can better understand the speciation mode of the Law of Complex Magnitudes by observing its actions at the system's highest level of specificity, the four-phases of the converging decimal sequence. What is driving change at this level is the increasing need of the sequence to slow its convergence to the .08 limit as it approaches infinity. The sequence begins with a phase of rapid inflation, going from zero to .0769 in just seventeen stages. But already within this first phase a Sabbatical pattern is being set up in terms of a seven-member unit of the number of steps between each of the stages, such a "week" being composed of the following sequence of steps: 13, 13, 12, 13, 12, 13, 12. With the second phase, the decimal sequence divides between those decimals that are sequence advancing and those that are sequence retarding, all the 12s going over to the advancing column and the 13s to the retarding column. The second phase carries the sequence forward from the 18th to the 83rd stage, at which point it has advanced to .0789. In the pattern of steps for the second phase there were four retarding 13s and three advancing 12s for each decimal week. But at stage 84, which initiates the third phase, this pattern changes *abruptly*, with the first of the advancing 12s going over to the retarding column. Then again abruptly at the 296th stage, the final fourth phase is initiated with the shift of the second of the 12s to the retarding column. This can be considered the final phase because it arrives at the minimal patterning necessary to define the Sabbatical structure that has been the single, most dominating principle of patterning in this sequence. And it does so in a manner that clarifies this structure, defining its remaining weeks by six retarding and only one advancing decimal, the latter now a true Sabbatical marker. But in addition to defining this final pattern of Sabbatical sequence advancement, the fourth phase also makes it possible to recognize a megacycle of weeks, one beginning around the middle of the second phase, at the 44th stage, and extending through the 328th stage appearing in the fourth phase. Nor is its final patterning of the sets and larger cycle likely to remain fixed. Rather, the wealth of patterning arising in this higher order sequence, one ultimately deriving from a simple formula applied repetitively to three initial fractions, is likely to continue to surprise us with its emergent novelties. At what magnitude the sequence will shift to a new mode of regularity and what this new mode will be are unpredictable. What can be predicted is that at a very precise magnitude of numerically defined expansion an older, long-maintained patterning will suddenly yield to a new pattern, the periods of each new level of complexity being increasingly large.

While the phyletic level of such shifts of magnitudes follows much the same procedure, it differs in an important regard. If such phyletic shifts can be correlated with those between the modes of generating expansion, between the diagram and the periodic sequence and between that and the converging sequence, then what we see in addition to the shift to a new form of patterning is also one to a higher order of simplification. Such a radical shift can only arise if a prior magnitude has reached a relatively high degree of both regularity and complexity. It is the combination of a level of complexity overwhelming to the power of the system to generate greater growth in that form with the development within it of such regularity as will permit a radical simplification of its complexity that alone can drive the system to make such a radical shift to a higher order. It is because the Sabbath Star Diagram became too complex to permit much further construction at the same time as it became regular enough to permit its numerical extrapolation that calculation could replace construction. At this first level of numerical abstraction it could be seen that the numbers derived from the diagram and abstracted from its geometry were yet capable of generating new evolutionary change in one of its aspects and that the whole system could be simplified to the propagation of just this one continuing source of systemic evolution. The development of algorithms for determining the numerical constituents of this central diagram function and its decimal expression allowed the system to develop to the point that it could be further simplified to just a single formula.

At this point all aspects of the system tied to the geometry of the Sabbath Star Diagram could be sloughed off, just as a snake discards its old skin or a butterfly its cocoon, and the system continue in the transfigured form of an independently generated periodic decimal sequence. However interesting it might be to continue the geometric construction of the Sabbath Star Diagram at immense levels of space and complexity, the results could not justify the effort. It would be like painstakingly measuring the threads of a cocoon after a butterfly has escaped it; the life has moved on to another plane. But after a certain evolution of this higher-order systemic level, it too achieves a regularity subject to a further simplification. Rather than the two-thousand-page computer printout of the sequence taken at each formula iteration to 1,500 decimal places, the pertinent information regarding the central function of the periodic decimal sequence, expressible as a still higher-order decimal sequence, could be reduced to just ten pages and these organized in still briefer charts to reveal new evolving patterns.

The system has now been taken to the stage similar to that of the diagram in its algorithmic phase. The converging decimal sequence of its highest evolved phase has entered a phase of final regularity at the same time as it is becoming too costly to continue its exploration through a mode of generation still tied to an earlier phase of systemic evolution. What is now required is the discovery of a formula by which the converging sequence can be generated independently. To continue to explore it through the horse-and-buggy technique of taking the primary periodic sequence to immense new numbers of decimal places does again not seem to promise sufficient reward for such an undertaking. Whether such a formula for independent generation can be found I do not know, but it is only such a new radical shift in the mode of generation that offers any hope for a new level of systemic evolution meaningful enough to merit further exploration. Meanwhile, we can rest content that the system has been taken far enough to serve as a most precise model for the theory of complex systems, to a magnitude complex enough for us to see the approaching convergence at infinity.

We have seen that at both the species and phyla levels of a complex evolutionary system changes of patterning occur at certain magnitudes of expansion that remain relatively fixed until the threshold is reached of another magnitude, and this descriptive level of definition may be as far as we should go. But even such a description raises the deeper question of the source of such complex and regular patterning at these magnitudes. It seems quite impossible that all this profusion of detailed patterning could arise from just a few simple starting conditions, in the case of the two decimal sequences under consideration of just three sequential fractions and a simple reiterative formula for the further propagation of this sequence.

The same problem is also emerging from the new astronomical discoveries that reflect systemic characteristics similar to those discovered at the farthest reaches of the Sabbath Star System. The problem about the discovery of "evenly distributed clumps of galaxies stretching across vast expanses of the heavens" is that it has "raised further doubts about concepts that try to explain how, over time, gravity alone could have produced a universe marked by conglomerations of galaxies."[14] It is the enlisting of gravity to explain the development of macroscopic structure that has most bedeviled scientific cosmology.

The theory of a quantum-based inflationary epoch near the beginning of cosmic evolution was first developed by Alan H. Guth in the early 1980s to solve certain crucial problems that had developed in the big bang cosmology of an expanding universe first proposed in 1929 by Edwin P. Hubble. But "the theory of inflation predicts that the explosive expansion of the universe 10^{38} second after the big bang should have produced gravitational waves. . . . Furthermore, the fantastically rapid expansion of the universe would have stretched the graviton wavelength from microscopic to macroscopic lengths. . . . to 10^{23} kilometers, which is the size of the present-day universe."[15] Another cosmologist has shown the obvious difficulties of such an importation of gravity to the quantum realm and then its extrapolation to macroscopic, indeed cosmic, scale: "The most serious is the lack of a complete, manageable quantum theory of gravity. . . . all attempts to quantize Einstein's general relativity, have met with failure. . . . Another question that workers confront is the applicability of quantum mechanics to the entire universe."[16] Though my own model demonstrates a similar inflationary phase early in the development

of each of the decimal sequences of the Sabbath Star System, the quantum-mechanical basis of cosmic inflation raises as many problems as does the big bang cosmology it was designed to solve, for as this cosmologist had earlier shown: "the hot big bang model does not adequately explain the origin of large scale structures, such as galaxies."[17]

The latest important news from outer space, the discovery by two teams of astronomers in 1998 that the expansion of the universe is accelerating has required the hypothesis of a repulsive force of dark energy that not only constitutes two-thirds of the cosmic contents, though it cannot be observed, but has a most arcane source: "The best known possibility is that the energy is inherent in the fabric of space."[18] This refurbished form of the "cosmological constant" Einstein first developed and then repudiated has entered a quite metaphysical realm of speculation, as has been noted: "The force caused by the constant operates even in the complete absence of matter or radiation. Therefore, its source must be a curious energy that resides in empty space. The cosmological constant endows the void with an almost metaphysical aura."[19] Some cosmologists have given this dark, repulsive energy of space the name of "quintessence," the ethereal fifth element thought by Aristotle to pervade space, and have even suggested "that quintessence springs from the physics of extra dimensions,"[20] the extra dimensions that string theory declares to be curled up at the deepest points of space.

From 1929 to 1998, astronomers have been discovering remarkable features of the universe that cosmologists have attempted to explain by theories that never quite solve the problems they are addressing because of their misapplication of discoveries in the quantum realm to the evolution of cosmic galactic structure, this in spite of the fact that quantum mechanics and relativity theory have thus far resisted unification. For differences of scale *are* significant of different realms of complexity with their own emergent properties, as the noted cosmologist Martin Rees has importantly shown:

> But the difficulties of interpreting the everyday world and the phenomena that astromomers observe stem from their *complexity*. Everything

may be the outcome of processes at the subatomic level, but even if we know the relevant equations governing the microworld, we can't in practice, solve them for anything more complex than a single molecule. Moreover, even if we could, the resultant "reductionist" explanation would not be enlightening. To bring meaning to complex phenomena, we introduce new "emergent" concepts.[21]

So it is to complexity theory that we must finally turn for a deeper understanding of cosmic evolution.

Quantum cosmologists continue to believe that "theories must now be developed to create a new mechanism at the beginning of the universe that could account for the huge structures."[22] But the problem with explaining the evolution of both the Sabbath Star System and the universe solely on the basis of starting conditions is that such conditions cannot account for the specific structures manifested at discrete scales throughout these systems. In both cases it seems rather to be the synergistic interaction of systemically bound elements with specific magnitudes of expansion that is responsible for the emergence of a progression of complex patterning. As the Einsteinian curvature of space in response to mass first revealed space to have a "fabric," and the acceleration of cosmic expansion now seems to demonstrate that "the energy of our universe is dominated by empty space,"[23] so magnitudes would seem to be not truly empty but "morphogenetic,"[24] containing curled up within them, much as some theoretical physicists have envisioned their elementary "strings," a potential program, rather than energy, and one capable of generating forms. That is, magnitudes would seem to be generative of forms specific to their size when an expanding complex system crosses their threshold. A complex magnitude, then, is one that can imprint its own ordering on the raw materials of reproductive components as they expand through such discrete stages.[25]

What is being argued is that the physical universe with all its subsystems, and this includes all real or ideational systems that can be generated within it by its conscious components, is characterized by a morphogenetic infrastructure whose organizational principle is that of size, that at certain magnitudes,

whether of time, space, number, temperature, or whatever, certain structures become manifest that change a pre-established pattern in ways that were *not precisely programmed from the beginning*, which require a period of evolution to such a magnitude to *add* new patterning algorithms. To continue this analogy, the cosmic computer that allows all natural or ideal complex systems to evolve in size is able to provide such additional instructions for the morphogenetic operations of each magnitude whenever a complex system evolves to its level of organization, such operations while differing for each such system and being unpredictable beforehand, having a repeatable, deterministic character. Perhaps this cosmic computer has an ultimate program that provides for such stepped instructions for each possible combination of members that cross the threshold of a complex magnitude, but this is a power not available to the files created within it. As far as we can see, complex systems, and this may well include the universe, begin with a few simple components and a reproductive code capable both of increasing these numbers and endowing this increase with a primitive but unique organization. The development of more complex structures, however, would seem to be a function of the synergy between the primitive structure of a system and the complex magnitude to which it has evolved.[26]

Whether the Law of Complex Magnitudes is regarded as simply descriptive or as causative, it does seem to define the way evolving complex systems work. But though we can say that at certain magnitudes new patterns of regularity emerge, we either cannot say how they could have emerged from the starting conditions or how the magnitude has such a power of organization. It is finally a question of which inexplicable cause one prefers. But as it does not seem likely that the consensus quantum-astrophysical cosmology of the big bang will be able to account from the beginning for the immense regularities that have come into focus through the latest astronomical technology, it may be useful to consider the feasibility of the alternative being here proposed. And certainly such an understanding of the morphogenetic potential of complex magnitudes is no more difficult a concept to accept than the recently noted explanation of two-thirds of the contents of the universe as derived from empty space.[27]

This may well be an opportune time for such a consideration since we seem to be entering a postmodern phase not only of culture but also of the received scientific wisdom, its reductionism neither able to explain the growth of complex structure nor its meaning. But those scientists who have fought such reductionism through the study of nonlinear open and/or chaotic systems that defy entropy have also overgeneralized the cosmological implications of their partial studies, studies focused experimentally on just those areas of turbulence that stress the chaotic, stochastic aspects of dynamic systems.

What we have seen to be true at all levels of the Sabbath Star System, and what also seems to be increasingly clear of the universe, is that such chaotic features only occur at either primitive or transitional stages in a larger systematic movement toward regularity. To be sure, both chaos and complexity theorists have emphasized rather than denied the structural constraints emerging in chaotic systems, but they have still upheld such unstable systems as the model for a new cosmology. As physicists would like to bootstrap their way up through the physical hierarchy on the behavior of the quanta their violence has orphaned from their proper atomic structures, so with the brave new chaosists, who would make irregularity not the exception but the rule and the universe a house of unstable but somehow never toppling cards. Both would agree that the whole structure of the universe emerged from some self-organizing nucleus that contained all the ingredients necessary for its further evolution, differing only in whether they emphasize the deterministic or unpredictable aspects of such evolution. But just as people could not live and grow without air to breathe and gravity to ground them, without an environment both nourishing and constraining to further and shape their growth, so would there seem to be a cosmic environment whose infrastructure contains both the program of laws and the power for all potentialities that can bring any viable complex system, including that of the physical universe, from early irregularity, through various phases of growth, to a final mature regularity, one that may retain instances of irregularity but is governed both by its larger regularities and the direction of its overall evolution.

In this chapter and particularly in the previous section, experimental evidence has been provided to support the theory of complex systems that has just been offered as well as a more philosophical explanation of a cosmic mechanism that might account for its operations. I do not think that this explanation is any less "scientific" than current assumptions about physical laws and forces. It just shifts the focus of causation from a strictly past origin to one that is progressive, a shift that should help to solve some theoretical questions about the physical universe now unanswerable.[28]

But there are other questions for which only a metaphysical answer is possible, those relating to questions of ultimate cause and direction. Aristotle not only told us that the whole is greater than the sum of its parts but that it has four "causes": a material cause, a formal cause, an efficient cause or "entelechy," and a final cause, the "telos." As the material cause of a complex system would be its components and the formal cause the distinctive principle or program of their reproductive relationship, so the entelechy that permits it to grow toward self-realization would seem to involve the Law of Complex Magnitudes, the law governing the successive changes of patterning its structure undergoes at the specific increases of size characteristic of all evolution. All three are really required for an adequate scientific theory of cosmology. It is with the final cause that we have to leave the realm of scientific inference for that of poetry, the realm of imaginative power that can clothe the unknown with the fitting myths that can make sense of the available pieces of evidence through a deeper intuition into their generative source and so invest the whole with meaning. It is this extra step that has here been ever taken in interpreting the experimental mathematics of the Sabbath Star System, that hermeneutic method called the Science of Expressive Form by which its geometric or numerical features were not only established but systematically associated with the mystical cosmology of the Jewish esoteric tradition. And as we stand at the conclusion of this long investigation, one almost as expanded as the system it was exploring, we should look to what teleological message it can finally deliver.

One place we might start is the Lurianic concept of the Tzimtzum, the idea that the physical universe is expanding through a finite circular space left vacant by the retraction around it of the substance of infinity,[29] the circle of the Tzimtzum that has here been placed around the Sabbath Star of the upper Do at the midpoint of the seventh-world diagram. Thus any expansion of the Sabbath Star Diagram beyond this point can be considered an expansion into the infinity of Ein Sof, the Limitless One. But what the Sabbath Star System also shows us at its highest level is an apparent movement toward convergence, a movement that, with some difference, can be associated with the view of greater astronomical distances as reflecting ever earlier periods of time. As was earlier argued, the three major phases of the Sabbath Star System can be viewed as marking a progressive return through the same dimensions from which we came, a progression from the two-dimensional geometry of the Sabbath Star Diagram, through the infinite periodic decimal sequence that can be likened to the one-dimensional line, to the infinite converging sequence that will culminate in a nondimensional point at infinity. Thus in going forward, the further we approach the infinite, the further we may also be approaching the beginning, the point of convergence being that of the once and future points between which all the dimensions of space, time, and consciousness are strung. But the end will not be the same as the beginning, for both we and the infinity we will be rejoining will be changed by our voyage.

The cosmology of ultimate convergence is a persistent feature in most religious traditions, but the understanding of it that may well be the most illuminating is that of one of the greatest thinkers of our age, Pierre Teilhard de Chardin:

> Because it contains and engenders consciousness, space-time is necessarily *of a convergent nature.* Accordingly its enormous layers, followed in the right direction, must somewhere ahead become involuted to a point which we might call *Omega.* . . . Far from being mutually exclusive, the Universal and Personal (that is to say, the "centred") grow in the same direction and culminate simultaneously in each other. . . . each particular consciousness remaining conscious of itself at the end of the operation, and even (this must absolutely be understood) each particular consciousness become still more itself and thus more clearly distinct from others the closer it gets to them in Omega. . . . a grouping in which personalisation of the All and personalisations of the elements reach their maximum, simultaneously and without merging. . . .[30]

This mutual personalization of the All and of the elements is also the essence of the Hebraic secret doctrine of the son, a doctrine we have seen to emerge throughout the analysis of the seventh world as the central message of the Sabbath Star Diagram and its higher system levels. We have followed the further evolution of the Sabbath Star System through realms unknowable except to those who will participate in its creation as its twice-born divine sons. For the model of twice-born Ze'ir Anpin, of the divinely renamed Abraham, Sarah, and Jacob, and of Enoch transmuted into Metatron, is one to which all can aspire. In chapter 12 it was shown that the measure of the cosmic body by which man can become "a son of the world to come" will bring him into the tenth world, the octave of the Sol tone of man and center of that second octave in which the ascendant son becomes one with the divine personality of his higher self. And it seems not too much to hope that the son of man, as Ezekiel was called, can continue to evolve with his infinite source, retaining his complex spiritual identity as they move together to explore all the undreamed of possibilities of worlds without end, an exploration that requires the cosmically acquired personality and imaginal body of the cosmic child, of all those sons and daughters whose evolution can fill the infinite with the divine personalities by which the Ein Sof can know itself. And each such divine child can also be inspired by the knowledge that there are an infinite number of joyous facets to learn about the various layers of its consciousness and, fortunately, an eternity in which to learn them.

APPENDICES

A New Universal Model

APPENDIX A

Scientific Implications of the Hexagram Matrix

The main portion of this book has been devoted to a form of experimental geometry that not only provides a new model for kabbalistic cosmology and soul psychology but also for complexity theory. What is more, the pure geometry of this expanding diagram, though derived from the kabbalistic Tree of Life Diagram, has a universal character; it is capable of modeling other domains that are felt to be isomorphic to its features. Though the modelings of these other domains have been reserved for appendices, their inclusion in this work is important for establishing the universality of the diagram, especially for those domains that are like the Kabbalah in their multilevel structuring. This first appendix will apply the simple hexagram matrix first manifested in the fourth-world diagram to the domain of quantum physics; the second will apply the fourth- through sixth-world matrices to the hierarchy of systems levels, with special attention to the sixth-world matrix modeling of society; the third will extend this systems modeling of the fourth- through sixth-world matrices to the three levels of language, its modeling of the levels of the word, the sentence, and the work going far to explain the hermeneutic method of geometric interpretation employed here, that called the Science of Expressive Form; and the fourth will apply the construction elements of the third through seventh worlds to a modeling of human history based on the gender associations of these construction elements. This first appendix can be related to the analyses just prior and following it, extending its prior scientific modeling of complexity theory to the older perspective of quantum theory and doing so in ways that will be further supported by the study of general systems theory in the next appendix.

This is not my first attempt to apply the Sabbath Star Diagram to the modeling of quantum physics. I devoted chapter 9 of *The Secret Doctrine of the Kabbalah* to a modeling of all aspects of quantum physics by the triangle level of the matrix, showing how the triangular interface in the matrix provides a model for quantum theory that can organize and explain all of particle physics with great subtlety and new illumination. But the hexagram matrix has further implications for science. We shall begin this investigation by considering the way in which the hexagram matrix, especially in its lateral aspect, can provide a model coherent with the formulations of quantum physics and then see what this model can add to the standard formulations of modern science.

Unlike the earlier and later worlds of the diagram, the fourth world defines that cosmic turning point characterized by the existence of material solids. Thus the fourth-world diagram, in addition to providing the model of Nefesh consciousness, should also be able to model the archetypal nature of matter. In chapter 4, we saw that the Fa/Fi Sabbath Star identified with the material level of evolution did prove to have a structure that cast significant illumination on the functioning of material reality. Now we shall see what further illumination of the physical nature of reality can be achieved through analysis of the hexagram matrix. And we shall discover remarkable similarities in some of the conclusions that can be drawn from these two different ways of modeling the evolutionary level of matter provided by the Sabbath Star Diagram.

The matrix provides us with an independent microstructure and macrostructure as well as with their interface. The brief summary of the triangle matrix, given in chapter 8, showed that in their independent natures the microstructure could be identified with force and the macrostructure with form, and this can be considered to be as characteristic of the hexagram level of the matrix as it is of its triangle level. But what the hexagram interface adds to the earlier triangular description is the special distinction between the two types of microhexagrams, some of which are enclosed within macrohexagrams of their own color and some of which are not. In terms of quantum physics, it could be said that such enclosure transmutes a microhexagram from an undifferentiated constituent of a quantum field into a particle. Nobel-prize-winning physicist Steven Weinberg has said: "*the essential reality is a set of fields* . . . all else can be derived as a consequence of the quantum dynamics of those fields."[1] We can identify the microstructure with the quantum field and the macrohexagrams that enclose certain microhexagram elements of that field as that which produces the "quantum dynamics of those fields" that manifest "all else," particularly the form of particles. This distinction is particularly applicable to the lepton branch of quanta. By observing just the macrostructure, all that appears are the forms of these particles, the individual electrons. By observ-

ing just the microstructure, all that appears are patterns of waves. It is only the interfacing of the two that permits us to see the same microhexagrams in their dual forms as waves and particles, or from the macroscopic perspective, as energy and matter. Thus electrons, which not only can exist in the free form of electric current and the bound form within the atom but that also appear as either waves or particles depending on whether their momentum or position is being observed, can be precisely modeled by this aspect of the hexagram matrix, and one could say that their wave character is a product of observations at the level of the microstructure and their particle character of observations at the level of the macrostructure.

Viewing the quantum field as having an underlying character that persists through all the local condensations and dissolutions of its particle forms is closer to the matrix model than is Weinberg's definition of these fields. Such definitions have tended to treat the fields and particles as complementary manifestations of the same mass and spin, with only one quantum particle being allowed for each field and that serving to represent the whole field in its concentrated form. Indeed, the tendency has been to transfer essential reality from the field to the quanta and treat the field only as a pattern of the probability for finding a quantum particle at a particular point in space. But something like the concept of a quantum field as a continuous medium would seem to be emerging with the concept of the "multicomponent field," as explained by Heinz R. Pagels: "every field corresponds to a distinct quantum particle with a specific mass and spin. . . . But imagine several fields each with exactly the same mass and spin. In this case physicists continue to speak of a single field but a field with several "internal" components. . . . the multicomponent field."[2] Such a multicomponent field can be identified with the microstructure shown in plate 3, that of the interfaced matrix lateral system, the macrohexagrams enclosing field quanta in the form of certain microhexagrams would represent that which contributes the extreme intensity indicative of a particle at that point of the field. But plate.3 also shows another aspect of quantum theory through its color discrimination of one lateral axis into two comple- mentary spirals. To continue with Pagels' description:

> So one can think of a field at a point in space as describing the creation or annihilation of its quan- tum particles with a specific probability. If this mathematical description of the creation and annihilation of quantum particles is carried out in the context of relativistic quantum-field theory, one finds that one cannot have the possibility of creating a quantum particle without also having the possibility of creating a new kind of particle— its antiparticle.[3]

As can be seen in plate 3, every turquoise macro- hexagram has a scarlet counterpart, and these may be said to represent the dualism of matter and anti- matter that is always simultaneously created out of the quantum field.

Though it is the triangle matrix that was else- where offered as a comprehensive model for quan- tum theory, what the hexagram matrix can add to that fuller modeling of quantum theory is the sug- gestion of another dimension necessary to complete the quantum description, a dimension of form through which alone it is possible to explain *why* the field achieves a concentration at a particular point in space, why there are, in Einstein's words, "regions of space in which the field is extremely intense."[4] But if the hexagram matrix is suggestive even on the quantum level, its primary use would seem to be to model the distinction between the material microstructure of the quantum realm and the more complex level of organization that defines the macroscopic forms of matter. Even Pagels admits that such a distinction both exists and that it pre- vents the possibility of explaining all functioning at the higher levels of material organization solely on the basis of quantum interactions, that, in fact, Weinberg is wrong when he asserts: "all else can be derived as a consequence of the quantum dynamics of those fields." Pagels shows such derivation to be impossible

> because of a kind of "causal decoupling" between different organizational levels as one moves from

the microcosm to the macrocosm. For example, to understand chemistry one must comprehend the rules obeyed by the valence electrons in the outer parts of atoms. The details of the atomic nucleus—the quarks inside the protons and neu- trons—are "causally decoupled" from the chemi- cal properties of the atom. Another example from molecular biology of this "causal decoupling" is the fact that the biological function of proteins is decoupled from how they are coded for in the genetic material. Science abounds in examples of this "causal decoupling"—an important separa- tion between the material levels of nature which becomes reflected in the establishment of separate scientific disciplines.[5]

Between the quantum level and that of macroscopic objects, it is heat, the subject of the separate scien- tific discipline of thermodynamics, that represents the most significant evidence of such "causal decou- pling." As Ilya Prigogine and Isabelle Stengers explain:

> Heat *transforms* matter, determines changes of state, and leads to a modification of intrinsic prop- erties. . . . The study of the physical processes involving heat entails defining a system, not, as in the case of dynamics, by the position and velocity of its constituents (there are some 10^{23} molecules in a volume of gas or a solid fragment of the order of a cm^3), but by *a set of macroscopic parameters* such as temperature, pressure, volume, and so on. In addition, we have to take into account the *boundary conditions* that describe the relation of the system to its environment. . . . The aim of the theory [of thermodynamics] is not to predict the changes in the system in terms of the interactions of particles; it aims instead to predict how the sys- tem will react to modifications we may impose on it from outside.[6]

On the macroscopic level characterized by thermal properties, matter has been transformed intrinsically so that it now exhibits boundary conditions, the sign that it has become subject to the higher orga- nizational level of stable form.

With this return to the basic distinction between the instability of the quantum level and the relative stability of the molecular level of matter, we can better appreciate what the hexagram matrix can contribute to our understanding of material reality. For what it defines is precisely a dimension of form that lifts some elements of an underlying quantized force field into the domain of macroscopic solids, that it is form which causally decouples the macrocosmic from the microcosmic levels of matter.

Those who have tried to construct cosmic models based solely upon the discoveries of quantum physics have ended up with a vision of reality as limited as that of the "fundamentalist materialist" who, believing only what he can touch, discounts the whole realm of the spirit. If subatomic particles are considered the "basic building blocks" of material reality, it aught to be apparent that there is no way by which the known universe can be adequately constructed from them. The paradoxes that seem to control quantum functioning are the results of experimental violence done to nature.[7] If it be objected that conditions within the cyclotron can be naturally duplicated by conditions within the interior of the sun, it should again be obvious that if the laws that pertain within the cyclotron were all that were required to construct material reality, our earth would be another fiery star like the sun. But there is surely "something" that differentiates conditions in the interior of the sun from those on the exterior of the earth. Though all elements may be composed of the same atomic and subatomic particles, a bird spying a worm on a rock knows which to sharpen its beak on and which to eat. There would seem to be a higher ordering principle that, through different configurations of number and position, a form of mathematical and geometric programming, can cause identical electrons and protons to behave with consistently maintained differences.

John A. Wheeler would seem to come close to the matter, in both senses, when he says: "There is nothing in the world except empty curved space. Matter, charge, electromagnetism, and other fields are only manifestations of the bending of space. *Physics is geometry.*"[8] Wheeler's concept of "superspace," the somehow substantial fabric of space-time, seems to contain two elements, the "quantum foam" of which the "empty space" is composed and the "undulations" by which it is "curved." That is, the superspace is composed of an aspect that, though having no more solidity than those bubbles that are all that can actually be detected in the cloud chambers of quantum physics, can be associated with the material and an aspect that is purely formal.

If it is, in fact, this purely formal aspect of reality that is responsible for what we know as macroscopic reality, then it is a curious residue of materialism that causes both the spiritual interpreters of quantum physics and their spiritual authorities to reject the macroscopic level of reality as Maya or illusion simply because it is not as material as it appears. For the macroscopic is formed by something as real as the microscopic, though it may, like it, be ultimately as nonphysical, a purely formal power that, in the words of Shakespeare, gives "to airy nothing / A local habitation and a name."[9] There is that which forms and that which is formed, and it is ironic that the spiritual fundamentalism of some quantum physicists causes them to negate the reality of the realm of macroscopic multiplicity when it would appear that it is this macroscopic realm that is truly the product of mentally defined entities, mathematical and geometric factors so subtle, so purely formal, as to escape detection even by the spiritual seer.

It is the presence of such formal entities or factors that would seem to be responsible for those laws of nature studied by the macroscopic sciences, such as thermodynamics and chemistry, not to speak of biology, laws that are as absolute on the macroscopic level as are the newly discovered laws that govern the quantum level and that somehow are expressed through something much like the programs that were studied in chapter 15 and related to the concept of "complex magnitudes." It would further seem that we are dealing with laws deriving from two different systems levels, and that both, though immaterial, are equally real and necessary for creating those conditions that can support not only the life but also the perceptions of the quantum physicist. It would finally seem that these two levels, by which both consciousness and material reality can be analyzed, whether or not they are equated, function in this world through an interfacing for which the matrix of the Sabbath Star Diagram may well be the best model. The lateral half of the matrix provides a model of the interrelationship of the macroscopic and microscopic levels of reality in which a structure of forms gives us the appearance of macroscopic solidity and in which a structure of force presents paradoxical appearances as both particle and wave.

In this discussion of the interfaced lateral system of the matrix, we have seen that its basic distinction between unrestricted microhexagrams and those restricted by an interfaced macrohexagram of its color could provide an archetypal model for all the major distinctions of physics, on the quantum level between an underlying force field and the quanta emerging from and returning to this field, or even between the force field quantized as bosons and the fermion particles that feel its force, or as a systems model between the lower level of freely interacting quanta and the higher level that can organize such quanta into stable form. And as the microstructure and macrostructure of such a systems model present such contradictory pictures when studied apart from each other, so it might finally be pointed out is the theory of quantum interactions incomplete to the extent that the particles it studies in the high energy accelerators are orphaned by such experimentation from the controls to which they are normally subject within the constraints of atomic form, that higher level of form symbolized by an interfaced macrohexagram and denied by an exclusive focus on the level of the microstructure.

But if the physical world can be thus fully defined by the distinctions within the lateral system, what then of the unrestricted central microhexagrams that appears in the full fourth-world matrix in either of its forms? On the analogy to the lateral system, these unrestricted microhexagrams would seem to represent a form of energy, one that, on the macroscopic level, can interpenetrate physical particles but is of a different nature from the form of energy signified by the comparable unenclosed lateral microhexagrams. Viewing plates 7 and 8 (also figures 8.1 and 8.2) as providing a model of the physical world, it would seem that we are here dealing with a form of energy that escapes the measurements of the physical sciences but for whose interactions with matter there is accumulating evidence. Such a form of energy has been studied by parapsychologists both here and in Russia.[10] On the human level, it may be considered a form of psychic energy, one that can affect matter—bending nails, destroying cancer cells in a test tube, and so on—or simply bypass the physical and temporal obstructions to its power to perceive and communicate. On the non-human level, it may constitute a more spiritual or subtle component of physical reality, what the *Sefer Yetzirah* defines as a moral fifth dimension[11] and that would seem to explain the concept of Providence as it functions to maintain the balance of physical and historical forces.

The matrix diagram suggests, then, that in addition to the solid physical world we perceive, there are two forms of imperceptible energies, a grosser form that can be detected by instruments of physical measurement and a more subtle form that can only be caught in the net of statistics and the immemorial chronicles of miracles. In the fourth world, the grosser lateral elements appear in the dual forms of particles and waves, for the quantum microstructure level, or of matter and energy, for the macrostructure, while the more subtle individualized central elements appear only in the form of energy. The appearance in the fifth world of interfaced central macrohexagrams, however, suggests that there is some kind of subtle structure that can be built at that level out of central energies.

Such a possibility seems consistent with the accounts of such explorers of astral spaces as Robert Monroe and John Lily,[12] accounts of astral projection into psychic environments that appear solid and frequented by external entities though subject to different laws of continuity and control. Though some have argued, from this evidence, that there is no difference between consensus reality and either astral or dream perceptions, that all life is a dream composed of astral projections, that as Shakespeare said, "We are such things / As dreams are made on,"[13] the Sabbath Star Diagram suggests that these are separate realities composed of different energies and, perhaps, analyzable in terms of different forms of numbers.

It may be possible to associate the lateral system with real numbers and the central system with what are called imaginary numbers, numbers containing the $\sqrt{-1}$. If such an idea may be entertained, then we may speak of fourth-world "imaginary energies" and fifth-world structures composed of "imaginary mass," such as Gerald Feinberg's tachyons, proposed particles traveling faster than the speed of light. Through such imaginary numbers, it may, indeed, be theoretically possible to construct the fabled castles in the sky and so explain not only the astral adventures of Monroe and Lilly, to name only the more recent and respected of psychic travelers, but the institutionalized religious concepts of such spiritual environments as heaven and hell. Only, we would have to remember that "imaginary" does not here mean unreal but rather the real power of some individual and collective psychic entities to project themselves into structured realms that are subject to different laws than those that pertain to matter.

If physical particles can be thought of as the product of an energy field and some form of structuring code, then it may be possible to give a similar analysis for psychic appearances. We have only to "imagine" a field of psychic energy and individuals or meditative communities with the mental power to form these energies into structures through modes of concentration or imaging. Such a possibility is, indeed, enshrined in kabbalistic stories of the mental creation of the golem, a project for which the *Sefer Yetzirah* is supposed to be a manual. But leaving aside such stories of psychically created robots capable of doing household chores and frightening the Goyim, it would still seem valuable to provide some explanation of the phenomenon of psychic visions that neither rejects them as unreal hallucinations nor makes them the model for all modes of perception.

Such an explanation would seem to be provided by an understanding of the central and lateral systems of the Sabbath Star Diagram and their differing dispositions in the fourth and fifth cosmic worlds. If we remember that the fifth world is already present for those individuals who have fully developed the Ruach level of the soul but that its reality cannot be communicated to the individuals who have not progressed beyond the fourth-world given endowment of the Nefesh soul level, we can understand the differences between the experiences of the paranormal at these levels. Thus the Nefesh individual may experience an occasional premonition, haunting dream, or happy coincidence, the product of a subtle mode of energy that may be represented by the fourth-world central microhexagram, while the Ruach individual may experience an astral projection into a realm filled with psychic structures and entities, a product of a higher capacity to structure subtle energies that may be represented by the fifth-world interfacing of a central microhexagram and central macrohexagram. It might be further suggested that such lateral energies as electromagnetism and gravity could be a mean or link between the realm of solid macroscopic particles and the realm of such paranormal subtle energies.

In addition to the lateral system, by which all phenomena capable of physical measurement may be analyzed, the Sabbath Star Diagram also contains a second, central system, then, by which a fuller description of reality may be achieved that includes both subtle and gross forms of energy without the necessity of reducing one to the other. But it would be wrong to identify the central system simply with the spiritual and the lateral system with the physical since the dual systems of the matrix may be applied equally to the nature of consciousness and matter.

What is being suggested here is that in our normal world of physical nature, there exists not only the physical matter and energy that can be measured by physical means but also a more subtle form of energy, perhaps that dark energy, discussed in chapters 1 and 15, that is now thought to compose two thirds of the cosmic mass and to be derived from space itself. But if the central microhexagram can also be thought to signify the new physical category of dark energy, then the collective central macrohexagram at the center of the fourth world could also be correlated with its counterpart of dark matter. It might again be suggested that the detectable physical energies signified by the lateral microhexagram could also carry that undetectable physical energy characterized as "dark" and thought to be causing the cosmic expansion to accelerate. In this context it should also be remembered that in the sixth-world matrix the central system represents, in terms of light units, the most powerful expression of this system, this sixth dimension perhaps being the most potent source of dark matter and energy, the two categories recently hypothesized to explain the missing matter and energy that have been calculated to exist and that string theorists do derive from "the physics of extra dimensions."[14] But to return to the single central microhexagram of the fourth-world matrix, it might finally be said about these subtle energies that though they would seem capable of acting independently of gross physical energies and certainly by different rules, it may be that they are also carried in the core of these physical energies as normal constituents of matter and so can help to explain such paradoxical physical appearances as those that occur at the quantum level or at the outer reaches of astronomical space-time explained by relativity theory. In any case, the fourth-world matrix of the Sabbath Star Diagram can provide a model for the distinctions made by modern physics that can also include both paranormal and still darker factors and so may be considered more complete. As the final sections of chapters 1 and 15 were concerned with the dark energy now thought to be accelerating the cosmic expansion, the end, as always, being prefigured by the beginning, so may this final contribution of my work to the scientific model of the universe shed new light on its darker areas.

A Systems Model of Sociology

THE SYSTEMS HIERARCHY

In this work the Sabbath Star Diagram has been developed according to its own discoverable laws, which the final chapter showed could provide a new mathematical model for complexity theory with its own cosmological implications. But the primary effort of this Science of Expressive Form has been the second-order mythological interpretation of its geometric elements in terms of the Jewish mystical tradition from whose main diagram, that of the Tree of Life, it was derived. The Sabbath Star Diagram has a dual structure comprised of construction elements and of the matrix that they produce, and this structure has a more universal validity since it is capable of modeling other domains, all such domains as can be modeled by the same aspect or level of the diagram providing reciprocal illumination of these analogous areas. This and the next appendix will provide just such modeling by the matrix of the Spiral Tree of fields not normally associated with the Kabbalah, this appendix using this three-world matrix to provide a new model for sociology and the next using it to provide a new model for linguistics. Finally, the last appendix will adapt the construction elements to a new gender modeling of human history. What all of these more secular fields share with the kabbalistic cosmology and soul psychology previously modeled by the diagram is an embedding of its particular subject in a multileveled structure, whether simultaneously or sequentially understood. Such a structure has been characteristic of general systems theory, and this modeling of society will begin with a brief review of such systems theory.

The conceptual foundation of general systems theory goes back to Aristotle, but it has been given a modern redefinition by Ludwig von Bertalanffy that allowed it to be applied to many scientific and social disciplines. Its definition of a system as a whole that is more than the sum of its parts and itself functions as the part of a yet more ordered whole is coherent with the properties of the matrix, and these properties, in turn, cannot only demonstrate but also refine its principles.

The first and probably most important aspect of the matrix involves its interface of a macrostructure and a microstructure, each following its own orientation and subject to distinctive laws. At its most elementary level, that of the matrix triangles, this interface reveals an essential aspect of systems theory, the systemic interface of macrodeterminacy and microindeterminacy. As explained in chapter 8, the macrotriangles can be associated with a deterministic form and the microtriangles with the freedom of force. For the primary distinction between these matrix particles concerns the number of their expressed lines of symmetry, the macrotriangles being conceived of as held rigidly in place by their three symmetry lines while the microtriangles are understood to have a three-dimensional potential for free spin on their single-expressed line of symmetry.

Paul A. Weiss presents much biological evidence "to confirm the validity of this principle of determinacy in the gross despite demonstrable indeterminacy in the small for practically any level and area of the life sciences."[1] For Weiss, the stability of natural systems is dynamic rather than rigid because it features both a microindeterminacy that can never be lost and a separate level of macrodeterminancy that cannot be reduced to the sum of the system's parts. In Ervin Laszlo's explanation "Systemicity is imposed as a set of rules binding the parts among themselves."[2] And as Weiss puts it: "it is arguing in circles to pose that it is feasible to compound that which 'regulates' from the sum of that which is being 'regulated'—the macroregularity of a formative field pattern, from the microproperties of spatially disarrayed work units."[3]

Most systems theorists distinguish three main stages in the systems hierarchy, which Laszlo defines in the following manner: "Because the patterns of development in all realms of nature are analogous, evolution appears to drive toward the superposition of system upon system in a continuous hierarchy, traversing the regions of the suborganic, organic, and supraorganic."[4] Though Laszlo is most concerned to show how the same mechanisms appear in analogous forms in all three of these levels, correlations with the matrices of the fourth through sixth worlds can go further to define the distinguishing features of the three main stages of evolution if these stages are somewhat differently understood. Rather than Laslo's suborganic, organic, and supraorganic, I would define the three evolutionary stages to be correlated with these matrix stages as the *impersonal*, *personal*, and *transpersonal*. While the last stages of both groupings are comparable, the first two are divided not in accordance with the emergence of organic life but of that personal consciousness given only to humans. Another way of defining these stages would, then, be as subhuman, human, and suprahuman, though the earlier names are more revealing of meaning and will be retained. The following analysis will utilize the mythological identifications already given to the matrices of the Spiral Tree. This is particularly true in terms of the transpersonal realm associated with the sixth-world matrix, a realm whose systemic organization is truly unvisualizable in terms of materialistic categories and can only be rendered through the structural archetypes of myth.

But we must begin our discussion of these three systems levels with the fifth-world matrix, now observed as the true model of the "personal," of the human, for it reveals the characteristic that, for Ludwig von Bertalanffy, the founder of general systems theory, is the defining characteristic of man:

> the basic fact in anthropogenesis is the evolution of symbolism. Without this unique characteristic, any number of biological and behavioral developments would not have been sufficient to make man human. Apart from satisfaction of biological needs man shares with animals, he lives in a universe not of things but of symbols. . . . This is the reason why, by and large and neglecting transitions, we find three great realms or levels in the observed world: inanimate nature, living systems, and the symbolic universe (culture, Hegel's objective mind, T. de Chardin's noosphere, Sorokin's meaningful super-organic realm, etc.), each having its characteristic immanent laws.[5]

Von Bertalanffy's triple-level systems hierarchy is identical with Laszlo's, but his identification of the latter's "supraorganic" level as the "symbolic universe" opens a new way of understanding both this higher level and the whole of the hierarchy in the "personal" terms I earlier defined. For "the profoundest result of symbolism," Bertalanffy affirms, is that "It creates the 'I' and the 'world.'. . . Only with symbolism an organized 'universe' arises."[6] The supraorganic can, then, be identified with the transpersonal, the product, on at least one level, of that personal symbolizer who is uniquely human.

But if this higher level can be accepted as composed of systems of symbols, then it would seem that the level below it, which can be controlled by such a "symbolic universe," cannot be identified with all "living systems" but only with that capable of being influenced by symbolism, that *"animal symbolicum"*[7] of Ernst Cassirer, man. Such an implication is borne out by the connotations given in chapter 9 to the elements of the fifth-world matrix, for their structure was earlier considered a model for the controlled functioning of the symbolic imagination. In that model of the fifth world, the central macrohexagram was identified with the faculty of the imagination, the lateral macrohexagram with the self-conscious will, and the various lateral microhexagrams with auxiliary powers and four levels of mastery in the use of the symbolic imagination. The fifth-world matrix defined the structure of personal consciousness in terms of its use of imaginative symbolism, providing an interface between the impersonal subsystems of organic matter that compose its human level and the symbolic transpersonal systems in which it participates and which, in turn, constrain its freedom of action.

If the fifth-world diagram is particularly well suited to model the human level of symbolic activity, this is because such activity is a sign of personal consciousness, and it is as a model of personal consciousness that this matrix is most expressive. It is not simply that it offers just the combination of macrohexagrams that can best model the union of personal will with imaginative or symbolic capability definitive of the self-reflexive nature of personal consciousness, but that it also has the most important diagram position between the fourth and sixth worlds that can allow it to function as the interface between these different domains, that which it contains and that by which it is contained. If they can be viewed as the inner and outer domains that border on the individual consciousness, then the Sabbath Star Diagram becomes capable of modeling a most interesting speculation by Freud:

> What consciousness yields consists essentially of perceptions of excitations coming from the external world and of feelings of pleasure and unplea-

sure which can only arise from within the mental apparatus; it is therefore possible to assign to the system *Pepts.-Cs.* [the perceptual system or consciousness] a position in space. It must lie on the borderline between outside and inside. . . . Let us picture a living organism in its most simplified possible form as an undifferentiated vesicle of a substance that is susceptible to stimulation. Then the surface turned towards the external world will from its very situation be differentiated and will serve as an organ for receiving stimuli. Indeed embryology, in its capacity as a recapitulation of developmental history, actually shows us that the central nervous system originates from the ectoderm. . . . The sensitive cortex, however, which is later to become the system Cs., also receives excitations from *within*. The situation of the system between the outside and the inside and the difference between the conditions governing the reception of excitations in the two cases have a decisive effect on the functioning of the system and of the whole mental apparatus. Towards the outside it is shielded against stimuli, and the amounts of excitation impinging on it have only a reduced effect. Towards the inside there can be no shield; the excitations in the deeper layers extend into the system directly and in undiminished amount. . . .[8]

Freud's insight into the significance of the spatially defined border area of the brain for the formations of conscious thought is essentially geometric, endowing such a structure with the unique capacity to define the self. But for Freud, this border does not simply distinguish between the self within and the non-self without; it is understood to contain lower levels of psychic evolution as well whose effect from within is unmediated by any border constraints. And so is it also with the nesting worlds of the Sabbath Star Diagram, where the past is retained as form within the present as it will be retained within the future. From the perspective of the fifth world, there is no remaining demarcation between the fourth- and fifth-world matrices, both the impersonal realm of subconscious instinctual psychic drives, or of autonomic bodily functioning, and the personal realm of the symbolizing consciousness being incorporated into the single functional unit that permits the exercise of free thought. But there would still be the matrix border of the fifth world to distinguish between the human self within and the symbolical, societal, or divine non-self without, as in the analogous cortical shield of the skull.

In terms of this Freudian model, the function of fifth-world consciousness can now be understood to be the sensitive mediation between the claims of the inner and the outer domains that represents the proper exercise of free choice in the definition and expression of the aware self. Such an exercise of personal freedom, which recognizes the legitimate rights of the body to adequate rest or unpolluted food and air as well as the legitimate rights of society to establish laws necessary for preserving the peace and safety of its citizens, will gradually arrive at a temperate lifestyle and law-abiding form of public responsibility that is the truest definition of the level of Ruach consciousness identified with the fifth world. In such Ruach or Messianic consciousness, the law is understood to be written in the heart, in that internal monitoring of "feelings of pleasure and unpleasure," arising from its ever more sensitive as well as responsible responses to internal and external demands, which can individualize the general rules to fit precisely the personality involved. Thus use of the symbolizing consciousness would seem to have an inner corrective that makes only its Ruach use truly self-rewarding and so can lead the fallen consciousness to the level of spiritual development that, the diagram suggests, was ideally programmed to be the complement of such personal imaginative power. But whether or not the lessons of Ruach consciousness are learned by those who have prematurely usurped its power, it is the fifth-world matrix, at its various levels, that would now seem to be the proper model for the position of all human symbolizing in the systems hierarchy.

We have seen that application of the systems concept to the fourth- and fifth-world matrices was reciprocally illuminating, this approach providing a new way of conceptualizing the diagram and these matrices providing precise modeling for the systems hierarchy. But it is when we come to the transpersonal level that the diagram becomes most illumi-nating of the nature and implications of viable systems at the symbolic level that can be correlated with the sixth-world matrix. As we have seen, this is the world earlier characterized as the wholly spiritual World to Come that can be associated with the level of divine personality, whether interpreted in terms of the five Partzufim, of the cosmic heart and mind, or of Neshamah consciousness. And it is the spiritual implications of such social systems as may best be correlated with the transpersonal, supraorganic, or symbolic level of the systems hierarchy that has haunted and most disconcerted the systems theorists of society. For it is at this nonphysical level that the "problem" inherent in the whole systems approach becomes hardest to avoid.

Such avoidance is, nonetheless, characteristic of systems theorists. Thus von Bertalanffy argues:

> Among systems features are . . . . evolution toward higher organization, teleology and goal-directedness in various forms and ways, etc. The fact that such features—omnipresent in the biological, behavioral and social fields, object of empirical observation both in everyday life and scientific research—are not covered by traditional physicalistic concepts has often led to their being considered as of a metaphysical or vitalistic provenience, or even to deny their existence and anathematize their investigation—in contradiction to common sense and to actual practice in the biosocial realms.[9]

But having defined the problem, his only solution is to hope for a future answer from the very approaches that have hitherto proved inadequate: "We are not willing to make a new 'vital force' or 'entelechy' out of presently unsolved questions; but we have to look forward to a new breakthrough, possibly in the way of further generalizations and unification of thermodynamics, information theory and molecular genetics."[10] Weiss, however, who comes from the last of these disciplines, has shown the futility of expecting such answers from science: "What science has been able to establish is only what life is *not*; the positive assertions of what it is or might be are still a matter of diverse factional beliefs rather than scientific knowledge, and possibly are even doomed to remain so. . . ."[11]

One who did recognize the essentially spiritual nature of all aspects of society and human culture was Thomas Carlyle:

> Of Man's Activity and Attainment the chief results are aeriform, mystic, and preserved in Tradition only: such are his Forms of Government, with the Authority they rest on; his Customs . . . the whole Faculty he has acquired of manipulating Nature. . . . Where are the LAWS where is the GOVERNMENT? In vain wilt thou go to Shoenbrunn, to Downing Street, to the Palais Bourbon: thou findest nothing there but brick or stone houses, and some bundles of Papers tied with tape. Where, then, is that same cunningly-devised almighty GOVERNMENT of theirs to be laid hands on? Everywhere, yet nowhere: seen only in its works, this too is a thing aeriform, invisible; or if you will, mystic and miraculous. So spiritual (*geistig*) is our whole daily Life: all that we do springs out of Mystery, Spirit, invisible Force; only like a little Cloud-image, or Armida's Palace, air-built, does the Actual body itself forth from the great mystic Deep.[12]

The spirituality that Carlyle saw as informing "our whole daily Life" may be identified with what is considered to be the immanent form of a supra-physical power, one defining and operating through the natural laws of the cosmos rather than transcending and violating these laws; and its operations are clearest in social and symbolic systems, which cannot be defined solely in terms of their physical or visible components and artifacts. Although careful not so to characterize them, even von Bertalanffy cannot define his "symbolic universes" without some recourse to vitalistic symbolism:

> the symbolic universes created by man gain autonomy or, as it were, a life of their own. Symbol systems, so to speak, are self-propelling. They therefore have an autonomy or inner logic of development. Myth, Renaissance painting from Giotto to Titian, music from Bach to Richard

Strauss, physics from Galileo to Bohr, the British Empire, or the evolution of Indo-Germanic languages—they all follow their respective immanent laws, which are not psychological laws that characterize mental processes in their creators.[13]

The "life" of a symbol system derives from the "immanent laws" defining its systemic organization and not from the lower level of its symbol-using human creators or members; for as earlier shown, he defines the three major systemic levels as "each having its characteristic immanent laws."

It is as a model of such immanent laws, in general, and of those characteristic of the transpersonal level, in particular, that the sixth-world matrix can be most illuminating, and for the reason that its formal structure defines the major elements of social or symbolic systems in precise functional terms while the definitions of these elements in terms of kabbalistic mythology provide a neutral terminology by which these functions can be discussed. Such mythology can be considered "neutral" because its use need not imply an acceptance of its literal truth. Indeed, the function of mythology is precisely to give conceptual form to that which cannot be conceptualized in the terms of normal, physically based, discourse. And since the unvisualizable cannot be represented by that which can be visualized without distortion, it is less important how this mythology is ultimately to be understood than that it provides the symbolic forms without which no understanding is possible. This mythology can be used, then, both by those who credit it as pointing to some form of spirituality beyond it, that is, to signifying the existence of something literally like its figurative connotation, and by those who refuse to define the unknowable beyond the figurative and thus perhaps endow it with an even greater character of mystery, though one that has been denied its aura. The final difference between these two uses of mythology is simply that the former provides a more complete theory than the latter. But however this mythology is ultimately to be understood, use of it to define the nature and functioning of social systems, both open and closed, stable and unstable, is so precise and leads to such remarkable conclusions for the systems understanding of sociology that analysis of it will have to be considerably extended. My major excuse for such extension is that this follows the trend of most systems theorists in devoting the major portion of their attention to the special problems and fascination of transpersonal systemic organization. The only difference is that the present analysis, while not insisting on a spiritual interpretation of its data, will not avoid the use of the specifically spiritual formulations of kabbalistic and biblical mythology that not only provide a most precise method of understanding social phenomena but perhaps also their most complete description.

SOCIAL SYSTEMS AND THE SIXTH-WORLD MATRIX

Unstable Social Systems

If the sixth-world matrix can be correlated with the "immanent laws" characteristic of the transpersonal social relationships in which human beings normally participate, then the implication of this is that the sixth-world diagram, with all its connotations, must be understood to model only that level of the transpersonal that is immanent in the cosmos. This is particularly important in defining the level at which the Partzufim, identified with this world, are to be understood to operate. Conversely, the Partzufim can be understood to constitute a mythological description of the way the immanent laws function in the cosmos to define the processes of transpersonal systems. What the Partzufim can first help us to appreciate is the difference between unstable and stable systems.

The structure of unstable transpersonal systems would seem to be best modeled by the matrix elements beyond the border of the first phase of the sixth-world diagram, as analyzed in chapter 11 in terms of plate 13 and figure 11.4, particularly that Sabbatical configuration just beyond the macrohexagram signifying Tiferet both as harmonious balance and the Partzuf of Ze'ir Anpin, a configuration whose number is suggestive of the bliss of rebirth but that is here centered on a Tohu, the condition of formlessness. But we must now understand these extraborder elements as not strictly constituting a

social evil so much as that chaotic instability which is the core significance of these elements. By moving to that illusory center of rebirth beyond the stable contours of the matrix border, what can be considered the firstborn form of Ze'ir Anpin would experience such an envisioned rebirth only as a form of recreation, the vagrancy of a vacation. Since the only relationships that can develop any prolonged form of even fluid stability, such as a standing wave, will be those based on affinity, such relationships may be said to feature another aspect of Ze'ir Anpin, the normal association of either his upper three Sefirot or just Tiferet with the heart of the cosmic anthropocosm, with the cosmic heart. In this modeling of firstborn Ze'ir Anpin, we can begin to understand the archetypal nature of those unstable relationships based upon pure affinity or love and lacking any system of superordinate constraints.

As Chaucer shows, this is, in fact, the only condition in which love can operate: "Love wol not be constrained by maistrye: / Whan maistrye comth, the God of Love anoon / Beteth his winges and farewel, he is goon! / Love is a thing as any spirit free"[14] What the diagram here provides is a model for understanding how Cupid-(firstborn)Ze'ir Anpin-Love enters unpredictably into affinity couplings to give them an unstable heightening that becomes immediately destabilized by the introduction into it of any further constraints, even those arising from the dynamics of that system. Let us now see how this model can be applied to three forms of affinity systems, those between lovers, friends, and ideological associates.

In each case, it is the attraction of affinity that brings the members into association with each other and leads them into an exchange of information about each other that, whether resulting in carnal or symbolic knowledge, brings them to the state of meaningfulness that is definitive of participation in the sixth dimension. With lovers and friends the exchange of intimate information about their essential natures leads to the self-validating experience of meaningfulness, the more intimate the exchange the more meaningful the experience. With friends and ideological associates, it is the affinities discovered within the symbolic systems being exchanged that contributes to the experience of meaningful exchange. In each case a moment of communion may develop that lifts the participants into a higher experience that can be called love but is more properly characteristic of that state known as grace, the state in which the transcendental seems to become evidential. It is, in fact, a feature of the sixth world that it can only complete its circuit through entrance into that "other side" identified with the transcendental dimension of the seventh world, whether in terms of the single or double Cherub-Tree illustrated in chapter 12. And it is the access to transcendental experience provided by the transpersonal systems of the sixth world that explains the attractive force within all forms of social groupings. Social systems may be said to succeed in their ultimate purpose when they bring individuals to that enhanced state of their being that comes from recognizing themselves as parts of a whole larger than themselves.

It is just this dual significance of transpersonal systems that is revealed in the biblical definition of the new society to which Israel has been called: "And the Lord went before them by day in a pillar of a cloud, to lead them the way; and by night in a pillar of fire to give them light" (Exod. 13:21). The sociological implications of the Exodus experience will be dealt with more fully at a later point in this discussion, but for the moment it can be simply noted that this moving pillar provides just those qualities of direction (the way) and meaning (light) with which society becomes endowed in those rare historical moments when it seems to reveal the transcendental in apprehensible form.

Returning to the moment of communion that sometimes seems to lift an affinity group into a transcendental dimension, it is possible to represent such powerful moments of coming together through the mythological concept of Yichud, coupling, in this case of Ze'ir Anpin and the Nukvah. It is just such a coupling that is kabbalistically understood to take place on the Sabbath and that mythologically explains the transcendental holiness experienced by the observant. Now if the ecstasy experienced by affinity groups, that sense each member may have of being lifted out of his or her limited self into a larger and more meaningful identity, can be compared with the Sabbath experience, then such groups may also be understood to share with the Sabbath its most distinguishing quality of rest. The unstable systems formed by affinity groups, whether of kindred personalities or ideology, are neither devoted to nor capable of producing work. They represent, rather, the vagrancy of feelings, ever pursuing that delight existing only in freedom.[15]

But the very dynamics of this pleasure inevitably lead such systems beyond their fragilely maintained stability into a new state either of total disorder or of higher organization. The power that builds up through the increasingly coherent resonance of the group can finally carry it over a watershed into a turbulent climax that finally takes it over the edge with an enormous power like that of a waterfall, to lie quiet at its base in a still pool. This hydraulic model has clear application to the sexual experience of lovers. And the same pattern appears in friendly associations where a moment of perfect communion can make continuity more rather than less difficult, its very unreproducibility creating obstacles to the future ease of communication by filling such postclimactic meetings with a sense of letdown only slightly relieved by nostalgia. It appears as well in ideological affinity groups, where casual discussion of shared values may develop first into a theoretical program outlining desirable changes and finally into some climactic action, the staging of a rally through the momentary assemblage of a horizontal, affinity network that can only come apart after the single event to which it is geared. In all cases, the moment of final engagement produces a vortexlike process of increasing structure that destroys the system's former freedom without endowing it with the true stability needed for its perpetuation.

But the aftereffects of such climaxes need not be negative. Positive results can also develop, as in the conception of a baby or the toppling of a repressive government. Such a new human or revolutionary baby cannot, however, be nourished by the free associations through which it was conceived. Thus though subsystems far from equilibrium can produce a giant fluctuation that can destabilize the larger system, they then can do no more than drive it to new forms of stability that are not those of non-equilibrium. The producers of progeny or revolutions must now develop the more organized social structures through whose stability their new creations can flourish. Social revolutionaries always provoke catastrophic instability at risk, the greatest risk perhaps being that they will then have to organize the society anew and lose their former freedom from accountability! Similarly, the creation of a child forces its parents to become a stable socioeconomic unit capable of providing for its physical needs as well as its safety, health, and education. It is all of these features that are the dividends accruing from the stable organization of society we are now to explore.

Stable Social Systems

We have seen that a significant correlation could be made between the functional nature of unstable social systems and the elements beyond the matrix border of that first half of the sixth-world diagram correlated with the divine personality of Ze'ir Anpin or the heart of the anthropocosm, of the cosmic heart. But if these matrix elements can be correlated with unstable social systems, then it seems consistent that the complete and properly bordered sixth-world matrix, that illustrated in plate 11 and figure 10. 2 of the Spiral Tree, should be correlated with stable social systems. And here we come to a remarkable aspect of such a correlation, the fact that the mythological connotation of the additional second half of the sixth-world matrix is precisely that of the cosmic mind.

When we arrive at the stage of social organization that exhibits the power to attract free individuals to function within the constraints necessary to fulfill its larger collective purposes, it becomes even more necessary to use vitalistic metaphors to explain its functioning in intelligible terms. We have already seen such usage in the previously quoted words of von Bertalanffy that bear repetition here: "the symbolic universe[s] created by man gain autonomy or, as it were, a life of their own. Symbol systems, so to speak, are self-propelling. . . . they all follow their respective immanent laws, which are not psychological laws that characterize mental processes in their creators."

The *locus classicus* of this concept in sociological discourse is the following statement by one of the founders of sociology, Emile Durkheim:

> The totality of beliefs and sentiments common to average citizens of the same society forms a determinate system which has its own life; one may call it the *collective* or *common conscience*. No doubt, it has not a specific organ as a substratum; it is, by definition, diffuse in every reach of society. Nevertheless, it has specific characteristics which make it a distinct reality. It is, in effect, independent of the particular conditions in which individuals are placed; they pass on and it remains. . . . It is the psychical type of society, a type which has its properties, its conditions of existence, its mode of development, just as individual types, although in a different way. . . . [T]he psychic life of society . . . [can be considered "psychic" in so far as it consists] in systems of representations and actions.[16]

With the introduction of Durkheim's concept of the *conscience collective*, the idea that society has not only "its own life" but a "psychic life," we come to the most astonishing correlation between the features of organized society and that portion of the Sabbath Star Diagram that other considerations have specified to be its matrix model. For the highest level of the sixth-world matrix was precisely correlated with the cosmic mind.

However this be understood, its implications are most illuminating with respect to the autonomous functioning of social or other transpersonal systems sufficiently stable to feature such autonomy, a "mind of its own." For if the total cosmic system may be said to have such a "mind," then it would seem that any transpersonal system that can be modeled by the same matrix configuration correlated with such a cosmic mind could be said to contain the whole of that mind, as any portion of a hologram contains the whole though its context within that whole gives it a greater specificity of particular details. Thus the "mind" of any particular transpersonal system may be said to give its own specific form to the archetypal structuring of the cosmic mind, in genetic terminology, to be the "phenotype" of the cosmic genetic code. Even that tiniest form of stable organization exhibited in a grain of sand has been found to contain the whole world in little; and if the poet's witness to a universal code informing all elements of the world and explaining its coherent systemic functioning can be accepted with reference to its material components, how much more so of those systems of symbolic coding composed of the stuff of mind.

For social organization does involve just such coding of information as can counter entropy and so may be said to demonstrate power. In this regard, the diagram is again instructive since that portion of the matrix defining the cosmic mind, whether in total or in any of its particular transpersonal forms, represents, in terms of "light units," the most powerful configuration in the matrix, eleven light units, as compared with the six that may at most be attributed to the individual psyche identified with the fifth-world matrix if both its mind and heart elements are included. A study of light units in the matrix may help to explain the attractive power of social integration. For entrance into society, counting now both the first and second half of the sixth-world matrix, may be said to endow a member with a tremendous additional factor of sixteen units. And herein is the secret of the attractive force of society, that compliance with its system of constraints, rather than diminishing the individual, is, indeed, empowering.

Sociological analysis has long featured discussions of the role of power in society, discussions that largely tend to view it in negative terms as a coercive adjunct to some superior source of legitimized authority. But it would seem that this is a false distinction. A true understanding of social organization can only be achieved if we recognize its identification with power in its purest sense, that essential quality shared by all forms of power, whether they be physical, social, or spiritual. If language may be considered to enshrine the deepest understanding of the culture that employs it, then it may be said that what language brings together should not, by any wise person, be driven asunder. In the case of power, it is impossible, in fact, to say whether it is the physical, social, or spiritual use of the term that should be taken as metaphor. And it may well be that it is the social and physical uses of the term that are metaphorical, that the metaphor so linking certain social and physical phenomena both to each other and to some more inclusive reality can provide a key to the deepest meaning of the conceptual cluster known by the word *power*.

Let us, then, begin this consideration of the social meaning of power by observing the scientific definition of its purest physical cognate, the power that is the subject of the field of mechanics. As is well known, the mechanical definition of power is the ability to do work. If we can accept as the primary meaning of power, in all its domains, the ability to produce work, and that in the most efficient and effective manner possible, then such ability would clearly seem to be a property of social organization. The first thing we can say, then, is that *it is power that organizes* and, conversely, that organization inherently contains and builds up power. Such a definition of organization is compatible with the identification with information proposed for it in information theory. Since it is a major premise of this theory that the buildup of information acts to counter entropy or disorder, information becomes identifiable with the very order that constitutes its negentropy. But since the production of entropy is also accompanied by a loss of energy to a system, its dissipation as heat, the implication is that the buildup of informational order is accompanied by the converse of entropic energy loss, the buildup of systemic power.

Once power has been identified with organization, the next step is to identify its method of functioning. And here I would propose as a principle that *power organizes through establishing a system of constraints*. The way in which constraints convey the presence of power can be visualized either in terms of the mathematical metaphor of "attractor surfaces" or of the source of this imagery in the physics of magnetic attraction. In his mathematical explanation of how "constraints can be visualized as attractor surfaces," Conrad H. Waddington shows that,

"If the system starts from any condition, which will be represented by a point in the multidimensional phase space, the trajectory from that point will first of all move to the nearest attractor surface, and then move along that surface."[17] Similarly, if a magnet is placed beneath a paper and iron filings are strewn over that paper, these filings will arrange themselves according to the magnetic field produced by the magnet.

Now, the reason social constraints can be visualized as attractor surfaces is that they offer the most efficient means of empowerment to one willing to align his or her behavior in compliance with their direction. And so, as with magnetic power lines, they do attract the free energies of individuals into that ever fuller integration with society that can reciprocally enhance individual effectiveness, giving it, as it were, an additional charge of magnetic power. It is through such social integration that individuals can learn to recognize the true nature of their freedom, such freedom, whenever it appears, as is always the sign from the systems point of view that its possessor is a component of a larger whole. And as the freedom of all components must submit to the constraints of the larger whole to which they belong in order for that collectivity to achieve the enhanced benefits provided by such higher organization, so is it also that individual human freedom can only function effectively by recognizing the constraints inherent within its chosen medium and using those constraints to give proper form to its purposes. It is the old kabbalistic principle that force can only achieve effectiveness, existence, by submitting to the constraints of form. And it is just this generative union of force in form that is represented mythologically by the continuous Yichud of Abba and Imma within Arikh Anpin, one that, in the Sefirot of the Spiral Tree with which we are now concerned, represents the mentality of the anthropocosm, that cosmic mind earlier said to inform and be specified by all transpersonal systems, society probably being the most important. Since energy cannot achieve any useful purpose until it has been constrained by an appropriate form, it is only through such constraints that it can be translated into power, the ability to do work. The establish-

ment of such power lines of constraints, by attracting the self-enhancing participation of lower individual energies, can thus organize those energies into a more effective power to work for the welfare of all.

One sociologist who has understood this primary significance of social power as the capacity to accomplish work is Talcott Parsons. Despite the serious lack of agreement he notes about the meaning of political power, he follows the tradition of Hobbes in arguing:

> There is, however, a core complex of its meaning, having to do with the capacity of persons or collectivities "to get things done" effectively. . . . Power then is generalized capacity to secure the performance of binding obligations by units in a system of collective organization when the obligations are legitimized with reference to their bearing on collective goals and where in case of recalcitrance there is a presumption of enforcement by negative situational sanctions. . . . But for power to function . . . to mobilize resources effectively for collective action, it must be "legitimized" which in the present context means that in certain respects compliance . . . is optional.[18]

In discussing Parsons, I cannot do much more than simply note the general coherence of his analysis with that being here offered. But in one respect his lack of general distinction between the way in which power can be used by "persons or collectivities" can lead to some misunderstanding of the nature of systemic social power. If "Power . . . may be formulated in terms of the conception that A may have power over B," which involves "the 'right' of A, as a decision-making unit involved in collective process, to make decisions which take precedence over those of B, in the interest of the effectiveness of the collective operation as a whole,"[19] then no real distinction is being made between the *conscience collective* and its individual interpreters on the power hierarchy within a society. But the power that even a socially cooperative individual may acquire through an effective collaboration with the power structure that results in his promotion is not the same as the power exercised by the society itself as an autonomous transpersonal system. The proof of this is in the well-known corruptibility of individuals who do achieve great power through their canny use of the structure of such transpersonal power. Individual power, in fact, functions in a manner inverse to that of the transpersonal. Here it is the private sector that is the true domain of competition while the public sector is that which must "care" for the welfare of the whole, not only making sure that the nonproductive members of society are provided for, in a manner that would seem to incorporate the characteristics of love, but also ensuring the more general welfare by regulating the potentially damaging products of the private sector and by establishing the stable order that can protect its members from threats to their safety coming both from within and without the boundaries of society.

In distinguishing between the public and private sectors of society, the sixth-world matrix can again be instructive, its structure enabling us to differentiate precisely between the largely centralized form of the political power structure, dedicated to establishing the order necessary for the production of work, and the lateral form of the private sector, which is largely responsible for the economic forms of such work as well as for the politics and culture of a society. And it can distinguish as well between those forms of lateral freedom that work within and are necessary to the functioning of the whole and those whose freedom from all constraints is generally countercultural and may involve such forms of deviance as were considered in the previous subsection, forms that may become or be considered dangerous to society. This latter is particularly true, as we shall soon see, in relation to the scarlet component of what chapter 12 defined as the Double Spiral Tree, shown in plate 16, the counterpart at the left of the sixth-world diagram of the turquoise component to its right. What is more, the structure of the society that can be modeled by the form of the sixth-world matrix associated with the upper six Sefirot of the Spiral Tree would seem to be that which is "open." That which does not, as this, follow the turquoise lateral path to final union with the blue Keter but rather the red central path culminat-

ing in the red Keter, comprised of seven rather than ten total macrocomponents, would rather seem to provide the model for the antithetical closed society. In the earlier discussion of this matrix distinction in chapter 10, its ten-macrohexagram form was identified with the ten Sefirot of the Tree of Life Diagram and so with the Jewish mystical tradition of the Kabbalah, while its seven-macrohexagram form was identified with the seven chakras of the system of Indian yoga. And now in the present context of open versus closed political systems, the Jewish tradition again would seem to favor the open.

This is, indeed, the meaning of the central historical event on which the nation of Israel was founded, that of the Exodus from Egypt. It is from the closed system of Egypt, whose Hebrew name *mitzrayim* derives from the root meaning narrow, that Israel was with violence divinely brought forth to follow the difficult path of freedom: "And it came to pass, when Pharaoh had let the people go, that God led them not through the way of the land of the Philistines, although that was near . . . But God led the people about through the way of the wilderness of the Red sea. . . . And the Lord went before them by day in a pillar of a cloud, to lead them the way; and by night in a pillar of fire to give them light . . ." (Exod. 13:17, 18, 21). The new society of Israel is to be defined not by the direct but more roundabout approach to social order that first establishes the condition and practice of freedom, a condition that makes possible the contractual assent of covenant to the subsequent introduction of the ever more fully elaborated regulations and the structure of hierarchical authority that would direct this freedom into the proper fulfillment of the ends for which such a society was founded. In the conclusion to this appendix, these ends, characterized by the divine pillar providing direction and meaning, will be more fully discussed. But first we should consider the diagram analog to the more circuitous route by which Israel was led away from the closed society of Egypt to the discovery of the new consensual basis of an open society ruled by laws superior to any of its judges or kings, that is, a society ruled not by the will of individual persons but by a system of law and one in which its members complied voluntarily with its constraints. This diagram analog is the path followed by the sixth-world Sefirot of the Spiral Tree, which introduces an extensive lateral dimension into its definition of society. In fact, what distinguishes the open from the closed form of society in diagram terms is precisely this inclusion of lateral elements within its structural framework, elements excluded from the more narrowly centralized diagram structure identified with its closed form.

In this discussion of open social systems we have so far considered only the structure of power that could be associated with the collective mind of society, that whose light-unit power is largely central in its matrix components and that occupies the upper portion of the diagram. But it is the right side of the diagram, featuring only lateral elements, that can truly be said to define its heart. We meet again with those elements also defining the cosmic heart and the divine personality of Ze'ir Anpin. In the first half or right side of the sixth-world diagram given in labeled form in figure 10.3, the macrohexagram of Tiferet is flanked with those of Chesed and Gevurah, thereby reinforcing its association with the principle of balance. But the extremes of what can be considered liberalism and conservatism would also seem to find their allowed positions within the institutionalized forms of freedom that may be associated with this exclusively lateral area. These three macrohexagrams may clearly be associated with the ideological categories of left, right, and center as they appear in the forms of political parties and of news media, both vital adjuncts of the political process in an open society. Unlike the freer form of unstable affinity groups earlier considered, which may be thought to function outside of the structure of social institutions, the institutionalized forms of free association and expression are characterized by the stable organization necessary for them to accomplish their work within the marketplace of ideas. This is also the case with the economy, where individual businesses battle it out for success in a free market. Even in the less competitive field of the arts, the clash of styles is a sign of the freedom necessary for artistic creativity, though it may also function both within and without the border of social stability. It is, then, this lateral aspect of society whose free condition generates

the culture and productive capacity of an open society, that creative element, whether in political ideas or economic entrepreneurship, which can enable the society to evolve peacefully to an ever greater satisfaction of the needs, both physical and spiritual, of its members. It defines the true cultural heart of society.

In those lateral areas that may be said to define the private sector of society, the role of centralized governmental power is ideally confined to such regulations as are concerned to protect the people from products and practices deemed dangerous to the health and welfare of individuals and the environment. It is protection that is the main function of government, the establishment of a condition of stable order that can ensure the general safety of its citizens and that requires the maintenance of extensive administrative agencies as well as of the police and army.

But in addition to these functions, centralized government would also seem to be best constituted to provide other essential services such as health and education. The experience of England and Canada with its national health service shows that it is possible to provide basic medical treatment at lower cost through governmental control, even if this means that those physicians who are in this profession less for reasons of a healing vocation than for money will leave it for more lucrative fields. And higher education can achieve the same excellence in public as in private institutions, as a comparison of the University of California at Berkeley with Yale University should demonstrate. As it is the government that has final responsibility for social welfare, so it would seem well suited to provide those services of health and education whose practitioners have what might be called a vocation for these fields. For it is as "public servants" that individuals are ideally attracted to government service, to serve the greater good. Conversely, the experience both in the capitalist West and in such a county as communist China that greater productivity can be assured by freer market conditions seems to suggest that the production of goods is best left to the private sector.

In contrast to the division of functions between the public and private sectors possible in an open society, what distinguishes the nature of a closed society in diagram terms is its exclusion of such lateral elements. Politics, economics, and culture have all come under the direct administration of government, and there is no institutionalized, and thus protected, place for freedom. But the lateral elements continue to exist on the side of the diagram to the left of this model of closed society at its bottom, again better viewed in plate 16 of the Double Spiral Tree. Whether these be understood to represent noncooperative pockets of freedom within or beyond the territorial boundaries of such a society, in the former case representing a political underground, economic black market, or other countercultural forces, the response of the government is the same, repression of internal dissidents and military conquest of temptations to freedom across its borders. The use of force to overcome either ideas or the weak, particularly if they be combined, is always the sign of a closed mind, even if it represents the leadership of a so-called free society. And its effect in either case is to make a repressive society or culture vulnerable to the insidious effects of that which cannot be officially allowed, effects all the more dangerous because the suppressed forces cannot help but become warped into such unnatural forms of vice and violence as may be further modeled by that Sabbatical configuration beyond the matrix portion of the negative Spiral Tree to the left of the diagram, a configuration betokening a license not as benign as its counterpart to the right. If an individual or a society, either in its political structure or cultural norms, follows the wrong path to social stability, that which in diagram terms goes out with the central and back with the lateral rather than the reverse, the effect of the earlier suppression of any behavior that might be deemed deviant is to make it more susceptible at a later more decadent stage to the corrupter forms that this suppressed material has had to take in order to maintain its underground existence. Thus the effect of governmental or cultural suppression is to produce an underground world of vice and crime, on the one hand, and of revolutionary ideas and forces, on the other. Where the inclusion of lateral elements by open societies and minds allows them to evolve through adapta-

tion to the new, their exclusion by closed societies and minds leads to an inner corruption that can only be scourged through revolutionary change.

If God led the people by a circuitous path to the establishment of a society based upon freedom within law, it was because such an open society could best fulfill the highest purposes of social organization, to give direction and meaning to human life, the very purposes expressed in the pillar of divine guidance that may be said to inform the very soul of society. That such purposes can be ascribed to society follows from the modeling of transpersonal social systems by the sixth-world matrix; for the sixth world represents the dimension of meaningfulness, that in which the whole pattern of the Sabbath Star Diagram first becomes clear, and any subject or systems level that can be identified with it must be shown to partake of this essential element if such modeling is to be justified. How social participation gives meaning to human existence, and in the highest of biblical terms, will be the concluding subject of this systems analysis of society.

SOCIAL MEANINGFULNESS

In the preceding analysis, it was suggested that society enhances individual meaningfulness both by giving individuals the sense that they belong to and can serve a greater whole and by rewarding the service that works most effectively within the social system with empowerment. So also does Durkheim define the ideal purposes of society, beginning with the implications, for a worker, of his functioning within society:

> He feels that he is serving something. For that, he need not embrace vast portions of the social horizon; it is sufficient that he perceive enough of it to understand that his actions have an aim beyond themselves. From that time, as special and uniform as his activity may be, it is that of an intelligent being, for it has direction, and he knows it. . . . the morality of organized societies . . . only asks that we be thoughtful of our fellows and that we be just, that we fulfill our duty, that we work

at the function we can best execute, and receive the just reward for our services. . . . This is far from being on the verge of realization. We know only too well what a laborious work it is to erect this society where each individual will have the place he merits, will be rewarded as he deserves, where everybody, accordingly, will spontaneously work for the good of all and of each.[20]

Man enters society to fulfill his double need to connect and contribute to something larger than himself and also to have his unique contribution acknowledged, not simply to escape from his isolated individuality but also to affirm it and, even more importantly, to have it affirmed, and that not merely by other individuals in their personal capacities but by what Durkheim calls the *conscience collective.*

All social relationships, from the simplest dyadic interactions to the more systemic interrelationships of man and society, are marked by this basic human need to belong to a larger acknowledging whole. When King Lear said, "Allow not nature more than nature needs, / Man's life is cheap as beast's" (2.4.261–62), that "more" that Lear and the mankind for which he speaks requires and that only society can provide is the acknowledgment of his individual significance. But though people ask this of all their relationships, this need can never be fully satisfied by the personal, only by the transpersonal. It is not by hierarchical superiors in their personal capacities that we wish our merits to be acknowledged, since this is always somewhat fortuitous and subject to corruption, as is also the case with lovers, but by the *conscience collective* itself and this because it can do no other. The need for such public acknowledgment has never been more baldly stated than by Milton, as when he said:

> I seem to survey, as from a towering height, the far extended tracts of sea and land and innumerable crowds of spectators. . . . Of all the lovers of liberty and virtue the magnanimous and the wise, in whatever quarter they may be found, some secretly favor, others openly approve, some greet me with congratulations and applause; others who

had long been proof against conviction at last yield themselves captive to the force of truth.[21]

However megalomaniac may be the terms in which Milton wishes those services to the republic to be acknowledged for which he suffered blindness, these terms contain the two conditions necessary for such acknowledgment to be truly meaningful, that it be a response that seems to reveal the necessary functioning of the system as a whole and that it be deserved, the reward of merit. Both of these conditions require further consideration.

Given the possibilities of social corruption it must overcome, the occurrence of any such true acknowledgment must have a quality of grace. But this is not only on account of its actual unpredictability, rather because of the purity of transpersonal power. To understand this, it is necessary to distinguish between the nature of personal and transpersonal power. In the sense that I have been using it, a person has power if he can organize resources so that they will result in a value-added product. This is because he is deriving his power from the same organizational capacity as does his transpersonal social model. And if he works within the constraints of the social system, he will increase his own as well as the collective power. It is because the experience of such power is always rewarding that it can be perverted to the purely personal purposes that are corrupting both to the individual and to the proper functioning of the system. To the extent that a person finds the exercise of power to be psychologically rewarding, it is just so far justified by what it reveals of his ability to make the system work for him by his understanding of how to work within its constraints. To learn how to work within a system, however corrupt, is always rewarding, endowing the individual with a sense of earned power as well as with its more tangible benefits.

But the lessons and proper functioning of society do not end there. For if that power is gained from an already perverted system, is gained through the personal corruption of the system rather than merit, or is then perverted to serve purely personal ends, its psychological reward will be gradually drained of meaning. This is because, as Durkheim so wisely recognized, the psychic life that can be attributed to society as a whole is characterized by the quality of "conscience," a moral quality that informs all of its systemic functions to ensure that, on the psychic if not physical level, we reap as we sow, that the ultimate reward society can provide, the experience of meaningfulness, will accrue only to those who have contributed their very best to the common good and whose contribution is marked by no moral failure in their use of transpersonal power that might sully its purity. There is no cheating our personal hologram of the *conscience collective*. Its accounts are exact and will only under the strictest conditions of service to the common good and moral probity give us an experience of meaningfulness so great and self-validating that it makes all cognitive questions of ultimate purpose and individual survival irrelevant and grants us heart's ease.

Sociologists are fond of speaking of social power in terms of A's power over B, as though the sum of all such interactions can explain the functioning of power in society. But where A and B are both social units, A's power can only represent that perversion of systemic power to personal use whose consequence is the frustration of society's highest aims, not meaningfulness but what Durkheim calls "anomie," the state resulting from a loss of the sense of social connectedness that can finally lead to suicide. Since one is only driven to suicide when his life has become totally void of significance, if such a draining of individual significance can be laid to the disintegration of the social sense, then it is from society that one's sense of personal meaningfulness is derived. But where A has personal power over B, its exercise will be as dehumanizing to both as is their sociological reduction to the status of letters. A will be defeated by the *conscience collective* since his lack of proper procedure will deprive his life of meaning. But B will be defeated by A's perversion of the system so that it cannot grant him the acknowledgment he deserves whether or not it publicly rewards him. For if his acknowledgment is owing to any such chance factors as must attach to any other social unit whatever its hierarchical position, such factors as A's personal liking or need for a publicity symbol, then B will lack the particular feature of sys-

temic macrodeterminacy that can alone legitimize his sense of accomplishment, that proof of an abiding structure of just order to which he has proven worthy. Thus the social system will only work for both of them if A uses his hierarchical power over B transpersonally and not personally. Only as a true transpersonal agent can A award B the proper and uncorrupting benefits accruing to him from the unwearying contribution of his talents to the greater whole, such transpersonal acknowledgment as can be the source of personal meaningfulness and the great reward of membership in society.

Thus for the system to work as it is intended, to give that highest benefit for which individuals venture out of the cave of their hearts both to accomplish serious work and to present that work for social acknowledgment, both A and B must so serve the public good that the hierarchical distinction between them becomes insignificant beside the priestly character of their equally required services. To achieve the sense of meaningfulness that is the final blessing of social participation, both must perform their services to the transpersonal source of their derived personal power in such a manner of moral purity as can fill both them and their works with holiness. As J. H. Hertz has noted, it is just such an association of holiness with community that, according to Moritz Lazarus, is enshrined in the language of the Bible: "The philosopher Moritz Lazarus calls attention to the fact that whenever the duty or ideal of holiness is spoken of in the Torah, the plural is invariably used (*e.g.* 'Ye shall be holy,' Lev. XIX, 2), because mortal man can only attain to holiness when co-operating with others in the service of a great Cause or Ideal, as a member of a Community, Society, or 'Kingdom'."[22] Thus it is that society can become a means toward the achievement of that group holiness that, whenever successful, can transform any secular society into the biblical ideal of "a kingdom of priests, and an holy nation" (Exod. 19:6), and this without loss of its secularity.

When any society so fulfills its purposes that all are cared for with the spiraling increase in general value that results when the best efforts of all its members are encouraged, it can be said to achieve a state of holiness in which its rewards seem informed with a truth beyond themselves. In such a state society seems to become a clear glass through which one may glimpse a larger cosmic system like it in its blessed capacity to acknowledge personal contributions and worth. For resonating through every transpersonal social acknowledgment and enabling it to convey the experience of meaningfulness is that sense of higher approbation again never better expressed than when Milton has his God say to a loyal angel: "Servant of God, well done" (*Paradise Lost*, 6.29).

The glory of those moments in which society works perfectly to reward merit is that it seems to reveal a larger pattern of meaningfulness, a still higher dimension that not only endows society with its capacity for just order but is itself so informed, following the same systemic laws to be observed in the workings of society. The transcendental experience conveyed through stable social systems adds to the feeling of social solidarity the bliss of acknowledged personal accomplishment. It does not simply represent a return to undifferentiated being but also that growth in individuality that Durkheim derives from the necessary division of labor in complex societies.[23] It represents both a return to being and a progression in becoming, in becoming that which the sixth-world diagram also represents, what in different contexts was characterized either as a Neshamah Master or a divine personality. For the discipline of serving humanity through society is one that can develop the consciousness to the highest degrees of holiness, whether or not such a master of transpersonal social power ever consciously understands his experiences of meaningfulness in transcendental terms.

It was at a time when Jewish institutional religion no longer seemed to reveal the existence of divine forces functioning in any terms that were either comprehensible or meaningful, in this being in one way different from the surrounding Christian Churches, that the predominantly Jewish founders of sociology turned to society as a source of higher truth that might inspire dedication and answer a quasi-religious need for ultimate explanation. It has been said that for them, and particularly the followers of Marx, society proved to be a god that failed.

But as the just completed analysis should have shown, this was not because society is a false god, properly understood, rather that its human agents proved inadequate to its highest demands for priestly, transpersonal service. It was Durkheim who recognized the truly religious character of society, that it represents the highest reality that can be examined and understood but which does not necessarily comprehend the whole of the truth:

> according to the well-known formula, man is double. There are two beings in him: an individual being which has its foundation in the organism and the circle of whose activities is therefore strictly limited, and a social being which represents the highest reality in the intellectual and moral order that we can know by observation— the individual transcends himself, both when he thinks and when he acts. . . . A society is the most powerful combination of physical and moral forces of which nature offers us an example.[24]

Though he normally preferred to confine his analyses within the secular framework of observable social phenomena, in the case of those "collective representations" that constitute the unobservable element within society, particularly the *conscious collective*, he seems to recognize a form of evidence for an order beyond that of society and one with which societal order is in essential accord. This is especially true of the religious beliefs within the collective conscience of society:

> A collective representation presents guarantees of objectivity by the fact that it is collective: for it is not without sufficient reason that it has been able to generalize and maintain itself with persistence. If it were out of accord with the nature of things, it would never have been able to acquire an extended and prolonged empire over intellects. . . . It is precisely this principle which is at the basis of the method which we follow in the study of religious phenomena: we take it as an axiom that religious beliefs, howsoever strange their appearance may be at times, contain a truth which must be discovered.[25]

Since there is a "nature of things" beyond society, and one whose truth may prove to be strangely consistent with religious beliefs, Durkheim concludes that those explanations restricting themselves to the secular view of society, rather than adopting a further spiritual perspective, may well prove inadequate: "when it is recognized that above the individual there is society, and that this is not a nominal being created by reason, but a system of active forces, a new manner of explaining men becomes possible. . . . To be sure, it cannot be said at present to what point these explanations may be able to reach, and whether or not they are of a nature to resolve all the problems."[26]

The foregoing analysis of society has argued the largely Durkheimian position that it is only an ideal understanding of society that can explain the integrative forces operating demonstrably within it. But history has also shown that the ideal of such a perfectly functioning society has yet to be realized, that whether or not it is understood to represent the divine in immanence, it is a god that has consistently failed. Such failure can, however, also be explained by the diagram. We have seen that the most coherent methods of modeling the hierarchy of system levels postulated in general systems theory in terms of the matrix was that in which the fourth-world matrix was assigned to all levels up to that of prelapsarian man, that of the fifth world to man the symbolizer, and that of the sixth to such transpersonal symbolic systems as society. But such a modeling is, indeed, ideal since it places socialized man in the fifth world of Ruach consciousness. Now, what marks such consciousness is precisely that identification of the self with the needs of the Other that would permit the proper functioning of society. It is not the God in society that has failed man, for like any natural system society is always capable of recovering its balance and health if that by which it was polluted is replaced by new sources of vitality. It is rather man that has thus far failed to realize the potential of society to further his spiritual development from the Ruach to the Neshamah level, this precisely because he enters it not with Ruach but Nefesh consciousness, with an *ego* still competitive with and hoping to gain power over *alter*. With the

threat of terrorism and nuclear destruction hanging over the world, it is now more imperative than ever that man develop his consciousness beyond the level of reptilian responses that continue to represent his normal social functioning and so also that of the social institutions developed by him, that he learn to live up to the program of which he forms a most significant part rather than still preferring to rest at incomplete stages of development, entering into society in a state of Nefesh consciousness.

Nations, national economies, and individual corporations, whether or not their particular stable systems are open or closed, still interact in accordance with the laws of the jungle, those laws whose fitness to reptilian consciousness did not prevent the extinction of the dinosaurs. Nor is a clear solution available. For the very unbalanced development that has permitted man to develop instruments of mass destruction he could not certainly control does not bode well for any world government he might now establish. If man does not develop to the point where he can dismantle his nuclear arsenals, there is no assurance that a world government he might establish to control the use of nuclear weapons, should it ever be given the power it would require to function effectively, would not become the corrupted dystopia envisioned in so much futurist literature. It can only be hoped that the nuclear and ecological threats that might spell man's extinction will rather prove to be the catalysts to his development of a higher level of social consciousness, one that could not only make the dream of one world a reality but enable all of its component social systems to function with that truly holy character ever attributed to the Millennial Kingdom.

The modeling of general systems theory by the Sabbath Star Diagram here undertaken has brought us to a subject not previously considered in this study, that of sociology. But where modern sociologists have been concerned to deny all metaphysical implications of social functioning, the study of society just modeled in terms of these theories has once again, and in spite of the protestations of their proponents, introduced metaphysical elements that tend to confirm the very cosmological claims it has been the business of modern culture to try to eradicate. As this analysis has shown, society reveals a structure of power whose proper functioning leads not only to the endowing of human lives with meaningfulness but also to the further revelation of a cosmic structure in which society itself is embedded and which must feature a similar structure of meaningful order to explain its own workings.[27]

The geometric system of the Sabbath Star Diagram offers a revealing model through which the orderly functions of an evolving cosmos can be apprehended in all its wealth of details and all the majesty of its design. For like the society it has here been modeling, it is itself a transpersonal symbolic system the study of whose geometric significance can provide ever deeper insights into the structure and meaning of the cosmic reality for which it may truly be said to contain the code, the very mystery of its own expressive forms providing precisely the light capable of illuminating at least a portion of the larger cosmic mystery. And as both society and the diagram modeling it reveal a structure of control beyond them, so does the socializing of man reveal his freedom to be subject to similar constraints, that he is part of a systems hierarchy reaching backward to the atom and forward to beyond the stars.

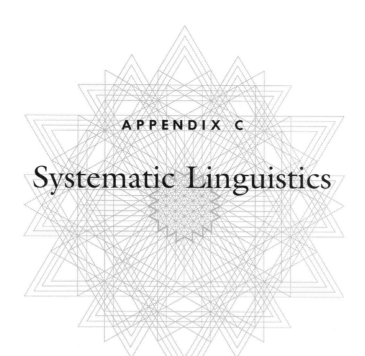

APPENDIX C

Systematic Linguistics

THE THREE LEVELS OF LANGUAGE

The following study of structural linguistics both supports and extends the earlier definition of the hermeneutics of diagram interpretation that chapter 2 has named the Science of Expressive Form as well as the effort of these appendices to show that the Sabbath Star Diagram cannot only model the Kabbalah but has more universal applications. It is with Emile Benveniste that the notion of level enters into modern linguistic analysis and, in so doing, makes possible such a systems approach to language as was applied to society in appendix B. And its modeling of the systems hierarchy of language reveals, most importantly, that at each of its levels language makes the same connection between an aspect of the temporal and of the spatial that is both extraordinary and can help to explain its capacity to interpret geometric forms.[1]

For Benveniste, there are two main levels of "articulated" language, that of the sign, which he largely equates with the word, and that of the sentence. In studying "language as an organic system of linguistic signs,"[2] Benveniste stresses that "a linguistic unit will not be acknowledged as such unless we can identify it within a higher unit."[3] But since "Meaning is indeed the fundamental condition that any unit on any level must fulfill in order to obtain linguistic status,"[4] it is the word, "as the smallest free unit of meaning,"[5] that defines the lowest linguistic level, and this even though it is composed of still lower but nonautonomous units. The two necessary aspects of linguistic units involve an important relationship: "Form and meaning thus appear as conjoined properties, given of necessity and simultaneously, and inseparable in the functioning of language."[6] We shall return to this understanding of language but must first conclude Benveniste's analysis of the two primary language levels he recognizes, particularly his definition of the word as having a "double nature":

> The word has an intermediary functional position that arises from its double nature. On the one hand it breaks down into phonemic units, which are from the lower level; on the other, as a unit of meaning and together with other units of meaning, it enters into a unit of the level above. . . . this unit is not a longer or more complex word—it belongs to another class of notions; it is a sentence. . . . A sentence constitutes a whole which is not reducible to the sum of its parts. . . . The word is a constituent of a sentence; it brings about its signification; but it does not necessarily appear in the sentence with

the meaning which it has as an autonomous unit. . . . Here is the last level our analysis reaches, that of the sentence. . . .[7]

The sentence, like the word, "constitutes a whole which is not reducible to the sum of its parts," the defining characteristic of a system, and, as in general systems analysis, it is the higher level, that of the sentence, that controls the freedom of implication of the lower, determining the specific referents of its multiple-meaning constituent words. But though Benveniste does not take his own analysis to any level higher than that of the sentence, in his final discussion of what is for him the "last level," he opens up the possibility of a yet higher linguistic level: "with the sentence we leave the domain of language as a system of signs and enter into another universe, that of language as an instrument of communication, whose expression is discourse. . . . the sentence is the unit of discourse.[8]

It is Paul Ricoeur who, adopting Benveniste's analysis of linguistic levels, takes the final step to a full definition of the third linguistic level to which Benveniste's discussion had seemed to point, that of discourse. But in developing its truly systemic nature, he has had to shift his attention from the indeterminacy of spoken discourse to the more structured form of discourse that is the written text or work, the latter being the term that he finds more meaningful:

Composition, belonging to a genre and individual style characterize discourse as a work. The very word "work" reveals the nature of these new categories; they are categories of production and of labour. . . . Let us use the term "work" to describe the closed sequence of discourse which can be considered as a text. . . . the text is not only something written but is a work, that is, a singular totality. As a totality, the literary work cannot be reduced to a sequence of sentences which are individually intelligible; rather, it is an architecture of themes and purposes which can be constructed in several ways. . . . Moreover, as the notion of singular totality suggests, a text is a kind of individual, like an animal or a work of art.[9]

As the meaning of a word cannot be reduced to the sum of its phonemes and that of a sentence to the sum of its words, so a meaningful work of discourse cannot be reduced to the sum of its sentences; its meaning inheres in the structure of that singular totality marking the ascent to this third and highest linguistic level. Though we shall not pause at this time to explore the richness of Ricoeur's definition of discourse, we can see that with this extension of Benveniste's notion of linguistic levels Ricoeur has reconceptualized linguistics in terms of three levels that are clearly parallel to the three main evolutionary levels posited by general systems theory, levels that not only can be modeled by the matrices of the fourth, fifth, and sixth worlds of the Sabbath Star Diagram but can also gain in implication through comparison with the modeling of the three systems levels given in appendix B. Let us see, then, what illumination can be provided for the field of structural linguistics by modeling the primary level of the word by the fourth-world matrix, the intermediate level of the sentence by the matrix for the fifth world, and the final level of the discourse by that for the sixth world, being particularly concerned to see how such modeling can reveal a central duality within all the levels of language.

THE MATRIX MODELING OF THE WORD

If the fourth-world matrix is to be correlated with the linguistic level of the word, then it is best to understand it, as does Benveniste, in terms of the structure of the sign as it has been defined by the field known as "semiotics." Founded in the early twentieth century by the Swiss linguist Ferdinand de Saussure, semiotics emerged as a major intellectual force in France, profoundly influencing the anthropology of Claude Lévi-Strauss, the psychoanalytic theories of Jacques Lacan, and the criticism, both of literature and popular culture, of Roland Barthes. From these French roots, it has spread to other disciplines and countries but always retaining something of the theoretical suppositions of its original linguistic model as developed by Saussure, most importantly that "Language is a system of signs that express ideas."[10]

For Saussure the linguistic sign is composed of two elements, the signifier and the signified:

> The linguistic sign unites, not a thing and a name, but a concept and a sound-image. The latter is not the material sound . . . but the psychological imprint of the sound. . . . The linguistic sign is then a two-sided psychological entity. . . . The two elements are intimately united, and each recalls the other. . . . I propose to retain the word sign [*signe*] to designate the whole and to replace concept and sound-image respectively by signified [*signifié*] and signifier [*signifiant*]. . . . The bond between the signifier and the signified is arbitrary. . . . arbitrary in that it actually has no natural connection with the signified.[11]

Benveniste has noted a flaw that enters into Saussure's understanding of the arbitrary nature of the sign once he identifies the signifier not with a thing but a concept; for Benveniste argues that, on the basis of Saussure's own analysis, "Between the signifier and the signified, the connection is not arbitrary; on the contrary, it is necessary. . . . The mind does not contain empty forms, concepts without names."[12] He supports this by citing Saussure's own image of language:

> There are no preexisting ideas, and nothing is distinct before the appearance of language. . . . Language can also be compared with a sheet of paper: thought is the front and sound the back; one cannot cut the front without cutting the back at the same time; likewise in language, one can neither divide sound from thought nor thought from sound; the division could be accomplished only abstractedly. . . .[13]

As Benveniste further shows, the bonding of concept to sound-image is intrinsic to language and neither could exist without the other:

> The signifier is the phonic translation of a concept; the signified is the mental counterpart of the signifier. . . . The choice that invokes a certain sound slice for a certain idea is not at all arbitrary;

this sound slice would not exist without the corresponding idea and vice versa. In reality, Saussure was always thinking of the representation of the real object (although he spoke of the "idea") and of the evidently unnecessary and unmotivated character of the bond which united the sign to the thing signified.[14]

Benveniste's critique of Saussure is not radical in that he accepts the arbitrary character of signs; he only would remove this arbitrary characteristic from the concept to the "thing signified." Though even here he recognizes a problem, he prefers to sidestep the issue, and with him, we too shall temporarily defer consideration of this central issue:

> It is indeed the metaphysical problem of the agreement between the mind and the world transposed into linguistic terms, a problem which the linguist will perhaps one day be able to attack with results but which he will do better to put aside for the moment. To establish the relationship as arbitrary is for the linguist a way of defending himself against this question and also against the solution which the speaker brings instinctively to it. For the speaker there is a complete equivalence between language and reality.[15]

Though Benveniste has shown only that the relationship of signifier to concept signified is necessary, in what follows we shall share his uncritical speaker's instinctive understanding of a further bond of necessity between the concept and the thing signified, the latter being further understood to be conceptualized in terms of a visual image.

We shall return to the significance of the image in the development of language, but first we must consider the implications of these two aspects of the sign so defined. If the signifier can be identified with a sound image and the signified with a visual image, then words involve the meaningful bonding of two wholly dissimilar domains, that at the heart of at least primary words or names is that seeing of similarity between dissimilars that Aristotle ascribed to metaphor: "a good metaphor implies an intuitive perception of the similarity in dissimilars."[16] How the signifier can be, in Benveniste's words, "the phonic translation of a concept," when by concept we understand image, is a question we shall leave for later discussion, but that the mind can make such meaningful translations of images into sounds and vice versa is demonstrable in the elementary processes of language. And they not only suggest how linguistic sounds can translate geometric forms but mark these processes as essentially metaphorical.

The further development of vocabulary through metaphorical transfers from signifiers whose referents are sensible images has been pointed out by many, among them Julian Jaynes:

> It is by metaphor that language grows. The common reply to the question "what is it?" is, when the reply is difficult or the experience unique, "well, it is like—."... In early times, language and its referents climbed up from the concrete to the abstract on the steps of metaphors. . . . Understanding a thing is to arrive at a metaphor for that thing by substituting something more familiar to us. And the feeling of familiarity is the feeling of understanding. . . . Moreover, things that in the physical-behavioral world do not have a spatial quality are made to have such in consciousness. Otherwise we cannot be conscious of them.[17]

All denominations, then, retain some link to the spatial images through which corresponding sound slices first became capable of generating meaning. And however dead the metaphoric content of abstract words may become, their meaningfulness rests on some original metaphorical connection with a concrete image or process that can still be traced through their etymologies.

Paul Ricoeur also recognizes that later metaphoric processes may be the same as those originally responsible for the development of language when he asks: "could we not imagine that the order itself is born in the same way that it changes? Is there not . . . a 'metaphoric' at work at the origin of logical thought, at the root of all classification?"[18] In his main development of a theory of metaphor as the vehicle for "the creation of meaning in language,"[19] Ricoeur is primarily dependent on the earlier work of I. A. Richards, Max Black, and Monroe C. Beardsley, who all tend to view this production of meaning as the result of a metaphoric transfer.

But through the work of Marcus B. Hester and such earlier figures as W. K. Wimsatt and especially Wittgenstein, he later comes to question this earlier analysis and return to the central importance of the image to metaphor as first defined by Aristotle:

> the question remains whether one cannot or ought not to attempt the reverse, and *proclaim the image to be the final moment of a semantic theory* that objected to it as a starting point. . . . What remains to be explained is the *sensible* moment of metaphor. This moment is designated in Aristotle by the lively character of metaphor, by its power to "set before the eyes." . . . Like the icon of the Byzantine cult, the verbal icon [Wimsatt's titular phrase] consists in this fusion of sense and the sensible. . . . So the problem is to bring to light a liaison between sense and sensa that can be reconciled with semantic theory. . . . The most satisfying explanation . . . is the one that Hester links to the notion of "seeing as" (which is Wittgensteinian in origin). . . . The "seeing as" is the intuitive relationship that makes the sense and image hold together. . . . In this way, the non-verbal and the verbal are firmly united at the core of the image-ing function of language.[20]

With this reentry of the image into semantic theory, and the admission that metaphoric processes involving such imagery function at all stages in the development of language, we can now return to the original definitions given here of the signifier as the sound slice and the signified as the image that together produce the metaphoric meaning distinguishing the linguistic sign or word.

With these preliminary definitions, we can now demonstrate the very process with which this lowest linguistic level is concerned, the naming of things represented to the mind as spatial images. What the "ideal" or past-modeled form of the fourth-world matrix presents us with in plate 7 and figure 8.1 are two major and two minor elements, the former two being the collective central macrohexagram and the individuated lateral macrohexagram, while the latter two are microhexagrams, one central and one lateral. Now if the fourth-world matrix is to model the linguistic domain of the sign, then it would be best to define its two major elements in terms of their correspondence to the two major elements of the sign, the signifier and the signified. The next step is to determine the right assignment of sign aspects to macrohexagrams on the basis of some sense of similarity between their distinguishing characteristics. Since it is the signifier as sound image or slice that provides the form through which thought can become differentiated into concepts, it seems appropriate to assign the signifier to the color-individuated lateral macrohexagram. Similarly, it is the collective central macrohexagram that seems best suited to model the full complexity of the signified, that reality underlying and giving rise to the visible image by which it can be most immediately apprehended. If the lateral elements are given the turquoise color of the single Spiral Tree, then we can distinguish between the six central colors, which compose the collective central macrohexagram, whose extensions are shown in plate 4, and the two red elements it contributes to this Spiral Tree, the whole of this macrohexagram representing the reality to which the sign points and its red elements the sense data, primarily visual, by which the reality of the thing forces itself upon our consciousness. The signified would then represent both the visual image that largely determines our concept of a thing and the ontological claim that this image has a necessary connection to its referent. What I have here contributed to the semiotic definition of the sign is a restoration of the ancient and to some thinkers continuing understanding of the visual image as the source of thought and the origin of verbal meaning, that within the conceptual aspect of at least those signs that are primary words is a visual image.

To return again to plate 7 or figure 8.1 of the simpler past-modeled fourth world matrix and its original psychological analysis in chapter 8, it will be remembered that the collective central macrohexagram was identified with the collective unconscious, the individuated lateral macrohexagram with individual self-consciousness, the lateral microhexagram with the instinctive faculty, and the central microhexagram with the intuitive faculty, and a flow pattern was further established that went out with the lateral and back with the central, the two movements together defining a circular pattern. Now, if this structure is applied to the semiotics of the word, there are implications for language that can be drawn from each one of these circumstances.

To begin with, the earlier association of the central macrohexagram with the signified as image can be related to the concept of a collective unconscious through Owen Barfield's understanding of verbal signification as "collective representations," a term he derives from the anthropologist Lévy-Bruhl. For Barfield, the way the phenomenal aspect of things, that is, their images, attain verbal meaning depends upon the way such representations are collectively understood by a cultural group, such understanding shifting the signification of the same words over time within a linguistic community:

> Collective representations . . . are common to the members of a given social group, and are transmitted from one generation to another, developing and changing only gradually in the process. . . . It is indeed possible, when thinking of the relation between words and things to forget what "things," that is phenomena, are; namely, that they are collective representations and, as such, correlative to human consciousness.[21]

It is collective human consciousness, then, that determines the significations of verbal sounds; and it may well be that the collective origin of language may be ascribed to this aspect of the sign. But the matrix tells us that its other aspect, the signifier, is as intimately connected with the individual.

Benveniste has shown subjectivity to be inherent in the nature of language: "It is in and through language that man constitutes himself as a *subject*, because language alone established the concept of the 'ego' in reality. . . . 'Ego' is he who *says* 'ego.' That is where we see the foundation of 'subjectivity,' which is determined by the linguistic status of 'person.'"[22] This linguistic definition of the individual is, for Benveniste, the complement of its social aspect:

Viewed from the standpoint of the linguistic function, and by virtue of the I-you polarity, individual and society are no longer contradictory but complementary terms. . . . Society is not possible except through language; nor is the individual. The awakening of consciousness in the child always coincides with the learning of language, which gradually introduces him as an individual into society. . . . language always realizes itself in *a language* in a definite and specific linguistic structure which is inseparable from a definite and specific society. Both are *given*.[23]

The "givenness" of language, the fact that the linguistic resources of his society are available to an individual as his birthright, can be further related to a specific feature of the earlier analysis of this fourth-world matrix as model of the unfallen or primitive Nefesh soul, namely, that this is the level of soul considered to be man's by birth, to require no personal effort of acquisition. But in making the verbal sounds whose correlations with meaningful images are a cultural given, man, like the sounds he makes, becomes a *signifier*. This is no trivial pun but serves to underscore the isomorphism between language and the language groups through which it is developed and without which they could not exist, an isomorphism that matrix modeling helps us to see.

Such modeling suggests that individuality is a property of the linguistic signifier and collectivity of the linguistic signified, a characteristic that the polysemic nature of words exemplifies. For as Ricoeur and others have shown, "polysemy is a feature of words, several senses for one name."[24] The individual word does not change, but its senses grow and shift as individuals select from its collective meanings those with which to make the metaphorical transfers necessary to develop new understanding. In so doing, the circle of language usage is completed in a manner that conforms to the matrix model.

As Benveniste has shown, the speaker "instinctively" selects the appropriate word to represent a particular aspect of reality: "For the speaker there is a complete equivalence between language and reality." This follows from Benveniste's understanding of the "necessary" connection of signified to signifier for a native speaker. We may say that the impulse to thought produced either by perception or reflection elicits the words appropriate for the expression of such thought in a manner that may be understood to be instinctual in the human use of language. And this movement out from the object perceived to the word by which it can be signified can be associated in the model with the lateral microhexagram, which emerges directly from the center of the central macrohexagram and touches the lateral macrohexagram. Conversely, the central microhexagram, which emerges from the center of the lateral macrohexagram to touch the central macrohexagram and close the linguistic circle, has a meaning again appropriate to its function in this circle, that of intuition. For it is in applying the word instinctively elicited by perception of an object back to that object that the individual gains an intuition of the meaning of that object, the meaning that develops from the metaphoric seizure of the similarity between the sound and the image that together represent the reality that is the ultimate referent of language.

The relationship of these microhexagrams to the opposite class of macrohexagrams whose centers they touch is especially interesting. It suggests first that the phenomenal object that appears as image is somehow also responsible for producing its phonic signifier, that it is, indeed, as Benveniste said, its "phonic translation." And it also suggests that the generation of meaning is a direct product of those sounds that are the denotative aspect of words. I have elsewhere shown at length that the sound that gives form to a word is ultimately derivable from the object it signifies, that their relationship is, as Plato deduced, natural rather than arbitrary.[25] And so is it from the formation of this verbal sound that the mind gains an intuition into the nature of its perceptions that renders them meaningful. Reference was earlier made to Benveniste's distinction between the form and meaning that are conjoined properties of linguistic units, and it would seem that these properties can, in the case of that lowest unit of the sign, be directly associated with the microhexagrams currently under discussion, the form of a word being identified with the lateral microhexagram and its meaning with the central microhexagram. But since these microhexagrams appear to emerge from the macrohexagrams that represent aspects of the sign seeming to be opposed to them, we are faced with the curious situation that the signified appears to be the source of the form of the word and the signifier of its meaning, a circumstance that may perhaps explain better than anything else the living quality of language, with its constantly evolving forms and meanings that are ever more capable both of describing and operating upon reality.

In the continuous circle of linguistic creation just described, the creative relationship of the macrohexagrams to the opposite microhexagrams just projected can gain a new dimension of meaning through consideration of the identifications of these macrohexagrams in terms of the Sefirot of the Spiral Tree. For in their terms, these macrohexagrams do, indeed, signify creation, the central macrohexagram correlated with the feminine Sefirah Malkhut and the lateral macrohexagram with the sexual Sefirah of Yesod, masculine when considered in relationship to Malkhut as its sexual mate. In ancient sexual mythology, it is the male who is always recognized as the source of generation, of the seed, while the female is understood to provide the vessel in which that seed can develop into its true form. However imperfect such physiology may be, it does here provide a model for the understanding of linguistic creation. For that macrohexagram formerly identified with the generation of meaning from verbal sound is now seen to be equated with none other than the great Sefirah of generation, Yesod, and that which was identified with the birthing of verbal forms can now be equated with the female Malkhut, a Sefirah that also has a collective connotation insofar as another of its identifications is with the Community of Israel. Moving out from the communal repository of language to individual usage and returning with an increased power of signification, the complexity of language development can be precisely modeled by a matrix of geometric forms as polysemous as the linguistic signs whose structure they are being asked to elucidate.

There is one other aspect of the Hebrew tradi-tion that is particularly pertinent here, the meaning attached to the Hebrew term for word, *davar*. In his linguistic study of this word, Thorleif Boman has shown that Hebrew draws no distinction between words and the reality they signify: "*dabhar*—'the word in spoken form,' hence 'efficacious fact,' is for the Semites the great reality of existence."[26] Susan A. Handelman further develops this understanding of *davar*:

> Though *davar* means both *thing* and *word* in Hebrew, it is crucial to point out that *thing* did not have the Greek connotations of *substance*. As I. Rabinowitz puts it, "the word is the reality in its most concentrated, compacted, essential form.". . . Names are not conventional, but intrinsically connected to their referents; the name, indeed, is the real referent of the thing, its essential character—not the reverse, as in Greek thought. One does not pass beyond the names as an arbitrary sign towards a non verbal vision of the thing, but rather *from the thing to the word*, which creates, characterizes, and sustains it. Hence *davar* is not simply *thing* but also action, efficacious fact, event, matter, process.[27]

It is clear that the Hebrew conception of the word is at least more consonant with the subtle modeling of the sign provided by the matrix than is that of modern linguistics, and more consonant as well with what appears to be a truer understanding of the relationship of language to reality. Handelman's depiction of *davar* as implying a movement "*from the thing to the word*" is particularly close to what the matrix seems to show concerning the emergence of sound forms from the reality signified. When the linguistic sign is interpreted from the perspective of *davar*, it is not simply the relation of signifier to signified that proves necessary but also that from the whole sign to reality. The signified becomes both linguistic and extralinguistic, and the signifier bound by necessity to a dynamic reality made ever more creative through the power of the word, a necessary relationship whose philosophic implications, as earlier noted, I have elsewhere developed.

Before concluding this discussion of the primary

level of the word we should return to a statement by Benveniste: "The awakening of consciousness in the child always coincides with the learning of language, which gradually introduces him as an individual into society." This progression would seem to take us from the fourth-world matrix produced by past modeling to that produced by future modeling, the more complex matrix of plate 8 and figure 8.2 that adds two lateral microhexagrams, those identified with emotion and analytic reasoning, and both would seem to be implied by the progression from the child's learning of language to its transformation into an "individual" signifier. But once this is accomplished, such an individual begins to move into the realm of the symbolizer best modeled by the fifth-world matrix, whose analysis will again show the remarkable coherence between language systems, general systems, and the Sabbath Star Diagram matrix.

The final consideration of semiotics must address the fact that the arbitrary character assigned by Saussure to linguistic signs, and by inference all other signs, has produced a "science" whose critical tools have been used not to arrive at universal truths but in a deconstructive process aimed at demystification. This can be seen most clearly in Roland Barthes' treatment of mythology. Unlike the simple denotative nature of the linguistic sign, myth takes us to a secondary, connotative level of signification:

> myth is a . . . *metalanguage*, because it is a second language, *in which* one speaks about the first. . . . We know that in a language, the sign is arbitrary. . . . The mythical signification, on the other hand, is never arbitrary; it is always in part motivated, and unavoidably contains some analogy. . . . In fact, what allows the reader to consume myth innocently is that he does not see it as a semiological system but as an inductive one. Where there is only an equivalence, he sees a kind of causal process: the signifier and the signified have, in his eyes, a natural relationship. . . . things appear to mean something by themselves. . . . Men do not have with myth a relationship based on truth but on use.[28]

Though myth reveals a "motivated" relationship of signifier to signified rather than the arbitrary relationship attributed to the linguistic sign, recognizing it as a semiological system allows the semiotic mythologist to treat it as an epistemological construct and so to rob it of its claim to true meaning. The primary emphasis of modern semiotics has, in fact, not been with arbitrary but motivated signs—myths, dream imagery, social rituals, and literary texts—but the thrust of such analysis has been to reduce transcendental claims to the problematics of epistemology, to man-made codes void of universal significance.

So too for Barthes the plurality of interpretations to which a classic literary text is susceptible destroys the truth value of any or all of its connotative meanings: "Let us first posit the image of a triumphant plural, unimpoverished by any constraint of representation (of imitation). In this ideal text, the networks are many and interact, without any one of them being able to surpass the rest."[29] Criticism of a classic literary text is thus a game of illusion: "Structurally, the existence of two supposedly different systems—denotation and connotation—enables the text to operate like a game, each system referring to the other according to the requirements of a certain *illusion*."[30] In defining his method, Barthes, nonetheless, does make some claim for the functional validity of his readings: "the meanings I find are established not by 'me' or by others, but by their *systematic* mark: there is no other *proof* of a reading than the quality and endurance of its systematics. . . ."[31]

It should be clear by this time that Barthes' method of reading the classic text can be applied directly to the "reading" of the Sabbath Star Diagram, that this diagram can qualify, in fact, as the ideal text posited by his theory. But once a self-generating geometric construction is substituted for language as the model for a theory of signification, the assertion that all connotative meanings must be based on arbitrary social conventions collapses. Rather than being arbitrary, the geometric "sign" returns this word to its original meaning as a conveyer of portents and omens, as an oracular source of truth. Nor does the theoretical plurality of mythic readings to which the diagram is susceptible destroy the truth value of such mythological interpretation. A geometrically based semiotics simply distinguishes between first-order and second-order signs of truth, between geometric denotation and mythic connotation. It does not consider the myth consumer to be innocent for whom "things appear to mean something by themselves" when those things are diagrams constrained by the laws of geometric construction and the meanings to which they give rise can be applied systematically. To call such readings myths and admit to the possibility of equally valid alternate readings does not contradict their truth value. For the geometric semiotician, the ability of the diagram to model the functional relationships within a secondary field establishes the validity of the new structure that it thus gives to this field, and the fact that it can be applied to all manner of conceptual domains with illuminating results does not destroy but confirms its own validity.

The fact that such a linguistically based approach can be applied to analysis of the various features of the Sabbath Star Diagram shows that this diagram is, indeed, a form of language. And since for Saussure "language is a system of signs that express ideas," this means that the geometric system that informs this diagram is also one capable of expressing ideas, ideas that can be systematized by the second-order metalanguage of mythological interpretation. Because such analysis must differ radically in its conclusions from those arrived at by a semiotics that views linguistic signs as arbitrary, I have chosen to distinguish the geometrically based semiotics demonstrated in this study by a new name as the Science of Expressive Form. And both the discovery and analysis of the Sabbath Star Diagram here undertaken should lay the foundations for such study of geometrically based mythology as an organ of truth.

THE MATRIX MODELING OF THE SENTENCE

In moving from the level of the word to that of the sentence, we may also be said to be moving from the Saussurean category of language, *langue*, to that of speech, *parole*. For it is at the level of the sentence

that communication through speech may properly be said to commence. The essential communicative function of speech would seem to correspond to a defining characteristic of the fifth-world matrix that is its model, for this is also the world and model of the Ruach soul, the level of soul that reaches out to community because of its inherent empathy for the other. The relationship of speech to community is different from that of language, understood as the system of signs. The latter was earlier shown to be the creation of the community, the sounds and meanings of words being given to the individual. But speech, involving the predicative function of sentences, is the creation of individuals addressed to community. Thus the Saussurean levels of *langue* and *parole* show a correspondence with the categories assigned in appendix B to the redefined lower and intermediate levels of general systems, those of the impersonal and the personal also modeled by the fourth- and fifth-world matrices. Though individuals comprise communities and contribute to the development of their languages, these contributions are normally anonymous. But speech not only involves the assertion of a predicate; it also requires a subject, and in so doing it creates the personal level of linguistic functioning. It is in such linguistic functioning, moreover, that man ideally conforms to the Ruach model for human behavior. Evolving from the mechanical will of the animal Nefesh soul, man here develops that individuality and truly free will that arise from a mastery of the symbolic imagination conjoined to language. In using language at the level of assertion, he is defining himself as personal through the very act of communicating with and within a community, but his true Ruach use of this mastery will be within and for the benefit of society.

Benveniste has emphasized this communicative function of the sentence, which is the essence of speech, and with his discussion we can begin our closer examination of the sentence: "The distinguishable types of sentences can be reduced to a single one, the predicative statement, or proposition, and there is no sentence outside predication. . . . The sentence, an undefined creation of limitless variety, is the very life of human speech in action. . . . of language as an instrument of communication . . ."[32] The predicative power of language, its ability to say something about some thing and to some one, is elsewhere understood by Benveniste as involving the "assertive function" of the verb, and the sentence redefined as "a finite assertion." Of this he further says: "A finite assertion, precisely because it is an assertion, implies the reference of the utterance to a different order, and this is the order of reality."[33] Though I have argued in the preceding section that words, too, are nonarbitrary signifiers of reality, it is at the level of the sentence that most linguists would link language to reality. Benveniste had distinguished study of the word as the level of semiotics and of the sentence as that of semantics, and of these two levels Ricoeur also claims: "Semiotics is aware only of intro-linguistic relationships, whereas semantics takes up the relationship between the sign and the things denoted—that is, ultimately, the relationship between language and the world."[34]

Now, since the "relationship between the sign and the things denoted" was earlier said to involve a metaphoric perception of similarity within dissimilars, the next point to be made is that the assertion of such a relationship must also be intrinsically metaphorical. And, indeed, Ricoeur, following in the theoretical tradition of Richards, Black, and Beardsley regarding the emergence of meaning through metaphorical transfers, views "the *statement* as the sole contextual milieu within which the transposition of meaning takes place," that we must "speak from now on of the *metaphorical statement*."[35] For Black, the word is regarded only as "the *focus* of the metaphor, and the remainder of the sentence in which that word occurs the *frame*."[36] It is this "frame" that for Beardsley permits the logical opposition that gives a statement its "metaphorical twist":

> when a term is combined with others in such a way that there would be a logical opposition between its central meaning and that of the other terms, there occurs that shift from central to marginal meaning which shows us the word is to be taken in a metaphorical way. It is the only way it can be taken without absurdity. . . . The logical opposition is what gives the modifier its metaphorical twist.[37]

But it is not only because the frame of the sentence allows a focus word to be used in such logical opposition to others that the statement can only be taken metaphorically, or even that all of its vocabulary resulted from primary or secondary metaphorical processes, that I would urge a new view of the sentence as, itself, radically metaphorical. It is rather because the sentence, in its most essential character, involves a meaningful linkage of two radically dissimilar parts of speech, the noun and the verb. To say that something is or does something else, that is, to predicate, is to make a metaphorical linkage that conforms to Aristotle's own definition of metaphor: "Metaphor consists in giving the thing a name that belongs to something else; the transference being either from genus to species, or from species to genus, or from species to species, or on ground of analogy."[38]

The movement from genus to species is the same movement from subject to attribute that comprises the normal predicate-nominative form of sentence most closely conforming to the subject-predicate mode of Aristotelian logic, the reverse being the same logical case. As the movement to or from genus to species is normally linked by a copula, such verbs as "to be," so that from species to species can be understood to be linked by verbs of action, and the drawing of analogies also requires a copula. All predication, then, involves a metaphorical linkage of nouns by verbs that is even more deeply one of nouns with verbs, of nouns verbing and being verbed, of being becoming. The connection, the "metaphorical twist" that is actually true of all sentences, is made by the verb. The two main parts of the sentence are distinguished by Aristotle on the basis of time: "A Noun or name is a composite significant sound not involving the idea of time. . . . A Verb is a composite significant sound involving the idea of time. . . ."[39] As essentially a name, the noun indicates an object defined, it would seem, in relation to space since it is pointedly excluded from temporal reference. As that which contains a temporal referent, the verb indicates some form of process or change, for even the copula "to be" is marked by tenses. *Thus the syntax of the sentence performs the same metaphoric process that was discerned in the word, the linking of the dissimilars of time and space into a unity.* As the word united the temporal dimension of sound in the signifier with the spatial dimension of image in the signified, so in the sentence objects in timeless space become invested with the dynamic realities of process and relationship. On the basis of this analysis of nouns and verbs, we can now begin the matrix modeling of the sentence.

Again we have two main constituents of the domain to be modeled and two main elements of the model with which they should be brought into metaphorical correspondence if the model is to be deemed appropriate. The two main matrix elements with which the noun and the verb are to be correlated are both individuated macrohexagrams, one lateral and one central. The assignment of the noun to the lateral macrohexagram would seem to follow from the assignment previously made regarding the sign. Since verbal signs are essentially names or nouns, and since it is possible to recognize the particularity of a name even if its meaning escapes one and requires recourse to a dictionary, it seems clear that names are more closely associated with the signifier than the signified, and that the dichotomy between words and things comes closer to defining the distinction between signifier and signified, though both can be contained in the Hebrew concept of the sign as reflected in the word *davar.* If, then, the name can be more closely related to the signifier, and this was previously identified with the fourth-world lateral macrohexagram, consistency requires the name words on the sentence level to be also represented by a macrohexagram that is lateral. Once the noun has been assigned to the lateral macrohexagram, the verb can only be assigned to the central, with implications now to be considered.

The most striking implications come from the associations of these macrohexagrams with Sefirot, for on the Spiral Tree the fifth world's lateral macrohexagram is identified with Hod and its central macrohexagram with Netzach. It is Netzach that is immediately most interesting since its signification of Eternity not only places it in a temporal context but also that of the verb. Though all of the Sefirot can be associated with divinity, that which signifies the eternal seems most close. And the primary fact regarding the Tetragrammaton, is, of course, that it is a variant of the verb for "being," Chayah. Boman's analysis of Hebrew verbs and particularly of Chayah is pertinent here:

> The verbs especially, whose *basic meaning* always expresses a movement or an activity, reveal the dynamic variety of the Hebrews' thinking. . . . We have found that *hayah* contains a unity of "being," "becoming," and "effecting," that it dovetails neatly into a group of internally active (stative) verbs, and that it is best understood by us in the "being" of an active person. . . . the *hayah* designates existence; only that to which one can attribute a *hayah* is effective. . . . and so existence is identical with effectiveness: it is not at rest but is dynamic. . . . The Israelite knows that above all others Jahveh *is*. . . . to *Jahveh* is ascribed an unalterable (i.e. eternal) *hayah*, and this *hayah* is a dynamic, energetic, effective, personal being "who carries out his will.". . . in the analysis of divine being, no new meaning of the word "being" has been discovered.[40]

If no new meaning attaches to the divine Chayah, the implication is that there is no separation between the divine activity and that which animates the rest of existence, that the verb of being, whose eternal character abides in its dynamic union of being, becoming, and effecting, attests to a power of transformation that is in truth miraculous.

But if the correspondence of Netzach with the verb endows the activity it signifies with a divine quality, that activity is incomplete without the power of the name identified with Hod. It was Adam, man, who named the animals, and it would seem to be from this power that he was able to gain that dominion over them commanded of him in his creation. All primitive peoples have recognized that knowing the name of a thing gives them a power over it. And it is because no thought is possible without names, as shown in the previous section, that from the most naturalistic perspective the power of language to manipulate reality derives from its power of naming. It is extraordinarily fitting, therefore, that the defining characteristic of Hod should be power. Like the third chakra with which it may be compared, Hod is the powerhouse of the Sefirot, especially on the Spiral Tree, where it ideally commands more microhexagrams than any other and, in any case, is the most powerful lateral macrohexagram. In the earlier analysis of the fifth-world matrix as a model of the Ruach soul, it was Hod that defined the identity and will of the Ruach Master, and it was the transformative power of the imagination lodged in Netzach that he had to control to effect his purposes. This personal character of Hod is especially consistent with its new correlation with the noun, for it is the noun that constitutes the syntactical subject. In terms of this analysis, what the structure of the sentence shows us is that man, as subject, through the power of the name can master the divine power of transformation. The association of the human and the noun with the lateral macrohexagram and of the divine and the verb with the central macrohexagram is also most appropriate and revealing. For it is through the very structure of the sentence that space and time, the human and the divine, can meet and become one.

To complete this analysis of the power lodged in the sentence, we should consider the six lateral microhexagrams that appear in the fifth-world matrix (fig. 9.1) when built upon the past-modeled fourth-world diagram (fig. 8.1), the lowest two of which are also completed by the future-modeled diagram of the fourth world (fig. 8.2). Surprisingly, these can be applied to the sentence without change from their earlier significations. In the previous analyses of chapters 8 and 9, the first of these was identified with the faculty of the emotions and the second with the analytic faculty of the mind. These are clearly relevant to the nature of the sentence, for its assertions have both intellectual and affective content. But if a sentence is not only to have a meaning and a tone but also power, it must enlist that power of creative thought identified with the first of the exclusively fifth-world lateral microhexagram. Because Hod, like the first two of these microhexagrams, was largely completed by the "fallen" fourth-world diagram, it may carry within it some tendency toward the perversion of linguistic power for personal use. From these tendencies the four fully Ruach microhexagrams are wholly free,

and it is from these constituents that the highest powers of language are released, those revelatory powers capable of transforming man and his world.

In the previous analysis of the Ruach Master in the final section of chapter 9, it was shown that the number of these higher powers he was able to call upon depended upon his level of spiritual development. If we can now equate the Master of Names with the words he chooses, we can say that the first level of real power he can infuse into his words is such a creative use of language as we have seen to be largely metaphorical and that Aristotle equates with genius: "It is a great thing, indeed, to make a proper use of these poetical forms. . . . But the greatest thing by far is to be a master of metaphor. It is the one thing that cannot be learnt from others; and it is also a sign of genius, since a good metaphor implies an intuitive perception of the similarity in dissimilars."[41] Aristotle classes metaphor as a form of the noun[42] and sees in such noun usage a sign not only of the author's genius but by implication also of the author's presence in his words; and this similar union of the noun with the author as ultimate subject is also signified by the capacity of Hod to model both the Ruach Master and the linguistic noun. The writer of genius will, then, infuse his words with the creative power of his own mind, a power that enables his words to reach and move their readers or hearers.

But these words will move with still greater force if, in addition to his genius with words, with the ability to express "an intuitive perception of the similarity in dissimilars," he also has command of the second power of synchronicity, identified with the second of the microhexagrams completed by the fifth-world diagram. Such power gives him an intuitive grasp of the character and needs of the moment and enables him to shape his words into their perfect expression. By thus exactly meeting the taste and interests of his time, his words can be most easily assimilated by his intended audience and reach the greatest number of them.

But if he is not only to reach a suitable audience of his own time, large or choice, but also enable his words to speak to those of all time, to become a classic, he must command as well the third power of transformation identified with the third of the wholly fifth-world microhexagrams. With this power he will be able to perceive the universal truths within the particular forms of his contemporary culture and so handle these forms that, without losing their particularity, they become transparent conveyers of the universal, become, in Wimsatt's words, "concrete universals."[43] And the universal truths they express through the forms of ordinary, contemporary life are also able to reach more deeply into their auditors' souls, bringing them to a recognition of their personal implication in such universals that can produce transformative change.

Between the third and the fourth of the fifth-world microhexagrams there is a break in the lateral spiral that was taken to suggest that its power is not available to a master at the Ruach level but only at that Neshamah level whose matrix closes this gap. For this is the level of the highest creative power that is linguistically expressed in prophetic utterance, utterance that has the power to reveal not simply the universals informing all particulars but transcendent truths, and so powerful is the revelation of such truth that it can create new historical causes, transforming not simply individuals but whole cultures recreated in their names.

Though the full powers of language just considered require the incorporation of sentences in literary works, it is appropriate that the power dimension of language indicated by the matrix should be at the sentence level. For it is through the quality of the actual sentences written that a work, however profound its thought, either soars or falls flat, that its reading enlivens the reader with new inspiration and power or numbs and deadens his mind so that it becomes an enormous strain to get from sentence to sentence. The pleasure of reading arises from the constant input of added levels of implication beyond that necessary for the sheer conveyance of information, and it is such value-added knowledge, beauty, or feeling that reveals the working of the metaphorical process. For metaphor is akin to the very structure of the sentence and can release the full resources of its power.

In fact, the matrix model of the sentence reveals just that "twist" which Beardsley has attributed to the sentence structuring of metaphor. As was also shown

in chapter 9, the feedback pattern of the fifth-world matrix is not the simple circular pattern of the fourth but adds to this, in figure 9.2, a reverse circle that transforms it into the figure-8 pattern signifying infinity. Between the level of semiotics and that of semantics the twist that occurs is largely between those elements signifying time and space. Because the positions of the central and lateral macrohexagrams are reversed with respect to each other between the matrices of the fourth and fifth worlds and the flow pattern moves out with the lateral and back with the central, the twist that occurs in the fifth-world form of this flow pattern in its outward progress converts the temporality of the lateral sign "signifier" as sound slice into the spatiality of the lateral noun, and the pattern of return converts the temporality of the central verb into the spatiality of the central sign "signified" as image. And since it is also the function of the sign and the sentence to unify these same signifiers of time and space within their own levels, the additional unification through crossing that occurs between these levels would seem to underscore what may well be the most essential truth about the nature of language, that its ability to generate meaning depends on its capacity to reveal the similarity between the dissimilars of time and space, between sound and image on the level of the word and between things and processes on the level of the sentence, to show how they can be brought into unification. Thus at its highest level the medium also becomes the message, as McLuhan so pithily observed, its meaning like its structure revealing the same knowledge conveyed through both Pythagorean and Hebraic sacred science,[44] the transcendent truth that space and time are but two sides of the same reality that is constantly converting one into the other in the continuous dynamic process of creation.

THE MATRIX MODELING OF THE WORK

Moving now to the highest linguistic level of the text, that to be modeled by the sixth world level of the Spiral Tree given with its labeled elements in figure 10.3, it is clear that Ricoeur's conception of such written discourse as a "work" restores to it the structure that Roland Barthes had denied to it in defining his ideal text: "In this ideal text, the networks are many and interact, without any one of them being able to surpass the rest." In denying to a text a structure of meaning that controls and surpasses all its parts, Barthes is making the same error in linguistics as Prigogine, Varela, and others have made in the cosmological extensions of their scientific theories, the refusal to concede the higher structural elements that give the stable identity to a whole not to be found in the sum of its parts.[45] Without such structural unity a literary discourse is not a true work but just a conglomeration of sentences that, however interesting in themselves, never adds up to anything. As Ricoeur stresses in his previously quoted definition: "As a totality, the literary work cannot be reduced to a sequence of sentences which are individually intelligible; rather, it is an architecture of themes and purposes which can be constructed in several ways." It is interesting that Ricoeur uses the spatial metaphor of architecture to convey the sense of literary structure, for as the matrix model will show, there is again at this level a distinction to be made between the spatial quality projected by a sense of the whole and the temporality of the actual serialization of the writing and reading. And again there is a crossing of space and time as we cross the boundary into a higher level of discourse, the imagining of the whole associated with the largely central vertical portion of the sixth-world matrix and the serial sentences with its wholly lateral horizontal portion.

In crossing the frontier into the domain of the work, we are also moving from the systems level of the personal to that of the transpersonal. Here language develops, as it were, a life of its own on the purely symbolic level that transcends the author's limitations as well as his or her intentions. As in appendix B society was shown to have a similar mode of psychic life, so here, as Ricoeur says, "a text is a kind of individual, like an animal or a work of art." The nature of such transpersonal life has been best expressed by Milton:

> For books are not absolutely dead things, but do contain a potency of life in them to be as active as that soul was whose progeny they are; nay, they do preserve as in a vial the purest efficacy and extraction of that living intellect that bred them. . . . as good almost kill a man as kill a good book: who kills a man kills a reasonable creature, God's image; but he who destroys a good book, kills reason itself, kills the image of God, as it were, in the eye. Many a man lives a burden to the earth; but a good book is the precious lifeblood of a master spirit, embalmed and treasured up on purpose to a life beyond life.[46]

The transpersonal life of a book is not to be found in any of its discrete parts but is, as Milton calls it in the continuation of the above passage, "that ethereal and fifth essence, the breath of reason itself . . . an immortality rather than a life." All of Milton's terms have special relevance to the sixth-world matrix that is to model the linguistic level of the literary work. The sixth world is, itself, identified with the immortalizing World to Come of Jewish eschatology, and that part of its diagram matrix that can be associated with the organizing structure of a literary work was variously identified with the upper three mental Partzufim—Arikh Anpin, Abba, and Imma, transpersonalities, themselves—and with the cosmic mind. The three macrohexagrams at the top of the diagram may, therefore, be said to represent the mind of the work. Most important is the central macrohexagram identified with Keter, which, for the cosmic mind, signifies something very like that "eye" of Milton's "reason," itself the "image of God." For this macrohexagram was earlier identified with the divine mental power to see the cosmic design as a whole, a power of imaging in which the five surrounding central microhexagrams, identified with the inner forms of the five senses, were also thought to play a part. Flanking this central macrohexagram are the two lateral macrohexagrams of Chokhmah and Binah that the mind needs to explicate its contemplative image, Chokhmah to intuit its meaning and Binah to formulate its intuitive perceptions in conceptual terms, in which process they make use of the interrelated cognitive tools of geometry, number, and sound, as all are further related to language, identified with the three lateral microhexagrams that complete the matrix model of the cosmic mind. Though the lateral elements of the mind are clearly necessary for its most effective functioning, its power is concentrated in its central elements that, in terms of the counting system of "light units," equal eight units to the lateral three. The matrix for the mind of the sixth world was so fully detailed both to explain the greater power of its largely visual central elements and because it can also help to explain the subtle processes involved in the development by authors of their structural framework from that original impulse to creation in which the future work is seized as a whole. But the controlling structure that is the mind of the work and gives it its greatest power is an "ethereal" essence nowhere to be located in the work, though it permeates it as a whole. It is this that, like the corresponding collective conscience of society modeled in the previous appendix, provides a frame of meaning that controls the implications even as it heightens the significance of its concrete linguistic units, the sentences.

It is the wholly lateral portion of the matrix at the right side of the sixth world diagram, which chapter 10 associated with the cosmic heart, that can best be identified with the actual words and syntactical units of the work. It is here that the characteristics defining discourse as a work for Ricoeur—"composition, belonging to a genre and individual style"—come into operation. It is through the actual labor of composing the work in accordance with the constraints and supportive formulae of the genre chosen as most appropriate to its thematic meaning that the heart of the work is realized, most notably in the opportunity such composition provides for the expression of the author's individual style. Ricoeur had said that the architecture of a work "can be constructed in several ways," and it is through actual composition that these ways are progressively chosen and fleshed out, in the lateral play provided by the horizontal dimension of the sixth-world matrix. It is here also that the work develops its tone, that central orientation to life that may or may not coincide with the author's intended meaning but that is the final determiner of the kinship between work and reader, transmitting its own mes-

sage from the heart of the work to that of the reader to bond one to the other. This heart tone may be associated with one of the Sefirot-macrohexagrams constituting this portion of the matrix and associated with qualities of the heart, Chesed with mercy and an expansive, affirmative attitude, Gevurah with rigor or justice and a constrictive attitude, which may also be that of negation, and Tiferet as not only the balance between the two but expressing the ideal of balance, of serenity and order. With the further fine tuning of the degrees of these qualities represented by the pair of microhexagrams attached to each, the matrix for this level of the work provides a fine model illustrative of its affective contents, its power to move the reader through their shared sympathies. Through style, liveliness of observation, and emotional tone, the medium of the actual writing does have and project a message of its own, without whose endearing qualities the reader would not stay long with a work. For if this were enough, Barthes and the deconstructionist critics would have the day, and writers could go on interminably without need of thesis or fable. But, in fact, what distinguishes the best work of a writer from those that fail to arouse interest, that which endures from the stillborn, is not the quality of the writing, which for good writers is everywhere evident in all their works in proportion to their talent, but a commanding idea, whether in fiction or nonfiction, that can organize a mass of material in such a way that it is made to reveal a significant meaning.

In his treatment of tragedy, Aristotle has given what is still the best definition of this unifying element and its importance:

> We maintain, therefore, that the first essential, the life and soul, so to speak, of Tragedy is the Plot; and that the Characters come second—compare the parallel in painting where the most beautiful colours laid on without order will not give one the same pleasure as a simple black-and-white sketch of a portrait. . . . Third comes the element of Thought, i.e., the power of saying whatever can be said, or what is appropriate to the occasion. . . . Fourth among the literary elements is the Diction of the personages . . . the expression of their

thoughts in words. . . . [P]oetry and story, as an imitation of action, must represent one action, a complete whole, with its several incidents so closely connected that the transposal or withdrawal of any one of them will disjoin and dislocate the whole. . . . the poet's function is to describe, not the thing that has happened, but a kind of thing that might happen, i.e., what is possible as being probable or necessary.[47]

The brilliance of the occasional thought and the beauty of its language take third and fourth place in Aristotle's thinking to "the life and soul" of a work, which is that "imitation of an action" that forms it into such an organic whole as can reflect the universal conditions within reality. It is with the concept of imitation, *mimesis*, that Aristotle enables us to see more clearly how the metaphoric process is as much at work at the highest linguistic level as it is at its lower levels, and again that what this essentially involves is the linking of spatial image with temporal sound. That "imitation" is ultimately a faculty for imaging is shown most of all by Aristotle's propensity always to illustrate its nature in poetry in terms of painting, as again in his central analysis of the term: "though the objects themselves may be painful to see, we delight to view the most realistic representations of them in art. . . . [T]he reason of the delight in seeing the picture is that one is at the same time learning—gathering the meaning of things."[48] Mimesis involves the creative perception of things, that interpretative seeing of the artist through which "the meaning of things" is also revealed and form becomes expressive. So too in the poetic imitation of an action that action becomes profoundly symbolic of a more universal meaning. And it is through this symbolic meaning of the action as a whole that what seems to be temporal, the dynamic quality of action, is revealed to be spatial in its essence: "Just in the same way, then, as a beautiful whole made up of parts . . . must be of . . . a size to be taken in by the eye, so a story or Plot must be of some length, but of a length to be taken in by the memory."[49] For a whole "to be taken in by the memory" it must be perceived by the mind's eye as a timeless unity, that final impression in which all

the particulars fuse into the structure of meaning that it is then the task of the critic to explicate once again in temporal terms. If it is impossible to describe the totality of a work without recourse to spatial metaphors, this is because it does have the main quality of a visual image, that it can be "seen" by the mind as an atemporal unity. But this finally atemporal unity of a work is imitated by temporal means, both in the sounds of the words (silent in the case of written discourse but there) and the sequential unfolding of the sentences.

The relationship between this organizing structure and its member parts is the same for a literary work as appendix B showed it to be for society, and this because both are part of the symbolic domain that can be modeled by the transpersonal matrix of the sixth-world diagram. In this previous appendix we saw that the locus of power rests with the organizing forces and that its members can only be truly empowered by conforming to its structure. So too in a literary work the language can only achieve its fullest power in manifesting a significant controlling conception.

This unity of the temporal and the spatial in a literary work has a final significance in terms of Ricoeur's secondary conception of such a "work" as involving the labor of construction. A work that has such unity of action requires a rigor of discipline lacking to those authors and critics who may be said to be only playing around with words, delighting in disorder rather than order, in exemplifying the meaningless rather than in building meaning. In terms of the diagram, such writers may be said to have harkened only to those elements beyond the matrix border of the first half of the sixth-world diagram, whose features were analyzed in chapter 11 and shown in appendix B to model the spontaneous development of unstable structures. As was there shown, such freedom can only have enduring effects to the extent that a return is made to the stable matrix within its border, creative freedom now being enlisted in the service of a higher order of signification.

For in the labor of constructing a true "work," the meaning of "work" is restored to its original biblical meaning with respect to the Sabbath rest, the work of the six weekdays being defined in the desert as the gathering of freely given manna and the building of the Temple.[50] If the talent for writing may be considered a gift and its creative expression a product of inspiration, then it would seem that the actual writing of the myriad sequential details, with all the free play of the imagination that this entails, may be compared with that easy form of Sinai work, the gathering of manna. But this was not considered enough for Israel and it is not enough to develop and fulfill the full potentialities of humanity. Human beings also must labor to build that Temple alone fit to be a vessel for the divine Presence; and writing a true work of literature involves just such a shaping of a vessel for the transpersonal. Thus it was Milton's lifelong determination "that by labor and intent study (which I take to be my portion in this life) joined with the strong propensity of nature, I might perhaps leave something so written to aftertimes, as they should not willingly let it die."[51] Literature at its highest, and Milton's *Paradise Lost* is surely the most sublime "work" in the English language, thus represents nothing else than the building of the spiritual Temple to house the transpersonal elements of man. It is a temporal labor to transcend the temporal and it uses the temporality of linguistic sound to construct an incorporeal image of the divinity in man, his power of meaningful creation.

This appendix has traced the levels of language from the naming capacity that gives man symbolic forms for thought, through the power of speech to create a community of self-aware individuals, to its highest achievement, the building of such structures for the communication of thought as can immortalize the genius of man. And as we have followed the precise matrix modeling for each of these levels, we have also seen that each reveals a metaphorical linkage of the temporal with the spatial through which meaning is generated. In language, then, as in the construction of the Sabbath Star Diagram that has so precisely modeled its levels, we find the same linkage of space and time that makes the associative metaphoric process of language the fit instrument not only for interpreting reality but also the expressive meanings of geometry.

APPENDIX D

A Gender Model
of Human History

In the earlier appendices we have seen how the matrices for the fourth through sixth worlds of the Sabbath Star Diagram, which had initially modeled the hierarchical dimensions of the soul, could serve equally well to model either the "physical" elements of the fourth world of matter or the main levels of systems theory, first the alternative structures of open and closed societies and then the three levels of linguistics. Now we shall see how the construction elements of the third through seventh of these worlds, which had initially modeled the sequence of kabbalistic worlds, can equally well model the main epochs of human history, particularly in its African to Middle Eastern to European manifestations. In both modelings the application of the particular features of this model, both their expressive geometric forms and some resonance of the prior kabbalistic identifications with which they had been correlated, has resulted in a selection of data from these domains that can provide a new illumination of these fields. What these studies prove, then, is that the Sabbath Star Diagram is a universal model whose matrices can be applied to any hierarchically ordered domain as can its construction elements to any domain sequentially ordered, with illuminating results for both; and this further suggests that this self-similar, expanding construction contains something like the code for all forms of complex, multileveled, and fairly stable organizations such as the cosmos itself.

The particular study of the periods of European history on which we are now to embark derives from an interpretation of the sixth-world construction elements that identified the vertical construction elements with the masculine aspects of the Partzufim, the divine personalities, and the horizontal elements with their feminine aspects. This was a natural association once this world's identification as the World to Come seemed to preclude the chronological development characteristic of earthly time that had been featured in analyses of the fourth and fifth worlds. For this World to Come was understood to be inhabited both by the Partzufim and the Neshamah soul, much as the third world had earlier been considered to be inhabited both by the angels/demons and by the pre-incarnate Nefesh soul. And as the Neshamah soul was understood to function as the interior aspect of the sixth world and so to be modeled by its matrix, the Partzufim, as the more external, governing aspect of this world, could appropriately be assigned

444

to its construction elements, with other numerical reasons supporting this identification.

But once the vertical and horizontal construction elements were so associated with gender and these associations were further applied to relevant elements of the first half of the seventh-world diagram correlated with the musical octave, it became clear that this distinction had a greater significance, one revelatory of the final mystery of the Sabbath Star Diagram as of the cosmos it models, the relationship of such parentally defined construction elements to the matrix their interface produces, that which at every level of expansion can be considered their offspring. The hidden meaning of the diagram would thus seem to be none other than what I have defined as the secret doctrine of the son. And this further understanding was central to the final mathematical extrapolation of the diagram to infinity, with its own cosmological implications, in the final two chapters of this work.

But the gender associations of the construction grids were also seen to be equally applicable to all prior as well as future stages of the diagram, that the worlds culminating in horizontal elements, the third, fifth, and seventh, had an essentially "feminine" character, and those culminating in vertical elements, the fourth and sixth, an equally essential "masculine" nature. But where the second half of each of these worlds has the uniform character of its culminating element, the first half is markedly different. It maintains the orientation of the previous world but in a balance with the waxing nature of its own gender orientation, a balance differing, however, in terms of this culminating gender orientation insofar as the balance in "feminine" worlds has a ratio of 1:1 construction elements on the vertical and horizontal diagram grids while the ratio in "masculine" worlds is 3:1 in favor of the masculine or vertical grid. This is a difference that seems reflective of a major difference between the sexes, the general desire of women for equality and of men for dominance. This and other supports for the gender associations of the vertical and horizontal construction grids can be found in section 3 of chapter 6, and it is summarized in table 6.2 of that chapter, which it will be helpful to present again here.

Table 6.2. Gender Correspondences of the Cosmic Worlds

WORLD PHASE	ORIENTATION OF C.E.	GENDER	NUMBER OF C.E.
3A	V	M	1V
3B	H	F	1H
4A	H	M/F	1V-1H
4B	V	M	2V
5A	V	F/M	3V-1H
5B	H	F	2H
6A	H	M/F	4V-3H
6B	V	M	5V
7A	V	F/M	9V-4H
7B	H	F	5H

With this brief introduction to an important aspect of the Sabbath Star Diagram, an aspect that not only seems reflective of perhaps the most basic premise of the Kabbalah—the intrinsically sexual nature of cosmic functioning—but seems suggestive of a similar waxing and waning of gender characteristics in human history, we can now turn to such a new gender modeling of our history.

It seems best to begin this historical survey at the point where myth and prehistory can be seen to meet, in that timeless realm of the third world kabbalistically associated with Edenic innocence. There are two phases of prehistory, that from the origin of man to 10,000 B.C.E., the time of the last glacial retreat, and the next 6,000 years until the beginnings of Sumerian civilization. If we can identify the first epoch with the masculine vertical hexagram of the third-world diagram and the second epoch with its feminine horizontal hexagram, we shall gain a new perspective on these earliest periods of human cultural history. As the first epoch can be identified with the hunter-gatherer culture of all mankind prior to 10,000 B.C.E., so that which distinguishes the second epoch is, first and foremost, the development of agriculture, followed by the domestication of animals and such crafts as weaving and pottery. In both of these prehistoric epochs there is a basic division of labor along sexual lines, the women more associated with vegetation and the men with animals; in the first epoch the women are the primary food gatherers and the men the hunters, whereas in the second epoch the women are more closely associated with farming and the men with herding. It should be noted that these associations are supported by the earlier identifications given to fourth-world construction elements, that of the plants being horizontal and so now by definition feminine and that of the animals vertical and so by definition masculine. Before entering more fully into the gender modeling of these two prehistoric epochs by the third-world diagram, it would be interesting to relate this modeling to the biblical value scheme.

The Bible identified the original evil of the Fall with the first female, an identification that seems to be supported by the new correlation of the horizontal Fa hexagram with the female since this hexagram had previously been associated with the Fall. But if this hexagram is now to be identified with the second prehistoric epoch and that correlated with the development of agriculture, then the second biblical instance of evil can also be associated with the female, with the activity most identified with the second purely feminine phase of the third-world diagram, farming. For in the case of Cain and Abel, farming is identified with evil and shepherding with good. Now what can have caused the biblical association of agriculture with evil is that it is more likely than animal herding to disrupt the nomadic traveling that had most characterized the earlier hunter-gatherer culture from time immemorial. Not that the earliest plantations led directly to permanent settlements, being rather seasonal stopping places along the established hunter-gatherer routes, but that they eventually would. We shall shortly see that the Hebraic culture can be associated with the purely masculine second phase of the fourth-world diagram, and we have seen that the hunter-gatherer culture apparently favored in the Bible can be correlated with the first phase of the third-world diagram that is also masculine. But the similarity between these diagram phases is not as important as their difference, the fact that it is the second phase that defines a world as a whole. Thus while the patriarchal nature of Hebrew culture is consistent with the masculine nature of the fourth-world diagram, the

hunter-gatherer culture is still dominated by the feminine nature of the whole period modeled by the third-world diagram, whether or not it be credited with a matriarchal culture. Though the Bible unerringly stigmatizes the activities that we have seen can be variously correlated with the precisely feminine phase of the third-world diagram, what would seem to be more important than the phases of this very simple diagram is the simple parity it shows between the masculine and feminine, a parity that is the characteristic most distinguishing the feminine from the masculine worlds of the diagram. Thus we have the curious fact that the overtly patriarchal culture of biblical Judaism, particularly of the Mosaic books, went against the bias of its own historical phase to ally itself with the earliest human culture, one that both the diagram and some anthropologists tell us was oriented to matriarchal values. Its manner of doing this, however, was to co-opt feminine values while stigmatizing the female as the evil source of all that went against them. The God of the Hebrews announced Himself originally as a God of the Way, drawing first Abraham and then all the Israelites in Egypt away from their settled lives to wander at His behest in the wilderness, to follow the spirit to the sacred places informed by the divine Presence. And it was just such spiritually informed wandering as characterized the prehistory of mankind that its diagram modeling associates with the feminine. In speaking of the "feminine" character of this prehistory I am not speaking of governance so much as of values. For whether or not such societies were ruled by women, and anthropologists are today divided on this question, they seem to have been informed by values that can be related to the feminine, primarily the sexual mythology of generation and its special reverence for Mother Earth.[1]

Traveling over an earth whose divine femininity was both recognized and worshiped by them, the aboriginal clans developed an intimate knowledge not only of all the edible resources of their territories but also of all its geographical features, particularly of those places they held sacred because of some sense of inexplicable power they experienced in those precincts. Their wanderings became pilgrimages routed from one sacred place to another where they could petition their Mother Earth to be fecund and their Father Sky to send rain, where, above all, their own ritual ministrations could facilitate such a unification between these earthly and heavenly forces as would also serve to bless their own lives, enabling them to share spiritually in that higher cosmic harmony they also recognized to be also the source of all their earthly good. The seasonal visitation to all these holy spots, necessary for recharging both their own vitality and that of the earth, thus gave to their directed wanderings a spiritual as well as practical character, the wanderings themselves finally understood to constitute a spiritual path, a following of the spirit ever present along the ancestral tracks.

Later this would all be more highly developed into a sophisticated sacred science capable of extraordinary feats of engineering. In a period contemporaneous with the rise of Sumerian and Egyptian civilization, that which shall be identified with the first half of the fourth-world diagram, the areas of the earth not touched by such civilization achieved the apogee of the older earth-oriented culture. The megalithic stone circles and earth mounds, as of the straight tracks joining them, spanned much of the globe in the period of 2000 B.C.E. to 1500 B.C.E. From Peru to England, standing stones transported from great distances as well as earthworks were precisely sited to catch the sun's rays at the solstices or to mark off other lunar and astral periodicities. But it seems evident that this ancient science had a purpose beyond such astronomical calculations, calculations that had to precede the erection of such monuments and so imply another purpose capable of mobilizing the entire resources of societies that left few other relics of their existence. John Michell, a longtime student of megalithic monuments, has offered what would seem to be the deepest insight into this purpose:

It has already been suggested that the prehistoric civilization was founded on the universal control of those invisible currents which move over the surface of the earth, the fields of gravity and electromagnetic energy . . . that some form of natural energy was known in prehistoric times and that a method was discovered, involving a fusion of the terrestrial spirit with the solar spark, by which this energy could be disposed to human benefit. . . . From the rocks, mountains and headlands a mysterious current once flowed down avenues of standing stones over mounds and earthworks towards some central hill dedicated to Mercury, the terrestrial spirit. Below the hill an instrument of solar generation produced the spark by which the current became animated and recoiled in a wave of fertility through the hidden veins of the land, urged on by the music and clamour of the festive people. In the Australian desert the natives still follow every year their line of songs, calling out the spirit from the rocks as they journey down the old straight tracks between the earth's sensitive places, the last fading voices in a chorus once universal.[2]

The purpose that Michell has attributed to the megalithic monuments, such unification of earthly and solar energies as could be understood sexually in view of the fertility resulting from it and that also seems to inform the ritual practices of aboriginal peoples, can also be recognized to inform the construction and rituals of still later sacred monuments, most notably the Hebrew Temple. In discussing the mythology surrounding the Temple, Raphael Patai says of its cosmological role:

the Temple was the center of the whole universe, the navel of the earth; its foundations pressed down upon the Female Waters of Tehom, the primeval abyss, and its underground shafts reached down into its very depths. Also, the Temple was located on the highest peak on earth, very near heaven. . . . Therefore, the ritual performed in the Temple . . . had an unfailing, direct and immediate effect on the world, on the order and functioning of nature. . . .[3]

Reaching both up into heaven and down into the earth, the Temple joined these two with a resulting fertility that was also understood in terms of a sexual mythology: "it is the Temple, more accurately the Holy of Holies, which is represented as a

Nuptial Chamber, though not until a comparatively late period do we find the express statement that the couple whose Nuptial Chamber it was, were God and the Holy Matrona personifying the Community of Israel."[4] It is the sexual myth that characterized the cosmology of the most ancient stratum of human culture, and the spiritual science deriving from its understanding of cosmic functioning continued to inform the later spiritual traditions that were also its heirs, inspiring them at various periods to monumental constructions whose full purposes we are only recently beginning to fathom but whose effective technology has now been largely lost.

What we can learn from these later survivals and elaborations of primordial human culture, in concert with the testimonies of the few remaining aborigines, is an appreciation of the heart of its cosmology, that linguistic abstraction of the principles informing its wandering lifestyle whose higher cognitive power most distinguishes early human behavior from the similar communal wanderings of the lower primates. And this cosmology, with its attendant ritualization of the journey, is markedly matriarchal. As Robert Lawlor has defined such matriarchal society: "Every example of an Earth-Mother society reveals a ritual and culture completely preoccupied with sexual symbolism and meaning."[5] The symbolism is that of the mating of terrestrial and higher energies and its meaning is not only the earthly fecundity thought to result from such a union but also the spiritual transformation of the human celebrants whose journeying to holy places and rituals therein have aided such a cosmic fusion of the changing and changeless. Characteristic of such society is the bonding force of kinship traced through the female, its decentralization into small clans, and its horizontal wanderings.

The horizontal orientation of this culture and its dominance by the central feminine concerns of sexual mating and childbirth, by what also becomes the central feminine mystery of the generative union of opposites, clearly has correspondences with the model of the third-world diagram. This is a world defined by the horizontality of its culminating element, one whose various geometric features correlate it with the feminine, a world of utter simplicity except for the significant polarization of its two construction elements into those spatial orientations that characterize them as masculine or feminine. Each of these elements also brings distinctive new features to the diagram, the vertical male element the new form of the Sabbath Star and the horizontal female element a new complementary axis, though this latter is also capable of a forbidden Sabbath Star development. But if these primary features may be viewed as the signs of a sharp differentiation between the sexes, then the male character would be more associated with complexity, the female with creative originality. The complexity of the masculine social sphere is reflected in the long and arduous initiations that men must undergo in all primitive societies, initiations in which they are not only taught the courage and skill necessary for a hunter but the systematic cosmology and sacred science transmitted immemorially through their lineage. The creativity of the simpler feminine sphere is reflected not only in the physical fertility of women and the social cohesiveness they developed to protect their young but, especially in the second epoch identified more particularly in the diagram with the feminine, with their invention and perfection of the crafts of weaving and pottery, crafts whose products went beyond utility to artistic expression. It is women's arts, particularly the agriculture finally developed from their vast knowledge of vegetation, that eventually led to the permanent settlements that were to mark the new stage of history better modeled by the fourth-world diagram.

It was around 3300 B.C.E. that the Sumerians invented writing and so began that recording of events we call history. From that date or shortly before it to around 1200 B.C.E. man developed the first civilized societies, that is, societies built around cities. The tribal sense of belonging yielded to the sense of isolated individuality that is a necessary product of city living, of living in a place where you are no longer known and related to everyone. And so human culture passed from an essentially matriarchal to a patriarchal culture. In the new male-dominated society, what was important were not the distinctions and creative interactions between males and females but the distinctions only between men on the hierarchy of social power and the deadly interactions between men at war. From the time in the twenty-fourth century B.C.E. that the Akkadian Sargon conquered Sumer and established the first empire to the final destruction of Troy in the thirteenth century B.C.E., the Bronze Age civilization that succeeded the Stone Age culture was marked by wars of conquest, wars in which individual men could achieve the greater personal power and glory that alone seemed to validate the emergence of their individual egos even as it defined the nature of their manliness. But the ever more complex societies they established in Sumer, Babylon, and especially Egypt were also marvels of centralized power in which a scribal bureaucracy kept records of all the royal transactions, records necessary to maintain a complex economy as well as the rule of law. In addition to developing the wheel, sailboats, and irrigation canals, the culture of ancient Mesopotamia also produced the first great literary work, the epic of *Gilgamesh*, a touching account of the confrontation of heroic man with the tragic human condition already "modern" in its sensibility.

But if the third and second millennia can be modeled by the first half of the fourth-world diagram, then such an account of the purely masculine aspect of this epoch must be considered incomplete. For this is a diagram phase marked by two Sabbath Stars, the masculine Fa/Fi Sabbath Star, ideally in its past-modeled form, and the feminine Fi Sabbath Star, which is its culminating element. In the passage to the wholly masculine second phase of the fourth-world diagram the diagram model of the first half of this world defines a transitional phase, one still dominated by the ethos of the past age but bearing the seeds of the spirit that is finally to dominate this new era. As the oscillations of a pendulum do not proceed from one extreme to another without first coming back to the center that partakes of both, so is it with the gender oscillations of the Sabbath Star Diagram from world to world, a model of historical oscillation differing in this respect from the Taoist model of the yin-yang diagram, which shows no such transitional phases.

Such a transitional phase may be said to have two aspects. On the one hand, it reflects the waxing of the new spirit and waning of the old that surely exists in all such transitional periods, contemporaneous manifestations largely out of contact with each other. But on the other, there are also unique syntheses made between the old and the new. In the period now being considered, such synthesis was most marked in the area of religion. This is not only in the form that will become distinctive of the next wholly masculine historical phase, the syncretizing mode of the Hellenic pantheon or the Hebraic co-opting of matriarchal myths and rituals to a patriarchal monotheism. It is in the devotion of the newly released masculine energies to the feminine religious ideal, a devotion that was to lead to the development of a sacred science directed to the erection of religio-scientific monuments and temples.

It is in the third millennium, at a time when the Sumerians and Egyptians had invented their different forms of writing, that they also began such constructions, the Sumerians the ziggurats and the Egyptians the pyramids. The stepped ziggurat form was representative of the sacred mountain and, among other purposes, was the site of the sacred marriage ritual.[6] It is such a ziggurat that the Bible identified as the evil Tower of Babel, evil in the imputed motivation of its builders: "And they said, Go to, let us build us a city and a tower, whose top may reach unto heaven: and let us make us a name" (Gen. 11:14). It is the very verticality of the tower that seems to God to reflect a refusal to live within limitations: "and this they begin to do: and now nothing will be restrained from them, which they have imagined to do" (Gen. 11:6). As in the case of Cain, who also "builded a city" (Gen. 4:17), not to speak of the wicked "cities of the plain" (Gen. 19:29), the activities stigmatized as evil in the early chapters of Genesis are precisely those that reflect any departure from the older hunter-gatherer culture. The source of such evil was recognized to be agriculture, with the concomitant cities and temples that would derive from permanent agricultural settlements, the temples transmuting the former horizontality of the spiritually directed wanderings into vertical construction, and the cities simulating such a deviation from the heterosexual basis of the former culture as homosexuality, the sin of Sodom. But though the Bible rightly pinpoints the evil of the newer masculine culture as its promotion of the heroic ideal, that personal glory achieved through a defiance of limitation, the verticality of the Tower of Babel may have had a purpose different from an arrogant challenging of heaven. If the arguments of Patai and Michell can be admitted, then the purpose of the ziggurats would not have been to conquer heaven by force but to provide the medium for the fusion of the energies of the sky with those of the earth, the same fusion that would seem to have been the goal of the Stone Age rituals at the sensitive mountains, caves, and streams they seasonally visited.

The careful siting of ancient monuments at places of greater telluric energy, at high places or over underground streams, with shafts going deep into the earth as well as architectural features rising into the sky, indicates a development of sacred science aimed at an enhancing of natural energies and their manipulation for the ends of human society. Whether or not this be considered a coercive conquest of heaven, it does represent a direct development from the earlier spiritual technology of ritual petition at places of apprehensible power. In the pyramids, as in the stone circles, it represents both a development of the abstract rational faculties involved in geometric and numerical reasoning, which may be identified with the emergent masculine consciousness, and their direction to the ends of enhanced cosmic harmony and human empowerment, the spiritual goals of the earlier matriarchal culture. In terms of the table for this transitional first period, what is most interesting about its one vertical or masculine element is, first, that its Sabbath Star was earlier identified with the minerals and, secondly, that its ideal form was earlier considered to be past-modeled. These circumstances would seem to symbolize the issue at hand, the masculine construction of vertical stone works for purposes modeled on the past. And what it shows is that in its ideal form, a form most perfectly embodied in Old Kingdom Egypt, the whole complexity of the newly settled, enlarged, and centralized structuring of society was to be devoted to such spiritual science as could ensure the immortality of both individual humans and of their society. In this last they succeeded, for the 3,000 years that this Egyptian civilization endured is the longest of any such technologically advanced nation. Where the Mesopotamian societies distinguished between the secular and the sacred, their kings ruling under divine restrictions rather than as gods and their reigns most memorialized by conquests, in Egyptian society the pharaoh was regarded as the divine medium through which the immortality of his subjects could be achieved, the whole society being a theocracy that, after the Nubian conquest, engaged only in defensive warfare and devoted its resources to the building of sacred monuments largely devoted to the sexual cosmic myth, with its promise not only of earthly fertility but of human spiritual rebirth. The traditional view of the pyramids is that they were constructed solely as royal tombs, the preservation of the pharaoh's body being deemed to be necessary to ensure the immortality of his subjects. But some newer, more divergent opinions on their purpose would have it that, like the stone circles, they were intended to serve, either exclusively or in addition to their tomb function, as astronomical observatories, almanacs, geodesic maps, or initiatory chambers.[7] Whatever the case may be, the sophisticated geometry and engineering required to construct such a monument as the great pyramid, its dimensions including the transcendental numbers pi and phi and its measurements precisely proportional to those of the earth, indicate a high level of scientific knowledge. Thus if this knowledge was applied primarily to structures having a religious purpose, then this purpose would have to include the precise demonstration or utilization of the principles of that very sacred science responsible for their construction.

As the esoteric purposes of all ancient religious monuments, whether temples or pyramids, would seem to be the same as that imputed to the stone circles, earthworks, and tracks of the megalithic builders, the question is what we are to make of the virtual contemporaneity of such a Stone Age monument as Stonehenge with the Great Pyramid and "tower of Babel" of Bronze Age civilization. If Stonehenge is a late product of Neolithic culture, then the question arises as to why the impulse to build stone monuments and earthworks at power points long held to be sacred, and the development of a sacred science both capable of such construction and devoted to it, should have been delayed to the same time as also saw the construction of similar religious edifices in the Tigris-Euphrates, Nile, and even Indus valleys, as well as the mountains of Peru. As the construction elements of the fourth and later worlds of the Sabbath Star Diagram produce matrices that may be considered the "soul" of these worlds, may it be that historical ages are also characterized by such a Zeitgeist as can pull all peoples within the orbit of its particular orientation? If this is possible and the Sabbath Star Diagram can be viewed as a model of this history, then what the diagram for this stage is telling us is that the third and second millennia were marked by the growth of a masculine technology devoted, at its best, to fulfillment of the immemorial spiritual aims of the feminine culture preceding this time, that as it marked the beginnings of the individualizing thrust of the masculine energy that was to create a new world orientation, so did it mark a creative culmination of the older world orientation that only it could achieve.

The original analysis of the fourth-world diagram defined both "unfallen" and "fallen" forms of its construction, and it may be that both are pertinent to the present application of the diagram as a model of history. In addition to the past modeling of the unfallen Sabbath Star of the minerals, in association with that of vegetation, which can be most fully correlated with the settled, theocratic society of Egypt, the future modeling of the fallen mineral Sabbath Star, also in concert with that of the plants, might be correlated with the secular societies of Sumer, Babylonia, and Crete, agriculturally based societies whose expansion through military might was to lead to the downfall of them all. With the thirteenth-century invasion of Egypt by the "sea peoples" and the Mycenaean destruction of Troy, a period of history comes to an end and a new one begins whose most important components, at least for later Western history, will be those of the Hebrews and Greeks.

Again it might be pertinent to apply the distinction between the two forms of the wholly masculine second phase of the fourth-world diagram to the Hebraic-Hellenic duality. In this case it is the construction element identified with the animals that is at issue, its form in the past-modeled diagram being an unelaborated hexagram and its opposite a future-modeled Sabbath Star, the latter of which significantly enlarges the fourth-world matrix. Where the former symbolizes man's domination over the animal level of his nature, the latter seems equally symbolic of its transformed expression through an intellect both more analytically developed and alienated than that of its ideally developed counterpart. This distinction can be seen even in that characteristic uniting them as exemplars of the wholly masculine historical period that can be modeled by the second half of the fourth-world diagram, their mutual celebration of the wonder of man.

The most famous Hellenic expression of this new appreciation of humanity is in the second chorus of Sophocles' *Antigone*:

> *Numberless are the world's wonders, but none*
> *More wonderful than man. . . .*
> *The lightboned birds and beasts that cling to*
> *   cover,*
> *The lithe fish lighting their reaches of dim*
> *   water,*
> *All are taken, tamed in the net of his mind. . . .*
> *Words also, and thought as rapid as air,*
> *He fashions to his good use . . . from every*
> *   wind*
> *He has made himself secure—from all but*
> *   one:*
> *In the late wind of death he cannot stand.*[8]

Where the Hellenic text attests to a tragic component of man's special glory, in the parallel Hebraic text such a consideration is overwhelmed by the even greater wonder of man's special relationship to his divine Creator:

When I consider thy heavens, the work of thy fingers, the moon and the stars, which thou hast ordained; What is man, that thou art mindful of him? and the son of man, that thou visitest him? For thou hast made him a little lower than the angels, and has crowned him with glory and honour. Thou madest him to have dominion over the works of thy hands; thou hast put all things under his feet: All sheep and oxen, yea, and the beasts of the field; The fowl of the air, and the fish of the sea, and whatsoever passeth through the paths of the seas. O Lord our Lord, how excellent is thy name in all the earth. (Psalms 8:3–9)

A distinction between the Hebraic and Hellenic orientations and cultures, cultures that are equally to inform the succeeding phases of Western civilization, has been noted in chapter 8, but the primary focus here will be on their similarities. Perhaps the most significant is the emergence in each of individuals whose expression of their own ideas was so powerful as to lead to the preservation not only of their written works but of their names. Whereas the only historical names previously memorialized were those of rulers or conquerors and their preserved works those of architectural monuments, in this later period, dominated by the wholly masculine aspect of the human spirit, individuals of inspired genius emerge even from the lower classes to guide a culture from a sphere unrelated to the ruling power structure. Two shepherds, the Hebrew Amos and the Greek Hesiod, arose in the eighth century B.C.E. to proclaim their similar understanding of the divine as the exemplar of justice. Whether called by the name of Zeus or the Tetragrammaton, the divine ruler was shown to work through history to punish the wicked and reward the good as well as being particularly concerned with the establishment of just societies in which the oppression of the poor would especially be alleviated.

Such writings show a shift of concern from man in relation to earthly fertility to man in relation to man, the former devoted to the divine femininity of the earth and the latter to a society overseen from heaven by a masculine deity. This new concern for social justice was to lead in the following century to one of the most remarkable of historical coincidences, the discovery of the Book of Deuteronomy in the Jerusalem Temple in the same year, 621 B.C.E., as Draco published his comparable legal code in Athens. And as Jerusalem moved toward a new sense of community, so did Athens, developing its great institution of democracy that was both product and source of the flowering of individualism and analytic rationality that was to be the special gift of Hellenic culture to the world.

Thucydides has defined Athenian culture best in the words of the "Funeral Oration" he attributed to Pericles:

> Our constitution is named a democracy, because it is in the hands not of the few but of the many. But our laws secure equal justice for all in their private disputes, and our public opinion welcomes and honours talent in every branch of achievement, not for any sectional reason but on grounds of excellence alone. . . . we decide or debate, carefully and in person, all matters of policy, holding, not that words and deeds go ill together, but that acts are foredoomed to failure when undertaken undiscussed. . . . In a word I claim that our city as a whole is an education to Greece, and that her members yield to none, man by man, for independence of spirit, many-sidedness of attainment, and complete self-reliance in limbs and brain.[9]

The many-sided attainments achieved through such intellectual self-reliance can be seen in the great literature, philosophy, history, and art resulting from what Thucydides calls "the fearless confidence of freedom."[10]

The Hebrews were also ready to "proclaim liberty throughout all the land" (Lev. 25:10), an ideal enshrined in the great Exodus saga in which they were seen as escaping from Egyptian slavery to a promised land of liberty. And like their Greek counterparts, the Hebrew historians were also interested in discovering the patterns in history, one pattern being the advancement of individuals "on grounds of excellence alone," such advancement as can be seen in the stories of Jacob, Joseph, and David, among others, in which all laws of inheritance and succession are divinely toppled to make way for the triumph of individual talent. Finally, it is through the literary products of such talent that these remarkable peoples have continued to influence the thought of all the cultures of the world.

It is, however, in terms of their differences that Hellenic culture achieved a temporary triumph over the Hebraic. As the Hebrews were largely a captive or client nation for most of the period in question, their highest energies were primarily directed to such holiness as could enable the nation to survive and grow spiritually. Hellenic rationality, on the other hand, invested its literature with the tragic sense and its philosophy with no final good beyond human happiness. To give meaning to such individual mortal existence, the Greeks from the time of Homer embraced the ideal of honor, an ideal best pursued through war that allowed the hero to win a momentary victory in defeat. As Thucydides defines this climactic moment: "So their memory has escaped the reproaches of men's lips, but they bore instead on their bodies the marks of men's hands, and in a moment of time, at the climax of their lives, were rapt away from a world filled, for their dying eyes, not with terror but with glory."[11]

It is the heroic ideal that was finally to lead to the conquests of Alexander that would Hellenize all of Mediterranean civilization and points as far east as India, spreading the Greek rational spirit with its language and culture throughout the empire. From Sargon to Alexander, the masculine spirit of the Bronze Age was expressed through the wars of conquest that would create ever larger and more complex social orders on the devastated remains of previous imperial ventures, social orders that would also permit the life of the mind to develop in speculative, artistic, and practical ways that were to add new wonders and comforts to civilized existence.

If the fourth-world diagram can model human history from the Sumerian to Hellenistic periods, so can the span from 200 B.C.E. to 1200 C.E. be modeled by the fifth-world diagram. The first half of this period can clearly be correlated with the rise and fall of the Roman Empire, and the first half of the fifth-world diagram will prove a most illuminating model for this time. For though the second half of this diagram world is defined by wholly feminine elements, its first half features both masculine and feminine elements in a 3:1 ratio indicative of masculine dominance. Though it is possible to make a point-for-point correlation of the three vertical construction elements with the main periods of Roman history—those of the republic, of the Augustan Age, and of the later empire—it is the dominance of masculine

over feminine elements that is more significant. For it is in this period that the masculine energies first released in Sumer achieve their culminating expression. With the conquests of Julius Caesar not only is the Hellenistic world placed under Roman sovereignty but also most of Europe and England, making them now part of the story of Western civilization and the focus of its next important period. Over this vast domain, the Romans extended their own versions of the Hellenic worship of man, their most culturally revealing architectural expressions being not their aqueducts and paved roads but the triumphal arches with which they celebrated human conquerors. Their writings were also continuations of Greek themes, Lucretius and Cicero in the republican period developing the philosophies of Epicureanism and Stoicism, respectively, while in the Augustan period Virgil imitated the epic style of Homer, Seneca the tragic drama of Aeschylus, Sophocles and Euripides, and Plautus and Terence the comic drama of Menander, though the theater had long since been reduced mainly to gladiatorial contests. For a while, however, the achievements of Roman law and technology and the peace it established through its cosmopolitan reign made the pursuit of individual human happiness seem a reasonable goal.

But though not in a dominant form, this period also saw the resurgence of the feminine energies that were finally to dominate the following medieval period. During the wholly masculine period of Hebraic and Hellenic culture preceding it, the feminine element of human culture had persisted in an entirely hidden form. I have elsewhere argued that a long tradition of sacred science was practiced by the Hebraic priesthood,[12] but this was truly an esoteric, a hidden, tradition. So, too, with the salvific mystery religions of ancient Greece. Though Socrates claimed to be an initiate, and much of the orientation of such fertility religions may have entered into the philosophy of his student Plato, he never openly divulged their secret lore. But it is in the Hellenistic Alexandria of the Roman Empire period that all of these secret traditions do begin to be divulged and to cross-fertilize each other. It is to this period that the *Corpus Hermeticum*, the Egyptian esoteric works attributed to Hermes Trismegistus, can be dated, as well as the Greek Orphic Hymns, the Neoplatonism of Plotinus, and such expressions of the Jewish esoteric tradition as the biblical Book of Daniel, the Ethiopic Book of Enoch, the Merkabah texts, and finally the *Sefer Yetzirah*. And it is in this climate of salvific esotericism that the Jewish sect of Jesus also develops to become finally a world religion capable not only of surviving both Roman persecution and the sack of Rome but to emerge as the guiding force of the age succeeding it.

The division of history into the three stages of the Ancients, the Middle Ages, and the Renaissance was the creation of fifteenth-century humanists who saw their period as marking a rebirth of classical culture and the intervening period as negligible. But the gender modeling of human history by the Sabbath Star Diagram will make possible a different view of the Middle Ages and a predating of the shift from feminine to masculine energies to the twelfth-century. In one respect, however, the humanists were right, in their recognition of an affinity between the sensibility of their times and that of classical, primarily Roman, culture, the affinity of their dominance by masculine energies. And it is also true that between the predominantly masculine cultures of the ancients and the moderns, there does lie a "middle age," one whose values could not be appreciated precisely because it was informed by the contrasting ideals of a femininely oriented culture.

Though the period from the fourth to the tenth centuries was marked by successive waves of invasions and such imperial interludes as the Carolingian and Holy Roman Empires, its most enduring institution is that of the Church with the new values it gave to the largely barbarian peoples of Europe converted to its vision. The classical culture was largely lost on the people who survived the various invasions of the Goths and Huns and so were its structures of centralized control. In its place there developed that social structure most characteristic of feminine culture, decentralization. Though there gradually came to be kings of France, Germany, and England, the primary structure of society and repository of power was in the feudal fiefdoms, and the ideal of feudalism was the knight errant. This leg-

endary knight traveled around the countryside and through uncharted wildernesses to right wrongs and protect the weak, most importantly to protect and honor women.

Not only is this period marked by the decentralization and wandering characteristic of feminine spiritual energy, but also by the reemergence of woman as the ideal toward which the highest energies of man are to be directed. And this was not only true of the secular realm of chivalry. In religion, too, the feminine emerged again as a sacred symbol in the worship of Mary as the "Mother of God." The knight errant and later mendicant friars were not the only wanderers. The people also began to travel on pilgrimage routes from one sacred place housing saint's relics to another. The spirit of the age is perhaps best summed up in the words of Chaucer:

> *That thee is sent, receive in buxomnesse;*
> *The wrestling for the world axeth a fal;*
> *Here is noon hoom, here nis but wildernesse;*
> *Forth, pilgrim, forth! Forth, beest, out of thy*
> *   stal!*
> *Know thy countree, looke up, thank God of al.*
> *Hold the heigh way and lat thy gost thee lede:*
> *And Trouthe shal delivere, it is no drede.[13]*

If the spirit-inspired wanderings of peoples best characterize the purely feminine orientation, the culminating expression of such feminine cultural energy must wait for the next stage of interacting energies, for that stage, to be modeled by the first half of the sixth-world diagram dominated by its final feminine element, shows a 4:3 ratio of masculine to feminine members. It is the parallel that can be drawn between the period earlier modeled by the feminine-dominant first half of the fourth-world diagram and the outstanding feature of the twelfth century that argues in favor of this date as the transition point to the larger period to be modeled by the similar first half of the sixth-world diagram. This is the construction of the great Gothic cathedrals along the older pilgrimage routes.

As we saw in the earlier discussion, it was not the hunter-gatherer clans of the epoch oriented to feminine culture that erected architectural edifices at the sacred places on their treks. It was rather in the next phase that masculine energies were enlisted to preserve and enhance the ancient sources of spiritual power. It has been said that "the entirety of the Egyptian spiritual legacy was a formalized remembrance and repository of the Golden Age of the preceding matriarchal phase of evolution,"[14] and so may it be said of the High Middle Ages with respect to those earlier ages called "dark." As the period of decentralization begins to pass, its horizontality also expressed in such spiritual wanderings as are epitomized in the legendary quest for the femininely symbolic Holy Grail, new masculine energies now arise to give vertical expression to this same feminine ideal, to Notre Dame, "Our Lady." The great cathedral at Chartres, like those that followed it, was erected to glorify the Virgin Mary, and its construction likewise signaled the reemergence of the most sacred science of geometry. The masons were the heirs to a system of sacred science that also found expression in the Egyptian pyramids, the megalithic stone circles, and the temples of Mesopotamia, Palestine, and Greece, a system that required the construction of sacred spaces for the unification of the masculine and feminine forms of the divine, such unification as is implied by those differently sized spires of Chartres cathedral symbolic of the sun and moon.

The masons who built the great cathedrals, like the Knights Templar, were members of esoteric orders, but they were not the only evidence of this new flowering of esoteric learning. The hidden esoteric tradition within Judaism was also to break forth at this time in the kabbalistic writings of Provence and Spain, with their express sexualization of the cosmic myth, the former also the site of the Catharist heresy of spiritual love and the new Troubadour idealization of the feminine in courtly love. Seen in this context, Renaissance humanism does not mark a sharp break but rather a continuation of the progressive divulgence of the ancient esoteric traditions. The first work that Cosimo de Medici commissioned Marsilio Ficino to translate into Latin is the *Corpus Hermeticum*, followed by the complete works of Plato. In fifteenth-century Italy, the same mix of esoteric traditions that had come together in Alexandria again came into synthesis. In addition to those just named, his mix also included works in the Pythagorean and Neoplatonic traditions as well as the kabbalistic reformulation of Jewish esotericism. As in the earlier period, so now the occult arts of astrology and magic were the recognized adjunct of a cosmology that saw correspondences between the spiritual and the material through which the adept could influence nature. From the building of the cathedrals in twelfth-century France to the magical attempts of Giordano Bruno and John Dee in sixteenth-century Italy and England, there is an unbroken dedication of some of the best minds of Europe to sacred science, to such science as alchemy that sought the spiritual union of masculine and feminine elements of nature through which the operator's own soul could be perfected.[15]

The spiritual character of these five hundred years can perhaps be even better gauged by its Jewish component. For from the twelfth-century *Bahir* to the sixteenth-century *Eitz Chayyim*, this was the most generative period in the history of the Kabbalah, recovering and redeveloping the ancient Jewish esoteric tradition with both a complexity and clarity never before so largely articulated and one in which the suppressed feminine aspect of this tradition was fully elaborated. More than any other characteristic, it is the sexualizing of the esoteric Jewish salvific myth that most distinguishes the Kabbalah of this period from the older Merkabah writings, a sexualizing that, like the Christian Mariolatry of this same period, most clearly indicates the inspirational ideal of the feminine informing and giving its own cohesion to these five hundred years. As thus developed, the Kabbalah would also be adopted by Christians searching for the esoteric roots of their own tradition, Christianity having originally given overt expression to a Jewish esotericism, which I have elsewhere argued was conserved and developed by the Zadokite Hebraic priesthood,[16] in which Judaism was itself rooted.

In the subsequent developments of both Jewish and Christian history during the Roman Empire period and earlier Middle Ages, this spiritual flame had been somewhat obscured by the needs of both religions to construct legal and dogmatic frameworks in which their communities as a whole could develop, the Christian hierarchy being further absorbed with the demands of what became their own almost imperial order. Though biblical Christianity even more than biblical Judaism reflected the feminine spiritual temperament, with its emphasis on love and the suffering of injury, the institutional forms of both religious traditions were informed by the masculine imperatives of building ethical communities even during the most femininely dominant historical phases. But this historical energy finally led to the new outburst of esoteric spirituality that could rebalance the religious heart of this epoch. As we turn to the first half of the period modeled by the sixth-world diagram, it is important to note that when the same impulse touched both groups, the Jews had a preserved esoteric tradition it could draw on while the Christians had to turn to pagan classical sources, to the Hellenistic mix of Hermeticism and the various developments of the Pythagorean-Platonic tradition as these were remixed, by such as Pico Della Mirandola, with the new Kabbalah of the Tree of Life.

Viewing history from the perspective of its oscillations between periods of feminine and masculine dominance, we can chart a continuous flow of the feminine historical energy through the three different periods from 200 B.C.E. to 1600 C.E. It is first manifested as the countercultural force in the period of mixed masculine and feminine energies dominated by the masculine, the period to the fall of the Western branch of the Roman Empire; then it is the informing energy of the Christian-feudal period; and finally it is the dominant energy in the period from 1100 to 1600 to which we now turn that was marked again by the synthesis of masculine and feminine energies, of that special dedication of masculine rationality and construction to the feminine salvific ideal animating sacred science, the generative unification of opposites. As we can see, the significant difference between masculine and feminine dominance during the periods of mixed energies is that during such periods of masculine dominance these two forces are seen as opposing each other and do not interact, whereas during such periods of feminine dominance they are seen as complementary and interact creatively.

But as in the first mixed age of feminine dominance, so in the second this dedication of the masculine to the feminine ideal is only partial. The masculine also grows as a countercultural force that finally becomes the exclusive informing agent of the next phase. The effects of the humanist recovery of classical texts was not simply the replacement of scholastic Aristotelianism by Platonism but also the new rebirth of the Hellenic secular spirit, with its worldliness, freedom, rationality, and reverence for man. Pico della Mirandola not only wrote his kabbalist *Conclusions* but also his *Oration on the Dignity of Man*. But though Pico based this dignity on man's moral freedom, he still saw man's highest development to be that of the magus, the white magician or sacred scientist: "I glory in Man the Magus as described by Hermes Trismegistus."[17] From the assertion of such freedom to the full secularization of science would be but a short step, however. And though nature would still for a time be viewed as the Book of God, what would be studied would not be the sympathetic interactions of matter and spirit, as with sacred science, but the mechanical operations of cause and effect on the purely physical plane. By the end of the sixteenth century, Galileo would have verified the Copernican revolution in scientific cosmology to bring in the new modern world at whose end we are now poised.

The seventeenth century marks the beginning of the four-hundred-year period ending with the present that can be modeled by the second half of the sixth-world diagram. At its beginning Francis Bacon both heralded the progress in human conveniences that could be accomplished through the advancement of science and also issued a cautionary note. Writing still as a man of the Renaissance in his fictional *New Atlantis*, he would have his scientific academy run by priests who could monitor whether the inventions they developed would be for the benefit or endangerment of mankind, its saintly scientists being willing to suppress potentially harmful inventions:

> God bless thee, my son; I will give thee the greatest jewel I have. For I will impart unto thee, for the love of God and men, a relation of the true

state of Salomon's House. . . . The End of our Foundation is the knowledge of Causes, and secret motions of things; and the enlarging of the bounds of Human Empire, to the effecting of all things possible. . . . And this we do also: we have consultations, which of the inventions and experiences which we have discovered shall be published, and which not: and take all an oath of secrecy, for the concealing of those which we think fit to keep secret. . . .[18]

The invention of gunpowder by the thirteenth century made the establishment of such moral controls on scientific inventions an urgent necessity. But since the first mention of gunpowder occurs in the thirteenth-century works of the Franciscan scientist-theologian Roger Bacon,[19] a legendary magus,[20] and even priests have been known for destructive fanaticism, witness the fifteenth-century Dominican Savonarola, one wonders how successful any such monitoring by imperfect man could be. Francis Bacon was enough of a Machiavellian in his political essays, called by Blake "good advice for Satan's kingdom,"[21] to recognize the futility of such a hope. For it is in Machiavelli's sixteenth-century *The Prince* that the amoral Realpolitik of ends justifying means is given the perfect expression that serves as well to express the new masculine spirit of Renaissance secular individualism. It is such individualism, freed from the moral constraints that necessarily operate in any sacred science, that, whether operating in politics or in secular science, has left modern man vulnerable to the worst evils known in human history, in our time the holocaust of Hitler and the widening hole in the ozone shield as well as the ever-threatening though, until recently, receding prospect of nuclear destruction.

By the seventeenth century, the triple assaults on the old religion made by humanistic atheism, science, and the Reformation, with its splintering of Christianity into numerous sects, had left man in the state of radical doubt that defines the modern world. This doubt was given early expression by John Donne:

And new Philosophy calls all in doubt,
The Element of fire is quite put out;
The Sun is lost, and th' earth, and no mans
  wit
Can well direct him where to looke for it. . . .

. . . .

'Tis all in pieces, all coherence gone;
All just supply, and all Relation:
Prince, Subject, Father, Sonne, are things
  forgot,
For every man alone thinkes he hath got
To be a Phoenix, and that then can bee
None of that kinde, of which he is, but hee.[22]

So, too, did Shakespeare's Macbeth see life as "a tale told by an idiot, / Full of sound and fury, signifying nothing."[23] The continuity of this modern mood can be seen in Matthew Arnold's view of man "as on a darkling plain / Swept with confused alarms of struggle and flight, / Where ignorant armies clash by night,"[24] and Yeats's sense that "Things fall apart; the center cannot hold; / Mere anarchy is loosed upon the world."[25]

The masculinity of this final period has not been as uniform as the comparable period modeled by the second half of the fourth-world diagram, being interrupted during the first half of the nineteenth century by the Romantic movement, with its more feminine spirituality. But what this diagram also shows us is a great increase in complexity. Though the succession of diagram worlds may be viewed as oscillating between masculine and feminine dominance, they also show a direct increase in complexity from world to world. But the increase from four to six construction elements between the fourth and fifth worlds is not as dramatic as that from six to twelve such elements between the fifth and sixth worlds. As the fifth world moved the center of Western civilization from the Mediterranean to Europe, so in the sixth world does it spread out from Europe to embrace ever larger spheres of influence, by the nineteenth century the area from America to Russia, with all the further areas colonized by the European powers, and by the end of World War II all of the Northern Hemisphere.

But even more significant than the rise in area and population was the dramatic rise in power occasioned by the invention of the steam engine in 1769 that, applied first to the manufacture of iron, then of cotton, and finally to the railroads, made England into a great industrial power by the nineteenth century and the vanguard of an Industrial Revolution that would spread to Western Europe, to America, and finally beyond to change the lifestyles and aspirations of the rest of the world. By the twentieth century, the growth in science from Newton to Einstein would be joined with that of advanced technology to release the even greater power of the atom.

It is, then, the increase in power that most characterizes the historical phase modeled by the sixth-world diagram, and this is particularly interesting in terms of the earlier identifications given to this world. For it was this world that was identified with the Neshamah level of the soul, a predominantly mental level of spiritual power. So, too, was the fifth world identified with the Ruach soul level, whose highest level is love, as the fourth world was identified with the Nefesh soul level of the senses. Though the Kabbalah understands these soul levels to be hierarchically ranked and to represent ever higher levels of spiritual development, it would seem that without such spiritual development on the part of Western man as a whole, the stages of his historical evolution have still followed the primary orientations of what can be considered the "souls" of each these periods and of the diagram worlds by which these historical stages can be modeled.

In the first historical period from Sumer to Alexandria modeled by the masculine fourth world, the Nefesh senses would, indeed, seem to be paramount. As the secular societies from the Sumerians to the Greeks saw pleasure as the highest worldly good, so did the religious societies from the Egyptians to the Hebrews pay similar tribute to the ideal of holiness. Now what distinguishes holiness is precisely that it is a form of subtle energy that can be apprehended in and by the bodily senses, sensed. The holy man goes through a training that further sensitizes his system to such subtle energies until he becomes the empowered vessel for their proper transmission. As the historical period correlated with the fourth-world diagram can be related to the sensual nature of the Nefesh soul earlier identified with it, so can that correlated with the fifth-world diagram be related to the emotional nature of the Ruach soul. And as the highest expression of the former was considered to be holiness, so can the highest expression of the latter be recognized in the spiritual love of the monks and chivalric knights of the earlier Middle Ages. But as the Neshamah soul is identified primarily with the highest mental power, so is it the development and utilization of such "brain power" that most characterizes the historical period correlated with the final phase of the sixth-world diagram. Thus, though the three major periods of history correlated with the fourth- through sixth-world diagrams do not represent a growth of the human spirit as a whole beyond the Nefesh soul level, the culminating phases of the periods correlated with the fifth and sixth worlds do show the emergence of psychic levels most characteristic of the higher soul levels earlier identified with these diagrams, the medieval period a heart quality that may be associated with the Ruach soul and the modern period the mental quality of the Neshamah soul.

These partial correspondences suggest that there is a transpersonal force operating within human history to direct or inspire human spiritual development but that it has not been completely successful. This would seem to be due to man's free will, which has become more and more engrossed with the experiences of the senses and the fulfillments arising from its operations on the purely physical plane. This transpersonal force shows both a feminine oscillation between the dualities of the sexes and a masculine steady progress toward greater complexity, characteristics that have been fully manifested in human history. But the further ideal associations of this transpersonal force with levels of spiritual evolution has led only to the partial resonance of human culture during the medieval period to the heart ideals of sacred and secular love and in the modern period to the mental ideals of rational understanding and discovery, the former period reflecting a feminine phase of this transpersonal force and the latter a masculine phase.

It is because man has gained access in the modern period to a level of theoretical understanding and consequent technological manipulation that is properly the domain of the Neshamah soul but without the spiritual development that should be its concomitant that his advances have become so perilous to his future and even present welfare. His medical advances have been more than balanced by the devastating potentials of his ever more destructive military technology and his conveniences by the pollution of his earthly habitat. In this period the masculine pursuit of personal power has led first to the growth of the centralized European nations and then to their further imperialistic expansion, the British achieving an empire so vast that they thought in their pride they had conquered the heavens, could prevent the very sun from setting. But this growth has been so unbalanced in its technological advances that it now threatens the future of all life on this planet, whether through the insanity of a nuclear holocaust or the price of industrial waste products. With the building of the Tower of Babel God had feared that "now nothing will be restrained from them," but the madness of man's unrestrained march to oblivion seems on the verge of being arrested in time. With the end of the Cold War, the countries of Eastern Europe are moving toward democracy while those of the "West" are moving toward an ever broader social-welfare net. But the threat of terrorism with new weapons of mass destruction has made human existence ever more perilous. If we are now, indeed, moving into a new age, what can the regularities of the Sabbath Star Diagram tell us about its probable course?

If the new millennium we are now entering can be correlated with the first half of the seventh world, then we may expect some features similar to those of the parallel first half of the fifth world. For like the period of the Roman Empire, this will be a period of mixed masculine and feminine characteristics featuring masculine dominance. Thus the masculine imperatives of progress will continue to be operative until the whole world has been brought up to the level of prosperity now enjoyed by the industrial West, has become at least superficially Westernized.

This history has ignored all but the salient developments of Western culture. But as we enter the octave phase of the seventh-world diagram, we must finally acknowledge the great and less great civilizations that have evolved largely out of touch with the accelerated development of the West, the great civilizations of China, India, and, in the Americas, of the Aztecs and Incas, and the less developed cultures of the rest of the Americas, of sub-Saharan Africa, and such fringe peoples as the Turks and Slavs. Greatest was the long-lived Chinese empire with its examination-based civil-service bureaucracy and its religious philosophies of Confucianism, Taoism, and the Buddhism that linked it to the other great civilization of predominantly Hindu India. But whether they had the trimmings of advanced civilization or a more primitive economic basis and social structure, all these non-European cultures had, by the nineteenth century, been long gripped by a paralyzing medievalism of their own. Though this period had, as earlier figured, lasted only seven hundred years in Europe, in some other parts of the world it extended for millennia. In sub-Saharan Africa, the Bantu and other more evolved tribes, though not themselves very far from the Stone Age, developed various feudal kingdoms that warred against each other much like their counterparts in medieval Europe.

It would seem to be characteristic of feminine eras to last longer than masculine eras, a distinction well illustrated by the dual axes of the diagram. For since the horizontal (feminine) construction elements are spaced further apart than the vertical (masculine) elements, they would seem to represent longer time spans when translated into historical terms. This is certainly true of the prehistorical period of some 66,000 years modeled by the feminine third world of the diagram. And it would also seem that the more innovative period modeled by the masculine fourth world did not last long in most parts of the world before subsiding into a more prolonged period of varying rigidity, a rigidity most pronounced in the Indian caste system. As masculine innovation can unbalance the system in one direction, so can the correction of feminine stability unbalance it in the opposite direction, leading to an ever more involuted cultural sterility on the one hand, and an otherworldly monasticism on the other. Especially in the more prolonged periods of such involution in non-European cultures that can also be modeled by the feminine fifth-world diagram, the need for a new period of masculine evolution was as necessary as it was not forthcoming. It was only in the European West that the medieval period was foreshortened by the accelerated movement into a new period of masculine dominance so innovative that it would lift all of human culture with it—if it does not destroy it first.

In the historical period now before us, which can be modeled by the first half of the seventh-world diagram, it seems likely that the rest of the world will be pulled rapidly through a parallel sixth-world development to join finally with the West in the one world of the octave diagram, the period earlier identified with spiritual communion. It is not until the masculine aspirations for social and intellectual freedom, as well as for a lifestyle not only beyond subsistence but filled with all the wonders of Western technology, have been satisfied throughout the world that the rocket of this most spectacular of masculine-dominated periods will be spent. And it is not until such a time that the waxing countercultural force of a resurgent truly feminine mystique will again achieve dominance. If we can credit the traditional understanding of the prophetic nature of the Hebrew calendar, then the period in question will last some 230 years, bringing us to the year 6000 in the Hebrew calendar and the beginning of the Messianic millennium, the period that would now seem to be identifiable with the final feminine phase of the seventh-world diagram.

The fact that Messianic possibilities for humankind emerge at just the point in human history where the traditional numbers merge with those of the Sabbath Star Diagram, in the seventh division of a historical or cosmic evolution essentially Sabbatical in its structure, must give us pause. Apart from the wonder of it, it also raises a problem of modeling consistency since the Messianic Age was previously associated with the construction elements of the fifth-world diagram. But this apparent inconsistency reflects a similar inconsistency within the time frames of the Kabbalah, that between the concepts of the four cosmic worlds and the seven his-

torical Shemitot, the latter also seen within the larger cosmic cycle of the Jubilee. Both concepts appear almost simultaneously at the beginning of the fourteenth century, that of the four cosmic worlds in the *Massekhet Atzilut* and *Tikkunei Zohar* and that of the seven Shemitot in the *Temunah*.[26] In the present work the attempt to combine the four worlds of emanation of the earlier Kabbalah with the future stages of the Tikkun adumbrated by Luria in the sixteenth century led to the identification of the future Messianic Age with a fifth cosmic world and the World to Come with a sixth, these two traditional future stages being further extended to include a third that would bring the total to the seven consistent with a basic Sabbatical cosmology reaching from Genesis through the Hekhalot literature and the *Sefer Yetzirah* to the *Temunah*.[27] But when we arrive at this seventh world in terms of the new historical modeling being attempted in this appendix, we see that it converges with the traditional historical projection for the time of the Messianic Age. One explanation for this apparent inconsistency is, of course, that we are dealing with two different schemes, the first a scheme in which cosmic time is translatable into spiritual dimensions and the second one concerned with actual human history, the approximately 5,765 years of Hebrew time being the actual span of such history since the time of the development of Sumerian civilization.

But if we do wish to resolve this inconsistency, one way would be to regard the fifth-world Messianic identification as the ideal of human spiritual development and its seventh-world identification as the historical reality of mankind's delayed development. If the paradigm of human development is Ze'ir Anpin, the "short-faced" or short-tempered, Impatient One, then man has been true to this supernal model of divine personality, following an accelerated emotional and mental development without having progressed spiritually beyond the sensual and territorial imperatives of his still reptilian Nefesh soul. In the conflicting traditions of the Kabbalah, different aspects of the truth have been variously formulated that, in synthesis, would thus seem to yield a still higher level of understanding.

If, then, we are now within some 235 years of

the time in which human spiritual evolution is to undergo a quantum leap into higher consciousness, what can the seventh world of the Sabbath Star Diagram tell us about its contours when interpreted from the historical perspective? It can tell us first that this era will be dominated by the feminine historical energy, an energy that in the coming 235 years will continue to be largely countercultural though its influence will make itself increasingly felt. In the period just entered, then, the masculine energies devoted to worldly fulfillment will achieve their crowning success in the high level of material prosperity that will spread out from the North Atlantic community of nations to embrace the whole world, building a cultural empire of Western technology and values whose *lingua franca* will be American English. We can also hope that it will be a period in which the resources formerly spent on war will be devoted to health and education, causing a great improvement in longevity and the potentiality for a complementary inner development of the self. And though the needs of this spreading industrial civilization will require ever greater amounts of fuel to power its productivity, great efforts will be made to control the toxicity of their emissions. The feminine countercultural concern with healthy food and a healthy environment will act to limit, both through legislation and a changing public opinion, the ability of private corporations to pollute the public air and water for personal profit. But the demands of the undeveloped countries for a Western standard of living will not go unappeased and will pose a continuing threat to the environment throughout this period. During this same period in which the East and the nations of the Southern Hemisphere are becoming Westernized, the West will become increasingly interested in the spiritual ideas and techniques of the East, a process that has been growing since at least the sixties, the feminine spiritual energy developing in a cultural exchange for the masculine energy the West is exporting to the rest of the world.

Finally, in the year 6000, if the prophecies hold, a spiritual millennium will begin whose radical change from the earlier periods of human recorded history will only be gradually recognized, because it

has been gradually developing, but that will finally be uncontestable. It will nonetheless have the qualities that have ever characterized feminine cultures: decentralization, reverence for the earth, and spirituality. The cultural homogenization of the previous period will come apart as each ethnic group strives to recover its spiritual roots. In the previous period the territorial assertions of such groups, as well as the resistance to change of a minority, had already begun even as the majority strove to join a unified Western culture and global economy. But now territorial independence will be accompanied by a reappreciation of the distinctive forms each ancient culture had given to what can finally be recognized to have been a universal intuition into the same ultimate truths, distinctive forms whose accumulation of spiritual energy will be tapped once more with authentic belief. There will be no world government with coercive power but rather local and international networks formed on the basis of various mutual interests of trade, cultural exchange, and the needs of defense.

Not only will the likely political structure of this millennial society be decentralized but all its distinctive units will be alike devoted to the central concern of this age, the healing of the earth. Where earlier there had been an attempt only to level off the curve of environmental pollution, the primary concern now will be to reverse this process, first by the use of nonpolluting energy sources like the sun and wind, even if this means a universal reduction in some aspects of the general standard of living, and second by devoting the major efforts of scientific research to the development of new, more powerful and nontoxic sources of energy and new agents of antipollution that can neutralize the present toxicity of the land, sea, and sky. As the previous period can only be completed when the economies of the whole world have been brought up to the same efficiency of production, so this final period—which will develop more natural modes of farming and industry as well as new technical advances in energy production, perhaps a new sacred science capable of tapping telluric energy once more—will only be completed with the general spiritual evolution of humanity and the healing of the earth, a period that should well last a thousand years.

Finally, this is the period in which mankind, having satisfied its material desires, can move beyond the "future shock" of its sudden emergence almost 6,000 years ago into the cities that bound man's resultant individuation with alienation, an alienation he compensated for through an ego aggrandizement leading to incessant warfare. From this adolescent assertion of individual identity for its own sake, the human race can now grow up, can recognize itself as a part of a larger, mutually nurturing whole, and can now strive to satisfy the deeper spiritual needs that had gone unmet in the unrestrained pursuit of material power. Given the experience of humanity with this prior path, which has gone far to annihilating the race and fouling the planet, it seems not beyond reason to hope that in this projected millennium of earth-healing, the human race will also be able to heal itself and develop spiritually at least to the level of the Ruach soul that was earlier identified with the Messianic Age. Whether human beings will also in this time span be able to complete the whole course of their spiritual development on earth and reach the Yechidah level earlier identified with this culminating phase of the seventh-world diagram, one can more hope than expect, though it would nicely resolve the conflict between the use of the seventh-world diagram to model both the highest levels of the soul and the future of human history. And whether the more reasonable hope of mankind's achieving at least the Ruach soul level during the Messianic millennium will be a result or prerequisite of the appearance of an individual Messiah, one also cannot say, though it is such Messianic consciousness that will grip humanity at this time and bring with it the power to redeem humankind and its world.

As humanity moves from the postmodern present modeled by the masculine dominance of the first half of the seventh-world diagram to the Messianic future modeled by the wholly feminine second half of this world, it will gain the knowledge of that larger cosmic structure which not only can inform the human spirit with a new sense of wholeness but lift society to a new level of peace. Then shall the prophecy finally be fulfilled: "They shall not hurt nor destroy in all my holy mountain: for the earth shall be full of the knowledge of the Lord, as the waters cover the sea" (Isa. 11:9). The association of the Messianic millennium with the full transmission of sacred knowledge has been one of the most persistent features of this age in the literature. And the final association of the seventh-world diagram with the seventh millennium of the Hebrew calendar traditionally identified with the Messianic Age and with the characteristic of Da'at, Knowledge, also traditionally thought to inform this age, seems to be more than coincidental and to indicate that the Sabbath Star Diagram not only encodes the course of cosmic evolution but, from another perspective, human history as well.

As we come to the close of this gender modeling of human history, it is clear that the Sabbath Star Diagram does provide an archetypal structure that can be variously interpreted but that also imparts to each such systematically developed interpretation its own power of illumination. For this is what a good model can do, organize the diverse materials of its intended field of application so that they reveal a new structure and meaning. In the present case, the modeling of human history by the gender-differentiated worlds of the Sabbath Star Diagram has led to a reorganization of historical materials that seems to reveal an oscillation between masculine- and feminine-dominated epochs, with the further definitions of the mixed transitional periods between them and the increasing complexity of the whole of this oscillating development. Though such correspondence is, of course, a partial product of selection, it is only such selection that can find the pattern in historical events and so make historical understanding possible. But if in addition to providing us with a meaningful structure we take the model one step further and argue for its truth value, then we would have to assign a different level of causation to the pattern we can discern operating through human history, a transpersonal force, call it cosmic consciousness, that informs the "complex magnitudes"[28] of temporal process with its own successive structural characteristics and purposes. This is a bold thesis but it is one that reveals the very shifting of gender-defined historical energies that seems to be taking place even as I write. As the twentieth century, dominated by the masculine imperatives of power, has come to an end and a new millennium, as of a new astrological age, begins, I can do no better than to close this work with the lines with which Dryden greeted the close of the seventeenth century, the first century of the modern era:

All, all, of a piece throughout;
Thy Chase had a Beast in View;
Thy Wars brought nothing about;
Thy Lovers were all untrue.
'Tis well an Old Age is out,
And time to begin a New.[29]

Notes

CHAPTER 1

1. *The Zohar*, trans. Daniel C. Matt, Pritzker edition (Stanford: Stanford University Press, 2004), vol. 1, pp. 7, 8 (1:2a).

2. See *New York Times* (21 November 1978), sec. C, p. 1.

3. In chapter 2 we shall see, however, that it is the precise structure of the Tree of Life Diagram that makes it possible to develop the scientific model of the Sabbath Star Diagram. Such a derivation earlier appeared in chapter 6 of my book *The Secret Doctrine of the Kabbalah: Recovering the Key to Hebraic Sacred Science* (Rochester, Vt.: Inner Traditions, 1999), which, in chapter 8, also showed that the Tree of Life Diagram, if rotated sixfold around its Da'at point, will provide a geometric demonstration of a method of doubling the cube, a continuing problem for the Platonic Academy and a proof of the sophistication of Hebraic sacred science. In the first two chapters of the aforementioned book, I further attribute such a sophisticated sacred science to the Zadokite priesthood of the Second Temple, as well as showing that from a sixfold rotation of the Tree of Life Diagram around its Da'at point a diagram is produced that can be held to demonstrate the very generation of the "son" that I argue to be the core of this priestly esoteric tradition. All of these earlier published studies should show that the structure of the Tree of Life Diagram is not arbitrary.

4. For a fuller development and validation of this symbolic method of geometric interpretation, see the section of chapter 2 entitled "The Science of Expressive Form" and appendix C.

5. My understanding of the Sabbatical cosmos that will be fully developed in the present book appeared in two of my earlier books. It underlies my synthesis of quantum cosmology with the cosmology of Luria in chapter 10 of *The Secret Doctrine of the Kabbalah* and it is the foundation of my most recent book, *The Kabbalah of the Soul: The Transformative Psychology and Practices of Jewish Mysticism* (Rochester, Vt.: Inner Traditions, 2003), which develops a simpler theoretical model for the cosmos, one containing the most important features of the mathematical model to be here presented, as a framework for the psychological analyses that follow it, some of which will appear again with the more scientific modeling of their features in chapters 3, 4, 5, 8, 9, and 12 of the present work.

6. Josephus, *Jewish Antiquities*, trans. Ralph Marcus, 9 vols., The Loeb Classical Library, ed. T. E. Page et al. (Cambridge: Harvard University Press, 1963), vol. 8, p. 179.

7. See S. K. Heninger Jr., *Touches of Sweet Harmony: Pythagorean Cosmology and Renaissance Poetics* (San Marino, Calif.: Huntington Library, 1974), pp. 243–44.

8. Gershom Scholem, *On the Kabbalah and Its Symbolism*, trans. Ralph Manheim (New York: Schocken Books, 1969), p. 167. Scholem here dates the *Sefer Yetzirah* as written "some time between the third and sixth century." See also his *Kabbalah* (New York: New American Library, 1974), p. 25.

9. See *The Secret Doctrine of the Kabbalah*, and note 3 above, for my radical thesis that the Zadokite priesthood of the Second Temple not only developed what I have called "the secret doctrine of the son," a secret doctrine passed on by them to the small groups that in various forms, such as the Merkabah mystics, continued to pass it on for over a millennium until it emerged to become the core belief of the Kabbalah, but that these Hebrew priests also practiced a sophisticated sacred science that could demonstrate this belief system.

10. In the *Fragments* of Philolaus, the first Pythagorean writings, we read: "it is evident that the world in its totality, and its included beings are a harmonious compound of Limited and Unlimited elements," in *The Pythagorean Sourcebook and Library*, trans. Kenneth Sylvan Guthrie, ed. David R. Fideler (Grand Rapids, Mich.: Phanes Press, 1987), p. 168.

Some further explication of Pythagorean harmonic theory would be useful here. To give the simplest examples of this, there are the ratios of 2:1, 3:2, and 4:3 that define the important consonant intervals of the musical scale: the octave, the fifth, and the fourth, respectively. When these ratios are inverted and expressed as fractions, the corresponding string length will produce the tone whose distance from the tonic (Do) represents the above musical interval. In the first instance, if the string length is halved, it will produce the octave double of the tone of its full length. If the string is stopped at the $\frac{2}{3}$ point, it will produce the musical fifth, and if at the $\frac{3}{4}$ point the musical fourth. Now, another remarkable aspect about the numerical inversion between string length and tonal frequency is that the frequency ratios also express the order in which the harmonic overtones emerge. The second tone produced after the fundamental tone is its octave and expresses both the frequency ratio and order of 2:1. The third tone is to the second as the interval of the fifth, 3:2. The fourth tone above that third tone is the second octave, which is a musical fourth above the prior musical fifth, 4:3. To continue, the fifth tone above the fourth, 5:4, is the interval of the major third, and the sixth above that, 6:5, is again the musical fifth, which is a minor third above the previous tone defining the major third. Above this, and the last that we shall be considering is the seventh harmonic, with a ratio of 7:6, which is close to a minor seventh above the tonic and a septimal third above the previous interval. For a fuller treatment of the nature and meaning of Pythagorean sacred science, see chapter 3 of my book *The Secret Doctrine of the Kabbalah*. See also note 8 to chapter 2 below.

11. For my analysis of the Hebraic sacred science exemplified in the *Sefer Yetzirah*, particularly in its first sentence, see *The Secret Doctrine of the Kabbalah*, pp. 87–94, and for my solution to the problematical diagram implied in the *Sefer Yetzirah*, see pp. 252–94.

12. See Simone Weil, "The Pythagorean Doctrine," in *Intimations of Christianity*, trans. Elisabeth Chase Geissbuhler (London: Routledge and Kegan Paul, 1957), p. 162.

13. Gershom Scholem, *Major Trends in Jewish Mysticism* (1961; reprint, New York: Schocken Books, 1978), p. 218.

14. The important kabbalistic concept of the Sefirot will shortly be elucidated, but I should note a stylistic option chosen with regard to Hebrew words. Here and throughout I have mainly distinguished Hebrew from English words by the simple capitalization of their initial letters in the case of words that are used extensively in the text, italicizing only those Hebrew words that appear just once or twice.

15. Chayyim Vital, *The Tree of Life: The Palace of Adam Kadmon*, ed. and trans. Donald Wilder Menzi and Zwe Padeh (Northvale, N. J.: Jason Aronson, 1999), p. 14.

16. See John Michell, *City of Revelation* (New York: David McKay, 1972), p. 55.

17. See "Magen David" in *Encyclopedia Judaica* and Scholem, *Kabbalah*, pp. 362–68.

18. See Scholem, *Kabbalah*, p. 363.

19. Gershom Scholem, "The Star of David: History of a Symbol," *The Messianic Idea in Judaism and Other Essays on Jewish Spirituality* (New York: Schocken Books, 1978), p. 259.

20. Ibid., p. 264.

21. Ibid., p. 266.

22. Ibid., p. 271.

23. Raphael Patai, *The Jewish Alchemists* (Princeton: Princeton University Press, 1995), p. 60.

24. Ibid., pp. 66, 67, 68.

25. Ibid., p. 66.

26. For my comprehensive text-based history of this doctrine, see *The Secret Doctrine of the Kabbalah*, particularly pp. 30–73.

27. Patai, *The Jewish Alchemists*, p. 69.

28. Ibid., p. 140.

29. Ibid., p. 127.

30. Ibid., p. 28. See also Scholem, "The Star of David," p. 271.

31. Patai, *The Jewish Alchemists*, pp. 323, 324.

32. In the poem entitled "A Valediction Forbidding Mourning," ll. 25–36.

33. See the discussion of "spherepoint" geometry in Keith Critchlow, *Order in Space* (New York: Viking Press, 1970).

34. *The Zohar*, trans. Daniel C. Matt, vol. 1, pp. 109–10, (1:15a).

35. *Baraita de Ma'aseh Bereshit*, trans. Jack Hirschman, in *The Secret Garden: An Anthology in the Kabbalah*, ed. David Meltzer (New York: Seabury Press, 1976), p. 4.

36. *The Creation according to the Midrash Rabbah*, trans. with commentary by Wilfred Shuchat (Jerusalem: Devora, 2002), vol.1, pp. 4, 15.

37. The list in 1:4 is "The Torah and the Throne of Glory. . . . The Patriarchs, Israel, the Temple, and the name of the Messiah" (pp. 15–16), while the list in 1:8 only concerns the Torah: "the Torah preceded [the creation of the world] by these six things, viz, *kedem* [the first], *me-az* [of old] (Proverbs 8:21) *me-olam* [from everlasting] (ibid. v.22), *me-rosh* [from the beginning], and *mi-kadmei* [from the earliest times], which counts as two" (p. 39). The brackets in this quote are those of Shuchat.

38. *The Zohar*, trans. Daniel C. Matt, vol. 1, p. 17 (1:3b).

39. *Baraita de Ma'aseh Bereshit*, p. 6.

40. *The Zohar*, Pritzker ed., vol. 1, p. 110 (1:15a).

41. Isaiah Tishby, *The Wisdom of the Zohar: An Anthology of Texts*, Littman Library of Jewish Civilization (Oxford: Oxford University Press, 1997), vol. 2, p. 567 (*Zohar*, 1:86b, trans. David Goldstein).

42. Ibid., vol. 2, p. 573 (*Zohar Hadash, Bereshit*, 13d, *Midrash ha-Ne'elam*, trans. David Goldstein).

43. Unless otherwise specified, the Bible quotations are given in the familiar English translation of the King James Version.

44. See Hans Jenny, *Cymatics* (Basil: Basilius Presse, 1974), vol. 2, pp. 96, 100.

45. In private correspondence, Stanley Krippner, who has done much research in shamanism, replied as follows to my query

concerning a hexagram model for the shamanic worlds: "there is abundant evidence linking the *Fire* to the top of the vertical axis and *Water* to the bottom." For additional sources, see Michael Harner, *The Way of the Shaman* (Toronto: Bantam Books, 1982), pp. 3, 13, 30, 45–46, 49–50 (associations of water with the lower world); Mircea Eliade, *Shamanism*, trans. Willard R. Trask, Bollingen Series LXXVI (Princeton: Princeton University Press, 1964), pp. 5, 205, 335, 363 (associations of fire with the upper world), pp. 266–68 (associations of mountains with the upper world), and ·p. 39 (association of water with the lower world); and Joan Halifax, *Shaman: The Wounded Healer* (New York: Crossroads/ Continuum, 1982), pp. 84, 93 (associations of mountains with the upper world).

46. See, for instance, Scholem, *Kabbalah*, p. 15, and Joseph Dan, *Jewish Mysticism*, vol. 1, *Late Antiquity* (Northvale, N.J.: Jason Aronson, 1998), p. 40.

47. In *The Kabbalah of the Soul*, my development of a theoretical model for kabbalistic cosmology that synthesizes the main traditions of cosmology deriving from the Bible, the *Zohar*, and the Lurianic school led me to discuss the conflicts between the Zoharic and Lurianic models, pp. 20–28, that is pertinent here and can support my claim that the seven stages of biblical cosmology continues to be the most authentic form of Jewish mystical cosmology.

48. *The Zohar*, trans. Daniel C. Matt, vol. 1, p. 210 (1:34a).

49. For a summary of the holographic theories of David Bohm and Karl Pribram, see *Looking Glass Universe: The Emerging Science of Wholeness*, by John Briggs and F. David Peat (New York: Simon & Schuster, 1984), pp. 109–12, 244–68.

50. See Scholem, *Kabbalah*, pp. 120–22, 336.

51. BT Rosh Hashanah 31a; trans. Maurice Simon (London: Soncino Press, 1938), p. 146.

52. BT Avodah Zarah 9a; trans. Maurice Simon (London: Soncino Press, 1948), p. 43.

53. For further treatment of the *Temunah*, see Scholem, *Origins of the Kabbalah*, ed. R. J.Zwi Werblowsky, trans. Allan Arkush (n.c.:Jewish Publication Society and Princeton University Press, 1987), pp. 460–74.

54. *Sefer Yetzirah: The Book of Creation*, ed. and trans. Aryeh Kaplan, 4:4; p. 163. Kaplan has printed his translation as though it was poetry, with short lines beginning for the most part with capitals. I have here and later restored his translation to prose, adding commas where necessary and removing the initial capitals. All of the remaining quotations of the *Sefer Yetzirah* in this section are from this edition and give chapter and verse for this text.

55. For my solution to the geometric enigma of the *Sefer Yetzirah*, see *The Secret Doctrine of the Kabbalah*, pp. 252–70. See also my other treatments of the *Sefer Yetzirah* in this book, particularly the remainder of chapter 7 on my full development of the *Sefer Yetzirah* Diagram I develop from this solution, pp. 270–94, and my earlier treatment of sacred science, pp. 87–94.

56. Here I take exception to Kaplan's translation of the phrase *shevah olamot* of 4:15, appearing as "seven universes" on p. 185 of his translation, and have substituted the more cosmologically significant translation of *olamot* as "worlds." Similarly with his translations of the *olam* appearing in 4:7–14 as "universe," I have substituted the more traditional translation of "world" when discussing these verses. I am, however, most happy to use this translation since my introduction to the Kabbalah came through the classes I attended for fifteen months in Kaplan's home on this as yet unpublished translation of the *Sefer Yetzirah*.

57. *Pirke de Rabbi Eliezar* (Jerusalem, 1990), chap. 18, p. 42.

58. See the supercommentary of Rabbi David Luria on the previously noted page of *Pirke de Rabbi Eliezar*.

59. Scholem, *Kabbalah*, p. 229.

60. From section 1.90a, trans. David Goldstein, in *The Wisdom of the Zohar*, vol. 2, p. 568.

61. *Zohar* 2:164a–165a, in *The Wisdom of the Zohar*, vol. 1, p. 349–50.

62. Scholem, "Worlds, The Four," *Encyclopaedia Judaica* (Jerusalem: Macmillan, 1971), vol. 16, p. 641.

63. For a fuller survey of the four worlds in the Kabbalah,which also finds only three such worlds in the earlier sources, see Isaiah Tishby, *The Wisdom of the Zohar*, vol. 2, pp. 555–59.

64. See Heninger, Touches of Sweet Harmony: Pythagorean Cosmology and Renaissance Poetics, p. 146f.

65. Ibid., pp. 152, 160, 168–69.

66. Scholem, *Encyclopaedia Judaica*, vol. 16, p. 642. See also Kaplan, *Sefer Yetzirah*, pp. 185, 371n.

67. *The Zohar*, trans. Daniel C. Matt, vol. 1, pp. 107–9 (1:15a).

68. Ibid., vol. 1, p. 152 (1:20a).

69. See *The Secret Doctrine of the Kabbalah*, pp. 74–113, for my full treatment of the modes and meaning of sacred science, including further analysis of the *Sefer Yetzirah*.

70. "Fragments of Philolaus," Diels-Krans, 1, in *The Pythagorean Sourcebook and Library*, comp. and trans. by Kenneth Sylvan Guthrie (Grand Rapids, Mich.: Phanes Press, 1987), pp. 168, 171, 174.

71. Vital, *The Tree of Life*, p. 24.

72. In Lurianic cosmology the central point just functions to mark a location for the subsequent processes of Tzimtzum that define a finite space; though we here see that it also is composed of light. But, for Luria, the creative force of light enters the *tehiru* from the surrounding light circumscribing this cosmic space and descends in ever more material form to the center. For a fuller discussion of the conflicts between Zoharic and Lurianic cosmology, see my book *The Kabbalah of the Soul*, pp. 20–28, as well as its whole first chapter. Where the present treatment differs from this earlier synthesis is in recognizing that Lurianic cosmology also attributes light to the central point and in attempting to develop its synthesis between the Lurianic Tzimtzum and the earlier cosmology of the *Zohar* by placing the Zoharic expansion from a central point within the primary context of Lurianic theory.

73. Lawrence M. Krauss "Cosmological Antigravity," *Understanding Cosmology*, (New York: Warner Books, 2002), pp. 90, 91.

74. Mario Livio, *The Accelerating Universe: Infinite Expansion, the Cosmological Constant, and the Beauty of the Cosmos* (New York: John Wiley & Sons, 2000), p. 165. This passage was italicized in the original.

75. See chapter 10 of *The Secret Doctrine of the Kabbalah* for a full comparison of quantum and Lurianic cosmologies.

76. Livio, *The Accelerating Universe*, p. 166. This passage was italicized in the original.

CHAPTER 2

1. For my full analysis, with translation, of the Cordovero text on the Tree of Life Diagram, see *The Secret Doctrine of the Kabbalah*, pp. 13–20.

2. See Scholem, *Kabbalah*, pp. 420–28.

3. See Joseph Leon Blau, *The Christian Interpretation of the Cabala in the Renaissance* (1944; reprint, Port Washington, N. Y.: Kennikat Press, 1965); Frances A. Yates, *The Occult Philosophy in the Elizabethan Age* (London: Routledge & Kegan Paul, 1979); Philip Beitchman, *Alchemy of the Word: Cabala of the Renaissance* (Albany: State University of New York Press, 1998); and Scholem, *Kabbalah*, pp. 96–201.

4. Milton's lines are as follows: "Boundless the Deep, because I am who fill / Infinitude, nor vacuous the space, / Though I uncircumscrib'd myself retire, / And put not forth my goodness" (*Paradise Lost*, 8.168–71).

5. See, for instance, Aryeh Kaplan, commentary and translation, *The Bahir* (New York: Samuel Weiser, 1979), p. 155. But Kaplan does attribute this diagram to Luria in his edition of the *Sefer Yetzirah*, p. 29.

6. See above, chapter 1, note 3, for the implications I have elsewhere drawn of the remarkable effect of rotating the Tree of Life Diagram six times around this Da'at point.

7. I am using this term, as I have in my previous books, as the handiest signifier for that cosmic catastrophe mythologically explained by the disobedience of Adam. For even in the Genesis story, this disobedience was represented as having lasting consequences for the progeny of Adam. Though the Jewish tradition has rejected the Christian understanding of the Fall as entailing the doctrine of Original Sin, it shares with it the understanding that Adam's disobedience had, in the words of Milton, "Brought death into this world, and all our woe, / With loss of Eden" (*Paradise Lost*, 1.3–4). But in the later Jewish esoteric tradition known as the Kabbalah, whether that of Isaac Luria, in Chayyim Vital's *Pri Eitz Chayyim*, or the *Sefer ha-Temunah*, Eden is either placed in the prior cosmic world of Yetzirah or in the prior Shemitah of Chesed, respectively. The loss of Eden may be understood, therefore, to result in something like a "Fall." The Hebrew word used in this context is *yerida*, generally translated as "descent." Since in the Kabbalah Yetzirah, the locus of Eden, is regarded as a "higher" world than Asiyah, the world of solids we inhabit, the Adamic transgression thus was understood to lead to a cosmic "descent" or "fall." I should also point out that the leading scholar of the Kabbalah, Gershom Scholem has used the term "Fall" without explanation in *On the Kabbalah and Its Symbolism* (New York: Schocken Books,

1965), pp. 71–2, 115, and in *The Messianic Idea in Judaism* (New York: Schocken Books, 1978), pp. 23, 174; and it appears as an item in *The Encyclopedia of the Jewish Religion*, ed. R. J. Zwi Werblowsky and Geoffrey Wigoder (New York: Holt, Rinehart and Winston), p. 141.

8. In the *Timaeus* (35B–36B), Plato elevated the diatonic scale into a cosmic principle, one explaining the creation of the world soul. In his curious derivation of this scale, Plato begins by taking the multiples of even and odd deriving from unity: 1, 2, 4, 8 and 1, 3, 9, 27. It should be pointed out in passing that Plato identified the odd numbers with the concept of the Limited and the even numbers with the concept of the Unlimited on musical grounds, namely, that each odd number defines a new harmonic while the even numbers adumbrate the octaves of each harmonic pitch to infinity. To return to Plato's cosmological definition of the diatonic scale, he then arranges the sequences of even and odd numbers into a single series: 1, 2, 3, 4, 8, 9, 27. With the exception of 27, these numbers give him the harmonic intervals needed to construct the diatonic scale. As further shown in note 10 to chapter 1 above, 2:1 is the interval of the octave (Do_1-Do_2), 3:2 the interval of the perfect fifth (Do_2-Sol_1), 4:3 the interval of the perfect fourth (Sol_1-Do_3), and 9:8 the interval of the whole tone (Do_3-Re_1). Taking the latter three intervals and interjecting them within the octave gives him the following elements of the musical scale: Do-Fa (the fourth, also Platonically identified with the harmonic mean), Do-Sol (the fifth, also Platonically identified with the arithmetic mean), and Fa-Sol (the whole tone between the two fourths Do-Fa, Sol-Do). How the two tetrachords whose extremes are defined by these fourths are further subdivided determines the differences among the Greek modes. Among these arbitrary possibilities, the Pythagorean-Platonic choice is the diatonic or two-tone possibility, which divides each of these fourths by two whole tones plus a remainder, the "*leimma*" with a numerical proportion of $243/256$ (the difference of 13 between these numbers being one reason for the esoteric significance ascribed to the number 13), this remainder approximating the semitone. The first fourth from Do-Fa is thus filled in by the whole tone Do-Re, the whole tone Re-Mi, and the semitone Mi-Fa, the second fourth from Sol-Do being similarly filled in by the whole tone Sol-La, the whole tone La-Ti, and the semitone Ti-Do, the two tetrachords being separated by the whole tone Fa-Sol. My earlier different discussion of the derivation of the Pythagorean diatonic scale in *The Kabbalah of the Soul*, pp. 48–51, also provides an illuminating comparison of the diatonic and the twelve-tone chromatic scales, for which see the next note.

9. See *The Kabbalah of the Soul*, pp. 46–51, for my relation of the diatonic and chromatic scales that can explain the dominance of the first half of the tones in the first two correlated cosmic worlds (signified by Do and Re), the equality of the two half tones of the third world (signified by Mi and Fa), and the dominance of the second half of the tones in the fourth to sixth such worlds (signified by Sol, La, and Ti).

10. *The Zohar*, trans. Daniel C. Matt, vol. 1, pp. 20–21 (1:5a).

11. See Michell, *City of Revelation*, pp. 23, 25.

12. Thorleif Boman, *Hebrew Thought Compared With Greek* (Philadelphia: The Westminster Press, 1960), pp. 200, 201, 202, 204, 205.

13. Elliot R. Wolfson, Through a Speculum That Shines: Vision and Imagination in Medieval Jewish Mysticism (Princeton: Princeton University Press, 1994), p. 5n.

14. E. D. Hirsch, Jr., *Validity in Interpretation* (New Haven: Yale University Press, 1967), pp. 170, 204, 205.

15. Max Black, *Models and Metaphors: Studies in Language and Philosophy* (Ithaca, N.Y.: Cornell University Press, 1962), pp. 219, 238.

16. Ibid., pp. 222, 229.

17. As the Sabbath Star Diagram is such an analogue model, so is the simpler imaginative cosmic model I developed at length in chapter 1 of *The Kabbalah of the Soul* such an "invented" theoretical model. See also note 43 to chapter 1 above.

18. Black, *Models and Metaphors*, pp. 233, 237.

19. Ibid., p. 238.

20. Susan A. Handelman, *The Slayers of Moses: The Emergence of Rabbinic Interpretation in Modern Literary Theory* (Albany: State University of New York Press, 1982), p. 56. In an important analysis, the methods used in the Talmud to interpret the meaning of biblical law and proof texts are also shown by her to differ from the deductive modes of Greek logic precisely in that they follow a logic of their own that seems to parallel the associative processes of metaphorical thought intrinsic to language.

21. For a full treatment of this understanding of sacred science, see chapter 3 of *The Secret Doctrine of the Kabbalah*. See also note 10 to chapter 1 above and appendix D.

22. In *Sefer Yetzirah* ed. and trans. Aryeh Kaplan (York Beach, Maine: Samuel Weiser, 1990), p. 261 (1:5), a five-dimensional cosmos, which adds the dimensions of time and morality to the three dimensions of space, is defined in the following terms: "a depth of beginning, a depth of end; a depth of good, a depth of evil; a depth above, a depth below; a depth east, a depth west; a depth north, a depth south."

23. *Shiur Qoma*, trans. The Work of the Chariot, in *The Secret Garden*, ed. David Meltzer (New York: Seabury Press, 1976), p. 34.

24. James Gleick's book *Chaos: Making a New Science* (New York: Penguin Books, 1987), can clarify the way in which the whole system generated by the Sabbath Star Diagram may be viewed as an example of the new science of chaos. The distinction between the finished elements within the matrix border of a diagram expansion and the unfinished elements beyond it corresponds to an important concern of chaos theorists, appearing in "the patterns that people like Robert May and James Yorke discovered in the early 1970s, with their complex boundaries between orderly and chaotic behavior" (p. 114), and Mitchell Feigenbaum's belief that "his theory expressed a natural law about systems at the point of transition between orderly and turbulent" (p. 180). But both chaos theory and the Sabbath Star Diagram are more adequately defined in terms of the laws of complexity they demonstrate: "Physicist or biologist or mathematician, they believed that simple, deterministic systems could breed complexity; that systems too complex for traditional mathematics could yet obey simple laws; and that, whatever their particular field, their task was to understand complexity itself" (p. 307). The special feature of such complex dynamics is well expressed by Doyne Farmer: "The system is deterministic, but you can't say what it's going to do next" (p. 251). For the Sabbath Star Diagram this is particularly true of the relationship of construction to matrix elements. The progression of the former, from one degree of diagram expansion to the next, is absolutely regular. As will be shown in chapter 6, the rate of increase of such elements can be predicted on the basis of a numerical formula, and the overall outer form of each diagram expansion will be identical with that of the smaller form on which it is built. In Gleick's words, it will show "self-similarity . . . symmetry across scale" (p. 103), this being a characteristic of such geometric expansion as is classically considered "gnomonic," a characteristic of the Sabbath Star Diagram. But the matrices produced as a byproduct of such construction, at least in the earlier worlds of the diagram, are not predictable with respect to the shapes of their matrix borders. In chaos theory as in the progressive expansion of the Sabbath Star Diagram, "the first discoveries were realizations that each change of scale brought new phenomena and new kinds of behavior" (p. 115).

Not only is such scaling a feature of this diagram, each expansion involving a geometric increase in size, but also the concept of dimension with which each expansion is symbolically related. Though this two-dimensional diagram cannot, of course, manifest these dimensions geometrically, the correlation of expansion with dimension made throughout this study may, perhaps, be related to Benoit Mandelbrot's concept of "fractals," fractional dimensions, since each expansional "dimension" is fractioned into various intermediate levels of construction. In his fractal geometry, Mandelbrot also uses the hexagram importantly, especially in the snowflake form known as the "Koch curve." But I would take issue with Mandelbrot's rejection of the power of classical geometric forms to model complexity: "They represent a powerful abstraction of reality. . . . But for understanding complexity they turn out to be the wrong kind of abstraction" (p. 94). As the Sabbath Star Diagram will show, the classical shape of the equilateral triangle *can* provide a geometry able to model archetypal complexity.

But perhaps this is, after all, a new use of geometry, an experimental form yielding much the same results as those variously developed by Edward Lorenz in terms of hardware and Feigenbaum and others in terms of the software of computer graphics. The endeavor of chaos theorists "to create miniature universes and observe their evolution" (p. 178) is what I have also been able to achieve through exploration of the laws and possibilities of this one geometric construction. Like such theorists, who "could change this feature or that and observe the changed paths that would result" (p. 178), I also have not only explored the modes of construction permitted by the discoverable laws of this diagram but such forbidden modes as are allowed by the trivalent logic of its geometry, similarly observing "that any changes in certain features could lead to remarkable changes in overall behavior" (p. 178). The freedom to follow forbidden modes of construction is one of three forms of freedom manifested in the diagram, the others being the microstructural potential for free spin in the matrix and the ability to transgress the matrix border. This joint emergence of freedom and constraint in the Sabbath Star Diagram shows that its geometry can resolve the philosophical conflict between freedom and determinism in the same way that Farmer recognized it could be resolved by dynamic systems: "On a philosophical level, it struck me as an operational way to define free will, in a way that allowed you to reconcile free will with determinism" (p. 251).

Whether the Sabbath Star Diagram is one of the "systems too complex for traditional mathematics" or can be given the kind of numerical or algebraic formulation more acceptable to modern mathematics and science, I leave to others to determine. But perhaps such formulation is not necessary to demonstrate the scientific significance of this diagram. For geometry has its own truths to teach. In chaos theory, as in general perception, "if you can visualize the shape, you can understand the system. . . . shapes carry meaning" (pp. 47, 94). Indeed, as the chaos experimenter Albert Libchaber said: "what I'm interested in is the evolution of shape in space" (p. 19). And I too can say that what has interested me has been exploring the evolution of the shape of the Sabbath Star Diagram, convinced that this complex evolving form carried meaning of the most universal nature. If the claim of chaos theory is true, that "the laws of complexity hold universally, caring not at all for the details of a system's constituent atoms" (p. 304), then the Sabbath Star Diagram may well be the most archetypal model for such universal laws, containing no less than the code for all aspects of cosmic evolution. It may be enough, therefore, simply to have discovered and described the laws governing the self-generation of this diagram and to let the form of its geometry speak for itself.

Gleick characterizes dynamic systems as generating "complexity: richly organized patterns, sometimes stable and sometimes unstable, sometimes finite and sometimes infinite, but always with the fascination of living things" (p. 43). He further claims: "In our world, complexity flourishes, and those looking to science for a general understanding of nature's habits will be better served by the laws of chaos" (p. 308). It is just such cosmological implications of the Sabbath Star Diagram that I have been concerned to elucidate through the methodology I have called the Science of Expressive Form. But though Gleick seems to equate the laws of chaos with those of complexity, as we proceed with exploration of the Sabbath Star Diagram we shall see that such chaotic features of the diagram as we have just been

considering are properly a feature of the more primitive levels of this geometric system and that as it evolves to greater complexity it also gains in regularity. The way the Sabbath Star Diagram, and the still larger numerical system to which it evolves, can provide a new model for complexity theory that seems more consonant with the nature of the cosmos, one in which chaos is present but contained and the growth is towards increasing but never completely predictable regularity, will be the subject of the final chapter of this work, its fully developed Sabbath Star System offering a new model for this theory.

25. See *The Kabbalah of the Soul* for a fuller expansion of this model of "The Transformative Moment" in its second and fourth chapters, in which latter it is understood to be a moment of Neshamah consciousness.

26. Arthur E. Green, "The Role of Jewish Mysticism in a Contemporary Theology of Judaism," *Shefa Quarterly: A Journal of Jewish Thought and Study* 1 (September 1978): 40. Green has reiterated this hope in a more recent review in *The New York Times Book Review* (30 October 1988), pp. 32–33.

27. Yosef Hayim Yerushalmi, *Zakhor: Jewish History and Jewish Memory* (Seattle: Washington University Press, 1982), pp. 98, 99.

CHAPTER 3

1. Plato, *Timaeus*, p. 28 (27c–29d).

2. See *The Kabbalah of the Soul*, pp. 84–86, 342–44n.

3. As shown in chapter 8, there is an interfacing level of microtriangles, with only one line of symmetry expressed, in the matrix. For my application of this interfaced triangle matrix to the modeling of quantum physics, see chapter 9 of *The Secret Doctrine of the Kabbalah*.

4. See chapter 2, note 8, above.

5. John Anthony West, *Serpent in the Sky: The High Wisdom of Ancient Egypt* (New York: Harper & Row, 1979), p. 127. See also R. A. Schwaller de Lubicz, *Le Temple de L'Homme* (Paris: Caractères, 1957), vol. 1, pp. 221–22.

6. See *The Kabbalah of the Soul*, pp. 116–21, 202–13, and chapter 2, note 25, above.

7. For a comparison of the experimental geometry involved in the self-generated Sabbath Star Diagram and the new science of chaos, see the long note 24 to chapter 2, above.

8. Modern systems of trivalent logic have developed in response to the supposed proof of the limitations of logical analysis provided by Kurt Gödel's Incompleteness Theorems, a proof that Bertrand Russell has disallowed on the grounds that it violates the necessary hierarchy of classes, which excludes the possibility that a class can be a member of itself or be self-referential, as in the paradoxical statement of the Cretan Epimenides: "All Cretans are liars." But the fact that Epimenides, Gödel, and Russell are capable of making such logic-defying self-referential statements has been thought to have a further consequence on the axiomatic structure of logical theory, as Michael Guillen has shown in *Bridges to Infinity* (Los Angeles: Jeremy P. Tarcher, 1983),

p. 18: "Gödel's results stimulated the invention of non-Aristotelian logical systems, according to which a statement can be something other than true or false. The simplest of these is a so-called trivalent logical system, in which a statement can be either true, false, or merely possible. Such a system is based on a disregard for Aristotle's law of the excluded middle (that is, something is either true or false: there is no third possibility), and because it allows for the possibility that a theorem might be logically uncertain, it is consistent with Gödel's findings." But for Gödel's proof to stand despite the fact that it collapses the prime cosmic distinction between wholes and parts, classes and members, it must enlist the support of a restructured logic that can validate all that is merely possible regardless of how "illogical" such results may be. Thus the fact that Gödel can play tricks with logic is not taken to disqualify his tricks but the laws of logic that would restrain him from making them, laws that give to reason its power of logical deduction. But that the law of the excluded middle must stand despite the contrary fact that possibilities do exist that defy the simpler distinction between true and false can be demonstrated by the laws of construction inherent in the Sabbath Star Diagram, laws whose two overlapping categories make it possible to integrate Aristotelian and trivalent logical systems. Given the mazelike condition of the fourth world shortly to be discussed, it is understandable that Gödel and others should have mistaken the higher level rules that govern the functioning of our dimension by looking for these rules at a level at which they are not disclosed. See also Douglas R. Hofstadter, *Gödel, Escher, Bach* (New York: Vintage Books, 1980), pp. 17–23. For further elucidation of Russell's solution to the problem of classes, see especially A. J. Ayer, *Philosophy in the Twentieth Century* (New York: Vintage Books, 1984), pp. 22–31. For further understanding of Gödel, see also Rudy Rucker, *Infinity and the Mind* (Toronto: Bantam Books, 1983), pp. 169–84, 289–317. See also chapter 15, note 11.

CHAPTER 4

1. See Hans Jenny, *Cymatics*, vol. 2, pp. 95–131.
2. Scholem, *Kabbalah*, pp. 158–59.
3. *The Zohar*, vol. 1, pp. 83–84 (19b–20a).
4. Quoted in Scholem, *Kabbalah*, 159.
5. In *The Kabbalah of the Soul*, pp. 75–77, I applied this de Leon quote to the Yetziric stage of Tzelem formation, but it can be more precisely correlated with this Fa/Fi stage. There is some overlapping with chapter 2 of the aforesaid book and the present chapter, particularly on the Yetziric Tzelem and the final stage of man.
6. The traditional Jewish understanding of astrology is based on the distinction between the impermanent and permanent angels, the former of whom are thought to have been created on the second day to perform specific missions and the latter to have been created on the fifth day, after the fourth-day creation of the stars, and to be figuratively represented in the Genesis account by the birds. It is these permanent, named angels who are thought to ensoul the stars, its matter enabling them to retain their identity through time and through the stars to direct the workings of Providence. This traditional understanding is variously represented in such Midrashic sources as Bereshit Rabbah 1:3, 3:8, 50:2, 78:4, and Shemot Rabbah 15:22, 48:2, as well as in Maimonides, Bachya, and Abarbanel. Such references were compiled by Aryeh Kaplan and appear in his edition with commentary of the *Sefer Yetzirah*, pp. 169–74.
7. See Rabbi Moses C. Luzzatto, *General Principles of the Kabbalah*, trans. The Research Centre of Kabbalah (New York: Samuel Weiser, 1970), pp. 218–19.
8. Since the progression of the analysis in this section has made the subject of astrology unavoidable, I cannot close this discussion without addressing some of the questions regarding it. Whether or not the kabbalistic and general older esoteric understanding of the stars and planets as ensouled by conscious entities be allowed, it seems clear that these physical celestial bodies do influence conditions on the earth, as is the case of the moon's effects on the tides. Now, if the weights, periods, and angular aspects of the planets can affect the impressionable waters not only of the seas but also of the atmosphere and underground streams, then they certainly must have an effect upon the largely water bodies of which we boast. If the motion of the sea can seem to us stormy or placid, then these same gravitational effects upon our liquid contents will be translated to our symbolic consciousness as similar emotional moods. Since we inhabit a vibrational cosmos of resonating frequencies, our own 70-megahertz frequency will resonate most particularly to this frequency and all its overtones, and it will thus respond either to its harmony or dissonance with the frequencies with which it is constantly bombarded by the interactions of the celestial bodies.

But the final validation of modern astrology is geometric, for its interpretations are made largely on the basis of the angles of aspecting planets and their positions on a twelve-slice pie defining either the earthly rotation around the sun in terms of monthly "signs" or its daily rotation in terms of di-hourly "houses," and all in terms of precise mathematical computations having nothing to do with the actual constellations. If this study has accomplished nothing else, I hope it will at least have shown that geometric relationships have resonances that work mythologically on our symbolizing consciousness with positive and negative associations. The two main principles of aspect interpretation involve just such interpretations of angles, that the 120° "trine" and 60° "sextile" aspects signify harmony, and the 180° "opposition" and 90° "square" aspects signify tension. Most harmonious are the two grand trines of Fire and Air or Water and Earth that together produce the hexagram, the symbol of balance that is the basis of this whole study. That the equilateral triangle should signify harmony and the dualistic crossing of perpendiculars tension are associations we shall see to follow from the very nature of these forms.

I suggest that our deep-brain structures perceive the triangle as harmonious and the perpendicular crossing as tense because they inherently are so. The base of a triangle provides a stability that neither a perpendicular upright possesses nor a square without its triangular diagonals. There are characteristics inherent in the nature of number and geometric forms that are not arbitrary or man-made. The former can be easily demonstrated by a Rudolph Steiner kindergarten teaching device. If one takes a single ball, say a Ping-Pong ball, one can see that it is unlimited in the direction in which it can roll. If two Ping-Pong balls, each held in one hand and touching, are rolled together, their relationship will be smooth if they are rolled in complementary opposite directions but produce friction if they are rolled in the same direction. If three Ping-Pong balls are held in one hand are rolled together by the other, they can only be smoothly rolled in an inward direction to the center, that is, involved, or in an outward direction, that is, evolved. Four Ping-Pong balls, similarly placed together and manipulated as with three, cannot roll. Anyone who takes four Ping-Pong balls and does this experiment will never again doubt that numbers define inherent functions, and that geometry is, in the words of Wordsworth, "an independent world created out of pure intelligence."

Now, if the angles of an equilateral triangle are inherently harmonious while right angles inherently contain stress, then these qualities will inform all dimensions in which they participate. Thus harmoniously aspected planets will affect impressionable water surfaces in ways that produce states of physical harmony, and if these water surfaces are in sensitive, conscious structures like man, then in addition to states of physical harmony, the psyche will experience states of enhanced emotional, mental, and even spiritual harmony, depending on its development. In the opposite case, the psyche will resonate to the tension in squarely aspected planets. Thus the geometric relationships among the celestial bodies will produce temporal shifts in the cosmos of what can be called archetypal "moods" that will make one impression on minerals, another on vegetables, another on animals, and the most complex impression on man.

9. Steven Weinberg, *The First Three Minutes: A Modern View of the Origin of the Universe* (New York: Basic Books, 1977), p. 76.

10. For my synthesis of quantum cosmology with the cosmology of Isaac Luria, see chapter 10 of *The Secret Doctrine of the Kabbalah.*

11. For an application of the matrix to a similar distinction between the macroscopic and microscopic levels of matter, see appendix A.

12. The sources of the last two translations are as follows: Rabbi Aryeh Kaplan, *The Living Torah: A New Translation Based on Traditional Jewish Sources* (New York: Moznaim, 1981); and Rabbi J. H. Hertz, ed., *The Pentateuch and Haftorahs*, 2nd ed. (London: Soncino Press, 1972).

13. For further discussion of the correlation of the Do-Fi or tritone interval with the √2, see Ernest G. McClain, *The Myth of Invariance: The Origin of the Gods, Mathematics and Music from the Rg Veda to Plato* (New York: Nicolas Hays, 1976), pp. 40, 99, 117, 210.

14. I am indebted for this discussion of √2 to Robert Lawlor, *Sacred Geometry* (New York: Crossroad, 1982), pp. 28–31.

15. Dorothy Maclean, *To Hear the Angels Sing* (Elgin, Ill.: Lorian Press, 1980), p. 67.

16. *King Lear*, 5.2.11.

17. For this understanding of the hypothalamic function, see Robert Lawlor, "Ancient Temple Architecture," *Lindisfarne Letter 10: Geometry and Architecture* (Stockbridge, Mass.: Lindisfarne Press, 1980), pp. 94–98.

18. Moshe Chaim Luzzatto, *Derech haShem: The Way of God*, trans. Aryeh Kaplan, 2nd ed. (New York: Feldheim, 1978), pp. 37–41.

19. Ibid., 81.

20. For this double etymology of Israel, see the notes in Hertz, *Pentateuch*, p. 124, and Kaplan, *Living Torah*, p. 88.

21. R. A. Schwaller de Lubicz, *The Temple in Man: The Secrets of Ancient Egypt*, trans. Robert and Deborah Lawlor (Brookline, Mass.: Autumn Press, 1977), p. 49.

22. Ibid., pp. 51–53.

23. Julian Jaynes, The Origin of Consciousness in the Breakdown of the Bicameral Mind (Boston: Houghton Mifflin 1976), p. 84.

24. Ibid., pp. 104–6.

25. Ibid., pp. 184, 190–91, 297–98.

26. An article by Erica Goode, "Experts See Mind's Voices In New Light," *New York Times*, (6 May 2003), F1, 6, highlights the work of Dr. Ralph Hoffman, a psychiatrist at Yale: "Dr. Hoffman's group . . . found heightened activity in Broca's area, a region of the frontal lobe involved with speech perception and processing. . . . . In Schizophrenia, he [Dr. Hoffman] suggests, a loss of gray matter may intensify the link between Broca's area, involved in speech production, and Wernicke's area, responsible for speech perception. . . . the signals coming from Broca's may then become more salient, bombarding Wernicke's area with internally generated words and phrases that are in some way interpreted by Wernicke's as external speech" (F6).

27. Jaynes, The Origin of Consciousness, pp. 98–99.

28. Schwaller de Lubicz, *The Temple in Man*, p. 51.

29. See Scholem, *Kabbalah*, p. 156, which states that immortality is the reward only of the righteous: "The wicked, on the other hand, are cast aside and annihilated. . . ." See also Luzzatto, *Derech haShem*, pp. 97–99,

30. See P. D. Ouspensky, *In Search of the Miraculous* (New York: Harcourt Brace Jovanovich, 1949), pp. 31–33; and *The Secret of the Golden Flower*, trans. Richard Wilhelm with an intro. by Carl Jung (New York: Harcourt Brace Jovanovich, 1962), p. 31f.

31. The question of immortality is, of course, a much debated subject, and the Kabbalah does not offer any definitive answers. But if we entertain the Zoharic suggestion (see note 29 to this chapter above) as to the immortality exclusively associated with the Neshamah soul—it being generally considered that the Nefesh soul confers no permanent

immortality but maintains only a brief, ghostlike existence around the grave before dissipating and returning to the earth—what then is the destiny of the personally acquired Ruach soul? Here another kabbalistic doctrine is helpful, the doctrine of Gilgul or reincarnation. It may be the Ruach soul that undergoes reincarnation and that what is meant by the immortality of the Neshamah soul is that only its full development can maintain a permanent identity and overcome the cycle of Gilgulim.

32. Aristotle, "Metaphysics," *The Basic Works of Aristotle*, ed. and trans. Richard McKeon (New York: Random House, 1941), p. 693.

33. These are the closing lines of *A Defense of Poetry* by Percy Bysshe Shelley.

34. Pierre Teilhard de Chardin, *The Future of Man*, trans. Norman Denny (New York: Harper & Row, 1969), pp. 127, 245.

35. For a further understanding of such a concept of time as embodying something like the geometric concept of the "gnomon," of self-similar growth, see Robert Lawlor, "Ancient Temple Architecture," *Lindisfarne Letter 10*, pp. 62–63, and *The Kabbalah of the Soul*, pp. 126–27.

CHAPTER 5

1. See appendix B for a fuller treatment of this redefinition of the systems hierarchy.

2. Chayyim Vital, *The Tree of Life: The Palace of Adam Kadmon*, ed. and trans. Donald Wilder Menzi and Zwe Padeh (Northvale, N.J.: Jason Aronson, 1999), p. 32.

3. The larger cosmic structure provided by the model here being developed of the seven expansions of the Sabbath Star Diagram was given a simplified version in the first chapter of *The Kabbalah of the Soul*, an analysis that specifically addresses this conflict between the future orientation of Luria's thought and the limitations of his four-worlds model. The third chapter of *The Kabbalah of the Soul* also contains much of the material, divorced from the Sabbath Star Diagram and given a simpler modeling, that appears in the present chapter.

4. Kaplan, ed. and trans., *Sefer Yetzirah*, p. 261 (1:5).

5. C. G. Jung, foreword to *The I Ching*, trans. Richard Wilhelm and Cary F. Baynes, Bollingen Series XIX (Princeton: Princeton University Press, 1978), p. xxiv.

6. For my fuller development of the concept of the geometric dimensions as the dimensions of time, see *The Secret Doctrine of the Kabbalah*, pp. 390–95.

7. I have inserted the word *shofar* in brackets within this and other passages of the King James translation of the Bible whenever the Hebrew text specifies it.

8. But see the different gender definitions of these two axes in chapter 6 and appendix D.

9. Joseph Klausner, *The Messianic Idea in Israel*, trans. W. F. Stinespring (New York: Macmillan, 1955), pp. 384–85.

10. Ibid., p. 418.

11. Ibid., pp. 401, 497.

12. Ibid., pp. 470–71.

13. Ibid., pp. 504–5, 512.

14. Ibid., pp. 455–56, 498.

15. Ibid., p. 278.

16. Ibid., p. 238.

17. Ibid.

18. As Gershom Scholem has shown, in *Kabbalah*, p. 335, the millennium was understood to involve a slowing of time: "The messianic age will last approximately a thousand years, but many believed that these years would not be identical with human years, for the planets and the stars would move more slowly, so that time would be prolonged (this view was particular [*sic*] current in the circle of the *Sefer Ha-Temunah*, and it has origins in the Apocryphal books). It is obvious, on the basis of these theories, that the kabbalists believed that the natural order would change in the messianic era. . . ."

19. Moshe Idel, in *Messianic Mystics* (New Haven: Yale University Press, 1998), has shown "the deep bonds that exist between certain forms of messianism and messianic personalities and certain kinds of mystical experiences" (pp. 1–2), particularly in the case of Abulafia and the Hasidim, but he has not shown the mystical testimonies he has discussed to have defined the individual path to spiritual redemption in terms of the traditional stages of the Messianic Age, as I am now to do. I also wish to note his important treatment of the constellation of Enochian topics, involving Metatron, the son of man, and the Messiah, in his treatment of Abulafia in this book (pp. 85–94), evidence that strongly supports what I have called "the secret doctrine of the son." Where Idel finds this mystical internalization primarily in Abulafia and the hasidic Tzaddikim, Yehuda Liebes does the same for the *Zohar* in "The Messiah of the Zohar: on R. Simeon bar Yohai as a Messianic Figure," trans. Arnold Schwartz, in *Studies in the Zohar* (Albany: State University of New York Press, 1993). Liebes does connect this process with the recognized stages of the Messianic Age but only with that stage I have defined as its second stage: "The notion that it is the task of R. Simeon and his circle to uphold the world through the evil times that precede the coming of the Messiah—the period of the 'birth pangs of the Messiah'—is only one step away from the idea that his generation must take measures to induce the Messiah's coming" (p. 11). In his final assessment—"R. Simeon of the *Zohar* is a messianic figure who embodies the fate of the entire cosmos, its flaw, and its redemption" (p. 73)—he shows this central Zoharic figure to contain the same history that Luria will attribute to the Partzuf of the son, Ze'ir Anpin.

20. For my fuller treatment of such a master of power, see *The Kabbalah of the Soul*, pp. 263–72.

CHAPTER 6

1. See Robert Lawlor, *Sacred Geometry* (New York: Crossroad, 1982), pp. 57–59.

2. Theon of Smyrna, *Mathematics Useful for Understanding Plato*, trans. Robert and Deborah Lawlor (San Diego: Wizards Bookshelf, 1979), p. 13.

3. Yakof Koppel, *Sha'arei Gan Eden* (Jerusalem: Yeshiva Torat Chayyim, 1977), p. 38. Hebrew edition.

4. Dorion Sagan, "Gender Specifics: Why Women Aren't Men," *New York Times* (21 June 1998), sec. 15, p. 20.

5. Quoted in *Feminism: The Essential Historical Writings*, ed. Miriam Schneir (New York: Vintage Books, 1972), p. 4.

6. See appendix D for a full application of the gender identifications of these diagram worlds to a new gender modeling of human history. This application, like those in appendix B of the sixth-world matrix to the modeling of human society and in appendix C of the fourth- to sixth-world matrices to the three levels of linguistics, demonstrates that the Sabbath Star Diagram provides a universal model for hierarchically ordered systems.

7. The concept of the cosmic son will become the central message of the seventh world of the Sabbath Star Diagram, as variously developed in chapters 7, 12, and 13. It was these original analyses that led to the source study of this concept in the Jewish mystical tradition that appeared earlier as chapter 2 of *The Secret Doctrine of the Kabbalah,* the concept that informs the whole of that book as it shows it to inform the whole of the Jewish mystical tradition.

8. See Scholem, *Kabbalah*, p. 114.

9. Chayyim Vital, *Eitz Chayyim* (Jerusalam: Kitvei Rabbenu ha-Ari, 1958), Hebrew edition, vol. 1, chap. 4, p. 8..

10. Thomas Middleton and William Rowley, *The Changeling*, 5.3.168–72.

11. William Shakespeare, *King Lear*, 4.6.132–33.

12. John Milton, "L'Allegro," ll. 140–44.

13. See chapter 4 of *The Kabbalah of the Soul* devoted to such an interpretation of Neshamah consciousness as exemplifying that Transformative Moment developed in chapter 3.

14. See the chapter on power animals in Michael Harner, *The Way of the Shaman.*

15. See *Renewing the Covenant*, pp. 229–30 on Jacob's animal magic in association with what is there demonstrated to have been the biblical power word "Vehayah," normally translated "And it shall come to pass."

16. Francis A. Yates, The Occult Philosophy in the Elizabethan Age, pp. 20–21.

17. Vital, *Eitz Chayyim*, vol. 1, chap. 2, p. 5.

18. Ibid., chap.1; 1.3.

19. See *The Kabbalah of the Soul*, pp. 241–50, for a fuller discussion of sex as a spiritual path to divine knowledge, and pp. 251–63 of that book for a similar discussion of love as such a path.

CHAPTER 7

1. For my fuller treatment of the feminine correlation with the number 13, particularly in terms of the geometric proportion 13:26::26:52, all the numbers of which have significant Gematria meanings in the Kabbalah, see *The Secret Doctrine of the Kabbalah*, pp. 117–29.

2. *The Zohar*, ed. and trans. Daniel C. Matt, vol. 1, pp. 1–2 (1:1a).

3. *Sefer ha-'Iyyun*, trans. Ronald C. Kiener, in *The Early Kabbalah*, ed. Joseph Dan (New York: Paulist Press, 1986), p. 46.

4. Hertz, ed. and trans., *The Pentateuch and Haftorahs*, p. 364.

5. Scholem, *Kabbalah*, pp. 16–17.

6. Ibid., p. 100.

7. *Sefer ha-'Iyyun*, in Dan, *The Early Kabbalah*, p. 47.

8. See Scholem, *Kabbalah*, pp. 47–48.

9. "The Greater Holy Assembly" [*Idra Rabba*], in *The Kabbalah Unveiled*, trans. S. L. MacGregor Mathers (London: Kegan Paul, Trench, Trubner & Co., 1926), p. 147 passim.

10. Scholem, *Kabbalah*, pp. 137, 140, 142–43.

11. Joel Rosenberg, contributor, *The Jewish Almanac*, ed. Richard Siegel and Carl Rheins (New York: Bantam Books, 1980), pp. 523–25.

12. *The Zohar*, ed. and trans. Daniel C. Matt, vol. 1, p. 3 (1:1a).

13. *Explanation of the Four-Lettered Name*, in Dan, *The Early Kabbalah*, p. 55.

14. Ibid.

15. For further consideration of "The Name of Forty-Two Letters," particularly with respect to prayer, see my book *Renewing the Covenant*, pp. 58–62, 168–69.

16. See the full explication of Cantor's "transfinite cardinals" in Rudy Rucker, *Infinity and the Mind*, pp. 238–86.

17. Aryeh Kaplan, trans., in *Meditation and the Bible* (New York: Samuel Weiser, 1978), pp. 44–45.

18. See quote at note 17 in chapter 6.

19. But Wolfson shows in *Through a Speculum That Shines*, p. 99, that in a tradition going back to "*Hekhalot Rabbati*, the enthronement is a form of *hieros gamos*."

20. Abraham Abulafia, *The Rose of Mysteries* [*Shoshan Sodoth*], trans. Aryeh Kaplan, in *Meditation and Kabbalah* (York Beach, Maine: Samuel Weiser, 1982), pp. 109–10.

21. *3 Enoch or The Hebrew Book of Enoch*, ed. and trans. by Hugo Odeberg, prolegomenon by Jonas C. Greenfield (New York: Ktav, 1973, orig. pub. 1928), pp. 8–9, 13, 22, 25, 27, 28–9, 33, 39.

22. Scholem, *Kabbalah*, p. 380.

23. Ibid., p. 143.

24. *Chagigah*, 14b, as quoted in *The Secret Garden*, pp. 3–4. This volume also contains a useful translation of the *Shi'ur Komah* by the Work of the Chariot. The critical edition is that of Martin Samuel Cohen, *The Shi'ur Qomah: Liturgy and Theurgy in Pre-Kabbalistic Jewish Mysticism* (Lanham, Md.: University Press of America, 1983).

25. Vital, *Tree of Life*, p. 24.

26. Scholem, *Kabbalah*, p. 131.

27. For the diagram illustrated with ten Sefirot, see Z'ev ben Shimon Halevi, *A Kabbalistic Universe* (New York: Samuel Weiser, 1977), p. 10; for one illustrated with forty Sefirot, see Charles Poncé, *Kabbalah* (Wheaton, Ill.: Theosophical Publishing House, 1978), p. 63; and for one illustrated with fifty Sefirot, see Philip S. Berg, *Kabbalah for the Layman* (Jerusalem: Press of the Research Centre of Kabbalah, 1981), p. 164. In the same year that the Quest edition of Poncé's book was published, the identical diagram appeared

in Manly P. Hall, *The Secret Teachings of All Ages* (Los Angeles: Philosophical Research Society, 1978), p. 119. Though Ponce's copyright date is 1973 and Hall's is 1977, the simultaneous publication of what look like photocopies of the same diagram in both of these books, neither of which give their source for the diagram, makes it difficult to assign priority between them, and it would appear that both derived the Tzimtzum diagram of forty Sefirot independently from the same unnamed source.

28. See *The Kabbalah of the Soul*, p. 390, the concluding page of the section synthesizing quantum and Lurianic cosmology.

29. See Scholem, *Kabbalah*, p. 130.

30. Ibid., p. 132.

31. As quoted in Aryeh Kaplan, ed. and trans., *The Light Beyond: Adventures in Hassidic Thought* (New York: Moznaim, 1981), p. 193.

32. This Gematria equation was conveyed to me by a student of a student of the modern Israeli Kabbalist Rabbi Gedaliah Koenig, who either transmitted or originated it.

33. For a fuller discussion of these harmonic octaves that also correlates the first ten harmonics with the ten Sefirot in ascending form, see *The Secret Doctrine of the Kabbalah*, pp. 79–90.

34. For my fuller treatment of this Lurianic understanding of the progress of Ze'ir Anpin with quotations from the *Eitz Chayyim*, see *The Secret Doctrine of the Kabbalah*, pp. 277–84.

35. Scholem, *Kabbalah*, p. 346.

36. Kaplan, trans., in *Meditation and the Bible*, p. 45.

37. *Shiur Qoma*, trans. Work of the Chariot, in *The Secret Garden*, p. 34.

38. *The Zohar*, ed. and trans. Daniel C. Matt, vol. 1, pp. 215–16 (1:34b), 253 (1:47a).

39. *Shiur Qoma*, in *The Secret Garden*, pp. 34, 35.

40. Trans. Philip Birnbaum, in his edition of the *Daily Prayer Book* (New York: Hebrew Publishing Company, 1949), p. 138 passim.

CHAPTER 8:

1. For further information on general systems theory, see appendix B. See also an article by its founder, Ludwig von Bertalanffy, "The History and Status of General Systems Theory," in *Trends in General Systems Theory*, ed. George J. Kirr (New York: Wiley-Interscience, 1972). See also von Bertalanffy, *Robots, Men and Minds* (New York: George Braziller, 1967); Paul A. Weiss, *The Science of Life* (Mt. Kisco, N.Y.: Futura, 1973); Ervin Laszlo, *The Systems View of the World* (New York: George Braziller, 1972); and see all the contributers of the volume *Evolution and Consciousness*, eds. Erich Jantsch and Conrad H. Waddington (Reading, Mass.: Addison-Wesley, 1976).

2. Support for this view can perhaps be found in Buckminster Fuller's understanding that "energy will automatically triangulate via a diagonal of a square, or via the triangulating diagonals of any other polygon to which the force is applied. Triangular systems represent the shortest, most economical

energy networks." In *The Dymaxion World of Buckminster Fuller* by R. Buckminster Fuller and Robert Marks (n.c.: Anchor Books, 1973), p. 43.

3. For this full discussion of the triangle matrix, which includes its modeling of all the particles of quantum physics and concludes with a treatment of probability, see chapter 9 in *The Secret Doctrine of the Kabbalah*, pp. 332–79.

4. In the previously noted chapter 9 of *The Secret Doctrine of the Kabbalah*, the triangle matrix was decomposed into three, rather than four, colors to model the interface of the hadron (proton or neutron) with the three differently "colored" quarks of which it is thought to be composed. The four-color discrimination of the hexagram matrix here undertaken was a choice vindicated by the spectacular result of this decision that clearly emerges at the level of the sixth-world matrix but can already be justified by the richer results that emerge as well at the fourth expansion of the Sabbath Star Diagram from the discrimination of the matrix into four rather than three colors. It would seem, then, that the triangle matrix is best specified by three colors and the hexagram matrix by four, an important difference of levels.

5. See the remarkable book by Theodor Schwenk, *Sensitive Chaos: The Creation of Flowing Forms in Water and Air*, trans. Olive Whicher and Johanna Wrigley (New York: Schocken Books, 1978), especially pp. 13–67.

6. For this diagram, see Virginia MacIvor and Sandra LaForest, *Vibrations: Healing through Color, Homeopathy and Radionics* (New York: Samuel Weiser, 1979), p. 69.

7. We have seen that an illuminating conjunction can be made between the twelve Dinshah colors and the twelve semitones of the chromatic scale. The next step would seem to require a further association of both with the twelve personality types represented by the zodiac. In the earlier discussion of the matrix macrostructure, we saw that it was only at the fifth-world level identified with the Ruach soul that all twelve of the color spirals achieved stable individuated form. Thus true personality would seem to imply a spiritual development to the Ruach level of the fifth world, at which the program of the Sabbath Star Diagram specifies the full development of the symbolizing functions of man. Though the final section of this chapter will define both the unfallen form of the fourth-world psyche and the further development that may be correlated with its fallen state and thus be considered to result from a forbidden method of constructing this diagram world, the ideal development of personality can be seen to be defined by the diagram exactly at the point that can be correlated with the full manifestation of the zodiacal types. Though this double correlation of cosmic stages and astrological signs with the twelve-color spectrum would suggest a correlation of personality types with cosmic stages, since all twelve personality types are now present, and all follow the sun through its yearly cycle, mankind may be said to contain the archetypes of all past and future evolutionary stages within it. And since all of these stages may be further said to play their own appointed and necessary role in the evolutionary cosmic cycle, so all of these twelve varieties of

Ruach soul must have equal opportunities for that spiritual development necessary for them to contribute their special tone to the plenitude of divine harmony.

There is one further point at which at least the basic concept of astrology becomes useful in illuminating the final aspect of the twelve-color matrix with which we shall be concerned. This concerns the color scrambling that occurs as we move further and further away from the initial definition of the twelve-color spectrum given in terms of the central microhexagram. This color scrambling can be seen most clearly by focusing on the outer circle of the twelve fifth-world macrohexagrams shown in plate 6. If we begin with the magenta macrohexagram at the lower right and proceed in a clockwise direction through the circle of these differently colored macrohexagrams, the order of the remaining colors will be turquoise, red, indigo, yellow, purple, green, scarlet, blue, orange, violet, and lemon. This is quite a shift from the color order given in the following chart, as previously in plate 4. And what it means is that each interfacing of a microtriangle with the two macrotriangles that bisect it will be absolutely unique not only in its diagram position but also in its color relationships, an individualizing that might be said to give each microtriangle its own "horoscope." Thus the matrix can be seen to provide an archetypal model of the ordered process of individuation. And if the Sabbath Star Diagram can be further interpreted as a model encoding the evolution of consciousness in all its varieties, then the process modeled by its matrix is one through which each particle of individualized consciousness may be said to develop its own unique personality, a personality that makes its own contribution to the whole process of cosmic evolution of which it may also be said personally to partake.

In exploring the further astrological implications of the twelve-color matrix, the following table should be useful. This chart shows all of these correspondences, relating the cosmic with the solar cycle by equating Do with the sign with which astrology begins the solar cycle, Aries:

COLOR	TONE	WORLD	COSMIC STAGE	SIGN
Magenta	Do	1	Manifest Atzilut	Aries
Scarlet	Di	1½	Unmanifestable Atzilut	Taurus
Red	Re	2	Manifest Beriah	Gemini
Orange	Ri	2½	Unmanifest Beriah	Cancer
Yellow	Mi	3	"Unfallen" Yetzirah	Leo
Lemon	Fa	3½	"Fallen" Yetzirah	Virgo
Green	Fi	4	Garden stage of Asiyah	Libra
Turquoise	Sol	4½	Human stage of Asiyah	Scorpio
Blue	Si	5	Advent of Messiah	Sagittarius
Indigo	La	5½	Millennium	Capricorn
Violet	Li	6	World to Come	Aquarius
Purple	Ti	6½	2nd half of W. to C.	Pisces
Magenta	Do	7	Divine Communion	Aries or All

For those with knowledge of astrology, the above chart should prove suggestive. One could venture further and employ the full chromatic matrix diagram given in plate 6 as the basis of a new mode of astrology—or at least a new game: Find Your Microtriangle! The way this would work is that one would first have to find a microtriangle in the color of his or her sun sign that is bisected by two colors of particular significance in that person's conventional horoscope. One would have to be the color of his moon sign and the other could be the color for the sign of his ascendant, ruling planet, or important conjunction. Once such an appropriate microtriangle is selected, it could then be determined whether it represented a Nefesh or Ruach psyche and one in a stable or unstable configuration. Such specificities of analysis are in addition to the basic correlations of the color of the sun sign with a phase of cosmic evolution and with the primary distinction between a central or lateral dominant mode of consciousness. But beyond this complex interpretation of the microtriangle's color and position in the diagram, there are the further distinctions involving the colors of the interfacing macrotriangles, that element of the horoscope identified with the bisecting color at the left being related to the left brain and that identified with the color on the right with the right brain. Not only can the signs of the moon and the ascendant be interpreted in terms of the macrohexagrams in which they appear but it is also possible, then, to correlate them with a left or right brain orientation. Such a chromatic understanding of the matrix not only permits us to read the basic "horoscope" of every microtriangle but to do so with a precision as to the general level of soul development, the comparative levels of the sun, moon, and ascendant, and the right and left brain orientations that go beyond descriptions possible in normal astrology. Tests of this astrological system with various individuals have led to most intriguing results. But whether or not it can actually be presented as a valid form of astrological interpretation rather than simply an entertaining form of parlor game is beyond my competence to say. I would also suggest that this possible new mode of kabbalistic astrology be considered in the context of my earlier extended treatment of astrology in chapter 4, note 8.

8. William Shakespeare, *The Merchant of Venice*, 5.1.64.
9. See Scholem, *Kabbalah*, p. 229.
10. *Zohar Hadash, Midrash ha-Ne'lam* to Ruth, 82c–82d, trans.

David Goldstein, in Isaiah Tishby, *The Wisdom of the Zohar: An Anthology of Texts* (London: Oxford University Press, 1991), vol. 2, pp. 729–31.

11. See Rachel Elior, *The Paradoxical Ascent to God: The Kabbalistic Theosophy of Habad Hasidism*, trans. Jeffrey M. Green (Albany: State University of New York Press, 1993), pp. 103–24, for an excellent treatment of the two aspects of the soul in Habad Hasidism that, though termed the "divine soul" and the "bestial soul" are shown by her to be "not two separate souls but rather two sorts of consciousness or two separate types of interpretive apprehension" (pp. 104–5).

12. See *The Kabbalah of the Soul*, pp. 38–43, for a different cosmic modeling of chaos in its seven, three-dimensional, concentric spheres in which each cosmic world builds its shell out of a Lurianic Reshimu combining both the forms of Gevurah and the chaos of the broken Sefirot. See also pp. 95–98 of the aforesaid book whose consideration of the Torah of limitation includes a discussion of the law of the manna and the Ten Commandments.

13. Herman Melville, "Bartleby, the Scrivener," *The Norton Anthology of Short Fiction*, ed. R. V. Cassill and Richard Bausch, 6th ed. (New York, W. W. Norton, 2000), pp. 1193–94.

14. Nathaniel Hawthorne, *The Scarlet Letter* (New York: Penguin Books, 1986), p. 93.

15. Homer, *The Iliad*, trans. E. V. Rieu (Harmondsworth, Eng.: Penguin Books, 1950), bk. 12, p. 229.

16. Ibid., bk. 16, p. 305.

17. Ibid., bk. 9, p. 172.

18. Ibid., bk. 1, p. 34.

19. For my full treatment of the theory and the Elizabethan literary tragedies of courtly love, as well as such a treatment of the contrasting form that I have named "worldly love" and that now can be considered the form of "lateral" love, see Leonora Leet Brodwin, *Elizabethan Love Tragedy* (New York: New York University Press, 1971).

20. For this understanding of the love-death as a "flight forward," see Theodore Reik's penetrating psychoanalytic study *Masochism in Modern Man* (New York: Farrar, Strauss, 1941), pp. 115–24.

21. In *The Varieties of Religious Experience*, William James distinguished the same two religious sensibilities.

22. For my study of such religious practices, particularly those of kabbalistic meditation, Sabbath observance, and ritual prayer, a study derived from both the esoteric and exoteric traditions of Judaism and focused on suggestions as to effective methods of doing these levels of spiritual practice that can aid the process of spiritual development, see *Renewing the Covenant*.

CHAPTER 9

1. See chapter 8, note 7.

2. See Joseph Dan, *Jewish Mysticism*, vol. 1, *Late Antiquity*, pp. 40–53.

3. See chapter 1, note 41, on the shamanic upper and lower worlds.

4. P. D. Ouspensky, *In Search of the Miraculous*, pp. 42–43.

5. Joseph Conrad, Heart of Darkness, in The Norton Anthology of Short Fiction, p. 297.

6. Samuel Taylor Coleridge, *Biographia Literaria*, chap. 14, in *The Selected Poetry and Prose of Coleridge*, ed. Donald A. Stauffer, Modern Library College Editions (New York: Random House, 1951), p. 269.

7. Ibid., chap. 13, p. 263.

8. Ibid.

9. Abraham Abulafia, *Seder ha-Tzeruf*, trans. Aryeh Kaplan, in *Meditation and Kabbalah*, p. 80.

10. Abraham Abulafia, *Otzar Eden ha-Ganaz*, trans. Aryeh Kaplan, in *Meditation and Kabbalah*, p. 84.

11. The most serious adjustment of details between material appearing both in this book and *The Kabbalah of the Soul* involves the treatment of this heart center, which in that latter book was given a faculty of empathy serving to regularize this center with the others that each have such a faculty, the nature of this added faculty deriving from the definition of this center just given, though it here has no such corresponding central microhexagram in the fifth world. But the six construction elements of the fifth world are also regularized with the four of the fourth world to fit its simpler model.

12. See Rudy Rucker, *Infinity and the Mind*, pp. 1–2, 333.

13. See also the more extensive correlation of chakras to Sefirot made in chapter 5 of *The Secret Doctrine of the Kabbalah*, pp. 169–78.

14. Abulafia, *Otzar Eden ha-Ganaz*, p. 85.

15. See Karl H. Pribram and Diane McGuinness, "Arousal, Activation, and Effort in the Control of Attention," *Psychological Review* 82 (1975): 130.

16. For treatments of the attunement process utilizing a fuller form of this encoded process I have uncovered in the *Sefer Yetzirah*, see *Renewing the Covenant*, pp. 74–85.

17. In the appendix to *Renewing the Covenant* I suggested that the Hebrew word "Vehayah," the reverse of the Tetragrammaton, not YHVH but VHYH, was used throughout the Bible as a manifesting power word and could be used so today.

18. Jung, foreword, *The I Ching*, trans. Wilhelm and Baynes, p. xxiv.

19. For a discussion of rhythm entrainment, see Itzhak Bentov, *Stalking the Wild Pendulum* (New York: E. P. Dutton, 1977), pp. 21–24; and Michael Hutchison, *Megabrain* (New York: Ballantine Books, 1986), pp. 199–201.

20. Swami Muktananda Paramahansa, *The Play of Consciousness* (n.c., Calif: Shree Gurudev Siddha Yoga Ashram, 1974), pp. 30–31.

21. But I have interpreted the Sh'ma as signifying "Here: Israel, YHVH Elohaynu [the Lord thyGod] [and the unqualified] YHVH [are] one," for which see particularly *The Secret Doctrine of the Kabbalah*, pp. 68–73.

22. See *Renewing the Covenant*, pp. 55–57, for a discussion of writings of Dov Baer, the Mezhirecher Maggid and chief disciple of the Baal Shem Tov, in which he posits that only such an ascent to Ayin can explain the alchemy of transformation:

"This is how a miracle comes, changing the laws of nature. First the thing must be elevated to the Emanation of Nothingness. Influence then comes from that Emanation to produce the miracle. . . . This person can then lower it once again to the level of Thought, which is somethingness. At the end of all levels, he can transform it into gold." The translation here is that of Aryeh Kaplan in *Meditation and Kabbalah*, p. 302.

23. Abraham J. Heschel, "Toward an Understanding of Halachah," in *Conservative Judaism and Jewish Law*, ed. Seymour Siegel (New York: The Rabbinical Assembly, 1977), p. 150.

24. Abraham J. Heschel, *The Sabbath: Its Meaning for Modern Man* (New York: Farrar, Straus and Giroux, 1951), pp. 59, 60.

25. See chapter 3 of *Renewing the Covenant* for my full treatment of Sabbath observance.

CHAPTER 10

1. Chayyim Vital, *Pri Eitz Chayyim* (Jerusalem: n.p., 1988), Sha'ar ha-Lulav (Gate of the Lulav), Hebrew edition, chap. 3, p. 729.

2. Aryeh Kaplan, ed. and trans., *The Bahir* (New York: Samuel Weiser, 1979), pp. 110, 113, 126, 131, 174, 175, 176, 178, 179.

3. Kaplan, *Bahir*, p. 178.

4. A. E. Waite, *The Holy Kabbalah* (New Hyde Park, N.Y.: University Books, 1969), pp. 371–72.

5. Ibid., p. 349.

6. Ibid., pp. 383, 392, 394.

7. Kaplan, *Bahir*, p. 175.

8. Vital, *Eitz Chayyim*, vol. 1, chap. 1, p. 1.

9. For my full correlation of Sefirot to chakras, see *The Secret Doctrine of the Kabbalah*, pp. 169–74.

10. For my analogous new understanding of the talmudic concept of the "double heart" as unifying the more mental heart of the Neshamah soul with the more emotional heart of the Ruach soul, see *The Secret Doctrine of the Kabbalah*, pp. 163–84.

11. For my earlier treatment of the three levels of Yichud in which Malkhut participates, the sensual, emotional, and cognitive, see the final section of chapter 6.

12. In *The Kabbalah of the Soul* I similarly distinguished the main branch of the Kabbalah from most Eastern forms of mysticism (pp. 64–66), relating my long-held understanding to that recently appearing in a work of Jorge N. Ferrer, *Revisioning Transpersonal Theory: A Participatory Vision of Human Spirituality* (Albany: State University of New York Press, 2002). See my long note on his significant work, pp. 342–44n in my aforesaid book.

13. Dobh Baer of Lubavitch, *On Ecstasy*, trans. and ed. Louis Jacobs (Chappaqua, N.Y.: Rossel Books, 1963), pp. 111, 127, 128.

14. See *The Kabbalah of the Soul*, pp. 37–42, for a treatment of the earliest portion of the *Zohar*, the "Sifra de-Tzeni'uta" (Book of Concealment), that defines itself as "the book that

describes the balancing of the scale," a balancing that it understands to be the first act of creation. This understanding that the principle of balance must precede the emanation of that which is to be balanced would also seem to be modeled by the three lateral macrohexagrams of the first phase of the sixth world diagram, since the macrohexagram correlated with the balancing Sefirah of Tiferet is manifested earlier in the construction of the sixth world diagram than those correlated with the extremes of Chesed and Gevurah.

15. See chapter 1, note 46, above.

16. See chapter 4 of *The Kabbalah of the Soul* for a full treatment of Neshamah consciousness as exemplifying such a transformative process as may now be more specifically identified with the functioning of the Neshamah heart.

17. See chapter 4 of *The Kabbalah of the Soul* for a treatment of the Patriarchs that includes an analysis of Jacob's "Transformative Moment" of insight, particularly pp. 208–10, 296.

18. See again chapter 4 of *The Kabbalah of the Soul* for a treatment of Abraham and Isaac as biblical Tzaddikim within a larger study of the Tzaddik, pp. 213–22.

19. For a full analysis of the triangle matrix as a model for probability, see *The Secret Doctrine of the Kabbalah*, pp. 334–38, 376–79.

20. Samuel Taylor Coleridge, *Biographia Literaria*, chap. 14, p. 264.

21. Coleridge, "Dejection: An Ode," ll. 88–90.

22. See Lewis Thomas, *The Lives of a Cell* (New York: Bantam Books, 1980), pp. 43–48.

23. Percy Bysshe Shelley, *A Defense of Poetry*.

24. Ibid.

25. For a fuller discussion of these three related sacred sciences in the *Sefer Yetzirah*, see *The Secret Doctrine of the Kabbalah*, pp. 87–94.

26. J. H. Hertz, The Pentateuch and Haftorahs, p. 9.

27. Scholem, *Kabbalah*, pp. 137–38.

28. See *The Secret Doctrine of the Kabbalah*, pp. 100–13, for my philosophic expansion of Plato's theory of natural language in the *Cratylus*.

29. See Rupert Sheldrake, *A New Science of Life* (Los Angeles: J. P. Tarcher, 1981).

CHAPTER 11

1. For an extended analysis of this political "god who failed," see appendix B.

2. Though the artist responsible for the additional drawing in figure 10.4 actually placed the head of Ze'ir Anpin a little higher than this position, it should be obvious that his head could be lowered to this precise location.

3. Vital, *Eitz Chayyim*, vol. 1, chap. 4, p. 8.

4. Abraham J. Heschel, *Between God and Man: An Interpretation of Judaism*, ed. Fritz A. Rothschild (New York: Free Press, 1965), pp. 140, 141, 142.

5. Gershom Scholem, *Sabbatai Sevi*, trans. R. J. Zwi Werblowsky, Bollingen Series XCIII (Princeton: Princeton University Press, 1973), p. 30.

6. Scholem, *Sabbatai Sevi*, p. 29.

7. Gershom Scholem, *Kabbalah* (New York: New American Library, 1978), p. 130.

8. Scholem, *Kabbalah*, p. 130.

9. For further understanding of such an identification of Ein Sof and chaos, see my theoretical cosmic model of seven concentric spheres expanding into the realm of Ein Sof, in *The Kabbalah of the Soul*, pp. 28–46.

10. *Sefer Yetzirah*, trans. Aryeh Kaplan, p. 261 (1.4).

11. Vital, *Eitz Chayyim*, vol. 1, chap. 1, p. 1.

12. Nosson Scherman and Meir Zlotowitz, eds., *Tehillim*, The ArtScroll Tanach Series (Brooklyn, N.Y.: Mesorah Publications, 1985), pp. 1197–98.

13. Trans. Scholem in *Kabbalah*, p. 346. See also his full discussion of Gilgul, pp. 344–50.

CHAPTER 12

1. William Irwin Thompson, "The Serpent's Ascent," *ReVision* 5 (Fall, 1982): 70, 72.

2. Peter Tompkins, *Mysteries of the Mexican Pyramids* (New York: Harper & Row, 1976), p. 387.

3. Scholem, *Kabbalah*, pp. 47, 95, 114

4. Exod. 23:21, as quoted in *Shiur Qoma*, in *The Secret Garden*, p. 35.

5. There were two ways in which the soul that had completed its progress through the Spiral Tree can be associated with the divine number twenty-six in terms of the concept of light unit parity, as that fruitful concept was first developed in the final section of chapter 11, one that also requires recourse to the talmudic concept of the light reserved for the righteous. Though it was pointed out that the rule of light-unit parity deduced from its appearance in the sixth-world matrix might be premature, since it was based on too few diagram expansions to support such a construction definitively, it was also realized that this concept of hidden light was an equal possibility for both of the alternate modelings of the fourth-world diagram. In either case, then, the fully realized Neshamah soul could be understood to involute to the center to gain its reward of hidden light. Chapter 14 will be largely concerned with the attempt to resolve the problems arising from the concept of light-unit parity and will finally validate a reformulated understanding of this weighing of matrix elements that will lead to the deepest understanding of the laws of the matrix.

6. *The Zohar*, trans. Daniel C. Matt, vol. 1, pp. 194–95 (1:31b–32a). See also the references to the kabbalistic concept of a "Lamp of Darkness," in Aryeh Kaplan, *Meditation and the Kabbalah*, p. 324.

7. Chayyim Vital, *Sha'ar ha-Gilgulim*, as trans. and quoted in Gershom Scholem, *Sabbatai Sevi*, p. 43.

8. Nehemiah Hayon, *Divrei Nehemiah*, trans. in summary and quoted in Gershom Scholem, "Redemption Through Sin," trans. Hillel Halkin, in *The Messianic Idea in Judaism and Other Essays on Jewish Spirituality* (New York: Schocken Books, 1971), p. 119.

9. Scholem, "Redemption through Sin," pp. 94–95.

10. Scholem, *Sabbatai Sevi*, pp. 301–2.

11. C. G. Jung, *On the Nature of the Psyche*, pp. 116–18.

12. *Tractate Shabbath*, 2 vols., Hebrew-English ed. of the Babylonian Talmud, trans. H. Freedman (London: Soncino Press, 1972), vol. 2, p. 152b.

13. Zalman M. Schachter [-Shalomi], contributor, in *The Jewish Almanac*, ed. Richard Siegel and Carl Rheins (New York: Bantam Books, 1980), pp. 594–95.

14. Scholem, "Redemption through Sin," p. 99.

15. Scholem, *Sabbatai Sevi*, p. 42.

16. Such associations receive interesting support from the biblical description of Esau: "and the first came out red, all over like an hairy garment. . . . And the boys grew: and Esau was a cunning hunter" (Gen. 25: 25, 27). What is interesting about this description is that it seems to have a medical basis. Harold M. Schmeck, Jr., in his article "The Complex Organ Known as Skin Continues to Surprise," *New York Times* (8 November 1983), C3, has described such a "genetic disorder called erythropoietic porphyria, which has been blamed for the medieval legends that gave us the werewolf. The illness stems from an inborn lack of an enzyme. This lack leads to an accumulation of substances called porphyrins in body tissues, making them painfully sensitive to light. Victims of the disease tend to be excessively hairy. Their teeth have a reddish hue when exposed to light because of the accumulation of porphyrins. Sunlight brings out the most painful symptoms of the disease, prompting its sufferers to stay undercover until nightfall." Esau's occupation as a hunter would require him to spend most of his time in the forest, out of the sunlight that could only aggravate the genetic disease for which he would appear to have all the symptoms. Thus Esau is born doomed to inhabit the shadow side of biblical narrative while the aggressive Jacob, who supplants this figure of darkness, carries the blessing of Abraham into the light of history.

17. Hertz, ed. and trans., *The Pentateuch and Haftorahs*, p. 125, note to Gen. 33:14.

18. See chapter 5 for a parallel discussion of such early exclusion of evil followed by a later inclusion of what had formerly to be rejected as evil in the modeling by the Sabbath Stars of the fifth-world diagram of the chronology of the Messianic Age. This is also related to the treatment in chapter 3 of the "Transformative Moment" as a therapeutic model.

19. For my fuller treatment of the Gematria Ben = 52, including the association of such a "son" with the covenantal counting of the fifty-two Sabbaths of the solar year, see *The Secret Doctrine of the Kabbalah*, pp. 119–48.

20. For the full treatment of my theory that the concept of the son constitutes the secret heart of the whole Jewish esoteric tradition going back to the Temple priesthood, see particularly the first two chapters of *The Secret Doctrine of the Kabbalah*.

21. For the phrase "son of the world to come," see *Shiur Qoma*, trans. The Work of the Chariot, in *The Secret Garden*, p. 34. I have preferred the translation by The Work of the Chariot in this instance to that of the more scholarly edition and translation of Martin Samuel Cohen, *The Shi'ur Qomah:*

Liturgy and Theurgy in Pre-Kabbalistic Jewish Mysticism, because it preserves the usage "son of the world to come" which Cohen suppresses but which is true to the original manuscripts. For a discussion of his private correspondence to me, dated August 8, 1984, on this matter, see *The Kabbalah of the Soul*, p. 341n. For more information on this question see note 26 below.

22. Henry Vaughan, "The Retreat," ll. 19–20.

23. Jill Purce, *The Mystic Spiral: Journey of the Soul* (New York: Thames and Hudson, 1980), pp. 8, 11, 16, 17, 25, 32; my brackets.

24. The phrase "son of the world to come," from the *Shi'ur Komah*, will continue to be featured prominently in further discussions of the Hebraic secret doctrine of the son and is further addressed in note 21 above.

25. *Shiur Qoma*, trans. The Work of the Chariot, in *The Secret Garden*, pp. 23, 24, 32.

26. This information was conveyed to me by Martin Samuel Cohen, editor of the scholarly translation of the *Shi'ur Qomah*, to which reference was made in note 21 above, in a private correspondence, dated August 8, 1984, with respect to this phrase "ben ha-olam ha-ba," which he does not translate as "son." For further discussion of this private correspondence, see *The Kabbalah of the Soul*, p. 341n.

27. Scholem, *Kabbalah*, pp. 16, 17.

28. See Theon of Smyrna, *Mathematics Useful for Understanding* Plato, p. 13.

29. As indicated in chapter 7, note 31, this Gematria equation has been taught by the modern Israeli Kabbalist Rabbi Gedaliah Koenig, who either transmitted or originated it.

30. *The Zohar*, trans. Harry Sperling, Maurice Simon, and Paul P. Levertoff, 5 vols. (London: Soncino Press, 1978), vol. 3, pp. 409–11 (2:141b–142a).

31. Scholem, *Kabbalah*, pp. 345, 346.

32. Purce, *The Mystic Spiral*, p. 23.

33. T. S. Eliot, "Little Gidding," ll. 242–44.

34. *Shi'ur Qomah*, ed. Cohen, p. 259.

35. The association of Enoch with Metatron is made in another Merkabah text, The Hebrew Book of Enoch, now known as 3 Enoch, for which see the section of chapter 7 entitled "The Working of the Chariot." For my fuller treatments of 3 Enoch see *The Secret Doctrine of the Kabbalah*, pp. 47–52, and *The Kabbalah of the Soul*, pp. 58–61.

36. Ibid., p. 238.

37. Scholem, *Kabbalah*, p. 380.

38. See chapter 7 at note 19 for this Abulafia statement.

39. *Shi'ur Qomah*, ed. Cohen, p. 133.

40. The winding of the Yechidah soul through such a six-leveled model may be found in the revised form of chapter 5 in my book *The Kabbalah of the Soul*, pp. 229–305. This chapter, entitled "The Six Paths to Divine Knowledge," originally appeared at the close of the present book. In this original form it added to the analysis of the Chayah soul's possible triple windings through the Double Cherub-Trees, a reconceptualized Sixfold Cherub-Tree that could summarize the three levels of both the human and supernal souls defined in

the *Zohar* while relating each to a "path to divine knowledge." Also using categories derived from Ezekiel's Throne vision, particularly of the Chayot, the "living creatures" whose four faces are of the ox (further taken in modern medical morphology to represent the bull), the lion, the eagle, and man, as well as of the prophet and the envisioned man on the Throne, the latter two elaborated in 3 Enoch under the names of Enoch and Metatron, these six paths are entitled as follows: "The Sexual Path of the Bull," "The Love Path of the Lion," "The Power Path of the Eagle," "The Cognitive Path of Man," "The Holy Path of Enoch," and "The Unifying Path of Metatron." The original inspiration for this analysis was our present model of a hierarchical Sixfold Tree whose windings always brought the soul back to Malkhut, at whose center is the point of Da'at, Knowledge, on the traditional Tree of Life Diagram that, in this alignment, was the source of the Sabbath Star Diagram, as explained in the chapter 1 of the present book. In *The Kabbalah of the Soul* I have taken those aspects of my psychological analysis that could be separated from the Sabbath Star Diagram and given a simpler modeling, in this case just of the six categories that could be derived from Ezekiel's vision, and have published them apart from their original modeling, both in the attempt to shorten the current work and to give some of its best analyses a more accessible form. This was certainly the case with the chapter on "The Six Paths to Divine Knowledge," but readers of this present volume who wish to follow the evolution of the soul to its completion would be well advised to read this chapter and book.

CHAPTER 13

1. Heinz R. Pagels. The Dreams of Reason: The Computer and the Rise of the Sciences of Complexity (New York: Bantam Books, 1989), p. 101.

2. See the concluding chapter of this part for my use of the full Sabbath Star System to model a new theory of complexity, a model that not only reveals this to be a complex system but challenges the conclusions of the main developer of cellular automata, Stephen Wolfram.

3. John Michell, with whom I discussed the twelve-pointed star of the seventh-world matrix when I had the pleasure of meeting him in 1989, indicated the association of the number twelve and of such a twelve-pointed star with the solar cosmology of the earliest kings, the subject of a since published book of his, with Christine Rhone: *Twelve Tribe Nations and the Science of Enchanting Landscapes* (London: Thames, and Hudson, 1990).

4. See Michell, *The New View Over Atlantis* (San Francisco: Harper & Row, 1983), pp. 167–70.

5. See Giorgio de Santillana and Hertha von Dechend, *Hamlet's Mill: An Essay on Myth and the Frame of Time* (Boston: Gambit, 1969).

6. Plato, *Timaeus*, p. 98 (section 37D).

7. These last correspondences require some final comment. For the Jewish esoteric tradition would seem to differ from the Greek in its gender associations of the even and odd numbers.

The Pythagorean-Platonic tradition based its gender associations of the even and odd numbers on harmonic grounds. The fact that each different harmonic emerges at an odd number while the octave doublings of each such harmonic emerge at even numbers led to the identification of the odd numbers both with the concept of Difference and the masculine and of the even numbers both with Sameness and the feminine. In the Kabbalah, however, the second Sefirah was identified with the paternal principle of Abba and the third Sefirah with the maternal principle of Imma. And now again in the identification of the vertical worlds of the Sabbath Star Diagram with the masculine and of its horizontal worlds with the feminine, this same correlation of the even with the masculine and odd with the feminine persists. Whatever the truth might be with regard to any absolute gender correlations of the even and odd numbers, it seems clear that the numerical associations the Greeks drew from the harmonics differ from those of the geometric worlds of the Sabbath Star Diagram, and that in this latter circumstance, as in the Tree of Life Diagram, the even is correlated with the masculine and the odd with the feminine.

8. For my innovative interpretation of the Sh'ma, which builds upon the general kabbalistic understanding that it concerns a divine unification to see this unification as also including the divine "son" Israel, see especially *The Secret Doctrine of the Kabbalah*, pp. 68–73; *Renewing the Covenant*, pp. 62–74; and *The Kabbalah of the Soul*, pp. 325–32.

9. It was this emergence in the seventh-world diagram of a light-unit total curiously close to the Gematria of Ben (son) = 52, one whose differences from 52 of 1⅓ could be related to the correlation of the two halves of the seventh-world diagram with the infinite and the finite, that gave me my first insight into the importance of the word *son* to kabbalistic cosmology as well as its meaning, that the cosmic son is he who can unify the finite with the infinite. For my full development of what I finally recognized to be the secret doctrine at the core of the Jewish mystical tradition, see *The Secret Doctrine of the Kabbalah*, particularly the textual history I provide for this Hebraic concept of the son in its second chapter.

10. All the illustrations in this book of the Sabbath Star Diagram as well as that of the Hexagram of Creation have been drafted personally by myself with the Superpaint program on the Macintosh II computer, this not only being the best program for this purpose available at that time, 1989–91, but one, though retired by its new corporate owner, that is still unsurpassed.

11. See Robert Herrick, "Corinna's Going a Maying," l. 2.

12. Gershom Scholem, *Origins of the Kabbalah*, ed. R. J. Zwi Werblowsky, trans. Allan Arkush (Princeton: The Jewish Publication Society and Princeton University Press, 1987; orig. German ed. 1962), p. 112.

13. George Chapman, *Bussy D'Ambois*, 5.4.150–55.

CHAPTER 15

1. I am greatly indebted to my mathematician colleague and friend, Dr. Maurice Mackover, for having discerned this formula as operating in my data, a discovery without which it would have been far more difficult, if not impossible, to program the computer to generate the infinite periodic decimal sequence that is the basis of this final investigation.

2. I am most grateful to Paul Karagianis, a systems programmer at the St. John's University Computer Center, for having programmed the university mainframe IBM computer with the three crucial fractions deriving from the seventh through ninth worlds of the Sabbath Star Diagram and the formula of their relationship discovered by Dr. Mackover, as explained in the previous note, by which the periodic decimal .074 could be generated at ever greater iterations and expansions of decimal places. As I went back to him time after time for increasingly larger such decimal places and iterations, finally to 1,500 decimal places with over 6,000 formula iterations, he would hand me ever weightier packs of computer print-outs with a smile and the words, "Have fun!" I have and much more. Through his help I have discovered a world of infinite complexity and meaningful order.

3. The distinction I am making is not one with which mathematicians would agree, who see them both as forming similar linear graphs and infinite decimals, the latter more properly represented by the decimal number .080000000 . . . . . But to those mathematicians who think that an infinite number of zeros after a decimal integer is no different from a periodic repetition of 074 that does add value to a decimal, I can only give the tart reply of King Lear: "Nothing will come of nothing" (1.1.92). If the distinction between the periodic decimal .074 . . . and the asymptote .08 has not been viewed as significant in formal mathematical terms, it may be because these categories of numbers have been divorced from true geometric thinking. The fact that both can be artificially translated into similar linear graphs obscures the real geometric difference inherent in these very different decimal sequences, that between infinite repetition and convergence at infinity, the extension of the first defining the essence of the line and the convergence of the second the essence of the point. If not yet significant in terms of number theory, it is significant in the cosmological terms that have been the main focus of this investigation.

4. Andrew Marvell, "To His Coy Mistress," opening line.

5. Edmund Spenser, *The Faerie Queene*, canto 8, verse 2, ll.16–18.

6. William Shakespeare, *Henry IV, Part One*, 5.4.81–82.

7. Natalie Angier, "Biologists Unravel Key Steps of Cell Division," *New York Times* (6 November 1990), C 1.

8. John Noble Wilford, "Galactic Evenness Gives Astronomers Pause," *New York Times* (25 February 1990), A 25. Wilford's article is based on the study by T. J. Broadhurst, R. S. Ellis, D. C. Koo, and A. S. Szalay, "Large-scale Distribution of Galaxies at the Galactic Poles," *Nature* 343 (22 February 1990): 726–28. In a review article on the findings of Broadhurst et al published in the same issue of *Nature* and entitled "Looking Backwards Past Zero," Marc Davis has also summarized the implications of their discovery: "not only have Broadhurst *et al.* found structure at the

largest scale they have studied, but they find periodic oscilla- tions of density. If the galaxy distribution is truly periodic, it is safe to say we understand less than zero about the early Universe" (p. 699). See also the front page article by Wilford, "Astronomers' New Data Jolt Vital Part of Big Bang Theory," *New York Times* (3 January 1991), A 1, A 19, which reviews the implications of a report published on that date in *Nature*: "A critical element of the widely accepted Big Bang theory about the origin and evolution of the uni- verse is being discarded by some of its staunchest advocates, throwing the field of cosmology into turmoil. . . . A new analysis of a highly accurate survey by the Infrared Astronomical Satellite now shows the universe to be full of . . . superstructures and companion supervoids. A problem is that these structures appear to be far too vast to have formed since the Big Bang. The analysis has led a team of British and Canadian scientists to conclude that 'there is more structure on large scales than is predicted by the standard cold dark matter theory of galaxy formation.'. . . they said the theory in its present form must be abandoned."

9. Jeremy Campbell, *Grammatical Man: Information, Entropy, Language and Life* (New York: Simon & Schuster, A Touchstone Book, 1982), pp. 102, 105, 108, 263, 264, 265.

10. Stephen Hawking, *A Brief History of Time* (New York: Bantam, 1988), p. 123. See also the whole of chapter 8 for his discussion of chaotic big bang cosmology.

11. Appendix B will be centrally concerned with the now largely bypassed "general systems theory" that still seems most coherent with the modeling of the Sabbath Star Diagram. I do regret that many of its proponents have adopted the model of "self-organization" that violates the basic under- standing of the earlier theory of systems defined by the dual levels of microindeterminacy and macrodeterminacy. Erich Jantsch, by developing a full-scale model of a "self-organiz- ing universe" in *The Self-Organizing Universe: Scientific and Human Implications of the Emerging Paradigm of Evolution* (Oxford: Pergamon Press, 1980), enables us to see the lim- itations attendant on the attempt to forge a complete theory from the work of Ilya Prigogine with dissipative chemical structures and of Humberto Maturana and Francisco Varela with "autopoietic" biological systems, both of which exhibit the same "self-organizing" features through which a form emerges that simply reflects a balancing of various interact- ing forces. We have seen that Hans Jenny showed a "cymatic" form to emerge from sound vibrations passed through certain media and that Theodore Schwenk showed the same to be true of flowing forms in water; and so have recent researchers shown a vast array of such "fluid" types of organization, from predator-prey populations to the growth of cities, storms, and cancers. But it is not just such poten- tially catastrophic effects as cancer, locust plagues, and nuclear war that must limit our enthusiasm for autopoietic systems, rather the very features that distinguish them from the model of general systems theory earlier advanced: "At each level of autopoietic existence, a new version of macro- scopic indeterminacy comes into play. . . . there is now the

macroscopic indeterminacy in the formation of structures" (pp. 48–49). That Jantsch means his new formulation to supplant the older version is clear when he says: "With a generalized theory of dissipative structures, the dynamic aspect of a general system theory moves into the foreground and the macroscopic quantization of structures becomes of importance as well as the creative role of fluctuations" (p. 56). Only rarely does he qualify his enthusiasm for such a "generalized theory of dissipative structures": "We may tentatively view dissipative self-organization as an 'interme- diary' phenomenon. . . . Things are certainly much more complicated than . . . has been concluded by equilibrium thermodynamics. But they can also certainly not be explained by a simple condensation model of structuration" (p. 59). With this more balanced assessment, I can certainly agree, and we have just seen that the Sabbath Star System reveals just such "intermediary" structuring in the transi- tional stages between major regular phases. For the data amassed here and elsewhere do prove the existence of a wide variety of unstable systems not comprehended by general systems theory while being inadequate to explain the control features that give the great majority of systems the stability enabling them to survive. It is only by recognizing that nei- ther stable nor nonequilibrium structures can provide a sin- gle model capable of explaining all aspects of both permanence and change that a fully adequate theory of gen- eral systems can be formulated, one in which the latter per- haps are associated with the dynamics of evolution while the former are responsible for the dominant phases of stability.

12. One conclusion that I draw from this culminating "Law of Complex Magnitudes" is that a "complex" system is one that increases in regularity as it grows in size, as is the case with an organism, while a "simple" system is one dominated by irregular or random instability, as with a storm. These lat- ter systems I consider "simple" because they can never achieve the stable, multifaceted organization of the truly complex systems whose generation of more highly evolved stable forms gives meaning to the cosmic process. This is the opposite of the definitions and consequent conclusions developed by Stephen Wolfram in his recently published, detailed study of cellular automata entitled *A New Kind of Science* (Champaign, Ill.: Wolfram Media, 2002). Wolfram again proves, though with far more systematic exploration and attempted analogies than ever before, that simple pro- grams with simple initial components can yield outcomes of remarkably intricate and often beautiful patterning. My book hopefully proves the same. But his choice of signifi- cant outcomes reveals the perhaps unfortunate truth that one's most rationally developed scientific or logical proofs are just the fancy dress in which we clothe our personal convictions or prejudices. Thus he dismisses, with the oft- stated words "obviously simple," the majority of uniquely patterned outcomes of slightly different initial components or rules if they show any beauty-generating regularity like nest- ing and bestows his more honorific term "complex" on the few programs, like rule 110, that produce pure randomness.

Further, he takes such production of randomness not only to be the "universal program" that can model the cosmos but derives from this his culminating "Principle of Computational Equivalence" that all such programs have equivalent computational sophistication, that is, that no single such outcome is more meaningful than another. Thus he seems convinced that he has demonstrated that cosmic functioning is essentially random and meaningless. I hope that my present book will just as scientifically prove the opposite.

13. Stephan Jay Gould, *The Panda's Thumb: More Reflections in Natural History* (New York: W. W. Norton, 1976), p. 185.

14. Wilford, "Galactic Evenness Gives Astronomers Pause."

15. Robert R. Caldwell and Marc Kamionkowsky, "Echoes from the Big Bang," *Understanding Cosmology* (New York: Warner Books, 2002), pp. 47, 48.

16. Jonathan J. Halliwell, "Quantum Cosmology and the Creation of the Universe," *Understanding Cosmology* (New York: Warner Books, 2002), p. 106.

17. Ibid., 102.

18. Jertemiah P. Ostriker and Paul J. Steinhardt, "The Quintessential Universe," *Understanding Cosmology* (New York: Warner Books, 2002), p. 73.

19. Lawrence M. Krauss, "Cosmological Antigravity," *Understanding Cosmology* (New York: Warner Books, 2002), p. 90.

20. Ostriker and Steinhardt, "The Quintessential Universe," p. 81.

21. Martin Rees, Just Six Numbers: The Deep Forces That Shape the Universe (n.c.: Basic Books, 2000), 177.

22. Philip J. Hilts, "Far Out in Space, a Giant Discovery," *New York Times* (12 January 1990), A22.

23. Mario Livio, *The Accelerating Universe* (New York: John Wiley & Sons, 2000), p. 166. The original statement was in italics.

24. The term *morphogenetic* signifies the generation of form, for which see the full development of this concept by Rupert Sheldrake in *A New Science of Life: The Hypothesis of Formative Causation* (Los Angeles: J. P. Tarcher, 1981).

25. This is an idea similar to that concerning the power of the geometric dimensions that I developed in *The Secret Doctrine of the Kabbalah*, pp. 390–95, in concert with an analysis that synthesizes quantum cosmology with Lurianic cosmology. It was there argued that the dimensions represent true powers, ultimately those of time, as well as different levels of consciousness coherent with such space-time organization. This concept of dimension can be synthesized with that now being offered for complex magnitudes by regarding the dimensions as the major phase shifts of the universal system and the complex magnitudes as those occurring within each of these dimensions. It is the same phyla-species distinction taken to a still vaster scale.

26. Such a morphogenetic concept of magnitude may perhaps answer the question raised by Ilya Prigogine and Isabelle Stengers in *Order out of Chaos* (Toronto: Bantam Books, 1984), p. 206: "Since size or the system's density may play the role of a bifurcation parameter, how may purely quantitative growth lead to qualitatively new choices?"

27. But in the final section of chapter 1, I showed how a main element of the theory of an accelerating cosmic expansion, the antigravitational power of the "cosmological constant," could explain the earliest and most influential of biblical concepts of cosmogony: "He stretches out the heavens like a curtain" (Psalms 104:2). How the scientific understanding of such an accelerating universe can be synthesized with the Sabbath Star System model for complexity theory is further suggested in the following note.

28. One such question involves the "standard cold dark matter theory of galaxy formation" that, as we are told in note 8 above, "in its present form must be abandoned." If, however, such cold dark matter could be equated with the formative force in a complex magnitude, and this understood to be actualized only when a complex system crosses its threshold, then there would be no need to account for this strange matter from the time of the big bang, and it could be reaccepted as part of the progressive process of cosmogenesis.

29. For my earlier contrast between quantum cosmology and the cosmology of Luria, see *The Secret Doctrine of the Kabbalah*, pp. 380–412.

30. Pierre Teilhard de Chardin, *The Phenomenon of Man*, trans. Bernard Wall (New York: Harper & Row, 1975), pp. 259, 260, 262–63.

APPENDIX A

1. As quoted in Heinz R. Pagels, *Perfect Symmetry* (Toronto: Bantam Books, 1986), p. 187.

2. Ibid., pp. 187, 188, 189.

3. Ibid., p. 193.

4. As quoted in Fritjof Capra, *The Tao of Physics* (Boulder: Shambhala, 1975), p. 211.

5. Pagels, *Perfect Symmetry*, p. 161.

6. Ilya Prigogine and Isabelle Stengers, *Order out of Chaos*, pp. 105–6.

7. For the principles I have adduced from sacred science that argue against the conclusions drawn by quantum physics from their experimental violence to the structure of the atom, see again my major study of quantum physics in chapter 9 of *The Secret Doctrine of the Kabbalah*.

8. As quoted in Michael Talbot, *Mysticism and the New Physics* (Toronto: Bantam Books, 1981), p. 77. See also pp. 65–86 on Wheeler's concept of "superspace."

9. William Shakespeare, *A Midsummer Night's Dream*, 5.1.16–17.

10. See, for instance, *The Kirlian Aura*, ed. Stanley Krippner and Daniel Rubin (Garden City: Anchor Books, 1974).

11. See Kaplan, *Sefer Yetzirah*, p. 44 (1:5).

12. See Robert A. Monroe, *Journeys Out of the Body* (Garden City: Anchor Books, 1977) and John C. Lilly, M.D., *The Center of the Cyclone: An Autobiography of Inner Space* (New York: Bantam Books, 1979).

13. See chapter 15, note 20.

APPENDIX B

1. Weiss, *The Science of Life*, pp. 21–22.
2. Laszlo, The Systems View of the World.
3. Weiss, The Science of Life, p. 43.
4. Laszlo, The Systems View of the World, p. 67.
5. Von Bertalanffy, *Robots, Men and Minds*, pp. 21–22, 30.
6. Ibid., p. 32.
7. As quoted in ibid., p. 22.
8. Sigmund Freud, *Beyond the Pleasure Principle*, trans. James Strachey (New York: W. W. Norton, 1961), pp. 18, 20, 22–23.
9. Von Bertalanffy, *Robots, Men and Minds*, pp. 69–70.
10. Ibid., p. 80.
11. Weiss, *The Science of Life*, p. 78.
12. From Thomas Carlyle, *Sartor Resartus*, chap. 8, "The Center of Indifference."
13. Von Bertalanffy, *Robots, Men and Minds*, p. 30.
14. From *The Canterbury Tales*, "The Franklin's Tale," ll. 704–7.
15. For my fuller treatments of love, see *The Kabbalah of the Soul*, pp. 251–63, and *Elizabethan Love Tragedy*.
16. Emile Durkheim, *The Division of Labor in Society*, trans. George Simpson (New York: The Free Press, 1964), pp. 79–80. My brackets.
17. Conrad H. Waddington, "Concluding Remarks," in *Evolution and Consciousness*, eds. Erich Jantsch and Conrad H. Waddington (Reading, Mass.: Addison-Wesley, 1976), pp. 244–45.
18. Talcott Parsons, *Sociological Theory and Modern Society* (New York: The Free Press, 1967), pp. 298, 308, 314.
19. Ibid., pp. 319, 320.
20. Durkheim, *Division of Labor*, pp. 372–73, 407, 408.
21. John Milton, from the beginning section of *The Second Defense of the People of England*, trans. Robert Fellowes.
22. Hertz, ed., The Pentateuch and Haftorahs, p. 315.
23. See Durkheim's statement, "far from being trammelled by the progress of specialization, individual personality develops with the division of labor," in *Division of Labor*, p. 403.
24. Emile Durkheim, *The Elementary Forms of the Religious Life*, trans. Joseph Ward Swain (New York: The Free Press, 1965), pp. 29, 495.
25. Ibid., p. 486.
26. Ibid., pp. 495, 496.
27. A great forerunner of systems theory, whose evolutionary thought is most consistent with my own, is Pierre Teilhard de Chardin. That *The Phenomenon of Man*, originally written in 1938, presents a systems view of nature is clear from the following: "if things hold and hold together, it is only by reason of complexity, *from above*. . . . The existence of 'system' in the world is at once obvious to every observer of nature. . . . Determinate *without*, and 'free' within" (pp. 43, 57). Teilhard also presents a systems hierarchy comparable to the three basic levels I have distinguished as those of the "impersonal," the "personal," and the "transpersonal." For Teilhard, the critical point of evolution is not that of conscious life, since he believes this to be present in some precursive form at all stages of matter, but of reflexive consciousness, of an individual "*center . . .* conscious of its own organisation" (p. 165). And beyond this threshold of individual reflection is the further threshold of the "hyperpersonal" (p. 254), otherwise referred to as the "noosphere," the sphere of mind, and "Omega": "over and above this particular phenomenon—the individual accession to reflection—science has grounds for recognizing another phenomenon of a reflective nature co-extensive with the whole of mankind. Here as elsewhere in the universe, the whole shows itself to be greater than the simple sum of the elements of which it is formed" (p. 178). It should be clear that as the whole of evolution up to the threshold of reflection can be modeled by the fourth-world matrix, and that of the individual centers of reflection by the fifth-world matrix, so the "noosphere," which is identified both with society and the collective soul of mankind, can be modeled by the sixth-world matrix. Indeed, Teilhard's understanding of the spiritual nature of society comes closer to the position I have here presented than that of any other systems theorist: "Our earth of factory chimneys and offices . . . this great organism lives, in final analysis, only because of, and for the sake of, a new soul. . . . what are the intricacies of our social forms, if not an effort to isolate . . . the structural laws of the noosphere? . . . there is really developing above us another hominisation, a collective one of the whole species" (pp. 215, 222, 306). Similarly, the involution to the center I projected after completion of the Spiral Tree is exactly comparable to Teilhard's concept of final convergence to the Omega point, as shown at the conclusion to chapter 15.

APPENDIX C

1. Emile Benveniste, "The Levels of Linguistic Analysis," *Problems in General Linguistics*, trans. Mary Elizabeth Meek (Coral Gables, Fla.: University of Miami Press, 1971), p. 101.
2. Ibid., p. 104.
3. Ibid., p. 103.
4. Ibid., p. 105.
5. Ibid., p. 107.
6. Ibid., p. 104, 105, 108.
7. Ibid., p. 110.
8. Paul Ricoeur, *Hermeneutics & the Human Sciences*, trans. John B. Thompson (Cambridge: Cambridge University Press, 1981), p. 136, 166, 169, 175.
9. Ferdinand de Saussure, *Course in General Linguistics*, trans. Wade Baskin (New York: Philosophical Library, 1959), p. 16.
10. Ibid., pp. 66, 67, 69.
11. Benveniste, "The Nature of the Linguistic Sign," *Problems in General Linguistics*, p. 45.
12. Saussure, p. 113. See also Benveniste, "The Nature of the Linguistic Sign," p. 45.
13. Benveniste, "The Nature of the Linguistic Sign," pp. 45, 47.
14. Ibid., p. 46.

15. Aristotle, "Poetics," *The Basic Works of Aristotle*, ed. Richard McKeon (New York: Random House, 1941), p. 1479 (1459a).

16. Jaynes, *The Origin of Consciousness*, pp. 49, 51, 52, 60.

17. Paul Ricoeur, *The Rule of Metaphor: Multi-disciplinary Studies of the Creation of Meaning in Language*, trans. Robert Czerny et al. (Toronto: University of Toronto Press, 1977), p. 22.

18. See the subtitle of Paul Ricoeur's *The Rule of Metaphor*, given above in note 17.

19. Ibid., pp. 207, 209, 211, 212, 213. My brackets.

20. Owen Barfield, *Saving the Appearances* (New York: Harcourt Brace Jovanovich, n.d.), pp. 33, 82.

21. Benveniste, "Subjectivity in Language," *Problems in General Linguistics*, p. 224.

22. Benveniste, "A Look at the Development of Linguistics," *Problems in General Linguistics*, pp. 23, 26.

23. *The Philosophy of Paul Ricoeur: An Anthology of His Work*, ed. Charles E. Reagan & David Stewart (Boston: Beacon Press, n.d.), p. 126.

24. See *The Secret Doctrine of the Kabbalah*, pp. 100–13, for my philosophic development of the ideas presented in this appendix concerning the linguistic complementarity of spatial and temporal referents, which becomes my explanation of the meaning of sacred science.

25. Boman, Hebrew Thought Compared With Greek, p. 184.

26. Handelman, *The Slayers of Moses*, p. 32.

27. Roland Barthes, *Mythologies*, trans. Annette Lavers (New York: Hill and Wang, 1972), pp. 114, 115, 126, 129, 131, 143, 144, 156, 157.

28. Roland Barthes, *S/Z*, trans. Richard Miller (New York: Hill and Wang, 1974), pp. 5–6.

29. Ibid., p. 8.

30. Ibid., p. 9.

31. Ibid.

32. Benveniste, "The Levels of Linguistic Analysis," pp. 109, 110.

33. Benveniste, "The Nominal Sentence," *Problems in General Linguistics*, pp. 133–34.

34. Ricoeur, *The Rule of Metaphor*, p. 74.

35. Ibid., p. 65.

36. Black, Models and Metaphors, p. 28.

37. Monroe C. Beardsley, "The Metaphorical Twist," *Philosophy and Phenomenological Research* 22 (March, 1962): 299.

38. Aristotle, "Poetics," p. 1476 (1457b).

39. Ibid., p. 1475 (1457a).

40. Boman, Hebrew Thought Compared With Greek, pp. 28, 46, 48, 49.

41. Aristotle, "Poetics," 1479 (1459a).

42. See ibid., p. 1476 (1457b).

43. See W. K. Wimsatt, Jr. *The Verbal Icon: Studies in the Meaning of Poetry* (n.c.: University of Kentucky Press, 1954), 69–83.

44. See chapter 3 of *The Secret Doctrine of the Kabbalah* that not only defines Pythagorean and Hebraic sacred science but draws the philosophic implications of their unions of the temporal and the spatial, of the finite with the infinite.

45. See note 11 to chapter 15 above on systems theorists who have been proposing the model of "self-organization" in violation of the most basic principle of systemic organization.

46. John Milton, near the beginning of *Areopagitica*, his great treatise against censorship.

47. Aristotle, "Poetics," pp. 1461–62 (1450a & b), 1463 (1451a).

48. Ibid., p. 1457 (1448b).

49. Ibid., p. 1463 (1451a).

50. See chapter 3 on the Sabbath in *Renewing the Covenant*, especially pp. 99–106, 132–34, for this understanding of Sinai work as the gathering of manna and building of the Temple.

51. John Milton, *The Reason of Church Government*, preface to book 2.

APPENDIX D

1. Cynthia Eller, in *The Myth of Matriarchal Prehistory* (Boston: Beacon Press, 2001), has presented evidence to dispute the views of other anthropologists that there was a period of prehistory in which there was matriarchal rule. But Robert Lawlor in his studies of the Australian aborigines and their implications has shown that within a patriarchal social structure there were separate male and female societies that transmitted different cosmologies; and this is approach I have accepted to define the distinguishing characteristics of the eras I am correlating with the feminine or masculine orientations. For Lawlor's understanding, see *Voices of the First Day: Awakening in the Aboriginal Dreamtime* (Rochester, Vt.: Inner Traditions, 1991) and also, *Earth Honoring* (Rochester, Vt.: Park Street Press, 1991), particularly pp. 43, 109.

2. John Michell, *The New View Over Atlantis*, pp. 197, 212–13. See also pp. 36–7, 90.

3. Raphael Patai, *Man and Temple in Ancient Jewish Myth and Ritual*, 2nd ed. (New York: Ktav, 1967), p. 221.

4. Ibid., p. 89.

5. Lawlor, *Earth Honoring*, p. 44.

6. For the relation of the Sumerian temples to the sacred marriage, see Patai, *Man and Temple*, p. 88.

7. See John Anthony West, *The Traveler's Key to Ancient Egypt* (New York: Alfred A. Knopf, 1985), pp. 91–100.

8. Sophocles, *Antigone*, trans. Dudley Fitts and Robert Fitzgerald, in *Greek Plays in Modern Translation*, ed. Dudley Fitts (New York: Dial Press, 1947), pp. 469–70.

9. The superb translation of Pericles' "Funeral Oration" by Sir Alfred Zimmern is contained in Thucydides, *The History of the Peloponnesian War*, trans. Sir R.W. Livingstone (London: Oxford University Press, 1943), pp. 111, 113, 114.

10. Ibid., p. 114.

11. Ibid., p. 115.

12. See *The Secret Doctrine of the Kabbalah*, particularly chapters 1 and 6–8.

13. Geoffrey Chaucer, "Truth," ll. 15–21.

14. Lawlor, *Earth Honoring*, p. 177.

15. For the importance in this period of the *Corpus Hermeticum* and, through Pico della Mirandola, of the Kabbalah, see Frances A. Yates, *Giordano Bruno and the Hermetic Tradition* (Chicago: University of Chicago Press, 1964), as well as such of her later books as *The Rosicrucian Enlightenment* (Boulder: Shambhala, 1978), which traces the fusion of this tradition and alchemy in the works of John Dee. For the equal importance of the Pythagorean-Neoplatonic tradition, see Heninger, *Touches of Sweet Harmony: Pythagorean Cosmology and Renaissance Poetics.*

16. See *The Secret Doctrine of the Kabbalah,* pp. 2–11 passim.

17. As quoted in Yates, *Giordano Bruno and the Hermetic Tradition,* p. 91.

18. Francis Bacon, *New Atlantis,* in *English Prose: 1600–1660,* ed. Victor Harris and Itrat Husain (New York: Holt, Rinehart and Winston, 1967), pp. 84, 91.

19. See *The Columbia History of the World,* ed. John A. Garraty and Peter Gay (New York: Harper & Row, 1972), p. 485. I am indebted to this work for much of the factual background information in this appendix.

20. For a glorified Elizabethan treatment of Roger Bacon's magical powers, see Robert Greene's play, *The Honorable History of Friar Bacon and Friar Bungay.*

21. William Blake, "Marginalia" from his copy of Bacon's *Essays,* in *Selected Poetry and Prose of William Blake,* ed. Northrop Frye (New York: Modern Library, 1953), p. 446.

22. John Donne, "An Anatomie of the World," ll. 205–18.

23. William Shakespeare, *Macbeth,* 5.5.26–8.

24. Matthew Arnold, "Dover Beach," ll. 35–37.

25. William Butler Yeats, "The Second Coming", ll. 3–4.

26. For this dating of the *Massekhet Atzilut* and Tikkunei Zohar, see Gershom Scholem, *Kabbalah,* p. 119. For his revised dating of the *Temunah* to "around 1300," see his *Origins of Kabbalah,* note 233 on pp. 460–61, and the comments of Werblowsky in the editor's preface, p. xiv.

27. See the concluding section of chapter 1 for the fuller historical development of a Jewish esoteric cosmology of "seven worlds."

28. See the concluding section of chapter 15 devoted to "The Law of Complex Magnitudes" that I have derived from the modeling of complexity theory by the fully developed Sabbath Star System.

29. John Dryden, "The Secular Masque" or "Masque of the Century," (written 1700), ll. 95–100. In addition to their more general applications, there are also the more specific references in these lines to the three English kings of the seventeenth century, James I, Charles I, and Charles II.

Index

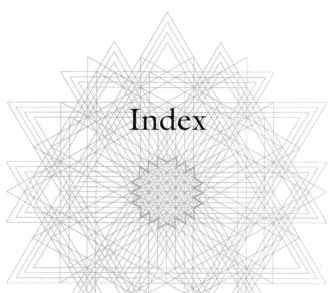

Aaron, 277, 279
Abba (Father)
  forbidden crossings and
    illusion of knowledge, 303
  fourth-world diagram, 64
  infinity, the final model of,
    377, 378
  linguistics, systematic, 440
  octave diagram, 201
  sixth-world diagram, 169,
    176
  sixth-world matrix model of
    the Neshamah Soul, 262,
    266
  sociology, a systems model
    of, 418
Abrabanel, Isaac, 105
Abraham, 254, 267, 278, 279,
  399
Abulafia, Abraham, 194, 240,
  247
acknowledgment, social, 423
Adam Kadmon, 35, 378, 467
  See also octave *listings;*
    seventh-world diagram
Adams, Abigail, 166–67
affinity, the attraction of,
  414–15
agriculture and a gender model
  of human history, 446, 449,
  451
Aharon of Karlin (Rabbi),
  172–73
Akiba, Rabbi, 195, 196, 203
Akkadians, 449
alchemy, 7–10, 18, 19, 485
Alexander the Great, 453
alienated individuality, 230
analogue model, 46, 47
androgynous cosmic
  son, 168
angels, 96, 97, 175, 204–11,
  322

animal stage of the Asiyah,
  112–18
Antigone (Sophocles), 451
Apocrypha, 133
Arafel, 193
Aravot, angels of, 204–11
architecture and systematic
  linguistics, 440, 441
Arikh Anpin (Long Face)
  forbidden crossings and
    illusion of knowledge, 303
  fourth-world diagram, 64
  infinity, the final model of,
    378, 379, 399
  linguistics, systematic, 440
  octave diagram, 190, 191,
    195, 201
  sixth-world diagram, 169,
    170, 172, 176, 179, 180
  sixth-world matrix model of
    the Neshamah Soul, 262,
    266
  sociology, a systems model
    of, 418
Aristotelian Final Cause, 149
Aristotle, 124, 396, 398, 430,
  436, 441–42
art/creativity, 232–33, 420
Asiyah, fourth material world
  of, 35, 47, 64, 97, 192,
  198, 261, 378, 379
  See also fourth world, the
    evolution of the
associative learning, 45–48
astral/dream perceptions,
  406
astrology, 471–72, 475
Attika Kaddisha, 186, 191,
  193, 196
attunement process, 247
Atzilut, first world of, 35, 37,
  61, 96, 170, 171, 191, 192,
  197, 198, 201, 261

"Auguries of Innocence"
  (Blake), 232
Aurobindo, Sri, 110
Auroville, 110
autopoietic systems, 481
ayin, 254
Azriel of Gerona, 18

Baal Shem Tov, 201
Babaji, 306
Baba Muktananda, 252–53
Bach, Edward, 110, 111
backward construction and
  seventh-world diagram,
  339–41
Bacon, Francis, 456–58
Bahir, 24, 263–64
balancing the scale, 477
Baraita de Ma'aseh Bereshit,
  12–13
Barfield, Owen, 431
Barthes, Roland, 428, 434–35,
  440
Beardsley, Monroe C., 430,
  436, 439
Benveniste, Emile, 427–32,
  434–36
Beriah (creation), 36, 37, 93,
  96, 170, 171, 192
Bible and a gender model of
  human history, 446
  See also Genesis creation
    account
Bible and significance of
  number 13, 184
bicameral man, 122–23
big bang cosmology, 396–97,
  480–81
Binah (understanding)
  forbidden crossings and
    illusion of knowledge,
    297, 307–9
  linguistics, systematic, 440

octave matrix of the Chayah
  Soul, 324
sixth-world diagram, 169
sixth-world matrix model of
  the Neshamah Soul, 259,
  281–83, 286
Tree of Life Diagram, 31,
  32, 42
Black, Max, 45–46, 430, 436
bliss, divine emotion of, 303–4,
  424
blue spiral, 341
Bohu (emptiness), 228, 229,
  234, 288–90, 294,
  298–300, 307, 324
Boman, Thorlief, 44–45, 433,
  437
Book of Jubilees, 20
borders, matrix, 130–31,
  156–61, 289–94
  See also beyond the border,
    temptations *under* fourth-
    world matrix of the
    Nefesh soul; forbidden
    crossings and illusion of
    knowledge
brain functioning and right/left
  sides, 240, 241, 411
Bridges to Infinity (Guillen),
  469–70
Broca's area, 471
Bronze Age, 449

Caesar, Julius, 453
Campbell, Jeremy, 391
Cantor, Georg, 189
Cardozo, Abraham, 320
Carlyle, Thomas, 413
Cassirer, Ernst, 411
catastrophic disorder needed to
  establish a new level of
  organization, 393–94
center, access to the, 91

central system in hexagram matrix, 215–16, 219–20, 230–34, 268, 279, 281, 291–92, 432–33
See also individual subject headings
cerebral intelligence, 122
chai force, 175–76, 190, 193
chakras, yogic concept of, 242–43, 267, 270–71, 282
chance, mysterious power to win against odds of mechanically determined, 249–51
chaos/disorganization, 302, 392, 468–69, 476
Chariot mystical tradition. *See* octave diagram
charisma, 296, 297
charity, higher counsels contravening impulses to, 302
charting the infinite future construction and matrix elements, relationship of, 362–72
double-octave decimal differences, 370–72
eighth-world matrix, 368–70
formulae for determining numbers of four matrix categories, 359–61
gender and construction elements, 362–64
ideally constructed numbers, 364
infinity, extrapolating the matrix to, 358–62
ninth world of Sabbath Star Diagram, 370
seventh-world diagram, 366–68
sixth-world diagram, 364–66
Chashmal, 192
Chaucer, 414, 454
Chayah soul. *See* octave *listings*
cherubs. *See* octave *listings*
Chesed (mercy)
forbidden crossings and illusion of knowledge, 295, 297–99, 301–3, 305–7, 309
fourth-world diagram, 31, 42
infinity, the final model of, 378, 379
linguistics, systematic, 441
octave diagram, 191, 193, 196, 201
sixth-world diagram, 169, 171–73
sixth-world matrix model of the Neshamah Soul, 258, 263–66, 268–70, 274–77, 279

sociology, a systems model of, 420
chi, 176
child, doctrine of the divine, 346
children, spiritual, 333
children and systematic linguistics, 434
China, 459
Chokhmah (wisdom)
forbidden crossings and illusion of knowledge, 297, 306–9
fourth-world diagram, 31, 32, 42
infinity, the final model of, 378
linguistics, systematic, 440
octave diagram, 206, 209
seventh-world diagram, 341
sixth-world diagram, 169
sixth-world matrix model of the Neshamah Soul, 259, 281, 283, 286
Christian and Jewish Kabbalah begin to diverge, 31
Christianity and a gender model of human history, 455–57
church and a gender model of human history, the, 454
clairaudience, 282, 283
clairvoyance, 282, 283
classic text and systematic linguistics, 434–35
closed society, nature of a, 421
Cohen, Martin S., 334
Coleridge, Samuel T., 239, 240, 281
collective representations, 431
collective unconscious, 220, 431
color and hexagram matrix, 217–21, 267, 268, 294–96, 403–4, 474–75
See also individual subject headings
community/master and Ruach consciousness, 145–47
compass (instrument), creative workings of the, 10–11, 13
complementarity of evolutionary levels of man/his God, 304
complexity theory, 390–99, 481–82
"Complex Organ Known as Skin Continues to Surprise" (Schmeck), 478
comprehension, mystery of, 282
computer generation/calculation, 336–37
concept bonded to sound-image, 429

Conclusions (Pico Della Mirandola), 456
conscience collective, 416, 422–24, 431
consciousness, creation account projecting virtual fields of higher, 19
constraints conveying the presence of power, 417–18
contraction of divine to a point and then withdrawal around that point, 24–25
Cordovero, Moses, 29–32, 317
Corpus Hermeticum, 453–55
corruptibility of individuals, 419
cosmogony, earliest source of Jewish, 24–26
cosmology prior to its adoption of four cosmic worlds doctrine, Kabbalistic, 20–26
counting as a cutting, understanding of, 284
covenant renewal, x
creations, concept of two, 20
creativity, 232–33, 246, 249, 448
cubic form defining created man's spiritual essence, 5, 21, 208–10
cymatics, 14–15

Da'at (non-Sefirah) element
fifth-world diagram, 139
fifth-world matrix model of the Ruach Soul, 245, 254
forbidden crossings and illusion of knowledge, 307–8
fourth world, the evolution of the, 92, 93
fourth-world diagram, 32–33, 42
fourth-world matrix of the Nefesh soul, 216
seventh-world diagram, 341, 343, 344
dark energy, 396, 407–8
davar, 433, 437
David, 277, 278, 333
death for love/honor, choosing of, 231–32, 291–92, 453
decimal sequence, 480
See also infinity, the final model of
de Leon, Moses, 102, 103
democracy, 452
Derekh ha-Shem (Luzzatto), 121
determinacy principle, 410
Devekut, 189, 195, 202, 204
diagonal to the side of a cube, relationship of the, 5, 21
diatonic scale, 36–37, 59, 64–65, 91, 108, 131, 181, 467
See also harmonic series; *individual subject headings*

dimension, the concept of, 482
directions of Sefirot relating to sexual positioning, 263–66
dissimilars and systematic linguistics, 438
Donne, John, 457
Do Sabbath Star, 153, 190, 191, 193
double-aspecting, 220–24
Double-octave decimal differences, 370–72
Double Spiral Tree, 319–29
Dov Baer, 269–70
Draco, 452
dream state and collective unconscious, 220
dual-aspected nature of all worlds, 346–47
dual movements of the mystical journey, 196
Durkheim, Emile, 416, 421–22, 424–25
dyad, the indefinite, 164

Eastern traditions, the soul and, 58
egocentric purification and Ruach consciousness, 145
ego satisfaction, destructive pursuit of, 229–30, 302–3
Egypt, 121–22, 209, 449–51, 458
8, biblical beginnings of number, 381
18, significance of the number, 187–88
eighth world of Sabbath Star Diagram
Bible identifying eighth day as special, 346
charting the infinite future, 368–70
dual aspected nature of all worlds, 346–47
infinity, the final model of, 374
Plates 19-21, 347
problem constructing, 346–47
pulsating star, 351–53
seventh-world diagram used to construct, 347
sixth and seventh worlds, observing borders of, 348–53
size of border design, 352–53
twelve-pointed star, 349
Ein Sof (Limitless Light), 170, 182, 184, 199, 203, 303, 305, 306, 318, 342, 382, 399
Einstein, Albert, 26, 396
Eitz Chayyim (Vital), 20, 31, 35, 171, 176, 197, 263, 264, 303–4, 311

Elijah, 134–36, 173, 195, 196, 203
Eliot, T. S., 334
Elisha, 254
Elohim, 13, 184
emanation process, 6, 23, 31, 42, 58, 96, 197–99, 305, 378
empathy, 241
Enoch, 194, 195, 202, 207, 346, 399, 479
erythropoietic porphyria, 478
Esau, 324, 325, 478
Esh M'Saref (The Refiner's Fire), 9
eternity and time, difference between, 342
ethereal essence and systematic linguistics, 441
ether element pervading space beyond earth's atmosphere, 337
even numbers, principle of, 164
evil and good, Yetziric, 96–97, 120, 220, 270
evolution, biological, 131, 394–95, 410
existential despair, 230
Exodus from Egypt, 419
expanding universe, 392, 393, 396–97
expansion and point/field of primordial light, 24–26
"Experts See Mind's Voices in New Light" (Goode), 471
exploitive power, self-defeating nature of, 293–94
expressive form, science of, 44–48, 241, 281, 398, 435
Ezekiel, 143–44, 190–92, 194, 201, 203, 207, 315, 319

Fa/Fi Sabbath Star, 66–81, 98–106, 118, 137–39, 143, 449
fall, fourth-world diagram and biblical description of the, 68–80, 467
fallen faculties, matrix modeling of the, 226–27
false Messiah/prophet, 235, 296–300, 320, 424–25
familiars, 173
Farmer, Doyne, 468
Fa Sabbath Star, 91–94, 97
Feigenbaum E. A., 468
Feinberg, Gerald, 407
feminine personality, 166–69, 433
See also gender model of human history
Fibonacci series of numbers, 163, 330, 331
Ficino, Marsilio, 455

fifth-world diagram
beyond matrix borders, 294–300
borders, matrix, 130–31
charting the infinite future, 364
fifth dimension, 127–28
fifth-world Sabbath Star to fourth-world diagram, 83–87
gender model of human history, 449, 451, 453
geometry of Sabbath Stars, 136–44
impersonal and transpersonal realm, 126–27
infinity, the final model of, 375
linguistics, systematic, 434, 435, 438
Messianic age, 131–44
overview, 126–27
Ruach consciousness, 144–47
shofar, the, 128–30
sixth-world matrix model of the Neshamah Soul, 270–72
systems theory, 410–12
fifth-world matrix model of the Ruach Soul
analytic faculty of Ruach mind, 245
brain functioning and right/left sides, 240, 241
chakras, yogic concept of, 242–43
creativity, 246
definition of fifth world matrix, 236–47
free will, 238–39
imagination, 239–40
infinite continuity, 242
meditation, 244–45, 247–49
mind and heart functions, 244
number of its constituents, 237–38
power, 241–42, 249–55
52 and seventh-world diagram, 344–46
Findhorn community, 111
finite and infinite, difference between, 342, 356
fire and water, concern with opposing qualities of, 10, 13, 18
Fi Sabbath Star, 66, 86, 103, 106–12, 132, 143, 175, 449
Fi/Sol Sabbath Star, 66, 81–83, 112–18, 121, 124, 131, 137, 140, 153
5 and 13, number sequence of, 183
five dimensional cosmos, 468
flight, spiritual, 306

forbidden constructions, 88–89, 93, 113, 159, 165
forbidden crossings and illusion of knowledge
border, meaning of matrix, 288–89
fifth-world matrix border, 294–300
fourth-world matrix borders, 289–94
introduction: Tohu or Tikkun, 288–89
light units, 308–12
sixth-world matrix border, 300–308
See also beyond the border, temptations *under* fourth-world matrix of the Nefesh soul
force used to overcome ideas/the weak, 421
four cosmic worlds, 6, 18–20, 23, 24, 47, 127–28
fourth world, the evolution of the
Asiyah and the minerals: first Sabbath star
introduction, 98–100
matter, esoteric interpretation of, 104–5
matter, physics of, 105–6
soul and its vestments, the, 100–104
Asiyah and the plants: second Sabbath Star, 106–12
Asiyah and the plants: third Sabbath star, 112–18
Asiyah and man: fourth Sabbath star, 118–25
definition of the Sabbath Stars, 90–91
Yetzirah, Sabbath Stars of, 91–97
fourth-world diagram
beyond matrix borders, 289–94
charting the infinite future, 364
and the fall, 68–80
gender model of human history, 453
infinity, the final model of, 375
introduction, 56–58
linguistics, systematic, 432, 438
redemption, sabbatical model of, 83–87
Ruach potential, 127
self-generating, 58–68
sixth-world matrix model of the Neshamah Soul, 270–72
Sol Sabbath Star, 59–67

transformative moment, 81–83
trivalent logic, 87–89
fourth-world matrix of the Nefesh soul
beyond the border, temptations
central personality, 230–33
conclusions/summary, 233–35
introduction to temptations of a fallen culture, 228–29
lateral personality, 229–30
dual spiral matrix in fallen/unfallen forms, 220–24
hexagram matrix, understanding the
central system, interfaced, 219–20
introduction, 214–15
lateral system, interfaced, 217–19
macrostructure, 215–16
microstructure, 216–17
42, significance of the number, 188–89
"Fragments of Philolaus" (Diels-Krans), 464
free will, 121, 238–39
Freud, Sigmund, 411–12
Friedmann, Alexander, 392
Fuller, Buckminster, 474
"Funeral Oration" (Thucydides), 452
future inspiring attuned spirits to new modes of being, 124–25
future-modeling, 56, 57, 73, 81–83, 91, 98, 127, 221–22, 347

galaxies, formation/distribution of, 480–82
"Garden, The" (Marvell), 111
Garden of Pomegranates (Cordovero), 29
Gates of the Garden of Eden (Koppel), 165
Gematria, 284–85, 310, 319, 326, 331, 344, 365, 378, 379
gender model of human history
aboriginal clans and wandering, 446–48
Bible, the, 446
conclusions/summary, 462–63
construction elements, 165–69, 362–64
feminine and masculine dominance, oscillations between, 456

feminine eras lasting longer than masculine ones, 459–60
fourth to the tenth centuries, 454–55
Greek and Jewish associations, differing, 479–80
Hebraic-Hellenic duality, 451–53
hierarchically ordered systems, 473
Messianic millennium, 460–62
monuments and temples, building, 447–51
Myth of Matriarchal Prehistory, 484
new millennium, 459
overview, 444–45
prehistoric epochs, 445–46
Rome, ancient, 453–54
seventeenth century to present, 456–58
6000 and a spiritual millennium, 461–62
3300 B.C.E.–1200 B.C.E., 448–49
transpersonal realm, 458–59
twelfth to sixteenth century, 455–56
generation gap, 371–72
Genesis creation account
cosmology prior to four cosmic worlds doctrine, 20–26
disobedience by Adam, 467
hexagram, 10–13
hexagram form, progressive revelation of, 13–20
octave diagram, 181
Pythagoreanism, 5
See also octave diagram
genus to species, movement to, 436
geometric interpretation, linguistic method of, 3–4, 44–47, 283–86
geometry providing an archetypal explanation of the functioning of cosmic consciousness, 4, 12
Geronese Kabbalists, 6
Gevurah (judgment)
fifth-world diagram, 135
forbidden crossings and illusion of knowledge, 295–99, 303, 305–7, 309
fourth world, the evolution of the, 120
linguistics, systematic, 441
octave diagram, 193, 199, 201
seventh-world diagram, 341
sixth-world diagram, 171
sixth-world matrix model of

the Neshamah Soul, 258, 263, 264, 270, 271, 274–79
sociology, a systems model of, 420
Tree of Life Diagram, 31, 42
Ghadiali, Dinshah, 219, 221
Gilgamesh, 449
Gilgul, 333
Gleick, James, 468–69
Gödel, Kurt, 469–70
Godhead divided into immanent/transcendent forms, 24
God's partnership with man, 304
Goethe, Johann, 246
Gog and Magog, the war of, 133–35, 138, 298
good and evil, Yetziric, 96–97, 120, 220, 270
government and a systems model of sociology, 420–21, 425
grace/rigor, delusive dangers attached to excessive, 302–3
gunpowder, 457
Gurdjieff, George I., 238–39
Guth, Alan H., 396

Habad Hasidism, 269–70
Handelman, Susan A., 47, 433
Ha-Nefesh ha-Chokhmah (de Leon), 102
Hannah, 333
harmonic series, 14–16, 19, 203
See also diatonic scale; *individual subject headings*
harmony and proportion, 275–76, 306
Hawking, Stephen, 392
healing and meditation, 247–49
heart
center, heart, 476
double, 477
linguistics, systematic, 441
and open social systems, 420
sixth-world matrix model of the Neshamah, 272–79
Heart of Darkness (Conrad), 239
Hebraea, Maria, 7–10
Hebraic-Hellenic duality, 451–53
Hekhalot literature, 21–24
hermeneutics, 45
Hertz, J. H., 285, 324, 423
Hester, Marcus B., 430
hexagon and hexagram, distinction between, 28–29
hexagram
of creation, 13–20
Genesis and the *Zohar,* esoteric key to, 10–13
Hebraic sacred science, 7–10

hexagon and, distinction between, 28–29
overview, 6
resonance deriving from overlaying of previous, 91
scientific implications of, 402–8
Tree of Life Diagram, history and structure of, 29–31
See also charting the infinite future; Tree of Life Diagram; *individual subject headings*
Hey, 378
hidden design, 2–3, 42
Hinduism, 178
Hirsch, E. D., Jr., 45
Hiyya, Rabbi, 22–23
Hod (splendor)
forbidden crossings and illusion of knowledge, 293, 295–97, 307, 311
linguistics, systematic, 437–38
octave diagram, 191, 193
sixth-world diagram, 170, 171
sixth-world matrix model of the Neshamah Soul, 258, 261, 262, 264, 271, 272, 279, 280
Tree of Life Diagram, 31, 33, 41
Hoffman, Ralph, 471
holiness associated with community, 423–24
honor/love, choosing death for, 231–32, 291–92, 453
horn, fifth-world diagram and form of the, 128–30, 135
Hubble, Edwin P., 396
hunter-gatherer tribes, 167, 446

iconography, Egyptian, 121–22
image and language development, 429, 430
imaginary numbers, 407
imagination, 239–40, 245, 252, 280, 292–93, 296
imitation and systematic linguistics, 442
Imma (Mother)
forbidden crossings and illusion of knowledge, 303
fourth-world diagram, 64
linguistics, systematic, 440
octave diagram, 201
sixth-world diagram, 169, 171, 176
sixth-world matrix model of the Neshamah Soul, 262, 266
sociology, a systems model of, 418

immanent laws, 413
immanent/transcendent forms, Godhead divided into, 24
immortality, 124, 242, 471–72
imperfection, dealing with, 231–32
impersonal realm, 126–27, 410, 411
incompleteness theorems, 469–70
India, 459
Indian cultures, Central/South American, 157
individuality, unrestrained, 229–30, 302–3, 457
individuality and systematic linguistics, 432
infinity, the final model of decimal sequence, converging
data exploration, 380–88
implications, exploring the, 388–90
decimal sequence, periodic, 373–80
finite and infinite, difference between, 342, 346
formulas needed for new discovery, 395–96
Law of Complex Magnitudes, convergence and the, 390–99
7 and 4, association of numbers, 379–80, 382
instinctive faculty, 431
intake/outflow, microhexagrams operating as organs of, 276
integration, attractive power of social, 417
interpretations and systematic linguistics, 434–35
intuitive faculty, 431
inward/outward aspects of supernal lights and worlds of creation, distinction between, 195
inward *vs.* outward hexagram construction, 161–62
Isaac, 23, 267, 278, 279
Isaiah, 202, 203
Israel and Exodus from Egypt, 419

Jacob, 173–74, 176–79, 201, 274, 279, 324, 325, 399, 478
Jaynes, Julian, 122–23, 430
Jenny, Hans, 14–15, 481
Jephthah, 278
Jesus' transubstantiation of bread/wine, 252
Jewish Alchemists (Patai), 7–9
Joseph, 188, 277, 278

Jubilee associated with concept of redemption, 129–30
Jubilee cycle, 20–21
Judah bar Shalom, 14
Jung, Carl, 220, 267, 321–22, 326
justice and the Neshamah Master, 277–79, 302

Kabbalah of the Soul (Leet), 46, 198, 199, 247, 464, 476, 479
Kaf ha-Kela, 322
Kaplan, Aryeh, xvi, 191–92, 263, 466
Karagianis, Paul, 480
Kashmir Shaivism, 178
Katina, Rabbi, 21
Kepler, Johannes, 280
Keter (crown)
    forbidden crossings and illusion of knowledge, 294, 297–99, 306, 307
    infinity, the final model of, 378
    octave diagram, 190, 193, 196, 198, 206, 209
    octave matrix of the Chayah Soul, 322, 323, 329
    seventh-world diagram, 343
    sixth-world diagram, 169, 170
    sixth-world matrix model of the Neshamah Soul, 259, 261, 266, 268, 279–83, 286
    sociology, a systems model of, 419
Khalid ibn Yazad, 9
Klausner, Joseph, 133–35
Koch curve, 468
Krippner, Stanley, 465–66

Lacan, Jacques, 428
La/Li Sabbath Star, 153
language as a cognitive power of the Neshamah mind, 283–86
"Large-scale Distribution of Galaxies at the Galactic Poles" (Broadhurst, Ellis, Koo & Szalay), 480–81
La Sabbath Star, 131–32, 134
Laszlo, Ervin, 410
lateral system in hexagram matrix, 216, 217–19, 229–30, 234–35, 268, 279, 293, 403–6, 420, 432–33
    See also individual subject headings
Lawlor, Robert, xv, 448
Law of Complex Magnitudes, 390–99, 481–82
Law of the Matrix Border, 300
Leonora, 267

letters, key to creation through division of Hebrew, 18, 21
Lévi-Strauss, Claude, 428
Lévy-Bruhl, Lucien, 431
light, contraction of divine. *See* Ein Sof; Tzimtzum
light, Lurianic distinction between inner and surrounding, 356
light units, 308–12, 342–46, 417, 478, 480
    See also charting the infinite future
light years, 342
Lily, John, 406
limitation, abiding within divine laws of, 229–30
limitation of our knowledge, all we can know is, 344
Limits, man deluded into thinking his dominion has no, 293
linguistic method of geometric interpretation, 3–4, 44–47, 283–86
linguistics, systematic
    levels of language, three, 427–28
    sentence, matrix modeling of the, 435–39
    word, matrix modeling of the, 428–35
    work, matrix modeling of the, 439–43
Li Sabbath Star, 149, 153, 155, 161, 185, 190
logical theory, 469–70
"Looking Backwards Past Zero" (Davis), 480–81
Lorenz, Edward, 468
love, courtly *vs.* worldly, 476
love/honor, choosing death for, 231–32, 291–92
Lurianic Kabbalah (Isaac Luria)
    Ari/lion system of cosmology, 6
    complementarity of evolutionary levels of both man and his God, 304
    conflict between Lurianic and Zoharic models, 466
    creations, concept of two, 20
    inward/outward aspects of supernal lights and worlds of creation, distinction between, 195
light, inner and surrounding, 356
light residing in darkness of the lower world, 320
linguistic expression, 285
    maturation levels, 171
    principles, three main, 30
    Reshimu, 305
    restoration, cosmic, 31
    soul's imprisonment, 102

soul taken forward to divine multiplicity, 58
Tikkun, 180
transformation of original divinity into Partzufim, 123
Tzelem, 95
Tzimtzum, 164
Lyrical Ballads (Coleridge and Wordsworth), 280

Ma'asekhet Atzilut, 6, 18, 23, 24
Mackover, Maurice, 480
Maclean, Dorothy, 111
macro/microdeterminancy, unity within a system of dual levels of, 392–93, 481
macrostructure, understanding the hexagram, 215–16, 403–6
    See also individual subject headings
magical transformation, accounts of, 252–53
magic made kosher/white through the Kabbalah, 175
magnitude, morphogenetic concept of, 482
Malkhut (kingdom)
    forbidden crossings and illusion of knowledge, 307
    infinity, the final model of, 377, 378
    linguistics, systematic, 433
    octave diagram, 190, 191, 198
    octave matrix of the Chayah Soul, 322, 325, 329, 334
    sixth-world diagram, 169–70, 173
    sixth-world matrix model of the Neshamah Soul, 260, 261, 263–66, 268, 269, 271, 277, 278
    Tree of Life Diagram, 31, 41
man stage of the Asiyah, 118–25
mantra, a, 247, 252–53
Marlowe, Christopher, 230
Marx, Karl, 424
masculine personality, 166–69, 377, 433
    See also gender model of human history
matriarchy, 448, 484
matter, esoteric interpretation of, 104–5
matter, physics of, 105–6
Maturana, Humberto, 481
maturation process, three-stage, 171
McLuhan, Marshall, 439
meaning and systematic linguistics, 441–42
meaningfulness, social, 414–15, 421–26

"Measure of the Body," 314, 329–34
Medici, Cosimo de, 455
meditation, 244–45, 247–49, 267–68
Melville, Herman, 230
men for dominance, 445
    See also gender model of human history
mental breakdowns, 302
Merkabah (Chariot) mystical tradition. *See* Octave diagram
Mesopotamia, 449, 450
Messiah
    communal response to the presence of the, 134
    false, 235, 296–300, 320
    gender identification, 168
    heralding in the, 136
    man, requiring form and participation of, 161
    See also fifth-world diagram
Messiah ben David, 133, 136
Messiah ben Joseph, 133, 135
Messianic Idea in Israel (Klausner), 133
Messianic millennium, 131–44, 460–62, 472
Messianic Mystics (Idel), 472
metaphor, 430, 436, 438, 439
Metatron, 194–95, 202, 203–4, 206–7, 210–11, 334, 346, 399, 479
Mexico, 209
Michell, John, 479
microstructure of hexagram matrix, 216–17, 403–6
    See also individual subject headings
Midrash ha-Ne'lam on Ruth, 223–25, 311
Midrash Rabba, 24
Milton, John, 424, 440, 443
mind, sixth-world matrix model of the Neshamah, 279–87
mind of its own, cosmic system having a, 416–17
mineral stage of the Asiyah, 100–104
Mi Sabbath Star, 63, 65–67, 70, 74–78, 81, 91, 92, 95, 99–102, 104, 132, 141
monad, the indivisible, 164
Monroe, Robert, 406
monuments/temples, sacred science directed to building, 447–51, 455
moral ambiguities, dealing with, 231
More, Thomas, xiii, 229
Moses, 192, 195, 203, 205–6, 209–10, 254, 275, 277, 279, 315

Mother, the (spiritual teacher), 110, 111
mountain form of Buddhist temple architecture, 157–58
mountain to another, Jewish history viewed as progressing from one, 16
Mount Sinai, ram's horn blown on, 129
Muhammad ibn Umail, 8
Muktananda, Baba, 252–53
musical sweetness unchaining the soul, 173
Myth of Matriarchal Prehistory (Eller), 484
mythology, 285, 314, 413–14, 434

naming ideas/things, 286, 430–31, 437
narcissistic inflation of ego, 229–30
Nathan of Gaza, 320–21
needy, Neshamah Master expanding capacities of the, 277
Nefesh Chayah, 70, 72, 80, 121, 226
Nefesh level of the soul
  animal stage of the Asiyah, 112, 113, 117
  Asiyah and the minerals: first Sabbath star, 100–104
  beyond fourth-world matrix borders, 289–94
  Fa Sabbath Star, 93
  Fi Sabbath Star, 103, 107
  fourth-world diagram, 57, 70, 80, 85, 87
  free will, 95
  gender model of human history, 458, 460
  hexagram, 19
  immortality, 471–72
  linguistics, systematic, 435
  man stage of the Asiyah, 118, 119
  Mi Sabbath Star, 90, 92, 95
  octave diagram, 196, 201, 207
  paranormal experiences, 407
  Ruach soul level, movement to, 124, 127, 144
  Science of Expressive Form, 47
  shedim (demons), 97
  social conditioning, 239
  Sol₂/Si Sabbath Star, 143
  vision, 280
  See also fourth-world matrix of the Nefesh soul
negative attitudes and disease/healing, 248–49
Negative Spiral Tree, 295–96, 323, 421

neoplatonic cosmology of emanation, 23
Neshamah consciousness/level of the soul
  Binah, 324
  fourth-world diagram, 124
  hexagram, 18, 19
  Midrash ha-Ne'lam on Ruth, 223–25
  octave diagram, 192–95, 202
  Partzufim, 173–80
  self-redemption, 323
  sixth-world diagram, 149, 157
  sociology, a systems model of, 424, 425
  systems theory, 412
  true soul, 327
  See also Sixth-world matrix model of the Neshamah Soul
Netzach (eternity)
  forbidden crossings and illusion of knowledge, 292, 295, 297, 307, 311
  linguistics, systematic, 437, 438
  octave diagram, 191, 193
  octave matrix of the Chayah Soul, 327
  sixth-world diagram, 170, 171
  sixth-world matrix model of the Neshamah Soul, 258, 261, 262, 268, 271, 272, 275–77, 279, 281
  Tree of Life Diagram, 31, 33, 41
New Atlantis (Bacon), 456–57
Newtonian physics, 393
ninth world of Sabbath Star Diagram, 353–57, 370, 374
nothing, production of something out of, 254
nouns, 436–37
nuclear weapons, 425
Nukvah (the Female)
  fourth-world diagram, 64
  infinity, the final model of, 377, 378
  octave diagram, 190–91, 193, 196, 197, 201, 202
  sixth-world diagram, 170, 173–76, 179
  sixth-world matrix model of the Neshamah Soul, 262–66, 268
  sociology, a systems model of, 415
number theory and diagram construction, 162–65

occult, Nefesh personalities who turn to the, 293
octave diagram

Aravot, angels of, 204–11
Chariot, the working of the, 189–97
construction elements, 181–86
forty position-defining construction elements, 202
harmonic series, 203
horizontal/vertical axes, 184–86
impurity at transcendent level of consciousness, 197
name, unification of the, 186–89
Tzimtzum, 197–204
octave matrix of the Chayah Soul
  cherubs and trees, 313–19
  Double Spiral Tree, 319–29
  gender model of human history, 459
  "Measure of the Body," 329–34
octaves and generation gap, 371–72
odd numbers, the principle of, 164
Odyssey, The (Homer), 128
Ofanim, 190, 192, 193, 201
On Ecstasy (Dov Baer), 269–70
open/closed societies, distinguishing between, 420, 421
Oration on the Dignity of Man (Pico Della Mirandola), 456
Order out of Chaos (Prigogine & Stengers), 482
Other Side, redemption through the, 198, 207, 295–96, 319–29
outflow/inflow, microhexagrams operating as organs of, 276
outward/inward aspects of supernal lights and worlds of creation, distinction between, 195
outward *vs.* inward hexagram construction, 161–62

Pagels, Heinz R., 403, 404
pagoda plan, 157–58
pain, disintegration of personality into, 305
Paradise Lost (Milton), 10, 31, 232, 294, 443
Paradoxical Ascent to God (Elior), 476
paranormal experiences/power, 293, 406–7
Pardes Rimmonim (Cordovero), 29–31
Parsons, Talcott, 418
Partzufim (divine personalities)

construction elements of sixth-world diagram, 169–80
fourth world, the evolution of the, 123
fourth-world diagram, 64
hexagram, 8
sixth-world diagram, 148–49, 165, 169–80
sixth-world matrix model of the Neshamah Soul, 261–67
See also individual personalities
past-modeling, 56, 57, 74, 81–83, 91, 127, 339–41
past retained as form within present as it will be retained within the future, 411–12
Patai, Raphael, 7–9, 447
patriarchy, 167, 446, 484
permitted/forbidden construction possibilities, distinction between, 88–89, 159
personalities. *See* Partzufim (divine personalities)
personal realm, 410, 411–12, 440
personal/transpersonal power, difference between, 422–23
Phenomenon of Man (Teilhard de Chardin), 483
Philo Judaeus, 4
Phoenix myth, 314
phonic translation, 432
phyletic transformation, 394–95
Pico Della Mirandola, Giovanni, 175, 456
Pirke de Rabbi Eliezer, 22, 24
plants stage of the Asiyah, 106–12
plateaulike matrix border, 221
Plato, 4, 58, 432, 455
Platonic solids, xv
poetry, 283, 286
police state, 299
politicians, 299
polysemy, 432
Portae Lucis (Rincius), 29
positive attitudes and disease/healing, 248–49
power
  bad/good use of, xi
  exploitive, self-defeating nature of, 293–94
  gender model of human history, 458
  light units and the illusion of, 308–12
  linguistics, systematic, 437–39, 442
  Ruach Master, 241–42, 249–55
  sociology, a systems model of, 417–23

prana, 176
predicate-nominative form of sentence, 436
Prelude, The (Wordsworth), 4
Prigogine, Ilya, 404, 481
Prince, The (Machiavelli), 457
prophecy, the power of, 299–300
proselytes, 134
Providence, 251, 262, 274, 277, 406
Psalm 104:2, repeated verse from, 24–26
pseudepigrapha, 133
psychic energy, 406–7
public/private sectors of society, distinguishing between, 419, 420–21
public responsibility, 412
Pulley, The (Herbert), 246
pulsating star, 351–53, 356, 372
punctuated equilibria, 394
Purce, Jill, 328–29, 333
purification and Ruach consciousness, egocentric, 145
Pyramids, 450
Pythagoreanism, Jewish esoteric tradition associated with, 4–6, 10, 23–24, 40, 45, 47, 128, 285, 464–65, 480

quantum mechanics, 393, 396–97, 402–8, 482
Quetzalcoatl myth, 314

Ra'aya Meheimna, 23
Rachel, 173–74, 176–79, 201, 267, 268, 274
reality, hexagram and physical nature of, 403–8
reality and language, equivalence between, 432
rectification accomplished through confronting Other Side, 198, 327
redemption
    Other Side, through the, 319–29
    proceeding in both directions simultaneously, 90
    sabbatical model of, 83–87
red spiral, 294–96, 419
Rees, Martin, 396–97
regularity emerging from initial irregularity, 362, 391–93, 397–98
reincarnation, 333
relativity theory, 393
religion and spiritual evolution, 233
religious beliefs within collective conscience of society, 424–25

religious claims of miraculous transformations, 252–53
Renaissance, the, 457
Renewing the Covenant (Leet), x, xiv, 246
repeating/retarding decimal sequence, 381–89
repression, 325
Reshimu, 305
resonance deriving from overlaying of previous hexagrams, 91
restoration. *See* Partzufim; Tikkun
revolutionary, the, 299, 416
Richards, I. A., 430, 436
Ricoeur, Paul, 428, 430, 439–42
rigor/grace, delusive dangers attached to excessive, 302–3
"Rime of the Ancient Mariner, The" (Coleridge), 280
Rome, ancient, 453–56
Romeo and Juliet (Shakespeare), 231
Rosh Hashanah, 129, 173
Ruach consciousness
    beyond fifth-world matrix borders, 294–300
    beyond fourth-world matrix borders, 289–94
    fifth-world diagram, 126–27, 142, 144–47
    fourth world, the evolution of the, 117, 124
    fourth-world diagram, 57, 85
    gender model of human history, 458, 462
    hexagram, 18
    linguistics, systematic, 438
    octave diagram, 190, 192, 201
    paranormal experiences, 407
    public responsibility, 412
    realized human level on which mankind should be functioning, 222–23
    schizophrenics, 234
    sociology, a systems model of, 425
    suicide, rising above drives to, 233
    sympathetic inhabiting of the partner's soul body, 327
    vision, 280
    See also fifth-world matrix model of the Ruach Soul
"Ruach Elohim Chayyim" (Breath of the Living God), 247
Russell, Bertrand, 469

Sabbath day, 254–55
Sabbath Star Diagram, xiii–xvi
    analogue model, 47
    combination of two geometric expressions of the Kabbalah, 2–3
    hexagram construction/progression principles, 39–44
    hexagram of creation, 19–20
    Kabbalah and the, remarkable coherence between, 3–4
    rules governing, 88–89
    self-generating geometric construction, 3
    seven worlds, movement beyond four cosmic worlds to, 20
    Tree of Life Diagram to, 464
    Tzimtzum, 199–201
    See also infinity, the final model of; *individual model of; individual subject headings*
Sabbatical cosmic structure, association of Jewish esoteric tradition with, 20–26, 181
    See also hexagram; seventh-world diagram
Sagan, Dorion, 166
Samson, 278, 302
Samuel, 302, 333
Sarah, 399
Sarug, Israel, 199
Satanism as danger to errant Ruach soul, 294
Satya Sai Baba, 252
Saul, 302
Saussure, Ferdinand de, 284, 428–29, 434, 435
Scarlet Letter, The (Hawthorne), 230–31
Schachter-Shalomi, Zalman, 322, 323
schizophrenia, 234, 292–93, 471
Scholem, Gershom
    Adam Kadmon, 187
    emanation process, 305
    four cosmic worlds, 23
    Geronese Kabbalists, 6
    inward/outward aspects of supernal lights and worlds of creation, distinction between, 195
    Merkabah tradition, 186
    Metatron, 194–95
    millennium, 472
    Pythagoreanism, 4
    redemption, 320, 321
    reincarnation, 333
    Reshimu, 305
    Sefirot, 317–18
    stars, soul of evolved humans in sphere of fixed, 357

236, enigmatic number, 330
Tzelem, 95
Tzimtzum, 197
Schwaller de Lubicz, R. A., 121–23
Schwenk, Theodore, 481
Science of Expressive Form, 44–48, 281, 398, 435
Secret Doctrine of the Kabbalah, The (Leet), x, xiii–xiv, 4, 5, 58, 171, 198, 209, 270, 283, 402, 464, 466, 480, 482
Secret of the Golden Flower, The, 124
Sefer ha-Bahir, 6
Sefer ha-Iyyun, 183, 186, 188, 314, 317, 318
Sefer ha-Temunah, 21
Sefer Yetzirah
    cubic form, 209
    expanding dimensions, 128
    five dimensional cosmos, 468
    gender model of human history, 454
    geometric enigma of the, 466
    language, 283, 285
    meditation, 247
    moral fifth dimension, 406
    nothing, production of something out of, 254
    obscurity, directions couched in, 5
    Pythagoreanism, 4
    Sefirot, the ten, 29
    seven worlds, 22
    space and time, Sabbatically structured cosmic, 21
    Tree of Life Diagram, 29, 31
    water and fire, concern with opposing qualities of, 10
Sefirot, the ten, 6, 29–31, 258–61, 263–66, 317–18, 473–74
    See also Tree of Life Diagram; *individual Sefirot*
self-consciousness, 431
self-organizing, universe as, 392, 481
Self-Organizing Universe (Jantsch), 481
semiotics, 284, 431, 434
    See also linguistics, systematic
semitones, 91, 108
sentence, matrix modeling of the, 435–39
7 and 4, association of numbers, 379–80, 382, 391
seven-day creation account, 18–20, 181
seventh-world diagram
    backward construction, 339–41
    border outlined, 340

charting the infinite future, 366–68
complete, 339
computer generation, 336–37
constituents of the matrix/total light units, 342–46
eighth-world matrix fashioned from, 347, 348–53
ether element pervading space beyond earth's atmosphere, 337
gender model of human history, 461
incomplete, 338
Pates 16-18, 337, 343
son, association of matrix borders with cosmic, 337
twelve-pointed star, 338–39
26 and 52, numbers, 344–46
See also octave listings
seventh-world matrix, 318–19
seven worlds, concept of the, 20, 21–24
sexual nature of cosmic functioning, 8, 35, 172–80, 263–66
See also gender model of human history
Sha'arei Gan Eden (Koppel), 165
Sha'arei Orah (Gikatilla), 29
Shadow Tree, 267, 321–22, 325, 326
Shakespeare, 406, 457
shamanic tradition, parallels between hexagram of creation and, 17–18, 275, 465–66
shedim (demons), 96–97, 120, 134
Shekhinah
infinity, the final model of, 377, 382
octave diagram, 188–91, 195, 196, 201, 210
octave matrix of the Chayah Soul, 334
sixth-world diagram, 175, 176, 179, 180
sixth-world matrix model of the Neshamah Soul, 262, 265, 268
Shelley, Mary, 124–25, 283, 286
Shemini, 389
Shevirah (breaking of the vessels), 30, 187, 198
Shield of David. See hexagram
Shi'ur Komah (Measure of the Body), 186–87, 195, 206, 207, 314, 329–34
shofar, the, 128–30, 135
signs/ideas and systematic linguistics, 428–32, 434, 439

Si/La Sabbath Star, 134, 141–42, 146
Si Sabbath Star, 132, 161, 207
Sitra Achra (Other Side), 198, 207, 295–96, 319–29
sixth-world diagram
beyond matrix border, 300–308
charting the infinite future, 364–66
eighth-world matrix and observing borders of, 348–53
gender and construction elements, 165–69
gender model of human history, 456
immanent laws, 413
infinity, the final model of, 376–77
linguistics, systematic, 440–42
manual for diagram construction
border, matrix, 156–61
covering position-defining hexagrams of all worlds, 159–60
do-it-yourself manual, 149–56
implications, 156–62
introduction, 148–49
inward vs. outward method, 161–62
matrix grid, 149–50
number theory and diagram construction, 162–65
Partzufim, construction elements and the, 169–80
public/private sectors of society, distinguishing between, 419
sociology, a systems model of, 414–21, 424
sixth-world matrix model of the Neshamah Soul
central and lateral spirals, 257–58
fourth/fifth-world matrix models of Nefesh/Ruach souls, 270–73
heart, 272–79
mind, the, 279–87
Partzufim, 262–67
path of the soul, Sefirot and the, 267–69
psychological model, spiral tree as, 269–70
Sefirot, macrohexagrams assuming an order parallel to, 258–61
spiral tree, completed pattern of the, 256–62
slavery, the shofar and freedom from, 129–30

Slayers of Moses (Handelman), 468
smell, sense of, 282–83, 296
snake and tree, iconographic association of, 314–15
social progress, delusional character of, 299
sociology, a systems model of meaningfulness, social, 421–26
sixth-world matrix and stable/unstable social systems, 414–21
systems hierarchy, 409–14
Socrates, 344, 453
Solomon, alchemical legends surrounding, 9
Solomon's Seal. See hexagram
Sol Sabbath Star, 59–67, 73, 91, 118, 120, 121, 124, 131, 132, 138, 141, 143, 207
Sol/Si Sabbath Star, 134, 142, 146, 196
Sol₂/Si Sabbath Star, 86, 143
Son, concept of the cosmic, 168–69, 337, 362–64, 366–67, 399, 473, 478–80
soul, the
creation categories, one the basic three, 21
as entities, souls as, 96
fourth-world diagram, 58
six-leveled model, 479
stars, soul of evolved humans in sphere of fixed, 357
26, associations with the number, 478
two types of interpretive apprehension, 476
Yichud, cosmic, 173–80
See also Nefesh level of the soul; Neshamah consciousness/level of the soul; octave matrix of the Chayah Soul; Ruach consciousness
space, bending of, 405
space and time, Sabbatically structured cosmic, 21
spatial vs. temporal quality of thought, 44–45, 442
stable social systems, 416–21
Star of David. See hexagram
stars, soul of evolved humans in sphere of fixed, 357
Stengers, Isabelle, 404
Stonehenge, 450
stretching and point/field of primordial light, 24–26
string theory, 393
subjectivity inherent in the nature of language, 431–32
suffering the sins of the world, passion of passively, 324
suicide, 233–34, 291–92

Sumerian civilization, 445, 448, 449, 453–54, 458
synchronicity, 128, 250–51, 274
syntax, 285, 436–37
Systemicity, 410
systems theory, 474, 483
See also sociology, a systems model of

tally, meaning of, 284
Talmud, 7, 20–21, 45–48, 468
tandra state, 254
Tanna Eliyyahu, 21
Tantric Buddhism, 178
Taoist view on gender, 168
taste, sense of, 283, 296
Teilhard de Chardin, Pierre, 125, 399
telos, 124, 398
temporal vs. spatial quality of thought, 44–45, 442
Temunah, 23
Tetractys, 5–6, 23
Tetragrammaton, 181–82, 206, 325–26, 378, 379, 437
Theon of Smyrna, 164
thermodynamics, 404
13, significance of the number, 317–18, 371–72
See also octave diagram
39, significance of the number, 202, 330–32
Thompson, William I., 314
thought, spatial vs. temporal quality of, 44–45, 442
Thucydides, 453
Tiferet (beauty)
balancing the scale, 477
forbidden crossings and illusion of knowledge, 295, 298–99, 305–7, 309
octave diagram, 191, 193
sixth-world diagram, 170–73
sixth-world matrix model of the Neshamah Soul, 258, 263, 264, 266, 274–77, 279
sociology, a systems model of, 414, 420
Tikkun (cosmic restoration)
animal stage of the Asiyah, 117, 118
creation, last three days of, 19
forward thrust of spiritual evolution, xi
free will, man's, 121
humanity, pivotal role of, 180
justice, 278
Law of the Matrix Border, 300
octave diagram, 189, 201
redemption, 58, 321
Sabbath Star Diagram and Tree of Life Diagram, relationship between, 261

short-circuiting of discipline characterizing path of, 297
sixth-world matrix model of the Neshamah Soul, 271
soul, the, 102
Tohu from, distinguishing, 229
transformation of original divinity into Partzufim, 123
Tree of Life Diagram, 30–31, 261
Tree of Return, 42
Tikkunei Zohar, 6, 18, 23
Timaeus (Plato), 36, 59, 342, 467
time, concept of hallowing, 254–55
time and eternity, difference between, 342
"Tintern Abbey" (Wordsworth), 110, 280
Ti Sabbath Star, 149, 151–55, 190, 191
Tohu (formlessness), 228, 229, 235, 288–90, 292–93, 300, 301–2, 304–5, 324
Tompkins, Peter, 314
Torah, 12
touch, sense of, 283, 296, 297
Tower of Babel, 450
transcendental experience, 415, 424, 443
transcendent/immanent forms, Godhead divided into, 24
transformation, accounts of magical, 252–53, 274, 476–77
transformative moment, fourth-world diagram and, 81–83
transpersonal/personal power, difference between, 422–23
transpersonal psychology, 235, 269–70
transpersonal realm, 410, 412, 413, 440, 458–59
transubstantiation of matter into a vehicle for spiritual experience, 252, 253
Treatise on the Dragons (Nathan of Gaza), 321
Tree of Life Diagram
Cordovero *vs.* Luria, 31–32
Da'at, relationship of ten Sefirot to, 32–33
hexagram construction/progression principles, 33–39
hidden design, not the, 2
overview, 8
to Sabbath Star Diagram, 464
sixth-world matrix model of the Neshamah Soul, 258–61
See also charting the infinite future; hexagram

triangle, threefold manifestation of unity in form of the, 11, 474
tribal belonging, 239
triple-level systems hierarchy, 410
trivalent logic, 87–89, 165, 469–70
troubadours and a gender model of human history, 455
turquoise spiral, 221, 236, 268, 296, 297–98, 322, 333, 341–43, 404, 419
twelve-color matrix, astrological implications of the, 475
"Twelve Color Spectro-Chrome System," 219, 221
twelve colors/semitones/personalities, associations between, 474–75
twelve-pointed star, 338–39, 349, 356, 479
26 and seventh-world diagram, 181–82, 344–46, 478
See also octave diagram
236, enigmatic number, 330, 332
Tzachtzachot, 314, 318
Tzaddikim, 197
Tzelem, 94, 95, 102–3, 121
Tzimtzum (contraction of divine light), 24–26, 30, 87, 164, 182, 197–204, 382, 399

Ungar-Sargon, Julian, ix–xi
unstable social systems, 414–16
"Upon Appleton House" (Marvell), 112

Varela, Francisco, 481
vision, central system and, 280
Vital, Chayyim, 6, 20, 127, 171, 320
vitalistic symbolism, 413
vocabulary, 285, 430
voices, divine, 123
von Bertalanffy, Ludwig, 410, 412, 413, 416
Vuv, 378, 379

Waddington, Conrad H., 417–18
Waite, A. E., 264–65
Wallis, John, 242
water and fire, concern with opposing qualities of, 10, 13
water of the sky and alchemistic symbolism, 8–9, 18, 19
Weinberg, Steven, 106, 403
Weiss, Paul A., 410, 412
Wernicke's area, 471
Western esoteric tradition, geometrically encoded knowledge in, 4

Western traditions, the soul and, 58
Wheeler, John A., 405
Wilde, Oscar, 323
Wimsatt, W. K., 430
winged serpent, imagery of the, 314, 315, 317
Wisdom of the Soul (de Leon), 102
"Witness Consciousness," 281
Wittgenstein, Ludwig, 430
Wolfson, Elliot R., 45
women for equality, 445
See also gender model of human history
word, matrix modeling of the, 428–35
work, matrix modeling of the, 439–43
world, spatial category of, 21
worlds, two tradition of Jewish esoteric cosmology combined under rubric of, 21–24

Yates, Frances A., 175
year, temporal category of, 21
Yesod (foundation)
forbidden crossings and illusion of knowledge, 307
fourth world, the evolution of the, 97
infinity, the final model of, 378, 379
linguistics, systematic, 433
octave diagram, 188, 190, 191, 193, 201
octave matrix of the Chayah Soul, 327
Sabbath Star Diagram, 34–38, 42
sixth-world diagram, 165, 169, 171, 173
sixth-world matrix model of the Neshamah Soul, 261, 263, 264, 271, 272, 278, 280
Yetzer ha-Tov/Ra (good/evil), 97, 120, 220, 270
Yetzirah, third world of, 35, 36, 41, 90, 91–97, 201, 261
See also Mi Sabbath Star
Yichud, cosmic, 172–80, 191, 193, 196, 201, 210, 262–66, 415
Yitzchok, Rabbi, 201
Yod, 206, 378
youth, spiritual, 333

Zadokite priesthood of the Second Temple, 5, 464
Ze'ir Anpin (Short Face)
forbidden crossings and illusion of knowledge, 303, 304

fourth-world diagram, 64
gender model of human history, 460
infinity, the final model of, 378, 379, 382, 399
octave diagram, 193, 201, 203–4
sixth-world diagram, 169–73, 175, 176, 178, 179
sixth-world matrix model of the Neshamah Soul, 262–64, 266, 276, 277
sociology, a systems model of, 414–16, 420
zeros after a decimal integer, 480
zigzag matrix border, 215, 221
Zodiac, twelve signs of the, 339
Zohar
conflict between Lurianic and Zoharic models, 466
cosmic construction, 101
creation, 382
Da'at (non-Sefirah) element, 32
doubling of the three primary soul levels, 333
Elohim, 13
four cosmic worlds, 18, 23
42, the number, 188
geometric descriptions of creation, 12
hidden design, 2, 42
Neshamah level of the soul, 124
obscurity, directions couched in, 5
octave diagram, 183, 184
Partzufim, 8
Sabbath Star Diagram, 43–44
soul, the, 223–25
13 and 5, sequence of, 183, 184
Tzimtzum, 198
worlds associated with more than one palace, 22